OUTDOOR RECREATION

OUTDOOR RECREATION

Douglas M. Knudson

Associate Professor, Forestry and Natural Resources, Purdue University

MACMILLAN PUBLISHING CO., INC.

NEW YORK

COLLIER MACMILLAN PUBLISHERS

LONDON

Macmillan Publishing Co., Inc.
866 Third Avenue, New York, New York 10022
Collier Macmillan Canada, Ltd.

Library of Congress Cataloging in Publication Data

Knudson, Douglas M
  Outdoor recreation.

  Includes bibliographies and index.
  1. Outdoor recreation—United States—Management.
2. Natural resources—United States—Management.
I. Title.
GV191.4.K67   1980   658'.91'790973   79–4691
ISBN 0–02–365350–7

Printing   1 2 3 4 5 6 7 8   Year   0 1 2 3 4 5 6

Preface

Scholarly study of the phenomena related to recreational use of natural resources has become the life work of many of the nation's brightest young academics. As professors, research scientists, executives, and government officials, they are leading the way in the understanding of an amazing but predictable revolution. The change is social, economic, and personal. It is welcomed by most. It is leading to greater mass leisure, with attendant heavy use of outdoor resources for recreational purposes.

The timeliness and importance of the study of outdoor recreation are highlighted by the increasing attention given it by governing bodies of public and private interests. Virtually every time the U.S. Congress, the Canadian Parliament, state and provincial legislatures, and local government councils convene, leisure-time use of natural resources is a major item of business. The board rooms of many major industries are intimately concerned with the leisure market, the largest single economic factor in North America.

The incredibly complex interactions of social, economic, and biological factors involved in recreational use of natural resources require the best minds and most eager talents in the nation. This book was written for college students who look forward to professional work in parks and recreation, forestry, wildlife, and related natural resource fields. Because recreation and open space have become major concerns of society and are shapers of national growth, students of public policy, land use, and environmental law will also find relevant information throughout the book.

Countless young people planning careers in parks and recreation or natural resource professions made their choices because they enjoy natural beauty, adventure, forests, mountains, and wildlife. They soon learn that the work requires considerable planning and management expertise. Professional reality is more related to planning and supervising the work of others and dealing with visitors and pressure groups than it is with tramping through the woods, scaling mountains, or handling wild animals.

All natural resource management is now strongly affected by recreation considerations. Recreational use of public forests, parks and refuges has become their single most important use, despite the value of timber, wildlife or other commodities. Even private industrial forests are heavily used for recreational and esthetic purposes. Public and private policies about resource management must continually account for the recreational values of the lands being managed.

The work of providing recreational opportunities has often been divided into two segments, referred to as *parks* and *recreation*. The artificial division has created schisms that have often inhibited development of the entire leisure services delivery system. The real unity of the parks and recreation profession seems intellectually obvious. It has been formally recognized by the National Recreation and Park Association. While specialization in program administration or resource management is important, the specialists need to comprehend the principles involved in the entire profession. Unified work is needed to provide edifying and satisfying leisure-time opportunities for a sophisticated population with increasing access to the out-of-doors.

This book is intended to describe the principles of administering outdoor recreation resources. Professionals in community recreation and park programs will find information useful in their areas as well as a means to better understanding the whole spectrum of recreation places available to the people of North America. Likewise, those who are interested in managing large industrial or public forests will find that the principles apply to their work.

The focus of the book is on natural resources and the private and public entities that administer them for recreational purposes. Due consideration is given the all-important recreationist who is the object of the management. The four parts of the book may be likened to the four major elements of the economic system: the visitors (demand), recreation places (supply), tools for recreation administration (management), and recreation resource policy (price surrogates).

Metric measurements and English equivalents describe areas and distances. The use of the metric system conforms with the practice of many federal agencies, most scientists, and with the policy of the Society of American Foresters in the U.S. as well as the nation of Canada. The most commonly used measurements in this text are hectares (1 ha = 2.47 acres or 10,000 m²) and kilometers (1 km = 0.6 miles or 1,000 m).

Illustrations in this book are highlighted by four original drawings by Fred H. Montague, Jr., of Foxbrook Studios, Monticello, Indiana. He is on the wildlife faculty at Purdue University. Photograph credits which are indicated by the initials of organizations signify loans by the following: U.S. Forest Service (USFS), Heritage Conservation and Recreation Service (HCRS), National Park Service (NPS), U.S. Air Force (USAF), Soil Conservation Service (SCS), U.S. Department of Agriculture (USDA), Bureau of Land Management (BLM), and The Nature Conservancy (TNC). Other gracious contributors of illustrations, credited by full names, include: Arctic Enterprises, Inc., Thief River Falls, Minnesota; Redwood Empire Association, San Francisco; Union Pacific Railroad; Walt Disney Productions, Anaheim, California; Yosemite Park and Curry Company; Michael Meyers Studio, Minneapolis, Minnesota; Florida Development Commission, Tallahassee; Hennepin County Park Reserve District, Minnesota; Bikecentennial, Missoula, Montana; Muscatatuck National Wildlife Refuge, Seymour, Indiana; U.S. Bureau of Reclamation; Elmer L. Onstott, Ferguson, Missouri; and Mary Vanderford, Naturalist, Hennepin Park Reserve District, Minnesota.

D. M. K.

Contents

OUTDOOR RECREATION

Introduction

Recreation is an integral and important part of the nation's total social, economic, natural resource, and urban environment. It is a basic component of individual and social behavior and aspiration. It is recognized as an important use of land and other physical resources. Large sums of both public and private investment go into recreation resources and programs and tens of billions of personal consumption dollars are spent on leisure-time pursuits.

Recreation has become a major national concern. Throughout the last half of the nineteenth century and the first decades of the twentieth century, the American people established the national park concept, promoted recreation in the national forests, started state and local park systems, set up active municipal recreation programs, and established many leisure-oriented volunteer agencies. Commercial and industrial interests expanded their services to a public that was gaining mass leisure and high average income.

These programs developed somewhat separately and sporadically over many years. Professional organizations and new public agencies sprang up, with relatively little unified direction, in the spirit of independence that has characterized the United States and Canada.

The decade of 1955–1965 was one of significant development of national, unified philosophy, policy, and public interest in recreation. It was a decade of thinking and talking. Because the nation faced increased leisure with insufficient facilities and preparation for its use, recreation became both a national problem and opportunity. There were many studies, books, and pamphlets, including the nationwide studies by the Outdoor Recreation Resources Review Commission (ORRRC). These developed philosophies and policies and urged their implementation. New laws were enacted and programs were initiated. The decade culminated in the unification of the major professional societies into a single federation, the National Recreation and Park Association, in which numerous branches of the recreation professions could discuss their common goals.

The period after 1965 brought the need for action and implementation. The thinking of the 1955–65 decade had to be activated, tested, and adjusted to changing reality. Many of the documents that were written in previous years had briefly described the management and policy decisions

1

Figure 1.1 Shenandoah River, Hazard Mill Recreation Area. (USFS)

needed for recreational productivity. Those often cryptic recognitions of problems and directions have to be translated into working rules, regulations, facilities, and programs. Predicting future recreation demands and meeting those demands are two phases of the same problem, requiring differing skills.

The ORRRC report (1962) is the basic policy-setting document for public recreational land management today. There is no similar report for other phases of recreation. Most recent governmental policy and legislation on recreation can be traced back to that 1962 report of a citizens' committee. The park and recreation professional in city, county, state, and federal agencies will continue to be affected by ORRRC recommendations for many years. His or her job will be to work with the results of those recommendations. They will be expected to amend and augment the basic concepts so they fit the local situation. The basic goal is to increase the recreational productivity of resources and personnel by effective programming and resource management.

The development of the outdoor recreation movement may be likened to the ages of man. After a long childhood when important foundations were laid, the recreation baby reached adolescence in the mid-1950s. After a short but intense crisis of adolescence, when planning and thought led to strong ideals and goals, the first stages of adulthood were entered in the late 1960s. With tentative public approval and new power, the plans and ideals are being carried out and modified. Full maturity is still a long way off. The vigorous young adult is developing solutions and gaining wisdom. The "correct" answers are not always available.

This book presents the story of outdoor recreation into its early adulthood. It explains a few known precepts and discusses areas that require further work. Its objectives are to

Interpret present and future significance of outdoor recreation.
Describe the philosophy, responsibilities, and operations of recreation agencies, from a systems viewpoint.
Present major concepts and techniques used in administering outdoor recreation resources and programs.

The focus of the book is on the land and its associated resources of forests, water, and open spaces (Figure 1.2). The overriding concern is with philosophies and methods of increasing the productivity of outdoor recreation resources to achieve optimum human welfare while also maintaining the health of the land.

FIGURE 1.2 Deer Lick Nature Preserve, New York. (TNC)

Recreation as Culture

Recreation is a major shaper of American land, cities, and counties today. It is a major movement of the present time.

Recreation interests affect not only the preservation of open space but also public agencies' policies, budgets, resource management practices, industrial locations, industrial land-use practices, highway development, and city design.

This is not to say that recreation is in command. Nations are shaped by many forces that interact. Recreation considerations and interests, however, are potent in their influence and are among the major forces affecting society today. Interestingly, the movement is one of popular origins and volunteer citizen strength, not of economic power brokers.

Its durability rests on the good will and enthusiasm of individuals who have little to gain but pleasure and satisfaction in a more handsome, livable environment (Figure 1.3). They often struggle with local, state, and federal government officials who consider recreation and parks to be minor frivolities. They face powerful economic incentives to oppose open space and they confront the plans of engineers, builders, and others who seek to usurp park and forest land.

The moves to preserve open space for recreation and to spend money on park development and programming are not easy. They are hard-fought

FIGURE 1.3   Yellowstone backcountry visitors, 1922. (NPS)

battles, often against competing interests. In local budgets, the recreation sector sometimes takes a back seat to transportation, welfare, and other basic concerns of mankind. But, all in all, recreation needs have grown so that they are strongly influencing the shape and character of America's landscape and the culture of its people.

In American society, work and its productivity have long been considered the norm by which one person is compared to another. They are standards commonly used to compare cities, states, and nations. The United States and Canada can be considered among the leading nations in the world, according to numerous measures of work: real income per capita, gross national product, output of almost all manufactured products, agricultural output, variety of products and services accessible to consumers, number of bathtubs (an old measure of affluence), TV sets, automobiles, miles of highway, percentage of houses with central heating and two inside bathrooms, and pounds of paper products used each year.[1]

Usually overlooked in comparisons among nations and individuals is the use of leisure time. Yet, most nations refer to their culture with pride. Culture is usually produced by either leisured individuals or by the society as a whole in its leisure. Culture traditionally includes art, music, literature, drama, religious attitudes and practices, and social customs and events.

There are no commonly accepted measures of culture, which is usually discussed in qualitative terms. It may change in concept among nations and even among individuals. Europeans have been known to declare that America has no culture. Others have said that it has a work-oriented culture. The values and characteristics that identify the United States are supposedly those associated with work, efficiency, and productivity. Work is said to dominate the national character.

If this is so, it is perhaps characteristic, yet ironic, that this nation leads the world in studies of recreation. We even make work out of our fun. This book, for instance, encourages greater productivity of services and resources in the recreation profession.

Whatever our attitudes toward work and play, it is undeniable that Americans are spending less time at work and more at play (Figure 1.4). A large segment of society is devoted to providing services and goods for leisure-time pursuits. Eastman Kodak, Coleman, AMF, Outboard Marine, Winnebago, Wilson Sporting Goods, and Kampgrounds of America are only a few of the enterprises that provide goods and services for outdoor recreation.

Recreation and tourism comprise a huge industry. In this country, most states rank expenditures by tourists as one of the primary sources of income to the state economy. Although only some of the tourist expenditures are

[1] Citizens of the United States use 84 metric tons of cultural paper per 1000 capita per year. Figures for other countries are: Canada, 55.3; West Germany, 50.5; Ghana, 2.1; Japan, 43.0; Continental China, 3.3; Sweden, 76.5; Brazil, 6.9; USSR, 8.9 metric tons (UNESCO, 1977).

FIGURE 1.4 Rivers offer some of the last natural landscapes in many midwestern areas. (HCRS)

for strictly recreational activities, there is no way to separate travel monies into their component parts. States spend considerable tax funds to advertise for more tourists, receiving several times those expenditures in sales taxes paid by the tourists.

More important than the money involved is the profound sociocultural development that is taking place in American life. A nation that has prided itself in its ability and enthusiasm for productive work has now made for itself large blocks of leisure time in which the compulsion toward work is minimized.

Man is a creative being. He seems to find satisfaction in developing, reorganizing, fabricating. He has long satisfied this creative desire in his work. Now, craftsmen have given way to assembly lines and prefabrication. In the 1950s, Walter Reuther, a leader in the American labor movement, observed that the day of creative work was gone; the laborer must now be creative in his leisure. Although professionals and certain executives are still called upon to be highly creative in their work, the vast majority of workers hold relatively routine jobs.

This extension of the mechanical age appears to be one that will rem for some time, although McLuhan (1964) suggests that eventual ch with the advent of the "electric age" will make a man more of a ger with broader, more creative responsibilities.

At any rate, the use of leisure time for creative activities today and will apparently remain so for some time. Rather tha the technology that has given man free time but dull wo

seeks to emphasize the role of recreation in stimulating and promoting creativity during leisure hours. Recreation is not a palliative but an opportunity for true cultural development. Recreation is not a way to pass time but an exciting social development opportunity. Leisure must be used for more than amusement and comfort. Cultures based on such shallow goals can hardly be expected to sincerely reward those who live in them nor will they survive for long as valid cultures. Recreational leisure would be well used if it provided the vague but vital rewards of 1) self-fulfillment, 2) physical and intellectual involvement, and 3) creative and cultural development.

The nation is undergoing changes other than just expanding its leisure time. The long-term obsession with growth—the bigger and better syndrome in which everything is measured by how many and how large—is being questioned by large segments of the population. Whereas religious leaders have for years been calling for a spiritual balance to our materialistic orientation, now several generations seem to have caught the idea that more is not necessarily better. Pollution problems accentuated this feeling with the fear of what "more," left unregulated, might do to life.

The near future may be an era of true cultural change and development. The United States and Canada have the chance, almost alone among large civilizations, to achieve mass culture on a leisure-time base.

The Professional Challenges

Professionals in the businesses and agencies supplying outdoor recreation are confronted by a complex system that seeks to satisfy diverse leisure-time interests. Administration of recreation services and resources is far more than the old stereotypes of organizing softball tournaments or living in fire towers. The professional must understand legal and policy matters, the philosophies of many land-managing agencies, economic and social impacts, biological principles, and other basic operational tools of the profession. There is a growing need to keep up with controversies about recreation resources plus the workings of governments and pressure groups.

Some of the policy and legal concepts that affect recreational professionals are the following:

Comprehensive recreation planning.
Land classification systems.
Federal revenue sharing.
Acquisition and development funding programs.
Land-use planning and zoning.
State and local financing.
Off-road vehicle impacts and policy.
Use of easements for recreation.
Mandatory dedication.

Designation of areas such as wilderness, wild and scenic rivers, national trails, nature preserves.

Differences in purposes and resources of the numerous local, state, and federal agencies that control more than one third of the nation's land, much of which is used for recreation.

Economic and social analyses of visitors, roles of private and public investment in outdoor recreation, and the economic consequences of outdoor recreation activity are part of the basic understanding needed for intelligent, informed decision making by professionals. Knowing how to deal with members of the public—many of them very well informed—in decisions involving citizen participation is of great importance to the modern park and recreation professional, forester, wildlife manager, or industrialist.

Biological principles of recreation area management apply to all types of recreation managers. The more intensively used the facilities—such as in camps and local parks—the more intensive is the need for understanding biological interactions, the carrying capacity of the site, and manipulative principles for managing the site within its natural parameters.

Knowledge of these and other principles is valuable to any well-rounded and informed professional. A person trained in parks and recreation or related land management should be acquainted with the entire system of recreation areas and the diversity of opportunities they offer. The advantages of understanding the whole picture are many. The different agencies and companies—federal, state, local, United Way agencies, industries, and private recreation businesses—interact in many ways.

The policies of these agencies usually complement each other so that citizens have choices among the widest array of activities and resources. State comprehensive outdoor recreation plans and various funding programs are designed to promote complementarity. The role of each agency is thus partly defined by the policies and strengths of other agencies and firms.

Another advantage of comprehending the broad field of parks and recreation is related to the employability of the professional. There is considerable potential for mobility throughout the parks and recreation field. A state park agency recently hired a young graduate in municipal recreation to serve as the recreation director in a state park; the job included explaining the goals of state parks to visitors. The National Park Service hires people from city park departments and state wildlife agencies, and vice versa. A YMCA director may become a recreation specialist for the Tennessee Valley Authority or the Corps of Engineers. Lateral mobility is so common that it is almost the rule; no professional can afford to be ignorant of the entire field.

A more selfless reason for a broad knowledge is that many professionals serve as volunteers and collaborators in other agencies. It is not uncommon that a federal or industry forester will serve on the park board in the community where he lives. Likewise, a county recreation director is likely to be invited to serve on a national park advisory committee. Both individuals may also serve on the state outdoor recreation planning advisory committee.

In any professional work, there is satisfaction in comprehending what is going on in the profession, above and beyond the immediate confines of one's particular, immediate job. The outstanding professionals are usually those who work hard in their own special task but who, at the same time, comprehend and communicate with people in the entire profession. To advance in the profession, the individual needs a considerable range of skills and knowledge.

Literature Cited

McLuhan, Marshall. 1964. Understanding Media: the Extensions of Man. New York: New American Library, 318 pp.

Outdoor Recreation Resource Review Commission (ORRRC). 1962. Outdoor Recreation for America. Washington, D.C. 246 pp.

UNESCO. 1977. Statistical Yearbook, 1976. Paris. 1074 pp.

A System View

The fundamental truth that recreation is essential to the cultural, moral, and spiritual well-being of our people has been reaffirmed . . . The challenge to use leisure time effectively and constructively demands full development of our national, state, and local recreational resources.

—JOHN F. KENNEDY

The big picture of the outdoor recreation system is a colorful kaleidoscope of diversity. Those who participate engage in dozens of different activities. Their numbers are growing, along with increases in leisure time. They use recreation resources of all descriptions, partly on the basis of what is close to home, partly by preference of activities. Some like remote wilderness areas large enough to challenge a hiker's sense of direction and skill of living without contact with mechanical devices—areas that are designated for preservation from the introduction of artificial elements. Other recreationists prefer highly developed amusement parks where mechanical devices and crowds dominate. Most people have wide-ranging interests and seek experiences at many levels.

A growing population has learned how to pave roads to beautiful natural places. Now it is learning to understand and appreciate those places. As the people gain appreciation, they gain civilization and culture. A fortunate few have opportunities to work in the parks and other recreation areas that offer significant opportunities for personal development and enrichment through leisure-time pursuits.

A persistent annoyance to state and national forest managers is the visitor who comments, "What a nice park you have here." Likewise, the uniformed county park employee is often called a forest ranger. It is a minor error and perhaps unimportant to the visitor in most circumstances. But forests, parks, wildlife areas, and a myriad of other facilities have distinct roles in the system of recreation properties. They are geared to serve a wide variety of individual recreation preferences in specific ways. When the differences are understood, the system works more efficiently.

The purpose of this chapter is to provide an overall view of the broad subject of outdoor recreation. It gives the student an opportunity to see how things fit together. It offers a big picture of outdoor recreation, serving as an orientation to the interrelationships that are discussed in later chapters. The many agencies and businesses offering recreation have different policies and areas. There are dozens of other federal, state, and local agencies which regulate, assist, and finance recreation. The park and recreation professional faces a large task in understanding these details and must keep up with the ever-changing policies, laws, and agency responsibilities.

Recreation in North America is in a rapidly changing period. This means that adjustments are constantly being made to meet a constantly growing and often shifting demand.

Throughout the world, societies are increasing their standards of living. Even in nations that are extremely poor, working hours in industrial and agricultural employment allow time for leisure. In reality, it was only with the Industrial Revolution that time became so precious a commodity it was carefully metered out and distinctly divided between work and pleasure. Agrarian societies experienced a flow of the seasons, with relatively more or less work and leisure depending on seasonal demands. Recreation by some name has been part of life since early times. Recently, it has become a major national concern of most Western nations and Japan.

Leisure-time activities have become the leading industry of the United States as measured by people's spending. The Economic Unit of *U.S. News & World Report* ("The boom in leisure," 1977) estimated that 1977 spending on leisure and recreation totaled $160 billion. By 1985, this was expected to rise to $300 billion. That estimate of activity has risen steadily since 1965, when it was $58.3 billion. It rose to $105 billion in 1972 and to $146.5 billion in 1976. That spending involves many types of activities and products, only some of which are for outdoor pursuits. It is indicative of a burgeoning interest in leisure-time activities in America. The leisure market is on the upswing and shows no indication of slowing down.

Throughout the world, as people become steadily more prosperous and industrialized, their interest in recreational activities is likely to grow, at least until the earth reaches the point of resource scarcity and human deprivation, which may come from a combination of overpopulation and high rates of resource consumption. If, through the adoption of wise population restraint and more efficient uses of existing resources, man can improve his condition, he will surely maintain his growing interest in spending leisure time outdoors. In fact, it may be that association with outdoor recreation resources will do much to stimulate man's comprehension of the finiteness of the resource base of this earth.

The outdoor recreation system can be described in terms of its basic elements and their interrelationships. The elements and economic correlates used here are as follows:

System Elements	*Economic Parallels*
Visitors and their characteristics	(Demand)
Recreation places and their administration	(Supply)
Plans and policies for recreation	(Price system)
Tools and principles of recreation administration	(Management)

Visitors

Outdoor recreation activities are defined here as virtually all those constructive leisure activities that occur in parks and other open space areas. They include everything from playground and playfield activities to wilderness trips and camping. Recent state planning efforts have focused on 19 typical activities, which give an idea of the range of activities:

Bicycling	Picnicking
Camping	Playfield use
Canoeing	Playground use
Fishing	Power boating
Golf	Sledding
Hiking	Snow skiing
Horseback riding	Swimming
Hunting	Tennis
Ice skating	Water skiing
Off-road vehicle riding	

These suggest many other activities that are of great importance commercially and socially, such as attending outdoor sports and cultural events, nature walks, sightseeing, visiting zoos and amusement parks, playing outdoor games and sports, and driving for pleasure. Then there are organized youth camps and festivals to attend, photography, bird watching, jogging, sailing, rock climbing, hang gliding, and walking for pleasure. These are important to many individuals and especially to the recreation area and program manager.

Participation is greatest for simple activities, such as swimming, bicycling, picnicking, walking for pleasure, sightseeing, and driving for pleasure. Where facilities are available (trails, pools, picnic sites, bike routes, and roads), these activities involve large proportions of the population. Most are inexpensive and uncomplicated, requiring little preparation and only basic skills common to most persons.

More complicated activities are popular among those who have proficiency or special interests, but a smaller proportion of the population takes part in them. Nevertheless, considerable public and private resources are wisely invested to provide for activities such as camping, golf, canoeing, wilderness visits, backpacking, and horseback riding. It is probably fortunate that the majority of persons does not participate in most of these activities; many campgrounds, wilderness areas, and riding trails already are overflowing on peak use days.

People tend to seek recreation most on weekends, with about three quarters of all participation occurring on Saturday and Sunday. This produces work loads on recreation professionals that are opposite to those of the rest of society. Most areas experience overcapacity during the week and in off-season periods.

The growth in recreational participation has been across the entire spectrum of supply, commercial through federal lands. Virtually all major activities have grown. A few have seen spectacular growth since 1960, including bicycling, backpacking, and tennis.

Will growth in participation continue? Probably. People have more free time, more real income, greater mobility, better education, greater exposure to new ideas and places, and more of other basics to increase opportunities to participate. There will be more people in the population base. With larger numbers of people and increasing rates of participation per capita, the demand for recreation facilities and services will continue to expand. This should stimulate the growth of private and public outdoor recreation systems, expand employment in the profession, and exert pressures to manage existing resources more intensively for recreation.

Recreation Places

Outdoor recreation opportunities are offered on lands that bear a proliferation of names: forests, wildlife refuges, parks, nature preserves, playgrounds, recreation areas, state beaches, wild rivers, and scenic trails. They are managed by many agencies. The land base is described in Figure 2.1, in terms of percentages of area. The bulk of the land open for recreation is in

FIGURE 2.1 Public areas used for outdoor recreation in the United States, excluding federal lands little used for recreation. (BOR, 1973)

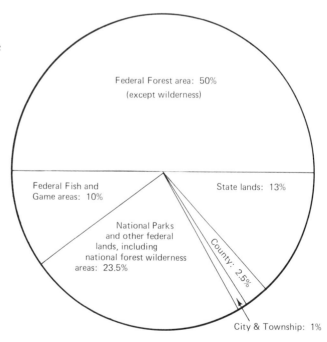

Federal Forest area: 50%
(except wilderness)

Federal Fish and Game areas: 10%

State lands: 13%

National Parks and other federal lands, including national forest wilderness areas: 23.5%

County: 2.5%

City & Township: 1%

multiple-use forests and range lands managed by the Forest Service and the Bureau of Land Management. Only small bits of these areas are especially developed for recreation. Most of it is land open for any who want to venture into it. These areas are much less intensively used than are local, state, and private facilities.

It should be noted that estimates of recreation resource areas are highly variable. Even state outdoor recreation plans do not provide consistent data. The most difficult to estimate are local and private lands. Therefore, exact figures describing recreation areas are often contradicted by different reports. In broad terms, it can be estimated that federal land is one third of all land in the nation, the majority of it in Alaska and low-productivity areas of the West. Almost 60 per cent of the nation is in private ownership, involving individuals, industries, and others. States own about 5 per cent, and publicly owned county and municipal land is only 1 per cent of the total land base. Indians control over 2.2 per cent of the nation, according to the Bureau of the Census (1977).

This book describes several common approaches to classifying recreation resources, so the student will be familiar with the terminology. One of the simplest classifications of recreation places was described by Clawson and Knetsch (1966), as follows:

> User-oriented areas—located and designed with the access and use by the visitor as the principal but not only consideration; include most city and county recreation areas, and many commercial areas (Figure 2.2).

FIGURE 2.2   Playgrounds are part of user-oriented recreation areas. (HCRS)

Intermediate areas—located and planned to meet needs of the users, but in areas dictated partially by the resource; managed with resource maintenance and use as balancing considerations; include most state parks, forests, reservoir projects, many fish and wildlife areas, and some commercial recreation areas.

Resource-oriented areas—located and planned with the resource base as the key criterion, with recreation use coming as a result of the resource; the large areas of national forests, most national wildlife refuges, national parks, national resource lands, and some large state properties fall in this category, as do forest industry lands (Figure 2.3).

The classification is quite useful, unless one becomes too literal. It is conceptual, helping people sort out the *relative* emphases of different classes of parks. Naturally, all recreation lands are a combination of user and resource orientations. Even most nature preserves, which are highly protective of the resource, provide for visitor use. Likewise, the most intensively used playground in Chicago will become unpleasant if attention is not given to maintenance of the land and basic facilities. A nature study center could clearly fall within any of the categories, depending on its location and purpose. Most state parks and forests are classed as intermediate; their locations are dictated partially by available natural resources and partially by the desire to serve the people of a region of the state or tourists. The classification is not always possible if based only on facilities or features; parks are often quite similar in appearance. The policy and purpose are also important in the classification.

The resource locations where recreation occurs may also be classified by ownership. They are managed by many private and public agencies. There is some communication among them, but they do not operate as a single unit. Rather, they resemble the free enterprise marketplace, each responding more or less independently to the apparent demands of the public that patronizes them or to fill in the gaps that exist in supply.

Private outdoor recreation businesses are the most important suppliers of recreational opportunities (Figure 2.4). They serve more people than do any of the public agencies. Commercial campgrounds, riding stables, beaches, resorts, and fishing lakes are among the major components of the private, for-profit businesses. Concessions in public parks and guide-outfitting services are other important recreation businesses. The huge recreation products industry is another component of growing importance to the economy. These facilities handle large numbers of people on rather small properties. They usually feature developed facilities and quite intensive concentrations of people on a relatively small land base. Although private lands comprise nearly 60 per cent of the nation, only about 10 to 20 per cent of that is readily available to public recreation.

Forest and other industries usually allow and often encourage recre-

FIGURE 2.4 Kings Island Amusement Park offers crowds and the dominance of mechanical devices.

ational use of their large holdings. They own about 13 per cent of the nation's forest land, most of which is highly productive of timber crops. Recreation is a secondary use that often provides small but important financial benefits to the forestry sectors of the industries. There are also rewards of positive relations with neighbors and the general public.

Among the public agencies providing recreation, city parks serve the most visitors on the least total area. Close-to-home recreation areas are naturally used most frequently. County parks are growing rapidly in number and size. They provide facilities that fall between city and state parks, with a rural or historical emphasis. Often, they are located on lakes or streams. Counties also can provide bike, hiking, and horseback trails and scenic roads, all connecting major recreation areas and communities. Special districts offer metro or regional parks in some localities. They are usually

FIGURE 2.3 Arches National Park, Utah, is a resource-oriented recreation area. (NPS)

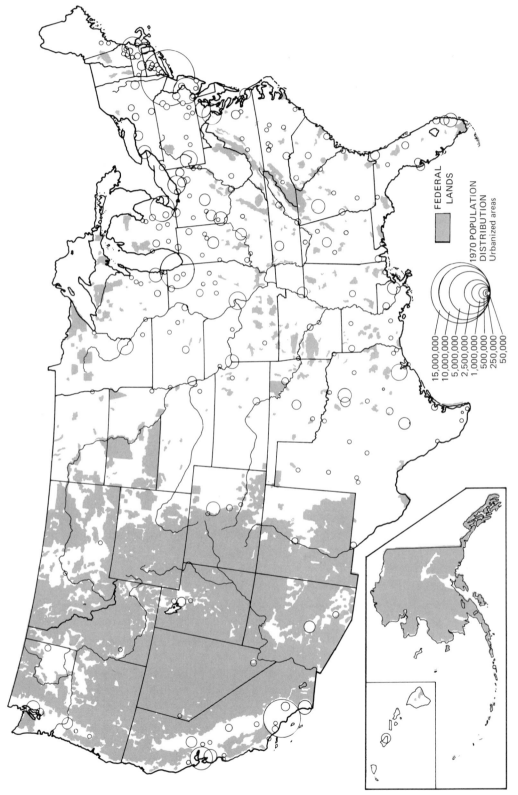

FEDERAL
LANDS

1970 POPULATION
DISTRIBUTION
Urbanized areas

15,000,000
10,000,000
5,000,000
2,500,000
1,000,000
500,000
250,000
50,000

FIGURE 2.5 Distribution of public lands in the United States is inverse to population distribution. (BOR, 1973)

large, natural parks near major population centers. They are often supported by special tax levies authorized by the state legislature.

States provide recreation at state parks, forests, wildlife areas, and several other categories of facilities that are called by different names in different states. They include recreation areas, beaches, state scenic rivers, state trails, nature preserves, fishing areas, and memorials. States attempt to balance the goals of providing places for recreational activities with those of managing significant resources for special or multiple uses.

The federal government manages about one third of the land of the nation. Most of it is open to dispersed types of recreation. Concentrated or developed recreation is provided in hundreds of campgrounds, picnic areas, and other visitor facilities. The principal managing agencies are the U.S. Forest Service, the Bureau of Land Management, the National Park Service, the Fish and Wildlife Service, the Army Corps of Engineers, and the Tennessee Valley Authority. The Bureau of Reclamation and the Bureau of Indian Affairs are also important in providing resources. These agencies provide some areas with special legal designations, including wilderness areas, wild and scenic rivers, and multipurpose reservoirs. The large bulk of federal resources available for recreation, however, is in the multiple-use forests and range lands of the Forest Service and the Bureau of Land Management. About 80 other agencies provide financial, coordinating, planning, and other services. The Heritage Conservation and Recreation Service has the central role in providing federal financial and technical assistance, as well as coordinating the planning for recreation at the local, state, and federal levels.

Plans and Policies

It seems that there is an inverse relationship between concentration of apparent demand and supply of land resources to recreation. In North America, most of the people live in the East. Most of the wide-open public spaces are in the West (Figure 2.5). Urban areas often have the most interesting local parks (Figure 2.6), but they suffer from low per capita acreages. The poorer neighborhoods often have the least parkland. Cities constantly seek to add to their recreation space.

The problem of maldistribution of resources and people was formally recognized in 1962, with the issuance of the report of the Outdoor Recreation Resources Review Commission (ORRRC). That report served as the nation's first comprehensive look at outdoor recreation areas. By presenting statistical data, it revealed the areas of greatest need and thus could be used in the allocation of resources.

That first nationwide plan recommended that the states develop comprehensive recreation plans. Since 1965, each state has written analyses of recreation supply, demand, and needs, followed by recommendations per-

FIGURE 2.6 Skating in Central Park, a user-oriented facility.

taining to all sectors within the state. These statewide Outdoor Recreation Plans are repeated every three to five years.

A Nationwide Outdoor Recreation Plan was prepared in 1973 by the Bureau of Outdoor Recreation. Like the ORRRC report, it reviewed policies and programs and compared existing resources with current and projected participation rates. It recommended actions to ensure availability of critical types of resources. A third plan of nationwide scope was issued in 1979. Again assessing the national picture, the latest plan included different tactics and greater involvement of public comment. Subsequent plans are to be prepared every five years by the Heritage Conservation and Recreation Service of the Department of the Interior.

In 1970, a special review of federal lands was reported by the Public Land Law Review Commission. Its recommendations described interrelationships and priorities among the many uses of federal properties. Recreation was a major concern.

Special laws and policies affect planning and management of recreation resources under all jurisdictions. Local parks have various federal sources of financial assistance, if planning and application procedures are properly followed. Local and state land use and zoning plans affect local and private recreation.

The decision of the Forest Service to provide mostly dispersed recreation and forest-type developed areas is an example of a policy that ensures diversity of opportunities and environments for recreation.

The Wilderness Acts of 1964 and 1975 have considerable impact on federal land management agencies. So do the various planning acts of recent years. The requirements to produce environmental impact analyses and to involve the public heavily in decision making call for skills and efforts far different from those of the past.

Increasing public interest in environmental study has led to establishment of nature preserve systems in many states. Related policy questions arise as to how much hunting and fishing should be allowed in fish and wildlife areas. Emotional interest in wildlife without knowledge of the natural dynamics of animal populations has led to requests to halt all hunting.

These and many other policies directly affect the professional recreation area administrator. The conduct of business is not a simple application of technical or economic principles. It also requires sensitivity to public opinion and to changing policies.

The Tools of the Profession

Planners, administrators, program leaders, and interpreters of recreation areas use a large number of conceptual, biological, legal, and organization skills to efficiently supply a variety of leisure-time opportunities.

First, the professional should be knowledgeable about the numerous agencies and types of businesses that offer recreation. Their policies, limitations, and modes of operation will be useful information. Although any individual is likely to work for only two or three agencies during a career, interactions among professionals of many organizations are frequent and important.

The planning process and regulations are vital tools. Projecting demand, inventorying supply, and calculating needs are important elements. Financial and technical assistance and in-house funding are often associated with planning. Few professionals can exist without knowing the numerous sources of money and in-kind services that a business or agency can tap.

Gaining the cooperation of volunteers is another cost-saving measure; knowledge of the goals of the numerous citizens' organizations is a key professional tool.

Administrative tools also include personnel management, resource classification, and visitor analysis techniques. Among these techniques are approaches to estimating the quantity and quality of use on a property. That is basic to budgetary calculations, maintenance scheduling, programming, and decisions to spread use.

Management of the biological resources requires numerous skills and considerable basic knowledge of the natural resources and their reactions. Naturally, some administrators will be more expert in biological concepts, whereas others will be strong in programming aspects. All need to understand the concept of carrying capacity as a cornerstone of the management of people and resources. The impacts made by people and their machines are fundamental to how many of them can be allowed on a property and still retain the quality of the resource. The use of fire in resource management is a controversial matter, as is timber harvesting for the enhancement of beauty. Even the methods used to manage wildlife areas have become a subject of growing public criticism.

The professional must have knowledge of legal and policy matters to operate effectively. Three processes that are basic to all recreation operations are the legal liabilities associated with ownership of land, public involvement in decision making, and the environmental impact review. The use of eminent domain and other land acquisition techniques, the issuing of bonds, and negotiation of easements are among the tasks that most professionals will face sooner or later.

Recreation service tools include interpretation, activity programming, zoning, design of facilities, and providing publications. The list is formidable. Certainly, the young professional will develop expertise in only a few of these at a time. They are introduced here so the student understands the scope of the basics involved.

In summary, supplying recreation resources requires 1) a thorough knowledge of the potential visitors, 2) an acquaintance with the various agencies providing recreation, 3) familiarity with the policies and regulations affecting agencies and businesses, and 4) ability to use the professional tools of the trade. Administration of recreation resources is not a test-tube science. The required skills call on many disciplines and an alert intelligence.

Literature Cited

Bureau of Outdoor Recreation. 1973. Outdoor Recreation: a Legacy for America. Washington, D.C.: U.S. Department of the Interior. 89 pp.

CLAWSON, MARION, and JACK L. KNETSCH. 1966. Economics of Outdoor Recreation. Baltimore: Johns Hopkins Press. 328 pp.

Outdoor Recreation Resources Review Commission. 1962. Outdoor Recreation for America. Washington, D.C. 246 pp.

Public Land Law Review Commission. 1970. One Third of the Nation's Land. Washington, D.C.

The boom in leisure—where Americans spend 160 billions. 1977. U.S. News and World Report 82(20):62–63.

PART ONE

The Visitors

C H A P T E R 3

The Recreation Experience

A person who lives 70 years will spend the equivalent of 27 years in leisure. The sum total of recreational experience will determine much about the character and quality of the person's life.

The bottom line in the recreation and parks business is "the experience." The sensations, satisfactions, personal challenges, and memories of a recreational outing help comprise the experience. These are the products of programs, scenery, and facilities. Recreation is all about how people feel, how they react, and how they enjoy themselves (Figure 3.1). This can be translated into individual and social welfare.

Recreation experiences are highly individualized. Most esthetic, emotional, and physical responses are special to the person, even though they are enough alike to be shared with others of similar experience.

Recreation is related to an individual or group *choice* of activities or inactivity taking place during *discretionary time.*

The word *recreation* comes from the concept of creating again, recollecting, or reforming in the mind. The idea of refreshment of spirit and strength after toil has led to the word being used to mean diversion, play, or amusement. The most commonly applied antonym to recreation is work.

Outdoor recreation is commonly referred to in terms of activities of a recreational nature conducted in the open air (Figure 3.2). A wide variety of types of activities are classified under the heading of outdoor recreation. A classification of these includes the following:

Traveling activities
  Walking and hiking
  Biking
  Horseback riding
  Driving for pleasure
  Sailing
  Canoeing
  Boating
  Water skiing

Social activities
  Games and sports
  Camping (to a growing degree)
  Picnicking
  Swimming

Esthetic/artistic activities
  Photography
  Sightseeing
  Painting and crafts
  Nature study

High adventure
  Survival trips
  Backpacking
  Mountaineering
  Rapids running
  Certain levels of other activities

Survival replay
  Fishing
  Hunting
  Camping
  Some games

The ultimate concern is not with these activities for their own sake, but with the effects they have on the health, growth, and satisfaction of the participants. Psychologists will be discussing this in great detail over the next few decades.

The words *recreation* and *leisure* are often used together. Leisure is basically a time concept, whereas recreation is an activity concept. Leisure

FIGURE 3.1 The charm of fishing is that it is the pursuit of what is elusive but attainable, a perpetual series of occasions for hope.

Figure 3.2 Both cross-country and downhill skiing have recently brought many people outdoors in the winter, stimulating local rural economies and presenting natural resource managers with new challenges. (USFS)

is free time, or discretionary time. Recreation is a type of use of such time.

DeGrazia (1962) has used the word *leisure* in an unusual psychological sense. He claims that leisure is really a state of mind in which one is freed of the compulsions of work, time, and unrefreshing thought patterns. What he defines as "true leisure" is one kind of experience from the use of leisure time. The planner and administrator must recognize that the frequency of such experiences among the public is a real measure of success for which they should strive.

For simplicity and practicality, leisure can be thought of as time in which a person is relatively free to choose his activities. Recreation can be considered as play activity or passivity pursued in leisure time.

The Recreation Experience

In the twentieth-century economy, the vindication of spiritual freedom became the generation's most urgent business, and the arena in which this spiritual battle would be lost or won would be a field of leisure that in a fully mechanized world might come to be all but coexistent with the field of life itself. (Toynbee, 1954)

Recreation is unavoidably connected to the pursuit of happiness. Philosophers have written volumes about the definition and logic of happiness. It is one of those words that everyone understands but no one finally defines.

Recreation is about "the good life," a curious, enigmatic phrase (Figure 3.3). The good life and happiness are universally appealing enough that statesmen, businessmen, theologians, and recreation experts all join forces to help us reach them. Peace of mind, self-fulfillment, fun, worship, a true sense of relaxation, physical development, and appreciation are all part of the pursuit of happiness and the good life.

Outdoor recreation is one approach to the pursuit of happiness for most people. Theoretical philosophy aside, most resource managers are providing the setting, facilities, and programs that offer opportunities for happy experiences and values. President Calvin Coolidge expressed the national value of recreation in a 1924 address to the National Conference on Outdoor Recreation:

The physical vigor, moral strength, and clean simplicity of mind of the American people can be immeasurably furthered by the properly developed opportunities for life in the open. . . . From such life much of the American spirit of freedom springs.

FIGURE 3.3 Horseback riding is desired by many but readily available to only a few—part of "the good life." (USFS)

The Visitors

Defining the Recreation Experience

There are numerous approaches to explaining the recreation experience. The National Park Service defines it in terms of the special qualities of each park.

A description of a recreation experience by Clawson and Knetsch (1966) suggests that it consists of the following four parts for any individual, broken down by time into a sequence of phases:

1. *Anticipation.* The period of foreseeing and awaiting a trip or occasion involves imagination and develops enthusiasm. Events may never occur but still contribute to one's happiness through anticipation.
2. *Planning.* Actual preparation for the event includes gathering equipment and supplies, packing, and preparing other logistics. Sometimes this involves physical training.
3. *Participation.* The activity and the events surrounding it extend from departure to return. It is the core of the experience, the time of encounter with the resource and activity opportunities. It may be relatively short in time.
4. *Recollection.* After participation, an experience is not usually over. Participation is relived, through pictures, stories, and memories. At times, the experience develops new significance and gains embellishments during the recollection phase.

This temporal definition of recreational experience suggests that information, maps, and pictures are important parts of any experience. For many activities, equipment has become a major element in pre- and post-action phases. Some climbers and fishermen seem to get more satisfaction from their equipment than from the actual events.

LEOPOLD'S COMPONENTS OF RECREATION

A more normative description of the different types of outdoor recreation has come from Aldo Leopold (1966). He classified recreation into components or levels of experience. These are related to the effects of mass pursuit of the experiences on the environment and on the value of the experience. For some, mass pursuit has little effect on the environment but interferes with the quality of the experience. For others, activities include consumption of the resource base but may or may not be critically affected by the number of participants. Leopold's components follow.

Collection of physical objects.
Feeling of isolation in nature.
Fresh air and change of scene.
Perception of natural processes.
A sense of husbandry.

Several or all of these components can make up any single recreation experience. On a hunting trip, for example, a man seeks a trophy. He may also feel isolation in nature, perceive natural processes of animals and plants preparing for winter, and enjoy the fresh air and change of scene. He may also exercise his sense of husbandry by selecting his trophy animals with consideration for the future of the herd and by cleaning up a previously messy campsite. This classification deserves further comment and study.

Collection of physical objects may be described as a trophy-seeking type of recreation. It includes activities as basic as the re-creation of the survival hunt, with anything from hand capture to complex and expensive artillery and finely balanced fishing mechanisms. The trophy may be a fish, a deer, or a sea shell, but it may also be an abstraction, such as a photograph or other type of certificate. Seeking, capturing, and displaying the trophy all bring satisfactions to the user. With mass pursuit of consumptive activities, natural resources are depleted and artificiality increases. More use depletes natural game and fish populations. In response, states augment natural populations with hatchery-reared fish, imported incubated birds, and transplanted elk. Artificially imposed seasons and bag limits restrict and control trophy seekers so as to prevent mass resource depletions. Put-and-take shooting preserves and safarilands in the United States are extremes. Are souvenir shops the ultimate expression of artificiality in the pursuit of trophies? A photograph does not dilute the resource photographed, although activities associated with mass photography may destroy some part of the surroundings.

The feeling of isolation in nature may also be called solitude. In an urbanized society with a growing population, this appears to be of growing importance. Mass pursuit of solitude creates a problem: is there enough nature to go around? A scarcity of wild places where one might isolate himself from other men and their effects increases interest in the relatively few places left. Identification of such places, officially or unofficially, leads to increased demands for their use. Because solitude is a delicate thing, easily shattered, this component of the recreational experience is diluted or destroyed by mass pursuit. Restricted use of wild areas will be increasingly needed if this type of experience is to be available.

Recreation for fresh air and change of scene is one component that Leopold claims suffers little dilution from mass pursuit. People who wish to get out and around on foot, bicycle, automobile, or horse (Figure 3.4) do relatively little damage to the resource. The presence of other people would not affect this component of their experience. In extreme cases, overmobility can pollute the fresh air, obscure the scene, and cause erosion. Mass use of roads by observers of fall foliage makes enjoyment of the change of scene a safety hazard for drivers. Mass use of parks in Chicago, San Francisco, and New York by bands of young people escaping the monotony of the rest of the city has diluted the pleasure of a trip through the park for many other citizens. The overcrowding of parks results in

FIGURE 3.4 Fresh air and change of scene is often the goal of cyclists. This is Bombay Hook, Delaware.

unsightly areas and a lack of facilities that destroys the recreational experience for others.

Perception of natural processes is the component of recreation often derisively referred to as nature study. It is more than watching birds with binoculars. It is more than identifying spring wildflowers. It is the perceiving—the understanding—of the ways in which nature operates. The relatedness of all elements of the environment provides the key to perception. The rhythm of natural changes provides the beat. When man perceives the processes, he understands better the Creation and feels the refreshment of recreation in its deepest sense. There is no consumption of resources in this perception, even by large numbers of people. Mass perception involves no dilution of the experience by the individual. Indeed, it may heighten the experience by offering social reinforcement. Leopold (1966) suggests that perception of natural processes should be the focus of recreation management efforts: "To promote perception is the only truly creative part of recreational engineering. . . . All of the other acts we grace by that name are, at best, attempts to retard or mask the process of dilution."

Exercising a sense of husbandry is, to Leopold, the most satisfying component of the recreational experience. Its prerequisite is perception of natural processes. Its realization is to work for conservation of resources

FIGURE 3.5   Wilderness areas offer solitude in nature. (USFS)

with your hands. Mass pursuit of husbandry would maintain or enhance the resource base and would not dilute the individual experience. Again, enhancement of the experience may come from social reinforcement and from satisfaction of seeing rapid progress. Usually, however, husbandry is not a mass recreational pursuit but is delegated as work to professionals and laborers who manage recreation resources.

Table 3.1 summarizes these concepts.

Yet another approach is used for planning and analyses. The United States Forest Service defines recreation experiences in terms that give guid-

TABLE 3.1 Effects of mass pursuit of recreation components.

Component	Effect on resource	Effect on experience
Objects collection	Depletes and requires artificialization	Dilutes or destroys; becomes more artificial when available
Feeling of isolation	Reduces number of places of solitude	Dilutes or destroys; artificial controls required
Fresh air and change of scene	Relatively little consumption or damage, except in extremes of pollution and paving	Little dilution except in extreme cases
Perception	No consumption of resources	No dilution of experience
Husbandry	Maintains or enhances	No dilution; may improve

ance to the supplying of facilities. These classifications range from primitive to modern demands on the forest, described below (Bertolino, 1976).

Primitive: 1. Recreation opportunities to satisfy basic needs to a near maximum extent. High degree of basic outdoor skills are involved. Feeling of physical achievement at reaching opportunities without mechanized access is important to the user (Figure 3.6). Adventure and challenge are

FIGURE 3.6 Backpacking has experienced dramatic growth in participation, but even so less than 5 per cent of the population take part in this activity.

afforded through minimum controls. There is a high degree of opportunity for isolation and a feeling of being a part of nature.

2. Recreation opportunities to satisfy basic needs to a near maximum extent as tempered by motorized access. A feeling of achievement for reaching the opportunity through challenging motorized access is important. Few controls are evident to the user. Opportunities to socialize with others are important, although less so than would be true at more primitive experience levels.

Intermediate: 3. Recreation opportunities satisfy basic needs to an intermediate degree. Moderate degrees of outdoor skills are involved. Controls and regimentation afford a sense of security, although some taste of adventure is still important to the user. Opportunities to socialize with others are of about equal importance as isolation. There is a feeling of being close to nature.

4. Recreation opportunities to satisfy basic needs to only a moderate degree. A moderate degree of basic activity skills suffice. User seeks a sense of security. Regimentation and fairly obvious controls are important. User is aware of opportunity to meet and be with other people—is obviously not isolated. Opportunity exists to be gregarious within relatively small groups. Some opportunity to use contemporary skills such as snow and water skiing are important.

Modern: 5. Recreation opportunities to satisfy basic needs to a modest degree. Skills required for basic outdoor activities are minimal. Feeling of security is very important to the user. Learning or beginning skills suffice when supplemented by administrative controls. High degree of opportunity to be gregarious. Abundant opportunity to develop and use contemporary outdoor skills such as snow and water skiing. A feeling of being next to nature rather than closely associated with it.

Moral Unease

Americans have historically had a slight philosophical difficulty in enjoying leisure time. This stems partially from necessity and partially from social philosophy.

Early Americans faced many practical needs that precluded leisure time. The business of survival on an expanding frontier occupied most of a person's time and energies. Isolation in the relatively free winter months kept recreation confined to the home and nearby church.

The notion that play is evil is often attributed to the Puritans—the same people who invented holidays, bundling, and social dancing. Industry had a bigger role in promoting the work ethic.

The Industrial Revolution affected attitudes toward leisure. Whereas Aristotle taught that the use of free time in contemplation and citizenship activities was an important means toward self-fulfillment, idleness was detested in the industrial ethic. The Industrial Revolution flowered in the United States to its fullest form. No wonder, then, that the so-called work ethic reached its fullest manifestation in the philosophy of American workers.

Slowly, the concept of leisure as an evil is dying out. Now, Americans choose to enjoy leisure. However, work as a good and leisure as an evil still persists as a subdued attitude.

Leisure has become a reward. It is rest, respite, and recuperation. It is a period of recuperation to help man work better, but not yet an end in and of itself. There is a trend toward more of an equalization attitude—leisure balancing work. Leisure time is not strongly directed in the United States, but there are many organized activities that the child or adult with free time can pursue.

The contemporary religious attitude toward leisure and recreation is positive. The idea of ministry now includes the development of richness of life in leisure. Creative recreational involvement of people has great potential for total growth, socially and spiritually. The promotion of religious joy in creation can probably do more for personal development than restrictive dos and don'ts of moral law.

On February 8, 1965, President Lyndon Johnson gave the first Message to Congress on Natural Beauty. Diamond (1966) observed that "only a few years ago a message with a title like that would have been laughed off Capitol Hill." Attitudes and concerns change with time. President Nixon's energetic statements and actions to clean up the environment would have been unacceptable during the early and mid-1960s. In the early 1970s, popular opinion prevailed against opposition by some industries and municipalities to environmental quality improvements. A similar change of attitude toward recreation as a public concern has been developing. The use of leisure time in outdoor recreation is a long-accepted fact. Now the provision of tax monies for high-quality recreational experiences is a major effort of businesses and governments at all levels. It became a part of presidential politics in 1976, when both candidates emphasized the need for measures to improve the quality of recreation resources and opportunities.

Leisure counseling is a growing field of private and public service. Recreationists, no longer considered as idlers, are advised as to how best to use their leisure time. Even in recreation, people hesitate to try new things out of fear of looking ridiculous. Americans strive for success even in leisure. Fear of failure permeates even recreation experiences.

WORLD ETHIC

Among the perceptions of true civilization are awareness and sensitivity to life around us. One of the early ways people can become sensitized is through recreational experiences in natural surroundings.

Parks and forests are places that preserve the possibility of perspective:

Perspective of time: nature's time; our time, rhythms of life by which we can evaluate our own.

Perspective of space: how big are we?

Perspective of culture: what has our culture done to itself, to the resources we live upon, to us (Figure 3.7).

Parks, wilderness, and recreation give context to our lives, and context is indispensible for a life full of value.

INTENSITY OF EXPERIENCE

If we accept the premise that recreation is normative, i.e., that it aims at socially and individually constructive use of leisure, then we can accept the opportunity of providing activities that meet deep needs. Survival, exploration, and wars have, in the past, offered man intense physical and emotional experiences from first-hand involvement. Manhood and womanhood were tested against strong, obvious adversaries.

In recent times, even the exploration of the moon caused little physical or emotional strain to the well-conditioned astronauts. The challenges of earning a comfortable income and of supporting a family are dulled by general affluence. The ease with which certain goals are attained makes the goals seem trivial.

Desk jobs replace those requiring physical labor. Machines turn laborers

FIGURE 3.7   A sense of the past, its pace and its problems, enrich the understanding of young and old. (NPS)

The Visitors

into seated lever pullers. The power is greater, but human exertion is less. If youths and adults seek intense experiences, they usually have to find it in their leisure time.

Many persons are eager to take risks, but the opportunities are relatively few. Perhaps the possibility of unfettered risks is one of the most fundamental appeals of the wilderness.

The tendency is for recreation programs to follow the same path as the rest of society. The principle of offering activities that are achievable and therefore satisfying is too often translated into activities that are easy. Safe playgrounds are made unchallenging, in over-response to protective instincts. Children's camps are too often all-electric, have hot and cold running water, and sell ready-made craft projects which prevent any outbreaks of creativity and resourcefulness. With notable exceptions, family camping has lost its zip as it has broadened its constituency. With the new dominance of sleeping compartments on wheels, even the emotion of camping with imagined spiders and snakes is blunted.

Man's most intense encounters with himself have often been in the wilderness. The United States and Canada have preserved a few representative wilderness areas. Some states and counties have done the same. The emotional commitment of proponents of preservation of such areas is traceable to their intense and usually satisfactory experiences in such environments.

The exhilaration and self-fulfillment of reaching a mountaintop after an arduous climb are sought by many young people through drugs, sex, and beer. Why? Possibly because the mountain climb is neither available nor encouraged. Drugs are easier, quicker, and the taker cherishes the promise of gaining public attention, even if it is negative. Available wholesome, constructive alternatives may help reduce the efforts of many toward self-destruction.

GREGARIOUS RECREATION

Outdoor recreation experiences may be solitary in the wilds or social in the midst of cities. Gregarious activities involve the mass of people and add considerably to the quality of life of any community.

One form of gregarious recreation that is well understood in Latin countries is *social strolling*. It is peculiar to towns or cities and seems to have two requirements—a public place and a sizeable collection of people. In Latin America, it is usually the town square where people walk. By some common understanding, the walking begins at a certain hour regularly and ends at a reasonable time in the evening. It is popular with young people as a courting procedure and with older couples as a social event.

The practice is not limited to quaint villages. The Champs Elysées in Paris and the promenades in New York City's Central Park and in Brooklyn's Prospect Park are scenes of gregarious recreation, as described in this delightful passage by Frederick Law Olmsted (1871):

Purely gregarious recreation seems to be generally looked upon in New England society as childish and savage, because, I suppose, there is so little of what we call intellectual gratification in it. We are inclined to engage in it indirectly, furtively, and with complication. Yet there are certain forms of recreation, a large share of the attraction of which must, I think, lie in the gratification of the gregarious inclination, and which, with those who can afford to indulge in them, are so popular as to establish the importance of the requirement.

Consider that the New York Park and the Brooklyn Park are the only places in those associated cities where, in this eighteen hundred and seventieth year after Christ, you will find a body of Christians coming together, and with an evident glee in the prospect of coming together, all classes largely represented, with a common purpose, not at all intellectual, competitive with none, disposing to jealousy and spiritual or intellectual pride toward none, each individual adding by his mere presence to the pleasure of all others, all helping to the greater happiness of each. You may thus often see vast numbers of persons brought closely together, poor and rich, young and old, Jew and Catholic. I have seen a hundred thousand thus congregated, and I assure you that though there have been not a few that seemed a little dazed, as if they did not quite understand it, and were, perhaps, a little ashamed of it, I have looked studiously but vainly among them for a single face completely unsympathetic with the prevailing expression of good nature and light-heartedness.

Is it doubtful that it does men good to come together in this way in pure air and under the light of heaven, or that it must have an influence directly counteractive to that of the ordinary, hard, hustling working hours of town life?

You will agree with me, I am sure, that it is not, and that opportunity, convenient, attractive opportunity, for such congregation, is a very good thing to provide for, in planning the extension of a town.

Natural Resources as Part of the Experience

Enos Mills (1917) promoted the saving and use of scenery, declaring that "no nation has ever fallen for having too much scenery."

Parks of unusual scenic value do much to promote love of country. The inspiration received from visiting special places maintains morale. It instills appreciation of the selfless acts of previous generations. The fact that beautiful areas have been preserved does much to develop a confidence in mankind. Imagine the listlessness that a country of wholly functional, plowed fields, grazed pastures, and colorless cities would produce. A drab country can produce a drab people. A beautiful nation can help keep the human condition above that of the animals.

The 1909 Plan of Chicago called for natural scenery as an important ingredient of recreational experiences. It was noted that, even then, those who could afford and arrange it constantly sought refreshment in natural, rural scenery. The value is in the contrast of the natural with the works of man's hand. "He who habitually comes in close contact with nature develops saner methods of thought than can be the case when one is habitually shut up within the walls of a city" (Burnham and Bennett, 1909).

The outdoors has a tonic effect on the human spirit. In the USSR, "psychological relief rooms" have been set up in many factories, to reduce the grievances of workers. On their breaks, the laborers can relax, listen to music and bird songs, and watch landscape slides projected onto large screens. The rooms have colored lighting that changes in intensity while pleasant aromas fill the air. A scientist reported in *Pravda* that "after a session in these rooms, people feel refreshed and work at their jobs with renewed energy" (Knight, 1978).

In view of the importance of natural surroundings, the management of recreational resources becomes vital because of two factors. First, a wish to perpetuate the use of the recreational resources is assumed. This allows current use and future use. It involves keeping the wilderness wild and preventing consumption of the whole resource base. It is the philosophy of the forester to allow *sustained use* of recreational resources, in the long run. The second factor is that of *mass use*. No more is the occasional hiker or the lone huntsman using the forest and the range. Today, masses of people seek the out-of-doors for recreational activities of all sorts. Without management, *mass use* preempts *sustained use*, at least at anything near to the present level. A goal of the recreation resource manager in most agencies is to provide experiences on a sustained use basis.

Literature Cited

BERTOLINO, BART. 1976. Recreation site carrying capacity—Hoosier National Forest. In: Knudson, D. M., Managing Recreational Resources for Century III. West Lafayette, Indiana: Purdue University. pp. 77–80.

BURNHAM, DANIEL H. and EDWARD H. BENNETT. 1909. Plan of Chicago. Chicago: Commercial Club. 164 pp.

CLAWSON, MARION and JACK L. KNETSCH. 1966. Economics of Outdoor Recreation. Baltimore: Johns Hopkins Press. 328 pp.

DEGRAZIA, SEBASTIAN. 1962. Of Time, Work, and Leisure. New York: Twentieth Century Fund. 559 pp.

DIAMOND, HENRY L. 1966. The politics of beauty. Parks and Recreation 1(2):138–141, 154.

KNIGHT, ROBIN. 1978. Why workers want to flee U.S.S.R. U.S. News and World Report 84(21):57–58.

LEOPOLD, ALDO: 1966. Sand County Almanac. New York: Oxford University Press. 269 pp.

MILLS, ENOS A. 1917. Your National Parks. Boston: Houghton Mifflin. 532 pp.

OLMSTED, FREDERICK LAW. 1871. Public parks and the enlargement of towns. Journal of Social Science 2(3):1–36.

TOYNBEE, ARNOLD J. 1954. A Study of History, Volume 9. London: Oxford University Press. 759 pp.

C H A P T E R   4

Characteristics of Visitors

There is no clear method of measuring the value of a recreation experience except by circumstantial evidence. If visitors don't complain, if they speak enthusiastically, and if they come back, one assumes that they found the experience worthwhile. Recreation is a discretionary activity. If it does not seem worthwhile, the individual can choose to avoid the experience or to participate somewhere or somehow else.

By knowing more about the people they serve, recreation professionals should be better able to provide wanted activities. People will accept only things they want; therefore, activities must be offered for the public taste. Without public support, programs would fail. Because participation leads to success, outdoor recreation areas and programs are products of the people.

Who are the visitors, their backgrounds and experience?
Where do they come from?
How many are there? In what kinds of groups do they come?
What do they enjoy doing?
Why do they choose one spot and not another, one activity over another?

It is important that a recreation resource administrator understand the visitors to the property as well as those who don't come. To efficiently supply the appropriate recreational services and facilities and to reduce opportunities for friction, the professional can study the patron and the potential patron. It is helpful to comprehend their preference, their socioeconomic characteristics, their work situations, their probable desires for services, their attitudes toward a park and an agency's general policies, and their future demands on the resource (Figure 4.1).

Recreation suppliers have been particularly poor at understanding visitors, especially in government agencies. With growing demand, there has been a seller's market situation. Sometimes, heavy investments have been made in public facilities with subsequent low use. In most cases, however, supply has met with quick response from users who have little choice of alternative recreation areas. This phenomenon of latent demand finding an outlet is referred to frequently, but erroneously, as new supply creating

FIGURE 4.1 Women have participated increasingly in outdoor recreation, once considered primarily a masculine area of activity. (1897 watercolor, HCRS)

its own demand. The demand for something is there; by offering a place and program, the supplier appears to have created a demand.

Recreationists are affected by the environment. The forest, water, and desert have impacts on people. Also, people have impacts on the resources used for recreation.

The administrator must comprehend how his resources affect the visitor. How can he manipulate them to produce the greatest positive benefit to present and future generations? How can he avoid negative impacts on the visitors? He is in the pleasure business. People seek pleasure outdoors with some desire for freedom, as a contrast to regimented daily living. The administrator must find the level of control that produces the best net positive effect.

The corollary principle is that the visitor's impacts on the environment must be kept at a manageable level. Control of human behavior requires delicate and unobtrusive, yet effective, channeling of movements to confine impacts. Encouragement of responsible social and environmental behavior is the most important and most efficient tool of the recreation resource manager.

How do you know how people will respond? Why is one person an effective motivator of cooperation, while another incurs the wrath of his visitors?

Understanding the visitor, his desires, motivations, fears, sociological background, and experience in the outdoors is a helpful basic step. It is not the only factor. Meeting situations with appropriate action is the crux of management. To understand the visitor requires the perceptions available from sociology, psychology, communication, and/or plain, old common sense. The research literature is full of studies of visitors. Their attitudes, preferences, activities, reasons for visiting a place, their willingness to pay for opportunities, and their socioeconomic status have been recorded and analyzed by sociologists, economists, planners, and foresters (e.g., Clark, Hendee, and Campbell, 1971; LaPage, 1967; Lee, 1977; Cheek, Field, and Burdge, 1976; Taylor and Knudson, 1972; Lucas, 1964). Still, relatively little is known about visitors in many of the activities. General popularity of activities has been described in several nationwide studies related to national outdoor recreation plans and in many state outdoor recreation plans. These are somewhat variable in methodology, so generally do not provide data that can be compared over time or across states. Nevertheless, some useful concepts help to explain recreation use patterns and motivation.

Theoretical Bases

Scientists have proposed at least three theoretical approaches to explaining recreation visitor preferences and behavior. These approaches are not competitive; they explain different aspects of behavior. They are all tentative. The first is that participation can be predicted or explained by various socioeconomic characteristics of individuals. This approach has been widely used in making projections of use for national and state plans. A related concept, which is intuitively easy to accept but still not well analyzed, is that an individual's recreation preferences and behavior are a function of the social group (family, friends, club) with whom he participates. The third idea is that supply tends to influence demand; that is, participation patterns are a function of the available resources.

Clearly, all of these have validity if the test of common-sense reasoning is applied. Any complete theory of recreation behavior will contain elements of all three. A brief review of each follows. Only a few of the authors who have contributed to these views are mentioned.

1. SOCIOECONOMIC FACTORS

Since the ORRRC report (1962), the basic working theory of recreation demand studies has been related to participation. It suggests that outdoor recreation participation (kinds and quantity) is a function of a series of socioeconomic factors of the population in question. It took the following form in the 1973 nationwide outdoor recreation plan (Adams, Lewis, and Drake, 1973):

$$P = f(INC,ED,LOC,CENRG,AGE,RACE,$$
$$SEX,MARS,FAMSZ,HAND,D/W,VD)$$

The variables considered were

P = the probability that an individual will participate in various outdoor recreation activities
INC = family income
ED = educational level of the head of household
LOC = rural or urban resident
$CENRG$ = Census Region (Northeast, North Central, South, West) of residence
AGE = age of the individual
$RACE$ = white or nonwhite
SEX = sex of the individual
$MARS$ = marital status
$FAMSZ$ = size of the individual's family
$HAND$ = whether or not the individual is handicapped
D/W = number of days worked per week by the individual
VD = number of vacation days taken per year

As students of statistics will note, the development of the functional variables in this manner presents problems. Some of the independent variables are dichotomous (yes–no), whereas others are continuous. That limits the value of the probability statement, because no quantity of individual participation is determined in relation to quantities of other factors.

The results of these analyses in the ORRRC report in 1962 and in the 1973 Nationwide Outdoor Recreation Plan were inconclusive, except as general descriptive statements. Statistically, the variation in participation was not heavily related to the variation in the socioeconomic variables. Thus, socioeconomic variables, as measured, do not adequately explain the outdoor recreation participation patterns of people. Much of this is probably attributable to the manner of measurement of such variables and not to any lack of connection. Further work or more refined measurements and inferential analysis may help in making more reliable statements about socioeconomic variables as predictors of recreational behavior. Intuitively, one feels that the relationships seem to exist.

In many state plans, results of surveys of participation rely on the memory of people over the past year. Wisconsin and a few other states used a year-round telephone interview system that produced data on participation over the few preceding weeks. This difference in approach bears further examination. The latter system seemed to produce more detailed results at a higher cost. The basic problem has been the cost of conducting, analyzing, and testing results.

2. GROUP FACTORS

Another approach to comprehending the preferences and behavior of recreationists is to study the use pattern of social groups (O'Leary, Field, and Schreuder, 1974, and Burch, 1969). It suggests that family groups may choose different types and quantities of recreation than do groups of men, or teenagers, or individuals. Presumably, the experience, pressures, and characteristics of the group cause the individuals in it to behave in certain patterned ways that could be identified.

Cheek (1971) noted that the social group is the most common unit of participation among people who go to parks. Participation by social groups was compared to participation by individuals. Field and O'Leary (1973) subdivided social groups into friendship groups (peer groups), family units, and a combination of family and friends. The most frequent group appearing in western park and nonpark leisure places was the family unit. All of these social groups were rated as being more frequent visitors than the individual visitor. For those individuals who participate in outdoor recreation, swimming and walking were the main activities (ORRRC, 1962).

Other research indicating similar data distinguishes between the interaction units of "singles" and "withs," noting that recreational settings and events are often organized not on the basis of individuals but in terms of participating units (Goffman, 1971). Similar group units or teams expect to find other group units or teams participating in like activities in the area they visit.

A theory of recreational behavior could be predicated on the idea that groups of participants determine how the individual behaves. It may provide a broad distinction among expected behaviors. At least the property manager and programmer can use the concept to try to interpret and anticipate use patterns of people according to group phenomena. The development of a distinct workable theory of recreational behavior as a group phenomenon seems to require more thinking and substantiation with time-sequence data on use patterns and group dynamics.

3. Supply Influencing Demand

The third concept of supply affecting demand is hardly an academic theory, but more of a practical assumption that has been sensed rather than enunciated. Its importance has been profound as perhaps the dominant concept applied to recreational resource development. The phenomenon of latent demand finding an outlet is a real one. Almost any standard facility that is built or area designated has been used. By offering a place and a program, the suppliers appear to determine the preferences of consumers. Just why this occurs is not clearly understood, but it seems to be related to a large pent-up and growing desire for various kinds of recreation. New people entering the market are surely influenced in what they do by the resources and the opportunities that are available. The danger in this theory is that, presumably, the supplier can do no wrong. However, there are certainly some facilities that would be more used than others. Businessmen who enter the recreation field must study what activities and facilities are in greatest demand over the long run, or they may eventually be without customers.

Expressed Preferences

A 1933 study of 5,000 adults, mostly in eastern cities, revealed the activities in which they would most like to take part, if given the opportunity. These were, in order: tennis, swimming, boating, golf, and camping. Driving for pleasure (motoring) and ice skating were other favorites (Butler, 1937).

A similar study of 2,000 persons was conducted in 1977 for the American Forest Institute (Opinion Research Corporation, 1977). Respondents reported what they had participated in during the past 12 months, what they expected to do in the next 12 months, and which types of facilities they thought should be expanded (Table 4.1). The 1933 study indicated wishes, whereas the 1977 questionnaire dealt with reality, but the results are not far apart. The facilities most desired for expansion were picnic areas, campgrounds, bicycle trails, accessible hiking trails, beaches, and remote hiking and bridle trails. The last was by far the most desired by respondents aged 18 to 29.

Table 4.1 compares data from the Opinion Research Corporation and the 1972 survey done for the Nationwide Outdoor Recreation Plan (NORP). These two are not directly comparable, but the lesson from this presentation is that data must be used cautiously. Virtually every survey is different, so the data presented may be quite different. The NORP information concerned only a three-month summer period and involved about 4,000 interviewees. The 1977 study used estimates of participation by 2,000 persons over 12 months. The consistently higher participation rates of the 1977 study cannot be attributed to any one factor, such as changes in

FIGURE 4.2 Sightseeing is one of the most popular participation activities. (HCRS)

TABLE 4.1 Estimates of per cent of persons in the U.S. participating in outdoor recreation activities in two studies.

Activity	1977 (ORC) Participated last 12 months	1977 (ORC) Expected to participate next year	1973 (NORP) Participated in past summer
Driving for pleasure	58%	55%	34%
Walking for pleasure	56	52	34
Sightseeing	50	46	37
Swimming	43	40	*
Picnicking	42	39	47
Indoor sports	42	42	(not available)
Outdoor sports	41	38	22
Attend sports	38	39	12 (outdoor)
Fishing	32	32	24
Nature walks	27	28	17
Bicycling	26	27	10
Outdoor drama, concerts	22	24	7
Developed camping	20	21	11
Hiking, accessible trails	19	20 ⎫	
Hiking/backpacking on remote trails	10	11 ⎬	5
Mountain climbing	5	6 ⎭	
Tennis	17	19	5
Jogging	17	17	—
Canoeing/sailing/rowing	14	16	*
Power boating	14	13	*
Hunting	13	14	3
Remote camping	11	14	5
Golf	11	12	5
Motorcycle/trail bike riding	11	10	5
Ice skating	9	12	—
Sled/toboggan	9	11	—
Water skiing	8	9	—
Horseback riding: accessible trails	6	7 ⎫	
Horseback riding: remote trails	5	6 ⎭	5
4-wheel, off-road	6	6	2
Downhill skiing	5	8	—
Snowmobile racing	4	5	—
Rafting	3	4	—
Aerial activities	3	4	—
Cross-country skiing	2	3	—
None	8	9	—

* Swimming: 18% outdoor pools, and 34% other outdoor bodies of water.
Boating: 3% canoeing, 3% sailing, 15% other boating.
ORC: Opinion Research Corporation (1977).
NORP: Nationwide Outdoor Recreation Plan (Adams, Lewis, and Drake, 1973).

The Visitors

FIGURE 4.3 Sailing is an activity that has grown rapidly with the production of inexpensive rigs. (HCRS)

participation over time. Rather, the differences may be at least partly the result of the sample design and size and types of questions asked.

Participation patterns in specific activities seem to be influenced strongly by the region of the country in which one lives. There is more per capita participation in the northeastern part of the United States than in other regions in canoeing, sailing, swimming, and attending outdoor concerts and plays (Figure 4.3). This does not suggest that these are the most popular activities in the Northeast but, rather, that interest in them is considerably greater there than in the rest of the nation. In the North-Central area, the following activities are more favored than elsewhere: hunting, bird watching, horseback riding, golf, playing outdoor games and sports, attending sporting events, and picnicking.

In the South, the activities are fishing and water-skiing. In the West, residents are more likely to drive four-wheel-drive vehicles off the road, photograph birds and wildlife, and hike than are residents of other regions (Figure 4.4). The West also has the distinction of having the highest per capita rate of participation in total outdoor recreation (Adams, Lewis, and Drake, 1973). Interest in other activities such as camping is spread evenly over several regions (Figure 4.5).

FIGURE 4.4 Rock and mountain climbing are among the most glamorous recreation activities, pursued by fewer than 5 per cent of the population. (NPS)

URBAN USE PREFERENCES

One problem with many studies of users is that they are done on the spot in recreation areas—often the wilderness area of the researcher's choice. That can provide useful information to the manager but the sample should not be construed as a cross section of the public.

A study of urban residents' attitudes (National Park Service and Bureau of Outdoor Recreation, 1977) revealed a number of attitudes and life patterns that emphasized the need for more recreational facilities close to home. This reinforced the studies of the general public in the ORRRC report (1962), the NORP studies, and several state studies. Urban residents preferred small, close-to-home parks as the highest priority, even though they also appreciate large scenic areas. Both indoor and outdoor sports were considered among the most critical needs. Team sports, but not organized league teams, were preferred. Tennis and swimming facilities were also in high demand. Supervised play areas for children and separate facilities for senior citizens were considered desirable.

The Visitors

Figure 4.5 Visitors from Germany use commercial campgrounds and a Mercedes tour-camp bus for 20 people on a deluxe vacation.

In cities with significant water frontage, increased access to the river, lake, or ocean was strongly desired. Middle- and upper-income people asked for more specialized facilities such as equestrian centers and trails, marinas, and physical fitness trails. Low-income residents requested close-to-home places for social activities, along with traditional recreation. Programming and supervision were considered important, with provisions for quality equipment, good staff, maintenance, security, and safety.

Citizens and professionals in the park and recreation agencies of the 17 major urban complexes studied were virtually unanimous in their opinion that existing resources within the cities and counties were either marginally adequate or less than adequate.

Amenity Packages

Except for short-term, close-to-home activities, recreationists tend to participate in several activities at one time. For example, a family taking a boat to a large lake might identify boating as its primary objective. The whole activity package would be likely to include fishing, picnicking, swimming, and short hikes along the shore, as well as boating. Another group with a boat may also participate in water-skiing, picnicking, swimming, sightseeing at nearby attractions, and playing softball.

From a list of 17 recreational activities and facilities, campers in Indiana indicated their first, second, and third choices of other recreational activities in which they preferred to participate during camping trips (Green and Wadsworth, 1966).

TABLE 4.2 Activities complementing camping.

| Recreation activities | Number of campers indicating activity preferences | | | |
	First choice	Second choice	Third choice	Total
Swimming	252	112	51	415
Hiking	150	144	97	391
Fishing	82	105	89	276
Playground	12	53	54	119
Boating	12	40	51	103
All other activities	34	74	154	262

Source: (Green and Wadsworth, 1966).

Swimming is the most preferred activity, followed by fishing and boating. Playground facilities for children and hiking complete the five most preferred activities or facilities. The three water-based activities were first choice on 59 per cent of the replies.

Camping is a family activity, so playground facilities are highly desired. Hiking is popular because the skill level and special equipment requirements are low. The remaining activities had little preference and, unless tastes and preferences change, should not be included in the product mix until facilities for the first five activities are provided.

These data make it evident that even in a specialized group of campers there is no single amenity package that will satisfy all. The recreation facility planner and manager cannot meet all desires but can develop facilities that provide several activity opportunities of general popularity. Different packages are associated with different principal activities. Picnicking, for example, is often accompanied by field games and swimming. Providing such combinations or packages of opportunities is a key professional judgement that must be made.

Recreation and the Many Minorities

Should the kind of recreation offered by public and private groups be decided upon the basis of majority vote? Should only the mass recreation facilities be paid for out of taxes? If so, there would be no wilderness areas. There would be no bowling alleys either (only 20 per cent of Americans are bowlers). There might not be any theaters or cultural centers. There might be a few city parks left, but no scenic rivers, hiking trails, bicycle trails, or state parks.

The studies of activities over the years reveal that the public has diverse interests. There are few, if any, outdoor recreation activities participated in by the majority of the population in any one year, according to surveys.

Yet, most people participate in some form or another of recreation (Opinion Research Corporation, 1977), although most surveys do not report nonparticipation figures.

In providing any recreational activity, an agency or business is serving a minority of the public. The majority may object that only kooks or crazies would participate in hiking, camping, or jogging and only kids would ride bikes or play softball. If public officials listen only to what the majority wants, there would be no recreational facilities. An often-heard argument is that a particular proposal for recreation land will serve only an "elite" group. As can be seen from figures on use patterns, only a small percentage (if that can be called elite) will use some of the nation's most common facilities: golf courses, boating lakes, water-skiing areas, hunting areas, tennis courts, skating rinks, and ski slopes. It should be noted, however, that 5 per cent of a population of 225 million is more than 11 million people. Five per cent of a county of 100,000 is 5,000 individuals, many of whom participate often. Thus, businesses and public agencies serve large numbers of participants in most recreational activities.

As has been the policy over the years, providing a number of different opportunities is desirable to meet the varying preferences and capabilities.

How are decisions made? The land manager must allocate public lands for different recreation experiences. He must resolve issues that are not resolved definitively by society at the voting booth or by representatives in the legislature.

One of the problems is to balance the quantitative demands of majorities or large minorities with the qualitative demands of minorities without treating either unfairly. It seems quite logical that purely democratic voting standards may not be appropriate criteria for decision making about recreational use of all lands. If they were, there would be a minimum of diversity and a narrow range of opportunities. Recreation would be reduced to the provision of the lowest common denominator of facilities.

On the other hand, if public agencies listen only to the needs of a few powerful people, a disservice can result by offering inadequate diversity. Democracy is served by providing a diversity of opportunities.

Applications of Research Findings

Using data from numerous studies, some conflicting, the professional must apply some common sense. What is known about most recreationists?

First, as an oversimplification, consider an average camper, even though it can be proven that there is no "average camper." There are obvious variations around the mean plus a danger of saying the average is a stereotype, but repeated studies show that a large share of male campers have common characteristics. They are:

Caucasians.

Urban residents.

Sedentary during most of the year.

Fairly prosperous (middle to upper income).

Well educated, but may be uninformed about the outdoors.

In their own cars.

Pulling a wheeled vehicle for sleeping (two thirds to three quarters of campers).

On vacation or a long weekend trip.

With their families.

Looking for water for swimming, boating, fishing, watching.

Looking for friendly people.

Expecting service and needing leadership.

Seeking a deep, satisfying experience.

Searching for creative activity.

Campers are the most frequently studied recreationists, partly because they stay in one place for a long time. Data on other types of participants are not so well defined. In general, users of rural parks have many of these same characteristics—white, middle-class, urban families seeking a different type of experience. Most come from within 200 to 400 kilometers (125 to 250 miles).

USE PATTERN

A study in London of city park users revealed that two thirds of the visits were to large parks of more than 20 ha (50 acres). Eighty-six per cent of the visitors participated in passive activities such as walking and sitting. Twelve per cent of the adults interviewed came primarily for children's activities, 6 per cent participated in various sports, and 3 per cent came for entertainment. Visitors considered the scenery and quietness of the parks to be the most important elements. Half of them wanted facilities for children in the parks (Whitaker and Browne, 1971).

DISORIENTATION

Use patterns are often disrupted and pleasure is impossible for people who cannot enjoy an area because they do not feel at home. Many American people do not know how to enjoy themselves out-of-doors. They have no roots—no sense of kinship with the land. They are relative strangers in a wild or semiwild environment. They are incurious. They are apathetic. They don't care about scenic beauty or about the birds and the bees. Or they are literally afraid. What little knowledge they have about things in nature is colored by misinformation and distorted by fear. Adult counselors in a day camp have been afraid to sit on the ground because of ants! They go for fun and adventure. It is more important to know why many citizens have no active interest in the birds and the bees and little or no respect for public property than it is to know what they like, what they want to do, and how to satisfy them.

The answer relates to people being out of their element. An urban ghetto child may be completely at home and fearless in the bewildering jungle of the city. He comprehends the order of things, what he can do, and what to avoid. He has many people with whom he interacts. People and their work dominate the scene. Pimps and thieves may be his heroes. Basketball and street games may be his major outdoor recreation—all very structured. Suddenly he is transported to a place with trees, water, and grass, little structure and rumors of snakes, bears, and Indians. Man's works seem inconsequential here. His role models and his world of order is not here. No wonder he is afraid. It takes a while to sort out the natural world. Gray (1969) summarized this problem:

There is a growing recognition of the fact that people are unequal in their need for community-supported recreation services. It requires substantially more effort to get results in a culturally-deprived area of the city than it does elsewhere.

SUMMARY

To properly serve the public, the recreation resource manager needs information about the life-styles, habits, and characteristics of the public that uses recreation facilities. Not everyone is interested in the same activities and not everyone participates with the same people. A number of studies have offered systematic characterizations of outdoor recreation participants. Each study has its limited scope and special conditions, but together they provide some general concepts.

People tend to participate in groups, mostly families. The group seems to affect their patterns of recreation. Analysis of group preferences, needs, and activity package choices can guide the land manager and program supervisor in planning future facilities and programs.

There are also certain characteristics of broad social classes of people that can allow the planner to anticipate relative needs for quantities and types of recreation.

People often need orientation. They also may genuinely desire opportunities that resource suppliers have not perceived. Attention to the visitors, their behavior, and characteristics is an important strategy for efficient land management. The land is to be managed for people's use.

Literature Cited

ADAMS, ROBERT L., ROBERT C. LEWIS and BRUCE H. DRAKE. 1973. Outdoor Recreation; a Legacy for America: Appendix "A"—An economic analysis. Washington: U.S. Dept. of the Interior, Office of Economic Analysis. 239 pp. + appendices.

BURCH, WILLIAM R., JR. 1969. The social circles of leisure: competing explanations. Journal of Leisure Research 1(2):125–147.

Bureau of Outdoor Recreation. 1973. Outdoor Recreation; a Legacy for America. Washington, D.C.: U.S. Dept. of the Interior. 89 pp.

BUTLER, GEORGE D. 1937. Municipal and County Parks in the United States, 1935. Washington, D.C.: U.S. Dept. of the Interior, National Park Service. 147 pp.

CHEEK, NEIL H., JR. 1971. Intragroup social structure and social solidarity in park settings. In: Research in the Parks; Transactions of the National Park Centennial Symposium (Annual meeting of the American Assoc. for the Advancement of Science). U.S. Dept. of the Interior, N.P.S. Symposium Series, No. 1 (1976): pp. 139–147.

CHEEK, N. H., JR., D. R. FIELD and R. J. BURDGE. 1976. Leisure and Recreation Places. Ann Arbor: Ann Arbor Science Publishers. 172 pp.

CLARK, ROGER N., JOHN C. HENDEE and FREDERICK L. CAMPBELL. 1971. Values, behavior, and conflict in modern camping culture. Journal of Leisure Research 3(3):143–159.

FIELD, DONALD R. and JOSEPH T. O'LEARY. 1973. Social groups as a basis for assessing participation in selected water activities. Journal of Leisure Research 5 (Spring):16–25.

GOFFMAN, ERVING. 1971. Relations in Public; Microstudies of the Public Order. New York: Basic Books. 396 pp.

GRAY, DAVID E. 1969. The case for compensatory recreation. Parks and Recreation 4(4):23–24, 48–49.

GREEN, BERNAL L. and H. A. WADSWORTH. 1966. Campers; What Affects Participation and What Do They Want? West Lafayette, Ind.: Purdue Univ., Agric. Exp. Sta., Research Bulletin No. 823. 23 pp.

LAPAGE, WILBUR F. 1967. Camper Characteristics Differ at Public and Commercial Campgrounds in New England. Upper Darby, Pa.: U.S. Forest Service Research Note NE-59. 8 pp.

LEE, ROBERT G. 1977. Alone with others: the paradox of privacy in wilderness. Leisure Sciences 1(1):3–19.

LUCAS, ROBERT C. 1964. The Recreational Use of the Quetico–Superior Area. St. Paul: U.S. Forest Service Research Paper LS-8. 50 pp.

National Park Service and Bureau of Outdoor Recreation. 1977. National Urban Recreation Study; Technical Reports, Volume 1. Urban Open Space, Existing Conditions, Opportunities and Issues. Washington, D.C.: U.S. Dept. of the Interior. var. pag.

O'LEARY, JOSEPH T., D. R. FIELD, and G. SCHREUDER. 1974. Social groups and water activity clusters: an exploration of interchangeability and substitution. In: Field, D. R., J. C. Barron and B. L. Long (eds), Water and Community Development. Ann Arbor, Michigan: Ann Arbor Science Publishers. pp. 195–215.

Opinion Research Corporation. 1977. Public Participation in Outdoor Activities and Attitudes Toward Wilderness—1977. Washington, D.C.: American Forest Institute, Research Recap No. 10. 4 pp.

Outdoor Recreation Resources Review Commission. 1962. Outdoor Recreation for America. Washington, D.C. 246 pp.

TAYLOR, CHARLES E. and DOUGLAS M. KNUDSON. 1972. The Camper in Indiana State-Operated Campgrounds. W. Lafayette: Purdue Univ., Ag. Exp. Sta. Research Bulletin No. 888. 11 pp.

WHITAKER, BEN and KENNETH BROWNE. 1971. Parks for People. London: Seeley, Service & Co. 144 pp.

The Visitors

Social and Economic Foundations

Subsistence Success

For centuries the mass of mankind has focused its energies on subsistence. Food, shelter, and clothing still are in short supply for two thirds of humanity. Many of the remaining one third seem to be concerned about subsistence, although survival is not as critical to them as is quality and the prestige it can bring them. Bigger houses, better and more varied clothing, higher-priced food, and an automobile are among the major objectives of families who are striving to improve their scale of living. The quality of life is thus expressed in terms of "better" essentials.

One might well ask what else there is to this earthly existence. The existential question to some must be "after survival, then what?" Or is man so easily fulfilled? Is he so unimaginative?

Of course not. The struggle to survive does not really lock us into an existence without play, recreation, or relaxation. Even people who live on the margin of an economy find time for personal expression, for religion, and for cultural participation. They always have, except in the most desperate events. Traditions of games and sports have been passed down, reshaped, and sometimes commercialized. Their origins are often in ancient societies, which long ago developed a balance between leisure time, work time, religious time, and subsistence time.

Recreation is not foreign amidst the realities of the world. It is integral to life. Constructive use of leisure is part of the continuum of life's concerns and basic desires.

Subsistence is the first essential of life—a prerequisite. While subsistence is being achieved and this lowest threshold is routinely overcome, the development of the human condition and spirit becomes vital. Without such development and enrichment, subsistence becomes fruitless.

The quality that parks and recreation bring to human life is not confined to those societies or people who have achieved a certain level of prosperity. Recreation is not a postindustrialization phenomenon. It is an enrichment

FIGURE 5.1 (following pages) Grand Canyon is one of the leading tourist attractions for both American and foreign visitors. (Union Pacific Railroad)

of all lives. Although some planner or government official may assign low priority to public recreation spending, the people will find recreation, regardless. The official who refuses to spend public monies to provide recreation spaces until some other economic priorities are reached is impoverishing the quality of life of the people.

This is not to argue that recreation spaces do not increase as personal and national income rise. Recreation desires usually do not command the urgency of sharp hunger pangs. The point is that recreation is an integral part of life at all levels of prosperity.

Social Development and Recreation

Primitive man, so-called by presumably civilized people, enjoys work and leisure with little worry about the differentiation between them. His survival duties may be blended with his pleasure duties, if indeed there is such a distinction. Anthropologists suggest that providing food, shelter, and clothing requires an average of 6 hours per day for man and woman alike in many primitive societies. The time differs with the seasons and the weather. The rest of the time is dedicated to games, harvest festivals, seeking the goodwill of superior beings or symbols, and enhancing clothing, weapons, and tools with artistic decoration. Superstition and fear enter into a great part of life, restricting and guiding activities and exploration. Whether long trips are considered work, adventure, or fun is difficult to verify, but travel has played a part in most civilizations. Contact with other cultures and places has been a prime motivator in the changes of all civilizations.

In preindustrial agrarian societies, play was also an integral part of life. Daily work was often less structured than today. Work was arduous and the hours were long, but there were many festivals and holidays. Today, we enjoy many of these—Brazil's Carnival and New Orleans' Mardi Gras, Thanksgiving, Halloween, and many religious observances, all descendants of religious or agrarian festivals. They usually combine survival, celebration, and social gatherings, so they are much more than simple respites from labor.

In industrial society, time became important to work. "Time is money" became true because the worker had to tend the machine or the process constantly. The longer the machines and the assembly line were operating, the more goods were produced and the greater the potential for profit. Disattention from work and leaving the machines unattended resulted in wasted production opportunities. This rationalization of work resulted in the defamation of leisure as idleness. Play was considered counterproductive. In societies trying out new methods of increasing productivity, idleness almost became equated with evil. In the early part of the twentieth century, a few industrial employers discovered that some recreational activity was good for morale and loyalty to the company, so they promoted certain activities—but to increase productivity.

Contemporary man can produce goods and profits more rapidly than they can be consumed. He has free time. He still has an ethical outlook that elevates work and looks down on free time. The work ethic requires that a man seek ways to use his free time constructively, not idly.

The social economy has developed so that now man is relatively free from servitude to the industrial machine. At least, there are ample opportunities for leisure pursuits. This freedom stems from the technologically based ability to produce food with little labor—one man can produce enough to feed about 50 people. The nation has a large capital structure so that much of the capital-based work is on a maintenance and replacement basis. This releases large numbers of workers to produce consumer goods, to provide services, and to work in related businesses. Assembly-line technology and automation have released human energies from work.

As a result of these and other developments, the nation has changed from a 12-hour day for six or seven days per week, with little or no vacation, to the legal maximum of an eight-hour day for five days, with vacations of at least two weeks for nearly all workers. This maximum has been reduced by labor contracts for seven-hour days, four-day weeks, and steadily increasing vacations.

The recent and current situation in the industrial world might be partially characterized by the following assumptions.

1. The work ethic is too rigid an attitude, as a result of increased productivity. Technological progress has outstripped sociological mores, producing guilt feelings about seemingly unproductive free-time pursuits.
2. Few people are educated to use free time constructively. Many tend to use it in unpurposeful ways and even in activities that are detrimental to the individual or to society.
3. Many assembly-line and automated jobs require little physical effort, mental challenge, or comprehensive thinking. Pride of craftsmanship and personal identity with products are virtually lost to many workers. These losses must be replaced by constructive accomplishments in free time if individual and social health are to be maintained.
4. Man is a physical animal and requires exercise to keep his body in tone and to maintain protective and survival abilities. Most jobs do not offer opportunities for adequate physical exercise.
5. The crowded conditions of city life and the stress of modern living produce tensions and mental problems. The manner in which free time is used either accentuates or relieves the problems. Yet, the major portion of the population is concentrated in crowded and growing urban situations with little room for expansive recreation places.

Population

Sheer numbers of people affect the amount of recreation participation. Growth in population in the United States has been one of the factors accompanying recreation development.

Several indicators are used to predict population trends. The Census Bureau provides many of these on a nationwide and a sectional basis. Data are also reported for the 281 Standard Metropolitan Statistical Areas that include the largest cities of the nation.

One key factor is the fertility rate. It is an indication of the number of people to be served in the next generation. In December, 1972, the Census Bureau reported that the nation's fertility rate was at a new low— just over two births per woman (2.05). The previous low was 2.19 in 1936. The modern high was 3.77 in 1957. Since 1972, the rate continued to drop to 1.79 in 1975, then leveled off, and fluctuated slightly. Net population increases will now slow noticeably in the years ahead, until increases may almost stop (near-zero population growth).

If this proves to be a long-term trend, the recreation professional should expect the following consequences:

An older population.
A shift in public spending, with less to schools and more to health care, pensions, and social ills of cities.
Continued growth in firms providing services and luxury goods.

If fertility rates stay at two children per woman, there would be major shifts in the age mix of the nation. Table 5.1 shows how this would change proportionately by the year 2000.

All age classes will increase over the next quarter-century. However, large increases will be in the middle and upper age brackets. The population distribution among ages will see major changes in the young, whose relative proportion will decrease by seven per cent, and the 35–49-year bracket, which will be six per cent more important than at present.

TABLE 5.1   Population projections by age class proportion at 2.00 fertility rate.

	Total	0–19	20–34	35–49	50–64	65+
1972 population (millions)	209	76.8	45.6	34.8	30.7	20.9
Percentage	100%	37%	22%	17%	14%	10%
2000 population (millions)	264	80.7	54.9	60.9	39.1	28.8
Percentage	100%	30%	21%	23%	15%	11%
Percentage change		+ 5%	+20%	+75%	+27%	+38%

The Visitors

TABLE 5.2 Number of households.	1964	56 million households
	1974	70 million households
	1984 (est.)	86 million households

Source: U.S. News & World Report, Feb. 25, 1974.

To the park planner and administrator, this would mean that programs and facilities for the future should be designed for better service to the people in their middle years. Their desires and preferences should be studied with sensitivity. If they are not being served at the present time, the reasons and remedies should be carefully studied.

Another facet of population is the number of households. Much recreation is based on family participation. A rather startling upsurge in households is now occurring (Table 5.2).

These facts are more meaningful to the recreation planner than are pure population figures. The Bureau of the Census and the popular press provide numerous analyses of various aspects of population.

In some cases, population data may be adequate for planning purposes for the short run. Some state plans have assumed that participation rates and patterns will remain virtually the same on a per capita basis over five-year periods. Therefore, projections of participation have been based on projected changes in population of a state or a region of a state. This approach requires only that current participation rates in various activities be calculated and expected population changes estimated (Bureau of the Census data). Then per capita participation is multiplied by expected population to yield a participation estimate five years hence. This method has appeal because of its simplicity. Just as other methods, it cannot predict innovations. As in most other methods, it does not use trends from past points in time. Its cost is low; its statistical sophistication is low; the method's results may be just as good as those of other estimates with greater apparent validity or sophistication.

Analysis of population data and trends is a basic tool of parks and recreation professionals. Use of census statistical data should be practiced until one is proficient at interpreting the myriad of tables.

Urbanization

Large movements of people to the cities began after the Civil War. In the space of one century, the nation changed from predominantly rural to urban. A nation that had 92 per cent farmers when it was established in 1776 is now more than 92 per cent nonfarmers (Table 5.3).

In the years since World War II, suburban sprawl has been the characteristic feature of urban growth (Figure 5.2). The sprawl was associated with availability of family automobiles, cheap energy, and unprecedented,

TABLE 5.3 Population in cities and towns of the United States.

Census year	Per cent of total population in cities	Number in cities	Total population
1790 (first census)	5.1	202,000	3,929,000
1870	25.7	9,902,000	38,558,000
1970	73.5	149,325,000	203,212,000

Source: Bureau of the Census, 1977.

widespread economic prosperity. Historical and natural resources around growing cities rapidly disappeared, with little concern by the citizens or the developers, both of whom were usually unfamiliar with the areas in which they were moving.

Americans, especially urban Americans, are threatened with anonymity and rootlessness. For thousands of years, children have retraced the steps

FIGURE 5.2 Suburban sprawl eats up rural land as central cities lose their affluent residents.

The Visitors

of their parents. They were initiated into stable ways and ritualized routines. They maintained a basic familiarity with place and family. Today, in an urban, mobile society, there is not only a radical rupture with the past but a trauma of preparation for an unknown future. This is not just a defining characteristic of today's society; it is a principal root of its disorientations.

About 75 per cent of the nation's people live in cities larger than 50,000 (or metropolitan areas of them). Approximately two thirds of the population live on less than 2 per cent of the nation's land. Until 1970, the trend was toward greater urbanization. People were leaving the country and going to the city. Many rural counties and small towns were losing population at alarming rates. Young people were getting their public school educations at the expense of country taxpayers, but were then moving to metropolitan centers during their productive, taxpaying years. This meant that smaller counties and cities were faced with less tax revenue to use for education, recreation, roads, and other amenities of life.

The period after 1970 was one of turnaround. From 1970 to 1975, population in non-metropolitan areas grew faster than in the cities and suburbs. While the national population increased 4.8 per cent, metropolitan areas grew at 4.1 per cent and rural areas increased at a 6.6 per cent rate (Slowdown for "strip cities," 1977). Rural communities lost a net of three million people during the 1960s. In the first half of the 1970s, there was a net gain of 1,840,000. At the same time, the proportion of the population living in the 23 largest metropolitan regions dropped slightly, from 72.7 per cent to 72.3 per cent. These one-million-plus urban areas still accounted for 65 per cent of the nation's total population increase in actual numbers of people.

The new rural residents are not evenly scattered about the country. Many are employed in the metropolitan areas but choose to live in nearby rural counties, some of which are becoming urbanized. This leaves many of the remote counties with the same problems (and blessings) from net out-migration as existed previously. Continuation of the new trend back to rural areas may be temporary and dependent upon low-cost commuting. The growth dip of the 1970s was associated with an employment slump in manufacturing enterprises. The picture may change with economic improvement, allowing urban area growth to resume its predominant role.

DEFINITION

There are several interpretations of what an urban area is. An *urban area* is defined by the Census Bureau as any community with a population of 2,500 or more. About 70 per cent of the nation's population lives in urban places of that definition. Many of the places do not fit the normal image of urban areas; with a rural atmosphere and populations of a few thousand people, they contrast sharply in character and problems with major metropolises.

The Census Bureau also identifies *urbanized areas*, which include at least one central city of over 25,000 population and the surrounding closely inhabited territory. These more closely fit the average citizen's concept of what urban means. About 60 per cent of the nation's population lives in such urbanized areas.

A third category of urbanization is defined as the *Standard Metropolitan Statistical Area* (SMSA). It includes an integrated economic and social unit with a large population nucleus. The *central city* or its equivalent must have a population of at least 50,000. It can be a city of 25,000 plus neighboring city-like, heavily populated areas with a combined population of 50,000 in a single economic-social community. The SMSA always includes the county in which the central city is located plus adjacent counties that are metropolitan in character and economically and socially integrated. This definition includes much rural land. The SMSA is the most commonly used term of reference for many purposes. About two thirds of the nation's population lives in the 281 SMSAs.

Still another level of identification of urban concentration are the *Standard Consolidated Statistical Areas*. Each one is comprised of two or more SMSAs which have a high degree of geographic integration and intermovement. They include several central cities and the adjoining counties. There are 13 such centers, as listed in Table 5.4.

The term *urban* thus includes collections of people with as few as 2,500 inhabitants and as many as 7.5 million. The Standard Metropolitan Statistical Areas vary from cities of 50,000 to 10,000,000, perhaps approximating what most people would conceive of as urban.

Among writers about demography and land use, the informal term *megalopolis* provides an even larger-scale definition of urbanization. Huge urban conglomerations are formed from the growing together of city and suburbs joining with adjacent suburb and city (Figure 5.3). Each of these groupings is called a megalopolis. These are roughly outlined, connected

Name	Population
Boston–Lawrence–Lowell	3,500,000
Chicago–Gary	7,600,000
Cincinnati–Hamilton	1,600,000
Cleveland–Akron–Lorain	3,000,000
Detroit–Ann Arbor	4,700,000
Houston–Galveston	2,200,000
Los Angeles–Long Beach–Anaheim	10,000,000
Miami–Fort Lauderdale	1,900,000
Milwaukee–Racine	1,600,000
New York–Newark–Jersey City	17,000,000
Philadelphia–Wilmington–Trenton	5,600,000
San Francisco–Oakland–San Jose	4,500,000
Seattle–Tacoma	1,800,000

TABLE 5.4 Standard consolidated statistical areas of the United States.

The Visitors

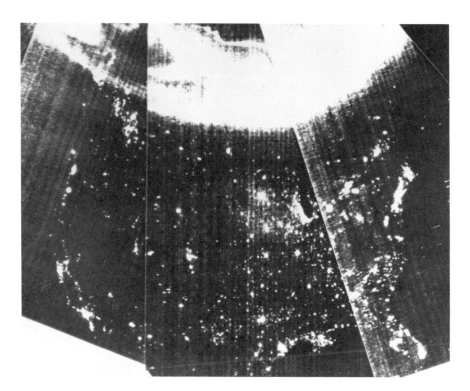

FIGURE 5.3 A composite of satellite pictures of the United States at night. The lights produced by all urban centers can be clearly seen, accentuating the interconnection of metropolitan complexes. (U.S. Air Force)

metropolitan strips that have been spreading over the countryside for years. About 23 strip megalopolises have been identified in the United States. Almost three quarters of the nation's population inhabits these massive, urban conglomerates. The largest can be called Bowash, stretching from southern Maine to the North Carolina border. The first four are so sweeping in their extent and so complex in their political jurisdictions that no one would consider them as rational units. The largest major populated strips are listed (Table 5.5) with their estimated 1975 populations.

There is an apparent relationship between the concentration of people into urban areas and their need for recreation places. In the early years of this century, when 70 to 75 per cent of this nation's population was rural, the need for public parks and recreation programs was not so evident. Most people had their own lands, creeks, trees, and swings for leisure-time pursuits. They were in daily contact with the open air, the opportunity to work physically, and the variety of the seasons. Much of the population was pursuing the goal of fulfillment of individual personal dreams on personal property.

In the rush to the cities, there has been increasing need for alternative

TABLE 5.5 Megalopolis areas in the United States.

1. Bowash	Atlantic Seaboard—12 states & D.C.
	Boston, New York, Philadelphia, Washington, Richmond
	64,000 sq. mi. 46.6 million people
2. Mid-America	Lower Great Lakes—Green Bay to Syracuse
	96,000 sq. mi. 39.8 million people
3. Pacific	California—Sacramento to San Diego
	20.5 million people
4. Sunland	Florida—Jacksonville, Tampa, Miami
	7.2 million people
5. Piedmont	North Carolina, South Carolina
	Raleigh, Charlotte, Greensboro, Greenville
	4.3 million people
6. Western Gulf Coast	Texas—Houston to Galveston
	3.0 million people
7. Eastern Gulf Coast	New Orleans to Mobile
	2.9 million people
8. Mid-Texas	Dallas to San Antonio
	2.9 million people
9. Central Dixie	Atlanta to Chattanooga
	2.8 million people
10. Twin Cities	Central Minnesota
	2.5 million people
11. St. Louis	Missouri, Illinois
	2.4 million people
12. Puget Sound	Western Washington
	2.2 million people

Urban area definition by Jerome Pickard, Appalachian Regional Commission for *U.S. News & World Report* (Slowdown for "strip cities," 1977).

expressions of the human spirit (Figure 5.4). Sigurd Olson (1973) described the need philosophically:

We look at the slums, at the never-ending traffic, the shrinking space and growing ugliness, and are appalled. Is this the great American dream?

. . . Somehow, someway, we must make contact with naturalness, the source of all life. The frontiers are still too close to forget . . . Civilization has not changed emotional needs which were ours long before it arose.

Ecological studies of cities reveal that maladjustments (insanity, property crimes, juvenile delinquency) occur more in urban than in rural areas. The highest incidence of maladjustment occurs in blighted areas. Maladjusted behavior is reflected from generation to generation in blighted areas, irrespective of different ethnic and racial groups that migrate into and out of them. This may suggest that there is some relationship of place with behavior. Does the place help produce the behavior? Until the factors involved in such circumstantial evidence are clearer, there is no obvious conclusion, despite a plethora of sociological hypotheses. It is clear that in many parts of blighted urban areas the social fabric has disintegrated.

Figure 5.4   A return to
nature and simple activities is
highlighted by the rapidly
growing popularity of Nordic
skiing. (Mary Vanderford)

In the 1970s, America's cities found themselves in difficult financial
straits. Somehow, Canada's metropolitan areas have done better. In both
countries, recreation services face numerous financial obstacles as well as
the sociological problems of serving the interests of diverse populations.
Careful monitoring of the problems and the opportunities for improving
the situation is one of the principal duties of the administrator of urban
recreation services.

Occupation Factors

Occupations in the U.S. are tending toward the white-collar jobs, which
now comprise about half of all jobs (Table 5.6). American economic activity
is becoming increasingly characterized as tertiary or service-oriented.

TABLE 5.6   Occupation groups as proportions of all employed persons in the United States.

| Occupation | Proportion of the work force by year | | | |
	1960	1965	1970	1977
White-collar workers	42.8%	44.8%	48.3%	50.2%
Blue-collar workers	36.1	36.9	35.3	33.1
Service workers	13.3	12.6	12.4	13.7
Farm workers	7.8	5.7	4.0	3.0
	100	100	100	100
Total workers (thousands)	66,678	71,088	78,627	89,258

Data source: Bureau of the Census, 1977.

Primary economies employ most of their workers in hunting, gathering, and agricultural activities, conditions long since past in the United States and Canada. *Secondary* societies are much more interdependent. Workers specialize in producing individualized items, depending upon other people (seconds) to produce other things they need. In a *tertiary* economy, few laborers are needed to produce things, as cybernetic systems allow mechanical and electronic devices to control many productive functions. Automation in agriculture and in industry results in the employment of the greatest proportion of the population in service or supervisory occupations.

Two characteristics of occupations appear to be important to outdoor recreation. The first is a general challenge to the leisure services sector of society. The second is related to empirical data that suggest different patterns of recreation are associated with different occupational classes.

The challenge arises from the nature of much of today's work. Although the work place is pleasant, the job is physically easy, and the pay and benefits are good, many jobs lack challenge. They fail to stimulate the individual's sense of craftsmanship or feeling of accomplishment. The assembly-line process that proved so efficient took away the autonomy of the individual, giving him dull, repetitive, seemingly meaningless tasks. Specialization of functions has spread into all types of work, producing discontent among workers at many occupational levels. This very situation has created many exciting opportunities and new freedoms, but most of these are available during leisure time. The great challenge is to construct a worthwhile civilization centered around leisure rather than around work.

From the study of recreation data, researchers have tentatively identified activity patterns that can be useful to the creative resource manager. People who have been found to be more active participants in recreation activities are usually in higher- or middle-income brackets, young age categories, high education levels, and have paid vacations.

Burdge (1969) hypothesized that these factors could be measured in simplified terms of occupational prestige. He notes that specific forms of recreation were common to persons in the highest or lowest occupational prestige levels. Generally associated with Level IV, the lowest prestige level (unskilled workers), were activities such as watching television, fishing, playing poker, attending drive-in movies, spending time in a tavern, and attending parties. Level I, the top of the occupational prestige ladder (professional and high-level management), included people who attended concerts, played bridge, read books, and worked in a flower garden. Golf was the most common activity for skilled workers (Level III), and white-collar workers (Level II) favored attending football games, weekend trips, and social gatherings. People in Levels III and IV had no other characteristic outdoor recreation activities. Level I persons participated heavily in winter sports, most water-related activities, and nature walks. Prestige Level II persons tended to enjoy fishing, hunting, bicycling, horseback riding, canoeing, boating, and hiking. Picnicking was the one activity that was about equally popular with all four groups.

The phenomenon of higher income and education groups being heavily represented as recreation participants is most marked in national forests and parks and wildlife refuges that are distant from population centers. Vaux (1975) discovered that wilderness users were mostly either students or had incomes of $15,000 to $25,000. More even representation occurs in city parks, which are readily accessible to all people. It should be noted, however, that some cities have apparently discriminated against the poor and racial minorities in their park building programs, so there may be some lack of participation by these groups simply because of lack of available facilities near their homes.

Several factors account for higher participation by educated and prosperous people in away-from-town recreation areas. The factor most commonly discussed is the cost of travel to get to the places. Although this is undoubtedly one of the considerations in a family making a decision to travel, especially if they have no automobile, there are other reasons that should be tested more thoroughly. One is lack of information or understanding. Often, a person without a strong education will not know or try to find out about new places. Because he has not been exposed to the ideas, he may be hesitant to explore the possibilities of recreation in a national forest or state park, unless he lives close enough to know about it. Because of the nature of his work, he may not have the energy to want to drive long hours to discover a campground or a remote mountainside. Finally, because he may be a member of a racial minority, he may have genuine fear of taking his family to a place where white people might make an experience unpleasant or even dangerous. It was only in the mid-1960s that the last signs came down that assigned "coloreds" and "whites" to their "appropriate" places and facilities. It is only the courageous black father who grew up under such separation who is willing to subject his family to the risks of abiding prejudice in the still-white domain of public campgrounds, picnic areas, and beaches in our rural parks and forests. Gradually, the change is occurring as people of various races find that they can enjoy the outdoors while using the same facilities.

Income

An assembly-line laborer in Wayne, Michigan was quoted in *U.S. News & World Report* (Jan. 9, 1978) as saying that he planned a ski trip to the Rockies and a visit to Egypt and Israel in 1978, and "I'm having steak for dinner."

There were income setbacks in 1977–78 in farm areas and steel towns but these are generally looked upon as temporary; living standards are improving and people are seeking out recreation.

Median family income has seen an almost constant rise in the past 40 years, even in terms of constant purchasing power dollars. In 1976, the median family income was just under $15,000. Full-time, year-round workers earned an average of $13,859 for men and $8,312 for women in 1976. (America's changing profile, 1978). In terms of 1976 dollar value equivalents (constant dollars), family income averaged $7,850 in 1950 and $14,958 in 1976 (Table 5.7). Thus, despite inflation, there has been a near doubling in family purchasing power over a quarter century.

Changes in income, national product, and other dollar figures are measured over time in terms of current dollars or constant dollars. The latter uses a base year's purchasing power, relating all other years to it in terms of relative purchasing power. Ideally, the constant dollar figures reflect only the change in the real volume of commodities and services, discounting the effects of inflation.

To measure availability of money per person, the figure *disposable personal income per capita* is the closest overall statistical approximation to consumer purchasing power. It is calculated by subtracting tax and nontax payments from personal income. Figures from 1969–1977 show steady gains, even though this period was characterized by considerable inflation and economic uncertainty (Table 5.8).

It is clear from these figures that Americans have greater means to

TABLE 5.7 Money income of families in the United States, in current and constant dollars.

Median family income	1950	1960	1970	1976
Current dollars	3,319	5,620	9,867	14,958
Constant dollars (1976)	7,850	10,803	14,465	14,958

Source: Bureau of the Census, 1977.

The Visitors

TABLE 5.8 Disposable personal income per capita.

Year	Current $	1972 $
1969	3,111	3,515
1970	3,348	3,619
1973	4,285	4,062
1975	5,077	4,014
1976	5,511	4,137
1977	6,037	4,293

Source: Council of Economic Advisors, 1978.

enjoy life than ever before. The affluence is better distributed, as well. The number of people falling below the poverty level (a flexible figure, dependent on family size, location, and inflation), has decreased absolutely and relatively (Table 5.9).

Recreational purchasing power has probably increased more rapidly than overall purchasing power. That is, the individual now can obtain a greater quantity and variety of recreation opportunities for a given proportion of his paycheck than ever before. The boost in recreation values per dollar is a result of providing more opportunities at steady or lower prices. Skiing and Hawaii and Florida vacations were impractical for most people 35 to 40 years ago. Today, they are available and relatively cheaper than before. Camping used to be confined to large public land areas and Boy Scout camps. Now there are campgrounds in almost every county of the nation. Better roads cut travel time, and transportation costs have stayed fairly steady, in real costs, despite escalated gasoline prices. New activities such as snowmobiling, scuba diving, and hang-gliding were almost unheard of until they recently became accessible to many. There are not only more dollars available for recreation but they will buy more opportunities.

Many characterizations of visitors to campgrounds, wilderness areas, riding stables, and other facilities have reported that most participants are moderate- to upper-income people. These suggest that comfortable, affluent people participate at a higher rate than the poor. Likewise, observa-

TABLE 5.9 Persons below the poverty level.

	1959	1970	1976
All (millions)	39.5	25.4	25.0
Per cent	22.4%	12.6%	11.8%
White (millions)	28.5	17.5	16.7
Per cent	18.1%	9.9%	9.1%
Blacks & others (millions)	11.0	7.9	8.3
Per cent	56.2%	32.0%	29.4%

Source: Bureau of the Census, 1977.

Social and Economic Foundations

tions in national parks suggest that a disproportionate share of wealthy people visit these special places.

However, when more than descriptive relationships are examined, the studies are inconclusive. The quantitative relationships between income and recreation participation are not distinct. Some studies have concluded that income has a significant impact on participation (Mueller, Gorin and Wood, 1962). Others (Lindsay and Ogle, 1972) saw little use for income as a predictor of participation. A thorough analysis of one aspect of income and participation was done for the 1973 nationwide plan (Adams, Lewis, and Drake, 1973). Low income elasticities suggested that participation was not strongly affected by individual prosperity. At least in terms of overall participation, people are not limited by finances. Changes in income would be more likely to affect the activity mix rather than total participation. Income may not serve as a determinant of taste but as a limit on their expression (Lucas, 1964; Taylor and Knudson, 1973). It should be noted that many of the studies of income factors contain inherent analytical problems caused by incomplete data or inappropriate study design. More work specifically related to this factor seems warranted.

Adams, Lewis, and Drake (1973) revealed that the greatest participation in most activities was in the large, middle-income ($8,000–15,000) population. However, the highest participation in hunting and off-road use of four-wheel-drive vehicles was by lower-income groups, whereas sailing, golf, and wildlife photography were participated in by more upper-income people. As income increases, a person may tend to abandon some of the old activities for new adventures he can now afford. At this point of knowledge, generalizations about income and participation should be avoided.

Leisure Time

Henry Ford invented more than mass production of automobiles. He helped invent mass leisure. In 1926, Ford factories instituted a 40-hour work week. His principle was simple. Greater leisure with relatively high earnings would increase the demand for cars. Ford was the exception at the time. Even the 48-hour work week was not totally accepted then.

Time has gained a new dimension in the twentieth century. The leisure dimension is a growing part of everyone's time budget. The growth in leisure time is directly related to the work week and to vacation benefits. The changes in these since the turn of the century have been dramatic throughout the world. Seventy-hour work weeks in factories and stores were not unusual at the turn of the century. The typical industrial worker of 1913 in the more developed countries was working 10 hours per day, 60 hours per week (Evans, 1969). That was in a noisy and grimy factory. There was no vacation with pay and relatively few holidays. Welfare facilities in the plant were limited to a minimum of sanitary conveniences required by law. Only a few companies promoted company-based recreation or social events. The home was overcrowded, located in drab surroundings, lacking comfort and amenities. Leisure-time activities were centered at the pub or tavern, at working men's clubs, and cultural events such as lectures.

Laborers now rarely work 48 hours; most countries have adopted a 40 to 44-hour standard. Vacation with pay amounts to two, three, and sometimes four weeks for laborers. Plants are better lit, better ventilated, less noisy, and management makes efforts to make work pleasant and easier. Protection of health and safety is a prime concern, with some places providing subsidized meals and recreational opportunities. Homes and leisure-time opportunities of great variety have enriched the lives of workers. The change has been a virtual revolution, developing in a period of about 50 years (Table 5.10).

The most striking reform is the vacation with pay. In the early 1920s, vacations were granted only to a privileged few. With the Depression of the 1930s and the growth of labor unions in the same period, the amount of vacation grew rapidly. Evans (1969) reported that by 1938 North American and most European countries had practices or law specifying at least one week of vacation. A half dozen Latin American countries had legislation providing for two weeks. Now, vacation with pay has become part of the life for workers almost throughout the world, usually with a minimum of two weeks.

The eight-hour day was advocated in 1817 by Robert Owen and some early trade unionists. The first meeting of the International Workingman's Association in Geneva in 1866 adopted the slogan "eight hours' work, eight hours' leisure, eight hours' sleep" (Evans, 1969). The aim must have

TABLE 5.10 Average hours worked by U.S. laborers in manufacturing, 1890–1975.

Year	Average hours worked*	
1890	60.0	
1900	59.0	
1910	56.6	
1920	51.0	47.4
1925	50.3	44.5
1930	—	42.1
1935		36.6
1940		38.1
1945		43.5
1950		40.5
1960		39.7
1970		39.8
1975		39.4

* Left column is from a Paul H. Douglas Study (Bureau of the Census, 1975). Right-hand column is from a Bureau of Labor Statistics study, 1909–1971, and monthly reports (Bureau of the Census, 1975, 1977).

seemed utopian. An eight-hour day had been secured in only one place in the world—the building trades of Australia, in 1856. A 12-hour day was permissible for men and the 10-hour work period was typical.

After World War I, industry and labor realized that productivity was higher when workers had more rest. The International Labor Organization recognized and promoted the importance of an eight-hour day or a 48-hour week. The latter was achieved in the United States by 1929 (Caro, 1974). During the Depression, the movement to a 40-hour week spread. Now the 40-hour week is enforced by law in the United States and Canada, as well as almost all of Latin America. European nations range from 40 to 48 hours as a legally imposed maximum without overtime.

The fears of many people have been that workers with leisure would put it to bad use. There are exceptions, but for the most part these fears seem to have no grounds. The new freedom, mobility, and income have been used by the workers to forge a widely diversified culture of leisure-time activities.

During the same period, there was a revolution in home gadgetry and convenience as well. This has done much to free women from the drudgery of incessant housework. The work of the modern homemaker has changed. Women have been freed to choose a wide variety of activities. Today, in more than half the families in the United States women hold jobs, many of them out of choice rather than necessity.

Leisure time is usually defined as discretionary; the individual has a choice of how to use it. Most obligations are removed. Clawson (1964) defined time in a simple, workable manner in terms of three blocks:

1. Subsistence time: that required to obtain food, clothing, housing, and transportation. This is mostly work-related for members of the labor force.
2. Existence time: that required for sleeping, eating, and personal maintenance.
3. Leisure time: anything left.

Small blocks of leisure time occur throughout the day and evening. They have an important effect on recreation use of local parks and playgrounds. Much of this time is spent in the backyard, in front of a TV set, reading, and in other activities. Sometimes recreation is combined with existence activities, such as combining a lunch period with a visit to a nearby park.

Larger blocks of leisure occur on weekends and holidays, producing major impacts on forest recreation sites outside the immediate neighborhoods. Vacation periods supply the largest blocks of discretionary time available to most adults and produce the greatest impacts on remote recreation resources.

Retirement and layoff periods are two special situations in which huge blocks of leisure time are made available to people. These also have very important impacts on recreation resources.

Future patterns of work may have strong impacts on recreation. During the last two decades, considerable speculation has surrounded the continued reduction of the work week. As fewer people were required to produce and to monitor the production of goods and services, it was generally predicted that there would be a rapid move toward a four-day work week or a six-hour work day in many manufacturing industries. This would, of course, extend the time people would have available to use recreational facilities and programs. It would probably affect the nature and quantity of recreation supply, by increasing and/or redistributing demand for facilities. A three-day weekend could extend the stay of existing campers, or it might stimulate new interest in camping among many people who now make one-day visits. Flexible work schedules, allowing a choice of work days and weekend days could result in spreading visitor use more evenly throughout the week. If people choose a short work day but six days of work, the major impact would be on local parks, with less use of away-from-home areas.

No clear pattern or trend away from the traditional five-day, 40-hour week has developed. Experiments with a number of variations have been tried in the 1970s, with no clear preference having emerged. It is likely, however, that with more time, there will be gradual changes in work patterns, which will have profound effects on leisure service delivery systems.

Mobility

Henry Ford's mass-production methods put automobiles under a large portion of the population. That completely altered weekend recreation patterns for many people, allowing them to reach rural parks and beaches. In a way, Ford created the traffic jam. Long lines of his cars chugged along inadequate roads on summer Sundays toward beaches that were already overcrowded. Eventually, roads and beaches expanded, but so did the number of Fords and other cars and the number of owners who seek recreation. They drove farther into the remote areas that had been the domain of only the adventurous with a week or more to spare (Figure 5.5).

Today the private automobile is the conveyance for all but a small percentage of recreation trips away from home, accounting for more than 90 per cent of recreational travel. Citizens of Canada and the United States drive half of the passenger cars of the entire world. In this country alone, there are about 100 million automobiles in use. About 75 per cent of American families have at least one automobile. These vehicles are driven on nearly five million miles of local, state, and federal roads.

FIGURE 5.5 A campsite at Mammoth Hot Springs, Yellowstone, 1922—the new mobility. (NPS)

The development of the interstate highway system, now approaching completion, has made once distant resources accessible to large numbers of people. Highways have made tourism a major contribution to states and communites that were hitherto isolated from most of the nation.

Although driving dominates recreation travel, a large number of people fly. In 1975, private pilots in the United States flew more than one billion hours for personal purposes, above and beyond business, commercial, or instructional flying. There were 368,000 private pilots and almost half that many learning to fly. Commercial plane passengers who rent or borrow automobiles also put pressure on outdoor recreation resources.

Earlier, trains and ships were important in delivering persons to resorts and national and state parks. Municipal buses are vital to users of many municipal parks. Lack of access to many local parks by buses has caused considerable concern.

Mobility has a strong effect on recreation. Because it is primarily a collective characteristic, it usually does not describe individual participation behavior.

Transportation is a management issue and tool. Overcrowding of parks by private automobiles has stimulated plans for use of various forms of group transport.

The Visitors

Education

Better educated people tend to participate more in outdoor recreation. Those with a college education prefer more recreation per person than those with high school or less, except for hunting, fishing, and that category in all studies entitled "other activities."

However, the number of participants in total is less for college-educated people for all activities except sailing. Thus, education is not a prerequisite to participation but seems to stimulate increased activity. Whether the education itself is the reason or not cannot be ascertained. College-educated people usually have higher incomes and different types of jobs than those with less training.

More people will get higher education in the future. The trend has been steadily upward. Enrollment is expected to increase from 10 million students in college in 1976 to more than 13 million by 1985 (Bureau of the Census, 1977). With the advent of TV study kits, electronic teaching off campus, and other forms of obtaining an education at low cost and with convenience, the educational level should continue to rise throughout the century.

High school completion has been achieved by 65 per cent of the U.S. population over 25 years of age. A total of 15.4 per cent of that same age group had completed four or more years of university training (America's changing profile, 1978).

Age

One final way to classify users and their preferences is by age groups. Frequency, intensity, and variety of recreation participation changes over the years. Physical ability, training, and strength are prerequisites for many activities. As ability waxes and wanes with age, people tend to participate more or less in various activities. There are many notable exceptions. With increasing interest in providing for older citizens, there is a remarkable resurgence of activity among them, demonstrating that they are capable of many activities that younger people also enjoy.

Six main classes of London, England, park visitors and their preferences have been identified in Table 5.11.

For other activities, there is some distinction among preferences by broad age class (Adams, Lewis, and Drake, 1973). Young people under 25 years old participate more per capita in off-road vehicle riding, horseback riding, water skiing, swimming, tennis, and other games. People over 65 consume more activity days per capita in remote camping, hunting, fishing, bird watching, hiking, walking for pleasure, attending sports and cultural events, and driving for pleasure than did other age groups. Nevertheless,

TABLE 5.11 City park activity preferences by user age classes—London, England.

Age classes	Preferences
Small children with mothers	Sand pits, play facilities, easy access
4 to 12-year-old children	Animals and birds, interesting play areas, room for ball games
Teen-agers	Swimming, sports, entertainment, space to flop around in
Young adults	Places to court, to take young families, to walk, picnic, relax on grassy areas
Middle-aged	Want to walk, sit, talk, especially at lunch near place of work
Elderly	Easily accessible parks near home to sit, talk, and watch younger people.

Source: Whitaker and Browne, 1971.

the number of individuals participating in most activities tends to decline with advancing years. From a sample of 4,000 people, it was shown that the probability of participation in all but two activities (sailing and bird watching) is inversely related to age (Adams, Lewis, and Drake, 1973).

These data suggest a simple approach to description of recreational participation patterns in a temporal sequence of an individual's life. Man finds adventure and recreational excitement in different activities throughout his life.

The young explore, then dig, build, and invent games. They need places to be flexible.

The teen-ager seeks action and limited new scenes, places for trying self-orientation and testing of one's own skills and powers. At the same time, learning of new skills is essential. The teen wants to know how far and how fast he can walk. Big explorations are planned. Inspiring scenery becomes more important as the late teens are approached. People seek new places to know. Intense physical activity leads to occasional reflection and sober philosophizing.

The 20s are years of more intensive mind-stretching. Activity and reflection are not totally separable. Ranging as far as possible, the young adult seeks to know as much about the world as possible. Seeing great scenes is important, along with exhibition of skills acquired earlier and practiced now. Specialization is developed in some.

The 30s and 40s are dominated by children, accompanying them through learning, exploring, and stretching phases. A few of the learned activities are practiced, some revived. Now, some sedate forms of socialization develop.

Then, activity seems to decline with age, except for some individuals. As some approach and enter retirement, they enjoy walking, golfing, fishing, and camping much more than before. Without the cares of watching children, they develop new interests.

The Visitors

With retirement, these people often pursue activities with intensity, developing skills in sports and hobbies that had received only limited attention before.

Youth had its day in the 1960s. They held the spotlight, galvanized the mass media, had their say, and got the vote. The over-65 group has now added its voice, demanding attention. Politicians, businessmen, and recreation professionals are paying attention. The Congress has added numerous Social Security benefits. Every session of the Congress sees hundreds of proposals introduced to help older Americans.

The reason is simple. One of seven persons of voting age is 65 or older. The ratio is increasing because the 1.5 million additions to this group each year are living longer. They vote more than other age groups— 70 per cent or more cast ballots in the average election—and they influence children and grandchildren who vote. Businessmen listen. Even though incomes are reduced, older people still require food, clothing, recreation, and transportation. Companies that tailor their goods and services to the special needs of the elderly have usually found it to be profitable. Examples include retirement cities, homes, hobby products, sports equipment, and clothing.

They can strongly affect recreation programs and facilities. They have time for recreation, on a prolonged basis. They camp, travel the world, use recreation centers where available, and serve as volunteers in recreational programming, design, and consulting. These people are among the most talented and most experienced in the nation. If given meaningful work opportunities, they often respond enthusiastically. As customers of recreation offerings, they have time and more discretionary income than would be expected.

Summary

The existence of leisure time and the widespread interest in outdoor recreation is a function of the productive and prosperous industrial economy that has developed in the Western nations and spread around the world. Leisure phenomena and organizations are a part of the whole system of physical, social, and economic and value conditions that exist in the nation and the world.

Because of the favorable conditions that have developed, a large portion of the earth's population is enjoying the beginning of a state of freedom that allows the development of an individual quality of life in a high-quality environment. The average citizen has enough free time and enough income to choose from a wide variety of leisure-time pursuits, many of which require open spaces and facilities supplied by private or public enterprise.

In the last 10 to 20 years, national policymakers have given considerable attention to recreation. President Nixon (1970) summed up the general political importance of recreation in his first environmental message:

Increasing population, increasing mobility, increasing incomes, and increasing leisure will all combine in the years ahead to rank recreational facilities among the most vital of our public resources. Yet, land suitable for such facilities, especially near heavily populated areas, is being rapidly swallowed up.

Social and economic factors have produced a society able to enjoy leisure. This chapter reviews the social conditions related to leisure time and outdoor recreation. The factors described are those identified by national plans and other research as important to recreation. Although all the relationships between these factors and recreation participation have not been determined, most researchers and professional administrators agree that changes in these factors have been accompanied by changes in the interest in outdoor recreation.

The factors considered and their apparent relationship to recreation participation are

Population—increasing numbers produce increasing activity.

Urbanization—urban people tend to participate more than rural residents.

Leisure time—more free time allows more participation.

Family income—rising income of the general population has accompanied rising recreation participation; differences in participation among income groups is variable, but middle-income groups participate more per capita.

Education—persons with more education participate more.

Occupation—occupational group seems to be related to types of activities.

Age—probability of participation of individuals is inverse to chronological age, but some older people participate much more often in certain activities than do other groups.

These and other socioeconomic factors can be analyzed in several different ways. So far, the most valuable use is to describe the social situation to help provide basic understanding of the recreation environment. Another use of these characteristics is to try to predict or explain future participation in recreation. This approach has been used in nationwide and state plans; otherwise, it has been of academic interest. A third use of data might be to analyze individual or group recreation participation patterns. A few such analyses have been tried but require more work. The collection and management of accurate data are big tasks.

With a population of about 220 million people and a civilian labor force of 100 million, the United States economy is in a long, steady growth pattern. With several interruptions (of sometimes major consequences), this growth has been continuous since the nation started. Based on analyses of the social and economic situation, it appears that outdoor recreation will continue to grow as an economic, social, and political factor in the economies of the United States, Canada, and most of the other countries of the world.

Literature Cited

ADAMS, ROBERT L., ROBERT C. LEWIS and BRUCE H. DRAKE. 1973. Outdoor Recreation: a Legacy for America: Appendix "A"—An Economic Analysis. Washington: U.S. Dept. of the Interior, Office of Economic Analysis. 239 pp. + appendices.

America's changing profile. 1978. U.S. News and World Report 84(20):56–57.

BURDGE, RABEL J. 1969. Levels of occupational prestige and leisure activity. Journal of Leisure Research 1(3):262–274.

Bureau of the Census. 1973. 1972 Census of Governments; Volume 1, Governmental Organization. Washington, D.C.: U.S. Dept. of Commerce. 476 pp.

Bureau of the Census. 1975. Historical Statistics of the United States: Colonial Times to 1970. Washington, D.C.: U.S. Dept. of Commerce. 1200 pp.

Bureau of the Census. 1977. The Statistical Abstract of the U.S. (1978). Washington, D.C.: U.S. Dept. of Commerce. 1048 pp.

Bureau of Labor Statistics. 1932. Park Recreation Areas in the United States, 1930. Washington, D.C.: U.S. Dept. of Labor, BLS Bulletin No. 565. 116 pp.

CARO, ROBERT A. 1974. The power broker. New York: Vintage Books. 1246 pp.

CLAWSON, MARION. 1964. How much leisure, now and in the future. In: James C. Charlesworth, Leisure in America: Blessing or Curse? Philadelphia: American Academy of Political and Social Science, Monograph 4.

Council of Economic Advisers. 1978. Economic Indicators, March, 1978. Washington, D.C.: Joint Economic Committee, 95th Congress. 38 pp.

EVANS, ARCHIBALD A. 1969. Work and leisure, 1919–1969. International Labour Review 99(1):35–59.

LINDSAY, JOHN J. and RICHARD A. OGLE. 1972. Socio-economic patterns of outdoor recreation use near urban areas. Journal of Leisure Research 4(winter):19–24.

LUCAS, ROBERT C. 1964. The Recreational Use of the Quetico-Superior Area. St. Paul: U.S. Forest Service Research Paper LS-8. 50 pp.

MUELLER, EVA, GERALD GORIN and MARGARET WOOD. 1962. Participation in Outdoor Recreation: Factors Affecting Demand Among American Adults. Washington, D.C.: ORRRC Study Report No. 20.

NIXON, RICHARD M. 1970. President's Message on the Environment, February 10, 1970.

OLSON, SIGURD F. 1973. A longing for wilderness. In: Wilderness, USA. Washington, D.C.: National Geographic Society, pp. 9–16, 25–28.

Slowdown for "strip cities": reversal of century-old trends. 1977. U.S. News and World Report 82(9):39–42.

TAYLOR, CHARLES E. and DOUGLAS M. KNUDSON. 1973. Area preferences of midwestern campers. Journal of Leisure Research 5(2):39–48.

VAUX, H. J., JR. 1975. The distribution of income among wilderness users. Journal of Leisure Research 7(1):29–37.

WHITAKER, BEN and KENNETH BROWNE. 1971. Parks for people. London: Seeley, Service & Co. 144 pp.

CHAPTER 6

Economic Impacts of Outdoor Recreation

This chapter describes the economic importance of outdoor recreation in society, the measurement of economic impacts, and specific examples of the effects of recreation developments on local economies. These matters are important because most resource managers must explain the economic values of projects and areas to the public and to their superiors.

It is often claimed that a reservoir, park, or other development will have positive economic influence on the commerce of an area. The Chambers of Commerce of most communities have a tourism promotion committee that seeks ways to bring in more tourist dollars. These groups usually are counted among the supporters of public water projects and major parks. In specific cases, there is reason to question the general assumption that a new recreational development is an economic and social blessing. Several large reservoir projects have been shelved after local residents analyzed all the costs and found that they were greater than the community was willing to pay. These costs are sometimes not explicit cash outlays but involve loss of local rural atmosphere, private farm land, disruption of roads and school districts, and increased local expenditures for protective services including police, fire, and emergency medical equipment.

Recreation Economics

Most states rank tourism as one of the major sources of income to their economies. The impact is obvious in such states as Florida, Hawaii, and Colorado (Figure 6.1). It is also important to the economies of industrialized states such as Michigan, New York, California, and New Jersey, where resorts brought in more than $3 billion a year, before gambling was allowed in mid-1978. Kentucky designed its state park system specifically to attract tourists who would help boost the economy. Michigan spends $1 to $1.5 million a year on promotion of its tourist attractions, which draw in $1.5 to $3 billion a year. Attraction of tourists from other states depends mostly upon lakes and streams, parks and forests, big game, amusements of outstanding quality, resorts, and festivals. Management of these resources and programming of use are therefore essential parts of the states' economies.

FIGURE 6.1 Colorado's Rocky Mountains help make tourism a mainstay of the state economy. (USFS)

The effects of tourists on the economy are several. The apparent flow of money increases. Resident tourists from inside the state spend their money on recreational goods and services; a good portion of this is spent near their places of residence, but as much as 20 to 25 percent may be spent while in travel or on a recreation site. This travel expenditure helps distribute wealth to various sections of a state. Because many recreationists live in high-income, suburban and urban centers and they seek outdoor recreation in the scenic, less populated areas of the state, they assist in providing income to residents of those areas that are often economically deprived.

Tourists from outside the state likewise bring in a certain amount of their recreation money to spend on services and goods provided by people of the state. This influx of dollars is an addition to the state's economy and also often has the effect of aiding in distribution of wealth. Little is known, however, about the actual incidence of benefits from the expenditure of recreation dollars. The net impact of dollars spent in an area is not necessarily proportional to the number of visitors. The local impact depends upon the type of recreation facilities available, the characteristics of the ownership, and the length of stay of visitors, as well as the type and fame of the supporting services—gasoline stations, restaurants, sleeping accommodations—available to the visitor. If the owners and employees of a recreation enterprise do not live in the region, their incomes will be, to a large extent, spent outside the region, thus bringing relatively little economic impact to the immediate area. If visitors come into an area to backpack, they will spend relatively little money in the area. The principal income in such a case would be associated with government expenditures to maintain and patrol the trails and associated lands.

Most backpackers prepare their trips ahead of time, so even supply stores in the region of the trails would benefit only a little, unless outfitting, guiding, and transportation of hikers are required or popular.

On the other hand, if owners and employees live in an area that has a variety of recreational facilities, the dollars spent by recreationists will be more numerous and may be multiplied in their effect several times by respending in the community. This recycling of dollars in a community, region, or a state is called the *multiplier effect.*

Economic Impacts

Southern Florida is an enormous empire of leisure that is catering to mature Americans. Its beaches promise fun and sun. Retirement communities promise everything life could not deliver elsewhere—freedom from crime, congestion, indifference, and aggravation.

The young are also attracted to the state, at least during part of the year, seeking warmth on the sands of the state's several thousand kilometers of shoreline or the diversion of its several hundred major tourist enterprises.

Retirement recreation is represented primarily by the people over 65 years of age who comprise 16.5 per cent of the state's population (11 per cent nationwide). From 1950 to 1977, there was an average net gain of 222,000 population per year. Almost half of these were 55 years old or more. The population tripled between 1950 and 1976. The economic impact is not easily measured in total, but Social Security payments add $4.4 billion per year to Florida's economy. Military pensions add $724 million more annually (Wooten, 1978). Agriculture is important in the state, but the farm value of Florida's entire citrus crop is one sixth that of annual Social Security payments. The new residents bring cash and put it in banks.

Year	Spending for leisure (billions of dollars)
TABLE 6.1 Spending for leisure in the United States.	
1965	$ 58.3 billion
1967	71.0
1969	82.6
1972	105.0
1977	160.0

Source: U.S. News & World Report composite from various sources.

They bring a need for housing, so the cash-rich banks have poured millions of dollars into real estate developments.

Each new retiree adds one job to the state employment picture. Predictions for 1975–1980 foresaw a 25 per cent increase in trade employment and a 38 per cent increase in service employment. A growing leisure industry now produces equipment and apparel for an active and fairly prosperous retirement community that demands products for travel, boating, jogging, and golfing, the top recreational activities of the retirees.

Tourists add more impetus to the state. In 1977, 31.5 million tourists spent $11.5 billion in Florida. This produced 500,000 jobs for residents. It added $500 million in tax revenues, which is one fifth of the state's total (Wooten, 1978).

Americans spend scores of billions per year on leisure-time activities, according to annual estimates by *U.S. News & World Report*. This portion of economic activity in the United States regularly exceeds national defense costs. It is more than the outlay for construction of new homes. The total spending on spare-time activities surpasses the total of corporate profits. It is more than the gross value of the United States exports. The aggregate income of American farmers is far less than leisure spending.

Leisure-time products and services clearly comprise a major component of the national economy. It is still growing. It is expected to more than double in the 1970s. The growth in the past few years has been spectacular: from $58.3 billion in 1965 to $105 billion in 1972 and $160 billion in 1977.

The character of spending identified as leisure-related varies among sources. The various stock market reporting services have been frustrated in attempts to identify leisure or recreational industries; each service has its own, variable combination of firms which they consider to be the leisure market. The identification problem has two major aspects: 1) identifying the products and services that are leisure-oriented is difficult for certain classes, such as motels, restaurants, and films, and 2) many companies produce recreational equipment as part of their total operation but do not separate these as distinct economic units.

The *U.S. News & World Report* subdivided 1972 leisure-time spending in the following groups, with their contributions to the total:

Recreational sports equipment and activities	$50 billion	48%
Vacations, recreation trips in the United States	40	38
Travel abroad	7.5	7
Vacation land and lots	5.5	5
Second homes	2	2

ECONOMIC WORTH OF OPPORTUNITIES

Although economists spend long hours trying to figure out the value of a recreation experience and have difficulty defining the economic value of parks, the public has demonstrated its support of parks in a very tangible way: parkland is maintained despite opportunities to sell it. One way to evaluate the worth of a park is in terms of what it would bring on the real estate market, even if that is not a viable alternative. Central Park in New York, with 750 or more acres of open space, is worth several fortunes in terms of real estate. If it were priced at a modest $500,000 per acre, it would be worth more than $375 million. For 130 years, the people of New York have agreed that it is worth more as a park than as a source of temporary revenue from its sale.

Turkey Run State Park in Indiana was bought in 1916 from a lumber company to preserve the big trees and the scenery. At that time, the state and volunteer funds paid exceeded the commodity value of the trees. Recently, a logger offered $75,000 for three mature walnuts in the park, but the intangible value of those trees is, by policy, considered greater than the market value for timber.

The U.S. Congress annually allocates about $900 million per year for a land acquisition and development fund for new forest and park lands for recreation. In contrast, to develop new timber resources, it has come up with only $5 to $10 million per year for federal tree-planting efforts over the past few decades, even though there is a chronically severe lag in public reforestation efforts.

A small woods in the Midwest was recently donated by an aging brother and sister to be a nature preserve. Foresters estimated that the 28 acres of woods had a timber value of more than $300,000 at the time of the donation. Keeping the woods intact for study and pleasure was worth more to the donors and to the state than was its commodity value. Hard-headed businessmen, lawyers, and economists in The Nature Conservancy saw it the same way. So did bureaucrats, who contributed federal funds to fence it and build a house for a guard on the edge of the property.

ECONOMIC ANALYSIS TOOLS

In the outdoor recreation market, there are three general problems that hamper economic analysis, according to traditional theory. They are collective utility, nonmarketability, and a mixture of private and public supply of recreation services (Strand, 1967). *Collective utility* implies that more than the consumers benefit, so traditional markets underrate the value of recreation areas. *Nonmarketability* of certain recreation products or services exists because they are provided for the general public with no charge allowed. This also is the major reason for the public entering into the field of recreation, alongside the private enterprises that charge for certain profitable services. This disrupts free market prices.

Reaching national policy decisions about allocation of recreation resources and services requires more than the economic tools of the marketplace. These conditions do not necessarily mean that decisions will be erroneous or misallocated, but decision makers will have to impose criteria of political judgment and indicators, along with general economic information. Most of these judgments are made by either elected bodies or planners and administrators designated by elected officials. For these groups to reach effective decisions, they need to know the gains and sacrifices that will result to the common welfare from the different alternative actions they face. Evaluating the costs and benefits, in social welfare and economic terms, requires the use of several tools to analyze the impacts of recreation. At the present time, these tools are still being developed and refined. Any group of economists, sociologists, and planners will provide numerous opinions as to the most effective approaches to use. A few are presented here.

OPPORTUNITY COST VALUES

The opportunity cost approach to evaluating the worth of recreation participation is an estimate of the users' concept of the value of experiences. It may produce very high values, because it involves expenditures plus nontangible values. One such study in the South (Horvath, 1973) dealt with hunting, fishing, bird-watching, and other forms of fish and wildlife-related recreation. More than 12,000 household members were asked how much a day of such recreation was worth to them and how much money it would take to persuade them to give up a day of it. They were also asked how many days' pay they actually lost by taking time off and how much money they paid for travel, lodging, and other expenses for such recreation. Nonwildlife values such as scenery, photography, and camping were not included. The results indicated that people spent $4 billion per year in the South. They estimated that the recreation was worth $24 billion per year and they would not give it up for less than $31 billion. These answers were not meant to indicate willingness to pay these amounts. Rather, they are an estimate of the tangible and intangible values of wildlife-related recreation resources and opportunities to the users of them. The U.S. Forest Service has used figures from this study and others using similar approaches to evaluate alternative courses of action in its planning process.

METHODS OF MEASUREMENT OF IMPACT

A number of terms are encountered when estimates of economic impact are made. They signify different ways of calculating impact. Some are more complete than others, accounting for differences in total quantities. Each may also have a different data base, because outdoor recreation or the leisure-time market are quite variable ideas. The reader must beware in trying to perceive just what is being claimed. Among the various terms used are the following four common approaches to measuring the dollar benefits of recreation:

1. Expenditures or direct outlay in leisure travel, sports equipment, campers, boats, summer homes, package vacations; these may include indoor recreation products (televisions, magazines) also.
2. Tax impacts on the local area or state, in terms of total taxes gathered that are attributable to recreation activities; usually travel taxes are included to indicate contributions through motels, gasoline stations, and restaurants patronized by vacationers, based on surveys of travel patterns.
3. Percentage of personal income, gross national product, or other economic statistic attributable to recreation or leisure-time spending.
4. Direct plus indirect impacts, measuring the total effect of dollars spent on recreation, including the multiplier effects of direct expenditures stimulating new expenditures within a community or state under consideration.

These are just a few of the terms and approaches that are used. Anyone who must prepare an estimate of the value of recreation in economic terms is likely to become frustrated quite rapidly. Careful investigation reveals only that there are many approaches and none of them can be considered satisfactory. The best estimates are often those made for a specific area, involving careful surveys of recreationists plus input-output analysis of the local economy. These are quite expensive means of estimating impacts and are accurate only for the period of measurement. They usually are confined to a small geographic region.

The national *Survey of Current Business* and the *National Income and Product Accounts* are sophisticated national estimates of direct expenditures for consumption of many goods and services. Among these, recreation accounts for 6.8 per cent of personal consumption expenditures in 1975 (Bureau of the Census, 1977). Just what recreation involves is not clear; it is certainly more than outdoor recreation but, on the other hand, does not include food, transportation, clothing, or foreign travel. Other estimates are generally much higher. The conclusion of a search for national or state figures on the economic impact of outdoor recreation or just recreation is that there are no completely acceptable figures. By tracing the trends of any one statistic, there is a clear pattern of growth in recreation interest and expenditure, in dollar terms and in the proportion of total expenditures by consumers. The person presenting statistics must choose and specify, or it is necessary to conduct individual studies.

Benefit Cost Analysis

The U.S. Army Corps of Engineers and other major construction agencies are given direction in evaluating expected economic impacts of any proposed project. The evaluation is summarized in a benefit-cost ratio that estimates the value of returns to society (benefits) in relation to the total cost of the project, both calculated over the life of the project, not to exceed 100 years. A benefit-cost ratio of 0.75 suggests that for every dollar invested in a project, the public will eventually realize seventy-five cents of benefits. The Congress would not usually approve funding of such a project.

On the other hand, a ratio of 1.45 suggests that a project would produce benefits that exceed its costs. Such a project would probably get the nod over one calculated at 1.25, if political, personal, or other considerations are not involved. In this process, a recreation visit is given a fixed value. Interest rates are kept fairly low. All benefits and costs are calculated over the longer period and then discounted to the present value. A low discount rate means that benefits over a long period of time retain a fairly high value. The "interest" on borrowed money does not mount very rapidly. The Corps of Engineers and similar agencies are required to consider impacts of various types, not all of which figure into costs. Likewise, they calculate a wide variety of benefits beyond the direct ones.

The Multiplier Effect

By using what is called the multiplier effect, the total impact of an outside tourist dollar on a community or region can be estimated. The initial expenditures of visitors provide the first round of receipts. Some of the dollars received by local merchants must be paid out for supplies or materials involved in the sale, and some will stay as profits, or net benefit. Some will go as payments to nonresident suppliers or workers. Knetsch (1977) gives the example of a dollar purchase of gasoline versus a dollar's worth of lodging. More of the lodging dollar stays in the community in the form of payments to local labor and services, whereas imports of petroleum from outside the region take a major share of the gasoline dollar.

The money that stays in the community or region increases the spending power of those who receive the wages and profits of local owners. They spend some of the money in the area for groceries, rent, and clothing. Some of that money remains as profit and wages, and some goes outside for supplies and stock. The portions that remain in this continuing chain keep stimulating the next sector. The net effect can be expressed as a multiplier of the original dollar spent by the tourist. In a small region, one dollar spent may produce the effect of $1.53 in the region, as in the case of visits to Norris Lake, Tennessee (Garrison, 1974). If the whole nation is considered, a much higher effect is induced. For each dollar in visitor expenditures and operation expenditures at Olympic National Park,

$3.02 of income was generated in the United States economy (Beyers, 1970). There is very little leakage from the national economy, whereas there is considerable spending outside of a local economy.

In the Olympic National Park case, it was found that visitors spent $21.8 million total direct expenditures in the United States in relation to their visit to the park. Of this total, $18.3 million was spent in the state of Washington. Only $8 million of the total expenditures for trips to the Olympic park were actually spent on the Olympic Peninsula. On the national level, the $21.8 million total expenditures produced the effect of about $66 million.[1] If non-Washington residents are separated out, the expenditure in the national economy for trips to Olympic were $10 million, while $6.5 million of that was spent in the state. This infusion of capital and park service operations plus its multiplier effect supported the equivalent of 2,800 jobs in the state.

Knetsch (1977) notes that there are at least three ways to look at multiplier effects—the sales multiplier, the income impact, and the employment multiplier. Each looks at the effects of incoming dollars in terms of the impacts on the particular statistic of interest.

Recreation and tourism expenditures tend to be somewhat more labor-intensive than average, suggesting that they have a somewhat greater local impact on labor; more money could stay in the community. On the other side, expenditures are highly seasonal, and demands for labor are for low-wage occupations (Knetsch, 1977). Within the community, expenditures benefit innkeepers, taxi drivers, campground owners, tour guides, ticket agents, construction firms, cleaners and laundries, gasoline stations, and restaurants. Some members of the community receive little or no benefit from tourism but must suffer the increased congestion, disruption of privacy, and higher prices.

The Tax Base Argument versus Public Acquisition

When public land projects involving land acquisition are discussed, the tax base argument is always heard. If land is converted from private to public ownership, the property tax base of a county or municipality is reduced (most local governments rely on property taxes). Presumably, there is a concomitant reduction in net tax revenues and the county or municipality suffers a financial shortfall. Most units of government are facing rising costs and demands for more services.

Is it true? The first premise is a fact. Converting ownership reduces the land base in private, taxable hands. The second premise may or may not follow. Even though revenues coming in decrease, there may be no

---

[1] Beyers (1970) also included the effects of National Park Service expenditures in the calculation, which followed the same principle.

net reduction in the tax budget. There are various likely situations that might occur, involving combinations of the following:

1. Net loss: a reduction in tax income with an increase or no change in expenditures.
2. A reduction in tax income with a decrease in expenditures.
3. Little or no change in tax income with an increase or no change in expenditures.
4. Little or no change in income with a decrease in expenditure.

It is often assumed that, when public land is acquired, tax income is reduced and tax expenditures remain stable or rise. This may be the case, especially if the land being purchased is highly productive, easily accessible, or of a large acreage. However, if the acquisition is gradual or small, which is often the case, there may be little effect on local fiscal affairs.

Many public park and conservation projects are located on low-productivity lands that yield minimal property tax revenues. The people living there may earn so little that they are receiving more government income subsidies than they are paying back in taxes. If they relocate elsewhere in the same county or municipality, their incomes may go up, stay the same, or go down.

Public acquisition and development of the land for recreation may result in some new revenues being generated through sales taxes and licenses paid by visiting recreationists. State or federal payments to the local governments in lieu of taxes is another compensating factor that aids tax income.

A decrease in local tax expenditures may be the most dramatic result of public acquisition of remote properties with relatively small population. Figure 6.2 illustrates properties that contain about 25 private residences of persons who are neither wealthy nor poor. The county or town expends considerable money to maintain roads and drive school buses to these homes. The roads are neither travel arteries nor heavily used recreation roads, but are primarily for access to these homes. If these lands were purchased by the Forest Service and the people moved into town or along a major road, the following situation would exist:

School bus and emergency service costs could be reduced for the county.

Road maintenance costs could be reduced (Forest Service would maintain or abandon them if the county vacated them).

The acres of agricultural and forest land would be removed from the taxable property assessment rolls, and a Forest Service payment of a portion of receipts, prorated by acreage, would be paid to the county in lieu of taxes.

The former owners would have received the appraised value of their property plus relocation benefits, much of which would probably be

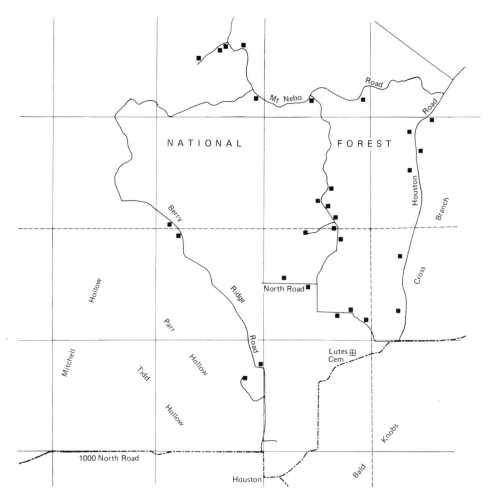

Figure 6.2 This map shows a rural road system that serves scattered homes within a national forest. County costs of servicing these properties may just balance tax revenues yielded.

reinvested in real property in the county. The move might affect the income status of the families; some might go onto welfare while others could go off of welfare.

The net result could be one of lower expenditures but little or no difference in the tax income to the county and schools.

Net benefits could accrue to the local tax base in a city, too, if a park were to replace housing. The property surrounding the park would rise in assessed valuation. In addition, the residents who remain would have the benefits of a park and open space, which might enhance the resale potential for their houses. City and school service costs would be reduced in most urban situations. These factors could be more than compensating for the removal of the properties. In fact, many houses in cities do not pay their own way. They cost the city and schools more in services than they produce in taxes. Thus, conversion of the land from private to public would cause no reduction in net revenues to the city. This, of course, can only be applied to a limited project and would produce different results if applied broadly.

A Wisconsin case study of impacts on local property taxes from public land purchase showed similar results (Rosner, 1977). The National Park Service and the state Department of Natural Resources acquired more than 10,000 acres from 1970–75 and planned to add another 7,000 acres by 1980 to the St. Croix State Forest-St. Croix National Scenic River in two northwestern Wisconsin counties.

In the study, it was assumed that all acquisition had occurred in 1974. The changes in taxes and resultant tax rates were compared with a no acquisition case. The effects of the National Park Service purchase of 2,877 river-frontage acres for the scenic riverway were compared to the state's purchase of 14,677 acres.

There are three types of local taxes: county, town, and school. With no acquisition, the county tax rates in 1974 would have been $3.06 per $1000 of equalized valuation in Burnett County and $3.92 per $1,000 in Polk County. If all 10-year acquisitions had been made in 1974, the rates would have been $3.08 in Burnett County and $3.93 in Polk County. This slight change—67 cents in taxes for the owner of a $25,000 house— would actually be spread over 10 years of purchases.

The results also indicated that there was little effect on taxes in any of the seven towns. In five of the towns, the total acquisition would produce a lower total tax rate. In one town, there was no change, and in the other, a small increase.

School taxes, which comprise 70 per cent of the total property taxes, were generally compensated by state aids which stabilize the district tax rate, despite changes in the tax base. In the district most heavily affected, there would be an increase in taxes for the entire 10-year acquisition of $0.05 per $1,000 valuation, or $1.25 in additional property taxes from the owner of a $25,000 home.

Rosner (1977) reported that public land acquisition did not affect the local tax rate for the following reasons:

1. The county tax base lost was a very small part of the total valuation of the school districts and the counties, equaling less than 1 percent of the valuation of each county.
2. The state offset lost school tax revenues with increased school aids (school district taxes were 70 per cent of the total tax rates in these counties).
3. The Wisconsin Department of Natural Resources has a policy of payment to counties for state forests in lieu of taxes. The National

Park Service had no such policy in 1974, but started them in 1977. Thus, the slight increase in taxes calculated for federal purchase in 1974 would be reduced or eliminated. Payments in lieu of taxes are the major reason that public purchase lowered the tax rate.

4. Any initial changes in local tax rates are partially offset by changes in shared state taxes and tax credits.

The compensating monies come from the various statewide taxes. All taxpayers of the state share in covering any costs incurred by acquisition of land for state forests. The Wisconsin property tax system generally ensures that local people do not pay the costs of public land programs through higher property taxes. Therefore, the local decisions about state lands can be made without concern about the effect on taxes. Instead, projects can be considered for their whole values—the effects on the environment, on the general economy, and on the community social character.

Induced Impacts of Major Recreation Investments

Some major investments in recreation attractions have the effect of inducing development around them. In this category are amusement parks, ski resorts, reservoirs, and some national parks. Most other recreational facilities induce little development by themselves or are part of the package that provides services wherever the development occurs.

The examples of Disneyland in California and Walt Disney World in Florida are interesting in that the company tried to benefit from its experience. At Disneyland, enough land was purchased to handle the theme park plus a huge parking area and a convention hotel. Just outside the park, many businesses sprang up. They came in all sizes, shapes, and qualities. The Disney Corporation had no financial or developmental control over its neighbors. Small family businesses and corporate chain firms profited from the Disneyland customers. Yet, they paid no financial tribute to the Disney firm; neither were they in any way bound to maintain any standards of quality, decor, or prices that the Disney group might wish to suggest.

When Walt Disney World was planned for Florida, the 100-acre theme park was placed inside of 27,000 acres purchased by the Disney Corporation (Figure 6.3). The State of Florida authorized the establishment of the Reedy Creek Improvement District to plan the unregulated and undeveloped land. There were no zoning or building codes, so the company could turn its imaginative designers, and architects, and plantsmen loose. Most service traffic is underground. The land around the Magic Kingdom is managed as swampland, forest, and pasture. By 1976, the staff had recorded 153 species of birds, 200 species of native plants, 36 kinds of mammals, but not a single franchised hamburger or ice cream store (Bloomfield, 1976). The $650 million (and growing) investment has produced spectacular re-

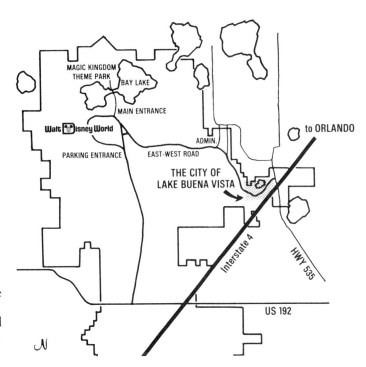

FIGURE 6.3 Map of Walt Disney World, showing large forestry and agricultural area buffering the theme park and related attractions. (© Walt Disney Productions)

sults, both in terms of controlling the immediate environment and in attracting customers.

However, the control does not extend to the whole region. In general, the developments south and east of Orlando are clean and of high quality, but there are economic and land-use changes nevertheless. More than 20,000 hotel and motel rooms were constructed along Interstate Highway 4 between 1970 and 1976. Several of the hotels produced serious financial difficulties for investors. Apartments and other developments were built behind the motels, displacing old orange groves. Several large, commercial campgrounds are located within easy driving distance of Disney World, providing overnight accommodations for the visitors who cannot or prefer not to stay in the large Disney-owned campground. Another major theme park—Sea World—is just north of the Disney property. Others have plans for development in the area. Most of the tourist facilities are neat, attractive, and in keeping with desirable development policies.

The induced development has had several other consequences. Ground water pollution has become a major problem. Providing service to people in the unincorporated areas is expensive and difficult, causing a drain on the county government. Roads may have to be widened beyond the best-laid plans, made before the 1971 opening of Walt Disney World. According to one analyst, "the original efforts to control land use by buying adjacent land were reasonable, but the boomtown growth of the Orlando region and the lack of land-use control outside Disney's site were unexpected and have to some extent defeated the original intentions" (Urban Systems Research & Engineering, Inc., 1976).

The problem of induced development distracting from the character of a place has long been present. Niagara Falls is perhaps the classic case. On both sides of the river, Canadian and American, tourist businesses sprang up as soon as the place gained popularity with tourists. At one time in the early 1900s, it was difficult to see the falls, because of all the hucksters and makeshift commercial shops that lined the sides of the scenic wonder, charging visitors to get good views of the falls.

Both Ontario and New York authorities managed to reduce the problem by using various legal and economic pressures. New York made a parkway and state park along one side, reserving some of the land as open space. Competition in terms of quality, coupled with complaints from irate citizens, helped clean out many of the less elegant commercial structures. Now, the honky-tonk has turned to restaurant towers and large buildings. One of the world's most famous natural wonders is viewed against a backdrop of two booming cities in two nations. The jurisdictional problems of agreeing on a procedure to systematize controls has proven to be difficult. A binational commission with impressive-sounding duties has identified and analyzed many of the problems but has found implementation of solutions to be both unpopular and clumsy.

Other places where major attractions have brought associated honky-

FIGURE 6.4 At the gate of the Great Smoky Mountains lies Gatlinburg, Tennessee, with its numerous tourist businesses. (NPS)

The Visitors

FIGURE 6.5 At the other side of the Great Smokies is the village of Cherokee, North Carolina, with its commercialism. (NPS)

tonk are the Great Smoky Mountains National Park and the Rocky Mountain National Park. On each side of the Smokies is a small town that lives off the visitors to the most frequented of the national parks. Gatlinburg, Tennessee, long known for its trinkets and low-budget businesses, has gradually improved the quality of its accommodations, restaurants, and shops. The hustle and bustle still provide stark contrast to the quiet wilderness of the park, breaking the mood for many visitors (Figure 6.4). On the other side of the mountain, Cherokee, North Carolina, brings enterprising Indians into contact with the white man's money, which the latter will spend for many curious souvenirs. Some have called the business center of Cherokee the site of the red man's revenge (Figure 6.5). At the eastern entry of Rocky Mountain National Park is the resort village of Estes Park. Its busy summer commerce is so commanding that many people return home to report that they have visited Estes National Park, perhaps barely noticing the sweeping vistas of mountains and glacier-carved valleys. The development has spread up toward the park, with motels and barbecues springing up on private land that is virtually surrounded by federal holdings. Hampered by a lack of funds for buying such inholdings, the National

FIGURE 6.6 "Civilization" makes a last-ditch effort to capture the visitor to Rocky Mountain National Park. (NPS)

Park Service watched helplessly as its margins filled with commercial structures, many of which clash with the natural environment of the park (Figure 6.6). On the park boundary, a 40-acre, treeless, private campground was opened in the late 1960s just outside the park gate and within 50 yards of the log homes of Park Service employees.

Telluride, Colorado, is an old mining boomtown high in the Rocky Mountains, about as remote from population centers as any town in the west. In the 1950s, it was clear that the boom left long ago. A small population was aging with the buildings. There was plenty of charm for those few who enjoyed rediscovering 10-cent movies at the old Opera House, the fascination of abandoned mines, and a rusting train engine called the Galloping Goose in the center of town. The place had no visible means of support. Tourists came, occasionally, but in very small numbers, and they found few traps for their money. Then, about 1970, someone decided that the slopes just south of Telluride's box canyon were ideal for skiing. They bought land and negotiated leases with the Forest Service. Condominiums, shops, and a resort atmosphere brought in visitors, even though they had to suffer long bus rides or drives from Grand Junction. The Telluride slopes produced a new boom, altering the architectural, economic, and social landscape of a town. The long-term residents still ask whether this boom will last or will dwindle to a new low, leaving behind empty apartments with shed roofs, resembling the old mineshaft buildings that long stood as monuments to the first boom.

The Visitors

Although the economic impact of such induced developments is undoubtedly positive, the question of quality and appropriateness is one that concerns community leaders, recreation officials, and many environmentalists. This is a question that will be discussed heatedly in the next 20 years, just as it has been over the past 50 or more. Local, state, national, and private parks face similar questions. The solutions will surely have drastic impacts on the businesses that are directly involved. It seems likely that unbridled private enterprise will not remain as free to build and operate as it has been. On the other hand, it seems unlikely that the government will totally control the businesses outside the parks. Despite cries of socialism that will arise, the government will surely not assume ownership of the firms, but the public will have some collective influence on the kinds, qualities, and locations of induced developments.

Literature Cited

BEYERS, WILLIAM B. 1970. An Economic Impact Study of Mt. Rainier and Olympic National Parks. Seattle: U. Of Washington, Dept. of Geography. 110 pp.

BLOOMFIELD, HOWARD. 1976. Mickey Mouse grows trees, too. American Forests 82(7):16–19,55.

Bureau of the Census. 1977. The Statistical Abstract of the U.S. (1978). Washington, D.C.: U.S. Dept. of Commerce. 1048 pp.

GARRISON, CHARLES B. 1974. A case study of the local economic impact of reservoir recreation. Journal of Leisure Research 6(1):7–19.

HORVATH, JOSEPH C. 1973. Preliminary Executive Summary: Economic Survey of Wildlife Recreation, Southeastern States. Atlanta: Georgia State University, Environ. Res. Group. 8 pp.

KNETSCH, JACK L. 1977. Outdoor recreation as a vector for economic development and other social programs. In: J. M. Hughes and R. D. Lloyd, Outdoor Recreation; Advances in Application of Economics. Washington, D.C.: U.S. Forest Service, General Technical Report WO-2. pp. 16–21.

ROSNER, MONROE H. 1977. Impact upon Local Property Taxes of Acquisitions Within the St. Croix River State Forest in Burnett and Polk Counties. Madison: Wisconsin Department of Natural Resources, Technical Bulletin No. 101. 24 pp.

STRAND, HANS. 1967. Outdoor Recreation from an Economic Viewpoint. Vollebekk, Norway: Norwegian Forest Research Institute, Vol. 22(84):161–187.

Urban Systems Research & Engineering, Inc. 1976. The Growth Shapers; the Land Use Impacts of Infrastructure Investments. Washington, D.C.: Council on Environmental Quality. 71 pp.

WOOTEN, JAMES R. 1978. Sunny Florida: foreshadowing our future? U.S. News & World Report (Jan. 9)84(1):34–35.

Recreational Equipment—
What Next?

In a midwestern state park, campers plugged in so many coffee pots, television sets, razors, and portable refrigerators that they blew out the park transformer. The volume of complaints suggested that this was a serious disruption of the camping experience for the modern outdoorsmen.

In 1978, Arctic Enterprises started production of 2,000 Wetbikes (Figure 7.1). This offers one more way for the recreationist to enjoy the combined pleasures of the machine and the outdoors. The Wetbike propels one or two riders across the waters at exciting speeds and makes sharp turns, all at less than 84 decibels. The machine was featured in a James Bond film and a TV soft drink advertisement, enhancing its attractiveness.

The ingenuity of manufacturers and the fascination of American consumers with equipment make the Wetbike one more in a continuing stream of vehicles, gadgets, and gimcracks that have had important impacts on outdoor recreation.

This chapter focuses on several of the more prominent types of recreational equipment and their impacts, as well as on the philosophical and management aspects of the various issues that have arisen. Recreational equipment includes bicycles, boats, camping equipment, off-road vehicles for summer and winter, and a host of other devices. Some major U.S. businesses thrive on the predilection of people for new devices.

Equipment

Technological playthings are part of the outdoor recreation scene. DeGrazia (1962) claimed that because people are unable or unprepared to use their leisure time for contemplative, constructive means, they surround themselves with technological devices. This may be an oversimplification, but it points out the disdain that many people have for those who bring many gadgets to recreation places. Leopold's (1966) philosophy suggests that equipment can become a distraction from the perception of natural processes. Edward Abbey (1968) was moved to describe visitors to national park campgrounds as TV-watching, motorbike-riding people who live in

FIGURE 7.1 The Wetbike, a 50-km/hr motorcycle for water, was first put in production in 1978, providing new challenges for riders and resource managers. (Arctic Enterprises, Inc.)

quilted aluminum, fiberglas, and plastic suburban villages, cook over charcoal briquettes, and compare electric toothbrushes.

It should be noted, however, that critics are selective about what they consider to be good equipment. The wilderness backpacker often looks down upon the masses who find pleasure in amusement parks. Yet, many backpackers pore over catalogs to find the latest, lightest gadget to stuff, stack, or cook. Mountain climbers often exhibit more pride in a new wrinkle on the sole of their boots than in the peaks they have conquered. And they sometimes pay more for that wrinkle than they do for the opportunity to climb Old Baldy.

The paying for resource use is always done more grudgingly than the paying for gadgets. Those who bring elaborate trailers or motor homes to campgrounds seem to be the most vehement protesters of camping fee increases.

Recreational equipment is part of the visitor, an extension of him. The administrators of recreation places must respond to what is coming and be ready either to accommodate it or ban it.

A major concern is the impact that any type of equipment will have on the environment. This is a key criterion that the administrator must use in making decisions about whether the equipment is appropriate. Systematic monitoring and documentation of soil erosion, vegetation, water quality, fish and wildlife, and overcrowding are increasingly important parts of the administrator's job.

Recreational Equipment—What Next?

FIGURE 7.2   Hang gliding became a popular sport that produced new problems for park managers in the 1970s. (NPS)

TYPES

Trailers, snowmobiles, and trail bikes are among the most discussed of the recreational equipment, but many other types of travel equipment have invaded parks and forests throughout the nation. Beach buggies on Fire Island National Seashore have killed the vegetation that holds the dunes, so they had to be strictly regulated, much to the chagrin of the local residents who use them for transportation and fun. Hang glider use in Yosemite required the assignment of rangers to special duty to enforce safety regulations at the Glacier Point jumping-off place (Figure 7.2). Jeeps in Canyonlands and many of the southwestern forests are popular and allowed but may be getting out of hand. Jet boats ply many western rivers and air boats have had to be controlled in the Everglades.

There were 7,700,000 outboard boat motors in use in 1976 in the United States. Half a million new ones are sold each year, with horsepower going up steadily. In 1960, the average horsepower was 27.4, but by 1976 the average outboard boat had a 42.1 hp motor (Bureau of the Census, 1977). The increase in numbers of more powerful boats has the effect of decreasing the recreational water resource, because greater velocity requires

102

Figure 7.3 Bicycling, long a popular means of transportation and recreation, experienced a massive resurgence of interest in the 1970s. (1887 lithograph, HCRS)

greater space per boat. This has the effect of lowering the carrying capacity of existing recreation resources.

Bicycles

Bicycles are now popular with all ages as recreational vehicles. Until 1970, they were considered a plaything for children and a few odd adults. Then, a sudden resurgence of interest among adults recalled the early years of the twentieth century, when bicycling was a popular activity among adults (Figure 7.3). The year 1972 was a significant one for American bicycle manufacturers. More than 40 per cent of the population owned them. More bikes were sold for adult use than for children in that year. American bike production passed Europe's then and, for the first time since World War I, more bicycles were sold than automobiles (Grove, 1973). In some localities, demand had quadrupled in three years.

As a result of the renewed interest in bicycle riding, new demands

Recreational Equipment—What Next?

were put on local and state governments for safe places to ride them. Light-weight, narrow-tired bikes do not operate well on gravel or dirt, so riders use paved bike lanes, streets, and highways. In most states, auto and truck-oriented highway officials have ignored the opportunity to use up to 1 per cent of federal highway funds for bike lanes of the type provided in most European countries. Oregon, California, and Arizona, however, took prompt action to provide for bicycle commuting and recreation. Numerous city governments responded to pleas for safety. Some realigned traffic lanes and painted a bike line on the streets; others built rather elaborate, isolated, narrow parallel roads. In general, county governments have been reluctant to spend money for places where a few city people might someday want to ride a bicycle. Plans in a number of counties include bike routes that connect the major urban and rural parks and historic sites, traveling the lesser-used roads and creek bank trails.

Camping Vehicles

Mass sales of outdoor recreational (camping) vehicles did not begin until about 1960. Although some trailers were being used in the 1920s, they were not mass-produced in any large quantities until 40 years later. The Recreational Vehicle Industry Association began recording data on shipments in 1961, when about 63,000 vehicles were produced and shipped for sales. Dramatically rapid growth ensued through the 1960s and early 1970s (Table 7.1). Then a slight drop occurred in 1973, changing the industry from boundless growth to one of overcapacity. Many of the small, poorly financed production firms dropped out. Many of the overexpanded, large firms had to cut back. At least three factors contributed to the decline in sales: 1) a temporary saturation of the buying market, which was experiencing a small back-to-basics move among young campers; 2) a widely publicized shortage of oil products and an increase in price, precipitated by an export restriction by oil-producing countries in 1974; and 3) an economic recession from 1974 to 1976.

At the peak of production in 1972–73, there were 650 manufacturers of recreational camping vehicles—travel trailers, camping trailers, truck campers, and motor homes. These companies sold about 550,000 units

TABLE 7.1   Recreation vehicle shipments, by type, in the United States.

Year	1961	1965	1970	1972	1973	1975	1978
Total (thousands)	62.6	192.8	380.3	582.9	528.8	339.5	389.9
Travel trailers	28.8	76.6	138.0	250.8	212.3	150.6	159.8
Motor homes	NA	4.7	30.3	116.8	129.0	96.6	157.2
Camping trailers	18.0	67.2	116.1	110.2	97.7	48.1	48.2
Truck campers	15.8	44.3	95.9	105.1	89.8	44.3	24.7

Source: (Bureau of the Census, 1977), data from Recreational Vehicle Industry Association.

FIGURE 7.4 Recent trends in camping equipment have brought many new campers to once remote scenic wonders, requiring new facilities and spaces. (HCRS)

per year during that peak time. In 1955, they produced less than 15,000 per year; by 1961, this had grown to 62,500 per year; eleven years later, they were producing almost that many vehicles each month.

In the early 1960s, tent campers comprised two thirds or more of all units in campgrounds. By the early 1970s, the proportion had reversed, with wheeled vehicles predominating.

The dramatic rise in production of recreational vehicles produced a need for revisions in campground design (Figure 7.4). Park roads and camping spurs had to be enlarged to accommodate the larger vehicles. Parking spurs had to be flat or nearly so. They required gravel, asphalt, or concrete surfaces to keep the vehicles from becoming stuck in the mud. Many of the wheeled vehicles had electric lights, heating, and appliances. They contained sewage and water systems. Some included telephones, television sets, gas-burning stoves, and refrigerators. Many private and some public campgrounds tried to meet the requirements of these rolling homes by installing direct hookups at the sites for electricity, gas, water, and, sometimes, sewage. Sewage dump stations for the popular self-contained systems became adjuncts to virtually all large campgrounds. Many places provided TV cable service to the campsite; telephone hookups became a sign of the deluxe campground. These services raised the campsite price, often beyond the means of tent campers. There are several campgrounds in Florida that do not allow tent campers to use the place. These are wheeled-vehicle resorts that charge up to $15 per night.

Off-Road Vehicles

One of the most touchy land management problems of the 1970s was the use of off-road vehicles (ORVs) on public lands (Figure 7.5). Rapidly rising sales of bikes, snowmobiles, all-terrain vehicles, buggies, and other devices conflicted with a concurrent sensitivity to the protection of natural values. Conservationists, bird-watchers, and other visitors seeking solitude in the forest or desert object to the noise of the immediate presence of ORVs. There is also a negative psychological impact from having a motor

FIGURE 7.5 Off-road-vehicle owners have difficulty finding appropriate places to ride. (HCRS)

The Visitors

vehicle suddenly overtake you after you have walked for several miles or days with a heavy backpack.

On the other hand, the ORV riders affirm the legitimacy of their sport and their right to use public land. They ask why one kind of recreation is acceptable and another is not. They point out their own sensitivity to the land, arguing that only a few miscreants ride bikes in a destructive manner or chase deer with snowmobiles.

Managers of recreation lands face major policy issues related to off-road vehicle use. The ORVs have become an important part of outdoor recreation. They operate in all seasons. The decision maker faces the following complex of factors:

1. People have strong feelings about ORVs—pro and con and all levels between.
2. ORVs cause considerable impact on the land, vegetation, and fauna, only some of which is obvious.
3. Machines used vary considerably in the impacts they cause.
4. People ride differently; there are few effective ways to control those who may be reckless or dangerous without restricting others.

Conflicts are inevitable between ORV proponents and traditional outdoorsmen. The vehicles quickly dominate the scene with their noise and speed. Increased velocity means there is a need for increased space per motorized person for the same amount of recreation time. Velocity preempts space. People who ride machines have a high appetite for space but a low consumption of details of the environment. They are often as much interested in the machine as they are in the natural world around them.

The off-road vehicle is an extender of man. One rider may equal the physical and esthetic impacts of many hikers in the same area.

Impacts on other uses are many. The conflicts that arise are characteristically felt most strongly by the participants in slower-paced activities. Usually, the ORV rider is not bothered by the presence of hikers, and the snowmobile rider is not upset if there are skiers or snowshoers in the area. Those on skis or snowshoes complain of the riders, however. They are relatively helpless against the faster, more powerful machines. Cross-country skiers complain of noise, lingering fumes, and the fact that one snowmobile can wipe out carefully prepared ski tracks.

Velocity and noise combine to use up space. Carrying capacity is lowered. Off-road vehicles tend to tyrannize other users, preempting their space and the quality of the environment. There are two types of visitor response to this situation. The first is accommodation or adjustment to the presence of ORVs by hikers, campers, seekers of quiet, and others. Just as the deer seem to become accustomed to the machines, people can learn to accept them, lowering their expectations of solitude and calm. The other response has been called the ISD syndrome—impairment, suppression, and displacement. These are usually sequential results of invasion of ORVs into an area (Badaracco, 1976). Impairment of the experience is the first step. It is well documented by complaints in writing to officials about how motorbikes ruined a camping trip or a hunting experience. Suppression occurs next, with a reduction in participation by nonmechanized visitors. This can eventually lead to displacement of these visitors, who totally abandon the site, having determined that their satisfactions are less than their frustrations.

The most common solutions to the conflict are zoning, exclusion, or the permissive approach. Zoning separates activities, assigning space for ORV use that is distinct from that reserved for quiet uses. Many private campgrounds have solved the conflict by building a minibike track away from the campground and requiring that all riding be done only there.

Different agencies respond in different ways. The Tennessee Valley Authority, at Land Between the Lakes, has set aside the Turkey Bay ORV Area, with a campground and staging area. The whole 950-hectare (2,350-acre) area is open to free-choice travel by trail bikes, all-terrain vehicles, four-wheel-drive vehicles, and whatever other ORV comes around. A study of the area by an outside observer (McEwen, 1978) found it to be highly popular with riders. After five years of use, the area had suffered relatively little damage to its stony soil, the timber, or wildlife populations.

The U.S. Forest Service has worked out forest-by-forest solutions for regulating the use of vehicles. On a few forests, ORV use is prohibited because of soil and water conditions. On others, riders have fairly free access to most of the trails, except in wilderness areas. In most forests, the ORVs are confined to designated trails that can withstand the use. General restrictions on forest use were issued in 1977.

The Army Corps of Engineers also regulates ORV use around its reservoirs, usually allowing use only on roads, including old rural roads. The same is true of the Bureau of Reclamation areas, national wildlife refuges, and the national park system.

The Bureau of Land Management (BLM), having long passively allowed recreational use of its lands, found itself besieged by ORV riders. Since 1972, it has undertaken a study and regulation program to bring all of its lands under a ORV use restriction system by 1987. The first permanent regulations were in 1977, banning or restricting and defining use of 30 to 40 million acres in the Southwest and Alaska.

Exclusion has been the policy in a number of state properties, permitting no ORV use within the state park, forest, or wildlife area. That is also the policy on most farms and many local parks. This has the effect of frustrating the owner who has paid a month's wages or more for a machine that he cannot ride on public land. Advertisements and his own emotions have led him to believe that he would have plenty of room to ride off into nature, challenging the hills, and splashing through streams. Thoughts of damage to the environment and irritation of other people are not part of the user's perception of ORV recreation.

In 1972, the federal government took a comprehensive interest in ORV use in federal lands. President Nixon issued Executive Order 11644, directing the Departments of Agriculture, Interior, and Defense and the Tennessee Valley Authority to

1. Establish policies and procedures to ensure that ORV use on public lands is controlled and directed so as to protect natural resources.
2. Promote the safety of all users of these lands.
3. Minimize conflicts among land uses.

This led to various studies by the agencies and to structuring of use to a greater extent. The ORV riders generally accepted the new restrictions gracefully, except when the studies resulted in closure of entire properties to all riding.

The Council on Environmental Quality was responsible for monitoring the ORV activities on federal lands. It recommended that a new executive order be issued to amend the first one. President Carter did so in 1977, in Executive Order 11989, which had three major provisions:

1. It excluded from the ORV category any fire, military, emergency, or law enforcement vehicles when used for emergency purposes or combat in national defense.
2. The agency head is permitted to close an area to ORVs immediately when he determines use will cause considerable adverse effects on the soil, vegetation, wildlife habitat, cultural or historic resources on public lands.
3. The agency head can adopt the policy that portions of public land shall be closed to use by ORVs, except those that are suitable and specifically designed as open.

As a result of this policy, many ORV riders and the industry became concerned. The policy gives managers greater control over riders—where and when they ride, and how many of them can use the area at one time. This structuring of the use may lead to acceptance of ORV riding as the legitimate activity that proponents claim it is.

Increased litigation will result from the expected structuring and closing of some lands. So will discussions with riding groups about the locations, size, times of use, and number of users of designated riding areas. The continuing debate on the nature of the ORV experience is not likely to die. Riders who seek the freedom and challenge of off-trail bushwhacking have already run afoul of Forest Service and BLM regulations that confine users to marked routes. Wendling (1977) predicts that these restrictions will lead to a decline in ORV use and/or a transfer of use to new private or local properties.

SNOWMOBILES

Silence no longer descends on the North Woods and meadows when the white blanket of snow falls in December. After three inches of snow, these once-deserted forests are turned into noisy playgrounds, receiving almost as many recreationists as they did in the summer. The key to this activity is the snowmobile, a track-and-ski vehicle (Figure 7.6). It is one of the most revolutionary gadgets of the century. Its quick speed over firm snow challenges racers; its flexibility and lightness carry families through the woods to explore back country and enjoy nature in the winter. It has changed the former lonely winter life of the North. Social and economic life is much more active. Money circulates faster. Tourists come in and residents come out. New businesses have started, and existing firms stay open and busy the year around.

In 1960, there were almost no snowmobiles available in normal channels of trade. Then a boom began, reaching its peak in 1971–72, when 500,000 units were sold in the United States and Canada. Sales dropped during two winters with little snow, partly because of increased regulations and partly because of oversaturation of the market. Sales stabilized at about 200,000 per year, with slow, steady increases. The U.S.–Canada market is dominated by six manufacturers producing 13 brand names.

The idea of snowmobiles is not new. The machine is an invention that took many years to become popular. Gilbertson in 1910, Kuhl in 1911, and Babst in 1920 are among the names claiming credit for the first snowmobiles. Joseph Armand-Bombardier of Canada made the machine a commercial success, switching from heavier snowcat machines to recrea-

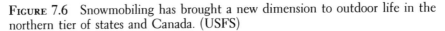

FIGURE 7.6   Snowmobiling has brought a new dimension to outdoor life in the northern tier of states and Canada. (USFS)

FIGURE 7.7 Snowmobiling has been allowed on unplowed winter roads in many forests and parks, including Yellowstone. (NPS)

tional vehicles in 1960, and then building a major new industry and sport around them.

His product was met with both enthusiasm and active concern. The enthusiasm was expressed by the purchasers, who formed more than 3,000 local snowmobile clubs and two national federations—the Western Snowmobile Association and the United States Snowmobile Association. The concern came from land managers and other citizens who discovered considerable theft, property damage, and abuses of wildlife by snowmobilers. Safety and health officials became alarmed at the number of accidents and deaths that occurred to snowmobilers on the roads, crossing neck-high wires, and venturing onto lakes and rivers. In addition, there are those who drink and ride, and some who run out of fuel long distances from home without adequate food or clothing. Snowmobilers experience serious hazards to hearing from high noise levels. The noise also irritates many who enjoy the quiet of the winter woods. The number of cross-country skiers has grown rapidly, with a pattern similar to that of snowmobiling, about 10 years later. The competition of these two groups for the same open spaces has produced new sources of conflict and demands for policies to separate them.

On many public lands, snowmobiles are confined to trails or unplowed roads (Figure 7.7). Local clubs often aid in the maintenance of trails, once the public agency has groomed and packed them. By concentrating use, much of the damage to plants and animals is avoided. Considerable research has been conducted on snowmobiles and their impacts (Bury, Wendling, and McCool, 1976). Many of the snowmobile studies are characterizations of the people who use snowmobiles. These produced information indicating, for example, that, among Michigan snowmobilers, 25 per cent were skilled workers, the family had owned 1.3 snowmobiles for 1.7 years, and earned an income slightly above average. The head of the house was a high school graduate, 43 years of age, with two children (Lanier and Chubb, 1971). This identifies the average user and may be of some value toward more effective management of users and resources.

Descriptions of the damage done by snowmobiles have been abundant, but few, if any, have documented the long-range impacts on the environment. It is dramatic when a snowmobiler runs a deer or fox to death, or guns down Alaskan wolves, caribou, or polar bears from the foam seat of his machine. Less obvious but more agonizing drama occurs when short chases merely tire the animal, leaving it with reduced energy reserves to survive the winter. More subtle yet is the effect of compaction of snow in fields. Voles and shrews live beneath the snow in tunnels. They cannot survive temperatures much below freezing, so they depend on the snow to insulate them. The insulative value of snow is a function of the dead air space in it. Compaction reduces the insulating power and prevents the animals from digging ventilation shafts to their tunnels. The death of voles and shrews reduces the available food supply for foxes and birds of prey, thus affecting the food chain and the composition of the entire community of animals and plants.

The effects of snowmobiles on white-tailed deer were studied in Minnesota during 1973 and 1974 (Dorrance, Savage, and Huff, 1975). Study areas were in St. Croix State Park, where the numbers of snowmobiles per day averaged 10 on weekdays and 195 on weekends, and in Mille Lac Wildlife Management Area, where snowmobiling was prohibited except by project personnel. St. Croix State Park was picked because snowmobile use was heavy on weekends but light on weekdays, so deer response could be contrasted between periods of light and heavy use. Also, the park is a wintering area for a large number of deer. Deer responded to relatively low intensities of snowmobile traffic. During periods of snowmobile use, the deer used larger home ranges. The movement of deer increased sharply when snowmobiles were operating in the study area. During severe winters, the movement of deer over even small parts of the home range is detrimental. Snowmobile use causes an additional drain on the deers' energy, which cannot be replaced because of inadequate winter food supply.

Two methods suggested to reduce the disturbance of white-tailed deer by off-road vehicle use are to locate route trails away from areas where deer concentrate in the winter and to avoid the use of particular trails on consecutive days (Dorrance, Savage, and Huff, 1975).

Damage to vegetation and soils by snowmobiles is worst in areas where snow is light, on windswept slopes, and under big trees. Often, serious erosion follows a snowmobile trail on a bare hillside.

Because of problems of noise, esthetics, misbehavior, and wildlife damages, snowmobiles have been banned from many private and public places. Glacier National Park outlawed them in 1975 in response to public outcry and the rising popularity of Nordic skiing. Yellowstone National Park and most national forests permit their use but under controlled conditions and on designated routes. The increasing shortages of places to ride has prompted snowmobile clubs to work assiduously to improve the behavior and the image of participants so as to reduce the impact of the small minority of riders who spoil opportunities for the majority. Many northern states have instituted a registration fee for operating machines. Fees usually go into a fund that is used to lease or acquire land for trails. In Indiana, a small fund is maintained by the Department of Natural Resources for December to April leases on private property. These cost approximately $75 per quarter mile per season, but are negotiable. Local clubs negotiate the leases, sending the completed agreements to the Attorney General for ratification. In some states, a major contributor to snowmobiling is the forest products industry, with networks of logging roads available through leases or agreements with local clubs or county governments.

TRAIL BIKES

The California desert is only one place where trail bikes are heavily used, but it is the most dramatic spot. The Mojave desert looks like a wasteland of sand, cactus, and creosote brush to most mechanized city people. Thousands of them go to the desert to ride their bikes and four-wheel-drive vehicles. Massive races are held annually on the land administered by the Bureau of Land Management.

Various studies have indicated that the impacts are numerous and serious. The desert ecosystem is tenuous. It survives by waiting and hiding— waiting for water to nourish the shallow-rooted plants, and hiding from the sun under the shade of any available shrub. Impacts that have been documented and compared to low-use areas include the following:

1. Direct killing of plants and animals.
2. Crushing of ground nests and breaking of shrubs with bird nests.
3. Collapsed burrows.
4. Harassment, producing an energy strain in an environment of high stress; incubating birds may abandon nests.
5. Vegetation indirectly destroyed by crushing and exposure of shallow roots, leading to deprivation of food and cover for animals and birds.
6. Mechanical disturbance of the soil upsets water storage, reduces water infiltration capacity, changes the thermal structure of the soil, and disrupts germination strategies of seeds, reducing the number of spring annuals.

Even light ORV use on the desert has an effect on the slow-growing desert biota. When riders skirt shrubs, the vehicles disturb the root systems, hasten erosion of top soil, and disperse and bury seeds and fruit used as food by small mammals and birds (Bury, Luckenbach, and Busack, 1977).

Habitat quality in the desert has been classified in terms of ORV impacts (Bury, Luckenbach, and Busack, 1977):

> Control areas: relatively free of ORV tracks.
>
> Moderate use areas: high shrub counts, about one half of the foliage disrupted, most shrubs intact at base; soil and ground disturbed between shrubs as ORVs travel around shrubs.
>
> Heavy use areas: reduced shrub numbers; ground cover essentially absent; creosote shrubs destroyed as ORV tracks go through shrubs, cut branches, and crush plants.
>
> Pit areas: most shrubs and ground cover absent or pulverized; soil compacted; much debris and litter in these camping and staging areas.

By extrapolating available data it is estimated that a square kilometer of creosote shrub habitat would contain about 6,650 terrestrial vertebrates weighing about 285 kilograms (kg). Heavy ORV use over that square kilometer would destroy 3,000 individual animals weighing 220 kg. In moderately used areas, the decline would be about 830 animals with a biomass of 185 kg. This decline in the prey would also produce a decline in more mobile predator populations (Bury, Luckenbach, and Busack, 1977).

Use of ORVs on the Mojave Desert has been intensive only since the late 1960s. In less than 10 years, administrators and researchers verified widespread negative impacts on the desert flora and fauna. In the desert, there is little chance for the ecosystem to rebound; it is not resilient. Therefore, many of the effects are cumulative. In addition to ecological damage, ORV tracks have marred cultural artifacts of great significance. Because the BLM is severely understaffed to handle heavy recreational use, it has not done thorough inventories or protection work on many of the cultural and scenic areas that exist in the National Resource Lands. Neither has it had the manpower to effectively regulate the use of ORVs.

Trail bikes have been used for years in the Rocky Mountains, starting with a few "tote-goats" by hunters in the late 1950s and building up to large numbers of users. Where use has been intensive, trails erode rapidly and there are evident impacts. However, the situation has not been as alarming as the desert use, partly because the mountain ecosystems are more resilient in most cases and partly because the use has not been as massive. On trails, horses and bikes do similar kinds of damage, with bike damage being more rapid in most cases.

Miller (1970) reported that motorcycle use did little damage on tree-covered areas of California national forests. The major damage was to meadows and stream banks. The bikes have proven useful in keeping fire-breaks up in the chaparrel of southern California. The associated erosion on these ridge-running breaks is a cost accepted by forest managers.

Monitoring Impacts

Impacts by off-road vehicles can generally be categorized as damage to the soil, vegetation, and water; damage to animals; and damage to the experience of other visitors. Some impacts are obvious to any observer but most require documented evidence of damages to back up policy decisions to bar or regulate certain uses. A monitoring system also can serve as an early warning system to the property manager of problems that are developing but appear to be little different from year to year.

Trail activities can be monitored by using transects across the trail between fixed points. A simple but accurate method is to put a nail in the base of small trees off the trail on both sides. Then, tie a string between the nails; the string serves as the transect line that is reproducible year after year. At fixed intervals, say every three to seven centimeters (cm) along the string, measure the vertical distance to the soil surface, and record the ground cover at that point. From this, a surface profile and a ground cover diagram can be drawn. Year-to-year comparisons can reveal changes in apparent soil loss (erosion plus compaction) and changes in ground cover next to the trail. The number of transects to be used depends upon the length and variability of the trail, but there should probably be at least 20 or 30 as a minimum. There should be parallel control measurements on an area not receiving such use, on similar soils and topographic conditions.

Other monitoring techniques should include written comments by visi-

FIGURE 7.8 Dune buggies have been outlawed on most state and federal parks. (HCRS)

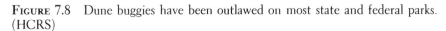

tors of all interests, a record of complaints, measurements and records of noise levels, traffic (pedestrian and other) problems, inconveniences, and recording of soil and vegetation conditions off of designated trails, roads, and campsites. Damage to grass, trees, and soils on steep hills should be measured by a regular monitoring program when it seems necessary and productive. A photographic record is often valuable. Repeat pictures taken from the same spot with similar lighting conditions often serve as valuable references of conditions before and after use. Water quality measurements are also important, even though they are sometimes difficult to take. Most water measurements are variable with the weather and the intensity of activity upstream immediately preceding the time of measurement, so there is high variability. This requires duplication of conditions or numerous samples over time to approximate average conditions. Studies of sediment deposits downstream or in lakes are among the least weather-dependent variables that can measure water phenomena.

Measurements of wildlife are particularly difficult, except in the case of direct kills. Impacts of noise on nesting birds, on animal distribution, and other wildlife factors have been hypothesized but not well documented. Monitoring impacts on wildlife is important, but there is presently no method that is recommended as practical.

Conclusion

In the future the land manager will deal with tremendous impacts on the environment. Recent developments of equipment are an indicator of what will probably come. Snowmobiles in operation went from virtually none to over one million within ten years. In the period from 1965, off-road bikes became similarly abundant. Four-wheel-drive vehicles changed from Forest Service utility vehicles to civilian playthings, invading old trails and roads to reach remote lakes. Backpacking, canoeing, cross-country skiing and numerous other sports came into vogue in the early '70s, with their participants demanding peace, quiet and a natural setting. Their desires conflicted with the motorized users; both claimed that they should have a right to use public lands. By the nature of their participation, the quiet activities required areas without the presence of the motorized equipment. In 1980, when Wetbikes are invading remote lakes, fishermen in canoes and rowboats are raising their hands in despair, asking "what next?" The resource manager must ask the same question, but before the surprise arrival. A broad-based philosophy and policy toward inevitable invention will help prepare for unreasonable responses. A vital aspect is preparation of public understanding through the land ethic called for by Aldo Leopold (1966):

When we see land as a community to which we belong, we may begin to use it with love and respect. There is no other way for land to survive the impact of mechanized man.

FIGURE 7.9   Use of airboats in the Everglades has long been a controversial subject. (NPS)

Literature Cited

ABBEY, EDWARD. 1968. Desert Solitaire: a Season in the Wilderness. N.Y.: McGraw-Hill. 269 pp.

BADARACCO, ROBERT J. 1976. ORV's: often rough on visitors. Parks and Recreation 11(9):32–35, 68–75.

Bureau of the Census. 1977. The Statistical Abstract of the U.S. (1978). Washington, D.C.: U.S. Department of Commerce. 1048 pp.

BURY, R. BRUCE, ROGER A. LUCKENBACH, and STEPHEN D. BUSACK. 1977. Effects of Off-road Vehicles on Vertebrates in the California Desert. Washington, D.C.: U.S. Fish and Wildlife Service, Wildlife Research Report 8. 23 pp.

BURY, RICHARD L., ROBERT C. WENDLING and STEPHEN F. McCOOL. 1976. Off-road Recreation Vehicles. College Station: Texas Agr. Exp. Sta., No. MP-1277. 84 pp.

DeGRAZIA, SEBASTIAN. 1962. Of Time, Work and Leisure. N.Y.: Twentieth Century Fund. 559 pp.

DORRANCE, MICHAEL J., PATRICK J. SAVAGE and DAN E. HUFF. 1975. Effects of snowmobiles on white-tailed deer. Journal of Wildlife Management 39(3):563–569.

GROVE, NOEL. 1973. Bicycles are back—and booming: National Geographic 143(5):670–681.

LANIER, L. L. and M. CHUBB. 1971. Michigan's 1970 snowmobile study. In: Chubb, M.(ed.). Proceedings of the 1971 Snowmobile and Off the Road Vehicle Research Symposium. E. Lansing: Michigan State Univ., Dept. of Parks and Recreation, Technical Report No. 8. pp. 55–71.

LEOPOLD, ALDO. 1966. Sand County Almanac. N.Y.: Oxford University Press. 269 pp.

MILLER, PHILIP. 1970. Case study no. XVI; off-road recreational vehicle composite. In: Public Land Policy and the Environment, Part II: Environmental Problems on the Public Lands. Springfield, Va.: National Technical Information Service, pp. 730–767.

McEWEN, DOUGLAS N. 1978. Turkey Bay Off-road Vehicle Area at Land Between the Lakes: an Example of New Opportunities for Managers and Riders. Carbondale: Southern Illinois University, Dept. of Recreation, Research Report No. 1. 28 pp.

WENDLING, ROBERT C. 1977. The Evolution of Off-road Vehicle Policy: Chaos or Rational Planning? Paper to Society of Park and Recreation Educators, Symposium on Leisure Research, Las Vegas, Nev.

PART TWO

Recreation Places

C H A P T E R   8

The Resource System

This chapter offers a brief, but comprehensive, look at the recreation places of the United States. The place where recreation is available is, in economic terms, the *recreation resource or supply*. Subsequent chapters describe each element of the supply system in some detail.

There are many ways to classify recreation resources. One is by ownership or jurisdiction. Private, industrial, city, county, state, and federal properties provide the framework of study for the remainder of this book.

Within each of these ownerships, there are many types of properties: parks, forests, fish and wildlife areas, nature preserves, nature centers, ar-

FIGURE 8.1   The places where recreation opportunities are available comprise recreation resources or supply. The first national monument in the United States was Devil's Tower, Wyoming, established in 1906. (NPS)

boreta, trails, memorials, scenic riverways, parkways, ski areas, golf courses, reservoirs, recreation areas, camps, country clubs, and many other designations.

All of these combine to offer a variety of recreational opportunities. Americans pursue recreation wherever possible. The basic requirement is a land base. Lands available for recreation are described here.

Types of Recreation Resources Available

1. Multiple-use lands, with timber production and/or grazing as historically dominant uses, often include recreation as a current major use.

Names of Areas	Administrator
National forests	U.S. Forest Service
National resource lands	Bureau of Land Management
State forests	Equivalent of: Division of Forestry, Department of Natural Resources of the state
County forests City forests	Local departments of parks and recreation or forestry
School forests	School districts
Industrial forests	Paper, plywood, and lumber companies plus other industries

2. Parks and recreation areas are specifically set aside either to preserve outstanding natural or historical resouces for public enjoyment or to provide recreation areas close to home or in other appropriate places.

Areas	Administrators
National parks, national parkways, national monuments, national historic parks, national recreation areas, national memorials, and others of national significance.	National Park Service
State parks and recreation areas, state beaches, state memorials of state significance	Equivalent of: Division of State Parks, State Department of Natural Resources
County or regional parks, park reserves; primarily for local use.	Boards of: county park departments or special park district authorized by state

City parks, neighborhood parks, block parks, mini parks	Boards of city parks and recreation departments
Township parks	Township trustees
School parks and recreation areas	Universities, school districts
Tree farm parks	Forest industry
Commercial parks and resorts, ski resorts, skating rinks, marinas, campgrounds, riding stables, amusement parks	Private enterprise
Club parks (Elks, Izaak Walton, conservation clubs)	Limited access for members of service or conservation clubs
Roadside parks, waysides	State highway departments, county highway departments
Local historical parks, structures	Private, nonprofit associations; local government, private enterprise.
Employee parks, country clubs	Industry or membership, exclusive

3. Fish and Wildlife areas are set aside to provide wildlife habitat, most frequently for migratory waterfowl, and/or opportunities for hunting, fishing, and wildlife observation.

Areas	*Administrators*
National wildlife refuges National fish hatcheries	U.S. Fish and Wildlife Service, Department of the Interior
State fish hatcheries State fishing areas State fishing and wildlife areas	Division of Fish and Wildlife, State Department of Natural Resources
Local fish and wildlife areas	County or city departments of parks and recreation
Sanctuaries, private refuges	Organizations, individuals
Shooting preserves	Industry (often restricted use), private enterprise, clubs
Fishing lakes (pay lakes)	Private enterprise
Hunting lease areas	Industry, private landowners lease to clubs

4. Water Project areas are designed to store water for various purposes, including recreation.

Areas	*Administrators*
Reclamation reservoirs, usually producing power and irrigation water	Bureau of Reclamation (most leased to other agencies)
Flood control multipurpose reservoirs	U.S. Army Corps of Engineers (many leased to other agencies)
Multipurpose reservoirs	Tennessee Valley Authority
Small watershed project reservoirs	State authorized soil and water conservation districts
City/county water supply reservoirs, lakes	Local water works or park, recreation, and conservation agencies
Power-generating reservoirs	Power and light companies
Private fishing/swimming lakes and ponds	Mostly family-owned recreation businesses and farms

5. Specially designated areas include the following:

Areas	*Administrators*
National wilderness preservation system (wilderness areas)	U.S. Forest Service, National Park Service, Fish and Wildlife Service, Bureau of Land Management
State wilderness areas or wilderness parks	State Departments of Natural Resources or special agency
"Pocket Wilderness"; wild preserves	Forest industries, Tennessee Valley Authority
State nature preserves	State Departments of Natural Resources
Privately owned sanctuaries, nature preserves (often open to the public)	The Nature Conservancy, Audubon Society, conservation clubs, individual families, other groups
Nature centers, environmental education centers, nature study areas	Non-profit organizations, schools, local parks and recreation departments, some state and federal agencies, a few corporations
Organization camps, sports camps (often use by reservation)	Churches, Scouts, Y's, Salvation Army, private enterprise
National wild, scenic and recreational rivers	U.S. Forest Service, National Park Service, or state agencies

State scenic rivers (various names)	State Departments of Natural Resources, sometimes county or local conservancy groups
National scenic trails	U.S. Forest Service, National Park Service
National recreation trails	Various groups, endorsed by Department of the Interior
State trails systems (often cross all classes of land ownership)	State Departments of Natural Resources

Table 8.1 describes the properties by the levels of government and general designations. Acreages of state, local, and private resources are highly variable among reports. These should be interpreted as approximate.

TABLE 8.1   Land ownership by levels of government and major recreation resources.

	Acres (millions)		Source
Federal	761	(all uses)	Bureau of the Census, 1977
National Park System	31		
National Forests	187		
National Wildlife Refuges	30		
National Resource Lands	470		
Other	43		
State	116	(all uses)	Bureau of the Census, 1977
Parks and Recreation Areas	9.8		Bureau of the Census, 1977
Forests	24.1		State Foresters Yearbook
Fish and Wildlife Areas	15.7		Bureau of Outdoor Recreation, 1973
Other	(NA)		
Local*	20		Bureau of the Census, 1977
County Parks	8.7		Bureau of Outdoor Recreation, 1973
City Parks	1.6		Bureau of Outdoor Recreation, 1973
Forests	(NA)		
Other	(NA)		
Industrial	40	(open to recreation)	U.S. Forest Service, 1979
Private forest and range land	208	(open to recreation)	U.S. Forest Service, 1979
	1,145		

Note: Figures are compiled from various sources, so do not always match. Federal figures are before Alaska national interest land reallocations.
* More than 78 different units of local governments were identified by the 1972 Census of Governments.

CASE—THE OREGON RECREATION SUPPLY COMPLEX

Most states contain the full range of recreation supply agencies. The mix in Oregon includes heavy participation by the Bureau of Land Management. Data are from various sources, dated 1970 to 1978. The Oregon supply situation is as follows:

Federal Areas
  U.S. Forest Service
    13 National Forests—6.7 million hectares
      550 campgrounds—7,000 sites
      2,250 picnic sites
      17 ski areas
      hundreds of miles of trails for hiking, riding opportunities for climbing, backpacking, hunting, fishing, other dispersed use
  Bureau of Land Management
    6.5 million hectares
      60 recreation areas—510 campsites
      532 picnic sites
      hunting, fishing, other dispersed use
  National Park Service
    3 areas—65,000 hectares
      Crater Lake, two historic sites
      lodge, camping, picnicking, nature walks, boat rides
  National Wildlife Refuges—7 units
  Corps of Engineers dams—13 lakes
    with associated water-based activities

Private Parks
  Power and timber companies
    12 firms with 50 areas—1,400 hectares
      500 picnic sites
      650 camp sites
  Commercial recreation areas
    about 200 campgrounds

County Parks
  300 parks—1,400 hectares
    1,100 campsites
    4,350 picnic sites
    water-based recreation
    trails

Municipal Parks
  Numbers not available

State Areas

    State parks—242 parks—36,500 hectares

       5,900 picnic sites

         water-based facilities

       3,841 campsites

    Safety rest areas—50 along highways

    State forestry parks—two units

       large state forest land area for dispersed recreation,

         tent camping, picnicking

    Fish hatcheries—32 sites

    State scenic rivers

Areas of Critical Concern

The 1973 Nationwide Outdoor Recreation Plan listed the following types of recreation resources as being of critical concern. They are defined as areas of great value to outdoor recreation on which uncontrolled development could result in irreversible damage.

Shorelines, beaches, and estuaries: Populations nearby are increasing rapidly; development and exclusive private use are occupying natural shorelines. Estuaries are being filled and built upon. Only 23 per cent of the shoreline is controlled by public agencies, excluding Alaska, where 99 per cent is public. (Alaska has 56 per cent of the nation's coastline.) Only 9 per cent of the non-Alaska shoreline is developed for public recreation. Another 16 per cent is used for private recreation. The plan urged federal, state, and local action to acquire these lands and to provide public access where appropriate (Figure 8.2).

Floodplains: About 5 per cent of the nation is occupied by the 100-year floodplains of rivers. Dams, floodwalls, dikes, and channel improvements have been built to reduce flooding hazards, at a cost of more than $7 billion (1936–1973) of public funds. In addition, considerable private money and increasing developments of the floodplains for structures have used up many of the acres of this flood-prone land. Zoning against certain high-investment uses of floodplains and the use of these areas for parks and trails have increased in the past few years. Reduction or elimination of federal insurance programs for most floodplain structures have also had a retarding effect on development. On the other hand, recreation financing programs have given some priority to park acquisition and development in some floodplains.

Wetlands: Drainage and filling of wetlands has long produced a deleterious effect on wildlife, especially waterfowl. There are numerous private and public programs to restore wetlands, but they have not been as vigorous as the private and public efforts to eliminate them.

Trails: Despite the 1968 National Trails Act, America is woefully

FIGURE 8.2   Public shoreline is one of the critical areas for future action to increase recreation supply.

short on designated places to walk through the countryside. During the Bicentennial year of 1976, there was considerable talk and planning for local trails. Most of these have not yet been developed. Even though federal highway funds were made available for the construction of bicycle trails along highway rights-of-way, only a few states have used the monies for that purpose. Completing the interstate system or repairing auto and truck trails has taken priority over supplying facilities for bicyclists or other slow-velocity travelers. Although some localities have made splendid records in providing trails for hiking, walking, biking, and horseback riding, the nation has fewer footpaths than virtually any other country in the world (Figure 8.3). England and Wales have more designated trails (mostly on private property) than the entire United States, excluding Alaska.

Special Natural Areas: Unique or valuable natural areas are important as representatives of native America for the curious and the scientific student. They are good places for environmental education and for general appreciative types of outdoor recreation. New nature preserve programs in several states have started to work with The Nature Conservancy and other private groups to preserve some of these areas. The Nature Conservancy acquires about 40,500 ha (100,000 acres) per year in 200 projects. These are managed by the organization or turned over to public agencies.

Recreation Places

Identification of National Natural Landmarks is coordinated by the National Park Service, which maintains the register but does not guarantee protection of the areas.

Natural Lakes: There are few large natural lakes in the nation—250 of more than 10 square miles. These are located in 23 states, with 100 in Alaska and another 100 in five states—Minnesota, Wisconsin, Michigan, New York, and Maine. Commercial and residential pollution and encroachment are reducing the recreational values of these lakes. There is need for an inventory and for protection of these resources, as well as for many of the smaller lakes.

Reservoirs: Large artificial bodies of water occur in 75 per cent of the states. Many of them do not provide for recreation as a legitimate use. Many other farm ponds and small reservoirs are available but undeveloped for recreation. The nationwide plan called for particular attention to the development of recreational opportunities on municipal water supply reservoirs. In the Northeast, there is an abundance of such water bodies that have traditionally been closed to recreational use.

Islands: The Bureau of Outdoor Recreation published an inventory of islands in 1970. It recorded 26,325 islands of 10 or more acres. Most

FIGURE 8.3 The national scenic trail system proposed in 1968 consisted of only the already existing Appalachian and Pacific Crest routes for ten years; the Continental Divide route was declared official in 1978, along with several historic trails. (HCRS)

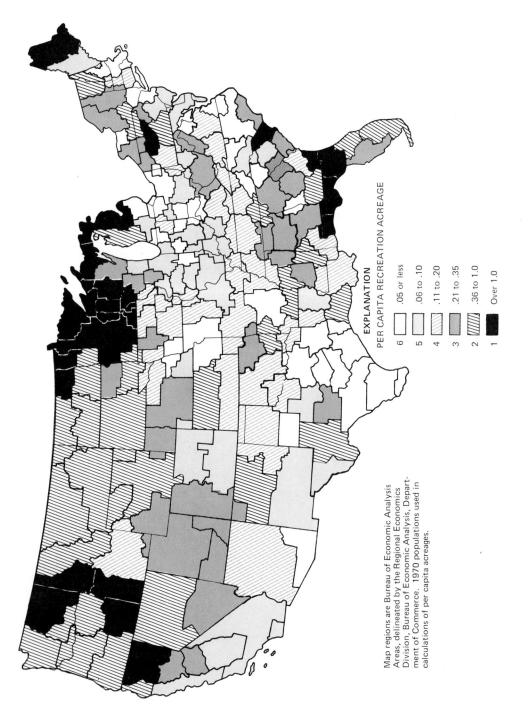

EXPLANATION

PER CAPITA RECREATION ACREAGE

6	.05 or less
5	.06 to .10
4	.11 to .20
3	.21 to .35
2	.36 to 1.0
1	Over 1.0

Map regions are Bureau of Economic Analysis Areas, delineated by the Regional Economics Division, Bureau of Economic Analysis, Department of Commerce. 1970 populations used in calculations of per capita acreages.

FIGURE 8.4   State and local park and recreation acreage per capita, by Bureau of Economic Analysis region, 1972. (BOR, 1973)

of the 11.6 million hectares (28.6 million acres) was in Alaska. In the rest of the nation, 0.6 million ha (1.5 million acres) of islands are publicly controlled. About 1.2 million ha (3 million acres) of private islands have recreational potential. Surprisingly, islands remain mostly undeveloped for recreational or other purposes. Recent attention to coastal islands of the southeastern states has raised interesting controversies between real estate speculators and conservation organizations.

Rivers and Streams: There are about 4.8 million km (three million miles) of watercourses in the nation. Ten per cent of that mileage has been dammed. Other stretches have been leveed and dredged or otherwise altered. The recreational and natural values of river protection have been recognized by law, but progress in effectively designating streams has been sluggish on state and federal levels. The recreational potential of these resources is tremendous.

Wilderness: In 1937, Robert Marshall wrote that "the universe of the wilderness is vanishing." Federally designated wilderness areas have recently produced much more debate and heat than seems appropriate. The wilderness resource has grown somewhat as an official entity on paper but not in reality. In fact, there are reductions in wilderness area left, except in some of the eastern states. States and forest industries have set aside areas and named them wilderness. Citizen groups and politicians are working hard to establish more areas in the national wilderness preservation system.

Historic Properties: These are included in the list of critical concerns because of their inherent uniqueness and the relative scarcity of nationally or regionally significant areas. The Historic Preservation Act of 1966 has stimulated the setting aside of many areas by private, local, state, and federal groups.

Arid and Semiarid Lands: These areas have long been abhorred and ignored. In recent years, they have become critical concerns because of the recreational impacts on them. The most dramatic impacts have been from the use of motorcycles and four-wheel-drive vehicles on the deserts of southeastern California and southern Nevada. The fragility of the ecosystems there and the difficulty with which they revive from impacts have prompted public action.

Mined Land: Strip mines were once thought to be wastelands. Now they have become occasional recreation places. With new state and federal laws requiring reclamation of surface-mined land, the recreation potential will increase, if appropriate planning and development occur.

Geographic Distribution of Resources

One measure of the availability of recreational opportunities is the parks and recreation area per capita. The nationwide recreation plan mapped the acres per capita available in 171 regions throughout the nation (Figure

8.4). This revealed that some regions had less than 0.05 acres per capita, whereas others had more than 1.0 acres per person. This does not include the large federal holdings in the West. Study of the map suggests that density of population has little to do with ability to provide state and local parks. Alaska has high per capita acreage, and some of the relatively remote sections of Texas have the lowest. The New York-New Jersey complex is low, as are southeastern Arizona and the Champaign, Illinois area.

Federal recreational resources are much less equitably distributed. More than 85 per cent of the federal lands are in the West and in Alaska, whereas nearly 85 per cent of the population is in the eastern parts of the nation. These federal resources cannot be moved, of course. Increasing eastern federal land holdings to any significant level is neither financially nor politically feasible. This situation will require intensive management of existing eastern lands. Vigorous initiative by state and local governments will be required if close-to-home recreation demand is to be met. Acquisition, development, and programming are the basic tools needed.

Land area alone cannot measure effective supply. The capacity of a resource to serve recreational needs is a valuable measure of the supply of recreation resources. For some activities, large areas are needed; but, for most, it is not the number of hectares but how they are used that is most important.

The following factors affect the capacity of an area: natural productivity of the soil and vegetation, design of the facilities and improvements, zoning of activities, types of activity mix, and programming. These can all increase the effective supply of existing properties. Strategic purchase of easements and development of linear parks for trails and streams can also help increase the power of the recreation dollar.

Literature Cited

Bureau of the Census. 1977. Statistical Abstract of the United States (1978). Washington D.C.: U.S. Department of Commerce. 1048 pp.
Bureau of Outdoor Recreation. 1973. Outdoor Recreation: a Legacy for America. Washington, D.C.: U.S. Department of the Interior. 89 pp.
MARSHALL, ROBERT. 1937. The universe of the wilderness is vanishing. Nature Magazine 29:235–240.
U.S. Forest Service. 1979. The 1980 RPA Assessment. Washington D.C.: U.S. Department of Agriculture, 1979.

C H A P T E R 9

Private Enterprise in Outdoor Recreation

Recreation for profit is a key factor in supplying opportunities. Two major kinds of enterprises exist—recreation service firms, such as campgrounds and ski resorts, and recreation real estate firms.

John Bintz is an apple farmer. His Michigan farm has hundreds of apple trees and a few added attractions. Beneath a big A-frame restaurant is a ski resort. Out in front is a homemade ski hill where 15 instructors train the youth of Bay City, Midland, and Saginaw to ski.

Skating-fishing ponds fill the holes from which the hill was built. This apple farm has a ski shop, a cider mill, a bakery, fruit farm sales, and a gift shop. Each of these enterprises is operated on an incentive program by a separate manager. Mr. Bintz, in mod clothes and a luxury car, coordinates everything. He puts on older clothes to help build or repair structures, to supervise improvements on a pond, or to pick apples.

Although Mr. Bintz is unusual for his energy and skill, he is representative of thousands of other entrepreneurs who are providing high-quality recreation opportunities. Most such firms are individually or family-owned. Some are major corporations.

Together, they are the largest factor in the outdoor recreation market in terms of total visitation. Although there are no accurate statistics on the visitor-hours handled by different sectors, all indications suggest that the commercial sector handles more total recreation participation than all federal agencies or than all state agencies; use of all local agencies may approximately equal the use of commercial areas.

Private recreation areas are extremely important to managers in the public sector. Without them, the pressures on public forests and parks would be intolerable.

The main purpose of most outdoor recreation enterprises is to return a profit to the owners. Although some of the operators seek primarily the joy of offering recreation opportunities to friends, even these must at least cover expenses to make the operations possible.

A general estimate of the relative profitability of various activities is listed in Table 9.1. This merely suggests areas where profits can be made, not that any business offering high-potential services will succeed.

The table refers to the general situation as perceived by the author.

TABLE 9.1 Financial potential for private supply of recreational facilities by activities and types of facilities.

Very high potential	Campgrounds for travelers
	Destination campgrounds
	Urban recreation facilities
	Organization camps
	Horse stables
	Amusement parks
High potential	Resorts
	Swimming lakes and pools
	Boating facilities
	Vacation center complexes (camping, swimming, boating)
	Downhill skiing
Medium potential	Nature study
	Picnicking
	Fishing
	Some hunting (preserves, leases)
	Off-road vehicle trails and courses
	Snowmobile trails and courses
	Interpretive activities
Low potential	Backcountry recreation use
	Large area activities—hunting, remote camping, boating
Almost no potential	Driving for pleasure
	Wilderness
	Wild and scenic rivers preservation
	Trails
	Special scenic/natural features preservation

There are quite profitable private enterprises operating in low-potential activities. The operators of outfitting and guide services near wilderness areas and wild rivers are examples. They do not provide the area but are, in essence, programmers of it. A number of scenic tourist attractions are owned and operated profitably. So are a few private nature centers and cultural/historic centers. However, nonprofit operations such as Colonial Williamsburg (Figure 9.1) have survived partly because of the continuing sponsorship, in this case by the Rockefeller family. With gradual withdrawal of sponsor money, the operation faces financial difficulties.

Types of Businesses

Commercial outdoor recreation enterprises offer many kinds of facilities, mostly of the developed type. Campgrounds are among the best known. Guest ranches, guest farms, and resorts are among the oldest elements of the industry. America's 650 to 700 ski resorts often have their base operation on private lands, with the tows and slopes using public lands, especially those of the U.S. Forest Service. Other recreation businesses include riding stables and trails, golf courses, fishing lakes, swimming lakes and pools,

FIGURE 9.1   At Colonial Williamsburg, history is reenacted in an authentic setting of prerevolutionary days. (HCRS)

off-road vehicle trails. There are shooting preserves and many leased hunting lands. Picnicking areas and ice skating rinks are other attractions. There are also marinas and clubs for boats and yachts and some commercial beaches. Outfitters and guides serve large public areas (Figure 9.2).

AMUSEMENT PARKS

Amusement parks are now incorporating natural resources into their plans and facing intensive maintenance and design problems. These facilities, which fall into the entertainment field as much as in recreation, have developed rapidly. There are 30 major theme parks and dozens of smaller parks, virtually all of which came into being since 1945, when Santa Claus Land was started in southern Indiana. The two Disney parks are the giants

Private Enterprise in Outdoor Recreation

Figure 9.2 Rafting expeditions on the Salmon and other rivers of the United States have become important concessions. (USFS)

of the industry, drawing one third of the total attendance at the major parks (Standard and Poor's, 1977). In 1977, Walt Disney World had more than 13 million visitors, producing $274 million in revenues.

Ski Resorts

Growth in ski resorts accompanied industrial growth of the 1960s. What used to be a rich man's sport or a poor man's necessity is now available to the middle classes and the rich. Skiing influences the location of major industries. The Martin Company, Eastman Kodak, IBM, Hewlett-Packard, and many major government operations have moved to Colorado, partly for the clean air and partly for the recreational opportunities in summer and winter. With them have come many new ski areas and many new complications for forest managers who are responsible for the land.

Ski developers are mostly in high finance. The Murchisons of Texas, Callaway Textiles of Georgia, LTV, Ralston Purina, and American Cement have major ski resorts in the West. Joseph Zoline and Swiss interests have

Recreation Places

TABLE 9.2 Selected major amusement parks in the United States.

Park	Location	Opening date	Owner
Disneyland	Anaheim, Calif.	1955	Walt Disney Productions
Cedar Point	Sandusky, Ohio	1957	Cedar Point, Inc.
Six Flags	(3 locations)	1959	Great Southwest
Busch Gardens	(3 locations)	1959	Anheuser-Busch
Sea World	(3 locations)	1964	Harcourt Brace Jovanovich
Kings Island	Cincinnati	1972	Taft Broadcasting
Magic Mountain	Los Angeles	1972	Newhall Land
Walt Disney World	Orlando, Fla.	1972	Walt Disney Productions
Carowinds	Charlotte, N.C.	1973	Taft & Kroger
Opryland	Nashville, Tenn.	1973	NLT Corporation
Great Adventure	New Jersey	1974	Hardwick, and others
Kings Dominion	Richmond, Va.	1975	Taft & Kroger
Great America	(2 locations)	1976	Marriott

Source: Standard and Poor's, 1977.

built an elaborate resort at Telluride, Colorado, investing at least $100 million.

These ski slopes are mostly located on national forest land. The district ranger or forest supervisor is responsible for administering the special use permits and analyzing the impacts of the ski slope. The Forest Service is now taking a much more active hand in guiding the development of ski slopes and is seeking to limit the number of people on a slope in a day. Construction of ski trails must leave the land undisturbed, reducing the possibility of bulldozing. The building or expansion of a ski resort has many other implications concerning land use and impacts on public lands, all related to the number of people attracted to the area in summer and winter. There are problems of water rights and water quality, roads, needs for camping facilities, pressures for trails, Nordic ski routes, avalanche control, and even pressures on timber harvest programs that will affect the scenery people come to enjoy.

RESORTS

The resort industry is old and widespread. It developed rapidly in northern states on remote lakes and rivers soon after World War I. As automobiles became available in the 1920s, the common man could reach the lakes of Minnesota, Michigan, and Wisconsin. The new resort businesses were small, usually owned and operated by families. These were in marked contrast to the existing large resorts that had developed on islands or on railroad routes. These older businesses were well financed and catered to the wealthy, who reached them by special train or boat.

After World War II, there was a quick revival among all resorts, but then a gradual decline set in. In Minnesota, the number dropped off by one third in the 1967–1977 decade (Blank, Simonson, and Larsen, 1977). The reasons are mostly related to other forms of recreation. The competition includes

> Artificial lakes built throughout the mid-south and central parts of the United States.
> Air conditioning.
> The new popularity of Florida, the Gulf Coast, and Texas.
> Automobile vacationing patterns, with shorter stays; average three-week resort stays in the late 1940s have dropped to less than one week.
> Camping popularity and availability; for example, about 40 per cent of Minnesota resorts now rent campsites.
> Lakefront second homes and year-round residences, sometimes involving converted resort property.
> Air travel allowing long-distance journeys, including resorts in Canada.
> New investment in destination resorts and other facilities all over the United States and the world.

North Country resorts have modernized to try to meet the competition, but there has been a shortage of massive amounts of capital to change the 1930s flavor of many of the businesses (Blank, Simonson, and Larsen, 1977).

About half of the resorts in this country are now owned by corporations, and 40 per cent, by families. The other 10 per cent are in the hands of clubs and partnerships.

CAMPGROUNDS

Private campgrounds have become more than sleeping camps. They are now resorts or recreation centers. The camper beside the highway makes relatively few demands, but even those transient camps must offer some recreational opportunities to be competitive. Swimming is perhaps the most frequently offered. In destination-type, resort campgrounds, swimming is particularly important. It is the most desired activity in a campground.

Other activities include a playground, with swings, teeter-totters, and other equipment. Game areas for badminton, horseshoes, ping-pong, and shuffleboard are common facilities. Indoor games often include revenue-producing banks of pinball machines and related mechanical devices.

The commercial campground industry involves big and small business. The most impressive recent trends are the development of chains of franchises and the tentative entry into the business of major corporations such as Gulf Oil, Holiday Inn, and Ramada Inns. Many of the latter have proven unsuccessful. The biggest element is still the family-operated campground, fishing lake, and other enterprises. Even the chains are mostly family-owned or partnership franchises, with only the name and central

FIGURE 9.3   A pole, a crawdad, and a fishin' hole—part of a KOA campground.

control under the management of major companies, such as Kampgrounds of America (KOA), United Camps, Safari Camps, Kamp Dakota, and Yogi Bear's Jellystone Parks (Figure 9.3).

Franchises: Franchises offer the advantage of advertising and management know-how for a price. The potential operator of a campground can purchase the name of the company and its services and usually gain a guaranteed territory. The cost is high. KOA, a few years ago, required payment of $10,000 as a nonrefundable franchise fee. Then there was a $4,500 "initial fee" and a $5,500 "completion fee." During operations, the holder of the franchise paid the KOA company 8 per cent on gross vehicle registration fees and an annual "renewal fee" of $300 (Creedman, 1973). The capital is the responsibility of the franchisee, but loans may be easier for investors who are associated with a nationally known firm. There is no evidence that well-managed franchised campgrounds are more or less profitable than well-managed campgrounds without a franchise name. However, over the years, the average investment in campgrounds and other commercial recreation facilities has risen. There are relatively fewer shoe-string operations run on a part-time basis. These are still important, but the business demands time and ingenuity to be successful.

Campground Associations: Recreation businesses have banded to-gether to promote their enterprises and to make themselves heard by state and local government. Campground associations are most frequently en-countered. They are usually organized on a statewide basis with voluntary membership. Less than half the private campgrounds are usually represented in the membership. The Vermont Association of Private Campground

Owners and Operators has member campgrounds plus associate members that are groceries, restaurants, and other service businesses, which promote the association members. The Delaware Campground Association has 19 members, which are listed and described on a state map in folders that are distributed at travel information centers and by mail. The member campgrounds range in size from 66 to more than 600 sites. The major values of these associations are three—joint promotion and information to the public; a collective voice in government affairs, such as planning advisory committees and legislative affairs; and the workshops and tours the groups sponsor. These workshop events are surprisingly open and informative. Members tell other members their successes and failures. They exchange ideas with their competitors, freely discussing their finances and tricks of the trade.

The major national association is the National Campground Owners Association. It is made up of state associations and individual enterprises. In the late 1960s, the Family Camping Federation made strong efforts to upgrade and promote private campgrounds but lost its impetus in the mid-1970s.

Economics of Private Recreation

The commercial outdoor recreation industry is a regional and national market structure identified as *monopolistic competition*. This term, confusing to many, means that there are highly competitive conditions among many sellers but that each seller offers a special product or service that can be differentiated from other, similar products. Thus, the monopoly element is the name, location, and character of the recreational facility plus the service offered. Such nonprice factors influence the buyers. The consumer can identify with his favorite place by its brand name. Most of the enterprises in the industry are small. There are many of them; it is thus a competitive industry. There are many sellers who offer close substitutes of service so the consumer has some choice. Entry into the business is relatively easy. Most American industries are in this monopolisitc competition type of market—restaurants, motels, retail establishments, service companies, and professional services.

A few, such as automobile and steel manufacturers are called *oligopolies*, with few sellers and large capital commitments to enter the market. Farther down the scale of concentration are *monopolies*, such as power and telephone utilities that offer the consumer only one source of goods or services and, therefore, are heavily regulated by the government to protect consumers. The other type of market structure is *pure competition*, which is best characterized by agriculture, with many sellers and virtually no differentiation of product.

Because the recreation industry is characterized by monopolistic competition, the managers can increase sales by using non-price factors related to the economic principles of that structure. Because entry into the business is fairly easy, there is little need for huge, corporate investments. The operation can be personalized. Ma, Pa, and the kids can start fairly small and build a business. Many firms, however, start too small and never build up enough. Most financially successful firms have invested at least $100,000 in land, facilities, and improvements (Degler and Knudson, 1972). The owner's personal touch has much to do with developing customer loyalty. Nonprice competition among these firms takes four forms:

1. Product adaptation—better, more attractive, cleaner, more spacious facilities and services, variety of activities.
2. Promotion—advertising and salesmanship.
3. Location—accessibility, scenery, and/or proximity to other attractions.
4. Quality guarantee—assurance of certain facilities, character, and dependability.

Promotion and quality guarantees are used heavily by franchise chains in the travel campground market. Promotional brochures, directories, and national advertisements help make the name a household word. The parent companies insist that a basic package of facilities and services is available so customers can depend on a given, acceptable quality. This characteristic of reliability and predictability has also been a key to the success of several major motel chains.

FINANCE

Financing of private outdoor recreation enterprises is one of the most serious problems faced by the industry. This has been a persistent problem nationwide, but, as the industry has developed, lending institutions have been somewhat more supportive. Problems that concern lenders are the seasonal nature of the businesses, the limited managerial ability of operators, the possible amplified negative effects of a downturn in the economy on recreational spending (possibly an erroneous assumption), and the limited equity involved in the mortgages (Shanklin, 1967). New owners must often put up personal collateral. As loan rates soared into the 10 per cent range, operators found it difficult to match interest payments with returns from the business.

FACTORS OF SUCCESS

There is a wide range of income differences among firms. These are based on many factors, none of which can be easily pinpointed. Among the factors identified with profitability is location. Accessibility to population centers, resort areas, and/or major highways seems to be important (Epperson, 1977; Degler and Knudson, 1972; Callahan and Knudson, 1966). Expe-

FIGURE 9.4 Caves are managed by private enterprise and all levels of government for recreation purposes. (NPS)

rience in the business seems to aid profitability. In southern Indiana, the most profitable firms had been in operation an average of 12 years. They had invested considerably more than less successful firms and had greater annual operating expenditures (Degler and Knudson, 1972).

The types of activities offered have an effect on profitability. In Indiana, where there are few large resorts and businesses are mostly family-oriented, the swimming lakes proved to be the largest money-makers. In Florida and Colorado, where the tourist business is of primary concern, campgrounds or sightseeing enterprises would be expected to be among the most profitable.

As in most business ventures, there is no guarantee of financial success in outdoor recreation. A mix of factors, not well identified by analysts, contributes to successful operations. A key ingredient is the mysterious but real element called management. The entrepreneurial ability of an owner-operator who dedicates his energies to pleasing customers and guiding the business is a major factor in success.

Truck drivers, farmers, and school teachers jump into the outdoor recreation business every year. At least three reasons motivate them (Lykes, 1968):

1. It looks like a good way to make money fast. This misleading appearance is debunked by the studies of economics of the business (Callahan and Knudson, 1966; Degler and Knudson, 1972; LaPage, Cormier, and Maurice, 1972). Returns to management and operator labor and capital are less than 10 per cent per year, based on the total amount invested. If manager labor were taken out, many enterprises would not have a positive income.
2. The investor owns a piece of property at a strategic location. That is a key to successful operation, if all other factors are positive.
3. A neighboring campground is doing well, and the investor believes he can provide complementary services or a better campground that will draw customers.

Another attraction to the business is its seasonal nature. Many people get into the business because they are recreation participants who think they can operate an ideal campground. The business is extremely demanding of time, especially during the season. The manager must be a Jack-of-all-trades. Patience and friendliness with people are essential. Good business sense also helps.

Commercial outdoor recreation areas are admirably helping to meet recreation demand, at no cost to the taxpayers. The industry, however, has serious troubles, especially the little firms. Researchers report low earnings. Government officially encourages private enterprise but competes through low-cost public facilities. Many operator-owners have dropped out of the business after 2 to 10 years of marginal operation. Financing and insurance are hard to get. Local, state, and federal governments have imposed difficult laws in regard to public health, sewage and water, safety, tax assessments, and liability.

Laws requiring racial integration at public places upset many owners who held racial prejudices or believed their customers would not accept integration. A large number of these avoided the law by creating "clubs," which governed the admission policies to the enterprise.

The problems of occupancy at campgrounds plague most operators. With the slowdown in camping during the week and on rainy or cool days, these firms are left with occupancy of 25 per cent or so. Operating costs do not drop accordingly, so profits decline or disappear. To reduce the impact of the low-occupancy days, many campgrounds offer season or year-round rates. Trailers are moved onto the site for the entire season,

FIGURE 9.5 Private enterprise recreation varies from down-home, shoestring fishing lakes to elaborate resort-ski lodges.

with the campers coming whenever they have time. That way, the owner is guaranteed a steady income and the campers have a bargain rate. The campground takes on the look of a trailer park, but regular customers often make special efforts to keep their place neat.

One key trouble of the private sector is the fees charged by many firms. They apparently feel they must keep prices close to those of public sites. However, the nonprice competition aspects of the industry allow flexibility in pricing, as quality and service are flexible. Campgrounds that have raised their prices have apparently not lost appreciable numbers of campers (LaPage, Cormier, and Maurice, 1972).

144   Recreation Places

Fees at private areas are usually higher than in public campgrounds. In 1977, U.S. Forest Service planning data indicated that the average fee for campsite use was $3.22 at public campgrounds and $4.60 at private parks. This suggests that the private areas must offer more services or somehow differentiate their product. One of the key differences is the personal attention usually received at private campgrounds. A family operation, with constant presence of the operators on the site, usually ensures more personal service. Other key factors are the electrical and sewage services that private enterprises offer in much greater frequency than the public areas. Many private campgrounds also have a grocery or snack service, and most have hot showers and flush toilets, even though these are sometimes in rather rustic buildings.

Differentiation of the product has taken some interesting turns as the campground business has grown. There was a big explosion in camping and private campgrounds during the 1960s and on into the 1970s. It was related to the rapid acceptance of recreational vehicles. The trend stimulated private campground operators to provide increasing luxury. Electricity and water are basics.

A Florida campground allows no tents, no children (except in summer), and no pets (kennel service available). It has 350 full hookup units, planned entertainment with a recreation director, square and modern dancing, 12 shuffleboard courts, paved streets with curbing, a concrete patio and walkway at each site, a laundry with soft water, mail delivered to the campsite, a barbecue area, a swimming pool, an air-conditioned recreation hall, and easy access to shopping. Nearby are golf courses, beaches and marinas, racetracks, dinner theaters, good restaurants, and an airport. Other features that many Florida camping resorts offer include tennis courts, a general store, a bait and tackle shop, ocean beach with shark nets, nature interpreters, telephone and television jacks, toll-free reservations, and credit card acceptance.

The campground administrator is really a city manager, even in the more rustic campgrounds. Above and beyond scenery, space, and programs, he must be concerned with roads, water supply and distribution, sanitary and sewer facilities, garbage, electricity, safety, protection, and information. Some campgrounds even offer banking, laundry, baby-sitting, stores, and church services.

A secret of business success is to latch on to something promising early, before anyone else knows about it. Get involved with a new product, idea, or activity at the beginning of its climb. Then ride it all the way to the top.

Profiting from the changes in society is how many millionaires acquired their first million dollars. They took the big risks and profited. Many others who take risks on new products, services, or ideas do not profit as much. Some lose their shirts. Of course, it isn't just taking risk that produces profits. It is taking risks that will pay off—calculated risks. It also involves considerable amount of careful product-market analysis, good accounting, sound customer relations, and a worthwhile product or service.

Many people jumped into the outdoor recreation business when it was seen that a trend was developing. They did not necessarily become rich. A few did. Many fell by the wayside, forgotten amidst the journalistic success stories.

Recreational Real Estate

One of the best ways to preserve the wilderness is for you to own it! It may sound like a paradox, but selling land often saves it . . . because people like you buy it. They take good care of their wooded acres and the natural beauty around them. In fact, conservation-minded people are our largest number of buyers, and we have sold thousands of acres of primitive land in Idaho, Eastern Washington and Montana. Shouldn't you set aside some mountain or meadow land now for recreation, camping, a cabin? Maybe for retirement. Low down payment. Terms available. Guaranteed road access, warranty deed and title insurance. As low as $1950 for land in the Northwest! 5–40 acre and larger tracts for recreation, retirement. P. O. Box 14006, Opportunity Station, Spokane, Washington 99214 *(Advertisement for Reforestation, Inc.)*

At least four million second homes have been constructed in the United States for vacation purposes. At least 10 million recreational lots have been subdivided for sale (American Society of Planning Officials, 1976). Florida and Texas lead the way among lots sold in interstate commerce. New Mexico, Arizona, Colorado, California, and northeastern Pennsylvania are other major locations.

THE SECOND-HOME PHENOMENON

Royalty and the rich have long enjoyed the privileges of owning country or coastal retreats to which they might repair to escape stress. Some of these houses have become well known: The Rockefeller retreat at Bar Harbor, the Queen's various castles in England and Scotland, the Kennedy compound at Hyannis, the Nixon San Clemente estate and the Ford condominium at Vail, Colorado.

Perhaps imitating the rich, millions of middle-class Americans and Europeans have bought second homes or vacation cottages. During the 1960s, such activity surged. Individual cottages in the woods and isolated cabins in the mountains are still the image of second homes, but high-density, platted developments in rural areas are predominant in the market.

Sales used to be made by a farmer, rancher, or small real estate company on a face-to-face basis. The U.S. Forest Service, starting in 1915, leased summer home sites in designated portions of the forests, a program now much deemphasized. In the 1960s, an aggressive, though disaggregated, real estate industry sold millions of acres by mail and telephone solicitation.

146

Many buyers agreed to purchase land without seeing it. Some of the larger companies offered free or partially paid trips to see the sites.

The tract lot purchaser often buys land in a fairly high-density, planned development. Some areas offer lots one quarter or one fifth of an acre in size. Rather than a cabin in the woods for hunting, the family purchases a portion of a potential leisure-oriented town that could be more crowded than its first home.

The motives seem to be twofold. First is the desire to own some vacation land, simply for the satisfaction of its use and/or ownership. Second is the belief in the eventual profitability of land investment.

A report in the early 1970s (Ragatz, 1974) indicated that five to seven million families owned some type of recreational real estate. Of these, more than three million had second homes.

Originally, the wealthy owners concentrated on Cape Cod, the east coast of Florida, Lake Tahoe, Estes Park, the northwestern shore of Lake Michigan, and other large estate areas. The new recreational communities are scattered throughout the nation, and they are for the vast middle-class population. Some are modest trailer towns beside reservoirs. Others are huge urban complexes that are suffering growing pains.

Many of the recent real estate developments have emerged as total planned communities. They are often designed to blend with and take advantage of the natural surroundings. Many of these communities are not accurately described as second home sites or retirement communities. Although these purposes may be primary, residents are settling into some of the recreational communities on a permanent basis.

Golf, tennis, and swimming are central recreational activities around which many of these communities are built. Several hire well-known professional athletes to serve as resident teachers and coaches. Some stage well-known tournaments. Their locations range from ocean islands to ski resorts high in the mountains. Examples include the chain of Club Mediterranean resorts scattered over the tropics and subtropics and ski resorts such as Vail, Colorado. The former are seaside resorts operated somewhat like a hotel with food and fun. The latter is a community with owned or rented cottages and condominiums, with an open-door policy for the skiing and commercial facilities.

A number of luxury-oriented resorts exist in the mountains and on islands off the Southeast coast. They cater to the affluent (Table 9.3), with homesites ranging up to $100,000, and standard design cottages, houses, and apartments from $40,000 to $250,000.

The investment in these resorts is not modest. At Fripp Island, in South Carolina, $800,000 was recently spent installing an irrigation system in the golf courses and improving it. Hound Ears Lodge and Club in the mountains of North Carolina completed plans for an $8 million condominium in 1977. The recreationists are willing to pick up the heavy investment

TABLE 9.3   Southeastern resort communities.

Name and developer	Facilities	House arrangements
Sea Pines Plantation Hilton Head Island South Carolina	Five-mile beach, 45 tennis courts, 4 golf courses, 2 marinas	Time-sharing condominiums
Palmetto Dunes Hilton Head Island South Carolina (Phipps Land Co., Atlanta)	Three-mile beach, 2 golf courses, fishing lakes, 11 swim pools, beach recreation center; racquet club (Rod Laver); boat-fish equipment rental; 14-mile navigable lagoon system	Resort and residential hotel— 360 rooms, condominiums, villas, homesites, condominium villas, 1-wk shares = $1,200 to $5,700
Fripp Island South Carolina (15 Savings and Loan Associations)	golf course, oceanfront beach, pool, restaurant, lounge, 21 tennis courts	Cottages, tree houses, golf villas, nature villas, oceanfront lots
Hound Ears Lodge and Club North Carolina (community of primary and secondary homes)	golf, skiing	Homes, guest lodge, rental chalets
Grandfather Golf and Country Club North Carolina	2 golf courses, tennis, horseback riding, boating, swim beach, trout fishing	500 homes and condominiums, one-acre lots, owners or condominium renters only
Kaawah Island South Carolina (Kuwait Investors)	Inn—150 guest rooms, restaurants, golf course, 9 tennis courts, racquet club (Roscoe Tanner), beach club (private), olympic pool	Residential cottages, villas, and townhouses
Seabrook Island South Carolina	golf course, tennis center, lake fishing, 3.5-mile beach	Homes, condominiums, tree houses, villas, beach club, pond cottages, golf villas, half condos on time-sharing rental plan, lots, 0.5–1 acre
The Landings Skidaway Island Georgia (Union Camp)	27 holes golf, tennis, pool, private club, marina	Residential only, 2,000 units maximum
Sandestin Florida (Charles Trust)	1.5-mile bay, 0.25-mile gulf, golf course, 10 tennis courts, racquet club, health clubs	Sheraton Inn—96 rooms, convention facilities, townhouses, villas, villages
Innisbrook Resort Florida (Gulf Hosts International, Inc.)	3 golf courses, 13 tennis courts, 5 pools, sailing, fishing, recreational program	Condominium apartments furnished

Source: Cheatham and Cheatham, 1977.

Recreation Places

costs. Despite the national economic conditions, Seabrook Island in South Carolina sold $3.8 million worth of homes and property in 1976. In the first half of 1977, sales were at $5.3 million and were expected to rise to an $8 million total by the end of the year (Cheatham and Cheatham, 1977).

In contrast with these beautiful, elaborate, high-investment operations are many marginal subdivisions of rural land that offer greater promise than performance.

The recreational real estate business is often a matter of paper. Title to pieces of land is assigned to persons who have agreed to send monthly checks to some office or bank. Many of the purchasers receive newspapers or magazines about the development but visit the land only rarely. The American Society of Planning Officials (1976) reported that lot sales exceeded construction of second homes by a rate of 3 to 1. Many lot purchasers intend to hold the lots as an investment for resale at an undetermined date. Speculative purchase is most highly concentrated in unimproved recreational subdivisions. Lot buyers who intend to build on and to use their properties for seasonal or permanent residences tend to purchase lots in subdivisions that have more improvements and amenities.

Overall, recreational subdivisions have fewer infrastructure improvements than first home properties. Two thirds of the projects have no central sewer system; one third have no central water system; most have only dirt roads.

Even well-capitalized firms such as Boise Cascade found themselves overinvested in land for resale. Their recreational lands division seriously cut into company assets, requiring the firm to abandon their extensive plans and to take major financial losses in the early 1970s. McCullough Corporation of oil and chainsaw fame had six major communities, several of which were successful. In 1977, the corporation abandoned recreational real estate as an enterprise.

The Department of Housing and Urban Development is responsible for enforcing laws governing interstate land sales. The laws are designed to protect the consumer against fraudulent practices of land developers and promoters.

Sales agents and developers must register their intention to sell or lease land by mail or other means in interstate commerce, in any subdivision of 50 or more lots. They must file a statement of record, describing the land and its ownership, and issue a printed property report to the purchaser at least 72 hours before a buyer signs an agreement to purchase or lease.

Title XIV of the Housing and Urban Development Act of 1968 (P.L. 90–448) is the legal authority for the program. This gave the Federal Office of Interstate Land Sales some teeth by requiring registration and full disclosure of plans and assets for most developments larger than 50 acres. The following year, the law was amended to require a 48-hour refund period for buyers, a property report for customers, and accurate information. Some of the developers have adopted a stiff code of ethics through the American Land Development Association. At least 20 states restrict use of shorelines, river valleys, and mountainsides for building. County zoning commissions, the traditional regulator of land use changes, haven't always been able to cope.

LOCAL IMPACTS

Impacts of recreational lot sales and subsequent house building have been outlined by the Council on Environmental Quality (1974). If the development, which is usually built to lower standards than most residential subdivisions, is used only for weekends and vacations, the impacts may be minor. Many problems arise when the recreational use becomes residential use and the leisure homes become permanent homes.

Leisure-home tracts are usually seen as beneficial to the local economy. Owners pay property taxes and spend money in the local economy. During their short periods of vacation residence, they demand some local public and private services, such as road maintenance, water and sewer service, police protection, and some added health care. The additional costs of these services to the existing government are likely to be lower than the property taxes they pay, as long as the subdivision remains in seasonal use. When residents become permanent, they require other services, often more costly, especially for schools and better roads, the cost of which may well exceed the revenues added.

Low-quality developments that become heavily used can pollute streams if septic systems are not designed for high use, overtax local water supplies, and increase erosion and siltation of streams. Because many recreational sites are in fragile ecosystems, such as dunes, marshes, and mountains, these problems may be quite acute.

A Wisconsin study of lake property owners (Klessig, 1973) revealed that the following services were desired by more than half of 1,183 landowner interviewees; the governmental unit most likely affected is indicated in parentheses.

Stocking of fish (state or federal government).
Enforcing building codes (county government).
Property tax information and discussion (county).
Inspecting private septic tanks (county).
Monitoring sources of pollution (county or state).
Pumping and servicing septic tanks (private).
Patrolling for vandalism (county).
Regulating skiing and boating (state).
Stabilizing water levels (state, county, or private).

Perhaps the most important consequence to recreation is the tendency for private lots to block off public access to prime recreation resources.

Many Midwestern and Eastern lakes are completely encircled by houses, with no access to the water for the public. An alarming amount of the nation's ocean beaches have been preempted by private cottages and estates, as well as by urban coastal strips. Parking and access to the public beaches is often made difficult by private land. Where public agencies have acquired ocean and lake frontage, the costs of additional acquisition for parking have often been prohibitive. A slightly different access problem has developed by historical accident in the mountain West. Private ownership of the valleys, often in the form of large ranches, blocks access from main roads in the valleys to public lands on the hillsides.

VALUES OF PARKS TO PROPERTY

The impact of recreational areas on the values of neighboring real estate is another important aspect of this question. Real estate values are heavily influenced by the proximity of properties to recreational areas. Lots and homes adjacent to open-space parks, golf courses, wildlife refuges, forests, and lakes usually bring a higher value on the market than do comparable offerings without such proximity.

The beauty of open space as an extension of one's lawn is a major factor. The convenience of access is another. Proximity to swimming pools, ballfields, playgrounds, and game courts are usually assets in real estate transactions, assuming that a residence is not so close that lights, noise, and traffic from the facilities are nuisances.

Recreational facilities and parks have become important in industrial locations. When firms move, the executives often consider the parks, pools, golf courses, mountains, and lakes with traditional factors such as transportation, raw materials, markets, and costs of labor.

THE PARK CITY

Cities can be parks (Rose, 1976). When the residential and travel environments are totally beautiful, enriching, and pleasant, the parks people will have moved from patch parks to park cities.

Attempts to achieve something similar have been most common on small-scale real estate developments. Apartment complexes, condominiums, lake housing, and small subdivisions sometimes are built around community recreational features and facilities. Builders and renters have found that swimming pools, golf courses, picnic areas, tennis, basketball, volleyball, and shuffleboard courts, and similar facilities help home sales and rentals. Owners usually pay fees for upkeep and programming and have exclusive use rights of such facilities.

Large-scale developments that incorporate leisure facilities into a major plan include the new towns of Reston, Virginia, and Columbia, Maryland. Both have problems, but they demonstrate that communities can be beautiful and offer ample outdoor recreation opportunities.

Literature Cited

American Society of Planning Officials. 1976. Subdividing Rural America; Impacts of Recreational Lot and Second Home Development; Executive Summary. Washington, D.C. Council of Environmental Quality.

BLANK, UEL, LARRY SIMONSON and DAYTON LARSEN. 1977. Minnesota's resort-tourism in critical transition. Minnesota Tourist Travel Notes 15(2):1–8.

CALLAHAN, J. C. and D. M. KNUDSON. 1966. Economic Aspects of Commercial Outdoor Recreation Enterprises in Southern Indiana. Lafayette, Ind.: Purdue Univ., Ag. Exp. Sta., Research Bulletin No. 814. 20 pp.

CHEATHAM, EDGAR and PATRICIA CHEATHAM. 1977. Is it still the good life? A new look at some of the south's well-known resort communities. Pace 4(5):6–11.

Council on Environmental Quality. 1974. Environmental Quality; the Fifth Annual Report. Washington, D.C.: 597 pp.

CREEDMAN, MICHAEL. 1973. A franchise is a hard way to get rich. Money 2(9):33–37.

DEGLER, GEORGE F. and DOUGLAS M. KNUDSON. 1972. Growth and Change in the Commercial Outdoor Recreation Industry in Southern Indiana. W. Lafayette, Ind.: Purdue Univ., Ag. Exp. Sta., Research Bulletin No. 892. 14 pp.

EPPERSON, ARLIN F. 1977. Private and Commercial Recreation. New York: John Wiley and Sons. 385 pp.

KLESSIG, LOWELL L. 1973. Lake Property Owners in Northern Wisconsin. Madison: University of Wisconsin Extension for Upper Great Lakes Regional Commission. 146 pp.

LAPAGE, WILBUR F., PAULA L. CORMIER and STEVEN C. MAURICE. 1972. The Commercial Campground Industry in New Hampshire. Upper Darby, Pa.: U.S. Forest Service Research Paper NE-255. 41 pp.

LYKES, IRA B. 1968. Report of planning and development committee (Family Camping Federation). Family Camping Leader 6(1):4–11.

RAGATZ, RICHARD L. ASSOCIATES, INC. 1974. Recreational Properties: an Analysis of the Markets for Privately Owned Recreational Lots and Leisure Homes. Springfield, Va.: Council on Environmental Quality, PB-233.

ROSE, LARRY L. 1976. People and urban parks. In: Knudson, D. M. (ed.). Managing Recreation Resources for Century III. West Lafayette, Ind.: Purdue University. p. 49.

SHANKLIN, JOHN. 1967. Financing of Private Outdoor Recreation. Washington, D.C.: U.S. Dept. of the Interior. 5 pp.

Standard and Poor's. 1977. Leisure-time Basic Analysis. S & P Industry Surveys, pp. L8–L38.

Industrial Recreation

This chapter deals with outdoor recreation opportunities provided by industries to the general public and to its employees. The major focus is on large firms. Most private recreation land is owned by individuals, some of whom are farmers and ranchers. Their contributions to recreation supply are also mentioned.

Industrial Lands for Public Recreation

Industrial lands provide significant recreation opportunities in some sections of the country (Figure 10.1). More than half of the 68 million acres of industrial forest and range lands are in the southern states. In 1978, Forest Service studies indicated that 73 per cent of corporate lands were open for recreation of some sort, to at least some people. Forty-four per cent is open to the general public without permission.

The redwood industries of California set up a Redwood Council in 1965 to help create a more favorable image of their work among an increasingly hostile public that was moving toward creation of a Redwoods National Park. Part of the effort was to set up Redwood Industry Recreation Areas, which included campgrounds, picnic areas, redwood groves, and nature centers. They hired a forester to promote these recreation places, even though they ran into problems with the sensitive liability laws of California.

Olin Mathieson, for years, has operated a demonstration hunting preserve and target shooting area, partly for the public and partly to promote the sports for which it manufactures arms and ammunition.

These are but a few examples of industrial policies that offer considerable recreational opportunities, particularly in the South and Northeast. Most of these firms are not primarily interested in the recreation business. It is a by-product of their timber-growing land. Some companies merely open their lands; others employ a staff to manage an extensive recreation program and a sophisticated policy. Collectively, they put considerable time and effort into the complex production of recreation services.

Industries holding large forest-water properties include wood-using industries such as paper companies and lumber companies; other manufacturing industries such as chemical, textile, and steel firms; utility and public service companies, such as gas and electric firms, water companies, and railroads.

Examples of the various types of industries follow:

Wood-using Industries: St. Regis Paper Company has a nationally advertised policy of allowing public use of many of its lands for hunting, fishing, and other recreational pursuits. Some of this land has developed campsites, picnic areas, boat ramps, and other facilities. Most of it is forest land where the recreationist can find acres of woods for dispersed types of activities.

Bowaters Southern Paper Company and its subsidiary, Hiwasee Land Company, have a three-phase program of providing public recreation.

1. Many of the lands are open to sportsmen. Hunting groups and the company plant food strips in pine plantations to enhance the chances of producing game.

FIGURE 10.1 Taking time to stop and smell the roses is worth the entry fee at Hershey Rose Gardens.

Recreation Places

FIGURE 10.2 Hunting in late fall is a major activity on forest industry lands as well as on public lands. (NPS)

2. The company constructs and operates facilities for camping, picnicking, and hiking.
3. A Pocket Wilderness Program sets aside areas of unusual natural and scenic interest as preserves, accessible only by trail and dedicated to public study and enjoyment.

These areas vary in size from 2 to 120 hectares. The first four were established in 1970, totaling 450 ha (1,100 acres).

Weyerhaeuser Corporation dedicated the nation's first tree farm and tree farm park in the state of Washington in 1941. In the West, it now has nine camping parks that charge only a nominal fee. In 1975, the corporation estimated that it permitted hunting and fishing on 90 per cent of its tree farm lands. Twelve employees were hired to manage wildlife and to protect the life of the streams in conjunction with high-yield forest policies. Innovations in the recreation field include free cross-country skiing with a maintained trail in Washington, a ski resort in Vermont, and the development of nature trails throughout its properties. In the South, Weyerhaeuser leases blocks of land to hunting clubs. High-yield forestry requires many roads, opening the forest in many spots to public visitation for various activities. In addition, the corporation has provided vacation homesites for its employees in some of the more scenic parts of its lands. General public use of the timber lands is allowed for hunting, fishing, and hiking within prescribed limits of safety and company interests (Figure 10.2).

Industrial Recreation

155

International Paper Company owns 8.5 million acres of forest land plus rights on another 7 million acres, according to its 1975 annual report. It employs 4,000 full-time woodlands people, including 500 professional foresters. It has 28 pulp and paper mills in the United States, Canada, Europe, and South America. Although its major goal is producing income for its stockholders, this company has the vision to see the importance of managing the forest for multiple use and of educating the youth of the nation about forestry and conservation. International paper manages its lands with five aims in view: as a source of vital wood fiber; to preserve scenic beauty; to increase recreational opportunities; to enhance production of game and wildlife; and to safeguard watersheds.

Other Manufacturing Industries: United States Steel has advertised that its lands open for public recreation total the same land area as Rocky Mountain National Park (about 100,000 ha) but are located closer to the people.

Numerous coal mining companies also open their strip mine lakes and surrounding reclaimed land to the public. Others have donated or sold such lands to states, municipalities, and private concerns for park development.

Land-holding Companies: Louisiana Land and Title Company and Gulf and Western Corporation both have forest and wetland areas available for public recreational use. They have also donated lands for public and private preserves or recreation areas.

Utility and Public Service Companies: Railroads made early efforts to enhance the communities they served by building parks near the depots. Across Nebraska and Colorado, some of these remain as attractive, small city parks. More recently, some of the western checkerboard properties that railroads were given by the government to encourage such use have been opened for recreation or traded to public recreation agencies. Burlington Northern, in cooperation with neighboring property owners, recently dedicated some of its Montana lands as a scenic river corridor, allowing public access and maintaining the land in its natural state.

Pacific Gas & Electric Company derives much of its electric power from hydroelectric plants in the California mountains. Since it is a monopoly, California law limits its profits to 6 per cent, so the excess can go into projects such as parks and recreation. The company maintains a recreation planning and development team of foresters, engineers, and recreation specialists. By regulations of the Federal Power Commission, this and other. utilities must make a recreation development report on their reservoir plans. Thus, PG&E now has a series of recreation areas around its reservoirs. These vary in development from simple fishing access with parking to rather elaborate, though rustic, picnic and camping grounds. The company moved into the cities in the early 1970s. Where it had booster stations or wide rights of way for power lines, it installed small parks, trails, and bike paths for local use.

MOTIVATING FACTORS

Industries are by nature motivated by money. This is one factor that stimulates entry into offering recreation, but probably not a dominant one.

On forest lands, recreation and timber production can be compatible. Slight modifications in logging patterns and planning of recreation use can produce positive results for both the companies and visitors. Recreation is one more benefit of the land.

Prior Use: Some companies have opened their lands simply because people were already using the land, so they felt it might as well be an official and positive policy. Often, formalizing the use allowed land managers to provide facilities and thus concentrate and systematize use, reducing impacts and litter problems.

Fire Control: Providing opportunities for neighbors to use the land may encourage them to take better care of it. Incendiarism has long been a serious problem in the South. A lock-out policy would do little to prevent fires; a let-in policy may promote a sense of stewardship and sharing among neighbors.

Economics: Recreation is a valid economic use of industrial lands. It has two primary values to the companies. First, recreation is a means of making money or protecting an investment. Second, the company presumably benefits through public relations and advertising by allowing recreational use of its lands.

Income from recreation uses may pay the costs of interest, taxes, and patrolling of timber lands. Annual tax costs are financial drains that are added to the compound interest costs of producing timber over 15 to 80 years. They can make the timber investment financially unprofitable. By keeping annual costs near zero, deductions against the final timber crop are reduced. The goodwill of neighbors is of economic importance to any large landowner. There is no way that the company can effectively patrol large holdings against trespass. Friendly neighbors with an interest in the property can be powerful deterrents to unfriendly acts.

The Connor Lumber Company in Wisconsin has turned its old steam logging train and three miles of track into a commercial and educational business. For a substantial fee, a visitor can ride through the woods to a logging camp that includes a store, animal rides, and other features. Here, one can pay for a ride through a swamp or for a wagon ride with a forestry lecture through some of the forest management area. This commercial operation is an enterprise of the company that produces extra revenue and revives logging history.

Eminent Domain: The power of eminent domain is one of the motivating factors in industrial concern about the public, although it may not be expressed openly. Business does not function by divine or self-imposed right but exists with the sanction of the people as a whole. The interests of the public are expressed through government, which can turn public opinion into legislation. Likewise, the government can turn privately owned land into publicly owned parks, forests, and scenic rivers. That has happened several times in recent memory, and the forest product industry managers are well aware of the lingering possibility.

In the 1940s, the State of Michigan turned about 12,100 ha (30,000 acres) of Connor Lumber Company forests into Porcupine Mountains State Park. Nearby Pictured Rocks National Lakeshore contains about 4,050 ha (10,000 acres) of land that was industrial forest until the 1960s. In Minnesota, Boise Cascade used to own 16,200 ha (40,000 acres) of what became Voyageurs National Park in the 1970s. The St. Croix and the Allagash Scenic Riverways were long managed as paper and power company lands; the new designations put new (and probably unnecessary) restrictions on the lands bordering the streams, with some of the land being transferred to the government. Redwood National Park was purchased from industrial owners who relinquished over 25,000 ha (65,000 acres).

In each of these cases, the companies were compensated for the value of the land that was transferred to the governments. In each case, the transfer was a major inconvenience and disruption of long-range company plans.

The process is perfectly legal and as fair as can be managed in an imperfect world. The U.S. system of land ownership, commonly known as fee simple, is really "free and common socage." This is based on a medieval English type of land tenure. It merely gives the "owner" the right to the land. If taxes are not paid, all right to the land vanishes. Whoever pays the taxes takes over the right to that land. This is one proof that any piece of land is not totally "mine." If the public interest in using the land exceeds the public interest in keeping it under private ownership, the corporate public body can declare that the land is to revert to public ownership upon payment of just compensation. This process, referred to as *condemnation*, is the imposition of the power of *eminent domain*.

Private corporations operate lands under franchise from public opinion; that franchise can be modified or withdrawn by the people's representatives in government at any time. One clear and simple self-interest reason that industry opens its lands for recreation is the hope that a friendly, well-treated public may be less prone to see reason to take lands or to pass restrictive legislation than would a hostile, uninformed public. That is a strong argument for industry-sponsored interpretive and educational programs as well. It is doubtful that friendly hikers and hunters would stop development of a park of the historical and scenic significance of Voyageurs. Likewise, careful management of the Allagash by private firms maintained the stream in its beautiful condition, but this drew passing appreciation and only a compromise management program. Nevertheless, a sense of public responsibility and the need for sensitivity toward the public are real parts of many industries' policies.

Public Relations: Another principal reason that industries open their lands to recreation is for improved public relations. At least one company has found that immediate good public relations may not be a result. Gripes rather than compliments seem to be most common from users of freely provided accommodations. Gripes lead to public pressure and management problems. Frequently, free or inexpensive accommodations lead to the assumption of public privilege and eventually to public rights (Wyman, 1976).

PROBLEMS

Opening forest lands to recreationists always produces difficulties. Two of these are mentioned here.

Costs: Industry faces many costs when its land is opened to the public. Wyman (1976) of Brown Paper Company listed some of the duties that befall a landowner who allows recreational use: collecting trash; providing tourist information; developing camping facilities; dealing with increased fire danger, deteriorating roads, traffic, vandalism, and criticism; and many others. Snowmobilers have parked cars on plowed logging roads, impeding trucking. Forty miles of Appalachian Trail that crosses company lands are now being touted by the government as a donation with cutting limits along it.

Legal Liabilities: Any business that invites or allows people to use its facilities and lands is open to some sort of civil suit for real or imagined damages. Unfortunately, some citizens and their lawyers seem eager to find reason to file suit against large corporations. If state laws are written or interpreted to favor the individual over the corporation, the recreational offerings of the firm can be in jeopardy. Because of one judge's decision, the California Redwood Association suspended its carefully developed recreation program that included advertising, fine facilities, nature trails, and access to back country. In order to reduce their liability, the association's member companies had to withdraw their tasteful advertising and, at least once every three months, had to notify visitors that they must leave. This technically qualified visitors as trespassers and presumably relieved the companies of most liability (see Chapter 32). Such a procedure was both distasteful and discouraging to a superb program. Many states have passed liability laws that reduce some of the onus on private landowners.

A LEASE PROGRAM

The Brown Company in New Hampshire has developed a program for snowmobiling that reduces company liability and provides large areas for the sport. The same type of agreement exists for other landowners throughout the state. The state government leases the land for the development, maintenance, and use of snowmobile trails by the public. The substantial fee paid by the state is financed through the $10 registration fee that snow-machine operators buy from the state each year. The lease has several conveniences for the landowner. The company is compensated for inconveniences and for use of the land. The state holds the lease, so the company incurs no additional liability. The company has very low expenses for fee collection. The state, through its Bureau of Off Highway Recreational Vehicles, manages the recreationists. The public has assurance of the right to use the land, can groom the trails, and is guaranteed continuous trail, with alternate routes set up if the company must use a particular road for winter trucking (Wyman, 1976). Thus, a company enters into contracts with the government and treats it as a business partner, rather than coming under state control by statute.

Similar arrangements have been made in Maine, where timber companies lease land to the state for the construction and operation of public campgrounds. Rather than accepting the liability for invitees and the management nuisances, these firms have transferred the onus of public use to public agencies.

Donations of Land

Lands donated by American corporations to nature preservation through The Nature Conservancy, 1970 to April 1, 1977, are shown in Table 10.1. Only gifts of 900 acres or more are listed. The list is illustrative, not exhaustive (Figure 10.3). In early 1978, Union Camp donated 16,600 acres of Georgia's Okefenokee Swamp to be added to the National Wildlife Refuge.

Companies sell or donate their lands for recreation or preservation for

TABLE 10.1 Industry donation to The Nature Conservancy, 1970–1977.

Donor	Acres
Union Camp Corporation:	
Great Dismal Swamp, Virginia	49,097
Turtle Island, South Carolina	2,000
Chowon Swamp, North Carolina	3,815
Crescent Lake, Florida	2,850
Georgia Pacific Corporation:	
Merchant Mill Pond, North Carolina	925
Huber Corporation:	
Crystal Bog, Maine	3,793
Cummer Company:	
Cummer Sanctuary, Florida	985
Brown Lumber Company:	
Crows Wings Lake, Minnesota	2,770
Weyerhaeuser Corporation:	
Great Dismal Swamp, North Carolina	10,957
Time-Life, Inc.:	
Sandlands, Texas	2,138
International Paper Co.:	
Genesis Point, Georgia	26,000

Source: Morine (1977).

FIGURE 10.3 The Great Dismal Swamp was donated to the Nature Conservancy by the Union Camp Corporation and is now preserved as a natural wildlife refuge and a state park. (NPS)

any of several reasons. There are financial benefits, through savings on income taxes, primarily. Lands were typically acquired very cheaply, but have now risen in value; if sold, they would produce considerable profit and a high capital gains tax. The land is probably not worth its fair market value for the company's commercial purposes. By donating the land for recreation or conservation, however, the company receives credit for a donation appraised at the fair market value. If the tax rate of the firm is 50 per cent, a donation would produce $0.50 in cash for every dollar of land value donated. The donation can be used as a tax shelter for up to 5 per cent of net corporate income.

Morine (1977) reported that The Nature Conservancy had administered 75 land projects for which 70 companies donated or sold 300,000 acres. These lands were appraised at a fair market value of $100 million, but the total cost of acquisition by The Nature Conservancy was less than $50 million.

The Union Camp gift to The Nature Conservancy of the Great Dismal Swamp is a good example of enlightened self-interest also serving the public interest, once the alternatives are examined. The corporation staff analyzed the property for 1) timber production, 2) conversion to agriculture, and 3) a gift for preservation. The economic, social, and land use figures showed that the highest and best use of the property was to give the land away so it could become a National Wildlife Refuge and so the company could take appropriate tax credits.

Noncorporate Private Lands

Many farms, ranches, and other individually owned properties are used for recreation on a permission basis. Holecek and Westfall (1977) studied the willingness of landowners in Michigan in the summer of 1975 to allow public recreation on their properties. They asked about hiking, hunting, and snowmobiling. A majority did or would allow all three on their land. Hiking was received favorably by 78 per cent, hunting by 66.5 per cent, and snowmobiling by 53 per cent. The outstanding expressed concern of the people who refused permission for any of the three activities was damages to the land or facilities. Assurance that damages would be minimal or compensated for might be of considerable value to the success of programs involving private lands.

Other concerns of landowners included control of the type and amount of use of the land. The use rates on the Michigan study lands were relatively low—one to five visitors per week for most properties. The other major concern was liability for injuries to the public while on the private land.

Although a majority of landowners (31 per cent were farmers, but 81 per cent lived on or near the land) allowed recreational use of their lands at no charge, only about one fourth of all those interviewed were interested in a public access program that would allow them to receive compensation from the government for permitting hiking, hunting, or snowmobiling. Perhaps it was fear of being overrun by either visitors or paperwork that prompted a negative response. Even those who favored the payment program would require only up to $4.00 per acre per year.

It appears that incentives other than direct monetary inducements might be useful in ensuring public access to private lands. These may revolve around ways to assure landowners that damages, control of use, liability, safety, and personal use will be handled financially or administratively in such a way that it will cause the least inconvenience for them. Holecek and Westfall (1977) recommended that continued education of the public on proper means to gain access to private land and proper behavior would be helpful in maintaining the already generous attitude of most landowners.

Recreation for Employees

Many industries have set aside outdoor and indoor recreation facilities for their employees. Programs range from simple exercise programs at lunchtime to elaborate facilities and large recreation staffs offering a myriad of activities.

Oneida, Ltd., in upstate New York, built the first-known executive golf course in the United States in 1898. Its first football team played in 1916. In 1917, it built a clubhouse with a bowling alley. Women's sports were included along with men's (Jones, 1978).

In the late 1800s, National Cash Register started a "Men's Welfare

League," and soon added one for women. The first activities were baseball and other sports. The depth and variety of the program has increased over the years. Now, the company has a large park in the heart of Dayton, Ohio, adjacent to the plant, with picnicking, boat rides, tennis, and Olympic pool with lessons in the summer, and many other offerings. There are two large golf courses, including a golf club with plush but inexpensive restaurants, and some "retreat" property where families and employee groups can get away for a while. A specialized recreation staff manages a diversified program throughout the year at the many facilities in the plant and outdoors.

The advantages of industrial recreation programs to the companies are generally perceived as the following:

Improved relations among the employees and between employees and management.

Good public relations in the community and among employee families.

Increased productivity and reduced absenteeism (Erwin, 1978).

Financing for these programs is handled in a number of ways. The most common is to give the program the revenues from coffee sales and vending machines. This produces a large amount of money in some companies. Other companies provide a direct subsidy. Still others require that employees pay a membership fee to participate. Special services, such as group travel, use of the company resort, woodworking, photography laboratory, and use of the rifle range are paid for by a fee structure that helps defray the expenses.

More than 1,800 companies belong to the National Industrial Recreation Association, which aims to upgrade the caliber of recreation programs. It was established in 1941 and produces newsletters, manuals, and the magazine *Recreation Management*, issued 10 times per year. Members include industries of all sizes, such as Texas Instruments, Ashland Oil, McLean Trucking, Hughes Aircraft, Ford, Dow, Kodak, Coors, Hartford Insurance, Cabrillo Medical Center, Salt River Project, B. F. Goodrich, and others.

SUMMARY

Forest and other industry and private land-based businesses are deeply involved in recreation operations, which take the following forms:

1. Public recreational use of lands and special facilities.
2. Donation of lands for preservation or other uses.
3. Recreation services for employees.
4. Special classification and management for natural areas, redwood groves, scenic rivers, and other special resources (Figure 10.4).

FIGURE 10.4 Canoeing takes visitors through primeval strips of natural surroundings—the hidden recreation resources. Many are within industrial properties, where riverside logging has been carefully planned to maintain the forest scene. (NPS)

5. Intepretation and public education.
6. Wildlife management.

Industry has tried many different ways of supplying these opportunities, including leases and specialized company recreation departments. The future will probably involve an increasing commitment to recreation resource management.

Literature Cited

ERWIN, JACQUELINE. 1978. People's Jewelry Company. Recreation Management 21(3):18–19.
HOLECEK, DONALD F. and RICHARD D. WESTFALL. 1977. Public Recreation on Private Lands—the Landowner's Perspective. Michigan State Univ., AES Research Report No. 335. 11 pp.

Jones, Ronald C. 1978. Oneida Ltd. Silversmiths; from commune to thriving business. Recreation Management 21(2):18–23.

Morine, David. 1977. We can work with you. American Forests 83(11):10–12.

Wyman, Brad. 1976. Roles and Responsibilities of the Public and Private Sector for Providing Outdoor Opportunities and Resources: Who Provides and How? Paper to National Recreation and Park Association Congress, Boston, Mass.

Local Recreation Resources

When Carlos Gonzalez has a day off work, he likes to take his close-knit family to a park close to home for a picnic and games. He might enjoy a longer visit to a large state park, national forest, or even one of the resort beaches out along the shore. That would be a very special occasion, though, for he doesn't own an automobile. There is little or no public transportation to those facilities. He doesn't really know much about those state, federal, and private areas, although he sees a television show about state parks now and then. Even if he borrowed a car, it would be difficult to find his way or to know what to take along. He is still struggling with English idioms and he isn't sure that other visitors would treat his family with respect. Finally, there is the always-present issue of money. The Gonzalez family, like one eighth of American families, earns less than the poverty level. This means that any outing must be inexpensive. They will stick close to home, even if parks are overcrowded and poorly maintained.

Local parks also serve the rich and the vast middle class. The majority of all recreation participation occurs close to home. With most of the population living in urban centers, the responsibility is clearly on intensively used local parks to absorb more use or to expand.

The present shortage of urban parks suggests a need to expand most systems close to home. Without them, overuse of natural resource areas may develop, devastating rural and wilderness resources that are within easy reach of the cities.

The park and recreation professional in a local system must run a big business. Budgets range from $100,000 to tens of millions per year. The real estate in local parks systems is worth millions of dollars in many cities. Equipment value often exceeds a million dollars in large systems. The professional is in charge of numerous employees. The customers come by the thousands on most weekends.

In a town of 11,500 and growing population, a full-time park and recreation director was hired in 1966. He conducted studies on community preferences to help plan growth of the small system. Now, his department offers 100 recreation programs, with a staff of five full-time persons, 100 part-time program specialists, and 65 volunteers. There are 14 parks with 100 ha (250 acres) of land and a 200-ha (500-acre) flood plain zone used

FIGURE 11.1   A refuge from urban artificiality was created in the mid 1800s. Central Park in New York City remains a bucolic island in one of the world's bustling cities. (HCRS)

as a scenic park. A new 16-ha (40-acre) park with a swimming pool cost $1,400,000. Cooperative agreements exist with schools, churches, businesses, a college, the court chambers, and owners of vacant lots. The director works with half a dozen citizen groups that plant trees, promote bikeways, and help operate an outdoor education area.

The New York City park system is many times more complex, covering 11,000 ha (27,000 acres) ranging from one-lot playgrounds to the 862-ha (2,131-acre) Pelham Bay Park in the Bronx (Figure 11.1).

A single park in Philadelphia (Fairmount) covers 1600 ha (4,000 acres). It contains the nation's oldest botanical garden, a horticultural hall, an aquarium, the nation's oldest zoo, several historical buildings, an outdoor concert center, and numerous other attractions. It protects the banks of the Schuylkill River and Wissahickson Creek.

With all of these complications, parks, with their trees, grass, and walkways, are to be "still eyes in the hurricane of the city," a place where we can "enlarge people's freedom in a limited space" (Whitaker and Browne, 1971).

History of Urban Parks

Parks have a long history in cities. They are integral to modern city plans. Over time, their roles have changed substantially, although a recommendation made by L. B. Alberti in 1484 (Whitaker and Browne, 1971) suggests there are many similarities of purpose:

A city is not built wholly for the sake of shelter, but ought to be so contrived that besides more civil conveniences there may be handsome space left for Squares, Courses for Chariots, Gardens, Places to take the Air in, for Swimming, and the like, both for Amusement and for Recreation.

Many of the European-type squares and malls that once dominated the cities have given way to industrial, commercial, and transportation facilities. Squares were the early public parks. They remain important to the cultures of the Iberian peninsula and the small cities of Latin America. The Place des Vosges, built in Paris in 1610, is still considered one of the most beautiful of squares.

Even earlier, public open space and gardens were important adjuncts to sacred groves and temples in classical Greece. Julius Caesar gave his private gardens in Rome to the public in a bequest, perhaps the earliest recorded private endowment to public parks (Whitaker and Browne, 1971).

During the Middle Ages, there was little concern with public parks. The predominately rural populations could find their pleasure in the rural landscape where they lived, under varying severity of control by the landowners. It was with the Industrial Revolution and growing urbanization that the need for public open space slowly became evident.

The birth of the modern movement for municipal parks began in Europe in the late eighteenth and early nineteenth centuries. Previously, planned and landscaped parks were the property of nobility or royalty. The commoners could walk in them only at the sufferance of the owners, usually on special holidays.

Parc originally meant enclosure for animals for the hunt. The large parks in London and Paris were used for hunting by members of the royal palace. Two of London's most prominent public gathering places of today— Hyde Park and Regent's Park—were used by Henry VIII for hunting wild boar.

In Germany, the conversion began in the late 1700s. The many princes developed public gardens and "people's parks." Several of Munich's beautiful parks were dedicated to public use in this period. In Vienna, Josef II gave Prater Park to the city.

Parliamentary committees in nineteenth-century England pointed out the benefits of parks to the health of the workingman, to alleviate the effects of the Industrial Revolution. This both recognized and promoted the conversion of royal parks to public parks. It also led to new park planning and development at public expense. During this period, many of the magnificent gardens and open spaces of England and France were opened for public use, including Greenwich Park, Richmond Park, and Kew Gardens. Dublin's Phoenix Park, with its 709 ha (1,752 acres) being the largest public park in Europe for many years, was an imperial hand-me-down.

The transfers were not necessarily made purely out of largesse or social concern. Olmsted and Kimball (1928) suggest that the growing London population was using the royal parks in gradually larger numbers, until it became evident that they were, in practice, no longer royal preserves. Thus, transfer to public ownership and maintenance was as much a surrender to reality as it was a generous gift. In France, the change was more abrupt, with the French Revolution opening many of the Parisian royal gardens.

Settlers of the New World set precedents for public parks on relatively small areas. William Penn set aside certain blocks of Philadelphia as commons and public squares. As Spain settled Mexico and points north and south, it required that new towns contain public squares (Olmsted and Kimball, 1928).

In 1858, the Central Park plan for New York City formalized and directly declared the philosophy and policy that large parks for the public were important parts of cities. Savannah, Georgia, was laid out in 1733, with numerous public squares as focal points and tree-lined streets—a park-city in its original concept.

The Boston Common is one of the oldest parks in the United States, but its original purposes as a village green were to provide grass for visiting livestock (Figure 11.2). It was established in 1634 and has been used for many purposes, including a cow pasture, parade ground, military training field and encampment for both British and American troops, and public

FIGURE 11.2 The Boston Common, a European tradition that evolved into a central city park.

hanging post where pirates, witches, and Quakers met their earthly end. It has served as America's version of Hyde Park for public speakers and their hecklers. It is also the site of community celebrations, demonstrations, music, and sports, as well as a place for people to stroll and enjoy the beauty of a wooded and grassy island in the midst of a bustling city.

Boston is the home of at least four other park firsts. Across the street from the Common is the Boston Public Garden, founded in 1852 as the first *public* botanical garden in the United States. It traces its origins to citizen efforts dating from 1824. John Bartram's private garden, in Philadelphia, is claimed as the nation's first botanical garden. The oldest public arboretum in the nation is the Arnold Arboretum, started in 1876. The "Emerald Necklace" concept of a string of green space around the city, bringing recreation areas close to every citizen, was introduced in Boston in 1888 by Charles Eliot and Frederick Law Olmsted. The idea has been adopted by many other cities. In 1892, the Metropolitan Parks Commission combined the efforts of several cities of the immediate Boston area to become the first place where the concept was carried out. In the same year, the Kansas City metropolitan parks system was begun.

Parks developed rapidly in the latter half of the nineteenth century, except during the Civil War period. The conservation movement, which set aside large chunks of federal forests, parks, and wildlife refuges around the turn of the century, accompanied the interest in local open spaces. World Wars I and II interrupted the addition of parks.

During the economic depression of the 1930s, there was considerable interest among federal agencies in assisting communities to improve their parks. Many of the anti-Depression public works programs were quite beneficial to city parks.

Perhaps this was most notable in New York City, where Commissioner Robert Moses put thousands of people to work improving and building parks. They were financed largely from grants and matching funds from the federal government. In 1932, New York's parks covered 6,000 ha (14,827 acres), or 7.28 per cent of the city. This was a lower percentage than any of the other 10 largest cities in the world or America. Nearly half of the acreage was poorly developed, and most of the designated parks were in run-down condition. There were 119 playgrounds in the city—one for every 14,000 children. By 1939, there were 255 new playgrounds, 10 new swimming pool complexes, and about 8,100 ha (20,000 acres) in parks, playgrounds, and parkways, new and refurbished. Regrettably, very few of these facilities were developed in Harlem or other poverty-stricken parts of the city (Caro, 1974).

After World War II, there was growing interest in recreation and parks. Additions to park systems came rapidly in a period of economic prosperity. After the passage of the Land and Water Conservation Fund Act in 1965, there was considerable growth in park acreage in urban and suburban areas.

There was also a concomitant abandonment of central cities by white, middle- and upper-income people who moved to the suburbs. They daily create monumental, sluggish rivers of automobiles that flood the central cities, occupying huge parkings lots. By taking their tax money and citizenship with them, they have gradually impoverished the central cities. The people who need local recreation services the most and can afford them the least are now left with inner-city parks that do not receive adequate maintenance or programming.

One challenge of the inequities of location is that available parks in urban areas must be intensively managed and efficiently used. Addition of new areas is another continuing and costly challenge. To expand the urban recreation resource base will require considerable ingenuity, political acumen, and financial wizardry. To manage it efficiently requires skill and imagination plus innovative facility design and programming.

Legal Foundations

Local government is complex. One must always keep in mind the many exceptions to generalizations about parks and recreation at the local level. In the United States, there are 78,218 local units of government, 65,914 of which have property taxing power and 15,781 of which are school districts. Organized county governments total 3,044; there are 18,517 municipalities; 16,991 townships exist in 21 states; and there are 23,885 special districts (Bureau of the Census, 1977). Many of these levels of government, including some school districts and townships, provide parks and recreation programs. The major concerns of this chapter are cities, counties and their equivalents, and special park districts.

ENABLING LAWS

All states in the United States empower some or all of their local governments to manage park and recreation systems. Most states do this through general enabling legislation. Others use charters and special laws.

An enabling law is an act of the state legislature (usually amended over the years) that does some or all of the following, with variations from state to state.

1. Empowers the local government to establish, operate, and maintain parks and recreation programs and agencies.
2. Provides for the establishment of a board to govern the operations.
3. Empowers the board to acquire lands and other real properties and to develop them, to employ a staff, and to issue bonds.
4. Establishes the mechanisms for operations in subordination to the local government, and other procedures.

LOCAL ORGANIZATION

In most states, city and county parks and recreation departments are operated as subordinate agencies of the local, elected government. They are not separate units of government and do not, by themselves, have the power to levy taxes. Instead, their budgets and operations are directed by the mayor or city/county manager, who, in turn, responds to the elected council and/or board of commissioners.

The internal organization of the programs is primarily combined park and recreation agencies (66 per cent). Considerable consolidation occurred in the 1960s, bringing together the old, separate parks agencies and recreation agencies into single units. Only 3 per cent of the cities reported separate park departments in 1976. There are departments of recreation in 18 per cent of the cities, some of which also integrate park functions. Most of the rest of the agencies combine park and recreation functions under such titles as Parks, Recreation, and Human Resources; Parks, Recreation, and Conservation; Parks and Public Works; Human Resources and Conservation; and Public Works Departments (Verhoven and Lancaster, 1976).

An example of a split program is in Madison, Wisconsin, which has a recreation board and staff separate from the park board and staff. The system is similar to that in Milwaukee. The recreation staff conducts its programs in the parks, as well as at schools and with other cooperating agencies. This allows independence and flexibility for both the park department and the recreation department. The system seems to work well in Madison. A key ingredient is the cooperative attitude of the professionals of the departments. If they see the community good in compatible ways, the inevitable minor disagreements will not develop into schisms. Another key ingredient is the support of the community. Should the citizens lose faith in either the park or the recreation department, or should the services of one be unsatisfactory, the loss of support could disrupt the efficiency of both. However, this split system seems to have a built-in safety factor. If one of the agencies should become corrupt or inefficient, the citizens could abolish it and shift its responsibilities to the other group, already in place.

City Parks

The term *city park* evokes various images in the public mind. It may be one of old men on benches, a softball diamond, or a picnic shelter next to an active playground. Some think of swimming pools and crafts classes, whereas others think of rose gardens tended by senior citizens. A city park is not easily defined. Most contain these and many other facilities. They often include open space, forests, or desert, beaches, and hills. Some contain zoos, rifle ranges, senior citizen centers, horse stables, trains, nature trails, museums, and scout camps.

City parks (Figure 11.3) vary in size from a single city lot wedged between two large buildings—vest pocket parks—to such a vast area as the 5,665-ha (14,000-acre) South Mountain Park in Phoenix. They range from highly artificialized areas with concrete surfaces and engineered equipment to an almost totally natural environment, disrupted only by trails, roads, and a few picnic spots.

There are city parks outside the city limits. Many cities are authorized

FIGURE 11.3 This tiny vest pocket park offers rest to passersby and views from inside the building.

to purchase land beyond the incorporated boundaries for park purposes. Denver and Pueblo, Colorado, have mountain parks that are 40 to 80 km (25 to 50 miles) from the cities. One of the Denver units is the large Winter Park ski area high in the mountains west of the city.

There is no typical city park. The special quality of each city park is that it serves its own clientele. The people of a neighborhood, a section of town, or the community at large have their own characteristics and desires. The park has its unique place. It need not serve the people of the state or of the nation. Therefore, the park's design, facilities, and programs can be planned for the fairly small local groups of people to be served. They can help decide. Local governments have this great advantage: they can serve the local people in direct response to their particular characteristics. Therefore, there is no reason that one city park should be a carbon copy of another.

COMMONALITIES

Despite the individuality of parks, there are certain facilities that are common to most park systems (Verhoven and Lancaster, 1976). The vast majority of cities with parks and/or recreation facilities have tennis courts (854 cities reported them), baseball and softball diamonds (822 and 812), and basketball courts (801). These figures are from 1,123 cities that responded to a large questionnaire (Verhoven and Lancaster, 1976). Other common facilities include the following:

Recreation centers	672
Athletic fields	616
Outdoor swimming pools	602
Outdoor ice-skating rinks	305
Boat-launching facilities	284
Day camps	294
Bathing beaches	215
18-hole golf courses	205
9-hole golf courses	137
Stadiums	195
Bicycle paths	179 (averaging 9.2 miles)
Outdoor theaters	162
Nature centers	141
Indoor Pools	121

Other categories include: Outdoor recreation centers (111), museums (107), zoos (100), marinas (94), resident camps (73), artificial ice-skating rinks (72), outdoor ice-skating rinks (64), portable pools (50), combined indoor-outdoor pools (26); and indoor tennis courts (32).

Municipal park and recreation employment is mostly seasonal, because of the heavy programming for children in the summer. Permanent personnel are employed by most cities. According to Lancaster (1976), 82 per cent of the cities employ a full-time executive; 15 per cent employ full-time activity specialists; 13 per cent employ full-time recreation program leaders; and 8 per cent employ full-time law enforcement personnel, most relying heavily on other law-enforcement agencies. Virtually all employ permanent park managers or maintenance personnel.

CASE STUDY: OGLEBAY PARK, WHEELING, WEST VIRGINIA

An often hazy industrial town along the upper Ohio contains one of the world's great city parks. The 590-ha (1,460-acre) Oglebay Park in Wheeling, West Virginia, was the bequest of Col. Earl W. Oglebay in 1926. In the previous year, Wheeling had established its first park, Wheeling Park, with its 164 ha (406 acres), so the city fathers pondered the Oglebay gift two years before accepting the responsibility for maintaining the exquisite farm.

The Oglebay mansion became an historical museum. Barns were converted to offices, informal museums, a restaurant, activity and meeting rooms, and opera training rooms. Sixty-five log cabins, built from cast-off telephone poles, are rented to vacationers. The beautifully landscaped park (Figures 11.4–5) contains three golf courses that double as winter sports areas, a riding academy with forested trails, an elaborate garden center-greenhouse-flower garden complex, an arboretum, a zoo, an organization camp, and a children's center with playground, observatory, and nature center. A small lake for fishing and paddle boats, a motel and restaurant

FIGURE 11.4 One of three golf courses in Oglebay Park, Wheeling, West Virginia.

FIGURE 11.5 Oglebay Park's large swim center features ample decks.

lodge with numerous meeting rooms, a large picnic area, tennis courts, swimming pool, social center, outdoor theater, and scenic drives round out the physical facilities.

A dazzling array of programs is offered. The philosophy of Colonel Oglebay was to combine recreation with educational and cultural activities. That is done through classes, camps, tournaments, high-quality performances, and seminars. The summer Oglebay Festival offers theater-in-the-park with four or five plays plus musicals and touring shows with top stars, Wheeling Symphony concerts, chorales, an opera festival, and various flower, art, and crafts exhibitions. A large auditorium offers a rainy-day alternative to the terraced outdoor amphitheater. Vesper services bring leading religious programs to the park.

Recreation Places

There is no charge to enter the park and wander its trails. Each activity and facility is revenue-producing, with an attempt at being self-sufficient. About 300 volunteers help in recreation programs and teach classes in all of the arts—painting, folk dancing, ballet, folk guitar, choral music, and drama. Their contribution of time and talent keep costs moderate, but the charges probably restrict poorer families from frequent participation. The generosity of the Oglebay family through the Oglebay Institute (founded 1930) operates the Mansion Museum, departments of creative and performing arts, and the nature education department.

Colonel Oglebay did more than give land; he set the tone of the place in his will. His nephew directed the development of the park, actively organizing programs and forming committees of volunteers. Oglebay Park is one of many throughout the nation that are the result of private philanthropy. Other philanthropists for local parks include the Mott Foundation in Michigan, which has contributed to many parks. J. K. Lilly left his large estate and arboretum for conservation purposes. It is now the 1,942-ha (4,800-acre) Eagle Creek Park of Indianapolis. Many additional famous and lesser-known philanthropists have enriched communities with parks.

There are many other large parks owned by cities. Several are famous or notable as models. Among these are many of the 50 designed by Calvert Vaux and Frederick Law Olmsted in the late 1800s, including Prospect and Central Parks in Brooklyn and New York City, Fairmount Park in

FIGURE 11.6 Hanna Park in Jacksonville, Florida, offers a large beach, camping, picnicking, hiking, and a large natural forested area.

Philadelphia, and Golden Gate Park in San Francisco. Lincoln Park in Chicago is an outstanding waterfront open space. Minneapolis has a system of parks around the city's lakes. Hanna Park in Jacksonville, Florida, is a large, new, natural park featuring broad beaches, coastal forest, campgrounds, nature trails, and picnic areas (Figure 11.6).

County Parks

Many urban counties have long histories of maintaining park systems. Rural and suburban counties were usually late starters and are experiencing rapid growth at the present time.

Essex County, New Jersey, is reported to be the first with a county park and recreation system, established in 1895. By 1935, 91 counties in the nation had their own park systems (Butler, 1937). The leading states then were California, 13 counties; Michigan, 12; and Wisconsin, 10.

County park systems throughout the nation are relatively new, small, and usually inadequately financed. The exceptions are some of the large urban areas, which long ago took a stand for a system of parks. An outstanding example is the Cook County Forest Preserve district, which manages 25,900 ha (64,000 acres) within the Chicago area. Los Angeles County, California, and Dade County, Florida, have extensive and interesting county park systems. The six counties in the Milwaukee area operate 125 park and recreation sites with 4,452 ha (11,000 acres).

Today, most of the urbanized and suburbanized counties of the nation have some form of park and recreation system. Many are new since the early 1960s. They complement the city park systems. There has been active land acquisition and rapid growth of the programs in these counties, using Land and Water Conservation funds and other open space acquisition funds. Many of these areas have received support because of the high-income residents of the semirural communities. Financing of park and open space has been mostly on the basis of mill levy taxes on property or a percentage of sales taxes.

The dramatic growth in county park systems is exemplified by the activity in the Los Angeles area. Orange County had a system of 250 ha (600 acres) in 1963; by 1977, it had expanded to 3,250 ha (8,000 acres). Riverside County increased its park acreage from 600 to 10,000 ha (1,500 to 25,000 acres) in eight years. Los Angeles County doubled the mileage of new public beaches and tidelands in seven years through cooperative agreements with the state and by mergers. That county now manages 28 areas of beaches covering almost 64 km (40 miles). Fifty million people visited these beaches in the bicentennial year (National Park Service and Bureau of Outdoor Recreation, 1977).

Denver and its surrounding suburban counties have increased their holdings by acquiring lands along rivers and arroyos (Figures 11.7 and 11.8).

FIGURE 11.7   Denver's arroyos have become linear parks, with bike and walking trails winding through the city.

FIGURE 11.8   Some of Denver's arroyos are confined in concrete canals—an alternative to the park approach.

Local Recreation Resources

FIGURE 11.9 The nation's largest county park system is in Maricopa County, Arizona. The 92,000 acres feature a large reservoir (above) in the hills and an archery range among the saguaro (left).

These are developed into linear parks featuring hiking, bicycling, and horse trails. Some of them connect suburbs with the downtown area, allowing Denver residents to travel by bicycle from one end of the county to the other. The central focus of development has been along the South Platte River, where the city and counties are buying up property that periodically floods anyway. This is being developed into a greenway that includes golf courses, picnic spots, and other recreational facilities very close to home.

The nation's largest county park system belongs to Maricopa County, Arizona, (Phoenix) with more than 37,000 ha (92,000 acres) of desert land, mountains, and ball fields. It includes a large archery range (Figure 11.9), a huge rifle range, and several reservoirs. The 160-km (100-mile) Sun Circle Trail follows canals around and through the city, offering hikers,

Figure 11.10 Prototype county park system for a population of 125,000.

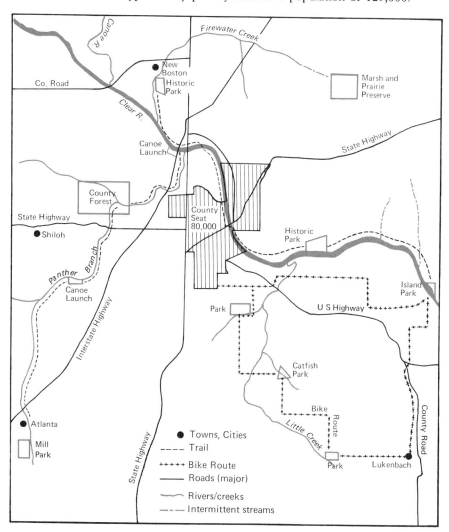

bikers, and horseback riders an unusual opportunity for recreation close to home.

Oregon's county park system complements the resources and programs of state and federal agencies. Twenty-nine of the state's 36 counties provide recreation facilities, generally close to population centers. There are about 300 county parks containing 8,500 ha (21,000 acres). These contain 4,350 picnic sites and 1,100 campsites. They also offer swimming, boating, hiking, fishing, sightseeing, and nature study.

A prototype county park system (Figure 11.10) might include the following types of properties, using the ORRRC resource classification.

   I. High-density recreation areas—limited number and area, usually as community activity centers (small parks) and beaches, comprise 5 per cent of system area.

  II. General outdoor recreation areas—picnic areas, festival grounds, campgrounds, playfields, comprise 25 to 50 per cent of the area.

 III. Natural resource areas—buffer and open space areas in parks, trail and river corridors, floodplain reserves, county forests and wildlife areas, lakes and reservoirs, comprise 50 to 80 per cent of the land.

 IV. Special natural areas—preservation for natural values or as nature centers, comprise 5 to 20 per cent of the area.

  V. Primitive—not represented.

 VI. Historic and cultural sites—historic areas, houses, monuments, museums, and signs at historic points, comprise 5 to 20 per cent of the area.

Special Districts

In some locations, regional park authorities that span several political jurisdictions have been successful. They are relatively uncommon but, where they exist, they provide significant open space resources.

The major reason for such districts is to reduce the complications of working across many local governmental jurisdictions. The Chicago Standard Metropolitan Statistical Area (SMSA), for example, contains 1,113 separate local governments. In the six counties are 171 separate park and recreation authorities. There are only 20 SMSA's with less than 10 local governments (cities, counties, town boards). The average is 91 per SMSA. Urbanized areas are particularly complex places to develop a system of long trails or large parks, because the numerous small towns are often unwilling to work with each other; coordination and funding would be problems even if they were of one mind. These districts do not usurp the function of the city park boards, but they do add a new dimension to the recreation opportunities for local citizens. By pooling the purchasing power of several communities through a common tax, large-scale projects can be developed and maintained.

A number of the large cities in Ohio have taken advantage of special state legislation enabling the formation of metropolitan park districts. They have thus supplemented their city park systems with regional parks. Most were established initially in the late 1920s. Cleveland's Metropolitan Park District had 4,050 ha (10,000 acres) of land by 1930, visited by 3.5 million people per year (Bureau of Labor Statistics, 1932). By 1975, visits were up to 17 million. Today, it remains a highly popular supplier of recreational opportunities. Cincinnati, Toledo, Columbus, and Akron are other centers around which large metro park systems have flourished.

EMERALD NECKLACE CASE

The Cleveland Metropolitan Parks District strings together 7,284 ha (18,000 acres) on its "Emerald Necklace" (Figure 11.11). The system is governed by a three-member Board of Park Commissioners, appointed by

FIGURE 11.11   Cleveland's Emerald Necklace surrounds the main metropolitan area. Rocky River park is the western strip.

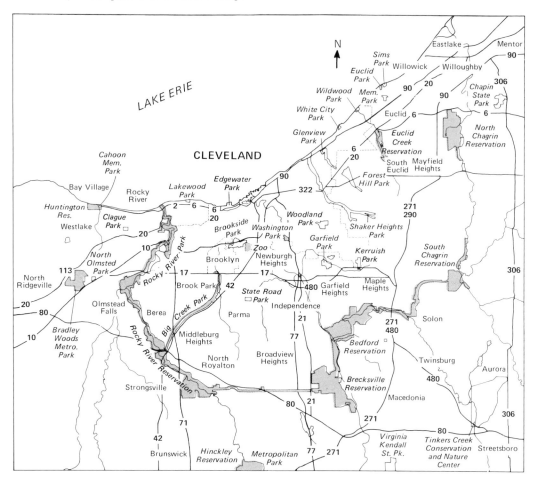

the Senior Judge of the Cuyahoga County Probate Court. They approve all land acquisitions and expenditures and oversee the use of the parks and their operating policies. The "necklace" is an almost continuous semicircular loop touching Lake Erie at both ends. Other separate blocks of land in Cuyahoga and neighboring counties are additional parts of the metro park system.

One of the units of the system is the slender, sinuous Rocky River Metropark. Its 2,300 ha (5,682 acres) of forests, bluffs, and creek bottoms wind along the Rocky River for 35 km (22 miles), accompanied by a scenic driving route, bike trails, and many places to walk. The park land lies in or on the edge of four suburbs. It was acquired from 1919 to 1975 at a total cost of $3,132,467.80. This park, as the others in the system, offers esthetic views of the natural stream bank, within easy access of most of the population of Cleveland and its suburbs; bus service goes to several places in the park from anywhere in the city.

Although most of Rocky River Metropark is a string-bean sort of property, stretched thin along the river corridor, it widens out in several places to form activity centers for interpretation, picnicking, winter sports, Camp Cheerful for handicapped children, several other youth facilities, a large swimming area, stable and riding rings, golf courses, two museums, and a small waterfowl sanctuary. One of the loop trails, called the Trail for All People, is built to allow blind people and wheelchair users to enjoy the woods. The park has an intensive program of activities throughout the year, organized by recreation specialists and interpretive naturalists. The entire system participates in radio and television programs and produces a monthly newsletter, *The Emerald Necklace,* which is sent to 38,000 patrons.

The system is notable for its 450-hour training program for park rangers who serve as conservation and law enforcement officers. They and the entire metro park system are geared to serve the people. Rocky River receives an estimated seven million or more visits per year. Its proximity to large populations, the relative ease of entry, and the fact that the park is kept clean and safe for visitors all contribute to make it a very popular and attractive park of the Cleveland area.

HURON-CLINTON METROPOLITAN AUTHORITY CASE

The Huron-Clinton Metropolitan Authority in Michigan, a regional park authority, was created to develop large park units and to preserve for public use the scenic beauties and recreational resources along the two principal rivers of the area.

Five counties were joined in a cooperative agreement by Michigan State Act No. 147, of 1939, ratified by the voters in 1940. The counties of Livingston, Macomb, Oakland, Washtenaw, and Wayne formed the metropolitan district to plan, promote, and/or acquire, construct, own, develop, maintain and operate, either within or without their limits, parks, connecting drives, and limited-access highways.

The Authority is governed by a seven-member Board of Commissioners, two of whom are appointed by the governor and each of the other five selected by officials of each county.

Financing comes from a tax levy, limited to one quarter of one mill,

FIGURE 11.12   The Hennepin County Park Reserve District serves the Twin Cities metro area in Minnesota. Park Reserves are natural recreation areas of 400 ha (1,000 acres). Regional parks are at least 40 ha (100 acres) and feature camping, boating, swimming, hiking, and picnicking. Riverside trail corridors and historic parks complete the 8,400-ha system. (Hennepin Co. Park Reserve District)

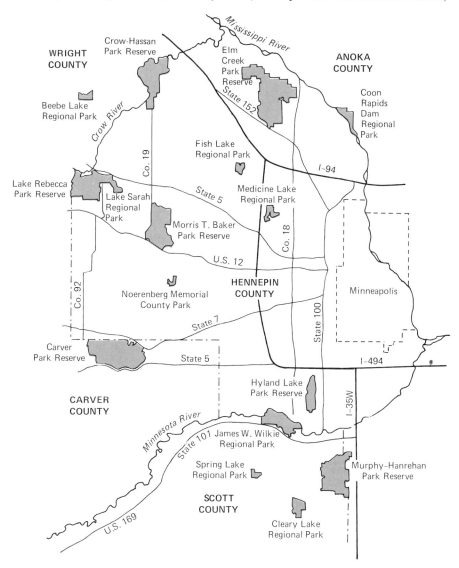

which is established by the Board of Commissioners on the regular county property tax in accordance with state assessments. This is actually an independent tax from other state and county taxes and does not pass through other hands than those of the commission.

During its first quarter-century, the Authority purchased 7,000 ha (nearly 18,000 acres) of land. It developed and opened for public use four large parks and four smaller ones. Approach roads and limited-access parkways were also developed.

Cooperation with other governmental agencies is, of course, an important aspect of regional development. The Huron-Clinton Metropolitan Authority has cooperated closely with and benefited from other agencies. Examples are a large dam on the Huron River, forming Kent Lake. The structure is on Department of Conservation land, under lease to the Authority. The U.S. Geological Survey maintains stream-gauging stations on Authority lands, paid for by the counties. The Detroit Metropolitan Area Regional Planning Commission and other planning groups in the district are important collaborators. County and state road commissions also affect decisions and plans of the Authority.

Another example of the metro park concept is the Hennepin County Park Reserve district that serves the Twin Cities metropolitan area in Minnesota (Figure 11.12).

Programs

Recreation programs are the activities offered in parks, buildings, and other facilities. In most local park systems, these are offered by the same agency that manages the parks. The activities may be organized events such as performing arts classes, tournaments, and nature programs or self-actuated activities such as sledding, skating, picnicking, and hiking. Experts in programming are trained in numerous activity-oriented recreation programs in various universities.

Most urban residents in the United States are served by full-time, year-round, recreation and/or park programs. A 1975 survey by the National Recreation and Park Association (Lancaster, 1976) of cities with more than 10,000 population revealed that 88 per cent of the 986 cities responding to the survey provide such services. All of the cities with more than 250,000 population reported that they had programs. Of the cities in the 50,000 to 250,000 category, 94 per cent offered year-round programs and facilities. Among smaller cities, better than 80 per cent have park and recreation operations all year.

Programming has a strong influence on the resources and on public support of the parks. Parks exist so people can enjoy them. Programs determine how that enjoyment occurs. Organized activities and sports were long considered an anathema to scenic city parks. Frederick Law Olmsted saw his parks as places for walking, riding, and relaxing in a naturalistic retreat from the harshness of the city. He had no patience with requests for organized activities. That attitude produced friction among people and produced playground and recreation movements that were distinct from the parks concept. These have now come together in most places—a sensible and civilized development.

In New York City parks, some imaginative programming ideas were instituted in 1965. The philosophy was that popular use of parks is the best policeman. Central Park had become unsafe by day and lethal by night. Prospect Park use had dropped to one third of its previous high. Programming ideas were tried; they produced no miracles, but urban life improved. These ideas may work elsewhere. The Metropolitan Opera put on free open-air performances throughout the city. Poets gave readings. There were costume parties, fashion parades, kite-flying contests, and side-walk decorating with chalk. A 100-yard canvas and an invitation to help paint it attracted 5,000 participants. In small parks in slum areas, 60 children's swimming pools were opened, and lessons were offered. Portable pools were used in other neighborhoods. These and other programs were initiated after community residents were consulted as to what was needed. New York parks have a listed information telephone that is used by more than 1,000 people per day calling for news about park events (Whitaker and Browne, 1971).

A significant number of cities do not provide services on weekends, when many citizens have their most extensive free time (Lancaster, 1976). Relatively few cities offer programs from 10 P.M. to 8 A.M., meaning that people working some shifts have no access to public recreation services.

In many cities, recreation programs do not operate effectively for citizens who work from 9 A.M. to 5 P.M., either. The programs seem to be designed for people who have leisure time from 8 A.M. to 6 P.M. This suggests that the programs may operate at the convenience of the staff, not the public. It also suggests one of the reasons why the bulk of most recreation programs occurs in the summer months and with children as the primary clients.

SCHOOL-PARK CONCEPT

The idea of using the same resources for schools and parks has long been promoted among park and recreation professionals. The school-park concept is alive and well in most cities. Schools represent a large taxpayer investment in land and facilities. Parks are close behind. Financial responsibility suggests that restriction of school facility use to traditional educational purposes is wasteful. Most state laws permit the use of school facilities for community recreation purposes. The Community Schools Act (PL 93–380) encourages further formal cooperation. Of 976 cities surveyed in 1976, 96 per cent reported cooperative arrangements with schools for recreational use. Some have no formal agreement. A few have arrangements for use of school buses; some receive funds through the school system. Almost half share joint planning of new facilities.

Park Administration

The first National Conference on Outdoor Recreation (1924) outlined the following essential conditions to operate a successful park and recreation system:

1. Sufficient funds.
2. Adequate facilities.
3. Use of trained individuals to administer the program.
4. Wise methods of administration.
5. Continued favorable public opinion.

Local parks are hard to manage as natural resources. In many cases, the city fathers give the park department the most worthless land in the city—the residue. These include floodplains, knobs of soil or rock, and poor soils that won't absorb water. Then they expect a park to be produced. Just before the magic of the park manager's green thumb starts to show, thousands of people come to play baseball and football, jog, walk their dogs, climb the slopes, picnic, and wash their cars. A few will attack any new grass with horses, off-road vehicles, and automobiles. If it survives long enough to develop beauty, then a flood the following spring will surely find its way to make an imprint. The public and the city fathers expect everything to look good soon after any disaster, however. Trees, flowers, shrubs, and hundreds of man-made facilities are all part of the problem of managing a city park. A single city park may have more problems than an entire national forest, according to foresters who have managed both.

WORKING WITH ELECTED OFFICIALS

Public recreation area management is always of interest to elected officals, especially if something goes wrong. Elected officials need to show results in two to four years—not progress or plans, but tangible results. Thus, a recreation specialist who produces with alacrity is valuable to the elected officials, as well as to the citizens of the community, state, or nation. Federal grant programs and economic assistance projects are designed to show results. The federal government is often much more interested in speed—getting something to show for its expenditures—than in priorities, feasibility studies, location, and design. That does not suggest that those matters are not important; they are often requirements for allocations of assistance. A project that meets these requirements and shows promise of completion in a reasonable time will win high priority and will help win repeat support.

Speed of construction depends upon the existence of detailed plans. Federal and local agencies need plans, often in a hurry. They look for plans to which they can assign their money. The key for the professional administrator of park and recreation resources is to be ready and to be able to get ready quickly. A large, stable planning force should be available and able to produce rapidly when called upon. In a large system, a planning group can be kept working continuously by assigning future projects and by preparing ideas. Once the plans are approved, then it is vital to be able to carry out the project quickly and efficiently. To do this, there must be a ready source of labor and the means to mobilize it. The successful administrator gets his people to work immediately, driving stakes and making commitments of land. There must be knowledge of the laws, the conditions, and legal complications with the properties. Unused public properties can be lined up and the work force ready to move as soon as there is a chance to do so. This avoids many complications and delays.

Robert Moses, as Commissioner of Parks of New York City, was highly successful in obtaining money and support from local, state, and federal sources, for more than 40 years. His success was the result, in great measure, of his ability as a problem solver and an achiever of works. Caro (1974) describes Moses' prowess as an appointed official who could satisfy the political needs of the elected officials. He understood that the mayor is confronted daily with many problems. Most of his advisors 1) have no solutions, 2) have impractical or unrealistic solutions, or 3) have no money for solutions. It was typical of Moses that, if given a problem one day, he was back before the mayor the next day with the following:

A solution, down to the last detail, often with blueprints or sketches.
Drafts of speeches the mayor could use to explain a proposal to the public.
Drafts of press releases.
Drafts of state laws needed, with advice as to who should introduce the bills in the legislature and to which committees they should go.
Drafts of City Council and Board of Estimate resolutions needed.
Constitutional questions and precedents.
A complete method of financing a project, all spelled out.

Clearly, Mr. Moses was an exceptional commissioner, with a great deal of energy and imagination. He had three other qualities that contributed to his ability to produce results: a substantial and well-trained intellect, ideas and plans that anticipated the needs and desires of the body politic, and a superb, obedient organization of planners, lawyers, and financial experts working for him. He did not wait for opportunities. He worked and planned for them. When they arose or when he created them, he was ready to seize them.

Once the solution was proposed, the plan made, and the project started,

Moses did not stop. The opening of any park, pool, or beach was always a major event (Caro, 1974). There was excellent news coverage, preceded by abundant advance publicity and involvement of the local community. The following sequence suggests how a swimming pool was opened in the midst of the Depression. The festival started in the early evening with a parade. In the parade were all the neighborhood political leaders, bands from the high school, the American Legion, the Knights of Columbus, and any others who might join, winding their way through the neighborhood. Priests of the neighborhood blessed the pool and the water in impressive ceremonies. Then swimming races and diving competitions were conducted by both neighborhood youngsters and Olympic stars from all over the United States. These serious competitors were followed by a swimming clown team. Then came time for more traditional entertainment, with singers and dancers of national renown. Finally, the mayor turned on the underwater lights, ordered the raising of the flag, cut the ribbon, and announced, "OK, kids, it's all yours."

Similar adroitness marked establishment of many national parks, national forests, state parks and wildlife areas.

Too often, golden opportunities to build great parks, little playgrounds, trails, or to preserve recreational riverfronts have gone a-glimmering because the park professional was too busy running programs rather than thinking ahead, planning, and creating opportunities. Every professional needs to be a practical dreamer and something of a schemer with a flair for public fanfare.

FINANCE

Among municipalities with more than 10,000 population, the average (mean) annual budget is $1,130,800, with about three quarters of that going to operational expenses, including salaries, rents, maintenance, and materials. This average is weighted by some large budgets, which cause the mean to misrepresent many smaller programs. The median (middle) budget is $264,300, suggesting that many communities allocate less than $150,000 per year. The distribution is shown in Table 11.1. Cities with more than 500,000 inhabitants spent an average of almost $30 million per year, whereas the small cities (10,000–24,000) had annual budgets averaging $229,000. The average in central cities ($4.4 million) is nine times higher than in suburban cities and almost 16 times higher than in independent cities (Verhoven and Lancaster, 1976). Geographically, the average budgets of cities in the West are the highest ($1.5 million), and North Central cities have the lowest mean ($700,000). Salaries and wages use almost 65 per cent of the average expenditures, with the rest almost evenly divided among operation and maintenance (nonsalary expenses), capital, and land acquisition.

Nationwide, less than 4 per cent of municipal budgets is spent for parks and recreation (Table 11.2). This compares to 8.7 per cent for police,

TABLE 11.1 Municipal park and recreation departmental budgets of U.S. cities over 10,000 population.

Population groups	Number	Mean budget	Median budget
More than 500,000	14	$29,618,800	$21,332,600
250,000–499,999	14	6,015,300	5,409,700
100,000–249,999	47	2,406,200	2,233,000
50,000–99,999	110	1,318,600	1,127,100
25,000–49,999	207	496,900	393,000
10,000–24,999	462	229,000	140,600
All cities Total	829	1,130,800	264,300
Operating		848,300	202,000
Capital		349,400	45,000

Source: Lancaster (1976).

4.8 per cent for fire protection, 11.9 per cent for education, 8.6 per cent for sewage and sanitation, 6.4 per cent for highways, 6.4 per cent for public welfare, 6.0 per cent for health and hospitals, and 2.9 per cent for housing and urban renewal.

The property tax is the principal source of revenue supporting local park and recreation agencies. Recreation services at the local level are usually heavily subsidized. Total annual revenues are less than total expenditures.

This cost dilemma, coupled with recent limitations put on property taxes, has resulted in many new programs being offered for a fee and new facilities being restricted to those that are partially donated or in cities with adequate fiscal or bonding reserves. Leisure services agencies compete with other municipal groups (police, fire department, others). In recent years, agency budgets have been held quite low, to the point of reducing the purchasing power of the dollars received. A few cities even pay operating expenses from borrowed income, which produces a deepening downward spiral of debt. In some cities, recreation and park services are still considered nonessential, or less important than health, fire, and police services. Therefore, when budgets are reduced, the deepest cuts are in park and recreation agencies.

TABLE 11.2 City government expenditures for parks and recreation, 1960–1975.

	(Millions of dollars)				
	1960	1965	1970	1973	1975
Total expenditures	$15,251	$20,680	$34,173	$48,021	$60,445
Parks and recreation	551	775	1,306	1,723	2,274
Percentage of expenditures	3.6	3.7	3.8	3.6	3.8

Source: Bureau of the Census (1977).

Local Recreation Resources

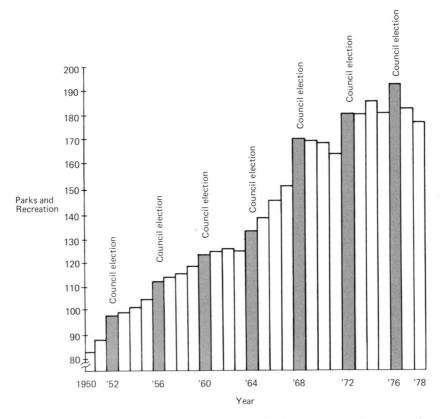

Figure 11.13 The West Lafayette, Indiana, budget goes up when councilmen are up for election. Major boosts every four years have sometimes been followed by decreases.

In large cities, outmigration of middle- and upper-income classes has diminished the city tax base for providing services. As the budget decreases, water, sewer, police, fire, and schools assume even higher funding priorities than does recreation. This often leads to the lack of maintenance and rehabilitation of parks. Despite this bleak picture, the politician who supports parks supports his incumbency. A study of most city budgets during election years, as contrasted with off-years, will verify that most councilmen are aware of the vote values of parks (Figure 11.13).

Many parks and recreation professors and textbooks have long advocated tax financing as the major means to pay for public recreation facilities and programs. Fees and charges are looked upon as discriminatory and justified only when special materials or services are involved, and then only when absolutely necessary. This ideal is logical, but reality is sometimes quite different from the ideal. Fees and charges provide significant operating income to most departments. The City Council of Indianapolis has directed that the park department make Eagle Creek Park self-supporting. A balanced budget for the park is required. Revenue comes from a riding stable concession, an auto entry fee, fees for swimming at the beach and for launching and rental of boats. Picnicking, hiking, and a nature center are free, except for special reservations or services. With restricted property taxes and escalating costs, it appears that a partial pay-as-you-go policy will become more common.

CHARACTER OF PARKS

The nature of urban parks and outdoor recreation has been questioned by Fred Smith (1972), a member of the ORRRC and the Public Land Law Review Commission (PLLRC) and an associate of the Rockefeller family. He notes that the urban resident of today is not just in from the country; he is a product of the new urban environment. He is a new creature, without roots in the natural world. He may feel no nostalgia for rural scenes.

The present design concept of many urban parks was intended to meet the needs of people who wanted a pastoral scene with trees and grass as a link to their rural past. The nostalgic purpose may be past, according to Smith. He suggests that the urban dweller who presumably most needs antidotes for urban frustrations is the person who uses the open spaces and green areas the least. Perhaps one reason is the need for action and for things to do, rather than nature appreciation. Nature parks in cities may be so foreign to the disadvantaged urban dweller that he will feel strained and uneasy in it, rather than relaxed and refreshed (Smith, 1972).

This argument suggests that the park concept developed in the nineteenth century might be reevaluated in terms of the clients it now serves. Although nature lovers have captured the recreation thinking of the time, they do not necessarily represent the majority of urban residents.

This should not suggest that existing parks be scrapped for game fields and activity carnivals. It does suggest a new look at emphases in programming and the evaluation of park services to all people.

MAINTENANCE AND REHABILITATION

A study of 17 urban areas by the Heritage Conservation and Recreation Service (HCRS, 1978) showed that 83 per cent of the neighborhoods sampled have at least one play area for small children; 74 per cent have at least one park. These are often not used or are underused because of broken equipment, poor maintenance, or poor design. Reduction in facilities has been greatest in low-income, core-city neighborhoods. Maintenance has generally been neglected or inadequate for the past 20 years. Rehabilitation of the run-down parks is a massive job, now that incremental investments in maintenance have been avoided. The fiscal distress of many core cities hampers allocation of rehabilitation money.

Assistance for major rehabilitation projects is available from several federal programs, including the Community Development Block Grants and the Land and Water Conservation Fund.

The Space Crunch

It is difficult to obtain open space in cities. In downtown Atlanta, a 1.7-acre site was valued at more than $9 million. The city acquired it by donation. In Houston, downtown Buffalo Bayou had some portions valued at $7 per square foot. Suburban residential areas were valued at $125,000 per acre, or $309,000 per hectare (National Park Service and Bureau of Outdoor Recreation, 1977). At these prices, there is little hope of expanding an urban park system by the purchase of land in fee simple. Other techniques for acquisition of partial rights are being used more heavily. They are described in the chapter on land acquisition.

Following are ideas for bringing recreation to neighborhoods without adequate resources. These have been tried successfully in a number of American cities.

1. Use land beneath and adjoining expressways and interchanges in cities. San Francisco, Los Angeles, Chicago, New Orleans, and many other large cities are criss-crossed by expressways that have long, elevated stretches. These cross streets, railroads, and open ground. Often, there would be no hazard to children playing in the open areas. A teen-ager from East Baton Rouge, Louisiana, wrote to her governor suggesting that vacant land beneath an interstate highway interchange be developed for outdoor recreation. The 30-acre area in the inner city was designed for picnic facilities, game fields, children's play areas, hand-surfaced courts, and passive recreation areas. In the New Orleans area, more than $600,000 of local, state, and federal funds were approved to build five such under-the-road sites for swimming, tennis, basketball, children's play, senior citizen's recreation, and other activities.

2. Alleys and streets can be converted to permanent neighborhood play areas. A street cut off by new freeways or other structures can become a charming, useful asset to the neighborhood. Present uses must be considered by providing substitute parking and emergency access. In 1971, Racine, Wisconsin approved closure of a five-block-long city street for conversion into a park. The new recreation mall includes ice skating, children's play, court games, baseball, and passive recreation. Landscaping was added to improve the appearance of the neighborhood.

3. Empty lots can be converted from junk-gathering eyesores to useful and attractive vest-pocket parks. Depending on the needs of the neighborhood's people, the minipark can provide a peaceful resting place to contrast with the hustle and bleakness of the city or a safe place to vent youthful energy in constructive play.

4. Where open space and privacy are at a premium, rooftop parks have become popular architectural devices. They are built as part

of apartment buildings, office complexes, and public buildings. On top of roofs, plants of all sizes are brought in for decoration and shade. Some are potted; smaller plants grow in shallow beds of soil. These parks may contain swimming pools, deck tennis courts, and other games. Some are strictly for viewing, strolling, and sitting. Most are restricted in access, but others are open to all visitors.

The key problem with small parks has been in maintenance and servicing. Unless neighborhood volunteers help maintain them, costs to a municipal government become very high, because of the logistics problems of moving personnel around to numerous small parks and supervising them. Intelligent management planning should help resolve this. A high level of dedication is required in some neighborhoods where the destructive propensities of a few residents require repeated repairs and replacement. Use of simple, inexpensive materials that are virtually indestructible is often a valuable preventive measure.

It is difficult to keep parks as open space. Central Park has long stood as a monument to the planning genius of Frederick Law Olmsted and Calvert Vaux. It has remained more or less natural-looking only at the insistence of numerous defenders and despite the repeated efforts to use it for something else. Besides the obvious temptation it offers building contractors, it has been used for a tavern-restaurant, a casino, a zoo, a museum, a skating rink, commemorative statuary, and playgrounds.

Serious proposals have been made to place the tombs of Grant and many other citizens in the park, to build a horse racetrack there, to hold a world's fair on its grounds, to put large ships in the reservoir, and to allow any number of commercial enterprises (Peet, 1954; Caro, 1974).

Robert Moses tried unsuccessfully to put an elevated thoroughfare over it, a parking lot on it, and a garage beneath it. He also brought it back from one of its many periods of disrepair and neglect.

Parks that are less hallowed than Central Park suffer similar indignities. Highways ate up thousands of acres of parks during the 1950s and early 1960s. They were publicly owned, in large blocks, and therefore easier to acquire than private property. Decreased enthusiasm for highway building and a rise in citizen sentiment for open space, combined with stricter requirements for route evaluation, saw a reduction in park decimation. However, public buildings, monuments, and parking lots are among the projects still proposed for park acreages.

Location

State recreation lands and local parks are often located inconveniently for most of the population. A principal reason is related to the cost of land. Most states, counties, and municipalities focus on acquiring cheap land or donations. Such sites are usually far removed from the densely populated areas. With tight, even reduced, municipal budgets in recent years, the acquisition of expensive inner-city land seems false economy if a larger acreage on the fringes can be purchased for the same cost. Once acquired, inner-city parks are often expensive to develop and to maintain. As a result, small plots of parks occur in the heavily populated areas, and large open spaces are on the edges of towns or far into the country. Transportation is a major factor in the ability to use recreation areas. Individuals without automobiles (most of them are urban) must rely on public transport, which seldom is routed to recreation areas. For citizens of the low-income Hunters Point area in San Francisco to reach the superb city zoo on public transportation requires five bus transfers and up to two hours' travel time each way.

Recreation Areas for Small Towns

The old hometown, with all its charm, warmth, and nostalgia, has suffered steady loss of economic and social vibrancy. When the valedictorian of the high school class goes off to college, he or she often says good-bye permanently to the community that paid for much of the first 12 years of education. The graduates leave for better opportunities elsewhere.

The talent drain leaves small towns without well-trained young leadership and knowledge. An age gap develops. Youth who need constructive recreation are matched by older people who must pay for such "frivolities," which weren't necessary when they grew up. The sociological problem is one difficulty. Another is money.

Parks are a problem for a community of any size. In a small town, the problem of finance is related to a critical minimum of tax money. Except by donation, a small town often cannot raise 50 per cent matching funds for federal programs assistance. They are often ineligible for other programs designed for large urban areas. The tax base declines because there are fewer prime earners and less new investment. Thus, maintenance and programming are often funded only minimally. Alternative sources of funding might involve a state department of rural parks, as has developed in some provinces of Canada.

In 1960, the Province of Saskatchewan began a new regional park program. This was a cooperative effort between the provincial and the municipal governments to assist in meeting outdoor recreation needs of rural and small town residents, as well as serving tourists to the province. More than 380 municipalities participate, forming various regional park authorities that are governed by representatives of the cooperating local governments. The Saskatchewan Association of Regional Parks and the Provincial Department of Tourism and Renewable Resources help coordinate the efforts to administer the 90 or so regional parks. These parks lie well outside the population centers in the agrarian southern portion of the province.

Most of the parks are on lakes or rivers. They offer swimming, fishing, camping, picnicking, boating, and golf. Winter activities are being developed in several parks.

Level of Responsibility

It is clear that urban areas face major opportunities and problems in providing outdoor recreation. Just how they will be handled and which level of government will take care of them are not so clear. There is a complexity of patterns within the diverse metropolitan regions of this nation. In an effort to generalize the trends that reflect economic, demographic, and social realities, the National Park Service and the Bureau of Outdoor Recreation (1977) reported broad trends observed over the decade of the 1970s:

1. Population growth is primarily occurring in the suburbs and on the fringes of the urban areas, although at a somewhat slower rate than during the 1960s.
2. Central cities are losing population and, with exceptions, the people remaining in the central cities are less affluent, older, members of minority groups, recent immigrants, and handicapped. Those who are able to do so move to the suburbs.
3. Inflation and lowered budget potential of the inner city are constricting central city budgets far more than those of the growing suburban areas.
4. Recreation as a city service is usually of low priority and is considered more of a frill than a necessity by some city governments.
5. Land for park, recreation area, and open space conservation is becoming increasingly scarce and expensive in the central cities and the suburbs. In the highly developed urban core, prices are high and going higher. Land ownerships are small and competition for land is intense. These conditions restrict the opportunity to acquire large open spaces within the urban areas.

The size of recreation areas in urban centers can generally be characterized as ranging from the smallest in the central city to the larger parks on the outside and the largest parks in the rural areas. This is contrary to the intensity of need for open space but reflects the economics of real estate development. Where parks and open space exist near the center of the city, it is evident that they were established at a time when the land was still essentially open space on what was then the urban fringe. Small parks in the central city are evidenced by Detroit's 388 parks that average about 12 acres in size, if the single large park of more than 1,000 acres is excluded. In neighboring Oakland County, state parks average more than 3,700 acres.

Historically, the federal and state governments have not taken an active role in supplying specific facilities close to urban residents. This has left most of the action up to counties and municipalities. Financial assistance from federal sources has been made available on a matching basis, especially in the 1930s when labor was readily available for park construction and since 1965 when various funds and services were made available by Congressional action.

It seems that city governments and the citizens who influence them have chosen not to dedicate adequate areas within the cities or near them to recreation. In a nation in which decentralized government has been a tenet of political philosophy, private enterprise and local governments are the agencies that should be expected to provide recreation at the local level, according to the needs of their citizens. They have the mandate to do so and have the power to tax citizens in a manner that will provide recreation areas close to home. Therefore, it seems that the blame, if any must be laid, rests with the local governments in not making adequate provision for their citizens. A lack of energetic, local initiative in government results in passing the responsibility to the next highest level. By keeping parks and recreation as a low priority, communities seem to assure increased state and federal interference in local recreation supply.

If municipal governments cannot or will not provide adequate recreation places, states have the next responsibility for the citizenry, including those in urban areas. State assistance in the development of large open spaces near or in urban areas is to be expected also.

Until recently, most states have not perceived their role to be one of providing recreation for urban dwellers. The major emphasis in states, much like that of the federal government, has been to preserve natural resources in rural areas. Some states have made efforts to meet urban recreation needs specifically, including the following:

> The state of Ohio manages 17 areas in the Cleveland region. It helped preserve the Cuyahoga Valley for the present Cuyahoga National Recreation Area, which contains several of the state properties.
>
> In the Chicago area, the state of Illinois maintains seven state parks, and Indiana has one state park that serves the Chicago-Gary urban complex.
>
> Near Los Angeles, the state invested more than $80,000,000 during the 1970s to purchase more than 30,000 acres of land in the Santa Monica mountains and the nearby seashore for open space, now managed in cooperation with the National Park Service. Likewise, in the San Francisco area, the state park system has several parks within one or two hours' driving distance of San Francisco. Recently, the state has directed greater efforts toward providing urban recreation, in terms of both land acquisition and financial assistance to county and local governments.

Nearly one quarter of Colorado's state parks are located in the Denver region.

Jones Beach and Robert Moses State Park on Long Island are other examples of state properties that serve an urban population, but it is notable that there are few facilities for mass transit to those two areas. When the area was designed, the access roads were built so that large buses and trucks could not use them.

Twelve state parks and recreation areas serve the Detroit metropolitan region.

Other states, however, have not done much to provide near-to-home state recreation facilities. Massachusetts, Missouri, Kansas, and Texas are among the examples of states that have few facilities in or near major urban centers.

Finally, the federal government can take on the job of urban recreation. If the people wish to have centralized financing and control over recreation areas, there is little doubt that senators and representatives will gradually agree to add increasing financial support and control over recreation areas near urban centers. That would be consistent with the pattern of centralization of many government services that has developed since the 1930s in the United States and Canada.

National recreation areas in and near cities, such as the Gateway in New York, Golden Gate in San Francisco (Figure 11.14), and Cuyahoga Valley between Cleveland and Akron, are signs that the National Park Service is taking an increasingly active position on the direct solution to recreation needs within cities. In 1978, new areas were added by Congress to accelerate the trend. These are managed by joint state and federal efforts. A variety of other resource-oriented properties happen to occur near urban areas and serve the function of supplying recreation opportunities to citizens of those areas. Such properties include the Indiana Dunes National Lakeshore, Fire Island and Cape Cod National Seashores, and the Delaware Water Gap National Recreation Area. Traditionally, national park areas have been established wherever there was a significant resource of scenic or historic value. Many of the historic areas are within cities but are limited to rather small spaces. The scenic areas are usually in remote places where private enterprise or housing has not already usurped the opportunity for development of a national park.

National Forests and Bureau of Land Management policies have not reflected an active and direct concern for urban areas. There is no reason to suspect that this is an active negligence of urban residents. It is merely a reflection of the policies that exist in resource-oriented recreation facilities. National Forests, fish and wildlife refuges, and the national resource lands have traditionally been wherever forests or wildlife habitat could be found and appropriately declared. That has generally been in relatively remote, rural areas at some distance from large cities.

FIGURE 11.14 Golden Gate National Recreation Area is a bayside strip of old forts, an airfield, and beaches around the northern and western edge of San Francisco plus large areas of land extending north and west from the Golden Gate bridge. (NPS)

Most of the public domain was the residue of lands, representing areas that no one else wanted to claim. When recreation demand rose, responsible agencies developed increasing numbers of recreation facilities on the lands they already owned. They are not villains for not providing recreation facilities in or near the cities. They simply provided recreation facilities where they had land and then held them open for anyone who wished to come to visit. There was no active desire to discriminate against the poor or other people without transportation. The Congress has never taken direct action to put these land management agencies into the urban recreation business, except for the urban national recreation areas.

With those exceptions, cities remain as the basic governmental jurisdictions that must provide public parks (Figure 11.15). Cities seem to be the logical suppliers of facilities for their own inhabitants, even if some of those inhabitants are in the city only during the day. It would seem that most cities with their large industries and high-density population could probably provide adequate recreation facilities. Historically, this has been the case, except that many of the cities were not sufficiently well

Recreation Places

organized or did not have sufficiently altruistic government officials who could see the value of recreation and open space. With the phenomena of post-World War II immigration into the cities by large numbers of rural poor and emigration from the cities by those with high incomes, federal assistance and local monies have been strongly directed to urban areas, but still most of the money has been spent in the suburbs and areas beyond the built-up zone. There has been emphasis on buying the least expensive land that is readily available. This has meant that parks are located at some distance from transportation systems and often out of the path of growth. Federal assistance programs are chiefly aimed at capital investments.

Many cities have pointed out the needs for maintenance and operating funds. Small, rural communities face the same difficulties of finding enough money to operate a park and recreation program. The tax base of inner-city areas and rural communities is low, because many of the residents have low incomes. Therefore, the contention is that the cost load should be spread.

There are several alternatives to this dilemma:

1. Let them go without if they can't pay or choose not to support the programs and facilities.

FIGURE 11.15 Local parks provide places for cultural events, among many other activities.

2. County park boards might take over the major responsibility for inner-city and suburban park work. By bringing all the park and recreation departments together into a county board, a more equitable distribution of facilities and services might result.

3. Establish metropolitan authorities to operate parks and recreation in the whole area, with assurances that the inner city gets an appropriate share of the monies and attention to correct any current imbalances. Of course, inner-city property will usually cost more than fringe properties, and maintenance costs may be higher.

4. The state can equalize some of the tax-base problems through its own cost-sharing program aimed at helping low-income or small tax-base communities.

5. The federal government may be called upon to share the load.

Summary

The future of local parks will apparently be much more complex than it now is. At present, there is a need for greater supply of recreation resources

Figure 11.16 Marinas and yacht harbors can be revenue producers for local park and recreation departments. Coyote Point Park is part of the San Mateo County Park Department, California.

close to home. Space is limited, costs are high, and inner-city tax revenues are deficient. More efficient use of available spaces, more rigorous maintenance, and stronger programming efforts are partial solutions.

Large cities and small rural communities are looking for new solutions. Federal funding helps somewhat but does not resolve the persistent shortage of funds. Alternatives that have been tried include expansion of the role of counties and special districts to cut across political jurisdictions for purposes of taxes and management. Some states have moved to serve urban areas more directly with close-to-home resources. Likewise, the National Park Service has moved into the cities on at least an experimental basis. Duke (1976) noted that greater federal activity in local parks will be very expensive, probably more so than if local control is maintained.

The real issues in local parks boil down to two words—*money* and *management*. The agencies and politicians worry about the source of the money, often relying on the time-worn ploy of seeking funds from a higher level rather than taking the responsibility for raising it locally for local services (Figure 11.16). Management is the key issue to the citizens, who will be paying the taxes, regardless of the agency involved. Their concern is how their recreational needs are served (Duke, 1976).

Local parks present a major challenge for the future, for agencies at all levels of government, and for private initiative. Imaginative, constructive, and active leadership is needed.

Literature Cited

Bureau of the Census. 1977. The Statistical Abstract of the U.S. (1978). Washington, D.C.: U.S. Dept. of Commerce. 1048 pp.

Bureau of Labor Statistics. 1932. Park Recreation Areas in the United States, 1930. Washington, D.C.: U.S. Dept. of Labor, BLS Bulletin No. 565. 116 pp.

BUTLER, GEORGE D. 1937. Municipal and County Parks in the United States, 1935. Washington, D.C.: U.S. Dept. of the Interior, National Park Service. 147 pp.

CARO, ROBERT A. 1974. The Power Broker. New York: Vintage Books. 1246 pp.

DUKE, NORMAN G. 1976. Urban parks—whose responsibility? In: Knudson, D. M., Managing Recreation Resources for Century III. West Lafayette, Ind.: Purdue Univ., Dept. of Forestry and Natural Resources. pp. 41–48.

Heritage Conservation and Recreation Service. 1978. National Urban Recreation Study; Executive Report. Washington, D.C.: U.S. Dept. of the Interior. 184 pp.

LANCASTER, ROGER A. 1976. Municipal services. Parks & Recreation 11(7):18–27.

National Conference on Outdoor Recreation. 1924. Proceedings (May 22, 23, 24). Washington, D.C.: Senate Document No. 151. 244 pp.

National Park Service and Bureau of Outdoor Recreation. 1977. National Urban Recreation Study; Technical Reports, Volume 1: Urban Open Space, Existing

Conditions, Opportunities and Issues. Washington, D.C.: U.S. Dept. of the Interior. var. pag.

OLMSTED, FREDERICK LAW, JR. and THEODORA KIMBALL (eds). 1928. Frederick Law Olmsted, Landscape Architect, 1822–1903; vol. two: Central Park, 1853–1895. New York: G. P. Putnam's sons. 574 pp.

PEET, CREIGHTON. 1954. Central Park, New York's big back yard. American Forests 60(7):10–11.

SMITH, FRED. 1972. Man and His Urban Environment. Rockefeller Plaza, N.Y.: Man and His Urban Environment Project. 57 pp.

VERHOVEN, PETER J. and ROGER A. LANCASTER, 1976. Municipal Recreation and Park Services. The Municipal Year Book 43:203–215.

WHITAKER, BEN and KENNETH BROWNE. 1971. Parks for People. London: Seeley, Service & Co. 144 pp.

CHAPTER 12

State Recreation Functions and Agencies

Historically, the role of the state has been to provide education, health, transportation, and police services for its citizens. Recreation facilities and activities were provided only passively or in exceptional cases. However, since the 1930s and particularly since 1945, the states have become involved in outdoor recreation. This rapidly expanding involvement, for example, resulted in the more than doubling of the state park area in the 25 years between 1950 and 1975 and about an eighteen-fold increase in expenditures for the same period (Table 12.1). In addition, recreation use on state forests and fish and wildlife areas has increased dramatically.

Although the state's role in managing outdoor recreation properties is essentially to provide facilities for its own citizens, it can also serve another important function. A well-developed outdoor recreation system can attract out-of-state tourists and thus provide much needed revenue to the state and for its citizens.

State Functions

State governments have now become the pivotal organizations in the national effort to supply adequate outdoor recreation resources. They are the keys in the allocation of financial and technical resources to efficiently develop increased facilities and services. State roles are much more than

TABLE 12.1   Changes in state park systems, 1950 to 1975.

	1950	1962	1975
Number of properties	1,725	2,544	3,804
Areas (1,000 ha)	1,885	2,334	3,983
Expenditures ($1,000)	36,399	106,151	649,000
Revenue from operations ($1,000)	6,646	26,466	115,000
Total personnel hired (number)	10,626	17,621	44,900
Professionals employed (number)	401	1,402	6,200
Attendance (1,000)	114,291	284,795	566,000

Source: Statistical Abstract of the U.S., 1968 and 1977.

TABLE 12.2 State functions related to outdoor recreation and typical agencies responsible.

Function	State agency
1. Manage state lands for recreation use (owned or leased)	
State forests	Division of Forestry, DNR*
State fish & wildlife areas	Division of Fish & Wildlife, DNR
State parks, recreation areas, beaches	Division of State Parks, DNR; and Division of Reservoir Management, DNR
State nature preserves, memorials	Appropriate divisions, DNR
State scenic rivers, trails, others	Division of Outdoor Recreation, DNR
2. Interpret natural processes and values	Division of State Parks, DNR
Encourage environmental education programs	Supt. of Public Instruction and cooperating agencies
3. Enforce state laws and regulations affecting hunting, fishing, ORV-riding, boating, other recreational activities	Division of Law Enforcement, DNR
4. Regulate welfare of citizens and resources, provide information, maps.	
Health, water quality (private, public areas)	State Health Department
Soils	Division of Soil Conservation, DNR
Geology	State Geological Survey, DNR
Strip mine reclamation	Division of Forestry or Reclamation, DNR
Flood plain uses	Division of Water, DNR
5. Prepare statewide recreation plan	Division of Outdoor Recreation, DNR
6. Coordination of federal and state funding programs, review of local and state plans	Division of Outdoor Recreation, DNR
7. Pass legislation enabling local governments to operate parks and recreation departments	Legislature
8. Promote tourism and offer information services	Division of Tourist Promotion, Department of Commerce
9. Provide highways, landscaping, and rest facilities	State Highway Department
10. Review environmental impacts of local, state, and federal projects	DNR, State Board of Health
11. Study, propagate, and distribute plants and animals for stocking public and private natural resource areas	Division of Forestry, DNR Division of Fish & Wildlife, DNR
12. Offer technical assistance to landowners on resource management for recreation, timber, wildlife, fish, other problems	Divisions of Forestry, Fish & Wildlife, Water, Geology, Entomology, Soils, other, DNR
13. Assure recreation services to special individuals (elderly, handicapped)	Land managing agencies, DNR and/or State Board of Health
14. Train professionals in recreation land management and programming; conduct research; provide information.	State universities

* DNR = Department of Natural Resources or equivalent. Names and organizations vary among states.

managing lands on which recreation is allowed. States are the keys to the planning process. They are in charge of distributing financial incentives. They help coordinate and promote outdoor recreation opportunities within their boundaries.

Table 12.2 describes the major functions related to outdoor recreation that the state governments now have, listed by the types of lands and agencies usually responsible.

The next portion of this chapter describes the land management agencies, the planning and coordination functions, and tourism. Finally, different approaches to state organization are discussed.

Land Management

The tradition of state governments protecting natural resources for the public good began in the colony of Massachusetts. The first reservation of wild lands for public survival and recreational benefit in North America apparently occurred in 1641. The Great Ponds Act, promulgated by the Massachusetts Bay Colony, set aside 2,000 bodies of water, each larger than 10 acres, as public resources, forever open for fishing and fowling. Thus, a total of 36,400 ha (90,000 acres) of water became a public fishing and hunting ground (Nelson, 1928). Today, Departments of Natural Resources, Conservation, or the Environment are the most common coordinators of state land management efforts. State forests, parks, and fish and wildlife areas exist in all states and in most provinces of Canada.

Three classes of state properties are common among virtually all the states, although there are differences in emphases of purpose. All are open for some types of recreation.

1. State parks and recreation areas are of state significance for scenic, historic, or tourism values. There are about 3,804 units in state park systems, covering nearly 4 million ha or 9.8 million acres (Bureau of the Census, 1977).
2. State forests are multiple-use areas, established as demonstration areas for timber management. Their recreation role has become significant. There are more than 1,000 state forests covering 9.7 million ha or 24 million acres (unpublished data, Indiana DNR).
3. State fish and wildlife areas are set up to provide habitats for animals. They are less used than forests or parks, but interest is growing in wildlife appreciation, hunting, and fishing. There are no reliable national data concerning state fish and wildlife areas. An estimate of 1972 conditions reported 6.4 million ha (15.8 million acres) in fish and wildlife areas (Bureau of Outdoor Recreation, 1973).

Other state areas are called by various names and are not common to all states. They include the following types of properties in some states:

4. State nature preserves are usually small areas featuring outstanding ecological or geological phenomena. They are managed to remain natural so they control visitation.
5. State memorials and museums commemorate historical structures, events, and people. They often cover small areas, and interpretation is the key to their use.
6. State waysides and highway rest areas are familiar to most travelers. They are usually managed by the Department of Highways.
7. State scenic rivers are preserved stretches of streams that are designated to be kept in free-flowing condition. The stream bank may be protected by easement, zoning, or purchase.
8. State trails are poorly developed outside of public property, but there is growing interest in long-distance trail development. Negotiations are complex and sometimes emotional.
9. Soil and Water Conservation Districts are legal subdivisions of the state, some of which develop small reservoirs. These are usually open to the public, often in collaboration with other state agencies.

There are wide differences among states in administrative policies for their lands. Some manage strictly according to the designation of their lands; most state parks are purely for recreation and preservation, in the mold of national parks. In others, parks and forest blend together in purpose, all being managed for recreation, timber, range, and wildlife. Some park systems are located for tourist trade, with uptown facilities. Some manage wildlife areas as pure refuges, with little or no hunting or fishing, although most open the areas to controlled harvest.

Alaska has large areas of undesignated land. Although it has a few state parks and forests, its greatest amount of property is the almost 104 million acres to be selected after statehood for future development. Little of this has been given special management classification yet. A number of western states were given school lands out of the public domain at the time of statehood and for special programs. These school trust lands are managed for income or held for future sale by public school systems and colleges, but usually are not open for recreation use.

To comprehend management in any state, it is important to study the organizational structure and policies of the various agencies involved in natural resource management and control. In many states, there are no organic acts for park and forest systems, so it becomes difficult to identify definitive documents that describe legal mandates and authority. The policy governing state recreation area management is a result of numerous laws, agreements, and leases with federal and other agencies, legislative appropriations, actions of appointed boards, and directives from state officials such as the governor, attorney general, or director of natural resources. Some policies develop through internal practice; they usually are written in regulations or policy manuals of the agency, but may be most accurately interpreted by directors of divisions or by property managers. State government has the advantage of flexibility and freedom for innovation.

State land holdings are especially important to outdoor recreation supply in the eastern part of the nation. Federal holdings there are few, and local parks are usually small in size. The states provide a large share of the areas with naturalistic environments where recreation can take place. Even in the mountain West, where federal forests and parks offer extensive wild lands for recreation, state parks have found an important role. They are often located on the plains or in the foothills, around small water impoundments. They provide warm-water fishing plus camping, picnicking, and other activities quite close to home.

Planning and Coordination

When the Land and Water Conservation Fund Act was passed in 1965, states discovered that recreation was one sort of land use planning with an advantage. The federal government induced state and local recreation planning by offering the "carrot" of matching funds for land acquisition and development. The requirement was that the state prepare an approved, comprehensive recreation plan. To accomplish this, governors usually named the director of the state Department of Natural Resources (or his equivalent) to be the liaison with the U.S. Department of the Interior. In many states, a division of planning or outdoor recreation was established to prepare the plan and coordinate the grant money, which was distributed to the state agencies and local communities. This involved technical assistance to local agencies and review of their plans and projects to establish eligibility for receiving matching funds.

The tasks of these divisions have often increased over time. Historic preservation funds and other recreation programs have been added. Out of the planning process have come proposals for scenic streams and trails. Implementation is often left to the outdoor recreation division. Likewise, this group is expert at reviewing federal documents, so it is handed environmental impact statements to study and on which to make official comment. Over the past 15 years, these fledgling planning-coordinating offices have become key elements in most state governments. A few states, notably Michigan, are still doing recreation planning work through collaborative efforts of several divisions of the Department of Natural Resources. Other states have assigned the planning function to an existing agency.

Tourist Promotion

The advertising of a state's attractions usually falls to a special division or office not directly connected to the management of natural resources. In Indiana, tourism is in the Department of Commerce. In Canada, Quebec

FIGURE 12.1 Yucca plant
bearing man's fruits. (NPS)

has a Department of Tourism, Fish, and Game, uniting recreation, tourism, and wildlife functions. This at least produces some unity in the efforts. Too often, one agency is promoting heavier use of facilities while managers of the other agency are fighting the effects of overuse (Figure 12.1). There is an increasing tendency toward informal coordination of efforts and communication among professionals in these agencies.

Tourist promotion efforts are concerned with all attractions in the state, private as well as public. Michigan has four regional associations, supported by tourist attraction enterprises, chambers of commerce, and some state funding. These produce their own regional folders and advertising. The state agency spends more than $1.5 million per year promoting travel to Michigan. It is estimated that the state takes in many times that amount in sales taxes from visitors.

Although the economics of tourism promotion is difficult to pin down, there is considerable public interest in and requests for information about recreation attractions in states. Surveys by tourist promotion organizations repeatedly show that the investment in publications, mass media advertising, and promotion through travel exhibitions is more than compensated by direct tax returns alone.

210

Principles of Administrative Organization

There are several principles that describe different aspects of organization. State government can be analyzed using these concepts. There is no pat formula for how they are to be applied.

1. **Scalar Principle:** The scalar principle is the concept of a continuous scale of authority, or chain of command. There is unity of command, with a direct channel from top to bottom. It is often referred to as *line organization*, meaning that there is a direct line or scale of authority, responsibility, and accountability. Authority and responsibility flow down through the links of the chain of command from the chief executive. Accountability flows back up. The scalar principle is illustrated in the short chain of command of line officers of an executive branch: Governor-Director of Department of Natural Resources-Director of Division-Property Manager. Basic operations and decisions are passed up and down this direct line. The scalar principle requires that each person in the line has only one boss. He may receive guidance and technical advice from others, but not orders. He is responsible to that boss and receives authority from him. In some government organizations, the chain of command gets stretched out with many links between the four mentioned here. This can have the effect of confusing or muddying communications or, at least, slowing down response time. The usual procedure to avoid these is to give staff officers informal line responsibility for day-to-day operations, while basic definitions and responsibility remain in the line. *Line* refers to the direct chain of command; *staff* refers to aides and technical advisors who laterally extend the scope of the line officer.

2. **Span-of-Control Principle:** When an organization becomes large, line officers face the problem of retaining full control over growing programs and numbers of personnel. A manager can effectively supervise three to seven subordinates if their work interlocks and needs coordination. A director of the division of state parks or forests faces a dilemma if there are 20 property managers under his command. In many cases, their work does not directly interlock, because they operate rather independently. That allows the director to work with them as replicates. However, in sharing equipment and sometimes manpower, coordination may become a problem. To solve the problem of too large a span of control, the line officer can adopt two approaches: a) lengthen the chain of command, putting three to five regional supervisors in charge of the property managers, these regional supervisors in turn to report to him, or b) use staff officers informally to keep the chain of command as short as possible. The latter is preferred in some organizations for its advantages of cohesiveness and responsiveness. Line officers set policy and major procedures and have final responsibility, but specialized staff members help coordinate on a day-to-day basis in relation to their specialties. Staff suggestions to down-line officers can always be appealed to the up-line officer.

3. Decentralization Principle: The key concept here is to place responsibility and authority to act at the lowest possible level. For this to operate, the lower line officers must assume the responsibility and be given authority. Decentralization requires controls, in the form of inspections, reports, and accounting. Delegating authority does not relieve the delegator of final responsibility. Delegation requires clarity, definiteness, and direction. It involves setting objectives, establishing minimum controls and criteria, and clearly setting deadlines.

4. Territorial Jurisdiction Principle: A single, responsible officer administers all the resources and activities in a geographical area. This is of particular importance in state property management, especially those where multiple uses are involved. One person is responsible for timber, wildlife, recreation, personnel, and other work on the property. He may have assistants and specialized staff to help with different problems, but his responsibility is clear and distinct. The alternative is to have a manager for timber, a manager for recreation, and so on, which usually results in confusion as to who is running the operation. Control by one person minimizes conflicts and provides coordination. It also requires that the person have a balanced view of the resources and an ability to administer them so that all values are given appropriate management attention. In most cases, line organization coincides with territorial jurisdictions.

5. Functional Segregation Principle: The functional segregation principle applies to staff positions for the most part, suggesting that specialists are assigned certain types of tasks, such as budget or interpretation, and other specialists don't butt in. Like territorial jurisdiction, this gives the specialist responsibility and accountability for doing the job. It allows superiors to evaluate the performance of the individual.

6. Coordination Principle: Within the organization, coordination is essential to harmonious functioning among the various specialists. This involves meetings of staff and line officers, field trips, inspections that help integrate operations, and reporting of the results of operations.

MODELS OF STATE ORGANIZATIONS

Each state has its own twist to the organization of its natural resources agencies. There are at least four identifiable approaches to administrative hierarchies for managing outdoor recreation resources at the state level.

1. Department with Specialized Divisions: The specialized division approach seems to be the most frequently encountered. The Department of Natural Resources or Department of Conservation is an umbrella agency with a director responsible to the governor. These departments coordinate the work of the divisions of forestry, wildlife, parks, and other property-managing groups with the work of planners and funding experts. Figure 12.2 illustrates the basic structure of the Indiana Department of Natural Resources, which is representative of many other states, including Minnesota and California.

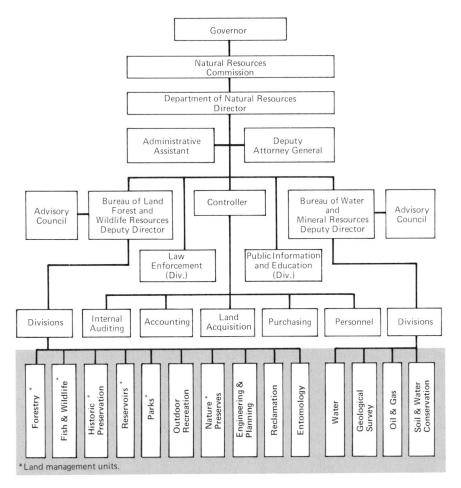

Figure 12.2 Indiana Department of Natural Resources organization chart.

2. Separate Specialized Departments: North Dakota has a rather disaggregated set of agencies working in the natural resource area. It has departments, agencies, councils, institutes, and other entities operating in parallel and, apparently, on an independent basis, without an umbrella agency. Recreation resources are managed by the State Game and Fish Department and the State Park Service. The State Outdoor Recreation Agency is responsible for planning and coordinating with local entities for recreational development. The governor has a Natural Resources Council that provides an interdisciplinary approach to natural resource management and planning by state agencies. In a state with a small population, this approach may be preferable to a structured hierarchy.

Idaho, likewise, has separate departments with no overall coordinating structure. The state has eight agencies related to natural resources, including a Department of Parks and Recreation, a Fish and Game Department, a

Department of Water Resources, and a Department of Lands that administers school land grants.

3. Unrelated Superior Agency: The outstanding example of an unrelated superior agency is in Oregon, where state parks and recreation is a branch of the Department of Transportation. Forestry and Fish and Wildlife are separate, independent departments, each reporting to the governor. Many of Oregon's numerous state parks are relatively small camping areas along the state and federal highways.

4. Individual Park Commissions: In some states, special situations have resulted in the establishment of special, independent commissions for the management of individual properties. Mackinac Island State Park in Michigan is an example. Its commission is part of the Department of Natural Resources but operates as a division separate from state parks. A similar situation exists in New York, where the Adirondack Park Agency was established in 1971 to administer the huge park and forest preserve. It is completely independent of other agencies, including the state office of Parks and Recreation and the Department of Environmental Conservation. The Palisades Interstate Park Commission is another independent agency, set up by joint action of New York and New Jersey.

These four types of arrangements are suggestive of the diversity that exists among the different states. Structures tend to change with changing needs (Figure 12.3) but some apparent anomalies persist for years.

An outline of a portion of the Washington state government follows as an example of the second model, separate specialized departments.

STATE OF WASHINGTON CASE

The following agencies are responsible for recreation at the state level in Washington (1978):

Department of Fisheries: responsible for food fish and shellfish plus most anadromous fish. The primary work is in saltwater. The department devotes most of its effort to salmon and tries to balance fish productivity with harvest by commercial, Indian, and sport fishermen.

Department of Game: responsible for game fish, including sea-run trout; the primary work is in fresh water. The department also manages and regulates wildlife activities, conducts research, produces game birds on eight game farms, manages 24 wildlife recreation areas (308,000 ha), where 60 per cent of the use is nonconsumptive and 40 per cent is hunting, trapping, and fishing. This agency also manages 36 facilities for fish rearing.

Department of Natural Resources: The forestry agency of Washington, manages 1.2 million timbered hectares (three million acres) for schools, counties, trusts, and the state. Another 810,000 ha (2 million acres) of tide and shore lands, including beds of navigable rivers, are managed for public benefit. The department regulates and protects private and public forests, and provides dispersed and primitive recreation opportunities. Trails,

FIGURE 12.3   State scenic rivers are new responsibilities for resource agencies in 25 states.

campgrounds, and a few natural area preservation projects are major recreation interests.

Parks and Recreation Commission: state parks host more than 35 million people per year on 200 properties, only half of which are developed and staffed. The system contains more than 33,000 ha (83,000 acres). Ten environmental learning centers and several interpretive visitor centers offer programs. There are also limited in-park, interpretive services.

Education	$254
Public welfare	120
Highways	82
Health and hospitals	46
Natural resources	17
Other	216
Total	$735

TABLE 12.3 State expenditures per capita, U.S., 1975.

Interagency Committee for Outdoor Recreation: set up in 1964 the IAC assists state and local agencies in the acquisition and development of outdoor recreation resources. In its first 12 years it channeled funding from three state bond issues, the federal Land and Water Conservation Fund, and a recent All-Terrain Vehicle fund from permit fees and fuel taxes.

The IAC also prepares the state comprehensive outdoor recreation plan and reviews local recreation plans. It coordinates distribution of grants-in-aid for outdoor recreation from state and federal sources. It also promotes user development through outdoor education and participation programs. The governing committee is five citizens and seven state agency heads.

STATE GOVERNMENT FINANCES

Nationwide, money spent on natural resources in 1975 was $3,554 million or $17 per capita (Bureau of the Census, 1977). Total state expenditures were $156,171 million, or $735 per capita (Table 12.3).

State government revenue in 1975 totaled $154,632 million, or $634 per capita. This came from federal sources, $36,148 million; from local governments, $1,680 million; taxes, $80,155 million (Table 12.4); charges and miscellaneous, $16,629 million; and liquor stores and insurance trust. More than half the tax revenues were from sales and gross receipts.

Source	Total (millions)	Per capita
Sales + gross receipts	$43,346	$204
Licenses	6,289	30
Individual income	18,819	89
Corporate net income	6,642	31
Property	1,451	7
Other	3,607	17
Total	$80,155	$377

TABLE 12.4 State tax revenue sources, for all states, 1975.

Source: Bureau of the Census (1977).

Recreation Places

Literature Cited

Bureau of the Census. 1977. The Statistical Abstract of the U.S. (1978). Washington, D.C.: U.S. Department of Commerce. 1048 pp.

NELSON, BEATRICE W. 1928. State Recreation. New York: National Conference on State Parks. 302 pp.

Washington, State of. 1978. 1977 Annual Report, Natural Resources and Recreational Agencies. Olympia. 91 pp.

State Recreation Resources

This chapter describes some of the history and the extent of state lands used for recreation. Financial and policy matters are defined for a few cases as illustrations.

When a young professional joins a state organization, there is a wealth of diverse talent and information available to help him or her. In the different state agencies, there are specialists in all aspects of resource management, planning, analysis, promotion, and, of course, politics.

Even the assistant manager of the smallest state park has access to data, advice, and information by telephone, letter, and personal contact. Resource management requires familiarity with the functions of the various agencies mentioned in the previous chapter.

State Lands Acquisition

State forests, parks, wildlife preserves, and other areas are approximately one seventh the size of federal areas. State lands, however, receive many more visits per year than do federal lands. Nationwide, state recreation lands can be divided into state forests with 10.5 million ha (26 million acres), state fish and wildlife areas with 3.7 million ha (9 million acres), and state park agencies with about 2.2 million ha (5.5 million acres), based on estimates by the U.S. Forest Service (1979).[1] A few states have not distinguished among these and manage their lands as natural resource areas or under other names.

Acquisition of state lands came about in a variety of ways, but most was not by full payment. Pennsylvania has acquired 3 million acres of forest land, with 1.9 million coming from tax-delinquent sources. Pennsylvania state game lands, now at 450,000 ha (over 1 million acres), were acquired similarly, as lands nobody wanted. The later discovery of oil and gas on these public lands resulted in revenues that were used to purchase additional inexpensive wild lands.

In Illinois, most of the state's recreation areas are fish and game lands,

[1] Estimates of land areas in state ownership vary widely among different reports. Alaska contains an additional 15 million ha which are not designated as forests, parks, or refuges.

scattered across the state. Because these were not productive for agriculture or useful for residential or commercial development, they were available at low prices. Washington State also bought its land from tax-delinquent, cut-over timber lands. The states of Florida, Mississippi, and Louisiana used private lands, leasing them from timber industries for hunting and fishing areas. Much of Louisiana and Mississippi fish and wildlife areas (Figure 13.1) are in floodplains and swamp lands (Bureau of Outdoor Recreation, 1970).

Before World War II, state forests and parks were mostly acquired from four sources: gifts, original state holdings (lands of the Colonies not turned over to the federal government), tax-delinquent lands, and federal lands turned over to the states. A number of parks had been bought directly from private owners, using state taxes and volunteer contributions to make payment, but these were in the minority (Bureau of Outdoor Recreation, 1970).

After World War II, emphasis on acquisition increased, and the states were required to appropriate increased funds for land purchase, not waiting for bargain opportunities to arise. Finance came from two principal sources—bonds and earmarked taxes. Bond issues have been the principal means of financing, accompanied by increasing annual appropriations. Several states have designated portions of special taxes as sources of capital development funds for parks and forests. Indiana, Wisconsin, and Nebraska,

FIGURE 13.1 Alligators play a vital ecological role in "weeding" dense, submerged vegetation out of limestone waterholes, thereby keeping swamp pools habitable for freshwater fish throughout lowland southeastern parks and refuges. (NPS)

for example, have revenues available from a cigarette tax that the legislature can appropriate for recreational capital costs. Nebraska uses this as its main source of funds to match Land and Water Conservation Fund grants from the federal government.

Other states use a portion of the state gasoline tax to acquire and develop property for recreational boating. Although only a few have taken advantage of them, state and federal highway monies are available for building bikeways.

Several federal laws made acquisition easier through matching grants. A great deal of land has been purchased for fish and wildlife areas as a result of the passage in 1937 of the Pittman-Robertson Act, which allowed federal monies to be put into wildlife restoration. In 1950, the Dingell-Johnson Act did the same for the habitat improvement of fisheries. The 1965 Land and Water Conservation Fund offered matching funds for recreational land acquisition and development.

The alternative types of acquisition are of interest to the administrator seeking economical solutions. Traditionally, acquisition of full title to large blocks of land has been used to form parks, forests, and fish and wildlife areas. For some purposes, outright ownership appears to be necessary. It facilitates management of any property, giving the agency control over its use and the design of the recreational and other facilities. There are several alternatives that can be used in certain circumstances.

Scenic easements have been quite successful in maintaining permanent, pleasant driving roads in Wisconsin. Many other states have laws that allow the establishment of scenic roads through conservation or scenic easements.

Public use access is another sort of easement. New York's fishing easement program has acquired permanent rights for public use along about 1,000 miles of its streams and their banks, since the late 1930s. In return, the state installs stream improvement devices, stabilizes banks, puts up fences to contain livestock where necessary, and improves and manages the fishing.

Mississippi, Louisiana, Florida, and Maine are using leases as an important tool in making land available for recreation. Each of these states has large blocks of land that are owned and managed by timber industries. While the trees are growing, certain types of outdoor recreation can be allowed at little or no detriment to the timber crops, if the use is managed properly. The states of Mississippi and Louisiana lease more than half of their fishing and hunting lands from forest products industries. The only danger in these arrangements is that of cancellation of the agreement. In 1967, Louisiana lost 130,000 acres to drainage and soybeans when the owners cancelled the lease (Bureau of Outdoor Recreation, 1970). Maine leases campgrounds from the large timber companies. The state is responsible for building the facilities and operating the campground, using company land at a nominal cost. That is almost a necessity, because timber companies own most of the northern half to two thirds of the state. This cooperative relationship is preferable to outright acquisition, which would be both costly and unpopular. Several timber companies have also preserved scenic forests along the principal tourist highways, thus adding to the recreational quality of their properties.

Easements and zoning are also used to establish scenic rivers and long-distance trails.

Professional Management

For years, many state parks, forests, and other properties were managed by political appointees, who often were deputy sheriffs, county chairmen of the party in power, or friends of friends. Seldom were they trained to manage resources; often they had experience in dealing with people. Most laborers on these properties are still politically chosen. Practices differ among states, with a strong tendency toward hiring professionally trained managers in most states.

Two characteristics of patronage management have been discontinuity and weak resource management. Discontinuity was a result of changing personnel every time there was a political change. Every four years, a new crew took over. This usually meant a slowdown by the old crew during the last year, with considerable loss of small tools. The new crew usually took the first year to get oriented. Thus, the administration was not always efficient.

Weak resource management resulted from a lack of trained managers. Political appointees usually keep the property neat and orderly. Visitors behave themselves. But there is no resource inventory, no plan for hazard management, no resource classification.

A professionally trained manager should be able to organize the custodial functions, a visitor use program, and a resource management program appropriate to the type of property. In addition, a wildlife enhancement and/or control program should be part of the management. Other elements include interpretation for visitors; a mapped inventory of unusual plants and animal habitats; a monitoring system for soils, water, vegetation, and special features; a mapped analysis of the carrying capacity for recreation and other uses by subdivisions of the property; a trail rehabilitation and maintenance plan; an activity zoning policy; and visitor use statistics by activity.

Property managers are under increasing pressure to accommodate new and traditional uses. Technical knowledge, common sense, and the ability to deal with people are all required.

State Forests

State forest lands were set up as timber management demonstrations. They are now multiple-use areas, with timber, recreation, wildlife, and water as the major benefits.

Recreation on most state forests is kept at a rustic, simple level (Figure 13.2). Campsites are usually designed more for tent campers than for trailer or motor home users. Trails are often fire lanes or logging roads. There are few developed recreational facilities other than campgrounds.

The recreational role of state forests has not been well defined in many states. Recreation and esthetic values are often treated as residuals or incidentals—matters to consider after the timber is measured and sold. That is partly the result of tradition and partly attributed to the relative ease of timber-related output measurement and decision making. As a result, recreational values are often ignored or occasionally lost in single-minded timber management plans.

FIGURE 13.2 Camping is popular in state parks and forests—West Virginia's North Bend State Park.

Recreation Places

TABLE 13.1 State forests in the United States, by region, 1975.

Regions and selected states	Number	State forests Thousands of ha	Thousands of acres
Total	1,030	9,737	24,050
Northeast	751	1,780	4,397
South	61	326	806
Midwest	167	3,134	7,741
Midlands	18	117	288
West	33	4,380	10,818
Selected states			
New York	442	293	724
Pennsylvania	19	810	2,000
New Hampshire	191	39	97
Michigan	33	1,527	3,772
Minnesota	56	1,215	3,000
Montana	7	80	199
Alaska	–	2,105	5,200
Utah	7	583	1,440
Washington	–	806	1,992

Source: Indiana Department of Natural Resources, unpublished data.

Many state forest managers, however, allocate a majority of staff time and operating funds to servicing recreational use. Some have set aside remote, primitive backpacking areas. Others are involved in managing beaches, long-distance hiking trails, horseback camps, and canoe routes. Increasingly, state forest managers are concerned with the recreational uses of their properties.

It is likely that the recreation role will increase, especially in the Northeast and the Midwest (Table 13.1). Those are the areas where public recreation lands are few and population is high and where state forests are mostly underutilized by the public.

Nature Preserves

In a few states, formal systems of nature preserves have been established, usually within the Department of Natural Resources or Conservation. In some states, the responsibility is under the state parks agency; in others, there is an independent organization that works with the other land-managing groups. The following statements are based on the Indiana system but seem to apply to most states where such preserves exist.

The purpose of nature preserves is to acquire and manage areas of outstanding natural significance. Nature preserves may be in public or private ownership. They contain unusual or typical plant, animal, geological, or scenic values. They are preserved as natural areas for the limited use of those interested in nature and for scientific and educational purposes.

Dedication of nature preserves is done by a natural resources commission, after staff study and planning for management of the property. If it is to remain in private hands, the owner must voluntarily agree to maintain the land in its natural state without commercial extraction or conversion to other uses. The department has authority to buy or accept lands as nature preserves. It may take fee ownership or easements.

Any unit of state or local government may dedicate nature preserves. The owner is responsible for preserving the character of the area, and the Division of Nature Preserves takes responsibility for inspections and direction. Nature preserves in state fish and wildlife areas, parks, and forests are set aside from other uses. One of their chief values is as reference points—places where natural forces are left to work without man's interference. After several decades, this value should be quite evident, as resource managers can document the results of natural succession.

Several states have undertaken an *ecological inventory* system that is strategic for nature preserve systems. It is called the Heritage Program, sponsored by The Nature Conservancy in cooperation with the state governments. It involves inventorying typical natural communities plus species and phenomena of unusual nature. These elements are identified and then located by occurrence throughout the state. The locations are plotted and filed, with inventory data attached. Cross-referenced indexes help identify the status of protection of natural diversity. Presumably, the Nature Preserves Division can establish priorities for additions to the system by identifying gaps in the present distribution of properties. This heritage program is not to be confused with the federal effort, which is called the national heritage program. The latter involves assistance monies to accomplish a similar type of objective. The two are compatible, with the state heritage programs geared to technical inventory and retrieval processes that serve as a basis for acquisition strategy.

The Illinois Natural Areas Survey (Department of Conservation) has long experience in researching, inventorying, and setting aside preserves. It was formed in 1858. Its nature preserve work was taken over by a Nature Preserves Commission in 1963.

There are more natural areas in Cook County, Illinois, than in any other county in the state. There the prairie, forest, and lake country come together. Many are school preserves. Others are in the Cook County Forest Preserves, and other bogs, dunes, and forests are held privately or by industry.

This suggests that the presence of people is not always negative to nature preservation. Some portion of a large population will seek to preserve natural conditions. With population stress, there is active concern for the scarce natural state. In the more rural areas, it is often assumed that an abundance of naturalness exists inexhaustibly, or there isn't enough local money for nature preservation, public or private.

The impacts of people on nature preserves is usually confined to trails. Most preserves are managed so that camping, picnicking, fires, motor vehicles, and horses are prohibited. Because of the small size and scattered location of these preserves, it is necessary to rely on volunteer overseers and the goodwill of visitors.

Fish and Wildlife Areas

All states have agencies responsible for the management of fish and wildlife resources. The operations of state agencies usually involve three major activities: 1) regulation of hunting and fishing, based on research and stocking programs; 2) assistance to landowners, including public agencies, on habitat management and wildlife population manipulation; and 3) management of public lands for fish and wildlife habitat.

The regulation of wildlife taking is ancient. There are references in Deuteronomy (22:6–7). Rulers have long reserved game for their own use. In monarchies, that often is still the case, even where representative governments allow licensed hunting. Hunting and fishing are usually by invitation or by paid privilege.

In the United States, all wildlife is the property of the people of each state; it is the responsibility of the state government. Certain migratory birds are controlled by federal law and by international treaty. Federal restrictions to protect endangered species are imposed upon state management. On federal parks and federal fish and wildlife refuges, the federal regulation of wildlife usually dominates. Elsewhere on federal, state, and private lands, the state fish and wildlife agencies have the principal responsibility for controlling wildlife, hunting, and fishing.

Wildlife management by regulation began during the colonial period. In the Northwest Territory, an important center of the fur trade, the General Assembly passed an act in 1799 to impose a bounty on wolves. Only in the mid-1800s did midwestern lawmakers impose seasons to protect big game animals. Meanwhile, many animals were extirpated or threatened, and habitat was disappearing fast because of land clearing and wetland drainage. In the last half of the nineteenth century, the foundations were laid for present controls of hunting and fishing, even though some bounties and rampant habitat destruction continued.

In the 1920s, the serious development of fish and wildlife areas began in the Midwest (Krauch, 1976). Major land use changes and commercial and slaughter hunting had reduced populations severely. Recreational hunters and fishermen were primary movers in introducing exotic species and setting aside refuges, preserves, and public hunting and fishing areas, in the late 1930s and 1940s.

State fish and wildlife areas are growing in popularity for diverse outdoor recreation. Camping, picnicking, hiking, and nature study are more popular than hunting and fishing, partially because the seasons are longer.

Like state forests, most fish and wildlife areas offer primitive facilities. The wild fauna get most of the pampering, and the visitor is made welcome on controlled terms. Interpretation of nature is of growing importance, although few state refuges employ full-time interpreters. Observation blinds, hunting pits, dog training facilities, and target ranges for archers and shooters are usually provided.

Stocking of fish in streams has been a politically popular activity, but often biologically unsuccessful. It has not improved the fishery population. Dumping hatchery-raised fingerlings off of bridges and stocking lakes had popular appeal, even though there was no evidence that fishing actually improved (Lockard, 1976). Stream and lake habitats are critical to the sustained productivity of fish, just as wildlife food and cover are necessary for land animals to survive.

Each year, 40 to 50 million sportsmen pay $200 to $300 million for state hunting and fishing licenses. They pay another $75 million or so in excise taxes on sporting arms, ammunition, and fishing tackle. Those two sources alone provide almost all of the funding for state fish and wildlife management programs, including efforts to manage nongame species and endangered species. The commitment and expressed concern for basic recreational resources—fish and wildlife—are an example of citizens supporting recreation area management with direct allocations of money.

A current issue is related to the incidence of these costs. Although acquisition and maintenance of fish and wildlife areas are paid for by sportsmen, the properties are now used less for hunting and fishing than for wildlife study, photography, hiking, picnicking, and camping. Although many of these users are the same people who become hunters and fishermen in season, the question of fairness is often raised. Should there be an entry fee or some other device to spread the cost to all visitors? The question has yet to become a serious policy issue in most states, largely because of the relative abundance of funds from existing sources. It is likely to be more seriously considered as fish and wildlife areas gain importance as diversified recreational resources and as costs for interpreters and facility attendants require a larger proportion of the budget.

State Parks

Colonel Richard Lieber, a leader of the state park movement, said in 1928 that a state park is

a typical portion of the state's original domain; a tract of adequate size, preserved in primeval, unspoilt, 'unimproved,' or 'beautified' condition. It is a physical expression of life, liberty, and the pursuit of happiness.

A state park must have either scenic or historic value or both, and is dedicated to the public for the intelligent use of its leisure time. (Michaud, 1966).

State parks differ from national parks in the appeal or significance of their features. When Richard Lieber, Stephen Mather, and others promoted the state park movement from 1916 to 1925, one goal was to respond to requests for national park status for local attractions. Lands that had state significance were recommended to states for acquisition and management.

Although Lieber's definition describes the nature of many, state park systems are highly variable in nature and extent. All 50 states have some sort of state parks. They range from highway-related areas in Oregon that average less than 160 ha (400 acres) in size to Alaska's huge natural areas that average more than 8,500 ha (21,000 acres) each. State parks range in character from wilderness areas to high-upkeep resorts such as the Kentucky resort parks with lodges, golf courses, and marinas. The states' fiscal dedication to their state parks roughly parallels their populations. However, 45 per cent of the total state park expenditures were made by six states—California, New York, Florida, Kentucky, Texas, and Pennsylvania (Table 13.2).

Acreage distribution is concentrated in relatively few states. Fifty-three

TABLE 13.2   Selected state park systems of the United States.

	Areas	Ha (1,000)	Acres (1,000)	Expenditures (millions of dollars)
Total	3,804	3,983	9,838	649
New York	209	1,206	2,978	68
Alaska	65	564	1,394	2
California	230	338	843	91
Pennsylvania	119	120	296	30
Illinois	186	116	287	13
Florida	115	115	283	43
New Jersey	106	102	253	20
Massachusetts	126	95	235	15
Michigan	93	91	224	11
Ohio	124	83	204	21
Connecticut	234	77	191	4
Delaware	9	3	7	2
Georgia	55	19	47	10
Hawaii	53	7	18	15
Indiana	20	27	66	11
Minnesota	92	71	175	7
Montana	130	14	35	2
North Carolina	34	28	69	9
South Carolina	48	26	63	8
Oregon	242	36	90	7
Texas	87	41	102	31
Washington	171	32	79	17
Wisconsin	73	44	108	7
Wyoming	48	64	157	1

Source: Bureau of the Census (1977) from National Recreation and Park Association data.

TABLE 13.3 Sample operating budget.

Otium State Park
Total = $249,344.55

Personal Services	
Salaried employees	$71,436.10
Biweekly-hourly employees	86,896.00
Workman's compensation	461.00
Other Services	
Postage	292.25
Light, heat, water, power	13,030.10
Gasoline credit cards	331.61
Local telephone	2,859.78
Long-distance telephone	663.87
Other services	18.00
Services by Contract	
Rentals	452.84
Repairs to motor vehicles	4,462.88
Repairs to office equipment	89.25
Maintenance, repairs, inspections	533.50
Janitor services, garbage or trash	1,244.75
Construction material, labor only	23.46
Materials, Supplies, Parts	
Stationery and office supplies	341.87
Livestock—forage, feed, medicine	191.65
Medical and lab supplies	42.47
Laundry, cleaning, disinfecting supplies	2,214.59
Motor vehicle fuel and lubricants	5,947.26
Heating fuel	3,940.12
Agricultural and botanical supplies for landscaping	550.00
Household supplies	148.26
Plumbing and drainage materials for repair	88.00
Research and testing supplies	36.64
Automotive equipment	2,181.94
Repair parts and supplies	111.28
Small tools and implements	22.26
Miscellaneous items	250.18
Equipment	
Pickup trucks	46,172.00
Mowers	2,595.00
Transportation equipment	1,375.00
Building and plant equipment	486.36
Grants, Subsidies, Refunds, Awards	
Medical and hospital compensation cases	897.33
In-state Travel	
Per diem in lieu of subsistence	36.00

per cent of the state park lands are in New York, Alaska, and California. The top 10 states contain 71 per cent of the nation's total acreage in state parks. New York's unusual Adirondack State Park is about 2.4 million ha (6 million acres) of more or less wild lands that belong to state, local, and private interests. It is the largest park in the nation, equal to Yellowstone plus Yosemite plus several others. It was established in 1892 and encompasses 800,000 ha (2 million acres) of state-owned Adirondack Forest Preserve, established in 1885. A policy of keeping the preserve "forever wild" was written into the state constitution in 1894 and reaffirmed many times since (Barnett, 1974). Around the preserve are 3.7 million acres of private land, over which the state has strong controls. Originally, a "blue line" surrounding the park enclosed the intended purchase area for the state park, but the cost of buying Saratoga Springs and other areas became prohibitive. Now, rigorous land use controls are imposed within the blue line area to keep the park in attractive condition, despite logging, mining, and resorting.

Finances

The budget for Otium State Park (Table 13.3) consumes a quarter million dollars each year. This is a 6,000-ha natural park with a pool, about 24 kilometers (km) (15 miles) of roads, three rather informal campgrounds, an inn, cabins, picnic areas, and numerous hiking and riding trails. It employs two managers, a naturalist, a maintenance foreman, and a clerk, year-round. A large summer staff is employed for three to six months. Professional staff and labor account for 64 per cent of the budget. Equipment to move and assist the workers takes up another 20 per cent, exclusive of repairs. The park charges a gate fee and camping fees. The inn, riding stable, and camp store are operated on a concessioner-lease basis with fees collected separately.

State parks usually operate at a deficit, although a few state legislatures appropriate only projected income from entry fees, concessions, and camping fees (Table 13.4). Nationwide, total expenditures are about six times the revenues from operations. The 560 million visitors in 1975 produced $114 million, and total (capital and operative) expenditures amounted to $650 million. Operations and maintenance cost $295 million, considerably more than income.

CASE STUDY—CALIFORNIA STATE PARKS

The California state park system is claimed to be the first in the nation. The claim is based on the Yosemite grant in 1864, which transferred federal lands to the state to be held for public use for all time. This was called a state park but was managed without rigorous policies or protection. In 1890, Congress established a national park around the state lands, and

State	Per cent recovered	Revenue per visitor
Michigan	116%	$0.60
New Hampshire	109	.62
Indiana	87	.40
Vermont	83	1.11
Alabama	75	.57
Oklahoma	69	.20
Wisconsin	65	.21
Kentucky	61	.47
Tennessee	58	.46
National average	39%	$0.20

TABLE 13.4 State parks with high percentage of operating costs covered by revenues.

Source: Buechner (1976).

by 1905, the state returned the Yosemite Valley and Mariposa Grove to the federal government as part of the park. The state's oldest existing state park is the Big Basin Redwoods State Park, formed through citizen action of the Sempervirens Club. In 1902, the governor appointed a commission to administer the park, then called California Redwood State Park (Figure 13.3). A comprehensive system of state parks was established in 1927 with the formation of a State Park Commission, provision for a survey of park needs, and authorization of a $6-million bond issue for extension of the system. A Division of Beaches and Parks was then established in the Department of Natural Resources.

Financing for acquisition has come from bond issues, gifts from individuals and associations, oil royalty funds, state appropriations, and federal matching funds.

Purposes of the California system are to protect, develop, and interpret for the inspiration, use, and enjoyment of the state's citizens areas of outstanding scenic, recreational, and historic importance. Areas of recreational importance refer primarily to ocean beaches and reservoirs.

Classification of units in the California state park system includes the following categories:

State parks: relatively spacious areas of outstanding scenic or wilderness character, often containing significant historical, archaeological, geological, ecological, and other scientific values, preserved as nearly as possible in their original or natural condition, and providing opportunity for appropriate types of recreation that will not destroy or impair the features and values to be preserved; commercial exploitation of resources is prohibited.

Scenic or scientific reserves: areas of outstanding natural significance, where the major values are in their geological, faunal, or floral characteristics. The purpose is directed primarily toward the preservation

Figure 13.3 California State Parks contain 25 units that preserve the redwoods. (Redwood Empire Association)

of outstanding natural features. Developments shall be for the purpose of making the areas available for public enjoyment in a manner consistent with the preservation of natural values.

Historical units: areas, usually limited in size, to preserve objects of historical and scientific interest and places commemorating important persons or historic events. Facilities are limited to those for safety, comfort, access, interpretation, and, sometimes, picnicking and other recreation. Certain historically linked agricultural, mercantile, and other commercial activity may be permitted, if properly regulated and if they enhance the historic scene.

State recreation areas: lands selected and developed to provide nonurban outdoor recreation opportunities to meet other than purely local needs but having the best available scenic quality. Camping, picnicking, swimming, hiking, horseback riding, boating, fishing, and hunting may be provided. The provision of such activities shall be the primary reason for operating recreational areas.

State beaches: areas with frontage on the oceans or bays designed primarily to provide swimming, boating, fishing, and other waterfront activities. Other coastal areas acquired primarily for scenic and scientific values shall be included in the classification "scenic or scientific reserves."

Wayside campgrounds: scenic, historical, or recreational areas suitable for overnight camping with convenient access to highways.

Underwater parks: areas of marine environment with outstanding scenic, ecological, geological, and natural scientific values. Certain selected areas may be preserved in their original or natural condition, and other areas may be designated for appropriate multiple uses.

CASE STUDY—CANADIAN PROVINCES

Most of Canada's provinces maintain systems of parks that are parallel in diversity to state parks in the United States. They vary in size from tiny urban parks to huge wilderness areas (Figure 13.4). The provinces have, in many cases, set aside large areas of land for future assignment

FIGURE 13.4 Large provincial parks in Canada contain immense areas for camping, picnicking, fishing, canoeing, and other activities. (USFS)

Recreation Places

of use. These are called reserves and are open to limited public use. The provinces have the option to develop them as parks without future, expensive land acquisition.

Two provinces are cited as examples: Quebec and British Columbia. French-speaking Quebec, with some citizens interested in being a separate nation, has a park system that is larger than the entire national park complex. Its 135,000 sq km (52,000 sq mi) of parks are mostly in the Laurentien Mountains. They contain complete holiday resort facilities for summer visitors and elaborate skiing facilities for winter. The major properties are very large, containing hundreds of lakes, wild fishing streams, and immense areas of undeveloped back country. The properties are called parks and reserves, the latter being less developed and maintained primarily for fishing. They may receive further development as demand increases.

British Columbia has more than 125 provincial parks, administered by the Park Branch of the Provincial Department of Recreation and Conservation and covering 21 million ha (8.5 million acres). There are three categories, based on the immediacy of development plans. Class A parks (the majority) are those of immediate value for recreation. They are protected by law against commercial exploitation or alienation. Class B parks are set aside for future use or for specific reasons. Carefully restricted resource uses, including timber cutting and mineral development, are permitted in these large wilderness parcels. Class C parks are smaller, local use parks, usually administered by rural park boards. They are the rural equivalent of city parks, usually offering picnicking, playgrounds, and small beach areas. A similar program in Saskatchewan goes under the name of regional parks.

Tweedsmuir, with spectacular Rainbow Mountain, is Canada's largest provincial park, containing 1,400,000 ha (5,400 sq mi). These and many smaller provincial parks and regional parks offer outstanding opportunities for recreation in a wide diversity of spectacular natural scenery.

SUMMARY

State (and provincial) recreation areas offer considerable recreational space close to home. At the present time, state parks are heavily used, but most forests and fish and wildlife areas offer a low intensity of development and uncrowded conditions. State parks receive large amounts of funding for recreation, but the other agencies receive little, even on a per capita visitor basis.

The large forest and wildlife areas in the eastern part of the nation will probably experience more pressure for recreational use, along with continued crowding of most state parks.

Demands on park, forest, and wildlife managers will require more careful efforts to inventory and monitor resource conditions, as well as to work with and for people.

New types of areas including nature preserves, long-distance trails, scenic rivers, state bike trails, and old canals challenge the ingenuity of recreation planners and managers.

Literature Cited

BARNETT, LINCOLN. 1974. The Ancient Adirondacks. Alexandria, Va.: Time-Life Books (The American Wilderness). 184 pp.

BUECHNER, ROBERT D. 1976. State park systems. Parks & Recreation 11(7):35–37, 98.

Bureau of the Census. 1977. The Statistical Abstract of the U.S. (1978). Washington, D.C.: U.S. Department of Commerce. 1048 pp.

Bureau of Outdoor Recreation. 1970. The Recreation Imperative. Washington, D.C.: U.S. Senate, Committee on Interior and Insular Affairs (1974 Committee Print). 389 pp.

KRAUCH, HERBERT C., JR. 1976. Wildlife management in Indiana, 1900–1940. In: McReynolds, H. E. (ed.), Fish and Wildlife in Indiana 1776–1976. Bradford Woods: American Fisheries Society, pp. 10–13.

LOCKARD, FRANK R. 1976. History of fisheries activities in Indiana, 1950–1976. In: McReynolds, H. E. (ed.), Fish and Wildlife in Indiana 1776–1976. Bradford Woods, Indiana: American Fisheries Society, pp. 17–21.

MICHAUD, HOWARD H. 1966. State parks. In: Lindsey, A. A. (ed.), Natural Features of Indiana. Indianapolis: Indiana Academy of Science, pp. 561–581.

U.S. Forest Service. 1979. The 1980 RPA Assessment. Washington, D.C.: U.S. Department of Agriculture.

CHAPTER 14

Federal Roles

Any young professional in the field of outdoor recreation soon confronts the federal alphabet soup. To be effective, he or she must decipher it and use it.

For anyone with the patience and determination, the rewards of understanding the federal bureaucracy can be great. The oft-maligned bureaucrats are usually very helpful and concerned with doing a good job for someone who has the courtesy and interest to learn the system and to deal with individuals.

The federal government administers one third of the land area of the United States. Another 2 per cent is held in trust for American Indians. This compares with about 5 per cent managed by state and local governments. Most of this nation was once under federal jurisdiction, acquired as indicated in Table 14.1. Table 14.2 indicates present ownership patterns.

The Dwindling Public Domain

There has been a consistent effort to reduce the federal estate, dispensing it to private, corporate, and state owners. Following federal acquisition of the large western lands, huge land allotment programs in the late 1800s

TABLE 14.1 Acquisition of the federal public domain (based on 1912 measurements).

Type of acquisition	Date	Hectares (million)	Acres (million)
Cessions by States	1781–1802	96	237
Louisiana Purchase	1803	212	530
Cession from Spain	1819	19	46
Red River Basin (details unclear)	1819 (?)	12	30
Oregon Compromise	1846	74	183
Mexican Cession	1848	137	339
Purchase from Texas	1850	32	79
Gadsden Purchase	1853	8	19
Alaska Purchase	1867	152	375

Source: Bureau of the Census (1977).

TABLE 14.2   Ownership of land in the United States (1974).

	Ha *(million)*	*Acres* *(million)*	*Per cent*
Total	916.9	2,264	100
Private	533.4	1,317	58.2
Indian	20.3	50	2.2
Public	363.2	897	37.6
Federal	308.1	761	33.6
State	47.0	116	5.1
County and municipal	8.1	20	0.9

Note: Federal and state figures include highway rights of way; Indian lands are trust lands exclusive of federally owned lands used by Indians.
Source: Bureau of the Census (1977).

followed settlement programs in the midwestern states. Settlers, loggers, railroads, and state education systems were deeded public lands by meeting minimal requirements of proving their interest in permanently managing it. In the 1890s it became evident that many individuals were taking advantage of the situation, filing false claims, cutting timber that wasn't theirs, and moving on to exploit new resources. Alarmed by the prospect of having little timber left to support the nation, presidents began establishing national forest reserves in the West. This activity reached its peak with Theodore Roosevelt and his chief forester, Gifford Pinchot, in the early 1900s.

The present-day national forests were carved out of the existing public lands to reserve some timber for the future. Only in the small eastern national forests were large areas of lands acquired from private owners, and these were almost all people who wanted to sell or who had abandoned their lands. Likewise, national parks and national wildlife refuges came largely from the public domain. Except for the Redwoods National Park acquisitions and many eastern parks, the land used was already public.

The Bureau of Land Management continues to turn federal land over to private interests. In Alaska, almost all the land was still federal in 1959, when statehood was declared. Homesteading continued to be very active through 1969, when unreserved lands were withdrawn from private appropriation until the settlement of native claims and other designation of federal lands could be completed.

More than 100 agencies, boards, and commissions influence the supply of recreational opportunities on federal lands. Only seven of these are the principal land management agencies offering recreational opportunities (Table 14.3).

Four broad classes of federal lands can be recognized. The largest land areas are managed on a *multiple-use* basis by the Bureau of Land Management and the Forest Service for recreation, timber, water, wildlife, and grazing. *Reserved lands* are the areas managed by the Fish and Wildlife Service and the National Park Service. *Water project* resources are related

F. H. MONTAGUE, JR.

to the reservoirs built by the Army Corps of Engineers, the Bureau of Reclamation, and the Tennessee Valley Authority. The fourth category of *special use* lands includes Indian reservations, military bases, and reservations of the Energy Research and Development Administration, with only portions of these being open to recreational use, sometimes under special conditions. The last category still has little national importance for public recreation, so the first three are emphasized.

Expenditures by the federal government for outdoor recreation was estimated at $1.5 billion in 1975 (Bureau of Outdoor Recreation, 1978). Although this was 190 per cent of the 1965 level, inflation, the increase

TABLE 14.3 Major federal programs affecting outdoor recreation.

Program	Agency
Land management	
National resource lands (190 million ha)	Bureau of Land Management
National forests (76)	U.S. Forest Service
National wildlife refuges (13)	Fish and Wildlife Service
National park system (13)	National Park Service
American Indian lands (52)	Indian Nations with Bureau of Indian Affairs
Reservoirs (7)	Bureau of Reclamation, Corps of Engineers
Land Between the Lakes, and reservoir-based land (0.4)	Tennessee Valley Authority
Financial assistance	
Surplus property	Heritage Conservation and Recreation Service
Loans to private enterprise	Small Business Administration
Land and Water Conservation Fund	Heritage Conservation and Recreation Service
National Heritage Program	Heritage Conservation and Recreation Service
Community development block grants	Department of Housing and Urban Development
General Revenue Sharing	Department of Treasury
Humanities grants	National Endowment for the Humanities
Manpower and labor training programs	Department of Labor
Employment for senior citizens	Administration on Aging
Planning	
Nationwide outdoor recreation plans, state and local plans	Heritage Conservation and Recreation Service
River basin planning	7 Regional River Basin Commissions
Technical assistance, advice	
Technical information, community development	Cooperative Extension Service
Small watershed program	Soil Conservation Service
Tourism data	U.S. Travel Service
Regulatory	
Environmental quality monitoring	Environmental Protection Agency
Power site recreation development	Federal Power Commission

in national parks, fish and wildlife areas, and the addition of BLM recreation responsibilities more than absorbed this cost increase.

The Land Agencies

The Bureau of Land Management is a relative newcomer to active resource management. It has long been a small, understaffed custodian of vast areas of the public domain, mostly arid lands that were sold or given away when-

FIGURE 14.1   A swimming hole in Shawnee National Forest, Illinois. (USFS)

ever possible. In the 1970s its legal mandate changed to permanent management. The agency's recreation work has been limited. Its properties are now called the National Resource Lands.

The Forest Service provides dispersed and developed recreation on large tracts of attractive, often mountainous land. Western national forests were established during the 1890–1915 period, out of the public domain. Eastern forests were purchased after 1911 to protect watersheds from erosion. Recreation has become the major use of most of these forests (Figure 14.1). Timber, water, wildlife, grazing, and mining are other important values.

The National Park Service administers outstanding preserves of natural, historic, recreational, and cultural significance for recreational and educational uses. The properties range in size from single city lots to million-hectare monuments. Up to 10 million visits per year are recorded at some individual urban recreation areas and Great Smoky Mountains National Park. Many of the nation's most famous places are in the national park system—Yellowstone, Sequoia, Valley Forge, the White House (Figure 14.2).

Federal Roles

239

FIGURE 14.2 Mount Whitney rises above Death Valley to 4,420 m (14,495 ft). It is on the boundary of Inyo National Forest with Sequoia National Park. (USFS)

The Fish and Wildlife Service manages lands primarily for the protection and enhancement of key wildlife habitat. Recreational use is not heavy at these often remote, often wet areas, but public use and interest are increasing rapidly.

A comparison of parks, refuges, and forests is given in Table 14.4.

The Army Corps of Engineers and the Bureau of Reclamation found themselves in the recreation business first by circumstance and now by

Recreation Places

law. They built dams to generate power, provide irrigation water, and reduce floods. These large bodies of water immediately attracted recreationists, second-home builders, resorts, and others. The Bureau turns its recreation operations over to other agencies, and the Corps has done so on only about one quarter of its projects. The lands around these multipurpose reservoirs are often managed for timber, wildlife habitat improvement, and grazing.

The Tennessee Valley Authority is a third major builder of dams. It manages recreation access areas and campgrounds, turns considerable land

TABLE 14.4 Differences among federal forests, parks, and refuges, before Alaska decisions.

	National forests	National parks	National wildlife refuges
Administration	U.S. Forest Service Department of Agriculture 155 units, 190 million ha	National Park Service Department of the Interior 300 units, 13 million ha	Fish & Wildlife Service Department of the Interior 300 units, 13 million ha
Recreation activities	Hunting allowed (regulated by state) Fishing allowed (regulated by states) Skiing concessions Summer home/resort permits	Hunting prohibited (with exceptions) Fishing allowed A few skiing areas No permits for non-commercial use, except historical	Hunting allowed on 184 units (regulated by state) Fishing usually allowed No skiing resorts No permits; farming by share cropping for wildlife food
	Off-road vehicles permitted on designated places	Off-road vehicles usually prohibited; some allow use on snow-covered roads	Off-road vehicles generally banned
	No entry fees; use fees for special facilities	Entry fees at many properties; camping fee	No entry fees; camping fee
	Camping, picnicking, hiking allowed nearly everywhere	Camping in 100 parks, picnicking at designated spots, hiking on trails	Camping limited, picnicking limited, hiking on trails
	Interpretation limited, mostly self-guided, several large visitor centers	Interpretation of major importance, conducted service	Interpretation important and growing
	Wilderness areas	Wilderness areas	Wilderness areas
Management philosophy	Multiple use—timber, wildlife, recreation, range, water, in best balance	Preservation of scenic, cultural, and recreational resources for appropriate recreational use	Enhancement of wildlife habitat, with heavy resource manipulation; recreation
	Timber harvest	No timber harvesting	Some timber harvesting
	Grazing leases	Only leases from land purchase negotiations	Some grazing leases
	Prospecting and mining	No prospecting or mining, with exceptions	Limited mining
	Visitor service concessions relatively few	Numerous concessions	Very few concessions

TABLE 14.5   Visitation to federal recreation lands, 1977.*

Agency	Total	Fee management units	Nonfee management units
	(Thousand recreation visitor days)		
Bureau of Land Management	60,225	39,915	20,310
Bureau of Reclamation	33,607	146	33,461
Corps of Engineers	162,751	11,238	151,513
Fish & Wildlife Service	6,010	1,123	4,887
Forest Service	204,797	25,646	179,151
National Park Service	92,029	79,596	12,433
Tennessee Valley Authority	6,980	542	6,438
Total	566,399	97,373	408,193

* In thousands of recreation visitor days. A recreation visitor day is an aggregate of 12 person-hours in any combination of individual or group use.
Source: U.S. Forest Service (1979).

over to local and state agencies, and assists private enterprise. Land Between the Lakes was developed as a national recreation demonstration area.

There are federal forests, parks, and wildlife refuges throughout the United States, but more than 95 per cent of the federal land ownership is in the western states, including Alaska. For every resident in the West, there are 16 acres of federal forest and range. In the northern states, there is 0.1 acre per person, and the southern states have 0.3 acre per resident (U.S. Forest Service, 1979).

Expenditures for outdoor recreation by federal agencies also favors the West, but heaviest investment per acre goes to the rest of the nation. The North received 26 per cent in 1975 expenditures; the South, 34 per cent; and the West, 40 per cent (Bureau of Outdoor Recreation, 1978).

The Forest Service provides about 36 per cent of the visitor hours on federal properties, even including the popular Army Corps of Engineers reservoirs (Table 14.5). Statistics for all agencies were calculated in terms of visitor days (12 visitor hours) to reduce the confusion of different units used by the various agencies. The Corps of Engineers had 29 per cent of the use, and the National Park Service hosted 16 per cent of the visitation, based on the conversions to visitor days.

Indian Lands

Many reservations are managed under federal trust by the Department of the Interior for the Indian Nations. Tribal councils are taking increasing initiative in governing the lands, including provision of recreational areas on reservations. Trust responsibilities include no financial obligation for recreation. Some tribes have set up their own park and recreation divisions under their Nation's Department of Natural Resources or as commercial enterprises.

Statistics on Indian lands are rather confusing. The Bureau of Indian Affairs statistics indicate that there are 21,210,000 ha (52,390,000 acres) of land under the agency's jurisdiction (Bureau of the Census, 1977). These are listed in three categories:

Trust allotted	4,063,000 ha	10,036,000 acres
Tribal, including tribal fee lands	16,962,000	41,896,000
Government owned	185,000	458,000

Recreation, timber, and range management have all begun to develop rapidly on many reservations. In the 1980s, significant progress is expected as well-trained Indians guide the tribes toward more intensive management of the resources. There will be an increase in outdoor recreational facilities for residents and for visitors.

Alaska

The conservation issue of the century is how to assign Alaska's federal national interest lands (Figure 14.3). Should they be preserved as parks and refuges, mostly in wilderness areas, or should they be managed for multiple uses, including mining, as they have been for many years?

Alaska was annexed to the United States in 1867 after purchase from Russia for $7,200,000. Nothing much happened there until 1898, except for establishment of an ineffectual civil government in 1884. In 1896, gold was discovered in Canada's Klondike region, bringing attention to the area. Prospectors in 1898 found gold in Nome and at many other places throughout Alaska. That caused an increase in the territorial population and a need to establish some kind of legal framework to deal with criminals and land ownership claims.

The General Land Office (predecessor to the Bureau of Land Management) controlled land in Alaska. National forests, national wildlife refuges, and national parks and monuments were established out of this public domain. So were homesteads, but they never amounted to much of the total land base. In 1959, when statehood was declared, the federal government still had 99 per cent of the 152 million ha (375 million acres) of land in one jurisdiction or another.

Under the statehood act, 42 million ha (104 million acres) were to be selected by the state government over time, primarily for commodity values and community expansion. Under the 1971 Native Claims Settlement Act (P.L. 92–203), the Eskimos, Aleuts, and Indians, who never signed treaties with the federal government, agreed to accept nearly 18 million ha (44 million acres) of federal land, patented to local and regional native

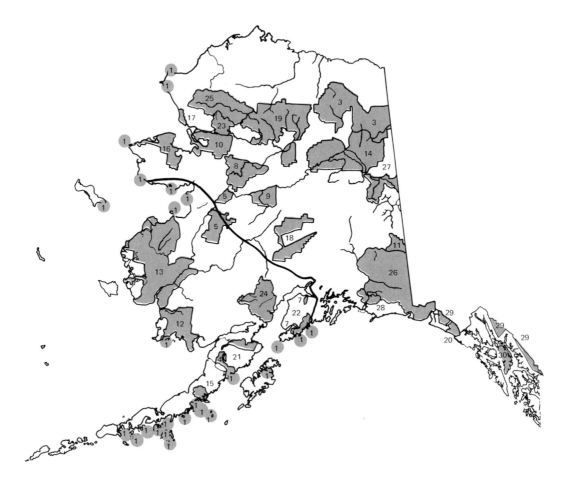

National Wildlife Refuge System	Millions of Acres		
1 Alaska Marine Resources National Wildlife Refuge	0.43	19 Gates of the Arctic Wilderness National Park	8.12
2 Alaska Peninsula Special Study Area	—	20 Glacier Bay National Park	0.59
3 Arctic National Wildlife Refuge	8.85	21 Katmai National Park	1.10
4 Becharof National Wildlife Refuge	1.03	22 Kenai Fjords National Park	0.41
5 Innoko National Wildlife Refuge	2.84	23 Kobuk Valley National Park	1.67
6 Kanuti National Wildlife Refuge	1.20	24 Lake Clark National Park	3.14
7 Kenai National Moose Refuge	0.23	25 Noatak National Ecological Preserve	5.96
8 Koyukuk National Wildlife Refuge	3.33	26 Wrangell-St. Elias National Park/Preserve	12.05
9 Nowitna National Wildlife Refuge	1.45	27 Yukon-Charley National Rivers	1.69
10 Selawik National Wildlife Refuge	2.09		
11 Tetlin National Wildlife Refuge	0.77	Total 41.77	
12 Togiak National Fish And Wildlife Refuge	3.84		
13 Yukon Delta National Wildlife Refuge	10.59	National Forest System	
14 Yukon Flats National Wildlife Refuge	8.45	28 Additions to Chugach National Forest	0.94
		29 Additions to Tongass National Forest	1.60
Total 45.10		30 Admiralty Island Wilderness Designation	(0.87)
		Total 2.54	
National Park System			
		National Wild and Scenic Rivers System	
15 Aniakchak National Monument/Preserve	0.49		
16 Bering Land Bridge National Preserve	2.34	33 Wild and Scenic Rivers 〜	Total 2.45
17 Cape Krusenstern National Monument	0.36		
18 Denali National Park	3.85	Iditarod National Trail —	Grand Total 91.86

FIGURE 14.3 The federal debate on assignment of Alaska lands for parks, forests, wildlife refuges, and wild rivers focused on these areas. (NPS)

corporations, as well as one billion dollars in start-up funds for profit-making ventures. This released the rest of the land for state and industrial development as well as management by federal agencies (Figure 14.4). Nearly 60 per cent of the state will remain in federal ownership. The settlement act recognized natural qualities as well as commodity values of the Alaskan lands. Section 17(d)(2) of the Native Claims Settlement Act required that the federal government study the matter of up to 80 million acres of the remaining federal holdings and recommend to Congress the additions that should be made to the National Park System, National Forests, National Wildlife Refuges, and the Wild and Scenic Rivers System. These became known as *d-2 lands*.

The study was submitted to Congress in 1973 by the Nixon administration. An alternative proposal to protect a larger acreage was submitted by a coalition of conservation groups. The State of Alaska proposed another plan, suggesting more multiple-use lands and less parks and refuges than the other two. A fourth plan was submitted by a Joint Federal-State Land Use Planning Commission after hearings and long evaluation. None of these was acted on directly.

In 1977, Congressman Morris Udall, chairman of the House Interior Committee, brought up a bill to designate 102 million acres mostly as preserve (park, refuge, and scenic river) lands and a little as national forest, where timber and mining operations are allowed. At the same time, he

FIGURE 14.4 At Kenai Fjords, Alaska, the Steller's sea lion's habitat was involved in the Alaska lands debate; it is now operated by federal, state, and native village jurisdictions. (NPS)

added sections that designated wilderness areas, further inhibiting commercial or extractive activities. The bill passed the House but a threatened filibuster stopped Senate action. Several other bills were introduced in the same session, including one by Alaskan Congressmen designating 20 million acres as parks, refuges, and scenic rivers. In that plan, the rest of the land would have been managed by the Forest Service, the Bureau of Land Management, or a joint federal-state arrangement.

The ninety-fifth Congress adjourned without taking the action required by the Native Claims Settlement Act. Since the legal deadline for action was December, 1978, the President and the Secretary of the Interior took matters into their hands. First, the Secretary declared that 44.5 million ha (110 million acres) of BLM lands were closed to development for three years or until Congress determined their future classification. This had the effect of preventing irreversible impacts from roads, mining or other activities on the land under consideration. Then President Carter issued a proclamation establishing 23 million ha (56 million acres) as national monuments. He used the 1906 Antiquities Act to set up two monuments on existing national forest lands, two new national wildlife refuges in the guise of national monuments, and 13 additions to the national park system. This action virtually ensured the preservation of the designated units in their natural condition. Congress was left with the opportunity to declare any of these units as national parks, national wildlife refuges, wilderness areas or wild and scenic rivers. There was little possibility for reversion of the lands to less protected status. The lands not declared as national monuments retained more flexibility for Congressional action. With the Presidential action preserving some of the most spectacular scenic, scientific and historic areas, the Congress could proceed at a more deliberate pace, settling the Alaska lands question over a long period of time. However, much critical wildlife habitat was left without definitive protection, causing conservation groups to urge rapid action.

The newly designated Alaskan areas are the largest, least disturbed areas in the nation. The December 1, 1978 proclamation more than doubled the size of the national park system and increased the land base of the Fish and Wildlife Service by 50 per cent. The new additions have corridors through the mountains to permit access to state and private lands and to allow the construction of certain roads and pipelines. The boundaries exclude some of the most promising known mineral deposits. Much of the range of two large caribou herds is protected by the designation. Refuge and park areas include the Noatak River basin, the nation's largest undeveloped watershed; much of the Brooks Range; additions of the Alaska Range to the park surrounding the continent's highest peak, Denali or Mount McKinley (Figure 14.5), and huge, flat wetlands, where many of the continent's waterfowl nest in the summertime. A glacier the size of Rhode Island and the probable entry route of man into the New World were also designated.

FIGURE 14.5 Mount McKinley or Denali is the highest peak in North America at 6,198 m (20,320 ft). It is included in Mt. McKinley National Park and the recently proclaimed Denali National Monument in Alaska. (NPS)

The recent discovery and development of oil in Alaska have done much to heighten interest in resource development and protection in the state. Intensive studies required for building pipelines and industrial structures revealed the fragility and complexity of Alaskan ecology. As recreational use of this land, remote to most Americans, becomes more popular, the management effort will have to be considerable. The tension created by the distribution of the national interest lands continues in the mold of the controversy over Hetch–Hetchy dam in Yosemite—development versus preservation.[2] There will be moves to open up parks and refuges for mining, since about one sixth of the known reserves of the state are included in such lands (Schaine, 1978). Like Yellowstone in 1872, many of the parks may not be heavily visited for many years. It is doubtful that their value or symbolism will exceed those of Yellowstone, but they surely will become important parts of our national wilderness treasure, highly prized by future generations.

The wilderness appeal of the last frontier of Alaska lies in its representation of the last outpost of natural America, with wolves, grizzly bears, caribou by the thousands, and sparkling lakes. It is our last expansive natural

[2] A 1912 dispute between John Muir and Gifford Pinchot over use of the scenic valley represented a major split in conservation forces. Muir opposed the dam, citing the esthetic values of the valley. Pinchot supported utilization of the valley for a reservoir to supply water to San Francisco. The dam was built and San Franciscans now drink Yosemite water.

Federal Roles

landscape. It is federally owned and it is fragile. Can it and should it be left in its natural condition?

The unforgiving nature of Alaska is a result of the short growing season and harsh climate. Shallow soils, underlain by permafrost, cover half of the state. Slow-growing timber in the interior and numerous animals that cling to life by ranging far and wide for the necessities of life all require that man exercise strict discipline in managing the land. That discipline has seldom been evident in American frontier history. Hard work, rusticity, and strong souls have characterized the people; but discipline in what they extract from the land or require of it has not been typical. With today's mechanical and technical power, restraint is required if Alaska is to remain anything but a land base.

Heritage Conservation and Recreation Service

Known as the Bureau of Outdoor Recreation for its first 15 years, the Heritage Conservation and Recreation Service (HCRS) holds no land. It is an advisory, planning, and coordinating bureau with a strong financial assistance program. It is part of the Department of the Interior.

The Bureau of Outdoor Recreation was established in 1962, by order of the Secretary of the Interior. Its Organic Act (Public Law 88–29) was signed May 28, 1963, by President John F. Kennedy. On January 26, 1978, the agency's name was changed to the Heritage Conservation and Recreation Service (HCRS). There were some shifts of responsibility and program between HCRS and the National Park Service.

The functions of the agency include the following: 1) a continuing inventory and evaluation of outdoor recreation resources and needs; 2) nationwide outdoor recreation planning; 3) special recreation studies and research; 4) Land and Water Conservation Fund administration; 5) surplus property transfers to park and recreation agencies from the General Services Administration; 6) review studies for national trails, national wild and scenic rivers, and water resources projects of the Corps of Engineers and the Bureau of Reclamation; 7) technical assistance to states, local governments, and private interests; 8) National Register of Historic Places and related historical registers; 9) National Natural Landmarks program; 10) National Heritage Program. Several of these programs are discussed in later chapters, and some are described in the following sections.

NATURAL LANDMARKS REGISTRY

The National Natural Landmarks program is a listing and recognition of outstanding natural features that are preserved by local, state, federal, or private groups. To be listed, an area must exhibit exceptional natural qualities and be recognized, nominated, and inspected by responsible authorities at the state level or nominated by the Secretary of the Interior. The

National Registry of Natural Landmarks is strictly a listing of the places that have high value and quality for illustrating or interpreting the natural heritage of the nation.

HISTORIC PLACES REGISTER

The National Register of Historic Places was established in 1966 (Public Law 89–655). By 1977, 14,000 properties were listed. The 50 per cent matching grants program, begun in 1967, had awarded $55 million to 1,600 projects, $14 million of which went to the National Trust for Historic Preservation. Another $35 million was budgeted for 1978 (Council on Environmental Quality, 1977).

Early emphasis for listing was on individual buildings and properties. Later, interest developed in entire districts. There are about 1,300 historic districts listed, 25 per cent of them in urban areas of more than 50,000 population. Half are in small towns, including all of Silver Plume, Colorado, and Sisterdale, Texas. In most areas, buildings are in residential and/or commercial use. Archeological districts make up 12 per cent of the total.

NATIONAL HERITAGE PROGRAM

New in 1978, the National Heritage Program is designed to conserve the best of the nation's natural and historic heritage. It allocates Land and Water Conservation Fund monies specifically to acquire and preserve scenic, wild, geologic, ecological, or historic areas of outstanding or special character. It also directs monies to assist museums in their interpretive and educational roles. The combining of historic and recreation functions through the heritage program and through transfers of historic registers was part of the rationale for the change of name from Bureau of Outdoor Recreation to Heritage Conservation and Recreation Service.

FEDERAL PLANNING

For many years, the National Park Service was responsible for nationwide recreation planning and reporting. However, there were virtually no funds and no mandate to conduct comprehensive plans. The Service prepared several publications concerning recreation and acted as spokesman about recreation, but it had no real coordinating function or financial assistance it could offer.

One of the most lasting contributions was the program of setting up national recreation demonstration areas in the 1930s and the 1940s. The federal government purchased land, helped state and local governments to develop it, introduced programming, and eventually turned it over for operation by the local jurisdiction. A number of state parks, fish and wildlife areas, and other properties were established in this manner.

Never had the tourism-related function of government been assigned to the agencies in the Department of the Interior. Often, federal tourism policy and recreation policy were not coordinated. This led to the proposal in Congress in 1978 to establish an independent Travel and Recreation Agency. This would consolidate the U.S. Travel Service and the Heritage Conservation and Recreation Service. The idea was to carry on research in travel and recreation, coordinate tourism and recreation planning at all levels, provide technical assistance, education, and clearinghouse services, and increase international promotion.

Environmental Protection Agency

Urban and rural environmental quality enhancement and maintenance are recognized as desirable social goals that improve the quality of life of individuals and protect them from unhealthy, unpleasant conditions.

Pollution of air, water, and land through industrial, governmental, or individual actions is undesirable and often produces injustices to innocent individuals and to society as a whole. Although short-range costs may increase somewhat as a result of reducing pollution, long-range social benefits should be considered liberally in evaluating the appropriateness of imposing pollution restrictions.

The National Environmental Policy Act of 1969 established federal policy to protect the health and welfare of the general public from the problems of pollution. The energetic work of the Environmental Protection Agency (established in 1970) has resulted in marked reduction of pollution to air and water. This has effectively increased recreational resources by making lakes and rivers clean enough to use for boating, fishing, and swimming.

Soil Conservation Service

The Department of Agriculture's Soil Conservation Service offers many advisory, technical, and financial assistance programs. Those that affect recreation and parks work involve conservation on private land, soil surveys, and the small watershed program.

Conservation assistance to private landowners involves all types of land-based activities, most relating to agricultural production. Through local soil conservation districts, technical agents are stationed throughout the nation to offer advice and information. They provide individuals, groups, and local agencies interested in recreation with data about soils, land use capabilities, reference to maps and aerial photographs, conservation practices, and technical advice on trees, grass, insects, diseases, water development, and a variety of other problems.

Soil survey results have been published for about one third of the nation. They are in the form of bound reports for each county (or other soil conservation district boundary) that has collaborated. The report book contains detailed analyses of the soils in the area, accompanied by maps showing the distribution of soil types over the county. Each soil type is described and its limitations and productivity are defined for recreation, wildlife, forestry, agriculture, and structures. This information can be used to identify portions of each property that are most suitable for specific uses. For example, building a pond on soil that has rapid internal drainage will require considerable investment in site modifications to ensure that the pond will hold water. A picnic area on poorly drained soil requires extra work. The soil survey is a valuable planning tool. If surveys are not available, the Soil Conservation Service will often do a property survey of soils.

The small watershed program, often referred to as Public Law 566, assists soil and water conservation districts and local communities to make structural improvements and to institute soil and water conservation practices in watersheds. Often this involves the building of small reservoirs to reduce flooding, increase local water supply, provide recreation, and improve fish and wildlife habitat. These are planned so as to protect the entire upstream watershed. More than 1,000 small watersheds have been assisted through this program. They offer diverse recreation opportunities, often managed by the state or local government.

National Recreation Areas

In 1963, the President's Recreation Advisory Council produced Policy Circular No. 1—"Guidelines for National Recreation Areas." It called for a system of national recreation areas with natural character above average in quality and recreation appeal, transcending that normally associated with state and local park and recreation properties, but of lesser significance than the outstanding scenic and historical elements of the National Park System. These were to be located in areas where recreation demand is not being met through other programs. Among the criteria suggested were that the aggregate gross area should not be less than 20,000 acres of land and water, except where total population within a 250-mile radius is greater than 30 million, or along rivers or coastal strips, and that outdoor recreation be the dominant or primary resource management purpose. National Recreation Areas (NRA) are managed by the National Park Service (16) and the U.S. Forest Service (7 units).

The NRA designation was originally assigned only to federally managed lands around reservoirs constructed by the Bureau of Reclamation and the Corps of Engineers. The name now also includes other lands, most recently urban areas. The purpose is to supply large areas of open space for outdoor recreation.

Examples of reservoir areas are the Flaming Gorge NRA (Forest Service, Utah, and Wyoming), Ross Lake NRA (National Park Service, Washington), and Whiskey-Shasta-Trinity NRA (Forest Service, National Park Service joint management, California).

Other national recreation areas are the Spruce Knob-Seneca Rocks NRA (Forest Service, West Virginia), Gateway NRA (National Park Service, New York), and Cuyahoga Valley NRA (National Park Service, Ohio).

An interesting and unusual national recreation area is Chickasaw, in Oklahoma. It resulted from the merging of the old Platt National Park with the young Arbuckle NRA under the National Park Service in 1976. This marked one of the few times a National Park was changed to another designation.

Literature Cited

Bureau of the Census. 1977. The Statistical Abstract of the U.S. (1978). Washington, D.C.: U.S. Department of Commerce. 1048 pp.

Bureau of Outdoor Recreation. 1978. Federal Outdoor Recreation Expenditures Study, 1975. Washington, D.C.: U.S. Dept. of the Interior. 73 pp.

Council on Environmental Quality. 1977. Environmental Quality—1977; The Eighth Annual Report of the Council on Environmental Quality. Washington, D.C. 445 pp.

SCHAINE, BENJAMIN A. 1978. Alaska land: a national issue; what is to be done with it? Vital Issues (Center for Information on America) 27(6):1–4.

U.S. Forest Service. 1979. The 1980 RPA assessment. Washington, D.C.: U.S. Dept. of Agriculture.

CHAPTER 15

National Park System

From the Statue of Liberty to Alcatraz Island and then on out into the volcanos of Hawaii, the National Park Service (NPS) manages some curious and wonderful pieces of land and history (Figure 15.2).

In Alaska, it protects the highest mountain peaks in North America in Mount McKinley National Park. In Florida, it protects a home for alligators and pelicans in the flat sea of grass called the Everglades National Park. Farther south in the Virgin Islands there is a Rockefeller-donated portion of a tropical island. In and around Washington, D.C., this agency cares for an urban and rural park system of 367 reservations, including the Catoctin Mountain Park that surrounds presidential Camp David. In New York and New Jersey, the San Francisco Bay area, the Cleveland-Akron area, Los Angeles, Atlanta, and the Indiana Dunes, the National Park Service strives to serve huge urban populations with quality outdoor facilities and programs. In the wild reaches of Glacier National Park in

FIGURE 15.1 National Parks are for people—tomorrow as well as today and yesterday. (HCRS)

Figure 15.2 The National Park System includes, (above) San Juan National Historic Site, Puerto Rico; (left) Acadia National Park, Maine; (opposite, top) Lake Clark National Monument, Alaska; and (opposite, below) the crater of Haleakala National Park, Hawaii. (NPS)

Montana and Katmai National Monument in Alaska, the National Park Service personnel do their best to protect grizzly and Kodiak bears, while allowing adventuresome souls to go out to enjoy the same habitat that these huge carnivores roam. George Washington's birthplace is a national monument in Virginia. In Missouri, George Washington Carver's birthplace and childhood home is another. Gettysburg National Military Park, the Golden Spike National Historic Site, and the Homestead National Monument are examples of recent American history preserved under the national park system. The Gila cliff dwellings in New Mexico and the Ocmulgee National Monument in Georgia are places that memorialize the culture of prehistoric residents of the United States (Figure 15.2).

The park system is experiencing rapid growth. With about 290 properties to manage in 1978, New properties recently added in Alaska doubled the size of the national park system. In the 10 years before that, 75 new parks were authorized. The problem with this expansion is that the NPS has sustained long droughts of employment freezes, especially during the 1970s. This means that increases in personnel and funding were necessary in order to catch up with the rapidly expanding land area to be managed.

National Parks History

Yellowstone was the first national park, established in 1872 by act of Congress (16 U.S.C. 21). Although the idea was new and thought by some to be outrageous, it passed the Congress with relative ease. The Senate vote on January 30 had almost no opposition. Only Senator Cole of California voted against the park. In the House, on February 27, there were 115 yeas, 65 nays, and 60 not voting. On March 1, 1872, President Grant signed the act, dedicating the 8,660-sq-km (3,344-sq-mi) reserve for a "pleasuring ground" (Mills, 1917). The campaign to protect Yellowstone's 300 geysers, high waterfalls, huge lake, and other wonders was brief and intense (Figure 15.3). On September 19, 1870, a campfire meeting in the park area had produced a proposal to set aside the land as a public park, open to all people. Cornelius Hedges, Nathaniel P. Langford, and William H. Claggett headed the park campaign. Ferdinand V. Hayden of the U.S. Geological Survey visited the area and took many photographs. Langford became the park superintendent who shepherded the dream into reality.

Other parks have some claim on first place, but none is as valid as is Yellowstone's. The Hot Springs Reservation in Arkansas, established in 1830, was made a national park in 1921. What is now part of Yosemite National Park was delineated by the federal government and donated to California in 1864, establishing the principle of managing land for its scenic wonders and recreation. In 1890, the federal area surrounding the state grant was designated as Yosemite National Park. In 1906, the state land reverted to federal control and was integrated into the national park.

Fourteen other parks and 22 National Monuments were established

FIGURE 15.3   Yellowstone National Park was named for the rock walls of the canyon through which its major river flows. As the world's first national park, it was followed by more than 1,200 parks in 140 nations. (NPS)

before the National Park Service was set up in 1916. The following were the early parks:

General Grant, California, 1890 (now part of King's Canyon).
Sequoia, California, 1890.

Mt. Rainier, California, 1899.
Crater Lake, Oregon, 1902.
Platt, Oklahoma (now part of Chickasaw NRA), 1902.
Wind Cave, South Dakota, 1903.
Mesa Verde, Colorado, 1906.
Lassen Volcanic, California, 1907.
Grand Canyon, Arizona, 1908.
Olympic, Washington, 1909.
Zion, Utah, 1909.
Glacier, Montana, 1910.
Rocky Mountain, Colorado, 1915.

Mackinac Island National Park was established in 1874 but became a Michigan state park in 1895. The Petrified Forest National Monument was proclaimed in 1906 by the President. In 1962, Congress established it as a National Park. A sample of other early properties now managed by the National Park Service includes the following:

Custer Battlefield National Monument, Montana, established as a national cemetery, 1879.
Chickamauga and Chattanooga National Military Park, Georgia, 1890.
Devil's Tower National Monument, Wyoming, 1906, the first national monument.
Gila Cliff Dwellings National Monument, New Mexico, 1907.
Jewel Cave National Monument, South Dakota, 1908.
Muir Woods National Monument, California, 1908.
Rainbow Bridge National Monument, Utah, 1910.
Sitka National Monument, Alaska, 1910.
Cabrillo National Monument, California, 1913.

Most of the national monuments were established under the terms of the 1906 Antiquities Act. That law gave the president authority to proclaim the designation of national monuments on any federal lands that had historic or prehistoric structures or other features of historic or scientific interest (Figure 15.4).

When the National Park Service was established in 1916, it inherited a group of properties that had been operated by a number of agencies, including the U.S. Forest Service, U.S. Army Corps of Engineers, and special commissions. By the end of 1916, there were 17 national parks and 22 national monuments under the aegis of the newly formed service. There were appropriated $500,000 to manage the parks and a ceiling of $19,500 to run the office of the director. The organic act set forth the enduring purpose of the agency to manage the parks so as:

To conserve the scenery and the natural and historic objects and the wildlife therein and to provide for the enjoyment of the same in such manner and by

258

FIGURE 15.4 Geological wonders are preserved in Devil's Postpile National Monument, California. (NPS)

such means as will leave them unimpaired for the enjoyment of future generations. (Everhart, 1972).

THE INITIAL CONCEPT

The idea of a nation's public park was an American invention. The concept of setting aside large pieces of land to retain their primitive, natural character was verbalized by Indian painter George Catlin. He wished a place where nature—including native Americans—could roam free and unfettered, free from the restrictive influences of the advancing technological civilization. His wish was partly realized with the establishment of Yellowstone National Park. (In Brazil's Amazon and a few parks in Africa, the full concept of reserves with unfettered people has been tried, not without serious management and cultural problems.)

Figure 15.5 Banff National Park, Alberta, Canada, has protected spectacular scenery since 1885.

The Idea Spreads

The national park idea spread rapidly. By 1917, Mills (1917) could report that most "leading nations" had established parks.

In Russia, Germany, Austria, and Poland, huge new parks were made after World War I from confiscated royal lands. President Kruger of what is now South Africa established a game preserve in 1898. After several enlargements, it is now the famous Kruger National Park, about 350 km long and 65 km wide. There are spectacular national parks and game preserves in many of the nations of Africa, notably Kenya, the Congo, and Zambia.

The Swiss National Park was officially recognized by the federal government in 1914. The initial concept (1906) was to set aside this 106-km² area as a large field laboratory to study alpine flora and fauna over a long time (Calahane, 1962).

260   Recreation Places

By 1972, when the United States celebrated the centennial of Yellowstone, the United Nations listed 1,204 parks or equivalent reserves in 140 nations (Curry-Lindahl, 1974).

Canadian National Parks

Canada has 29 large national parks featuring scenic values plus more than 20 national historical parks and sites. Banff National Park became the first unit of the system in 1885 as a 26-sq-km (10-sq-mi) reservation around its healing hot springs. In 1887, the Parliament expanded this to a 6.7-million-ha (260-sq-mi) Rocky Mountains National Park. The name was later changed to Banff, now known as one of the world's most beautiful mountain parks (Figure 15.5).

Neighboring Jasper (1907), Kootenay (1920), and Yoho (1886) National Parks plus nearby Glacier and Mt. Revelstoke National Parks, several provincial parks, and the extensive Rocky Mountain Forest Reserve combine to make an immense complex of public lands along the spine of the spectacularly scenic Rocky Mountains of Alberta and British Columbia. These parks are accessible by the Canadian Pacific Railway, the Trans-Canada Highway, and small aircraft.

Although the parks contain highly developed tourist service islands such as the Banff townsite, elaborate lodges and chalets, ski lifts, and other sports centers, they are primarily natural in character (Figure 15.6). The

FIGURE 15.6 Lake Louise lodge in Banff National Park attracts an international clientele to luxury amidst natural grandeur.

Canadian National Parks Act states: "The parks are hereby dedicated to the people of Canada for their benefit, education, and enjoyment—and shall be maintained and made use of so as to leave them unimpaired for the enjoyment of future generations."

This philosophy of natural museums closely resembles that of the United States. The Parcs Canada organization was originally known as the National Park Service of the Federal Minister of Northern Affairs and National Resources.

The largest of Canada's—and maybe the world's—national parks is Wood Buffalo in Alberta and the Northwest Territories. Its 4,481,000 ha (17,300 sq mi) contain 12,000 bison roaming at large, the most sizeable remnant herd on the continent. The park is not developed for the usual recreational purposes but serves strictly as a wildlife preserve. Visitors can reach the area by air, water, or, recently, by road.

National Park System of the United States

The National Park System is made up of many types of properties, only a few of which are called parks (Figure 15.7). An abbreviated list of classifications follows in Table 15.1 (1977 data). New areas were added in Alaska after 1978.

Urban Parks

Between Cleveland's heavy industry, Lake Erie's pollution, and Akron, where millions of rubber tires are baked each year, the federal government

FIGURE 15.7 Mount Rushmore National Memorial is one of the National Park Service's best-known historical areas, featuring the 20-meter-tall granite profiles sculpted by Gutzon Borglum. (NPS)

TABLE 15.1   Summary of the national park system, 1977.

Number	Name	Ha (1,000)	Acres (1,000)
37	National Parks	6,324	15,620
82	National Monuments	4,000	9,881
2	National Preserves	265	655
53	National Historic Sites	6	15
22	National Memorials	2	6
18	National Historical Parks	32	79
16	National Recreation Areas	1,414	3,493
4	National Lakeshores	80	197
6	National Seashores	241	595
4	National Parkways	65	159
6	National Rivers	151	374
1	National Scenic Trail	21	52
(300+)	National Capital Parks, White House, Mall, Visitor Center	2	5
Others:	National Memorial Park, National Military Parks, National Battlefields, National Cemeteries, other parks.		

is building the Cuyahoga National Recreation Area. Stretching the length of a 20-mile valley, it will connect the two urban giants. The project is a novelty. Officially called a recreational area by NPS, it is the Service's third major venture into urban parks.

National parks traditionally are established as natural or historical wonders set aside for preservation. Now the NPS is undertaking several urban projects that "put parks where the people are." But where people are, interests often conflict sharply, and land is at a premium. NPS is paying $41 million to buy 31,000 acres from 800 private owners to build the Cuyahoga National Recreation Area. It is an attempt to preserve the valley. Five more years and it would have been too late for the nearby refuge from the city. Similar efforts in the Santa Monica Mountains, along Atlanta's riverfront, and in other urban areas will require large investments.

The urban national recreation areas offer intensive recreation programs. They serve large numbers of visitors. They are quite expensive to purchase and operate. The debate will continue as to how much the National Park Service should dedicate its efforts and scarce resources to urban recreation areas of dubious national significance.

NATIONAL PARK POLICY

"The Constitution" of the National Parks is comprised of the following:

The separate Acts of Congress establishing and pertaining to each of the National Parks.

FIGURE 15.8   Mountain scenery and crafts are available to the slow-driving motorist who winds along the 500-mile Blue Ridge Parkway. (NPS)

The Antiquities Act of 1906.
The Act of 1916 establishing the National Park Service.
The 1935 Historic Sites Act extending the same principles to national monuments, military, and historic parks.

These are supplemented by many policies and programs that govern the rich and diverse system of special places (Figure 15.8).

The Preservation-Use Paradox

Balancing the *use* of parks with the *preservation* of the special resources is the key to effective management. It is not as difficult as it may seem in a dormitory discussion. It is a question of limited compromise—some controlled impact on the environment based on appropriate use.

RESOURCE CONSERVATION

Tilden (1975) described the values of natural areas in the national park system:

These are cultural treasures, as well as places for the refreshment of mind and spirit. They are the remaining "islands" in which life processes go on undisturbed, offering us the opportunity to understand a wilderness environment. In them one can observe the slow processes that have carved and shaped our earth and clothed it with plant and animal life. Without that comprehension, man cannot realize his own social life—so different, and yet with such vital correspondences!

National parks and their relatives are special places (Figs. 15.9 and 15.10). They have been set aside as the nation's outstanding examples of nature, history, and culture. The recreational areas perhaps are exceptions to this national significance criterion.

They are living museums. As such, they cannot also be playgrounds. Games have their place, but recreation in living museums is not the recreation of the saloon, the ball field, or the amusement park.

Some observers have noted that the park users of today do not always comprehend the purposes and behavior appropriate to these special places.

FIGURE 15.9   The forbidding spires of Silent City in Bryce Canyon National Park, Utah. (NPS)

FIGURE 15.10 Grand Teton National Park features one of the most beautiful block fault mountain ranges in the world, rising above almost flat Jackson Hole and the Snake River Valley, Wyoming. (NPS)

To them, any public park is a place where the public can do whatever comes to mind. Usually, this minority is not oriented to the diversity of recreation places or to the "rituals" of the "temples" of nature. Off-duty park rangers have a wealth of interesting observations about the confusion and the indignities these and other visitors perpetrate in the parks.

Solutions include increased interpretive efforts, which make arrival in the park special; preparation information, which does more than promote higher attendence; and training through city and state parks. It might not be remiss to require national park visitors to have passed tests in local parks on how to picnic and camp (Turello, 1975), as well as how to appreciate nature and history. These proposals point up the need for coordinated efforts among all levels of park administration to help people develop their recreational and appreciative skills and to increase their knowledge of the resources available. Leisure counseling is an activity-oriented approach to doing this. The agencies could develop cooperative approaches to preparing recreationists for intelligent use of their leisure time and recreation resources.

APPROPRIATE USE

The visitor use policy of the National Park Service clearly defines the concept that uses must be appropriate to the setting. In a national park, appropriate visitor use involves wholesome recreation in an outdoor, natural setting (Figure 15.11). That doesn't mean there can be all kinds of recreational use. Outdoor recreation involves a broad spectrum of activities, only some of which are appropriate to national parks.

A national park is not a scenic location for a golf course, amusement park, or spectator sport event. The test of appropriateness is whether the activity is inspired by the natural character and features of the park. Park use is on the upper end of the spectrum of outdoor recreational use, related to the significance of the areas. Overwhelming public use destroys the very resources that the Congress set aside to be preserved. This leads to the necessity for restrictions of use.

An extreme example of a restriction is in Muir Woods National Monument. The only public use in Muir Woods is by trail. All visitors can do is take a walk. There is no picnicking; there is no camping. The trail is paved to protect the trees from the impact of feet. The national monument was set aside to preserve samples of scientific phenomena and antiquity, and not primarily for public use.

"Parks are for people," says a popular political slogan. As most slogans, it is oversimplified and can be turned against the agency. Not everyone agrees that the present balance of resources and people is the best. Two extreme criticisms are examples.

Utah Governor Scott Matheson expressed his displeasure in a New

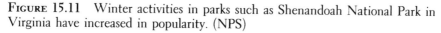

FIGURE 15.11 Winter activities in parks such as Shenandoah National Park in Virginia have increased in popularity. (NPS)

National Park System

York talk to travel and outdoor writers on November 15, 1977. He was quoted in wire service stories as charging ". . . the Park Service wants to keep the parks for the rangers and nobody else. . . . Who 'owns' our national parks, the people or the federal bureaucracy?" He wanted more access roads in Utah National Parks; he wanted an increase in park land available for recreation. He complained that much of the park land is wilderness and cannot be developed.

The Anchorage Daily Times, on May 7, 1975, said that the Mount McKinley National Park has not been adequately prepared for people. The criticism included the following:

The park service has built only one road in the entire park so that only a small part of the natural wonders of the area are accessible for most visitors. . . . Visitors are compelled to ride in buses provided by the park service. Last year one of the buses fell off the road and one person was killed.

The park service has removed signs that would help people enjoy the park. The signs gave directions and identified mountains, valleys, and animal areas. Signs marking trails for backpackers were also removed.

The one hotel in the park burned more than two years ago. It has been replaced with nothing more than temporary, makeshift accommodations. Like railroad cars for sleepers.

The programs and policies do nothing to strengthen bodies, except maybe strengthening them by surviving hardships of a visit.

The agency presents little to refresh the minds, uplift spirits, or enrich leisure. Indeed, most of the policies tend to deny those benefits to the people.

The park service appears to be deaf. Instead of improving its service to the people, it is trying to enlarge its real estate empire by doubling the size of the park.

More land for the park service would be like supplying more arms to an army that lacks the will to use them effectively.

Maybe it's time for the park service to surrender.

Certainly, some of the criticisms indicate a policy that may be somewhat dubious. The alleged lack of signs giving directions and identifying mountains does not seem to be consistent with policies in other national parks. The single access road has been reported as hazardous over the last few years. Heavy rains in the summer and the long winter season make maintenance of the road difficult and expensive. However, it is virtually a requirement for modern use of this huge park. Sleeping accommodations are a necessity in that the visitor must spend one or two nights in order to take the bus tours that go into the park. For this he pays somewhat of a premium and is offered no alternative solutions. Thus, there may be good

---

FIGURE 15.12 The world's highest combined waterfall of 739 m (2425 ft) is at Yosemite National Park, California, and is one of the outstanding features of the park. (NPS)

Recreation Places

reasons for Alaskans and other visitors to complain about conditions at this park. Responsiveness of the National Park Service may be limited by federal funding. This makes the park service look bad and, at the same time, makes people unhappy with the federal agency.

On the other hand, a strong push to make the parks more civilized and to attract more tourists for the benefit of the local economy is counteracted by people who seek maximum use. Proposals to run aerial cable cars up and down mountains and cliffs, as at European ski areas, were made for Yosemite Valley and the North Cascades (Figure 15.12). Wilderness proponents and traditional park advocates beat down the proposals, urged on the service by political spokesmen and concessionaires. Constant vigil is needed for protection of the natural qualities of parks against cute amusements and citified rides that will make money for their advocates.

Parks are for people—but not for everything that people can dream up. They are for people to see and sense the natural, historic, and cultural wonders, with minimal artificiality.

Park Management

The National Park Service management program is comprised of the following categories (Budget of U.S., 1978):

1. Overall management of park areas to accommodate visitors.
2. Maintenance of buildings and other facilities.
3. Interpretive programs to enhance the visitors' park experience (Fig. 15.13, 15.14).
4. Law enforcement to protect the visitors' well-being and reduce vandalism and other destruction.
5. Resource management to protect and preserve the unique natural, cultural, and historical features.

With the size of some parks, it is frightening to figure out how to administer them. Park management is concentrated on small areas. It is rare for 10 per cent of a national park to be frequently impacted by visitors. About 95 per cent of Yellowstone's visitors never get more than 100 m from the paved roads. Most of the impacted area is made up of visitor access and support facilities.

Effective control must be exercised over this 10 per cent or less. It is here that most maintenance and visitor programming activities go on. Even in wilderness areas, nearly all of the management activity is focused upon the campsites and trails—a miniscule portion of the wild land base.

The management of the rest of the area is by general patrol with focus on trouble spots. Most forest and park managers move on to another job before they see their whole property. This often-lamented fact is a

FIGURE 15.13 Free Government Guide and Lecture Service, Yellowstone National Park. Former President Gerald Ford was a seasonal ranger in 1936. (NPS)

FIGURE 15.14 Historical sites such as Fort Necessity, Pennsylvania, became a major official responsibility of the National Park Service in 1935. Costumed interpreters add color and a lively suggestion of the events of the time. (NPS)

result of a combination of practical necessity, higher priorities, and personal inertia.

It is easy to become familiar with a property, even while sitting in an office. Excellent aerial photographs and high-altitude imagery are readily available from government and private sources. Accurate topographical and shaded relief maps offer detailed information that easily orients the viewer to the lay of the land. A new employee can well use these maps, photos, and the most effective transportation available to become acquainted with the property soon after arriving on the scene. That usually takes personal initiative, because the old hands have either already seen the place or aren't interested.

With increasing attendance at national park system lands, management faces more problems:

More accidents, injuries, and deaths.
More poaching.
More vandalism.
More crowding.
More complaints about services.

There also are the consequences of environmental deterioration. During the last decade or two, park service budgets and personnel limitations put a squeeze on customary operating procedures.

Other issues face administrators of the national park system.

Human behavior—Hang gliding, off-road vehicle riding, and other inventive recreation plus illegal or disruptive parties and acts make park rangers into reluctant law enforcement officers.
Public access—especially to parks near urban areas.
Transportation—Within some parks, cars tend to dominate, leading to plans for collective transportation (Figure 15.15).
Mining—allowed on proven claims in many parks.
Backcountry and river permits—Overuse results in deterioration of the environment and the quality of experience, so capacities are fixed and forced, amidst some controversy.
Townsites—In Canadian parks and near U.S. parks, small towns provide tourist services but pose problems of expansion, visual quality, and high prices.
Concessions—Private businesses operating on NPS license become enthusiastic and politically potent, introducing incompatible elements, as shown in this 1975 ad for Ahwahnee Lodge in Yosemite (Sax, 1976):

It's not just another American convention hotel. . . . It's a great American castle. . . . All your worldly needs are provided for . . . when you go to the

FIGURE 15.15 Yellowstone and other parks were serviced by railroad concessions in 1926. Travelers were taken by train to the main gate and transported by stagecoach to the lodges. (NPS)

barber or the hairdresser or the gift shops. . . . This isn't no-man's land. Or primitive wilderness. This is civilization.

Inholdings—Private lands inside park boundaries are being bought as money becomes available, with some landowners voicing strong complaints about how they are treated.

Wildlife encounters—Bears find visitors in their territory, take natural measures, and are removed or shot as rogues; visitors want to see more wildlife, at no risk.

Regional recreation planning—Neighboring national forests and private lands are looked to for help in spreading the visitor load, but visitors prefer to stay in the parks.

Resource management—Forest insects, diseases, fire, and wildlife population control are major policy problems.

New Park Acquisition

Landowners at the Sleeping Bear Dunes National Lakeshore in northern Michigan have referred to an existing situation as inverse condemnation. The National Park Service has included 24,000 ha of private lands in the Sleeping Bear Dunes acquisition plan. In 1971, Congress appropriated $19.8 million for purchase of lands in the park. Only one sixth of the property had actually been purchased by 1978. Park officials blamed the shortfall on soaring land values in the two counties involving the National Lakeshore.

Land purchases were suspended when the National Park Service announced it had exhausted the funds appropriated for the park.

Persons whose property is within the proposed boundary of the park, but has not yet been purchased, feel that they are being treated unjustly.

The government is going to buy their property some day. The property is difficult to sell to private buyers because it is known the government wants it. However, the government does not want it now. The people would like to sell and buy some land outside the Lakeshore boundaries. They are in a bind that has no easy solution.

The superintendent of the Lakeshore says that if all of the $19.8 million had been appropriated in 1965 when the Lakeshore was first established, the park would be complete today. Quick and decisive action would have prevented the problem and kept the cost within bounds.

New Park Development

Declaring a national park does not make it one. Big Thicket National Preserve in southwest Texas was established by the Congress in 1974. More

Figure 15.16   The nation's oldest city, St. Augustine, Florida, was protected by the Castillo de San Marcos (1672–1695) which stands as a National Park Service monument to Spanish resistance against the English. The city fell to the British in 1763, was returned to Spain after the American Revolution, and then was ceded to the United States in 1821. (NPS)

Recreation Places

FIGURE 15.17 Yosemite National Park is renowned for photogenic rock monoliths, large trees, and wildlife. (NPS)

than three years later there was still no real national park as land acquisition proceeded quietly and slowly.

The United States Army Corps of Engineers surveyed, mapped, appraised, and studied the 12 units that make up the sprawling preserve delineated by Congress. In the meantime, NPS officials worked on the newly acquired land, getting it in shape for public use and interpretation of its features. In an area where hunting had been popular, the outlawing of hunting was bound to be unpopular. Therefore, the park service decided

FIGURE 15.18 Cultural artifacts and ruins are preserved in many southwestern parks such as Chaco Canyon National Monument, New Mexico, which contains 13 major Indian ruins representing the highest point of pre-Columbian Pueblo civilization. (NPS)

to eliminate hunting dogs but permit hunting on a controlled basis. Likewise, trapping was to be allowed under Texas law. No predators were to be hunted, but enforcement creates considerable animosity in a region where predators have traditionally been hunted.

The park service studied the area for its wilderness potential. It was looking at the river corridors, designing float trips along the 80 miles of rivers, developing campsites, constructing tramways to carry visitors on nature study tours, and planning for walks in primitive camping areas. Actual construction of facilities was planned for 1981, about 7 years following the act of Congress. In the meantime, 84,500 acres of Big Thicket were being prepared for public use.

This progress was actually quite rapid as compared to some other park developments. The Act of Congress does not make an immediate national park area accessible to the people.

Recreation Places

SUMMARY

The popularity of national parks has resulted in many new challenges to the professionals of the National Park Service (Figures 15.16, 15.17, and 15.18). Rangers, planners, interpreters, and maintenance experts are pressed to administer the huge new additions in Alaska and the intensively used urban parks while keeping up the quality of the older properties. In the face of citizen concerns about taxes, the challenge is difficult.

The National Park Service, established in 1916, manages its widely scattered holdings for their special natural and historical values while providing for use by visitors with varying perceptions of the values of the resources.

Literature Cited

The Budget of the United States Government, Fiscal Year 1978; Appendix. 1977. Washington, D.C.: U.S. Govt. Printing Office. 950 pp.

CALAHANE, VICTOR H. (ed.) 1962. National Parks—a World Need. New York: American Committee for International Wild Life Protection, Special Publication No. 14. 100 pp.

CURRY-LINDAHL, KAI. 1974. Projecting the future in the worldwide national park movement. In: Sir Hugh Elliott (ed.), Second World Conference on National Parks. Morges, Switzerland: International Union for Conservation of Nature and Natural Resources. pp. 82–94.

EVERHART, WILLIAM C. 1972. The National Park Service. New York: Praeger. 276 pp.

MILLS, ENOS A. 1917. Your National Parks. Boston: Houghton Mifflin Company. 532 pp.

SAX, JOSEPH L. 1976. America's national parks. Natural History 85(8):57–89.

TILDEN, FREEMAN. 1975. Who am I? Washington, D.C.: National Park Service, U.S. Dept. of the Interior. 41 pp.

TURELLO, DAVID. 1975. Park planning. Address to American Congress for Recreation and Parks, Denver, Colorado.

National Wildlife Refuges

The Okefenokee Swamp is reputed to house strange creatures that speak philosophically in comic strip balloons. "Pogo" is about as close as most Americans ever get to a national wildlife refuge.

The refuges are little known and among the least used of any major class of recreation resources in the nation. Many current visitors say "wonderful—keep it that way." Others see these lands as places for much increased use and opportunity to sensitize large numbers of people to the values of wildlife. The refuges are managed by the Fish and Wildlife Service of the U.S. Department of the Interior.

History

The Fish and Wildlife Service traces its history from 1900, when the U.S. Department of the Interior was given responsibility for birds under the Lacey Act. In 1905, a Bureau of Biological Survey was established as a forerunner of the present agency. Only in 1966 was a rather weak organic act passed to give comprehensive Congressional direction to the agency.

The National Wildlife Refuge (NWR) concept was started in 1903 with the establishment of tiny Pelican Island National Wildlife Refuge off the coast of Florida. President Theodore Roosevelt proclaimed it a refuge from plume hunters for nesting pelicans, herons, and egrets.

The system of refuges was slow in expanding. Its greatest growth is still occurring. The land area in refuges tripled between 1956 and 1974 to 13.7 million ha (nearly 34 million acres). It doubled again in 1975–1980, primarily as a result of new additions in Alaska.

Even before the latest Alaska additions, two thirds of the system's area was in Alaska (Figure 16.1). There has been a strong effort to establish refuges in every state; only West Virginia remains untouched.

Visits also tripled from 1956 to 1974. Permanent staff and funding increased in real dollars, but at a rate well behind visitor use. In 1978, after 75 years of existence, there were 386 national wildlife refuges. They are distributed from the Arctic Ocean to the South Pacific, from Maine to the Caribbean. They range from tiny, half-hectare islands to immense

FIGURE 16.1 Huge acreages in wildlife refuges in Alaska are required to protect the wide-ranging caribou and other animals whose food needs are met only by large grazing territories. (NPS)

FIGURE 16.2 Many people visit National Wildlife Refuges for nonconsumptive purposes such as nature study (Muscatatuck NWR).

areas in Alaska, measured in millions of hectares. The majority of the lands are in new Alaska refuges, protecting prime nesting grounds for many migratory birds and extensive range on low-productivity soils. Other large areas are western range and desert refuges, especially in Arizona and Montana.

The National Wildlife Refuge mission is described (U.S. Fish and Wildlife Service, 1976) as follows:

to provide, manage, and safeguard a national network of lands and waters sufficient in size, diversity, and location to make available, now and in the future, public benefits that are associated with wildlife over which the Federal Government has responsibility, particularly migratory birds and endangered species.

Wild creatures are the principal commodities, and fulfilling their needs is the principal responsibility of the refuges. All other assignments are subordinate to that obligation. The success of refuge operations is measured in the responses of wildlife to the management of the habitat.

Most of the land in the refuge system is federally owned and available for outdoor recreation. There are limitations on the types of recreation; it must not disrupt wildlife values (Figure 16.2). Hunting is allowed on nearly half of the refuges, during seasons set after careful study of the populations. Wildlife appreciation activities are popular and growing rapidly.

Land Ownership

There are differences in jurisdiction among the various units of the refuge system. Some areas are managed by private owners under easement. Under terms of the easement, the landowner agrees to protect wetlands from being destroyed through drainage, burning, and filling. The wetlands in the northern prairie states are prime breeding grounds. The Fish and Wildlife Service has had some difficulty in holding the owners to full compliance with the conditions of the easements on these privately owned lands.

Another arrangement is by cooperative agreements between the Fish and Wildlife Service, states, and other federal agencies. Interagency jurisdiction of lands involves 14 other agencies, with the Bureau of Land Management as the major cooperator. The Army Corps of Engineers, Bureau of Reclamation, and TVA also have important federal wildlife refuges superimposed on their water project areas. Likewise, Defense Department and NASA lands often involve wildlife refuges. Cooperative arrangements involve about 10 per cent of the entire system.

Most of the land is controlled outright by the Fish and Wildlife Service, acquired from private owners or reserved from the public domain.

Types of Refuges

Within the system, there are six designations of properties. There are no neat distinctions among them, only relative emphases of management and funding. The 13.7 million ha (33.8 million acres) before the Alaskan settlement were divided as follows:

1. Migratory Bird Refuges (waterfowl), 276 properties; 1.6 million ha. Examples: Bear River, Utah; Horicon, Wisconsin; Lacassine, Louisiana; Big Lake, Arkansas.
2. Migratory Bird Refuges (general), 68 properties; 1.7 million ha. Examples: Okefenokee, Georgia; Stump Lake, North Dakota.
3. Waterfowl Production Areas in Wetlands Management Districts, 0.6 million ha. More than two thirds are under easement, the rest are federally acquired, in prairie potholes of north central states.
4. Big Game Refuges, 16 properties; 3 million ha. Examples: Kenai Moose Range, Alaska; National Bison Range, Montana (for moose, bison, elk, caribou, pronghorn, reindeer, and bear).
5. Wildlife Ranges and Game Ranges, eight properties; 6.5 million ha. Examples: Cabeza Prieta, Arizona; Arctic, Alaska.
6. Coordination Areas or Wildlife Management Areas, 59 properties; 176,500 ha. These combine state and federal administration, usually in small areas. Examples: Beltrami, Minnesota; Killcohook, New Jersey.

In addition to these properties, the Fish and Wildlife Service has seven wildlife research centers; 25 administrative sites; 89 national fish hatcheries; and 11 fishery research and control stations.

Resource Values

A number of specific resource values are identified with the wildlife refuges:

1. Archeological resources are protected from indiscriminate collection. Scientists can request permits for survey and excavation, but they are issued sparingly.
2. Historic and cultural resources are identified and listed on appropriate registers when qualified.
3. Natural areas are identified and categorized into several different groups: National Natural Landmarks (HCRS), Biosphere Reserves (UNESCO), Research and Public Use Natural Areas, Research Natural Areas. Management practices on these areas are minimal, sometimes requiring cutting and burning to maintain subclimax vegetation

FIGURE 16.3 Active environmental education and interpretation programs promote perception of natural processes on National Wildlife Refuges (Muscatatuck NWR).

types considered as the *raison d'etre* of the designated area. Interpretation and appreciative recreation can be allowed on some of these natural areas (Figure 16.3).

4. Wilderness areas are designated by Congress after review and recommendation by the Fish and Wildlife Service. Ten years after the Wilderness Act was passed, the agency had studied nearly 30 million acres, proposing 104 areas for wilderness designation. Alaska added considerably more wilderness area to the NWR system.

Key Legislation Affecting National Wildlife Refuges

The *Lacey Act of 1900* gave the Department of the Interior authority and responsibility for game and other wild birds. With Canada, Mexico, and Japan concurring, the *Migratory Bird Treaty Act of 1918* protects migratory birds by controlling the possession, sale, transport, and importation of birds.

The *Migratory Bird Conservation Act of 1929* established a commission to approve recommended areas for refuges for migratory birds; it authorizes acquisitions, development, maintenance, investigations, and publications. The Act was amended in 1976 (Public Law 94–215) to allow use of MBCA funds for acquisition of partial interest in lands and waters. The *Migratory Bird Hunting Stamp Act of 1934* required a "Duck Stamp" of hunters.

Sale proceeds are used to acquire migratory bird refuges and waterfowl production areas. This law produced a big increase in refuges.

The *Fish and Wildlife Coordination Act of 1934* set up state-federal cooperation to require consultation with Fish and Wildlife agencies before building reservoirs or other water projects. It also authorizes conservation measures as part of water projects. The *Fish and Wildlife Act of 1956* established national fish and wildlife policy and the present Fish and Wildlife Service. It directs provisions of research, extension, and information services and calls for continuing acquisition of refuge lands and development of existing facilities.

The *Refuge Recreation Act of 1962* authorizes the administration of refuges and hatcheries for recreational use, when it does not interfere with primary purposes, and allows purchase of adjacent lands for recreational development. The *National Wildlife Refuge System Administration Act of 1966* constitutes an organic act, expressing the policy of Congress and providing guidelines and directives for the National Wildlife Refuge system.

The *Endangered Species Act of 1973*, which replaces acts of 1966 and 1969, authorizes the listing of endangered and threatened species and the ranges where danger exists; prohibits possession, sale, and transport; authorizes expanded habitat acquisition, including the lifting of a ceiling on Land and Water Conservation Fund monies; and authorizes a co-op program with states that have active programs.

There are also several international treaties (conventions) regulating export-import of fauna and binding the United States and other nations to provide refuges and to continue protection for certain species.

Recreation Use and Development

Wildlife refuges contain diverse ecosystems and, sometimes, dramatic displays of birds and mammals. They are places where people can see wild animals in their native habitats (Figure 16.4). Yet, use is quite low. These are not tourist areas, where visitor comfort and entertainment is of prime importance. Public use areas are established to provide access, unmanipulated nature, and potential for interpretation and education. The agency's policy is to emphasize a quality recreation experience over ability to accommodate quantity.

Although the wildlife refuges contain scenic beauty and ecological diversity, most of the properties do not contain spectacular scenery that draws crowds. To the trained naturalist, flat lands, swamps, estuaries, and rivers are among the most interesting and productive areas on earth. They are certainly attractive to the migratory waterfowl, for which many of the refuges were established. A visitor's snapshot of ducks and geese on water does not always draw the neighbor's admiration or instill a strong desire to visit the refuge.

If it is desirable to increase visitation to National Wildlife Refuges,

FIGURE 16.4 White tailed deer in the East and mule deer in the West are prime game animals, receiving considerable attention from hunters and other appreciators of wildlife. (Florida Development Commission)

there will have to be two or three major efforts to draw visitors. One is through interpretive programs that reveal the beauty of the place. Whereas the beauty of the Grand Tetons is obvious to anyone just standing there, most wildlife refuges have a subtle beauty that has to be understood to be appreciated. Interpretation is being increased on refuges. The second effort is to involve the visitors in memorable personal participation activities. If they can do something exciting or adventuresome, the experience will be remembered and transmitted. That will require considerable imagination and investment. A third possible tourist appeal is the provision of good camping facilities in or near appropriate refuges. The plan for operation of the system (U.S. Fish and Wildlife Service, 1976) has gone the other way, reducing the camping opportunities and focusing more on day use activities. This is likely to prevent the properties from becoming major visitor attractions.

TYPES OF USE

Consumptive recreational activities permitted in the National Wildlife Refuges include the following (U.S. Fish and Wildlife Service, 1976):

Recreation Places

1. Hunting, as long as it is "compatible with the objectives for which the refuge is established and is administered. . . ." Limits are set by state and federal regulations (Figure 16.5).
2. Fishing is permitted and is structured according to state regulations. Fishing is restricted when waterfowl are nesting, wintering, or breeding. Those refuges involved with flood control projects are generally the most used for fishing.
3. Fur trapping is permitted in 22 states. Primarily, muskrat and beaver are taken, along with raccoon, mink, and nutria. Raccoon at times have been purposely removed because of their predation on the eggs of various species of birds and other species such as sea turtles. Refuge trapping is conducted in accordance with state regulations.

Nonconsumptive wildlife uses include bird-watching, nature study, interpretive programs, dog training (for hunting), and environmental education.

Another major category of public use on refuges is nonwildlife-oriented recreation. Major types of activities in that category include boating, camping, hiking, swimming, picnicking, surfing, water-skiing, scuba diving, ice skating, horseback riding, and bicycling.

FIGURE 16.5 Hunting and fishing in season are popular activities on parts of many National Wildlife Refuges (Muscatatuck NWR).

RECREATION USE POLICY

According to the Refuge Recreation Act of 1962, the Fish and Wildlife Service has endorsed public use on refuges but noted that it is secondary to the management of wildlife. The refuges are open to the public, but no serious interference or competition with the prime objective will be allowed (U.S. Fish and Wildlife Service, 1976). Adjacent lands can be purchased for recreation.

The word *refuge* suggests a sanctuary, a place where birds and animals could be free of persecution by humans, their weapons, and machines. That concept was the original idea, but it has changed. The idea was inviolate for 21 years. Then, in 1924, the Upper Mississippi River Wildlife and Fish Refuge was established with built-in provisions for both hunting and fishing. In 1948, the Lea Act allowed purchase and farming of crop land to keep ducks off of private fields and authorized public waterfowl hunting. In 1949, a big change in policy came from the Congress. In revising the Duck Stamp Act, the legislators gave the Secretary of the Interior authority to allow public waterfowl hunting on 25 per cent of any refuge in the system. That rose to 40 per cent in 1958, with another duck stamp act amendment. Despite these changes, protection of and providing habitat for wildlife still dominate refuge purposes.

Big game hunts, under controlled conditions, are allowed on many refuges. These are usually conducted as needed to control excess population.

Fishing is generally allowed but restricted during bird nesting and migration seasons. Fishing is the most common recreational use of the refuges (U.S. Fish and Wildlife Service, 1976).

These uses sometimes conflict with bird watching, photography, and other study by visitors. The manager reduces conflicts by zoning areas for appropriate uses and by judicious timing of seasons and regulations.

A persistent question often faces preserve managers: how much recreation of various kinds is appropriate? Any diversion of funds or energies could be construed as interference with the usually underfinanced habitat management operation. However, many refuges have considerable recreation use and dedicate a significant amount of staff time to visitors. Without public visitation, sympathy, and support, the concept of refuges could face a bleak future.

THE SHOWPLACE CONCEPT

A key recreation question concerns what kinds of recreation to emphasize. A secretarial review committee (Leopold, et al., 1966) favored appreciative recreation without excluding consumptive forms: "the sorts of recreation appropriate on a National Wildlife Refuge should be oriented toward the appreciation, enjoyment and, in certain cases, the harvesting of wildlife and fish. . . ." The committee suggested wildlife viewing, hiking, sightseeing, nature observation, study, and photography, enhanced by tours, trails, observation points or towers, interpretive centers, and natural history exhibits. It strongly suggested that these types of recreation and ecological teaching should be emphasized on the refuges.

Appreciative and consumptive recreation are not mutually exclusive. Both can be accommodated in most refuges. However, if hunting inside refuges is as open as it is outside, then the refuge loses some of its distinctiveness as a display sanctuary. The Leopold committee recommended that hunting and fishing could be permitted, but neither for all species nor to the limit of surplus populations:

If all possible surplus populations are hunted, the refuge becomes little different from the rest of the countryside.

We take the view that the National Wildlife Refuges should be consciously developed as showplaces for all kinds of wildlife. All forms of disturbance, including hunting, should be so regulated in areas of visitor concentration as to favor an optimal display of wild birds and mammals, gentle enough to be easily seen by the visiting public. (Leopold, et al, 1966).

In the mission and objectives of the National Wildlife Refuge system, the concept of service to people is expressed in such phrases as "for the benefit of the people" and "public benefits." One objective is consonant with the appreciative concept (U.S. Fish and Wildlife Service, 1976):

To provide understanding and appreciation of fish and wildlife ecology and man's role in his environment, and to provide visitors at Service installations with high quality, safe, wholesome and enjoyable recreational experiences oriented toward wildlife.

The refuge system plans specific production goals by 1985 that include annual provision for 780 scientific studies; 288,000 activity hours of environmental education; 2,245,000 hours of wildlife interpretation; preservation and protection of 191 natural areas, 43 wilderness areas, and 65 special sites; 13,000 public programs; response to 1,276,000 public inquiries; 45 million activity hours of wildlife-oriented recreation, and 16 million hours of nonwildlife-oriented recreation.

To achieve these goals, the manager still focuses basically on the wildlife. It is the mammals, reptiles, fish, and birds that make these refuges of special interest. Populations of animals respond to the management of their habitats. In the final analysis, the key to providing wildlife-related recreation opportunities lies in the management of the land, water, and vegetative resources.

Management principles and practice are based on ecological theories. Diversity in food and cover is a major management goal. Wildlife requires a variety of food and cover, as well as the proximity of water. Refuge managers provide and manipulate croplands, forests, wetlands, and grasslands. Public use management is also applied.

Endangered Species

A judge in Youngstown, Ohio recently ruled that he could find nothing in the Constitution which guaranteed that pigeons had rights to life, liberty, and property (Shea, 1977). The city health department then proceeded to poison a flock of city pigeons. Most animals are in the same no-rights situation.

There are some animals, however, that do have the right to government protection of their lives, liberty, and habitat (Figure 16.6). Their rights have been guaranteed by the 1973 Endangered Species Act (Public Law 93–205, amended), which replaced the weaker acts of 1966 and 1969. It is a tough law, protecting the rights of any mammal, bird, reptile, fish, amphibian, shellfish, arthropod, or insect that is listed as threatened or endangered. Plants are also included, but action has been slow in listing them.

Congressmen who voted almost unanimously to protect the bald eagle, timber wolf, and beautiful Hawaiian birds have discovered that the rights of little-known fish and insects have stopped major water projects and highway construction. Predictably, this has produced some bills to reduce the stringency of the law.

The act is a measure "to provide a means whereby the ecosystems upon which endangered species and threatened species depend may be conserved . . ." (Public Law 93–205). Its basic goal is to reduce the rate

FIGURE 16.6   Wildlife refuges in the United States and Canada help protect threatened species and many more abundant animals.

Recreation Places

of man-induced extinction of species by giving animals and plants near extinction special protection.

To gain full protection against harassment, annoyance, harm, pursuit, hunting, trapping, collecting, or impairment of habitat, the species must be listed. The list is drawn up by the Secretary of the Interior through his Office of Endangered Species. That office must judge as to the relative threat or danger to a species, even though little may be known about candidates for classification. It is generally assumed to be wiser to list a species about which there is doubt then to forego listing. A species can be removed from the list if later discovered to be "safe," but it cannot be brought back from extinction.

Almost 200 species in the United States are on the list. By mid-1977, only six species had critical habitats officially designated. Habitat protection is considered the key element in preventing the disappearance of most endangered species.

Arguments against the Endangered Species Act usually center around the current usefulness of species to man. Species with little intrinsic value to humans are being given undue protection, it is said, especially if their preservation interferes with some other project of society. This usefulness-to-man yardstick seems shortsighted and arrogant, suggesting that if men do not have a current use for a plant or animal, then it has no inherent right to survive. If it gets in the way of draining a field, or damming a stream, or cutting a forest, should temporary human benefit prevail? Restraint in human action is sometimes the more noble route. It is neither good economics nor good ecology, and certainly poor stewardship, to pursue single goals of production to the detriment of other considerations, some of which are so precious as to have no price tag. The earth can produce goods and services in a way that spares us from having to choose between ourselves and other species. It requires wisdom and patience to find the way.

Managing Wildlife for Recreation

The dominant purpose of wildlife management is for recreation. Perhaps 90 per cent of wildlife management is aimed at recreation.

Wild mammals, birds, and fish have long been known for their recreational values. Elaborate preparations and expense are involved in going out in search of a few pounds of meat. The replaying of the survival drama of the hunt is now almost exclusively recreational. The explicit costs of the hunt are higher than the value of the food or hides returned for most hunters.

The preparations for hunting and fishing go far beyond the special clothing, weapons, and living gear that the participant gathers. State and federal governments have also gone to great expense to improve habitats

FIGURE 16.7 A Dall ram is one of the prizes of the Alaskan recreation scene. (NPS)

and food supply, build reservoirs, import and grow especially desirable game species, and provide campgrounds, roads, and parking places for the sportsmen. Although wildlife has traditionally been spoken of and managed as "game," hunting and fishing are not the only values of wild animals. Their esthetic, scientific, and ecological roles have become increasingly recognized (Figure 16.7).

Hunting and fishing equipment taxes and license revenues fund most of the wildlife management programs. A natural consequence is the emphasis on game species. Of the federal money dedicated to wildlife research and management, 97 per cent is spent on less than 1 per cent of the vertebrate species subject to federal control. State funding produces a similar imbalance. The money is spent on the few favored game species, such as deer, elk, trout, ducks, and geese (U.S. Fish and Wildlife Service, 1976).

Little is known about the other species, from a scientific point of view. Studies of their population dynamics and current status are almost nonexistent. Predators are usually still treated as vermin or threats to humans. Some bring bounties to those who shoot them. Songbirds and many other species appreciated by citizens are under no active conservation or management program. The educational and recreational opportunities offered by nongame species have received almost no attention or funding. Of course, many of these species have benefited from habitat improvements or protection intended for game species.

In his 1977 environmental message, President Carter encouraged the use of federal funds by the states for management of *all species of wildlife* and then asked the Secretary of the Interior to propose other measures. Suggestions for sources of revenue other than from hunters and fishermen include special taxes on binoculars, bird-watching licenses, stamps, and voluntary contributions. No sizable, steady sources of such funds have been developed.

Management Techniques

Techniques in managing for wildlife are related to either the populations or the habitat through land management.

Population management includes techniques such as wildlife census, marking and studying movements, and animal population control methods. These are applied selectively wherever possible. Animal population control methods include, in descending order of preference,

Habitat manipulation
Live trapping and transfer
Removal of surplus individuals through public hunting, fishing or trapping
Chemical and mechanical repellants
Physical or mechanical protection (barriers, fences)
Killing animals by other means (gassing, shooting, poisoning, seining)

Land management practices are ultimately the most efficient and necessary means of affecting animal populations.

Cropland management is aimed at providing food and cover to help sustain the population using refuges and to reduce the feeding pressures on neighboring private farms. Wheat, corn, barley, rye, sorghum, soybeans, buckwheat, rice, millet, alfalfa, and clover are grown on refuges. Where practical, share-cropping arrangements are made with private farmers. The refuge's share is left standing for wildlife feeding. About 20 per cent of the farmed acreage is tilled by refuge personnel.

Water management is used on most refuges to increase lake areas or maintain swamps (Figure 16.8). A green tree reservoir technique has been developed to provide water areas in the winter and green forest in the summer. Some species of trees can withstand fairly prolonged flooding in the dormant season. They need oxygen at their roots in the growing season. Low dikes are constructed around blocks of timber. In the winter, the areas flood and are used by ducks, geese, and other waterfowl, which have easy access to acorns and other edible seeds. The method was developed in the Southeast where water remains unfrozen most of the winter.

Figure 16.8 Wetlands are the most productive elements of the ecosystem, a fact requiring interpretation to drainage-prone Americans. (Hennepin County Park Reserve District)

Timber management is limited by policy, location, and growth conditions to less than 700,000 acres. Only 20 refuges have significant forest acreage. Forty-five others have managed woodlots. Here, sustained-yield forestry is practiced, using combinations of even-aged and uneven-aged silvicultural practices. On wildlife refuges, practices benefiting wildlife take precedence over achieving optimal timber outputs. Thus, individual trees are left standing when they have high food-producing capability (acorns, beechnuts, cones) and potential for dens (hollow spots). This means that trees somewhat past their prime wood-producing years may be left standing because of their superior benefits to wildlife, even though they are using space in which young trees might be growing vigorously.

Forest openings provide density of habitat. When natural clearings are inadequate, frequent spot thinning of the stand permits sunlight to reach the forest floor. This encourages grasses and forbs, which offer food and cover to wildlife.

Regeneration cuts on refuges usually approximate the shelterwood or seed tree models. Small clearcuts and selection cuts are used as conditions dictate. The cutting pattern is distributed in time and area to ensure habitat variety in the usual cruising range of the wildlife species of particular interest. Only about 1 per cent of the forest area is subject to regeneration cuts per year, to guarantee diversity of ages and habitats.

Grassland management on range areas seeks to spread use over the entire range. Improvement in plant composition is a key concern.

Prescribed burning is used in managing pine forests at various stages and in reducing wildlife hazards. Fire is used mostly in conjunction with selective thinnings and regeneration cuts.

SUMMARY

Over 300 National Wildlife Refuges are available for outdoor recreation, ranging from hunting, fishing, and bird watching to riding, hiking, picnicking and camping. The primary purpose of the refuges is to provide habitat and protection for wildlife populations; recreation is not allowed to supersede this goal. Most of the refuge support comes from hunting and fishing taxes, stamps and licenses, but the majority of the use now comes from other activities.

Although the vast majority of the refuges are in Alaska and remote parts of the West, the Fish and Wildlife Service plans on rapidly increasing recreation visitation. Among its goals are lighter emphasis on camping and much greater activity in the interpretive area. As showplaces for wildlife species, the refuges stand supreme.

Literature Cited

LEOPOLD, A. STARKER, CLARENCE COTTAM, IAN McT. COWAN, IRA N. GABRIELSON and THOMAS L. KIMBALL. 1966. The National Wildlife Refuge System. Report to Interior Secretary Stewart L. Udall. Transactions of the North American Wildlife and Natural Resources Conference 33(1969).

SHEA, KEVIN. 1977. The endangered species act. Environment 19(7):7–15.

U.S. Fish & Wildlife Service. 1976. Final Environmental Statement; Operation of the National Wildlife Refuge System. Washington, D.C.: Dept. of the Interior. Var. pag.

National Resource Lands

The Bureau of Land Management (BLM) is one of the best-kept recreation secrets in the United States. It is almost as if there were a plot to keep one fifth of the nation's land under wraps. The Congress and the people have long ignored the BLM's *national resource lands*. Only in 1976, was there strong congressional direction and public involvement.

This agency, however, has a longer history and broader jurisdiction than almost any other of the federal government land agencies. One of the agency's predecessors started in 1792, five years after the Constitution was signed. The General Land Office was the official holder, recorder, and dispenser of public lands in the expanding United States. This is the group that administered the Homestead Act. It gave lands to the railroads to open the West. It took title to Alaska, Oregon, and most other western states. It handles drilling on the outer continental shelf today.

These functions were inherited by the Bureau of Land Management, formed in 1946 by a merger of the General Land Office and the Grazing Service, which had been established in 1934 by the Taylor Grazing Act. The BLM combined the functions of custodian and manager of the grasslands, forests, deserts, and tundra that had not been claimed by the Forest Service, National Park Service, school grants, railroad grants, homesteaders, ranchers, speculators, miners, or states and their subdivisions.

The Bureau of Land Management is responsible for the residue of America's rich land bounty. Most of the BLM property looks like the residue—with some spectacularly notable exceptions. The exceptions include a few plots of grounds on the Las Vegas Strip and the highly productive timber lands of the reverted Oregon and California Railroad Grant, as well as beautiful mountain, desert, and arctic scenery.

The agency is not well known among the general public. Until recently, its major constituents have been ranchers who graze their cattle on the public lands for nominal fees, miners who prospect and stake claims on the lands, and a dwindling supply of homesteaders and settlers.

In recent years, recreationists have reached the national resource lands in large numbers. In the deserts of southern California and southern Nevada, the use of off-road vehicles has drawn national attention. Of special interest has been the controversial development of long, large cross-country motor bike races, involving thousands of riders. The Barstow to Las Vegas event has received considerable publicity. BLM restrictions and control of the races have increased with the study of impacts of use on the desert flora and fauna and with the vocal attention of environmentalists.

Legal Bases

In 1976, the BLM was finally given an official mandate from the Congress, in the form of an organic act—the Federal Land Policy and Management Act of 1976, signed by President Ford on October 21, as Public Law 94–579.

Attempts to develop basic legislation for BLM policies started in the late 1950s. Along the route, there were many partial directives from the Congress and a Public Land Law Review Commission report, which studied the many problems on all federal lands. One of the key laws was the 1964 Classification and Multiple Use Act. This, for the first time, gave the agency authority to classify and manage parts of the public domain as permanent federal land. Previously, the lands administered by the BLM were subject to transfer of some type or another. That law also officially recognized the multiple-use approach that had more or less been the operating policy of the agency in the field. Many outsiders, however, had criticized the agency for emphasizing grazing and mining activities almost exclusively. (Critics said "BLM" signified "Bureau of Livestock and Minerals.") By the time that the Classification and Multiple Use Act had run out its specified life, the BLM had designated about 200 million acres for retention and multiple-use management (Senzel, 1978).

The 1976 act officially ended the policy of transferring public domain lands into private ownership. It establishes the intent of the federal government to retain most of the 190 million hectares (470 plus million acres) under the control of the Bureau of Land Management or other federal agencies. The act also established direction for management on multiple-use and sustained-yield bases, which protects scientific, scenic, historical, ecological, environmental, air and atmospheric, water resources, and archeological values (Council on Environmental Quality, 1977).

Land use planning on these federal lands must be prepared promptly. Land areas of critical environmental concern are of special interest. The organic act finally gave the Bureau of Land Management authority to protect and manage its vast area and directed the Department of the Interior to proceed with developing regulations for full implementation.

This act also enabled qualified BLM lands to enter the National Wilderness Preservation System. After study of candidate areas, some of which are already administratively designated as primitive areas, the agency can

FIGURE 17.1   The BLM offers vast areas for riding, hiking, and exploration. (BLM)

submit recommendations for new wilderness areas to the Congress, through the president. The agency was given 15 years (to 1991) to review its potential wilderness candidates.

Recreation Use and Potential

The majority of recreational use on BLM lands occurs in dispersed areas (Figure 17.1). The most popular activities are primitive camping, summer and winter recreational travel, hunting, and fishing. On the national resource lands, the use is widely scattered. The key problems of recreation management by the BLM are maintaining control and establishing communication with the visitors. Sixty million visitor days per year are spent on 190 million hectares of land, mostly in dispersed activities. Most of that land is wide-open desert, range, or tundra (Figure 17.2). Access is easy from most western roads, but identification of the boundaries is virtually impossible for a visitor without a detailed map. Because much of the land is under grazing leases, ranchers tend to be protective of "their" territory and cautious about people who might disrupt their cattle or sheep.

Unlike state or national parks, there are no entry gates to most of the national resource lands. There are few highway signs announcing the visitor's entry into a particular management unit of the BLM. The principal places for visitor contact and information are at a few, scattered developed campgrounds and the district offices. The BLM has also worked through off-road vehicle organizations in southern California to inform riders of new regulations and to control race activities. Estimates of use of BLM lands must be extremely rough, because there are few or no controlled entries, except at campgrounds and boat-launching sites.

A strategy for contacting visitors will have to revolve around identification of key access points and popular attractions. At these points, information can be provided to perhaps the majority of visitors. Making maps and use information available in key urban areas and at all field offices will also help somewhat. Another important tool is increased development of interpretive materials and programs. The BLM is building its personal and self-directed interpretive offerings. It needs much greater commitment of resources to help people understand the natural process and wonders of "waste places." The desert, the range, and interior Alaska are virtually unknown to Americans. A major and prolonged interpretive effort is needed to develop public appreciation.

One major identifiable resource of the BLM with great potential is the trail. Long and short trails for hiking, nature study, horseback riding, and ORV riding could probably be among the most popular features on these public lands. What national fame the organization has for recreation stems mostly from the large motorcycle races in the Mojave Desert and the dog sled races across Alaska. Linear travel activities of major proportions

FIGURE 17.2 Grizzly bears require large wild areas and tolerant human neighbors, both of which are in short supply in the lower 48 states and much of southern Canada. (NPS)

National Resource Lands

can be offered on BLM lands because of the unusually extensive federal holdings.

A trail from Mexico to Canada across desert, small mountains, and high plains has been proposed. There would be minimal difficulty in laying it out across federal lands, with only occasional interruptions of private holdings. It might be well used in fall, winter, and spring. Adequate information on routes and water are necessities. Historical routes through the West are being studied by BLM and other agencies for potential trail developments.

Recreation is one of the major challenges for the "new" BLM. Policies and plans are now being revamped for the entire management program. Clearly, this agency has a tremendous opportunity to increase wide-open-space recreation.

Recreation Units

Most BLM lands are for a variety of uses; a few are identified primarily for recreational values. For administrative purposes, the BLM uses four designations for its land units devoted primarily to recreation purposes. Within these, the resource classification system proposed by ORRRC (1962) is used for planning.

1. *Recreation lands* are units of several thousand acres where outdoor recreation or wildlife is the primary use. They may have facilities or remain undeveloped. They may include all six of the ORRRC classes.
2. *Recreation sites,* usually less than 500 acres, have recreational use as the primary value. Generally, these areas are developed for concentrated use, such as camping, fishing, swimming, organization camps, and summer home leases. Some have historical or archeological features.
3. *Transfer tracts* are areas sold or leased for recreation purposes to state, local, or nonprofit groups.
4. *Buffer or scenic zones* are protective areas around recreation sites and transfer tracts. They are also established around lakes and along roads. These zones vary in width, from 80 to 1,000 meters. Uses not conforming with recreational values are prohibited within these zones.

Recreation and Public Purposes Act

The BLM sells or rents transfer tracts to states, counties, cities, and groups. Since 1926, the Bureau of Land Management and its predecessor, the General Land Office, operated under laws that allow public domain lands otherwise unreserved to be transferred for recreation. States, their subdivisions, schools, hospitals, research institutions, service groups (Scouts,

Y's), sportsmen's associations, and civic groups could buy land or lease it for recreation developments. The price is cheap. Under the 1954 revision of the act (Public Law 83–387), the Secretary of the Interior charges $2.50 per acre for purchase, or $0.25 per acre per year for leasing. The land has to be used as a park or other developed recreation area. It cannot be solely for hunting or sightseeing.

The 1976 Organic Act retained the program and amended it to set restrictions on the amount of land to be transferred in any year. The total that can be assigned to other groups in any state is 25,600 acres. State parks or related agencies can receive up to 6,400 acres of this, and nonprofit groups, up to 640 acres per year. Disposal of any piece of land larger than 640 acres requires a comprehensive land use plan and zoning regulations guaranteeing its long-range use for recreation.

Many western communities have benefited from this law. The Phoenix, Arizona, rural parks (city and county) are primarily results of use of this law. The state of Wyoming has used it in developing parks around small reservoirs. Other state and local agencies have joined nonprofit organizations to improve the recreation estate at low cost.

O & C LANDS

The BLM operates one of the richest timberlands in the world along the western edge of Oregon. Recreation areas are blended with intensive timber management and harvesting of the Oregon and California Railroad lands (O & C). These are checkerboard parcels of one square mile in size, amounting to 850,000 ha (2.1 million acres) and containing about 50 billion board feet of Douglas fir and other old-growth timber.

The O & C lands reverted to public ownership after the Oregon and California Railroad and the Coos Bay Wagon Road failed to live up to contracts. They had been granted the land as an incentive to develop a transportation system. It was the policy of the government to make such grants of strips of alternate sections of land to railroads that were helping settle and civilize the West.

In 1937, the Congress passed legislation providing for administration of the O & C timber lands on a sustained-yield basis and in cooperation with private landowners. The annual cut has been as high as one billion board feet. Fifty per cent of the gross receipts are paid to the counties in lieu of taxes, and as much as another 25 per cent is remanded to them as premanagement compensation. The agency has also invested heavily in the development of extensive recreation facilities.

The Alaska Frontier

The year 1978 was decision time for a large share of Alaska, as explained in Chapter 14. The 1971 Alaska Native Claims Settlement Act defined the time limit on determining how vast holdings of the BLM in Alaska would be managed. Since the year went by without congressional action, the President made decisions for "preserve" status for over half of the national interest lands and temporary reserve status for the remainder. This reduced BLM holdings by 21 million ha (52 million acres) and restricted use on another 23 million ha (58 million acres). The total area affected by these decrees is larger than the nine-state area from Maine through Pennsylvania.

Conservation groups backed the idea of preserving large areas of land but opposed their assignment to multiple–use conservation designations such as national forests or BLM national resource lands. Designation of lands as wild and scenic rivers and wilderness was promoted among recreationists and other groups interested in preservation. Many Alaska residents and industrialists were concerned about locking up large land areas for such nonconsumptive uses. Unemployment was high in the state and the economy was still in early growth stages. Many Alaskans saw the preservationists as enemies of economic progress.

Involved in the decisions on Alaska were concerns for wild animals (Figure 17.3), mineral ores, and timber, as well as recreation (Knickerbocker, 1978).

FIGURE 17.3 Brown bear fishing in Alaskan stream. (NPS)

Recreation Places

FIGURE 17.4   Hunting in Alaska is an essential part of the economy of many Eskimos, Aleuts, and Indians. Special provisions have been made to allow continuation of traditional hunting patterns. (NPS)

Much of Alaska's interior is relatively unproductive. A short growing season can produce lush growth on some soils. In many places, rainfall is low. Trees grow slowly and, sometimes, sparsely. Wildlife food supply is also spread out, requiring wide ranging by grazers. Grizzly bears roam over 100 square miles as home range. Caribou travel 1,000 miles annually in search of food. Protection of home ranges of these animals is difficult without vast areas under coordinated management. The controversial shooting of wolves and bears from airplanes has stirred the enthusiasm of preservationists to designate lands as parks or refuges, which have a long-time policy of protecting animals from hunting (except in some national wildlife refuges) as well as maintaining their habitat. Many of the Eskimos and Indians have asked that they be allowed to continue hunting for sustenance. This is permitted on most BLM lands and some National Park Service areas in Alaska (Figure 17.4).

The key issue is mining. The BLM is the key agency in administering the mining laws. Minerals brought Alaska fame and population. Prospecting continues as both a business and a hobby. The discovery of oil on the northern coast brought a pipeline and a construction boom in the mid 1970s. It is generally believed that there is more gold in the hills, as well as numerous other minerals. Mining is allowed in national forests and BLM lands but is severely restricted on parks and refuges. Therefore, industries and Alaskan economic interests have opposed "overprotection" of the state's resources, prefering the flexible multiple use policies.

Timber grows in much of the interior of Alaska. The Forest Service and the BLM have spent considerable effort in inventorying and estimating the growth of these forests, in cooperation with state foresters. Although coastal forests are highly productive, the growth rate in the interior is generally low. Still, there is raw material aplenty for forest industry. Scandinavian foresters have estimated that well-financed management could make forest land quite productive on a continuing basis. Fires have burned over huge areas, despite some efforts to control them. Insects and disease take tremendous tolls of timber and fiber each year. As the state develops, the economic possibility of salvaging wasted material and rationally managing a healthy forest resource becomes more real. Management on a multiple-use basis would provide for timber and mineral development, as well as rational allotment of wildlife, scenery, and recreation use.

The argument seemed to boil down to mistrust of multiple-use agencies by conservationists, as well as a strong desire to restrict hunting, mining, and logging. On the other hand, many local interests resent interference and restriction of economic flexibility by outsiders who may only come to Alaska for occasional brief visits. Whatever the outcome, the BLM will have less land in Alaska under its administration. Agencies with more manpower and funds will have some of the responsibility. This may allow the BLM to offer more protection against fire, insects, and disease on the land it does retain. It may also provide for more planning and management of recreation resources that still are underutilized.

Literature Cited

Council on Environmental Quality. 1977. Environmental quality—1977; the Eighth Annual Report of the Council on Environmental Quality. Washington, D.C. 445 pp.

Federal-State Land Use Planning Commission for Alaska. 1977. "The D-2 Book": Lands of National Interest in Alaska. Anchorage. 213 pp.

KNICKERBOCKER, BRAD. 1978. Ecology showdown for "last frontier." The Christian Science Monitor (Dec. 2).

SENZEL, IRVING. 1978. Genesis of a law, part I. American Forests 84(1):30–32, 61–64.

National Forests

In 1910, an employee of the U.S. Forest Service took a look at the national forest system in terms of the various values produced. Treadwell Cleveland, Jr., (1910) concluded that recreation alone was reason enough to manage most of the forest:

So great is the value of national forest area for recreation, and so certain is this value to increase with the growth of the country and the shrinkage of the wilderness, that even if the forest resources of wood and water were not to be required by the civilization of the future, many of the forests ought to certainly be preserved, in the interest of national health and well-being, for recreation use alone.

FIGURE 18.1   Backcountry camping in the national forests became popular following World War I. (HCRS)

FIGURE 18.2 The National Forest System. (USFS)

Mr. Cleveland's conclusion was written at a time when the national forests had just been established in the West and just before a law was passed to allow land purchase for them in the East. It was a time before outdoor recreation had become a major national concern and before the West was heavily populated. Even then, recreational use of the national forests was popular.

National forests are managed for multiple benefits, including timber, water, wildlife, grazing, and recreation. By almost any measure, recreation is the leading use of most of the forests at this time. Yet, the management function is to blend the uses, giving consideration to all of them.

Oregon Congressman James Weaver, chairman of the House Subcommittee of Forests, in 1977, pointed to a need to more intensively manage

FIGURE 18.3 Special biological areas are preserved by the Forest Service, including the ancient bristlecone pine stand forests of the Inyo National Forest on the border of Nevada and California. Some of the trees are estimated to be 4,000 years old. (USFS)

all values of the forests. He claimed that high-level yields of all renewable forest resources are possible, including esthetics, fish and wildlife, forage, outdoor recreation, timber, water, and wilderness (Weaver, 1977). That is the challenge for the forest manager on the multiple-use lands of the national forests—how to get more out of them to meet the fast-growing demands for wood, for high-quality water, for continued grazing rights on overgrazed lands, for wildlife, for wilderness preservation, and for many other forms of outdoor recreation. The water, wildlife, wilderness, and recreation values are all part of the people's leisure-time use of the forests.

People are coming to the forests in ever-increasing numbers (Figure 18.1). They are still discovering the national forests, even though the public already spends more recreation time on them than on any other type of federal land. The 205 million visitor days estimated for 1977 was more than twice the amount calculated for the national parks and 34 times that of the national wildlife refuges.

The national forests and national grasslands should be able to handle this kind of use and more. They contain tremendous amounts of land— almost 76 million hectares (187 million acres) of forests, grasslands, and alpine lands (Figure 18.2). That is several times the land base of the national park system or the wildlife refuges. Most of the Forest Service lands, featuring mountains, trees, streams and lakes, are scenically attractive to American recreationists.

The long-standing policy of the Forest Service to encourage outdoor recreation has produced a network of campgrounds, picnic areas, and wilderness preserves. Logging activities have left many roads and trails, which provide excellent access for hikers, hunters, fishermen, and ORV riders, as well as those just out for a Sunday drive on the improved roads. The forests contain numerous ski resorts, the nation's longest hiking trail system, a large proportion of the big game and fisheries resources, as well as outstanding scenery (Figure 18.3).

Facilities

The United States Forest Service offers a tremendous array of recreational opportunities and resources. Among these are the following:

100,000 miles of hiking trails.
15,000 miles of marked snowmobile trails.
54 per cent of the nation's vertical transport feet of ski lifts, numbering 674 installations.
225 winter sports sites.
The vast majority of the National Wilderness Preservation System.
81,000 miles of fishing streams.
Two million acres of lakes.
One third of the big game animals in the nation.

4,700 campgrounds with capacity to handle more than 400,000 persons at one time.

1,500 picnic grounds.

500 interpretive sites, 38 of which are major visitor centers or museums.

1,800 recreational residence special-use areas, with an average of 10 cabins per site.

Seven National Recreation Areas.

Driving for pleasure is a highly popular activity, and the Forest Service provides ample opportunity. The national forests contain nearly 400,000 km (247,000 mi) of agency roads, in addition to state and federal highways. There are 16,000 km (10,000 miles) of paved roads, 88,000 km (55,000 mi) of rock and gravel roads, 133,000 km (83,000 mi) of maintained dirt roads, and more than 158,000 km (99,000 mi) of what the agency calls primitive condition roads, popular with users of four-wheel-drive vehicles and trail bikes.

In addition, the unrestricted nature of national forests allows freedom to enjoy almost any legal recreational activity that does not damage the resource or disrupt other visitors or residents. Camping, picnicking, and other activities are possible virtually anywhere on a national forest. (Figure

FIGURE 18.4   The highest peak in northeastern United States, Mt. Washington, elevation 1,917 m (6,288 feet), is part of the White Mountain National Forest, New Hampshire. (USFS)

FIGURE 18.5 Nantahala National Forest, North Carolina. (USFS)

18.4). Such dispersed use was the early pattern, before campgrounds were developed to concentrate people, thereby reducing fire hazard, sanitation and cleanup costs, and a sort of recreational homesteading of prime sites by certain individuals. Now, there is increasing use of dispersed areas for these activities, and the Forest Service is encouraging it (Figure 18.5). Greater public care with fire and use of gas stoves produces less danger. On three National Forests in the Northwest, 622 undesignated, undeveloped sites show evidence of camping or other recreational activity, along 316 miles of road. A high degree of impact from repeated use was evident on less than 20 per cent of the sites (Hendee, Hogans, and Koch, 1976).

The dispersed use emphasis on national forests brings with it several management problems. Because most remote areas are not developed or designated, there is little chance to reinforce areas where heavy use will occur. Parking areas along roads may be graveled to help direct hunter and hiker use. However, other heavily used areas experience soil and vegetation impacts, leaving alternately dusty and muddy campsites. Trails become eroded, accelerating siltation of creeks and ponds and impairing fish production.

Recreation Places

Recreational Use of the National Forests

Recreational use of the national forests was estimated at almost 205 million visitor days (12 visitor hours) in 1977. The majority of this was in dispersed area use, with 131 million visitor days of use. Developed areas such as campgrounds, picnic areas, beaches, visitor centers, ski areas, and resorts hosted 74 million visitor days. Of the dispersed area use, about eight million

TABLE 18.1   Number of recreation visitor days for outdoor recreation activities in national forests, 1977 (thousands).

Activity	Total	Developed	Dispersed
Land-based:			
Bicycling	423	9	414
Camping	56,527	39,632	16,896
Motor biking	4,687	5	4,682
Hiking[1]	10,258	201	10,057
Horse riding	2,884	27	2,856
Hunting	14,517	19	14,499
Nature study	1,240	189	1,051
Picnicking	8,317	6,012	2,305
Pleasure walking	1,335	120	1,215
Sightseeing[2]	50,326	4,457	45,869
Other[3]	15,934	12,733	3,201
Total	166,448	63,404	103,045
Water-based:			
Canoeing	1,007	181	826
Sailing	214	47	167
Other watercraft[4]	4,719	1,148	3,571
Fishing	16,029	465	15,564
Swimming	4,422	1,869	2,553
Water skiing	803	48	755
Total	27,194	3,758	23,436
Snow- and Ice-based:			
Cross-country skiing	537	—	—
Downhill skiing	6,004	6,004	537
Ice skating	236	91	146
Sledding	62	61	0
Ice and snowcraft	3,038	91	2,947
Snowplay	1,277	368	908
Total	11,154	6,615	4,538
Grand Total	204,796	73,777	131,019

[1] Includes mountain climbing.
[2] Includes viewing outstanding scenery; auto driving and motoring; aerial trams and lifts; viewing works of man; Visitor Information Service.
[3] Includes spectator sports and activities; aircraft; team sports; games; other accommodations; gathering forest products; acquiring general knowledge and understanding.
[4] Includes ship, yacht, and ferry; powered boats.
Source: U.S. Forest Service (1979).

visitor days occurred in wilderness and designated primitive areas (not including RARE II roadless areas). Participation estimates in various activities are detailed in Table 18.1.

About one fourth of all the recreational use of national forests is in California (Figure 18.6). The large population in close proximity to forest lands (three forests surround the Los Angeles area) is partly responsible. Colorado and Oregon each account for 8 to 9 per cent of the use, followed by Washington, 6 plus per cent; Arizona, 6 per cent; and Utah, 5 plus per cent. National forests in these six states receive three fifths of the system's recreational use, even though there are national forests and grasslands in 41 states plus Puerto Rico (McGuire, 1977).

FIGURE 18.6 Big-trees *(Sequoia gigantea)* are protected in several national forests in California's Sierra Nevada, as well as in three national parks. (NPS)

Recreation Places

The national forests have long been managed for many uses, including recreation. Recreation has grown in the national forests at a rate and timing parallel to its relative importance among the general populace. The Forest Service started out to manage timber but soon found itself also managing for recreation, water, wildlife, and livestock grazing. The blending of uses came quickly, naturally, and with few difficulties. It gradually evolved into Congressional policy through the 1960 Multiple Use Sustained Yield Act.

Recreational use of national forests was recognized early in history. In 1891 Benjamin Harrison established the first forest reserve, the Yellowstone Timberland Reserve, now parts of the Shoshone and Teton National Forests. Eight years later Congress passed the first law officially recognizing and allowing recreational use of national forests. The 1899 law permitted the leasing of sites for sanitariums, hotels, and cottages near mineral and medicinal springs for health and pleasure.

National forests were first established by presidential proclamation. President Harrison took the initiative, designating 5.3 million ha (13 million acres) as forest reserves. His actions were based on a congressional act (26 Stat. 1103) giving him power to establish forest reserves from the public domain.

Grover Cleveland set up 10 million ha (nearly 25 million acres) more in reserves. Using the same law, Theodore Roosevelt transferred scores of millions of acres from the undesignated public domain into forests. Meanwhile, in 1902, the Congress chose to establish the Minnesota Forest Reserve, the first not set up by presidential decree. The Congress put a lid on Roosevelt's enthusiasm in 1907 by requiring Acts of Congress to create reserves in most western states.

In 1905, the Forest Service was established, and the forest reserves were transferred from the Department of the Interior to the new agency in the Department of Agriculture, under the leadership of Gifford Pinchot. In 1907, the lands became National Forests.

Roosevelt's presidency (1901–09) added a net of 53.4 million ha (132 million acres) to the National Forest system.

Eastern national forests came into being as a result of the Weeks Law of 1911, which established the policy of federal purchase of forest lands to protect the flow of navigable rivers. Most of the eastern national forests were acquired under authority of that act.

In 1915, the Term Lease Law authorized the Forest Service to issue term permits for summer homes, hotels, stores, and other structures for recreation or public convenience. This legalized a situation inherited by Pinchot's Forest Service in 1905; summer cabins and hotels already existed (Pinchot, 1947). Later, the agency did not encourage summer leases and restricted the areas where they could be offered, because of demands by the public for other, less exclusive, uses. Nevertheless, by 1973, there were

18,000 private recreation residences on Forest Service lands (U.S. Forest Service, 1973).

An upstart agency, the National Park Service, drew the attention of tourists and politicians in 1916. It had a wealthy, flamboyant director named Stephen Mather who led excursions through the parks and captured the public fancy.

This alerted the Forest Service further to the political punch of recreational use. Frank A. Waugh was commissioned in 1917 to study the potential of recreation on the forests. The landscape architect recommended that sightseeing, camping, and hiking should be considered equally with commodity products as uses of the forest.

Within the next year or so, Arthur Carhart became the first full-time recreation employee hired by the Forest Service. The young landscape architect from Iowa State University was assigned to District II, where he and community leaders developed a recreation plan for the San Isabel and Pike National Forests in Colorado. Then he tackled the White River (Colorado), Bighorn (Wyoming), and Superior (Minnesota) forests.

Carhart and his immediate superiors found some resistance to funding recreation, at times expressing their frustration in letters to the Washington office.* Gradually, interest developed in the agency hierarchy and in the Congress. A big spurt in use after World War I came from veterans who were accustomed to outdoor life and equipped with cars. The Congress first appropriated money for campgrounds in 1922, based on the value of developing such sites to reduce the hazards from campfires and garbage scattered throughout the forest in isolated campsites (McCall and McCall, 1977).

Steady growth of roads and the popularity of automobiles brought doubling and tripling of use of facilities through the 1920s. Even with the Depression, it was evident that forest recreation was a permanent part of the American way of life.

CIVILIAN CONSERVATION CORPS

Between 1933 and 1942, an army of Civilian Conservation Corps (CCC) workers did some remarkable things in the forests and parks of the nation. The 2,500 CCC camps and 500,000 men planted nearly a billion trees on eroded or silted-in land. They fought fires, improved ranges, and built recreation facilities that still stand as some of the most attractive structures in the forests. Elaborate networks of hiking trails and many campgrounds and picnic areas were built. They also repaired erosion scars along rivers and improved wildlife habitat. Out of the economic failure of the Depression came environmental improvements with a lasting effect.

* Many of the letters are collected in the Conservation Library of the Denver Public Library.

At the 1924 National Conference on Outdoor Recreation, H. H. Chapman (1924), professor of forest management at Yale University, said the following:

Forests have three primary uses; the first of these is for parks and recreation, the second for protection of watersheds, the third for the production of crops of timber to supply wood products for consumption. It is possible for the same forest area to serve all three of these functions at the same time. But for the forest on any one specific area or location to serve each of these three utilities simultaneously and with equal effectiveness is difficult and sometimes impossible.

. . . a sharp conflict has been waged for decades between advocates of the forest as a park or for recreation and those who would serve the public by supplying the innumerable demands of wood users. The cause . . . lies in the popular misconception that . . . there is no middle ground.

Chapman's three uses evolved into five major uses, recognized in the 1960 Multiple Use Act. Then, in 1964, Wilderness was added as a major legal responsibility, so some refer to it as the sixth resource (Figure 18.7). It is difficult to separate wilderness from recreation, water, wildlife, and forage, because all of these are products of areas designated as wilderness. Timber is the only product that cannot be removed. Manipulations of vegetation or streams are also restricted.

The 1960 Multiple Use Sustained Yield Act (Public Law 86–517) states

. . . it is the policy of the Congress that the national forests are established and shall be administered for outdoor recreation, range, timber, watershed, and wildlife and fish purposes . . .

'Multiple use means: The management of all the various renewable surface resources of the national forests so that they are utilized in the combination that will best meet the needs of the American people; making the most judicious use of the land for some or all of these resources . . . ; that some land will be used for less than all of the resources; and harmonious and coordinated management of the various resources, each with the other, without impairment of the productivity of the land, with consideration being given to the relative values of the various resources, and not necessarily the combination of uses that will give the greatest dollar return or the greatest unit output.

Two other major pieces of legislation have affected national forest management in recent years—The Forest and Rangeland Renewable Resources Planning Act (RPA) of 1974 and the National Forest Management Act (NFMA) of 1976. RPA established a process for periodically assessing the nation's public and private forest and rangeland renewable resources. It requires development of a Forest Service long-range program to help ensure the supply of these resources and the maintenance of a quality environment. The National Forest Management Act requires standards and guidelines to be developed for resource planning within the national forest system.

FIGURE 18.7 Near Phoenix, wilderness opportunities are available to a large population at a low cost in the arid Superstition Wilderness Area. (USFS)

The NFMA also ensures that public participation will be an integral part of management for the national forest system.

The first RPA report was submitted in 1975 (U.S. Forest Service, 1975). It recommended increasing the supply of recreation opportunities and services. Emphasis was to be on dispersed recreation, as opposed to concentrated, developed sites. Although developed sites would be maintained, the national forests have a unique opportunity to offer increased dispersed opportunities, whereas private and state agencies can offer more concentrated uses. The 1980 RPA (U.S. Forest Service, 1979) maintains the primacy of dispersed recreation.

Administrative Organization

In administering the national forests, the U.S. Forest Service has maintained a model of efficient operation within a complex, far-flung agency.

One key is that the chain of command has been kept short. Staff specialists aid in day-to-day operations, while line officers make key policy decisions.

The Forest Service is an agency of the Department of Agriculture. Its chief reports to the Secretary of Agriculture. He has always been appointed from among professional ranks.

The line officers are Chief, Regional Foresters, Forest Supervisors, and District Rangers. These four key levels are the line of communication from field operations to the top of the national policy ladder. Each officer has a specific territory that is his responsibility. Each has a staff with functional specialties. Authority is delegated and there are regular reporting and other control systems (U.S. Forest Service, 1970).

Forest Service Functions

The functions of the Forest Service are through three major activities: national forest management; research; and state and private forestry cooperation.

The Forest Service functions in outdoor recreation in these three principal ways: land management, research and information, and cooperation.

LAND MANAGEMENT

The land management function is the most commonly known. The agency is responsible for planning and managing the national forests and grasslands, comprising nearly 76 million hectares (187 million acres). Management is directed toward producing outdoor recreation facilities and opportunities of great diversity, in a quality forest environment, in conjunction with the production of other goods and services from the forests.

Among the many specific policies that govern the agency, the following help describe the goals of the Forest Service in recreation (U.S. Forest Service, 1978a).

Provide recreation opportunities within the national forest units of the wilderness system without impairing the basic resource.

Develop and maintain a system of road access and rights-of-way that provide a mixture of scenic and recreation opportunities.

Maintain trail uses for all—including the handicapped.

Give special emphasis to the protection and management of areas and trails that have been given special designation—such as National Recreation Areas, Wilderness, Wild and Scenic Rivers, and National Scenic and Recreation Trails.

Limit regulations, constraints, and supervision of recreation use to the minimum necessary for resource protection, visitor satisfaction, and safety.

Work with state wildlife departments to ensure sustained and diversified fish and wildlife populations to enhance recreation experiences.

Integrate landscape management techniques into all forest management activities to attain the best visual quality commensurate with cost and other needed land uses.

Utilize environmental education, visitor information, facility location, and site design to reduce user conflicts and resource damage.

Emphasize Visitor Information Service (VIS) activities.

Develop new and utilize existing simple, permanent organization camps through special use permits on national forest lands, to be used to bring people to the forest recreation resources and to provide bases for environmental education.

Direct Forest Service funded recreation development primarily toward those activities that are not potential profit-earning ventures for the private sector.

Where concessionaire operation is in the public interest, but profit potential is inadequate, government funds may be used to develop supporting facilities, such as access, boat ramps, and parking lots.

RESEARCH AND INFORMATION

The Forest Service maintains eight forest experiment stations throughout the United States plus the Institute of Tropical Forestry in Puerto Rico and the Forest Products Laboratory. In the recreation area, special interests have developed in the different stations. Considerable work has been done on wilderness use and management in the Minnesota and Utah units. On the West Coast, a series of studies on methods of blending timber harvesting with scenic values has provided guidelines for design of harvesting systems. Numerous studies on visitor behavior, resource impacts, and interpretation have advanced knowledge of recreation phenomena.

In addition to its research function, the agency has a separate information and education division and a Visitor Information Service, which provide support for national forest management activities.

COOPERATION

The Forest Service offers cooperation with private interests, local, and state governments through its branch of State and Private Forestry. The principal effort of this branch is related to funding and coordinating the work of state agencies that hire foresters in the Cooperative Forest Management program. States and federal governments share in the funding of these individuals who are assigned to assist private landowners in forest management. Most of this effort has been geared to timber management, but as landowners increasingly hold their properties for recreational and wildlife values, the field foresters are called upon for technical advice about managing the forest for these purposes as well.

The openness and cooperative attitude of the Forest Service is truly remarkable, as compared to similar agencies in some other nations. It is official policy to share knowledge, resources, and capabilities with public and private sectors. It works.

Effects of Recreation Use on Other Resources

A concern often expressed is that wilderness designation will cause distress to the timber market. That may be true locally for some firms, but there is only a small effect nationally. The national forests contain about 18 per cent of the nation's productive timberland plus many acres of reserved lands, noncommercial timber, grasslands, and alpine areas. Of the national harvest of timber, the volume that comes off of national forests amounts to almost 16 per cent (U.S. Forest Service, 1978b). About one fourth of this volume on national forests was under study in 1978 for possible designation as wilderness, although only a minority of the study land will reach wilderness status.

Expansion of other recreation uses would have minimal impacts on grazing, timber, watershed, and wildlife areas.

The area dedicated to developed recreation facilities and intensive use is less than one per cent of the total national forest area. It could be increased several-fold without making a significant impact on other resources.

The direct effects of recreation developments do not offer serious impacts on the timber supply. Wilderness designation cuts into some of it. Delays in wilderness study have frozen timber harvest activities on millions of other areas. The most dramatic effect, however, has been related to what the visiting public sees as abuse of the forest through timber management practices. The indirect, public opinion effect has been powerful.

TIMBER AND RECREATION

Recently a professional forester managing a national forest prescribed a clearcut in West Virginia. The prescription was not unusual. Since the early 1960s, the Forest Service had followed a policy of using clearcuts to improve forest quality. Most of the eastern national forests were in extremely poor condition when purchased. The trees presently being harvested are those that helped the land recover. The trees are the species that grew on poor sites. Most are not the species or genetic quality that should be left to regenerate the future high-quality forest. To improve both quality and species composition, then, it is seen as prudent to remove both the salable timber and the other trees of a quality that the loggers cannot use. The clearcut gives plenty of sunlight and growing room to valuable species such as tulip–poplars, cherries, walnuts, ashes, and white oaks.

Many visitors to the forest have objected to the practice of clearcutting, regardless of the good it is supposed to do. They believe that it is unsightly and some seem to fear that it is destructive of the forest soil and ruinous to the environment, despite reassurances to the contrary. Some even contend, in the face of most wildlife knowledge to the contrary, that the wildlife is destroyed.

Several citizen organizations took umbrage at the West Virginia clearcut. They like their forest beautiful, not cut over. They sued to prevent further clearcutting. They argued a point of law—in the 1897 Forest Service organic act there was a phrase stating that harvested trees must be large, mature, and marked individually. The citizens temporarily stopped clearcutting on the Monongahela National Forest and all the other national forests of the immediate vicinity when a federal judge agreed with them. The judge did not argue the merits of the silvicultural practices of clearcutting versus selective cutting. He merely read the law and suggested that it would have to be revised if clearcutting were to be continued. Similar challenges were temporarily successful in Texas and Alaska. Forest appreciators intervened in the management process through the courts. They were successful until the Congress reviewed the whole process and came up with a new law (1976 National Forest Management Act), which removed the 1897 prohibition on clearcutting.

This was a case of practice and science outstripping the law. Or maybe it was a case of ignoring the need to keep the law up to date, until a crisis arose.

It was also a case of the Forest Service being rather insistent on a practice that was at variance with the objectives of some of the forest owners who were unhappy. The owners were strong enough in their point of view that they threatened to severely reduce timber harvests across the entire nation. The Congress, representing all aspects of public opinion, finally made a decision to allow clearcutting. But Congress has also made many decisions that favor keeping certain tracts of forest in uncut, natural condition. The decisions continue to affect timber management. The Forest Service, a multiple-use agency, faces many demands from many interest groups. Its decisions must reflect sensitivity to the owners' desires.

Summary

Because of the size and the attractiveness of its holdings, the Forest Service has long been an important factor in the recreation supply system.

It has popular and high-quality developed facilities, as well as extensive backcountry areas. The Forest Service provides most of the wilderness areas in the nation.

Management for multiple products and services requires that the Forest Service consider all values in its planning. Theoretically, that produces an optimum blend of uses over large areas of forest. The growth of recreational use since 1920 has caused the Forest Service to consider recreation as a major endeavor, not an incidental by-product. Recreational visitors have strongly affected timber management policy.

Recreation policy first emphasized unstructured, dispersed use. Then, to control fires and pollution, campgrounds and picnic areas were designed to concentrate use. Now, realizing it can offer nearly unfettered recreational experiences on large areas, the agency is again emphasizing dispersed use.

Literature Cited

CHAPMAN, H. H. 1924. Compatibility of recreational uses with forest management. In: Proceedings, National Conference on Outdoor Recreation. 68th Congress, 1st Session, Senate Document No. 151, pp. 144–147.

CLEVELAND, TREADWELL, JR. 1910. National forests as recreation grounds. Annals of the American Academy of Political and Social Science 35(2):25–31.

HENDEE, J. C., M. L. HOGANS, and RUSSELL KOCH. 1976. Dispersed Recreation on Three Forest Road Systems in Washington and Oregon: First-year Data. U.S. Forest Service, PNW Publication No. 280. 20 pp.

MCCALL, JOSEPH R. and VIRGINIA N. MCCALL. 1977. Outdoor Recreation; Forest, Park, and Wilderness. Beverly Hills: Bruce. 358 pp.

MCGUIRE, JOHN R. 1977. Report of the Chief; Forest Service 1976. Washington, D.C.: U.S. Dept. of Agriculture. 36 pp.

National Conference on Outdoor Recreation. 1924. Proceedings (May 22, 23, 24). Washington, D.C.: Senate Document No. 151. 244 pp.

PINCHOT, GIFFORD. 1947. Breaking New Ground. New York: Harcourt, Brace and Co. 522 pp.

U.S. Forest Service. 1970. Organization and Management Systems in the Forest Service. Washington, D.C.: U.S. Dept. of Agriculture, No. FS-35. 79 pp.

U.S. Forest Service. 1973. National Forest Vacations. Washington, D.C.: U.S. Dept. of Agriculture, PA-1037. 54 pp.

U.S. Forest Service. 1975. RPA Summary (Draft); a Summary of the Program and Assessment for the Nation's Renewable Resources. Washington, D.C.: U.S. Dept. of Agriculture. 127 pp.

U.S. Forest Service. 1978a. The Forest Service Roles in Outdoor Recreation. Washington, D.C.: U.S. Dept. of Agriculture, Program Aid 1205. 13 pp.

U.S. Forest Service. 1978b. Draft Environmental Statement; Roadless Area Review and Evaluation. Washington, D.C.: U.S. Dept. of Agriculture.

U.S. Forest Service. 1979. The 1980 RPA Assessment. Washington, D. C.: U.S. Dept. of Agriculture.

WEAVER, JIM. 1977. A larger equation for forestry. American Forests 83(11):28–29, 45–46.

CHAPTER 19

The Reservoir Managers

More recreationists visit large flood control reservoirs than go to national parks. Reservoirs receive more individual visits than the national forests, but the total visitor days are fewer.

There are 49,500 dams in the United States, according to Corps of Engineers tallies (HCRS, 1978a). The few big ones are built under the direction of the U.S. Army Corps of Engineers, the Bureau of Reclamation, and the Tennessee Valley Authority.

Many of the medium-sized structures were planned with the help of the Soil Conservation Service (Figure 19.1). Most are small dams built by individuals and local governments.

About $10 billion is spent each year for federal water projects. Forty per cent goes to the water development agencies—Soil Conservation Service, Corps of Engineers, Bureau of Reclamation, and Tennessee Valley Authority. With few exceptions, water development refers to building structures, dredging, diverting, or draining water in ways that markedly alter natural watercourses and bodies. Much of this has provided new recreational resources of great significance.

The other $6 billion spent on water resources goes to 20 other agencies and cooperating local and state agencies. The largest programs are administered by the Environmental Protection Agency for water quality management and municipal waste water treatment.

Many small impoundments are used to supply municipal water. These are popular for recreation in much of the nation (Figure 19.2). In the Northeast, there is a reluctance to allow recreation on reservoirs, based on long tradition. The idea of people frolicking in the drinking water keeps many reservoirs closed, even though the water is treated later.

In the United States, there are about 22 million acres of still and running water accessible and usable for recreational purposes. This is only 23 per cent of the surface water; the rest is not useful for recreation because of inaccessibility, pollution, or other problems (HCRS, 1978b).

The Federal Water Project Recreation Act of 1965 recognized the reality of recreation benefits at reservoirs. It established procedures for considering the recreation, fish, and wildlife benefits and costs on Corps

FIGURE 19.1   On this small watershed project is a campground and boat launching area on a 57-ha (142-acre) lake in Orange County, Indiana. (Soil Conservation Service).

of Engineers and Bureau of Reclamation multipurpose water resource projects. Small reclamation projects, small watershed projects, and Tennessee Valley Authority projects were specifically exempted.

For years, large reservoirs had been used for recreation, including fishing and hunting. At some such lakes, the recreation benefits were primary. However, the constructing agencies had not been allowed to calculate the benefits from recreation or fish and wildlife when determining the values of appropriate developments for the project. The 1965 act provided that:

1. Full consideration shall be given to recreation and fish and wildlife enhancement as purposes in federal water resource projects, but not to exceed 50 per cent of the benefits or costs of such a multi-purpose project.
2. Planning of the recreational potential of the project is to be coordinated with existing and planned federal, state, and local public recreation developments.
3. Nonfederal administration is to be encouraged for the recreation

FIGURE 19.2   Municipal water supply reservoirs as in Prescott, Arizona, have long been used in many western states. In northeastern states, tradition has retarded acceptance of recreation on water supply reservoirs. (USFS)

and fish and wildlife enhancement features of most federal water projects.

In order for the recreation benefits to be counted in the project proposal, the nonfederal public bodies indicate in writing, before authorization of the project by the Congress, that they agree to administer project land and water areas for recreation, fish, and wildlife. They also agree to bear no less than one half of the separable costs of construction for recreation, fish, and wildlife and to bear all the costs of management, maintenance, and replacement.

This law was something of a mixed blessing to the two large reservoir agencies. The law recognized the benefits of recreation, which helps the justification of new projects by adding considerable value to the benefit side of the cost-benefit analysis. The additional costs are relatively small. On the other hand, the provision requiring state or local cooperation gives a veto power to local groups. This veto power has been used on occasion, as when the governor of Indiana announced that the state had withdrawn support for three projects in 1977. Even though the legislature had previously supported the projects in a formal resolution, the governor's retraction, reinforced by the legislature, effectively killed the construction, at least during his period in office.

Recreation Places

Legal Bases

WATERWAYS

The power of the United States to regulate commerce has been held to include power over navigation.[1] The Congress has the power to keep the navigable waters of the United States open and free and to legislate to forbid or license dams.

Navigable waters have been defined to include rivers presently being used or suitable for navigation; rivers that have been used or were suitable for use in the past; or rivers suitable for use in the future by reasonable improvements.[2]

Control for navigation is only one of the powers over water. Flood protection, watershed development, and power improvements are likewise considered parts of commerce control. For example, state laws cannot prevent the Federal Power Commission from issuing a license to build a dam on a navigable stream, because the stream is under the domain of the United States. Likewise, the flow of a navigable stream is not private property in any sense. Exclusion of riparian owners from the benefits of such a navigable stream, even without compensation, is entirely within the federal government's discretion.

The Constitution of the United States (Art. I, Sec. 8) gives the Congress the power to regulate commerce with foreign nations, among the several states, and with Indian tribes. The Secretary of the Army and the Secretary of Transportation (U.S. Coast Guard) have primary responsibility in exercising this power. The Secretary of the Army is involved because he is required by law to prescribe regulations on all matters not specifically delegated by law to some other department.[3] The Coast Guard is required to enforce all applicable federal laws upon waters subject to the jurisdiction of the United States, including promoting safety and providing aids to navigation and rescue on United States waters.

There are a host of regulations concerning navigable waterways, many of which might conceivably affect recreation activities and structures. These range from Coast Guard review of plans for bridges, new and old, to Corps of Engineers assistance for prevention of erosion of shores. They are best reviewed in summaries such as that by the Great Lakes Basin Commission (1975).

FLOOD CONTROL STRUCTURES

The Department of the Army has authority to study and construct for flood control needs. All surveys relating to flood control must include a comprehensive study of the watershed above the area flooded.

---

[1] *Gibbons* v. *Ogden*, 22 U.S. (9 Wheat.) 1, 189 (1824).
[2] *Rochester Gas and Electric Corp.* v. *Federal Power Commission*, 344 F. 2d 594, cert. den. 382 U.S. 832 (1965).
[3] 33 U.S.C. 3.

To have federal money spent on construction of local projects, the states and other interests must ensure that they will provide land, easements, and rights-of-way, hold the United States free from damages caused by construction works, and maintain and operate the works according to regulations issued by the Secretary of the Army. Construction of any water resources project shall not be initiated until each nonfederal interest has entered into a written agreement with the Secretary of the Army to furnish its required cooperation for the project.

The Secretary of Agriculture also has broad authority and responsibility for flood protection on watersheds smaller than 250,000 acres. He can authorize work on single structures smaller than 12,500 acre-feet of flood retention or projects that do not exceed 25,000 acre-feet capacity in a multistructure project. This work is done through the Soil Conservation Service under the Watershed Protection and Flood Prevention Act (Public Law 83–566). The Soil Conservation Service works as an investigator of the feasibility of these plans and as planner, cost analyst, and agent for agreements and financial assistance to local organizations. The local groups are usually state–authorized agencies, called soil conservation districts. They are made up of landowners in a subdivision of the state—usually a county—who can cooperatively approve and finance small watershed projects.

There are several other agencies involved in flood-related federal programs. The Small Business Administration can provide loans to aid small businesses that are affected by floods or other catastrophes. The Secretary of Housing and Urban Development administers the National Flood Insurance Program, in cooperation with the private insurance industry. Rate-making studies are aided by the Corps of Engineers, Soil Conservation Service, U.S. Geological Survey, the Environmental Science Services Administration, and the Tennessee Valley Authority. Federal flood insurance covers only losses caused by floods, defined as a temporary condition of partial or complete inundation of normally dry land areas from the overflow of inland or tidal waters, or the unusual and rapid accumulation of runoff or surface water from any source.

In most flood-prone areas, the most efficient attack on flooding problems is through nonstructural means. The focus is on land uses that are compatible with periodic inundation. The idea of keeping a floodplain for floods is economical and sensible, although it goes against the history of urban development. Most cities are built on or near floodplains. The approach of keeping most construction out of floodplains is institutionalized in many states and in community zoning regulations. This is reinforced by the National Flood Insurance Act of 1968 (Public Law 90–448). For states to be eligible for federal flood insurance, they must regulate land use in flood-prone areas. The law, supported by Executive Order 11988 in May, 1977, put new emphasis on land use regulation and policies as an approach to reducing flood damages.

Tennessee Valley Authority

In the valley of the Tennessee River, the hollows have been filled with water. The residents have no shortage of lakes.

The Tennessee Valley Authority (TVA) was established in 1933 as an experiment in governmental business. President Franklin D. Roosevelt proposed it as a corporation clothed with the power of government but possessed of the flexibility and initiative of a private enterprise.

Along the Tennessee River and its tributaries, a series of dams was built to control floods and generate hydroelectric power. The corporation was also given the duties of conserving the natural resources and improving economic and social conditions in the valley. Amidst controversy, it has done this, but it has never become totally self-sustaining. Tax money has supplemented the incomes from the sale of electric power and fertilizers. Dams were built to reduce floods and to generate electricity. Today, flood-plain zoning and steam-generated power have taken over. Recreation and navigation are now the key values of the lakes.

The recreation role of TVA had developed around the reservoirs and in the vast reforestation projects. The Tennessee River is now a series of pools, backed up by large dams (Figure 19.3). In the valleys of neighboring rivers, the Corps of Engineers also built large impoundments.

Three aspects of the recreation program are 1) operation of reservoir access facilities such as boat launch areas, marinas, campgrounds, and scenic

FIGURE 19.3   The Tennessee Valley Authority operates in seven states.

overlooks; 2) encouragement of private, local, and state recreation developments in the valley; and 3) the Land Between the Lakes recreation demonstration project. Forestry, fish, and wildlife efforts have made the area more attractive for recreation. More than 500,000 ha (1,200,000 acres) have been planted to trees, halting erosion and reducing fire, and wildlife and fish populations have increased tremendously.

TVA FACILITIES

TVA's own recreation developments provide access and basic services near reservoirs. Because one of the objectives of the agency is to improve economic and social conditions, it walks a narrow line between competition with private recreation operations and providing basic public access. There is continual examination of the question of whether campgrounds should be maintained by the agency and whether or not there should be a fee attached. Most were free in 1978. The agency was discussing the options of charging use fees, turning campground operations over to concessionaires, or continuing free use with stricter management. Informal camping at undeveloped sites has caused management problems in cleanup, safety, and resource protection. Closing such areas is a somewhat delicate matter when people have been using them for many years.

WILD AREAS

Small Wild Areas is the designation that TVA gives to lands set aside for nature preservation. In 1977, there were 17 of these preserves, seven of which were open to the public. They varied in size from 12 to 300 acres. TVA limits development to trails, parking lots, and signs. The areas preserve such natural features as waterfalls, caves, ravines, scenic views, and interesting plant life (Forestry, Fisheries and Wildlife Development Division, 1977).

RECREATION STIMULATION

Some demonstration boat docks and parks have led local, state, and private interests to provide more than 100 parks, 300 boat docks and resorts, 100 group camps and club sites, and about 400 lake access areas. Hundreds of millions of dollars have been invested by private and public interests in recreational development and equipment. The TVA staff has given technical and limited financial assistance.

Fishing has become a major sport in the area, drawing visitors from throughout the nation. Commercial fishermen take thousands of tons of rough fish such as catfish and carp, helping to maintain the quality of the sports fishery. The lakes also created new waterfowl resources. Large flocks of ducks and geese winter here. State wildlife management agencies supervise considerable shoreline area as refuges and management areas.

LAND BETWEEN THE LAKES

A multiple-use recreation area runs along a 40-mile ridge in western Tennessee and Kentucky. It started in 1964. It serves the nation as an experimental and demonstration area. Land Between the Lakes has 69,000 ha (170,000 acres) with 480 km of shoreline.

The property is near the mouth of the Tennessee River. It lies between TVA's Kentucky Lake, built in 1944, on the Tennessee River, and the Cumberland River's Lake Barkley, dammed in 1965 by the Corps of Engineers. The ridge, now federal land, was once used for marginal agriculture, grazing, and backwoods corn processing.

Most of the land has been planted to trees. The timber-producing potential of the area is low, so forest management techniques are geared toward wildlife and recreation enhancement (Figure 19.4). Wildlife food

FIGURE 19.4 TVA's wildlife division actively develops diversity in habitats at Land Between the Lakes. (HCRS)

and cover plantings dot the landscape. About 20 per cent of the area is kept open or cleared of scrub trees for scenic vistas, browsing ground for deer, and habitat for quail, songbirds, and small wildlife. Some timber from the elimination of large cull trees and pulpwood is harvested annually. This multiple-use management is intended to demonstrate integrated resource planning around recreation values, this being appropriate for much of the eastern United States and, especially, many areas upstream in the Tennessee Valley.

The outstanding recreation resource is the 480-km shoreline. Most of the recreation facilities are water-oriented, including the five large campgrounds and two group camps.

Because the reservoirs fluctuate in elevation, two stable lakes were dammed in small areas. Along the shore, it was necessary to eliminate the potential breeding habitat for anopheles mosquitoes. Beaches and access roads were built. Today, the area offers outstanding recreational variety.

Four state parks and a national cemetery are nearby. Several private and public marinas across the lakes offer services. The Land Between the Lakes is a huge area, long influenced by man but returning to natural conditions. Each year, it looks healthier and more natural.

Trails throughout the property vary from old, obscure traces to paved nature trails suitable for wheelchairs. The first interstate trail is a National Recreation Trail.

Off-road vehicle riders have a campground and free run of the Turkey Bay ORV area. Any means of ground travel seems to be provided for in this place. Horse trails and a long scenic auto tour are among the many opportunities.

An outstanding conservation education facility offers youth and adult programs. The 1,800-ha (4,500-acre) area on Lake Barkley has activity stations and trails plus learning centers and a youth camp.

The staff has approached its job enthusiastically and seriously. They test various methods of campground layout and trail surfaces. They bring in all sorts of groups to experience the area. They work with researchers and educators to check their methods. Land Between the Lakes is an exciting experiment in land management focused on outdoor recreation.

Army Corps of Engineers

The Corps of Engineers manages the largest water resource recreation program in the United States. Recreation certainly was not at the top of the list of reasons that the Corps got involved in water projects; but now, in terms of operation and maintenance functions, it has become a predominant function. In the past 30 years, recreation at Corps reservoirs has grown from an incidental amenity to a major program that serves hundreds of millions of people each year.

The statistics are so large as to be meaningless—400 Corps lakes with more than 4 million ha (10 million acres) of land and water, stimulating in excess of $100 billion in economic activity (Morris, 1973).

The reality is in the weekend tides of people that the recreation resource manager sees rolling into the property, rushing for the boat ramps and campsites. The Corps' branch of recreation resource management is the on-the-ground team that handles the crowds and cares for the land around most of the reservoirs. Most are professionally trained foresters or recreation resource specialists. They employ student summer help to handle the gates, the beaches, and the cleanup work. During the year, the team improves wildlife habitat, renovates camping, boating and fishing facilities, conducts and plans interpretive programs, and manages the timber.

The Corps of Engineers' involvement in recreation has grown gradually. Only in recent years has it become a full-blown, positive program. A brief history outlines key accomplishments leading to recreation planning:

1775: George Washington established the Corps of Engineers as part of the Continental Army.

1824: Congress assigned first civil works function, to remove sandbars and snags from major navigable rivers.

1890: Planning comprehensively for river basin resource development was developed by Col. Hiram Chittenden (who was also an early superintendent of Yellowstone National Park).

1936: Nationwide federal flood control responsibility was given to the Corps.

1944: The Congress authorized recreation management in the 1944 Flood Control Act: "The Chief of Engineers . . . is authorized to construct, maintain, and operate public park and recreational facilities and reservoir areas under the control of the Secretary of the Army and to permit the construction, maintenance, and operation of such facilities."

1962: The method of calculating recreation benefits in reservoir projects was outlined in Senate Document No. 97.

1965: Recreation was formally given full partnership status as a reason for building reservoirs, through the Federal Water Projects Recreation Act of 1965. (Public Law 89–72). Up to 50 per cent of the benefits of a reservoir could be from recreation.

In some states, the Corps leases land and water to a state agency to manage as a state recreation area. The Corps controls the water level, any hydroelectric operation, and manages the area around the dams. The rest of the area is operated by the state agency for outdoor recreation. Developed facilities are usually constructed jointly.

Boat ramps, beaches, picnic areas, and campgrounds are the principal developed recreation facilities. The lake is heavily used for fishing, boating, water skiing, and swimming. The bulk of the surrounding land is managed for wildlife-based recreation (hunting and observation) and, to an increasing extent, for hiking and riding trails. Wildlife management efforts include planting cover and farming wildlife food crops. The latter is usually done on a share-cropping basis, specifying corn, sorghum, soybeans, clover, and small grains. The farmer leaves a portion of each crop, usually in several strips, as wildlife food for the winter. Fallow strips are often left in weeds for cover.

The Corps of Engineers, just as other recreation agencies, has been responding to recreational growth over which it has no control. It must react quickly to sometimes unexpected demands. Over time, major shifts in the agency's role in recreation has occurred.

Once thought of as providing access to water only, the agency has now become a major supplier of camping opportunities. Most campers are of the destination type rather than travelers. The campers use the place as headquarters for a variety of recreational activities. They make some use of water, but their other activities demonstrate the desirability of trails, hunting areas, nature study areas, outdoor game areas, beaches, and other facilities.

BEACH AND SHORE ASSISTANCE

Beach and shore erosion is a problem occurring around many of the Great Lakes and along the seacoast. It is a natural process, sometimes exacerbated by the building of piers, jetties, and other structures that disrupt the natural currents and winds. The Army Corps of Engineers administers assistance for the construction but not the maintenance of shore protection and beach restoration projects. These often amount to the placement of considerable sand or rock along the beach in replacement of materials washed away and in a manner to reduce continued washing. On federal lands, the program covers 100 per cent of costs. On state and local parks and beaches, up to 70 per cent of the costs are covered by federal funds for the protection of beaches, protective dunes, bluffs, and other natural features, not including permanent human habitation. For construction or other works to protect against erosion, the program provides up to 50 per cent federal share. Federal assistance can be extended to private shores if there is public benefit such as from public use or from the protection of nearby public property.

In addition, the Corps of Engineers can investigate, study, and construct projects for the prevention or mitigation of shore damages related to federal navigation works.[4]

4 33 U.S.C. 426.

Bureau of Reclamation

At the turn of the century, the West needed water. Settlement had progressed rapidly. There just was not enough arable land with water to support the burgeoning population. A little water on the dry soils did wonders in growing crops.

The Congress came to the rescue by passing the Reclamation Act of 1902. That empowered the Reclamation Service to build dams, irrigation canals, and hydroelectric facilities in 17 western states. It now has well over 400 dams and has delivered water and power to farms and cities to change the West. Some of these structures are tourist attractions. Hoover Dam, Glen Canyon Dam, and Grand Coulee Dam are known throughout

FIGURE 19.5   Recreation services in a remote marina are provided at Lake Powell (Glen Canyon Dam) through a private concessionaire of the National Park Service. (Bureau of Reclamation)

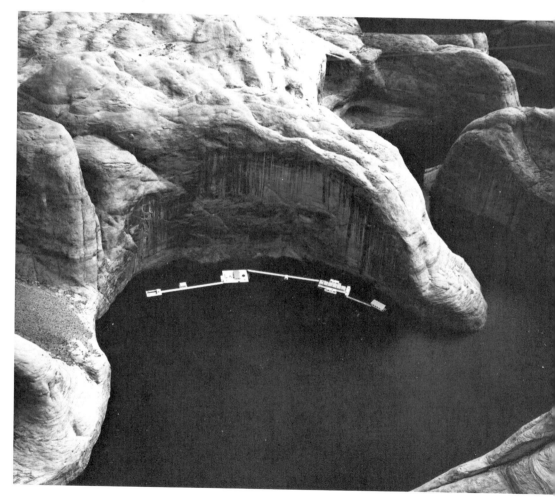

The Reservoir Managers

the nation. Most of the costs of these dams are eventually paid for by the users of the power and water produced.

The reservoirs are popular recreation sites, featuring boating, swimming, and fishing, of course. Float trips down the Green River and through the Grand Canyon are now regulated by the Bureau of Reclamation's water release from Flaming Gorge and Glen Canyon dams. The clear water of the Colorado as it flows through the canyon is a man-made phenomenon produced by the giant settling pond above Glen Canyon dam (Figure 19.5).

The Bureau of Reclamation has an important effect on recreation through its structures and through its planning of recreational facilities. But it assigns the management of recreational areas to other agencies, most notably the National Park Service and, sometimes, the Forest Service. Lake Mead National Recreation Area (Figure 19.6) is an example, with the park service handling visitors to the Reclamation lake.

This agency has done much to solidify public support for preservation of the natural environment. At the same time, it has produced some attrac-

FIGURE 19.6   Lake Mead marina includes a special dike and channel for low water access. (Bureau of Reclamation)

FIGURE 19.7   Camping sites accessible only by boat are features at some reservoir recreation areas such as Flaming Gorge in Utah. (Bureau of Reclamation)

FIGURE 19.8   Hetch-Hetchy Valley in Yosemite National Park as it appeared before flooding by a water supply reservoir for San Francisco. A long battle raged between John Muir's "preservation of scenery" philosophy and the "utilitarian" idea backed by Gifford Pinchot. (NPS)

The Reservoir Managers

FIGURE 19.9 Bighorn Canyon on the Montana-Wyoming border was dammed by the Bureau of Reclamation on the Crow Indian Reservation. (Bureau of Reclamation)

tive recreational lakes that have become quite popular with the public (Figure 19.7). In two cases where its ambitions were greater than the public would allow, it influenced public policy.

The first case started in 1950, when the Bureau of Reclamation revealed plans to place dams at Echo Park and Split Mountain in Dinosaur National Monument. These dams were part of the extensive Colorado River Storage Project, which helps supply electricity and water to Arizona and California. The Wilderness Society joined with other groups to protect the integrity of natural conditions in the national park system.

Many tools were used in this debate. The park groups used literature, films, and photographs to introduce people—particularly congressmen—to this little-known corner of Colorado and Utah. The pictures and arguments were featured in national magazines such as *Life*, the *Saturday Evening Post*, and *Reader's Digest*. They conducted float trips down the Yampa and Green Rivers to show first-hand the magnificence of the canyons that would have been flooded. Large sums of money from philanthropists supported the five-year struggle. Thousands of letters poured into Congress.

A half century earlier, the Sierra Club had gained some prominence for its losing role in the Hetch-Hetchy valley controversy in Yosemite National Park (Figure 19.8). Then, the need for water in the city of San Francisco was determined to be enough to justify the flooding of a beautiful valley within a national park. The preservation lobby in the Dinosaur National Monument case used before-and-after photographs of Hetch-Hetchy to convince legislators of the folly of flooding another national park area.

It was public reaction and the threat of encumbering the entire storage project that finally saw the deletion of the two dams, with a phrase stating, "that no dam or reservoir constructed under the authorization of the Act shall be within any National Park or Monument" (Nash, 1967).

This controversy brought about three important events. First, the value of wilderness, in opposition to more tangible resource values, was established in the highest legislative body of the land. Second, the Sierra Club moved out of the Pacific Coast region to become a national force. Third, the wilderness movement decided to take the offensive and to propose a positive wilderness bill after this exhausting defensive battle.

Parks and their rivers were not safe for long, however. The Bureau of Reclamation had long had its eye on the Grand Canyon as a lovely place for water storage. One dam was proposed for each of the national park system units—one in Grand Canyon National Park, one in Grand Canyon National Monument, and one upstream in Marble Canyon National Monument. The Sierra Club found that its best efforts were required to defeat this seemingly outrageous proposal. They used outings and float trips, books, exhibits, films, conferences, testimony before Congress, alternate bills, and advertisements in major newspapers to convince the public that one of the world's most famous natural wonders was not the place to dam the stream that was responsible for the canyon's beauty. The proposal was defeated and the three NPS units blended into Grand Canyon National Park, which provided even greater protection.

Outside of the national parks, the bureau continues to plan and build. The steepest and deepest and most picturesque canyons are usually the best places for efficient storage of water (Figure 19.9). Therefore, Lake Powell, "the jewel of the Colorado," is located in spectacular Glen Canyon.

FIGURE 19.10   At the present time, boaters can visit numerous areas of natural formations that are partly flooded but were visited by few people before construction of the reservoir at Glen Canyon. (Bureau of Reclamation)

Now a major tourist attraction and vacation spot, the unflooded canyon was scarcely known (Figure 19.10).

The struggle between groups eager to preserve places of natural beauty and the Bureau of Reclamation and the Army Corps of Engineers is a series of continuing battles.

Reservoirs and the Value Questions

Whenever a reservoir is built, adjustments occur. A high-use recreation area replaces a low-use creek bottom, with its farms, homes, timber, wildlife, and fish. Often, new timbered areas are started, wildlife enhancement procedures are initiated, and lake fish take the place of stream fish. New homes are built near the lake, and motorboats outnumber the fishermen who tramped the stream bank. Natural diversity and a free-flowing stream are replaced by a lake of flat water.

Reservoirs are not forever, though. Project life is indeterminate. The benefits calculated for more than 100 years for large reservoirs may not develop. The American experience with large reservoirs is relatively short. Some European impoundments have existed for several hundred years, but the slopes above them are forested and strictly controlled. Watersheds above many North American dams are plowed up every fall to bare their soils to the rain, wind, and snow for nine months. Construction and roads add their sediments to be carried down the stream and to spread out as they hit still water. Real estate and motorboats do not thrive near mud flats that form at the upper ends of reservoirs. The lake loses its power to hold back flood waters. The Corps of Engineers sometimes denies this, explaining that sediment-holding basins are built into the reservoirs, rather than attacking the problems of upstream sedimentation. In the long run, the reservoir has changed the landscape, which may be a cost that society deems worthy of paying. It is expensive and may be buying long-range problems. The generation since 1936 has made decisions to utilize most of the efficient dam sites in the nation. This generation of leaders has left few options to the next generation as to the appropriate use of those river valleys.

The current revolt against new dam projects reflects this concern. It appears that man has been on this continent for about 15,000 years. Yet, man makes decisions on a 30- to 50-year planning horizon. In 40 years, virtually irreversible commitments were made to impose serious, long-term alteration on many river valleys in the expectation of relatively short-term benefits. Such decisions are made in the name of progress and development; they have produced greater comfort, economic well-being, and recreation for some people.

The ultimate and unanswerable question—but one still worthy of consideration—is whether a future generation dependent on solar energy and nuclear energy will regard as wise the permanent alteration to produce hydroelectric power, to keep floods out of the floodplains some of the time, and to provide gasoline-powered recreation on flat water in place of pedestrian and canoe opportunities on flowing streams in natural valleys. The changes on TVA lakes suggest that benefits projected from 1935 were not valid by 1970. Good salesmanship is not always good foresight.

The arguments are not simple on either side, although they become oversimplified in expression. Progress is not bad, if we don't get too much of it. The call is for balance and long-range views. Economics and social welfare are often thought of in short planning horizons. Some claim that it is foolish to think beyond the next few years because there is no way to predict conditions in the future. If so, long-term environmental commitments of resources would seem unwise. The one responsibility is to provide environmental diversity that offers a healthy, productive resource base to coming generations, leaving them some options.

WEIGHING THE BENEFITS

In all new feasibility studies by the Army Corps of Engineers, the scientific, esthetic, and recreational values of impoundments are given consideration. Environmental impact statements are required for all major[5] projects by the Environmental Protection Agency (EPA). A weighing of benefit values against cost values is a key criterion that the Congress uses in deciding whether or not a project is worthy of appropriations. The values present problems.

Recreational, esthetic, scientific, and many of the impacts on biotic populations are intangible values. No dollar sign can be attributed to them directly. The cost-benefit equation necessarily becomes less reducible to purely monetary terms. Decision making then requires more judgment than is involved in formula responses. It also engenders more debate. Explanations are more difficult.

Because the Congress is heavily loaded with work and few local people can or will take the time to develop thorough bases for sound judgment, there is a constant attempt to quantify and simplify.

One means of measuring recreation benefits is by recreation expenditures. Presumably, the more that users of a new lake will spend on recreation, the greater are the benefits of the lake. Although money is no true measure of the value of recreational experiences, it at least indicates some of the sacrifice people are willing to undergo for them. The measure must include the impact of local equipment and supply purchases as well as entry, launching, and other fees at the reservoir. In addition, around new reservoirs, land values rise, new service businesses develop, bank activity increases, and the economic base of a community may change.

[5] The term *major* is undefined by the law. One regional office of EPA made unsuccessful attempts during 1971 to require formal impact statements for each timber sale made by the Forest Service.

The value added to the local community by such a project may be high. Some of the local people would be converted to boating, fishing, or hunting by a new local lake. There would be many, already converts, who would simply transfer their attentions to the local lake. They might actually spend less in the national economy, as a result of reduced travel time, even though their recreational satisfactions would be higher.

SUMMARY

Large reservoirs are built and managed by the Tennessee Valley Authority, the Corps of Engineers, and the Bureau of Reclamation. Smaller dams are often built with guidance from the Soil Conservation Service. Recreation is a principal use of virtually all of these reservoirs, even though most were built for other purposes. Municipal water and power supply impoundments are receiving increasing recreational use.

All recreation management responsibilities are contracted to other agencies by the Soil Conservation Service and the Bureau of Reclamation. TVA continues to manage small campgrounds and access areas, but private and public parks and forests offer numerous recreation opportunities close to the lakes. TVA also manages the large recreation demonstration area called Land Between the Lakes. The Corps of Engineers manages recreational areas around many of its projects but leases areas to states that cooperate in sharing recreation construction costs.

Reservoirs have made significant impacts on recreation use patterns. They have produced the anomaly of thousands of boats being pulled around the dry plains and deserts of Oklahoma and Arizona.

Reservoir construction plans have met increasing resistance from people interested in preserving natural streams and wild areas. The reservoir agencies and Congress face the difficult tasks of evaluating costs and benefits which range from construction estimates to esthetic values, plus no small amount of political strategy and sensitivity.

Literature Cited

Forestry, Fisheries, and Wildlife Development Division. 1977. TVA Small Wild Areas. Norris: Tennessee Valley Authority (brochure).

Great Lakes Basin Commission. 1975. Federal Laws, Policies, and Institutional Arrangements. Appendix F20 of Great Lakes Basin Framework Study. Ann Arbor, Michigan. 128 pp.

Heritage Conservation and Recreation Service. 1978a. Protection of Outdoor Recreation Values of Rivers; Task Force Report. Washington, D.C.: U.S. Dept. of the Interior. 13 pp. + appendix.

Heritage Conservation and Recreation Service. 1978b. Public Outdoor Recreation Benefits of Federal Water Resource Projects; Task Force Report. Washington, D.C.: U.S. Dept. of the Interior. 28 pp. + appendix.

MORRIS, J. W. 1973. Recreation surge. Water Spectrum 5(2):2–11.

NASH, RODERICK. 1967. Wilderness and the American mind. New Haven: Yale University Press. 256 pp.

Tools for Recreation Administration

Land Classification Systems

There are many ways to classify recreation resources. The advantages of the various approaches relate to the goals being pursued. Among the methods, at least five can be identified.

1. *Ownership or jurisdiction classes.* This approach was used in Section Two of this book, relating recreation offerings to the firms, individuals, or public agencies that own and manage them. This system does much to describe in a few words the goals and policies affecting the property.

2. *Designation classes.* Properties are called parks, forests, wildlife areas, nature preserves, memorials, recreation areas, parkways, trails, scenic rivers, lakes, or reservoirs. There are specific facility designations, such as wilderness, golf courses, country clubs, arboreta, ski areas, and camps that help define the character and features of the area. The most commonly understood classes are combinations of the jurisdiction and the designation, such as national forest, state park, and commercial campground, quickly describing the resource to people who have any familiarity with the resource system.

3. *Service area classification.* For people concerned primarily with planning, this classification approach refines the park and open spaces into size and service areas of public facilities, regardless of the agency managing it. It is used to define the character of supply and to point out the kinds of resources most needed. Variations of this approach have been used for years by the former National Recreation Association and the National Recreation and Park Association. A number of states and cities have adopted similar categories, referring to facilities in terms of whether they serve a neighborhood, community, or region, for example.

4. *Orientation classification.* This classification was described earlier. It defines management and policy purposes in rough groupings as to whether they are user-oriented, intermediate, or resource-oriented. This merely identifies management emphasis. It is most valuable in explaining the policies of an agency to interested visitors or in interagency discussions of proper roles for various resources.

5. *Resource classification.* Within a property, the land base can be classified into various resources related to its purpose and intensity of development. The six classes proposed by ORRRC (1962) are defined in the discussion that follows. The Forest Service has a different approach, the definition of which also follows.

The purpose of this chapter is to discuss some important classification systems so as to acquaint the reader with their purposes and uses. Each system has different advantages so there is no recommendation of one over another. It seems to be human nature to classify and to try to improve on the classification of others. Many variations of these methods will be encountered. Some people will feel strongly about a particular system and spend hours defending it. Classifications should be kept in perspective as *descriptive tools* that can be helpful in planning and management.

ORRRC Recreation Resource Classes

To guide recreational land planning and management, a set of six classes has been used by the Department of the Interior, most states, and local agencies. It was devised by the Outdoor Recreation Resources Review Commission. The classes are as follows:

Class I—High-density recreation areas.
Class II—General outdoor recreation areas.
Class III—Natural environment areas.
Class IV—Unique natural areas.
Class V—Primitive areas.
Class VI—Historic and cultural sites.

These six classes are defined and their characteristics described as follows:

I HIGH-DENSITY RECREATION AREAS
Intensively developed and managed for mass use.
Facilities: heavy investment concentrated in relatively small areas, many facilities usually present.
Use: exclusively for recreation: heavy peak load pressures (e.g., weekends).
Land use: often competes with residential construction and commercial uses, due to location near urban centers.
Examples: Beaches, boardwalks, swimming pools, highly-developed trailer camps, some mass-use picnic/game areas.

II GENERAL OUTDOOR RECREATION AREAS
Areas subject to substantial development for specific recreation uses.
Facilities: many, but usually fewer than in I—always some man-made facilities.

Use: This class accommodates the major share of all outdoor recreation day-use, weekends and vacations. Use is concentrated, but not as much as in I. Zoning may be needed.

Land use: competes with a wide variety of uses, due to locations in both urban and rural settings.

Examples: campsites, picnic areas, ski areas, resorts, coastal areas, hunting preserves.

III NATURAL ENVIRONMENT AREAS

Areas suitable for recreation in natural environments, intermediate between II and V.

Facilities: few and simple; user enjoys resources "as is" in an environment where man fends largely for himself; management emphasis is on the natural rather than the man-made. Access roads, trails, primitive camping areas, safety and fire provisions.

Use: generally dispersed, not concentrated; hunting, biking, fishing, canoeing, rustic camping, sight-seeing, snowmobiling, ORV use (family style).

Land use: often multiple use lands; largest class in acreage.

Examples: most national forest and BLM lands, buffers in National Parks. Most of state and county forests, fish and wildlife areas, most reservoirs.

IV UNIQUE NATURAL AREAS

Areas of outstanding scenic splendor, natural wonder, or scientific importance.

Facilities: few—acceptable only if they enhance protection of the natural feature.

Use: limited to observation and study in many cases. Management focuses on preservation of feature, not public demand.

Land use: areas often small, special; incompatible uses excluded.

Examples: Old Faithful geyser, Old Man of the Mountain, Bristlecone Pine area of Inyo National Forest, nature preserves.

V PRIMITIVE AREAS

Undisturbed roadless areas in a natural wild condition.

Facilities: none except trails, no structures, no machines.

Use: goal is to provide solitude from evidence of civilization; commercial uses prohibited except guide service; recreation facilities prohibited.

Use may be restricted in order to a) provide opportunity for solitude by user and b) preserve primitive conditions.

Land use: competes with several other wildland uses—timber production, grazing, power dam construction, mining. These uses and roads are generally excluded from primitive areas. (For reasons found acceptable by Congress, mining and grazing have been allowed to continue temporarily in some areas.)

Examples: Gila Wilderness Area; most of Rocky Mountain National Park; portions of Porcupine Mountain State Park, Michigan; Quetico-Superior Boundary Waters Canoe Area, Minn.-Ont.; Wood Buffalo National Park, Alberta.

VI   HISTORIC AND CULTURAL SITES

Sites of major historic or cultural significance, local, regional or national.

Facilities: emphasis is on restoration and preservation of the historic features; facilities usually relate to protection of features during visitor use and interpretation of the historical significance, providing suitable access.

Use: varies considerably, depending upon type and fragility of features; always appropriate to the historic feature. Overuse is prevented, not accommodated.

Land use: exclusive for appreciation of history and culture and associated recreation values of the site.

Examples: Mt. Vernon, Russell Cave (Ala.), Tippecanoe Battlefield.

This classification system is general in scope. It describes types of areas within a park or forest. Almost every park more than one hectare in size contains at least two of these land classes. Within any recreation property there may be specific subdivisions of one of the classes. For example, a Class I beach area may be zoned for beginning swimmers, another zone for advanced swimmers, another for divers, and yet another for rowboat launching and landing. In facility design and day-to-day operations, these activity zones are important. In general planning, system management, and policy making, the broader Class I is of greater relevance.

The classification system was first publicly proposed by ORRRC (1962). The Bureau of Outdoor Recreation reconsidered the system and adopted it officially. Many recreation plans used this system. It was endorsed by the Public Land Law Review Commission (1970) but not mentioned in the Nationwide Outdoor Recreation Plan (Bureau of Outdoor Recreation, 1973).

There is some debate as to the value of this classification system. Some individuals have difficulty with the rather broad definitions. They seem to seek precise categorization of every individual situation. Of course, any classification of immense resources into six simple classes is not designed

FIGURE 20.1   Mesa Verde National Park is one of the nation's most prominent historic and cultural sites, exhibiting the architecture and artifacts of a civilization that thrived throughout the Southwest in preColumbian times. (NPS)

Tools for Recreation Administration

as a precise tool. Although this classification scheme is sometimes ignored, viable alternatives are few.

Most campgrounds and picnic areas fall into Class II, but a few are so highly artificialized and well-equipped that they fall into Class I. Ski areas in general are in Class II, but some portions of them could be classed as I, if it were desirable to break down the area into tiny parts; other portions could be in Class III. When hair splitting gets out of hand, a decision must be made by judgement.

The first two classes are those in which the works of man and his presence in large numbers are evident. They are user-oriented facilities, featuring concentrated recreation. Classes IV, V, and VI are preservation classes in which the resource is of primary value (Figure 20.1). Use is allowed to the extent that the resource can withstand it. Class VI usually shows the works of man in past times and can often handle large numbers of visitors under controlled conditions. Classes IV and V often require restrictions on use to keep the resource in condition to provide the desired experience. Class III includes the vast majority of recreation land available in the nation. Most of it is multiple-use forests, range, or lakes open for dispersed recreational use. In Class III areas, the works of man occur mainly in the form of occasional logging, reforestation, reservoirs, temporary roads, and trails. Management of forest and range for timber, water production, grazing, and other values may be evident. Most of the land, however, does not show much evidence of manipulation except to the trained eye. It is here that great expansion of recreational opportunity exists. Some experienced western backpackers have learned that there is more opportunity for solitude in these nonwilderness areas of the national forests than in the well-known wilderness areas.

APPLICATION TO A NATIONAL PARK

The National Park Service has used land classification as a prerequisite for planning its properties. It is useful 1) to provide proper recognition and protection of park resources; 2) to plan for visitor enjoyment of values of the area; 3) as a basis for wilderness classification; and 4) as a basis for other judgments in the planning process.

The irreplaceable resources of the national park system are identified as Classes IV, V, and VI categories of lands. The distinctiveness of the natural and historical areas of the system are based on the existence of unique features (IV), primitive lands including wilderness (V), or historical and cultural values (VI). These are combined with Class III lands as buffer environments. Sufficient lands for the accommodation of visitors (Classes I and II) complete the complex that is a national park.

A specific example is shown in Figure 20.2, describing the classification of Zion National Park used in the master planning process (NPS, 1975). Study of the map indicates that the majority of the park is classed as primitive (V). Some or all of this may become legislative wilderness. Class

Tools for Recreation Administration

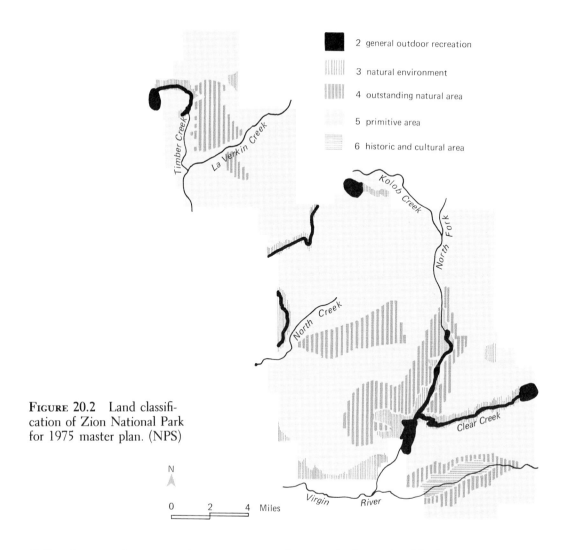

	2 general outdoor recreation
	3 natural environment
	4 outstanding natural area
	5 primitive area
	6 historic and cultural area

FIGURE 20.2 Land classification of Zion National Park for 1975 master plan. (NPS)

N

0   2   4 Miles

IV lands cover the spectacular canyon areas that are the key natural features of the park—a large area for Class IV. Class III lands are essentially the buffers for roads and trails, where roadside modifications must be made for safety and construction but near-natural conditions are maintained or restored. The ORRRC did not include roads in the system, but the NPS included roads as Class II. Class II areas are also the campgrounds, concession centers, and interpretive-administrative centers. A Class VI area is a pioneer Mormon valley settlement of historic interest.

Forest Service Experience Classes

The U.S. Forest Service uses a different classification system for some purposes. This system is interesting more for its own approach rather than as a substitute for the ORRRC classes. It is a type of development guide.

TABLE 20.1 Levels of experience in forest service recreation resources.

Environment modification	*Recreation experience*

1. Primitive

Minimum site modification. Improvements mostly for protection of the site, but rustic or rudimentary improvements may be provided for the comfort of the users. Use of synthetic materials avoided. Minimum controls are subtle. No obvious regimentation. Spacing informal and extended to minimize contacts with others. Motorized access is not provided or permitted.

Primitive forest environment is dominant. Rudimentary and isolated development sites beyond the sight or sound of inharmonious influences. Maximum opportunity for experiencing solitude, testing skills, and compensating for the routines of daily living. User senses no regimentation. Feeling of physical achievement in reaching site is important.

2. Secondary primitive

Little site modification. Improvements mostly for protection of the site but rustic or rudimentary improvements may be provided for the comfort of the users. Use of synthetic materials avoided. Minimum controls are subtle. Little obvious regimentation. Spacing informal and extended to minimize contacts with others. Motorized access provided or permitted. Primary access over primitive roads.

Near primitive forest environment. Outside influences present but minimized. Feeling of accomplishment associated with low-standard access is important but does not necessarily imply physical exercise to reach site. Opportunity for solitude and chance to test outdoor skills are present.

3. Intermediate

Site modification moderate. Facilities designed for both protection of site and comfort of user. Contemporary/rustic design of improvements is usually based on use of native materials. Inconspicuous vehicular traffic control usually provided. Roads may be hard-surfaced and trails formalized. Development density about three family units per acre. Primary access to site may be over high-standard, well-traveled roads. VIS (Visitor Information Service), if available, is informal and incidental.

Forest environment is essentially natural. Important that a degree of solitude is combined with some opportunity to socialize with others. Controls and regimentation provided for safety and well-being of user sufficiently obvious to afford a sense of security, but subtle enough to leave the taste of adventure.

4. Secondary modern

Site heavily modified. Some facilities designed strictly for comfort and convenience of users but luxury facilities not provided. Facility designs may tend toward and incorporate synthetic materials. Extensive use of artificial surfacing of roads and trails. Vehicular traffic controls present and usually obvious. Primary access usually over paved roads. Development density three to five family units per acre. Plant materials usually native. Visitor Information Services frequently available.

Forest environment is pleasing and attractive but not necessarily natural. Blending of opportunities for solitude and socializing with others. Testing of outdoor skills on site mostly limited to the camping activity. Many user comforts available. Contrast to daily living routines is moderate. Invites marked sense of security.

350

Table 20.1 continued.

Environment modification	Recreation experience
	5. Modern (urban)
High degree of site modification. Facilities, mostly designed for comfort and convenience of user, include flush toilets; may include showers, bathhouses, laundry facilities, and electrical hookups. Synthetic materials commonly used. Formal walks or surfaced trails. Regimentation of user is obvious. Access usually by high-speed highways. Development density five or more family units per acre. Plant materials may be foreign to the environment. Formal VIS services usually available. Designs formalized and architecture may be contemporary. Mowed lawns and clipped shrubs not unusual. (Class 5 sites only provided in special situations or close to large cities where other lands are not available.)	Pleasing environment attractive to the novice or highly gregarious camper. Opportunity to socialize with others very important. Satisfies urbanite's need for compensating experiences and relative solitude but less intensive than in class 1–4. Obvious to user that he or she is in secure situation where ample provision is made for personal comfort and the visitor will not be called upon to use undeveloped skills.

It deals with experience levels and the types of development offered. The levels run on a continuum from primitive experience with virtually no facilities to outdoor experiences with high security. The system is couched in terms that relate to the desires of the user. It has greatest relevance to Forest Service properties (Table 20.1).

Canada Land Inventory

There are seven land capability classes used in the Canadian recreation land inventory process. Land capabilities are differentiated strictly on the basis of the intensity of use or the quantity of recreation that it can supply. Class 1 is defined as lands that have high capability for outdoor recreation—one or more activities. Examples are large, outstanding bathing beaches and well-known ski slopes. Class 7 is defined as having very low capability for outdoor recreation; there may be some capability for specialized activities, or this class may provide open space. There are 25 subclasses that are related to landscape features. Examples are Subclass F, waterfall or rapids; Subclass O, land affording opportunity for viewing of upland wildlife; Subclass R, interesting rock formation. The capability classes are simple gradings from intense to light use capabilities. The subclasses are identifiers for features or characteristics of the area (Buhyoff, 1977).

This system is for simple reconnaissance surveys, valuable in identifying basic resource potentials. It has some similarities with reconnaissance approaches used by some agencies in the United States to inventory undeveloped lands.

Service Area Models

A descriptive model of types of parks and recreation areas is often used in local and state planning efforts (Figure 20.3). Its key elements define a principal area of service. This system is often used with space standards, such as that there should be five acres of community park for every 1,000 population in the community, or 10 acres of reservations and preserves for every 1,000 population. The classification (and the standards) must be interpreted flexibly for small communities.

The service area model used in the Indiana state planning process helps identify shortages of types of parks in various regions of the state. A slightly modified version of the park system model is described in Table 20.2. It ranges from large parks that serve the state or a region of it to miniparks that serve a block or small neighborhood. The district park might be typified

FIGURE 20.3 This prototype of various types of recreation resources illustrates the service area model. (from Indiana DNR)

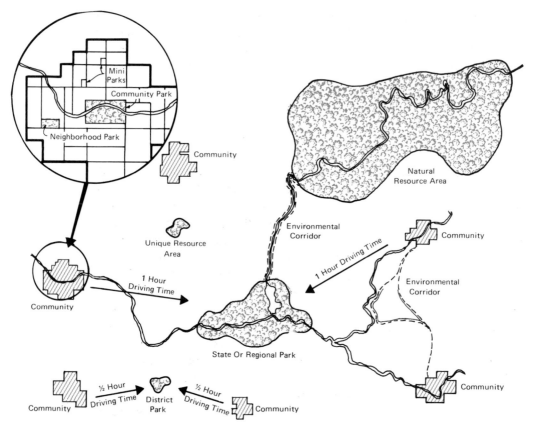

Tools for Recreation Administration

as a large county park. The community park would usually be the major city park(s). Other smaller municipal or county parks would serve neighborhoods. The optimum sizes are not rigid, but ideals; the parks that fall in these classes have wide ranges in size. Because of the mixture of size, service area, and character of the parks, it is difficult to fit many parks into the categories without stretching the definitions.

There are three classes that fall outside of the usual sequence and are treated as special areas. They are natural resource areas—the bulk of the recreation estate in public forests, fish and wildlife areas, and some reservoirs; unique resource areas such as historical sites and nature preserves; and environmental corridors such as trails, scenic rivers, and scenic drives. Although this system is usually applied to public parks, it can just as well include private and volunteer agency facilities, with some adjustments.

Dallas, Texas, provides an example of a similar park system classification (Doell and Twardzik, 1973). It includes playlots, playgrounds (neighborhood parks), playfields, large parks (more than 100 acres), parkways-ornamental areas-special parks, reservations-preserves, and regional recreation areas. This sytem is somewhat simpler than the Indiana classification, incorporating some of the special categories into broader classes. It does not include trails and rivers, but these could be fit into the parkway class.

Although there are many ways to classify recreation resources, none seems satisfactory for all situations. Thus, some variations will probably continue. Virtually all of them recognize a variety of recreation facilities ranging from tiny play or visual areas to large forests, refuges, and reservoirs. The park-type classifications are methods of describing what is already in place; therefore, they are somewhat imperfect. They can also be used to define what kinds of areas are desirable in the future, but there will be differences from the models. Local needs and agency policies will dictate the character of the resource and its facilities.

SUMMARY

Many recreation area classification systems are available for descriptive and planning purposes. None is perfect. All are general guides.

A once widely used system is the six-class approach recommended by ORRRC. It is fairly easy to understand, although there is some room for judgment. It classifies land *within* properties, so the resource manager can identify areas to guide development and management. The classification on a map can be very helpful in orienting new employees and informing the public of the management process. It helps systematize administrative policy.

Another popular classification is related to service areas of parks, identifying them as regional, district, community, or neighborhood. This approach allows a community, county, or state to get a quick grasp of the *kinds* of properties it has and what it may most need. Commercial and large natural resource areas can be added to obtain a more complete view.

TABLE 20.2   Elements of Indiana Recreation Model.

Element of system	Purpose	Character
State or regional park or recreational area	Preserve natural features and/or quality recreational opportunities in a natural environment	Outstanding scenic or historical areas; some are more for intensive recreational use
District park	Easy access, more intense activity, less extensive than regional park	Variety and openness, scenic views
Community park	activity-dominated, continued heavy use	Variety, high-use capacity
Neighborhood park	Facilities for all ages near home	High use and accessibility
Minipark	Protected for young in residence areas and space for adults in industry	Intensive use, unsupervised play; social interaction, quiet, passive
Natural resource area	Manage, conserve large natural resources	Forest multiple-use, wildlife habitat; hunting and fishing and related activity
Unique resource area	Protect and preserve historical or natural areas	Determined by feature to be protected and preserved
Environmental corridor	Provide lineal scenic corridors through and beyond populated areas	Variety and accessibility; easy movement

The use of recreation resource classification can be valuable to planners and managers to make their work more systematic, rational, and understood by superiors and the public.

Literature Cited

Buhyoff, Gregory J. 1977. Resource Based Recreation Planning; a Handbook in Projection Models and Inventory Systems. Blacksburg, Va. 93 pp.

TABLE 20.2   continued.

Undeveloped land	Service area	Opt. size	Facilities & activities
50–70%	60 min. driving time	approx. 2,000 acres	Picnic area, campground, golfing, winter sports, playfields, trails, nature study, food and lodging, water recreation
40–60%	½ hr. driving time	approx. 600 acres	Picnic area, campground, golfing, winter sports, playfields, trails: (hiking, bridle, vehicular, bike), nature study, water recreation
20–40%	15 min. driving time	approx. 200 acres	Picnicking, golf, winter sports, playground, playfields, trails: (hiking, bike, bridle), water recreation, nature study, community center
10–25%	5–15 min. walking time	approx. 25 acres	Playground, playfields, recreation building, swimming pool, picnic area
10–20%	5 min walking time	N/A	Playground, shelter, sitting area, small court area (horseshoes, shuffleboard)
approx. 95%	where resource occurs	approx. 4,000 + acres	Picnicking, camping, trails, water recreation, hunting, fish and wildlife
approx. 100%	N/A	1 mile or more	Hiking, observation and interpretation
All except access points & trails	varies		Camping, hiking, vehicular trails, bridle trails, bike trails, boating or canoe trails, launching ramps, nature study

Bureau of Outdoor Recreation. 1973. Outdoor Recreation; a Legacy for America. Washington, D.C.: U.S. Dept. of the Interior. 89 pp.

DOELL, CHARLES E. and LOUIS F. TWARDZIK. 1973. Elements of Park and Recreation Administration (third ed.). Minneapolis: Burgess Publishing Co. 332 pp.

National Park Service. 1975. Zion National Park; Draft Master Plan. Denver: No. NPS 804. 26 pp.

Outdoor Recreation Resources Review Commission. 1962. Outdoor Recreation for America. Washington, D.C. 246 pp.

Public Land Law Review Commission. 1970. One-third of the Nation's Land. Washington, D.C.

CHAPTER 21

Recreation Carrying Capacity

A foundation for recreation resource management is understanding of the principle of *carrying capacity*. Its use is for both planning and management in urban playgrounds and remote refuges.

In the mid-1960s, crowding of popular wilderness areas made wilderness management a problem for foresters (Snyder, 1966). Some wilderness areas were soon put on a restricted use basis.

In 1974, the Forest Service rationed use on the 10.7-mile Mount Whitney trail to only 75 persons per day. The number of hikers created problems on the trail to the high peak. It was not unusual to have more than 250 persons per day on this wilderness trail. Inadequate sanitation, loss of solitude, litter and waste along the trail, and destroyed vegetation were all signs of overuse or imprudent use of the existing facility.

Today, the backcountry of many forests and parks is restricted to a limited number of people. Most campgrounds have long been restricted as to the numbers of camping units allowed, after which the campgrounds are closed to further entrants.

Such restrictions are outgrowths of the use of the carrying capacity concept. The 1973 Nationwide Outdoor Recreation Plan (Bureau of Outdoor Recreation, 1973) called for identification of recreational carrying capacity for all federal land management units. It required management within those carrying capacity limits.

Impacts from Use

When people use an area for recreation, the area will suffer impacts. The vegetation will wear away, the soil will be compacted, erosion may develop, the brush will recede, and many of the trees will lose at least some of their vigor. If the area is used repeatedly for camping or picnicking, dust, mud, and need for sanitation facilities become serious problems. If use is over a whole forest, the wear may not be so evident, but fire danger and general littering are serious difficulties. So are water pollution and general appearance. Most of these impacts have been studied and recorded (Lutz,

FIGURE 21.1 Special construction measures are sometimes necessary for trail maintenance. Boardwalks across wet areas protect the resource from trampling and are convenient for hikers. (USFS)

FIGURE 21.2 Campground disturbance zones. (Adapted from McEwen and Tocher, 1976)

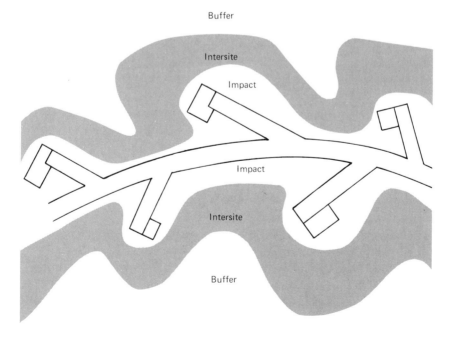

1945; Merriam et al., 1973; Helgath, 1975; Butler and Knudson, 1977). The recreation planner, to control this situation, uses several techniques:

Concentration of use in locales and channels.
Use of designated sites, trails, and barriers.
Reinforcement of ground surface with gravel, chips, walkways, and pavement (Figure 21.1).
Cultural techniques to aid growth of trees and grass, fertilizing, seeding, planting, and thinning.

A first step is recognition of areas of known impact (Cottrell, 1976). Three zones of differential impact in campgrounds can be identified (McEwen and Tocher, 1976). Figure 21.2 shows a heavy impact zone near parking spurs, a mildly disturbed intersite zone, and a buffer zone.

This chapter outlines the major factors related to carrying capacity, briefly describes applications of the concept, and lists a few of the measures that are used to detect and solve impact problems.

The Concept

Carrying capacity deals with the problems of site failure induced by use impacts. It is basic to the art of balancing use rates with resource resilience. It implies limits on the amount of use and abuse of any area. When limits are exceeded, site failure occurs.

Carrying capacity is the level of use a renewable resource can withstand and still remain productive. It is the highest level of yield that can be sustained over the long run. It might be described as the amount of use that a resource can take without its being used up. It is a long-range concept, in which the short-run actions must be considered in light of their long-term effect.

This is not a maximization concept, in the normal short-run view of maximization. It is an optimization problem in the short run, providing a constant use level which will produce maximum total returns over the long run.

A broad interpretation of carrying capacity states that it is the highest number of organisms (trees, cattle, people) that can live in an environment on a steady-state, renewable basis.

The concept is used in management of various resources. The idea of sustained yields of timber from forests rests upon the forester's ability to determine how much timber can be cut from a stand without impairing—in fact, while improving—future productivity of the area. His goal is to systematically harvest the timber in such a manner that the forest property will produce regular, sustained harvests of similar volumes of timber in perpetuity. Thus, timber harvest capacity is the amount of wood that can be removed from a forest without reducing the wood productivity of the forest in the future. This form of carrying capacity is often approximated roughly as *allowable cut* in a regulated forest.

Carrying capacity of a range is usually measured for livestock grazing. The basic environmental question is related to the productivity of the site in terms of the grass or browse mixture being grown. The grazing carrying capacity is a function of how much vegetable matter can be removed by grazing without reducing the yearly productivity of the range plants. For convenience of management, this rather cumbersome statistic is translated into the number of animal days that a portion of range can withstand year after year without declining. Grazing capacity is the maximum number of animals that can graze each year on a given area of range without inducing a downward trend in forage production, forage quality, or soil (Stoddard and Smith, 1955).

Translating this idea for recreation resource management brings in that often unpredictable element, the human user. This complicates things a bit, but the underlying idea remains of an optimal use level for maximum long-range benefits.

Many different phrases have been used to define recreational carrying capacity or recreation use capacity. They all relate to the upper limit of the number of people and the length of their use periods that a recreation site can absorb without losing its usability for the same kind and quality of recreation over time. More specifically, Chubb (1964) defined recreation use capacity as "the number of user-unit use-periods that the recreation site can provide each year without major, permanent biological or physical deterioration or appreciable impairment of the recreational experience."

The carrying capacity concept is never a complete, precise measure without problems. To determine a comprehensive carrying capacity, the manager must estimate optimal total effects of all viewpoints, to reach a highest value. That involves personal selection and weighting of criteria. Optimizing would be individual for each site (Bury, 1976).

Two variables that are difficult to predict are the following:

1. The variation in use rates and impacts from season to season, day to day, and hour to hour; the manager must decide whether he will manage and calculate for peak days or average days, rainy days, when impact on soils is greatest, or dry days.
2. The variation in site productivity from season to season, as affected by weather differences; in a year with good growing conditions, a site could handle more than an average impact. In a dry, hot year the site might suffer from use at an average carrying capacity level.

The manager must decide whether he should design and manage at 1) a conservative, low level and thus achieve underuse in even average years; 2) a medium level to achieve an overall averaging effect in the hope that poor growing years are not successive; or 3) a high level of use, sacrificing the resource on the assumption that either site management technology or recreation tastes will change so that altered conditions will be acceptable in the future. In the last case, carrying capacity will be violated as a norm for guiding management.

Factors Affecting Carrying Capacity

Carrying capacity is much discussed, but implementation of the concept has seldom developed beyond a seat-of-the-pants technique for outdoor recreation areas. Even the simpler timber and range management capacities are ultimately treated as rough estimates. Although the basic concept is easy to understand, putting it into practice as an exact measure is extremely difficult. The technique is often so rustic that the land manager can determine only that he has exceeded carrying capacity when the site begins to show signs of permanent deterioration. By then, it is often too late to alter designs and use habits, especially on public lands. This does not mean that the concept is useless. It is of great value as a guiding principle, even if quantification is imprecise.

The basic problem in developing a precise measure of recreational carrying capacity is the great number of factors that affect the number of recreation opportunities a site can provide on a sustained basis. To simplify the following discussion of such factors, they can be grouped into three major types:

1. Characteristics of the resource base: geology and soils, topography and aspect, vegetation, climate, water, fauna.
2. Characteristics of management: policy and management methods.
3. Characteristics of users: psychology, equipment, patterns of use.

CHARACTERISTICS OF THE RESOURCE BASE

The characteristics of the site can be analyzed into the following various elements of the environment. The site's deterioration is usually best indicated by negative changes in the vegetation on the site.

Geology and Soils: Vegetation in rich, fertile soil with evenly maintained moisture is far less sensitive to moderate use than plants that are barely able to support themselves in poor, gravelly soil. Good soil has high carrying capacity. Good soil and geology for various recreation uses are identified by several factors.

Drainage from the surface and through the soil must be adequate to keep the area reasonably dry during most of the recreational use season, yet not so rapid as to make the site droughty. Ponded and muddy sites have low carrying capacity during rainy periods because people will avoid them for picnicking, camping, and most other activities.

Soil must be on a suitable *texture* to reduce the effects of compaction and to allow vigorous vegetative growth. If it is too sandy, it is droughty; if too clayey, it ponds.

The *depth of soil* must be adequate for pit toilets, septic tanks or a sewage system.

Underlying rock must be suitable for the facilities being considered. A pond or reservoir built on porous limestone may have low recreational utility, if it holds water for only short periods after a rain. The slope of underlying rock may affect the direction of septic tank effluent flow more than will the slope of the surface soil. If the rock stratum slopes into a lake, the recreational carrying capacity of the lake for swimming, boating, and esthetics can be severely reduced by installation of septic tanks. Even trails have reduced capacity when constructed on sloping bedrock. In Taquamenon Falls State Park in Michigan, soil slippage from trails along a river gorge reduced their safety and utility.

Topography and Aspect: The terrain affects the capacity for many activities (Figure 21.3). Rough topography allows fewer campsites per acre than does smooth topography, assuming other factors are equal. The two principal reasons are that there is less usable ground, so the sites must be located only where the slope is suitable for camping, and the location of roads must follow the terrain and therefore occupy more space than on smoother ground.

The aspect of the slope of the land—the direction the slope faces—is important for some regions of the country. For example, in the southeastern United States, higher carrying capacity exists on slopes facing northeast, north, and east, because of their generally better soil fertility and cooler

FIGURE 21.3 Recreational carrying capacity of a nature preserve trail has been exceeded, producing severe erosion from the ridgetop.

temperatures. The same is true in the central Rocky Mountains, but the cooler temperatures may cut the useful season shorter, thus reducing carrying capacity for camping, picnicking, and other summer activities. Ski slopes that face the north and northeast receive less sun, so hold their snow longer and in better condition, resulting in higher annual carrying capacity.

Vegetation: Different types of vegetation have differing abilities to withstand use and abuse. As a general rule, narrow, leathery leaves, spiny plants, and grasses have relatively high resistance to direct impact. Some tree species respond negatively to recreation impact, whereas others are quite resistant.

Ripley (1962) did a preliminary study on recreation-related damages to tree species in the South. His results must be interpreted with care, because his criteria were incomplete and his evidence circumstantial rather than experimental. In general, he found that among trees in the South, hardwoods were more tolerant to heavy use than conifers. Although one would expect deeper-rooted trees to resist decline better than others, this was not a general pattern. There was no easily discernible pattern related to trees of similar site requirements. Of major species, Ripley listed the following in order of decreasing tolerance to heavy recreation use:

Hickory	Red oak
Sycamore	Black locust
White ash	Black cherry
Beech	Shortleaf pine
Yellow poplar	Hemlock
Red maple	White pine
White oak	Pitch pine
Black walnut	Virginia pine

Vegetation density is important to recreation carrying capacity. The natural vegetation growing in deep shade is often quite sparse and susceptible to damage. Camp and picnic sites under large trees can quickly lose their soft leaf or needle ground cover, becoming bare, eroded, or muddy. Soil compaction then reduces the vigor of the overhead canopy.

Tree shade and sod do not go together. A grassy campsite can be maintained under light shade, if shade-hardy grass species are selected. Often, a thinning of the trees will increase carrying capacity. In general, light tree cover produces a higher carrying capacity for the site than does a dense forest.

Vegetation is also a tool in providing special benefits to increase or sustain carrying capacity. Tree windbreaks on a beach or near a plains-state picnic area make them more useable; they may also help hold snow on a ski slope. Vegetation provides screens for privacy, shade for coolness, and cover for game.

Climate: A site may have deep, rich soil, suitable geological formations,

362

optimum topography, and resistant vegetation but still provide little recreation capacity. If the climate is unsuitable for recreation activities, the capacity may be zero. An obvious case would be snowmobiling in Florida.

The length of season affects carrying capacity. This is a function of latitude and altitude. The function is inversely related to summer activities—the higher the latitude or altitude, the lower the carrying capacity per year—and directly related to winter activities. This function relates to duration of use, not intensity.

Duration and frequency of use are also affected by rainfall patterns, fog, and storms. Mt. McKinley National Park has a low effective carrying capacity as a result of both a short length of season and frequent cloud cover that make its major attractions invisible and impossible to climb. Mt. Rainier National Park is often foggy, providing poor viewing for more than 50 per cent of the year. Hotel Paradise, located on the high, foggy slopes, went out of business as a private enterprise because of low visibility.

Rainfall affects carrying capacity at the other end of the scale, as well. Desert areas are quite fragile and vegetation quickly declines with recreational use. The season can be long, but unless people are dispersed over a large area and heavily used walkways are reinforced, a sand lot will replace the blooming desert.

Winter use is affected by snowfall. Carrying capacity for skiing and snowmobiling is a direct function of the amount of snowfall. Snow is the limiting factor for many enterprises; those on the southern or lower altitudinal edge of the snow belt live and die with the changing yearly snowfalls. In the summer, the number of rainy days and the duration of rains directly affect swimming, picnicking, and camping.

Rainfall is also closely related to reduction of carrying capacity. The most severe compaction and disturbance of surface soil usually occurs on rainy days.

Water: As a prime ingredient in the recreation mix, water bodies and streams must be considered in determining carrying capacity. Surface area and depth of lakes and streams are related to capacity for boating, canoeing, fishing, and water skiing. A polluted lake has a lower carrying capacity than one permitting full body contact.

Potable water must be available. Its quantity and quality for drinking, washing, and sewage may limit carrying capacity.

Ground water will directly affect the vigor and rusticity of vegetation of the area. Too much will increase compaction problems; too little or too uneven a supply will produce a droughty situation.

Thus, both as an attraction and as a support element, water is a critical factor affecting recreational carrying capacity.

Fauna: The presence or absence of wildlife and associated habitat directly affects carrying capacity for hunting, fishing, nature study, and sightseeing. The effect is related to the ability of the animal population to withstand depletion (bag limit) or disturbance, and to the attractiveness of the population to the public. The presence of poisonous or noxious fauna may reduce the overall capacity and attractiveness of an area. Scorpions, spiders, ticks, chiggers, and poisonous snakes indirectly affect the number of people an area can handle. Mosquitoes, gnats, and flies also can reduce the carrying capacity.

CHARACTERISTICS OF MANAGEMENT

The means by which a property is managed may increase or decrease its capacity to handle people. The policy and management practices may be imposed by law, by the philosophy of the responsible agency, or they may result from practical necessity. This is sometimes referred to as *institution capacity.*

Policy: Rules and regulations affect the number of recreationists that an area can serve on a sustained basis. State health laws and associated spacing standards are examples. In many states, campsites must be at least 50 by 50 feet. That allows about 15 campsites per acre. The policy of the Forest Service in the northeastern region is to design sites of 100 by 100 feet, allowing only three sites per acre. The type of camping experience to be provided dictates the number of people any area can accommodate. Wilderness camping, where solitude in a natural environment is planned, requires wide spacing for low densities. A social-oriented, trailer campground or a picnic area for large groups will be limited only by the durability of the facilities and health controls.

Certain campground associations, youth camps, and other groups help set carrying capacities by requiring members to comply with spacing standards.

Multiple-use land policies may place recreation in a secondary role, requiring that recreational use be low enough to allow normal timber growth. Most industrial lands are managed with this philosophy of setting recreational carrying capacity at a level compatible with high timber yield.

Management: Land management and engineering techniques can make a big difference in the carrying capacity of a site. Examples include the use of fertilizers, rotation of tables in picnic areas, and rest-recuperation of campgrounds. Hunting capacity may be increased by habitat manipulation such as timber cutting for deer, pond installation for ducks, flooding standing trees for fish. Swimming capacity of a deep, clear lake can be increased by adding beaches.

Design: The investment in design and the types of facilities chosen can affect carrying capacity. A swimming pool designed with a large deck can accommodate many more people than one with narrow decks. Scenic roads with large, well-designed lay-bys prevent traffic jams and aid viewing.

Reinforcement of impact areas can vastly increase carrying capacity in a specific place. The use of gravel or paving on roads, trails, picnic sites, and camp pads reduces erosion and allows pleasant use even when the soil is wet.

Simple design blunders often have reduced the recreational capacity of areas (Cottrell, 1976), such as allowing oil from parking lots to drain into a swimming lake; failing to reinforce areas of known impact; locating campsites in pristine, old-growth forests; and locating facilities improperly in relation to each other.

CHARACTERISTICS OF THE USERS

The third group of factors that affect the number of recreational opportunities a site can provide relates to the users. They are analyzed here in terms of psychology, equipment use, and social behavior. These factors help determine the type of amenity package and the quality of the environment that is most desired by the users. If the users are happy in an asphalt parking lot, carrying capacity per acre can be quite high. Those who seek a wilderness-type experience will impose a lower carrying capacity upon any site.

Psychology: Carrying capacity is partly dependent upon what the user considers as the desirable recreation experience. The planner or manager should be careful not to allow his own preferences to impair his objective analysis.

Many campers enjoy friendliness among people. They resent having to use sites "off in the woods somewhere." Camping is a social activity for many. Most trailer campers and boaters seem to like to be close together. In samples of campers, Reid (1963) and Taylor and Knudson (1972) reported that overcrowding was not a problem. Both studies showed that the most crowded areas produced high percentages of responses from campers who thought the areas had the right number of people. This was confirmed by other studies (Butler and Knudson, 1977).

The Wildland Research Center (1961) found that wilderness users have different preferences. A large majority (85 per cent) expressed a strong desire for the beauty of the *natural* scene. They were irritated by run-down, trampled, or artificial campsites. Isolation from other campers and large groups was the strong desire of 43 per cent. Thus, carrying capacity is generally different for wilderness users than for trailer campers.

Type of Equipment: Spatial needs vary with the equipment used. The larger the equipment, the lower the carrying capacity, other things being equal. Boats on trailers require twice the parking space of single cars. An increasing number of campers take up space of two and even three cars per unit. A pickup truck plus a trailer may disgorge a pair of motorbikes, a tent or two, plus a kitchen fly. All that is supposed to fit in a single-unit campground. With larger equipment, the number of units per acre is reduced drastically from the number needed to accommodate a small tent and a Volkswagen. The trend toward wheeled vehicle campers has changed either the carrying capacity or the type of experience offered in most existing campgrounds. A design that afforded tenters privacy and natural screening may today serve as a trailer city with little privacy and little visual screening. The capacity of the area remains the same, but the quality of the experience has changed.

Social Habits and Use Patterns. People's preferences and patterns of use strongly affect carrying capacity. For example, a highway-oriented campground is used mainly during the dark hours, with the visitors seldom spending more than one night. They may be little concerned about the naturalness or solitude of the area, but prefer convenience and ease of access. Carrying capacity may be quite high compared to a vacation-oriented campground, which seeks to hold people for a long time, offering a diversity of environments and some sense of privacy.

Boat fishing versus shore fishing likewise produces different carrying capacities for the same lake. Still hunting allows many more hunters on an area than stalk hunting, without a change in the danger to other hunters.

The relative attractiveness of a particular picnic site, viewing point, or campsite inversely affects its chances for recuperation. An area with equally desirable sites will have a higher carrying capacity than one with only a few highly attractive areas. In the latter, users will concentrate their impact on the few sites, making the useful life of the entire area shorter. The popular site deteriorates quickly, affecting the apparent carrying capacity of the whole area.

Such popular sites are usually related to distance from conveniences such as drinking water, toilets, roads, a fishing point, beach, or view.

The Consequence

The cost of increased use or congestion may be ecological deterioration of the recreational resource stock. If this happens, it may reduce both the quality of the recreation experience and the quantity of recreation that an area is able to provide. In effect, the stock of the resource has been reduced and the service flow from the resource has been diminished.

Knowledge of a site's ability to sustain use is necessary to avoid site failure. Site failure means that a particular property gives way or deteriorates irreversibly under the amount of use to which it is subjected. Site failure may be a result of either failing to choose a site adequate to the needs of the market—a planning failure—or failing to control utilization of the site to within its capabilities—a management failure.

The Limiting Factor Approach

All of the factors cited act in combination to determine the carrying capacity of a recreation area. One of them will be a limiting factor at a particular time. It will be the critical reason that an area cannot sustain more use, thus creating a ceiling of carrying capacity. If, by management, policy, or other changes, the limiting factor is removed, the ceiling will be raised to the next limiting factor, and carrying capacity will be increased. Successive removal of ceilings can raise carrying capacity to the point that further action becomes uneconomical, physically impossible, or otherwise impractical or undesirable. Once determined, however, it is the job of the administrator to control use so it will not exceed the capacity of the site.

Applications

Applying the concept of carrying capacity involves at least two processes: selecting new locations for new developments, and keeping tabs on existing sites and managing in response to the clues of potential site failure.

To select areas, the planner always looks at a variety of site factors. He seeks the optimal return from investment. If he has a choice between two or more sites of similar recreation potential, he can compare them on the basis of inherent carrying capacity. This comparison is based primarily on soil characteristics such as drainage, texture, and depth of profile; condition of the vegetation; and topography, as well as other factors previously mentioned. The planner should also seek special limiting factors and calculate the costs of overcoming them. The site that can offer the greatest productivity (carrying capacity) at the lowest cost in design, engineering, and hardening would be the most desirable.

To keep tabs on an already-developed site is the more common task. The manager watches for clues to future site failure. He should identify the factors that may be the most limiting and watch those most closely. When use exceeds the capacity, certain biological, physical, or social clues will become evident to the observant manager. Measured plots, transects, and photographs will aid the manager in year-to-year comparisons. The most sensitive indicator may be the ground vegetation on developed sites. By measuring the percentage of bare ground and the changes in plant species at the same time each year, the manager can determine whether or not there is a trend toward permanent deterioration. By analyzing his visitors, he may be able to detect changes in their attitudes. He may find that as a site deteriorates, old visitors disappear, to be replaced by others who are more tolerant of the conditions. However, on-site visitor opinion seems to be insensitive to even obvious rot in trees, bare ground, and crowding (Butler and Knudson, 1977).

When the manager detects permanent change that he deems to be undesirable, he has several recourses. He can do any of the following:

1. Restrict use, thereby reducing the impacts, and hope for recovery.
2. Eliminate use temporarily, allowing the site to recover (this method is highly overrated).
3. Use cultural methods to revive the resource (fertilize, seed, thin).

4. Change the design of the area to better reduce the impacts by channeling traffic more efficiently.
5. Make the sites artificial to a greater extent, so that people and vehicles have more opportunity to travel, sit and scuff on gravel, sand, or asphalt, thus reducing the impacts on surrounding natural elements.

Management Within Carrying Capacity

In administration and planning, control of the numbers of people is a key element. Only by controlling use can carrying capacity serve as an effective ceiling. The results of exceeding carrying capacity are not always evident immediately. Perhaps only after several years of overuse will a site show dramatic signs of deterioration. Then it is usually too late to replace soil and vegetation, and only at a very high cost can site rehabilitation be achieved.

To help control use, a number of devices are used. Hunting and fishing activities are controlled by laws and enforcement procedures that are based upon scientific knowledge of animal population dynamics. Limited seasons, bag limits, and licensing, coupled with strict enforcement prevent overtaxing both the game and the environment. For many species and some places, these forms of recreation are excluded altogether.

Beaches and picnic areas can be controlled by designing limited access and parking. Require parking in lots and make lots the size of the maximum number of visitors the area can support.

Campgrounds are frequently divided into lots or sites. Each site has a number and a designated, reinforced camping area, which define a rather clear territory per unit. In the absence of such designated sites, control by counting can be used. When the campground is filled to its carrying capacity, the gate should be closed to further use and campers turned away.

All areas are controlled somewhat by safety rules, such as for boats, beaches, and bridges. Zoning a lake or land area by type of use also aids in control. Hawaii's beach parks have a method of encouraging people to maintain the attractiveness of the properties; a $15 deposit is required of users, to be reimbursed if no damage or litter is left.

These and other management practices to minimize the effects of recreational use on the site should be based on a knowledge of an area's specific ecological conditions. There is much more research needed to establish guidelines and procedures for selection of campground and picnic sites so they can withstand heavy use with low-cost development and maintenance; management of native soil and vegetation to sustain vigorous growth and esthetic values; and improvement of vegetation and soil conditions where use has caused deterioration.

Specific types of actions to maintain site productivity for recreation areas have been recommended by various researchers. Those listed here should be considered general alternatives to be evaluated for any specific site.

Cultural Practices: Spread a thin layer of straw on bare spots immediately after a period of heavy use on the site. The straw imitates the natural condition of stems, catching wind-blown seed, and holding it against bare soil (LaPage, 1967).

Compacted soil may be loosened artificially by using a spading fork, harrow, or disk. Loosen only the upper soil layer to avoid damaging tree roots (Lutz, 1945).

In some cases, thinning the overstory will increase the resistance of trees and understory vegetation to abuse. Thin to protect the soil moisture values and to increase light to the ground cover, but do not reduce the amount of shade to intolerable levels for the visitors.

Amendments: Add organic matter to the soil to help maintain good physical and chemical conditions (Lutz, 1945). Where soil loss is severe, add new soil (Frissell and Duncan, 1965). Fertilize for vigorous ground cover.

Species Selection: Grow plants that are durable and can withstand heavy use (Magill, 1970). Use shrubs that do not produce good roasting sticks. Select sites with tree species that are vigorous and relatively resistant to use impacts.

Site Selection.   Establish recreation areas on soils that have good permeability, low erosion hazard, low compaction potential, and high organic matter content (Dotzenko, Papamichas, and Romine, 1967).

Rotation and Regulation: Close sites when establishing vegetation on them and every few years thereafter (Herrington and Beardsley, 1970). This procedure is one of the most recommended but often impossible because of economics and heavy use rates. Design the circulation system so sections of the campground or picnic area can be closed temporarily and the public diverted to new areas while the endangered areas are recovering for short periods (Lutz, 1945). This is possible during the week and in low-use parts of the year. Restrict the number of campers or picnickers to a certain level per season.

Reinforcement: Instead of planting new grass seed on an area, lay down sod with established turf (Cordell and Talhelm, 1969). Areas that will be intensively used can be paved or have sawdust, gravel, sand, or other materials spread over them.

Channel movements of visitors by using paths, elevated walkways, bridges, and artificial barriers such as posts, logs, rocks, fences, or guard rails; use natural barriers such as shrubs that are tough, brittle, thorny, and dense (Lime and Stankey, 1971, and Magill and Nord, 1963).

SUMMARY

The concept of recreational carrying capacity is based on the principle that there are limits to the number of visitors a given site can accommodate.

Beyond these rather elastic limits, the site deteriorates. Changes in design of site facilities, type of use, or management techniques may increase the carrying capacity.

Factors affecting the durability of a recreation site include characteristics of the site (geology, soils, topography, vegetation, climate, water, and fauna); management policy and practice; users, their equipment, and attitudes.

Administering the area to prevent site failure requires knowledge of these factors and the tools available to direct and govern use.

Carrying capacity is seldom reducible to a precise or a permanent number. It is a concept. It relates to resilience of a site, the kind of user, and the care by the manager. The concept is useful, as long as it is used in an elastic, dynamic manner. There *are* limits that nature imposes. Recreation productivity is subject to those limits. By understanding the limitations and how they can be ameliorated, recreation resource managers can efficiently provide quality recreational opportunities to visitors over long periods of time.

Literature Cited

Bureau of Outdoor Recreation. 1973. Outdoor Recreation; a Legacy for America. Washington, D.C.: U.S. Dept. of the Interior. 89 pp.

Bury, Richard L. 1976. Recreation carrying capacity—hypothesis or reality? Parks and Recreation 11(1):22–25, 56–58.

Butler, Elizabeth A. and Douglas M. Knudson. 1977. Recreation Carrying Capacity. Indianapolis, Ind.: Indiana Department of Natural Resources. 124 pp.

Chubb, Michael. 1964. Outdoor Recreation Land Capacity: Concepts, Usage, and Definitions. M.S. thesis, Michigan State University. 165 pp.

Cordell, H. K. and D. R. Talhelm. 1969. Planting Grass Appears Impractical for Improving Deteriorated Recreation Sites. U.S. Forest Service Research Paper SE 105.

Cottrell, Richard L. 1976. Site design for the future; lessons from the past. In: D. M. Knudson (ed.), Managing Recreation Resources for Century III. West Lafayette, Ind.: Purdue Univ. pp. 62–68.

Dotzenko, A. D., N. T. Papamichos and D. S. Romine. 1967. Effect of recreational use on soil and moisture conditions in Rocky Mountain National Park. Journal of Soil and Water Conservation 22(5):196–197.

Frissell, S. S., Jr. and D. P. Duncan. 1965. Campsite preference and deterioration. Journal of Forestry 63:256–260.

Herrington, R. B. and W. G. Beardsley. 1970. Improvement and Maintenance of Campground Vegetation in Central Idaho. U.S. Forest Service Research Paper INT 87. 9 pp.

Helgath, Shelia F. 1975. Trail Deterioration in the Selway-Bitterroot Wilderness. U.S. Forest Service Research Note INT-193.

LaPage, W. F. 1967. Some Observations on Campground Trampling and Groundcover Response. U.S. Forest Service Research Paper NE-68. 3 pp.

Lime, D. W. and G. H. Stankey. 1971. Carrying capacity: maintaining outdoor

recreation quality. In: Recreation Symposium Proceedings. Upper Darby, Pa:
U.S. Forest Service, Northeastern Forest Experiment Station, pp. 174–184.

LUTZ, H. J. 1945. Soil conditions of picnic grounds in public forest parks. Journal
of Forestry 43(2):121–127.

MAGILL, ARTHUR W. 1970. Five California campgrounds . . . conditions improve
after 5 years' recreational use. U.S. Forest Service Research Paper PSW-62.
18 pp.

MAGILL, ARTHUR W. and E. C. NORD. 1963. An evaluation of campground conditions and needs for research. U.S. Forest Service Research Note PSW-4. 8
pp.

McEWEN, DOUGLAS and S. ROSS TOCHER. 1976. Zone management: key to controlling recreational impact in developed campsites. Journal of Forestry 74(2):90–
93.

MERRIAM, L. C., JR. et al. 1973. Newly Developed Campsites in the Boundary
Waters Canoe Area: a study of five years' use. St. Paul, Minnesota: University
of Minnesota Agriculture Experiment Station, Bulletin 511. 27 pp.

REID, LESLIE M. 1963. Outdoor Recreation Preferences. Ann Arbor: Ph. D. thesis,
University of Michigan. 299 pp.

RIPLEY, THOMAS H. 1962. Tree and Shrub Response to Recreation Use. U.S.
Forest Service Research Note SE-171. 2 pp.

SNYDER, A. P. 1966. Wilderness management—a growing challenge. Journal of
Forestry 64(7):441–446.

STODDARD, LAURANCE A. and ARTHUR D. SMITH. 1955. Range Management. New
York: McGraw-Hill Book Co. 433 pp.

TAYLOR, CHARLES E. and DOUGLAS M. KNUDSON. 1972. The Camper in Indiana
State-operated Campgrounds. West Lafayette, Indiana: Purdue University
Agr. Exp. Sta., Research Bulletin No. 888. 11 pp.

Wildland Research Center. 1961. Wilderness and Recreation—A Report on Resources, Values and Problems. Berkeley: University of California, ORRRC
Study Report No. 3. 340 pp.

CHAPTER 2 2

Planning for Recreation

It is hoped, by studying the past and the present, planners can gather information that will help in planning for the future. Even when plans are carefully studied and well documented, they are but indications of what might happen. Robert Burns noted:

> The best laid schemes o'mice and men
>   Gang aft a-gley;
> An' lea'e us nought but grief and pain
>   For promis'd joy.

The gloomy realities need not deter the professional from trying. They do suggest that plans are mutable guides and nothing more.

Planning for land use and recreational development takes up a major portion of any professional's time. Today, there are more opportunities to prepare plans than there are to get the plans implemented, it seems. Too little of it is real planning.

Planning is a hallmark of a professional. The ability to gather and interpret meaningful data, project it into the future, identify problems, and bring a reasonable approach to solving problems on a sensible schedule with an affordable price tag is a characteristic much appreciated by an employer.

A planner suggests and analyzes courses of action but does not carry them out. The executor is the resource manager.

In North America, recreation planning has developed into some rather formal procedures and distinct types. Planning processes have developed in response to public and private funding programs that require certain types of planning efforts for eligibility to receive grants or loans. Each country has national planning efforts.

The Canadians have chosen to concentrate their national planning on the demand for outdoor recreation. The Canadian Outdoor Recreation Demand studies were an attempt to coordinate data gathering for the national studies and the provinces. There were four national surveys on participation between 1967 and 1972. There were two park user surveys and several other specialized surveys. In addition, the federal and provincial governments conducted facility inventories (Parks Canada, 1976).

From these, participation rates were calculated and used by individual public agencies to calculate future use possibilities. Projection of trend data suggested the recreation demand that may exist in the future. The information was based on 6,000 questionnaires the first time and fewer (because of funding limitations) on the second and third surveys. In an assessment of the Canadian program (Parks Canada, 1976), one principle was stressed as the key: "no survey should begin until one can be explicit about what the users expect to derive from it and how." That principle of spelling out objectives is the key to successful planning everywhere.

In the United States, there is a hierarchy of recreation plans. Comprehensive outdoor recreation plans are prepared at four levels:

1. Nationwide plan—sets out broad needs and policies, every five years.
2. State Comprehensive Recreation Plan—sets state goals based on supply and demand analysis, every three to five years.
3. Local—city, county, or other jurisdiction describing future park system five and 20 years ahead, renewed every five to ten years.
4. Project or site plans, which may be in several phases, each of which describes how a specific resource area is to be developed and used. On public areas, these would usually conform to requirements for Land and Water Conservation Fund eligibility.

The three levels of comprehensive plans are basically analyses and projections of supply and demand of outdoor recreation resources, with an estimation of needs for facilities to meet the future demand. Strategies or priorities for acquisition and development are often outlined.

Project or site plans are specific statements of policy, use, and development of individual parcels of land. They consist of graphic and narrative analyses of a property describing the facility, how it will be laid out, what the programming and maintenance will be, and how much it should cost.

In addition to the comprehensive and related site plans, each federal and state agency has its own system and property plans. Based on the Environmental Policy Act, any public project involving federal funds must carry with it an environmental impact assessment. The assessment suggests whether there will be major impacts that should be studied further through an environmental impact statement. In some cases, the rigorous requirements of these impact studies have guided the entire planning process.

Other layers of planning are called land use planning, area development plans, river basin comprehensive plans, and coastal zone management planning.

There also are special plans that affect federal lands such as Roadless Area Review Evaluations, the Public Land Law Review, and others.

A Fundamental Approach to Planning

There are certain elements to the recreation planning process that are common to many different approaches. These include the following:

Resource analysis—study the land base.
Visitor or potential user analysis—study the people.
Design of solutions, either as site plans, policies, or action plans—study the alternatives and their consequences.
Public participation and review—listen to the people with wisdom rather than emotion (Figure 22.1).

The planner who carefully develops these four basic elements will be able to adapt to virtually any of the numerous planning methods.

National Coordination and Planning

Efforts to coordinate recreation supply agencies and enterprises have been numerous but never very successful. The first major try at developing a coordinated recreation policy was in 1924, when President Calvin Coolidge called a National Conference on Outdoor Recreation. There were 128 public and private organizations that sent representatives. Study committees reported over the next four years. The final report (Senate Document No. 158, May, 1928) made strong recommendations that were partially ignored as the economic depression started.

Since then, administrative efforts to achieve greater coordination among federal agencies produced little except clarification of functions, communication, and recognition of the desirability of working together. No agency was given leadership responsibility for recreation. Eventually, the National Park Service developed the role of handling national analysis and planning, but without any financial or administrative teeth. It published some interesting descriptions of recreation resources in the nation (National Park Service, 1964). To study more comprehensive approaches, in 1958, President Eisenhower appointed the Outdoor Recreation Resources Review Commission (ORRRC).

Outdoor Recreation Resources Review Commission

The 1962 report of the Outdoor Recreation Resources Review Commission was the first comprehensive study of the nation's outdoor recreation, future demand, supply, and policy needs.

The ORRRC report defined a policy framework based on a division of responsibilities for public recreation among local, state, and federal gov-

FIGURE 22.1 The Corps of Engineers has long had plans to flood Red River Gorge, but responsiveness to citizen input has at least delayed the project. The gorge includes Natural Bridges Scenic Area in Daniel Boone National Forest, Kentucky. (USFS)

ernments. The private sector was recognized as a key element in supply. The guidelines for responsibility and jurisdiction are as follows:

1. Local and state governments are to take the basic responsibility for supplying recreational opportunities.

2. The federal government is to preserve areas of national significance.
3. The federal government is to offer financial and technical assistance, promote interstate arrangements, assume vigorous and cooperative leadership in getting all states to provide increased opportunities, and manage existing federal lands for broad recreation benefits.
4. Individual and private efforts are expected to continue providing places and activities, equipment, services, and other products, and leading in preservation of lands through nonprofit groups.

The ORRRC recommendations have been implemented to a remarkable degree. Various financial assistance programs have been developed, most notably the Land and Water Conservation Fund and the Open Space Act (since incorporated into the Community Development block grant program). The establishment of the Bureau of Outdoor Recreation, changed to Heritage Conservation and Recreation Service in 1978, has provided a federal focus on recreation planning and development that previously was lacking. The bureau produced studies that followed up the ORRRC report, most notably, the 1973 and 1979 nationwide outdoor recreation plans.

Other results of the ORRRC report at the federal level have been efforts to structure and start positive preservation of nationally significant features with natural, primitive, scenic, and historic values. Several new national parks and monuments have been established, including emphasis on National Seashores, National Lakeshores, and National Recreation Areas along water shorelines and near large urban areas, where needs were shown to be greatest. This gave a new dimension to the guideline on national significance. Congress took a good idea from the leadership of the Forest Service and made it firmer and broader with the passage of the Wilderness Act of 1964. A national trails system law and the Wild and Scenic Rivers Act set up machinery for recognition and establishment of significant corridors for recreation.

States and local governments have taken strong initiatives in directly supplying many types of outdoor recreation. All states have produced comprehensive outdoor recreation plans, conforming to the recommendations of ORRRC and making them eligible to receive matching Land and Water Conservation Fund monies. New state and local parks are being added to the recreation estate annually.

The ORRRC projections of participation alerted the nation to the need to increase facilities. Use of recreation areas has increased even more rapidly than predicted, producing stress on the natural environment, available facilities, and the professional staffs that manage the areas. To help meet the need, local governments have gone into debt through park bonds, to be paid off by those who benefit from the parks. A number of states have developed their own programs of financial and technical assistance to local governments.

The ORRRC report touched off a rapidly growing new interest in recreation by governments. It dramatically emphasized that a nation blessed with attractive, natural resources was falling short in making these available for recreation interests. At the same time, the people, with growing leisure, income, and mobility, were ready for a major effort to increase the supply of opportunities.

Public Land Law Review Commission (PLLRC)

From 1964 to 1970, a commission studied federal land policy and laws under the direction of the Congress through the Public Land Law Review Commission Act. Hundreds of foresters, range managers, lawyers, economists, and politicians examined the present and future problems and opportunities for lands including the public domain, the national forests, parks, wildlife refuges, and other properties.

The commission published its report in 1970, under the title, "One-Third of the Nation's Land." It contained 452 recommendations, many of them quite broad in scope and general in nature. The recreation section was prepared in continuity with the ORRRC report, starting out with a reiteration and support for the essential points of the ORRRC recommendations regarding the assignment of governmental roles and functions, as follows (PLLRC, 1970):

The Federal Government should be responsible for the preservation of scenic areas, natural wonders, primitive areas, and historic sites of *national significance;* for cooperation with the states through technical and financial assistance; in the promotion of interstate arrangements . . . and for management of Federal lands for the broadest recreation benefit consistent with other essential uses.

The states should play a pivotal role in making outdoor recreation opportunities available by the acquisition of land, the development of sites, and the provision and maintenance of facilities of state or regional significance; by assistance to local governments; and by the provision of leadership and planning.

Local governments should expand their efforts to provide outdoor recreation opportunities, with particular emphasis upon securing open space and developing recreation areas in and around metropolitan and other urban areas.

Individual initiative and private enterprise should continue to be the most important force in outdoor recreation, providing many and varied opportunities for a vast number of people, as well as the goods and services used by people in their recreation activities. Government should encourage the work of nonprofit groups wherever possible. It should also stimulate desirable commercial development, which can be particularly effective in providing facilities and services where demand is sufficient to return a profit.

The PLLRC focused its principal efforts on the policies and practices related to the management of federal lands. The commission noted that dispersed recreational use of national forests and BLM lands was compatible with other resource uses such as timber management and harvesting, watershed management, grazing, mining, and some occupancy uses, given proper planning and management.

Other recommendations were related to concern about overuse and incompatible uses of all types of federal lands. Regulation and rationing of use on a reservation system was called for, along with a general user fee.

The report was quite concerned with the classification and inventory of recreation resources, repeatedly recommending that more vigorous efforts along these lines be made. Standards were called for to help evaluate alternative recreation investment opportunities for public agencies, using the following factors for analysis: expected use rates, investment and administrative costs per unit of expected use, expected net impact on regional economies, the opportunity cost of uses of the land that will be foregone, impacts on the environment, and comparisons with alternative developments.

Access to federal lands through private properties has become a major problem in western states where large blocks of public land are remote from roads and access is possible only across private ranches. The commission called for the Congress and/or the states to provide for acquisition and construction of rights-of-way to public lands. It was also recommended

Tools for Recreation Administration

that block purchases of land be limited to new national parks, additions to the wilderness system for rounding out or protecting units, additions to the national trails, river systems, and of other areas of national significance such as national seashores. Additions to federal multiple-use lands for recreation purposes should be limited to inholdings only, according to the commission.

The report of the PLLRC has not received as much attention as seems warranted. Scholars and administrators have more or less ignored it, although its recommendations are still of great import and controversy. The chairman of the commission, Congressman Wayne Aspinall, was defeated in the primary election shortly after the report was issued, leaving no elected personality to direct and promote legislative efforts. The number of recommendations and the breadth of the report—covering all phases of management of federal lands—made it difficult to find a rallying point or to identify a crusade. Most interest groups could find things they liked in it; they also found items to which they strongly objected. There were arguments over what some of the recommendations meant. There was no single program for implementation (Senzel, 1978). However, the report raised or formalized many issues about recreation policy that continue to be of importance.

Nationwide Outdoor Recreation Plan, 1973

The Organic Act of the Bureau of Outdoor Recreation, Public Law 88–29, required that a nationwide plan be submitted to the Congress every five years. The law specifies that the Secretary of the Interior should:

. . . formulate and maintain a comprehensive nationwide outdoor recreation plan, taking into consideration the plans of the various Federal agencies, States, and their political subdivisions. The plan set forth the needs and demands of the public for outdoor recreation and the current and foreseeable availability in the future of outdoor recreation resources to meet those needs. The plan shall identify critical outdoor recreation problems, recommend solutions, and recommend desirable actions to be taken at each level of government and by private interests.

In 1970, Interior Secretary Walter Hickel presented to President Nixon a draft plan (a 1968 version was returned for revision) with a strong urban emphasis and a multibillion dollar price tag. The report was neither printed nor forwarded to the Congress, apparently because of its budgetary recommendation. Later, this document was printed for the record by the Senate Interior Committee, under the title "The Recreation Imperative" (Bureau of Outdoor Recreation, 1970). The report recommended that at least 30 per cent of the Land and Water Conservation Fund go to central cities, some as 75 per cent federal matching grants, and that there be grants for noncapital expenditures, including programming.

Instead, the Bureau of Outdoor Recreation printed and the President forwarded a plan in 1973, entitled "Outdoor Recreation, A Legacy for America" (Bureau of Outdoor Recreation, 1973). This did not have a price tag on it. It was basically a policy document suggesting traditional roles for federal, state, and local governments.

Included were an economic analysis of the national recreation situation in terms of supply and demand; reported studies of the situation by numerous small regions in the country, based on a survey of more than 4,000 people across the country; and an inventory of supply (Adams, Lewis, and Drake, 1973).

The survey in the summer of 1972 revealed that overall participation had increased, but little else had changed since 1960, when the ORRRC survey was made; people still participated most in the simple activities, although there had been some shifting in the popularity of particular activities.

This report pointed out recreation resources of critical concern and called for quick action to preserve them for recreation use. These included wilderness, shorelines, wetlands, floodplains, islands, lakes, rivers, and historic properties, among others. The report also revealed that only about 25 river basins were rated as slightly polluted. The rest had serious pollution problems.

The report contained recommendations that all federal and state agencies develop carrying capacity determinations for their properties and manage within them. It was also suggested that recreational use be reported in terms of visitor hours, reducing the confusion of current practice. Five years later, neither of these recommendations had been followed uniformly, even by the federal agencies. The BOR-HCRS, however, began estimating visitor hour and visitor day conversions for all agencies in 1976 (Bureau of Outdoor Recreation, 1977).

A large share of the report dealt with discussion and recommendations concerning the roles and responsibilities of government, business, and organizations in the provision of outdoor recreation. Although the general approach was along the same lines as ORRRC and PLLRC, there was more concern with including the private sector in planning and development activities. There were suggestions that states should both assist and promote quality among recreation businesses. In general, however, a *laissez-faire* attitude toward private business was followed.

Nationwide Outdoor Recreation Plan, 1979

The 1979 plan was developed through a series of task force reports on specific issues. These were submitted to the public and other government agencies for review and were revised subsequently, accompanied by public suggestions of issue papers to define the major issues as perceived by contributors. Based on intensive surveys of participation and preferences, the plan roughly calculated supply. The number of areas and number of acres for recreation are still difficult to produce, however. Even though states are expected to report complete data on recreation lands, the reports from the different states are not consistent enough to allow a national estimate that is reliable.

The 1979 plan, using demand and supply estimates for the future, predicted general needs and areas that required particular emphasis. Key among those was the need to increase emphasis on developing recreation close to home in urban areas. The plan recommended that more federal assistance be directed toward the cities for open space and called for a shift of some money for other than strictly outdoor facilities.

Other recommendations were for increased attention to federal and state wild and scenic river systems, identification of historic and natural resources through the Heritage Program, resolution of wilderness designation questions, access for the handicapped, and stronger efforts in developing the national trails system. The plan recognized the valuable contributions of volunteer, private groups in recreation resource management. It also called for an increased participation of the private-for-profit recreation sector in making state and federal recreation policy.

Environmental education was a major concern, with recommendations that the federal government should take action to promote stronger programs in federal and state recreation areas.

Off-road vehicle policy was examined, and energetic action was proposed to limit the negative impacts of these vehicles, and to provide appropriate places for them to operate.

State Recreation Planning

Every state prepares a comprehensive outdoor recreation plan, approximately once every four or five years. These plans describe the state's priority needs for recreation facilities and places. They indicate directions for the development of activities.

Authority for planning at the state level comes from the states' rights provision in the Constitution: that which is not a specific federal responsibility remains with the state.

The core of every state plan consists of three elements: projected demand, present supply of resources, and calculated needs.

Demand in virtually all state studies is not theoretical economic demand but an estimate of present and future participation. Participation figures are derived from surveys of residents and visitors to determine what they did, where, and how often. These are projected into the future, considering population and other socioeconomic changes. Demand is usually expressed in numbers of visitor occasions or visitor hours of an activity.

Supply is expressed in terms of area (land, water) or length (trails, rivers) of recreation facilities, or some other measure of capacity of the facilities. This comes from statewide inventories of public and private recreation places.

To calculate needs, existing supply is subtracted from projected participation. Because these are expressed in different terms, conversions are used. The supply is usually converted to the effective number of visitor occasions it can produce, considering capacity of the sites, visitor use patterns, weather and seasons of use, and the quality of experience to be offered (Hatke, Knudson, and Ziegler, 1977).

Based on calculations of needs by activity and region, identification of high-priority areas of the state and recommendations for focus on development are made.

Local Recreation Plans

A comprehensive outdoor recreation plan is a look at the supply, demand, and needs of a community or county. It starts with the present situation and includes estimates of future requirements to meet projected demands. Five- and 20-year time frames are commonly used. The plan then outlines how to achieve or approach the needs. In a local plan, specific actions and parklands are generally defined for the near future. Longer-range developments are outlined as specifically as possible, showing the general locations of new facilities.

Land and Water Conservation Fund plans emphasize land and facilities, because the fund is limited to acquisition and development. Maintenance and programming, along with indoor facilities, are also part of any planning process.

When the local area makes a plan, it has two basic methods for calculating needs and priorities. One approach is to use a procedure similar to the state plans. At the local level, it is easier to get a better handle on demand through interviews with a large proportion of the population. The needs calculation can be developed for regions of the city, remembering that availability of facilities strongly influences past participation patterns.

A second approach involves the traditional use of space standards. These are guidelines to suggest an amount of recreation space by population units. They were designed for cities by community recreation experts as early as 1906. They were revised through the National Recreation Association in 1934 and 1962, and by the National Recreation and Park Association in 1971 (Table 22.1). Most cities fall short of the standards, but Butler (1937) reported in 1937 that "there is fairly good acceptance among park and city planning authorities that each city should provide one acre of park and recreation space either within or immediately adjacent to its boundaries for each 100 population."

TABLE 22.1 Recreation space standards recommended by NRPA.

	Acres/1,000 pop.	Size range	Population served	Service area
Play lots	NA	2,500 ft² − 1 acre	500–2,500	Subneighborhood
Vest-pocket parks	NA	2,500 ft² − 1 acre	500–2,500	Subneighborhood
Neighborhood parks	2.5	5–20 acres	2,000–10,000	¼–½ mile
District parks	2.5	20–100 acres	10,000–50,000	½–3 miles
Large urban parks	5.0	100+ acres	one park per 50,000	Within ½-hour driving time
Regional parks	20.0	250+ acres	Entire smaller community; distributed throughout larger metro areas	Within 1 hour driving time
Special areas and facilities	NA	No standard applies: includes parkways, beaches, plazas, historical sites, floodplains, downtown malls, small parks, and tree lawns.		

Source: Buechner (1971). "The National Recreation and Park Association recommends that a minimum of 25 per cent of new towns, planned unit developments, and large subdivisions be devoted to park and recreation lands and open space."

States and cities have made their own revisions, as was revealed in a listing of the diverse planning standards by the Bureau of Outdoor Recreation (1967).

The standards approach has the faults of being too strictly interpreted and overly simple. It is still widely used, although not recommended by federal and state recreation agencies.

Agency Plans

In addition to the broad, comprehensive plans of the nation and the state, the various government agencies spend considerable effort on their master and action plans.

The National Park Service has done both system and park plans for many years. The system plans and analyses are infrequent. They identify the gaps in the park system and priorities for future acquisition. Individual park plans are called master plans (until 1975) or general management directives. They describe the key problems, trends in use, and major policy concepts for future management and development of the park. All recent plans have included an administrative classification of the lands, using the six recreational land-use classes of the Department of the Interior, recommended by ORRRC. Accompanying the master plans of the early 1970s were legislative proposals for classification of portions of the parks as wilderness, in consonance with the 1964 Wilderness Act.

The most complex are probably those of the U.S. Forest Service. Directed by the Resource Planning Act, this agency must make multiple-use plans that describe the apportionment and blending of uses on a national forest. Each use affects the others. Logging plans affect water yields, wildlife habitat, and recreational values. Designation of land for wilderness or special scenic values affects other recreational values and timber, water, and wildlife yields.

National Parks and Monuments have their own property plans for development classification and management. National Wildlife refuges have a national plan for management plus individual unit plans.

Accompanying these general property plans are action plans, such as interpretive prospectuses, wilderness study plans, circulation and development plans. The next step is working drawings and blueprints for construction of roads, trails, and other facilities. The Bureau of Land Management is also involved in multiple-use plans. Many state parks have a property development plan that is geared to the overall state lands plan required for eligibility for Land and Water Conservation funds.

Site Planning

A site master plan provides information, direction, and continuity in the management of a recreation property. The information provides the basic inventory of ecological, geological, and use data. Direction is provided by a statement of objectives, policy, and definition of the management practices. Continuity is offered by the purposeful scheduling of action plans to meet long-range goals.

The planning process has been described by many authors for many purposes. Each has its values and particular uses. Among the many approaches, the following is selected as an example, based on Peters (1978).

A master plan may follow seven basic steps.

1. Inventory the resources.
2. Analyze the inventory.
3. Determine the objectives and goals.
4. Prepare the master plan.
5. Gain approval of the plan.
6. Implement the plan.
7. Revise the plan.

The *inventory* is reported in texts, maps, charts, photographs, and, sometimes, collection of important specimens. Many resources are available for obtaining materials and information; some are listed in Table 22.2.

For any large property planning, three basic cartographic tools are of great value: A U.S. Geological Survey topographic map, recent aerial photographs covering the property with overlays, and a soils map. The maps

Tools for Recreation Administration

TABLE 22.2   Sources of inventory materials.

Materials	Local source
Maps	
Plat	County Court House
Topographic	U.S. Geological Survey, Department of the Interior
Geological	State Geologist or Department of Mines
Soils	U.S. Soil Conservation Service
Aerial photographs	U.S. Agricultural Stabilization and Conservation Service; area plan office; contract flights
Boundary description and neighboring landowners	County Court House, Auditor and Recorder, and/or document of establishment
Other legal information	County Court House, Surveyor, Recorder, Health Department, Assessor
Zoning regulations and maps	County Court House, Area Plan Commission
Hydrological data and maps	State Department of Natural Resources or Geology; Corps of Engineers or Bureau of Reclamation
History of ownership	County Court House, Deed Book and plat maps; neighbors
Agricultural history	U.S. Agricultural Stabilization and Conservation Service; Soil Conservation Service
Climatological data	National Weather Service
Soil survey and other soils data	Soil Conservation Service; Cooperative Extension Service

are for sale through some state offices, a few private sports stores and federal centers. The U.S. Geological Survey Distribution Center (Washington, D.C., 20242) can provide state indices. Aerial photographs can be ordered through federal agencies or county offices of the U.S. Department of Agriculture. Sometimes, local planning agencies have enlargements of such photos that can be blueprint copied at a low price. Transparent overlays of these photographs can be used to mark in features of special interest, such as a slope map, a vegetation map, a recreation use zone map, and a series of alternative development sketches.

The soil survey is available for about one third of the counties in the nation, those usually being of some agricultural importance. Where no survey is available, information may come from geological maps, local resource experts, and the state agriculture or forestry college. This information is useful to identify problem soils with poor or excessive drainage and to help select the best sites for trails and use areas.

The inventory should include field study to determine the condition of the vegetation and soils, special features to be protected, insect and disease problems, dangerous areas, a preliminary list of plant and animal species, the definition of the property boundary on the ground, outside land uses that may affect the property, encroachments, major ecological

Figure 22.2 Private property that abuts public parks sometimes intrudes on the visitor experience. (NPS)

communities, and other characteristics that may be of concern (Figure 22.2).

Analysis of the inventory is listed as a separate step because of the importance of going beyond the tedious recording of data. Too many park and recreation plans contain long lists of plants and animals that stand alone, with no incorporation into the plan or the environmental impact statement.

When the data are in, the planning team should examine them comprehensively. Putting all the lists, overlays, and base maps together is a start. Then the major characteristics of the property must be determined. Where are the problem areas, the areas worthy of special preservation efforts, the key attractive features? How might traffic flow, both vehicular and pedestrian? How will this affect the property, outside properties, and the transportation system?

The ecological balance of the plant and animal communities should be evaluated. The relative carrying capacity of the various identified communities can be estimated in terms of whether use would be disruptive.

Objectives and goals are usually sketched out at the beginning of the project. The clients, officials, and users can be consulted to prepare a final statement of goals. Often, planners fail to systematically consult with political officials, who later become disenchanted with the proposal presented.

The master plan is designed after reviewing various alternatives. Most planners present a set of alternatives to the public. These are reviewed in public meetings and one solution is chosen. That is presented in the

Tools for Recreation Administration

form of written rationale, maps and diagrams, and a timetable for implementation of the recommended steps. The master plan ("general management directive" in the National Park Service) should consist of more than the design of physical developments. The lands should be classified, land acquisition plans made, and provisions specified for trail development, wildlife species protection, research programs, and general operating policies dictated by the characteristics of the site.

Approval processes vary widely. Local and state projects usually require public presentation. Federally funded projects require public meeting on the plan and an environmental impact analysis; the guidelines are available from the Environmental Protection Agency or the state Department of Natural Resources. Public or congressional presentation often involves the planner's graphic materials being available for study some time ahead of a meeting, along with a written summary and/or the full report. At a public meeting, the planner or the property manager presents a verbal and graphic summary of the plan, answers questions (not defensively), and hears comments. With these oral and written comments, the plan is reviewed and revised as seems most advisable. Then the final draft is submitted.

Implementation is what keeps a plan from becoming a dust collector. A key job for a planner is supervising implementation of the work. Working drawings and detailed subplans will be developed as the plan is put into reality.

With time, *revision* of the plan is needed. No recreation plan is the Gospel. New developments will produce changes. The public or the agency may change its goals for the facility, requiring changes. Every planner thinks of his plan as a work of art, but it is a living, dynamic art piece. It doesn't just hang there; it is applied to an organic community with some of the most complex interactions known to ecology and sociology.

SITE PLANNING REPORT FORM

A complete set of site plans as used by the U.S. Forest Service consists of four parts:

I. *Detailed site map*—a surveyed and plotted map containing:
   A. Land lines and boundaries as well as ownership involved.
   B. A permanently established base line and evaluation control.
   C. The map scale.   (Usually no smaller than 1 in. = 50 ft.)
   D. Contour lines.   (Interval usually 1 or 2 feet.)
   E. Features
      1. Ponds, lakeshores, and streams (direction of flow and mean high watermark).
      2. Vegetation that will be preserved.
      3. Rock outcroppings or individual boulders if they will influence design.

4. Existing structures or utilities on the site or within 50 feet of boundary.
5. Telephone or power lines. (Indicate location of poles.)
6. Rights-of-way, easements, proposed highways.
7. Existing water supply and sewage systems.
8. Desirable view directions and prevailing winds.
9. Soil types and percolation data.
10. Proximity map.
11. Symbol legend.
12. Title block including proposed name for the area.

II. *Narrative report,* consists of three main parts.
  A. Analysis and discussion of the physical characteristics of the site as they may influence design and construction.
  B. Analysis and discussion of the physical and esthetic requirements of the use or uses and desired level of experience.
  C. Statement of design objectives—that which you intend to do with design to fit the desired uses upon the site within the capabilities of the site to withstand the use impact.

III. *General development plan,* usually made by tracing the detailed site map and adding proposed improvements. Contains:
  A. Overall design scheme.
  B. Type and placement of all facilities but not layout details.
  C. Road stationing.
  D. Survey control base line and description.
  E. Proximity map.
  F. Orientation.
  G. Legend.
  H. Aerial photo coverage.

IV. *Final construction plan,* conveys instructions to the contractor and includes:
  A. Road design.
  B. Water and sewage system designs.
  C. Grading plans including all contour modifications.
  D. Family unit layout and construction details.
  E. Construction drawings of all facilities and structures.
  F. Layout information for the location of all site improvements.
  G. All necessary specifications.

River Basin Planning

An attempt to look at the nation in ecological units of major watersheds was made in recent decades. The boundaries for planning units were the basins of large rivers and the Great Lakes. These cross many political jurisdictions, including state boundaries. In the case of some rivers, Canadian cooperation was sought in the federally sponsored effort.

The few plans completed have been comprehensive in nature, covering all resources. They provide excellent factual data and point out many of the problems of development that often will require interstate and international cooperation.

Once the reports are submitted, there seems to be relatively little done with them. Their comprehensive nature and lack of specific issue direction give little impetus to federal implementation. The problems of state and local governments working with other jurisdictions also impede progress. So far, these plans have offered excellent reference material and ideas that are often incorporated into other plans, but have not been used directly, except by the Corps of Engineers. That agency has used them as initial guidelines for exploring water control and development projects. Recent public opposition to many of these project proposals has made implementation of the long-range comprehensive proposals virtually impractical. With time, many of the projects have become quite costly. Analyzed on a cost/marginal benefit basis, many do not appear to be wise investments.

Land-Use Planning

Recreation plays a key role in land-use planning. During the 1980s, the concepts of land-use planning are taking on great importance. Local, state, and national regulations and legislation increasingly guide the way in which private and public lands are used (Figure 22.3).

The idea of restricting how land can be used is not new; people have insisted on restrictions of the more bizarre uses for years—junkyards, cattle or sheep in the city, burning noxious or poisonous materials in the local factory. As the severity of the restrictions has increased, moving from health and safety to qualities of beauty and attractiveness of the community, there have been some shocks. The decade of the 1980s will see these shocks turn land-use planning into a major controversy.

A key question is related to a definition of land-use planning. People tend to be nervous about any government-imposed activity that is ill-defined. Land-use planning as a concept is virtually impossible to define in specific terms that explain the impacts on individuals or industries. It is what the people make it. Basically, it is the determination of the appropriate uses of land, to make a livable, productive, pleasant environment at low or reasonable costs (Figure 22.4). In most of the nation, it is now manifested through zoning ordinances. In a few places, there are greenbelts (Figure 22.5), designed to surround the city, but which are now surrounded by urban sprawl.

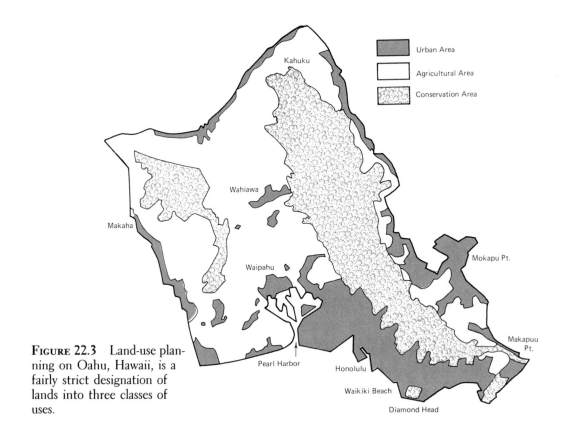

FIGURE 22.3 Land-use planning on Oahu, Hawaii, is a fairly strict designation of lands into three classes of uses.

Urban Area

Agricultural Area

Conservation Area

Kahuku

Wahiawa

Makaha

Waipahu

Mokapu Pt.

Makapuu Pt.

Pearl Harbor

Honolulu

Waikiki Beach

Diamond Head

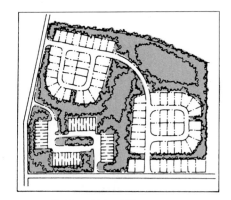

CONVENTIONAL SUBDIVISION

Number of lots: 108
Open space: 10%
Linear feet of streets 5,400
Linear feet of sewer lines 5,400

CLUSTER DEVELOPMENT

Number of lots: 108
Open space: 50%
Linear feet of streets 4,900
Linear feet of sewer lines 3,900

FIGURE 22.4 Land-use patterns in cities affect open space availability. Cluster development leaves open space and is cheaper to develop.

FIGURE 22.5 Ottawa, Canada has acquired greenbelt around its southern boundary. Some of the land is leased back to farmers. Part is a military reservation.

Land-use planning also addresses such questions as the following:

1. How much of the nation, state, or county should be maintained (or replanted) in forest, and what incentives is society willing to provide to keep that land in trees?
2. How much prime agricultural land should be kept in production, and how can urban sprawl be prevented from occupying these lands?
3. What restrictions on agricultural plowing, building, and other land-disturbing practices are needed to conserve top soil and reduce stream siltation, and should there be subsidies for real or imagined losses caused by restrictions?
4. What is the character of urban and rural residential development that is socially desirable; how can undesirable growth be controlled, and at what cost?
5. Where, why, and how should industrial development be located?
6. How much area in parks and open space should be provided, where

should it be located in relation to residences and places of work, what variety of services and environmental protection should be provided?

Parks, forests, and wetlands are likely to be important elements in any land-use plan. Nationwide, the United States loses 300,000 acres of wetlands per year. President Carter, in 1977 Executive Order 11990, withdrew much federal subsidization for destruction of wetlands. Most communities zone against structures in the flood plains (Figure 22.6).

Active protection of wetlands and floodplains as a rule, not an exception, should be federal, state, and local policy (Heritage Conservation and Recreation Service, 1978).

From 1967 to 1975, more than 3.2 million ha (8 million acres) of prime farmland was converted to urban development, reservoirs, public transportation, and other uses. This is an average of 1 million acres per year. Losses were greatest in the Southeast and the corn belt (Council on Environmental Quality, 1977).

Controls of land use are discussed in Chapter 25.

LAND-USE POWERS

There are four basic types of power that local and state governments can use to regulate or control land use (Council on Environmental Quality, 1976).

FIGURE 22.6 Counties without floodplain zoning often find attractive rivers cluttered with temporary and permanent housing.

Tools for Recreation Administration

1. The power of eminent domain allows governments to acquire any land, with payment of just compensation, for public purposes. Condemnation proceedings and use of the threat of them affects only a small portion of the land. This is discussed elsewhere.
2. The police power is the ability to regulate private activity to protect the health, safety, morals, and general welfare of the public. This is the power most used to guide or control the land development process at the local level. Regulations commonly relate to the zoning of types of development, subdivision regulations, building codes, housing codes, and environmental regulations.
3. The power of taxation, besides supplying revenues, can be used to encourage or discourage certain land uses for the public welfare. Lowered tax assessment for forests, open space, or farms is one method. Property tax exemptions for charitable, educational, and religious organizations is another. Encouragement of new industry is sometimes achieved by special tax arrangements. Commercial recreation might be encouraged by reducing property taxes.
4. The power to act affirmatively is potent. It allows governments to build facilities, designate and develop open spaces, scenic rivers, or parks, and to confer or withdraw benefits for concessions.

Citizen Involvement in Planning

Virtually all recreation planning efforts involve citizen input at some stage. Most federal programs require some sort of formalized, documented process of informing and recording responses of citizens.

Usually, the input sought is through organized groups, such as Chambers of Commerce, neighborhood action committees, conservation organizations, civic clubs, taxpayer organizations, and activity interest groups, such as campers, boaters, fishermen, hikers, and vehicle riders. Individual citizens are also given opportunities to speak or testify in writing.

The form of participation is highly variable. There is no one method that seems to be satisfactory. Public meetings usually must become rather rigid and formal to be completed in reasonable time. At such meetings, participants usually hear the outlines of the plan being considered, and then testify as to their views of the merits of the plan. The responsible agency then studies the various responses, makes appropriate modifications, and submits the revised plan for implementation.

Much more complex approaches have been developed by some consulting firms, some states, and a few federal agencies. These involve citizens in a series of meetings, from the beginning of the planning period to the final copy of the plan. It is believed that the long-term involvement allows more incorporation of citizen ideas, thus making the plan more responsive to the local area needs. It also means that the plan is likely to be accepted and implemented. By allowing groups and individuals with differing ideas to interact over the planning period, compromises and problems can be worked out to the satisfaction of all sides, at least more effectively than in opposing testimony at a single hearing. Two major difficulties of this heavy-involvement approach are 1) the citizens are required to spend many long hours in meetings and study at no pay; and 2) there is often discontinuity of personnel during the process, requiring considerable review and backtracking, and sometimes producing no less controversial results than simpler methods. In general, however, consultants who have learned to use this approach have been satisfied with it.

In state comprehensive outdoor recreation plans, there must be certification by the governor that there has been ample opportunity for public participation in plan development and revision. A process for involving citizen groups, recreation-related agencies, and the private recreation sector is required. So is distribution of information to the public through printed materials, regional workshops, and annual forums. A final public hearing is required for the plan.

The Bureau of Outdoor Recreation, in reviewing the success of the public hearing and involvement process (Bureau of Outdoor Recreation, 1977b), stated: "although we seek public involvement, we are not satisfied with the results to date. Often the only 'public' which participates is that organized around recreation and conservation issues. Other groups and the general public often are not adequately involved in the process."

This is the experience of many other agencies, suggesting that citizen involvement processes and use of the data they generate are still tentative and experimental. There is little question that citizens will continue to be involved in the planning process.

The involvement and consideration of citizen views complicates planning and makes it significantly more expensive. New techniques are needed to elicit representative response and to evaluate the public input.

Summary

Olmsted (1871) noted the cultural impact of setting aside open space in neighborhood and community parks of large urban areas, when he spoke of the "millions on millions of men and women who are to pass their lives within a few miles of where we now stand." Whether the people engage in pleasant and constructive recreation, as opposed to unhealthy pastimes, may be, in many cases, a question of opportunity and inducement offered by a park, pool, forest, or beach close to home.

The elaborate planning processes described in this chapter are aimed at determining where facilities are most needed and how they might best be provided. Government and private planners alike are caught up in a hierarchy of plans, at the national level, in state governments, local agencies, and private businesses.

Planning can prevent costly and unfortunate mistakes. It can direct public tax monies to the resources and people in need of assistance. An ultimate advantage of recreation and land planning is that it can allow people to anticipate future development and help assure freedom from the tyranny of unanticipated, incompatible developments. Through public participation, planning allows people to help determine their future recreation environment or lack of it.

Literature Cited

ADAMS, ROBERT L., ROBERT C. LEWIS and BRUCE H. DRAKE. 1973. Outdoor Recreation; a Legacy for America: Appendix "A"—an economic analysis. Washington: U.S. Dept. of the Interior, Office of Economic Analysis. 239 pp. + appendices.

BUECHNER, ROBERT D. (ed.). 1971. National Park, Recreation and Open Space Standards. Washington, D.C.: National Recreation and Park Association. 51 pp.

Bureau of Outdoor Recreation. 1967. Outdoor Recreation Space Standards. Washington, D.C.: U.S. Dept. of the Interior.

Bureau of Outdoor Recreation. 1970. The Recreation Imperative. Washington, D.C.: U.S. Senate, Committee on Interior and Insular Affairs (1974 Committee Print). 389 pp.

Bureau of Outdoor Recreation. 1973. Outdoor Recreation; a Legacy for America. Washington, D.C.: U.S. Dept. of the Interior. 89 pp.

Bureau of Outdoor Recreation. 1977a. Federal Recreation Area Visitation Report—1976. Washington, D.C.: U.S. Dept. of the Interior.

Bureau of Outdoor Recreation. 1977b. Urban Recreation; a Briefing. U.S. Dept. of the Interior. Mimeo., 58 pp.

BUTLER, GEORGE D. 1937. Municipal and County Parks in the United States, 1935. Washington, D.C.: U.S. Department of the Interior, National Park Service. 147 pp.

Council on Environmental Quality. 1976b. Untaxing Open Space; Executive Summary. Washington, D.C. 13 pp.

Council on Environmental Quality. 1977. Environmental Quality—1977; The Eighth Annual Report of the Council on Environmental Quality. Washington, D.C. 445 pp.

HATKE, TRUDY E., DOUGLAS M. KNUDSON and JEFFREY ZIEGLER. 1977. Total Seasonal Capacity of Indiana's Recreation Supply and Determination of Needs. Indianapolis: Indiana Dept. of Natural Resources. 20 pp.

Heritage Conservation and Recreation Service. 1978. Protection of Outdoor Recreation Values of Rivers; Task Force Report. Washington, D.C.: U.S. Dept. of the Interior. 13 pp. + appendix.

National Park Service. 1964. Parks for America. Washington, D.C.: U.S. Dept. of the Interior. 485 pp.

OLMSTED, FREDERICK LAW. 1871. Public parks and the enlargement of towns. Journal of Social Science 2(3):1–36.

Outdoor Recreation Resources Review Commission. 1962. Outdoor Recreation for America. Washington, D.C. 246 pp.

Parks Canada. 1976. Canadian Outdoor Recreation Demand Study. Vol. 1: An Overview and Assessment. Waterloo: The Ontario Research Council on Leisure and Federal-Provincial Parks Conference. 119 pp.

PETERS, TAMRA (ed.). 1978. Stewardship Guide for Preserve Committees. Arlington, Va.: The Nature Conservancy. 80 pp.

Public Land Law Review Commission. 1970. One-third of the Nation's Land. Washington, D.C.

SENZEL, IRVING. 1978. Genesis of a law, part I. American Forests 84(1):30–32, 61–64.

C H A P T E R   2 3

Estimating Use Rates

For some reason or another, counting people must be more difficult than measuring trees, deer, water, forage, and most of the things produced from the land or in manufacturing enterprises. The state of recreation use estimates is a hodge-podge.

Different agencies use different units of measurement. Each has its own sampling technique—or no sampling technique. They range from full counts to a year-end estimate of the approximate number of visitors during the year.

Different methods produce different results. In an Indiana park, one method produced an estimate of 160,000 visits in one year; another approach estimated 400,000 visits for the same year.

Estimates of recreation use of forests, parks, reservoirs, and most other recreation areas are in a fairly disorganized state of affairs. There is need to put things in order and get reliable estimates of recreation use (Figure 23.1).

This chapter is concerned with two phases of use estimates: current visitation to recreation properties and projections of future use.

Recreation use data are valuable for many purposes. The most obvious of these is for planning. When faced with the duty of preparing a statewide outdoor recreation plan, the professional planner, the administrator, and the politician have an obvious need for facts. To assess current participation in recreation and use of existing facilities, it would be nice to know that estimates of use are accurate and comparable.

At the present time, the planner is faced with the following situation. Most private recreation areas do not report numbers of users in any regular manner, even though they probably serve at least half (or more) of the recreation public. Local parks and recreation agencies do not have unified systems of reporting use; most do not make statistically based estimates of use, except in the loosest sense of the word. State properties report use rates, but these vary widely as to their reliability and as to the methods used in collecting them. Federal agencies likewise differ greatly in their reporting systems.

FIGURE 23.1 How many came? That is the most basic question of visitor use estimates. (Bureau of Reclamation)

From this chaos, the planner and decision maker are required to make some kind of judgment as to the needs for recreation and the relative popularity of different programs and facilities.

Use estimates are of value to administrators of individual parks and forests. With accurate data, they can analyze the changes in user patterns and preferences over the years. They can justify their decisions with facts, rather than by simply reporting a feeling that a course of action was desirable. They can use the figures for planning budgets, work schedules, and new priorities.

The greatest overall value of the estimates of the number of visitors can be summarized as communication. People interested in the administration of outdoor recreation can communicate with each other on a factual basis, which requires some regularity in terminology and sources of information.

Administrators, interpreters, and planners of recreation resource areas must report current use periodically. It is federal policy to encourage valid use estimates.

Tools for Recreation Administration

Units of Measurement

It was the recommendation of the 1973 Nationwide Outdoor Recreation Plan (BOR, 1973) that:

Each federal land managing agency will report annually to the Bureau of Outdoor Recreation, in accordance with the Land and Water Conservation Fund Act of 1965, as amended, on recreation use at each management unit, using the recreation visitor-hour as the standard unit of measure. When available and appropriate, agencies also should include recreation visit and activity-hour data.

A recreation visitor-hour is the presence for recreation purposes of one or more persons for continuous, intermittent, or simultaneous periods of time aggregating 60 minutes.

A recreation activity-hour is a recreation visitor-hour attributable to a specific recreation activity.

A recreation visit is the entry of any person into a site or area of land or water for recreation purposes.

States and localities should prepare similar reports on recreational management units for use in their planning programs.

The three units of measurement mentioned are supplemented by others. "Activity days" or "recreation days" are used by several organizations and used as an expedient in the first nationwide plan (BOR, 1973). This measure is the average number of hours of participation per day in a given activity. For example, walking for pleasure was 1.9 hours per activity day, boating was 2.8, and golf was 4.9 hours (Adams, Lewis, and Drake, 1973).

The preferred and recommended visitor-hour and the 12-hour visitor-day requires careful sampling and measurement and professional direction and checking.

Current Use Estimates

The nature of the problem suggests there must be a simple solution, but the apparent simplicity is deceptive. Most agencies do not use reliable methods of estimating visitation. The result is that many—probably most—estimates of use of outdoor recreation areas are reported with no statement of probability as to their approximation of reality.

There are at least five classes of estimates:

1. Pure guess.
2. Observational estimates by administrators.
3. A growing (seldom retreating) statistic, based on rough comparison from year to year (often a variation on class 1).
4. A sampling procedure, either using direct counts of people or counts of a related phenomenon.
5. A pure count of some kind of user data.

Because there is no uniformity in methods of collecting use data, any local or state government, attempting to examine use levels, encounters data that are not comparable. The consequences of the mix of present practices include:

1. Imprecise use data.
2. Lack of ability to assess the probability of the estimate as being representative of reality.
3. Inability to compare data among parks in the same system and among systems.
4. Different units of measurement, such as:
   Forest Service visitor-day = 12 hours of activity.
   National Park Service visits = entry into the park.
   Corps of Engineers activity day = participation in an activity sometime during the day.
5. Lack of information on use patterns.

Private Enterprise: No coordinated reporting system is used in private enterprises. The Internal Revenue Service is probably the only source that has any information and that is probably expressed in lump sum terms. Individual owners have excellent records of use; many do not, but can offer close approximations.

City and County Parks: Only a few city and county parks have comprehensive estimates of park use (Figure 23.2). Most have quite accurate figures on participants in organized programs such as softball leagues, youth clubs, and so on. Reports of use are made to city officials in annual reports. Reliability and thoroughness of estimates are highly variable.

State Parks and Forests: Measurement is highly variable among state parks and forests. Most have data only on the use of campgrounds and inns. Where entry gates are used and entry fees charged, estimates of state park use can be based on the sums of gate receipts from year to year. If gate receipts are up 10 per cent from the base year, then the number of entries is increased by 10 per cent. Some attempts have been made to use traffic counters. Both gate receipts and traffic counts require calibration to convert dollars or axle counts to people. These measures produce statistics on the number of visits.

State Fish and Wildlife Areas: Highly variable methods are used at state fish and wildlife areas, ranging from rigorous registration to occasional car counts during hunting season. Various registration procedures have been tried and merit further study.

Nature Preserves, Museums, Historic Sites: Registration is the standard method at nature preserves, museums, and historic sites. At outdoor or other unattended areas, the registration by users is highly sporadic. Most repeat visitors and local visitors seem to fail to register. Where there are

FIGURE 23.2 How long did they stay? At most local park facilities, carefully designed sampling procedures are the most practical approach to estimating visitor hours.

attendants in buildings, there can be 100 per cent registration. At museums, entry stiles and guards can record visits.

National Forests: Estimates of visitor-hours and visitor-days at national forests are made from calibrated traffic counters and checked by gate receipts only in certain developed sites. Use is allocated to activities by formulas derived from samples. In dispersed areas, estimates are more informal, based on field observation and calibrated samples. The agency's nationwide data system is perhaps the most sophisticated approach being used in the United States.

National Parks: Visit estimates (number of entries) are made for all units in national parks. Where there are no gates or control points, counts of users at selected points of the property are the basis of estimates. The users of the visitor centers are the most accurately counted.

Canadian National Parks use a tag and retrieve approach. Entrants in a park are tagged on sample days. Whenever the tag appears at another park, it is recorded. From this, an approximation of use patterns can be derived.

National Wildlife Refuges: The Fish and Wildlife Service has been reporting use in terms of the number of visits, but is now doing its planning in terms of activity hours, measured at entries, registration centers, and visitor centers.

Corps of Engineers Reservoirs: Calibrated traffic counts produce estimates of the number of visits, generally referred to as activity-days, at Corps of Engineers reservoirs. An activity-day is participation in an activity during part of a day, assuming that participation is detected by samples and counters. The activity-day approach produces very high numbers, not directly comparable to visits or visitor days. Part of this is because of the nature of the activity-day—one person can participate in several activity-days within a single day. The procedure for calibration of the figures is another factor that may be contributing to high estimates. The philosophy behind the procedure seems to be sound. The reliability of the estimates may vary from reservoir to reservoir, on the basis of maintenance of traffic counters and calibration accuracy.

A Variety of Experiments

Various approaches have been tested in efforts to estimate both mass use on developed sites and dispersed use on undeveloped sites. Lucas (1964) used traffic counters at major access points to the Boundary Waters Canoe Area. Cushwa and McGinnes (1963) tested a random sampling method for estimating hours of use and the number of visits on a 100-square-mile section of George Washington National Forest in Virginia. At randomly selected checkpoints and times throughout the year, visitors were stopped and asked to complete a questionnaire, indicating time spent in various recreation activities, as well as demographic characteristics. Both of these provided spot check estimates of use only for the periods when observers were in the field; there was no continuing measurement of season-long use.

In order to increase the efficiency of the sampling effort, it was necessary to develop a method by which the relationship between visitor use and one or more indicator variables could be determined. This would yield not only one-time use estimates, but continuous estimates, based on the cheaply measured indicator variables. Many different indicator variables have been used. They vary from traffic counters to the weight of garbage removed from recreation areas.

Numerous studies have shown the effectiveness of traffic counters and other devices to estimate recreation use on Forest Service properties (James and Ripley, 1963; James, 1966; James, 1967; James and Rich, 1966). The basic approach is to establish a relationship (usually a regression equation) between the number of traffic counts and the desired statistic, such as number of visitor days. To establish this relationship, both were measured on randomly selected sampling days during the recreation season. Then traffic counts were related directly to the visitor use statistic by a formula. That is, the traffic counts were calibrated to indicate the visitor use, rather than just the number of axle counts. The traffic counters then functioned all season, allowing conversion from the count to visitor-hours of use.

Herbert (1974) recommended the use of traffic counters in parks, based on one-hour calibration samples instead of the 12-hour daily units used by James. She also developed a procedure for estimating total park population at any instant. Madden and Knudson (1978) confirmed her finding and noted that either gate receipts or traffic counts could be used for measuring visits.

Other regression model sampling techniques have been tried with good results. A technique for estimating past and current attendance at winter sports is based on measurement of such indicator variables as lift and tow tickets (Bury and Hall, 1963). Methods for using indicators to estimate recreation use on large bodies of water are more difficult and costly (James, Wingle and Griggs, 1971).

In an effort to further reduce sampling costs, several researchers have developed methods for estimating use on a complex of developed sites. Bury and Margolies (1964) were able to estimate attendance for an entire complex of campgrounds, based on daily observation counts of attendance at a few supervised areas. Traffic counts, at one or more indicator locations in North Carolina, estimated season-long recreation use within a complex of untended, developed sites (James and Rich, 1966).

On scenic rivers, time lapse photography has been used to sample the numbers of visitors (Marnell, 1975). Cameras located at several places and automatic timers were operated on 12-hour sample days. By taking one frame every 12 seconds, it was possible to project a 12-hour day in six minutes.

Direct count samples can be made at intervals in small parks, visitor information centers, and other places where people can be easily seen and interviewed as to the length of their visit (Schreuder, Tyre, and James, 1975).

Calibration Sample Procedure

To set up a traffic-counter calibration for a recreation area, the following conditions and procedures apply. This produces first-time visit (for a day) estimates.

The basics of the method are a properly functioning, protected traffic counter across a road at a point where most of the park traffic will cross

FIGURE 23.3 What did they do? Activity analysis is a useful guide to management. (Hennepin County Park Reserve District)

it, and a calibration equation that converts mechanical traffic counts into number of visits (eventually number of visitor hours by activity). Each property requires a separate calibration.

To develop the calibration equation for entries, a sample of 45 one-hour observations can be selected for the season of interest (Madden and Knudson, 1978). If several seasons are to be considered, a second set of sample observations should be made.

For the summer season, randomly select one-hour sample periods from

Tools for Recreation Administration

throughout the summer. Stratification of busy and less busy hours may be useful.

Then during the sample hours, measure the total number of traffic counts during the hour, and measure the number of first-time visitors passing the traffic counter (assuming it is at the entry). The traffic counter will record all vehicles—buses, cars, bicycles, pickups with trailers, park employee vehicles, and service trucks. There is no need, however, to count any individuals in those vehicles except the first-time visitors. Count *all* first-time visitors—those with season passes, those who pay, and even any visitors who might get in free. In the visitor count, do not include employees, service drivers, or others who are not first-time visitors. Record for the hour the number of all traffic counts and the number of first-time visitors.

When the sample calibrations are completed, use simple linear regression to calculate the relationship between the number of traffic counts/hour *(x)* and the number of visitors/hour *(y)*. Then multiply both sides of the equation by 12 to obtain a daily estimate, assuming the bulk of the entries occur in a 12-hour period each day. By using the equation and traffic counter data for any day, an estimate can be calculated for number of first time visitors. More comprehensive measures of activity participation by traffic count can be developed by correlating entry counts to activity use pattern (Figure 23.3).

Areas that receive less intense visitation than usually experienced at state parks and recreation areas would require a larger sample, using longer sampling periods. This would reduce the possibility of observations at zero, which contribute little to the determination of the relationship between visitation and the indicator. Municipal, state, and federal parks, however, are particularly conducive to this technique, using one-hour samples.

APPLICATION

Use of the calibration equation is a matter of recording the number of traffic counts every day and then solving the equation for the time period of interest. It is crucial that the traffic counter be kept in good repair.

It is assumed that the calibration will be good for three to five years, if there are no major changes in facilities or use patterns in the park (James, 1966). There is a need to continue research and development of economical procedures for estimating visitor use. In the meantime, reasonable estimates can be made by using existing methods.

Projection of Future Use

Trying to estimate future events has made lucky men appear wise and wise men appear to lack foresight. No less a figure than Abraham Lincoln (and many of his successors) has made predictions that were far off the mark.

Lincoln, after studying data from the seven censuses from 1810 to 1860, predicted that by 1950, the United States population would reach 250 million, a definite overestimate. He also concluded that it would take 120 to 150 years to "civilize" the Great American Desert from the Mississippi to the Colorado Rockies. One generation did it, using the Homestead Act that Lincoln signed.

Outdoor recreation projections are numerous and interesting. Federal, state, and local governments estimate future participation in recreation to help set budget priorities. The financial community is concerned about how to focus investment capital. Standard and Poor's (1977), for example, reports that recreation is now regarded as a necessity, not just something to do with surplus income; the camping market was expected to hold up well even during an economic recession. This sort of information, based on projections, helps guide investor decisions.

Projections of participation are valuable in recreation agency investment decisions in two major ways. First, the number and location of new parks, reservoirs, or other land units should be partially guided by the geography of population growth. Second, within an area, the mix of facilities can be guided by projections. Should tennis courts be added? Is an investment in a nature center worthwhile? Because tennis and nature study show steady,

TABLE 23.1 Medium level projections of participant numbers relative to 1977.

Activity	Per cent of population participating	Index				
		1977	1985	1990	2000	2020
Camping (developed)	30	100	116	126	150	214
Camping (dispersed)	21	100	110	116	133	182
ORV driving	26	100	105	108	118	139
Hiking	28	100	106	109	117	146
Horseback riding	15	100	106	109	118	159
Nature study/Photography	50	100	106	110	121	145
Picnicking	72	100	107	112	124	150
Pleasure driving	69	100	105	108	116	135
Sightseeing	62	100	107	112	123	150
Canoeing	16	100	113	121	141	209
Sailing	11	100	127	145	185	298
Other boating	34	100	112	119	137	189
Swimming outdoors	61	100	109	115	127	168
Waterskiing	16	100	106	109	118	161
Cross-country skiing	2	100	120	133	161	241
Downhill skiing	7	100	125	142	179	289
Ice skating	16	100	114	123	144	212
Sledding	21	100	111	118	133	193
Snowmobiling	8	100	106	109	120	161

Source: U.S. Forest Service (1979), based on Heritage Conservation and Recreation Service 1977 participant survey.

Tools for Recreation Administration

strong increases in participation, these seem to be wise investments. Examination of a particular neighborhood or community can be helpful. If young families are moving into an area, provision of playground equipment and ball fields might be considered.

The analyst must somehow try to distinguish between short-lived fads and long-term trends. Facilities for fads can become expensive white elephants. By anticipating trends, an agency or business can offer its clients opportunities ahead of the crowd.

NATIONAL AND STATE PROJECTIONS

The national and state recreation plans make estimates of future demands. The approaches used by different states are quite variable, making it impossible to put them together for a national estimate.

The projections in Table 23.1 were based on the number of participants expected in future years (Hof, 1978). The projections indicate substantial growth in all activities. Winter sports are expected to increase fastest, more than doubling (collectively) by 2020. Water-based activities should almost double by 2020, with sailing making the greatest acceleration of all activities to triple in the next 40 plus years. Land-based activities are projected to 150 per cent of the number of 1977 participants.

There are at least three general approaches to predicting future use, each with a different basis (Clawson and Knetsch, 1966). They can be combined in some cases.

1. Extend trends in participation figures; that is, if a state park's use was 50,000 in 1950, 60,000 in 1960, 70,000 in 1970, 80,000 in 1980, it can be predicted that by 1985 it will be 85,000. This is simple to do. It requires historic data that are reliable and compatible, not always available. Projections should be limited to short time periods, because the method does not recognize changes in tastes or turns in rates of increase. If the use of Corps of Engineers reservoirs for 1950 and 1960 were extended to 2000, the prediction would have every citizen boating 2,500 times per year on a Corps reservoir.
2. Apply professional judgment to facts and trends in at least two ways:
   a) Satiety ceilings recognize that saturation occurs in use, such as the obvious case of reservoirs.
   b) Judgment of turning points, and probable future desires can sometimes be based on knowledge of other factors.
   Judgment does not mean a guess. It suggests that the prognosticator assemble all available data plus experience and knowledge of recreation phenomena and make a reasoned calculation of the likelihood of developments and changes. This has the disadvantage of being highly individualized. A well-respected authority's judgment may be accepted, but an expert young professional may have some difficulty.
3. Predict recreation use from study of related factors such as population,

income, mobility, age groups, and other data. Two techniques can be used:

a) Extend historical trends of related factors; then estimate use, based on correlation with use.

b) Generate relationships from cross-sectional data at one point in time, then project those relationships to meet future conditions (this is the method used by nationwide recreation plans and for cohort analysis used in some state plans).

The use of simple or multiple correlation/regression models is a common statistical technique employed for these predictions. They are based primarily on socioeconomic factors thought to be correlated with recreation participation.

Because the methods of approach three are widely used for national and state studies, they are discussed further.

The first of these methods requires historical data on related factors. They both require quantitative and meaningful measurements of association between changes in related factors and changes in use rates. It assumes that the past relationships will remain the same in the future. Unfortunately, the correlations between the factors and use patterns have not been close, perhaps as a result of the methods of measuring them.

Use of socioeconomic and demographic variables to predict or explain recreation participation was first done nationally for the Outdoor Recreation Resources Review Commission's Study Report 20 (Mueller, et al., 1962). Nine variables were judged to be major factors influencing demand and future participation. Others have been added as tests have continued over the years.

These include age, income, education, sex, place of residence, race, occupation, number of children, and marital status. These variables are measured by individual interviews or mailed questionnaires. The individual records his attributes and the amount and kind of recreation in which he participated over a recent period of time—two weeks, one month, or one year. Then, by regression and correlation analysis, the relationships between participation rates and the range of attributes can be calculated for the various recreation activities.

Socioeconomic Projections

The 1973 Nationwide Outdoor Recreation Plan used projections of demand based on a national telephone survey of more than 4,000 people (Adams, Lewis, and Drake, 1973). The relationships between the socioeconomic characteristics of these individuals and their rates of participation in different activities were established statistically. This means that participation rates were recorded for camping by income classes from the sample group. The same was done for camping by level of education completed, race, age, family size, and various other factors. When all of these were put together, a composite probability of participation for camping could be estimated for a population with any mix of these characteristics. That is, it could be estimated if it is assumed that the data base—the sampled people—were representative of the nation or region being studied. Adams, Lewis, and Drake (1973) made the assumption that the relationships established for the sample group also apply to segments of the population defined by their geographic residence. Then, each of 171 regions was characterized according to its socioeconomic characteristics. By combining these with the estimated participation equations, there was an estimated demand on each region. By projecting the developments in socioeconomic characteristics to a future year, the likely demand or participation for that year could be estimated. In actuality, this group found that changes in population were the most important factor affecting future participation. Family income was another important factor, but its effects were relatively small, compared to population.

For most activities, the 1972–1978 periodic national percentage increase in the quantity was between 10 per cent and 15 per cent (Adams, Lewis, and Drake, 1973). These matched with a projected increase in population of 9 per cent and in family income of 13 per cent. With a rise in family incomes, there was an associated rapid rise predicted for three of the expensive activities—golf at 24 per cent, attending outdoor sports events up 20 per cent, and boating with a projected increase of 18 per cent. Only one activity was projected to decrease in per capita terms—playing outdoor games or sports, expected to increase by only 5 per cent over the six years, whereas population went up 9 per cent.

The 1977 National Outdoor Recreation Surveys conducted by the Heritage Conservation and Recreation Service were based on interviews with members of 4,029 households throughout the contiguous United States. It emphasized what they reported as activities during the year.

Although whites participate proportionately more, this study showed that blacks were rapidly increasing their participation rates, in relation to the national average. Otherwise, characteristics of the participants have remained much the same over the past several decades. Most are urban residents from high- or middle-income groups, with the largest number 18 to 44 years old. This type of analysis can be quite helpful for administrators of recreation resources to anticipate continued changes.

AGE GROUP COHORT ANALYSIS

It is clear that there are shifts in recreation participation and in activity selection with progressing age. Youngsters seem to increase the diversity and at least maintain the participation rates as they advance into and through their teens, trying new activities as they go. Thereafter, a gradual decrease in total participation seems to occur with age, accompanied by changes in the types of leisure activities chosen.

Researchers in different places and at different times have found different relationships between age class and activity. Mueller, et al. (1962) reported that of the variables considered, age had by far the strongest relation to nationwide outdoor recreation participation. This was confirmed by studies of camping in more restricted geographic areas (Green and Wadsworth, 1966; Stovener and Guedry, 1968; Christensen and Yoesting, 1973; and White, 1975). Certainly, style of camping appears to be related to age, with older campers tending to prefer less rugged forms of shelter and conditions (Burch and Wenger, 1967).

Other studies have related changes in participation to activity preferences rather than the total level of participation—at least in comparisons of adults of various ages. With greater age, people tend to participate more in sedentary and less strenuous activities, often alone or in small groups. There are fewer leisure activities that appeal to one as he grows older.

Cohort analysis, principally by age groups, is one approach to projecting future participation. A version of this approach is widely used by school boards and universities to predict school populations, based upon the population of children in different age groups. Future population can be predicted by using actuarial tables and school attendance rates. Universities can project 18 years ahead as to the potential student population, but then most rely on judgment and different statistics to calculate the proportion of the population that will actually attend a given school.

Applying the concept to recreation participation, projections can be made from a single point in time. The analyst determines the recreational preferences mix of various age groups in 5- to 10-year age classes and identifies differences between age groups. It is assumed that persons entering these groups in the future will follow similar patterns.

Then, Census data and assumptions about birth and mortality are applied to the present populations. By projecting the numbers in the age classes through their life cycle, and applying the changing recreation mix, estimates of future use by activity can be made (Dippon, 1977). Table 23.2 shows a simplified example. This is a refinement of the process of using total population projections to come up with total participation figures. It approximates reality more by recognizing the different participation patterns in different age groups and accounting for future changes in numbers of people in the different age groups.

RELEVANCE

Many major studies of users have been conducted in the 1970s, with at least 65 completed in the United States. Often, these were done to meet a requirement in the planning process. The surveys have not been consistent in methodology. Partly, this is because of weak sampling techniques in the early studies, and partly, it is related to a shortage of funding.

There is a strong need for researchers and data gatherers to be closely attuned to the purposes for which the data will be used. This requires

Age	Participation rate*	Projected participation in future			
		1975	1980	1985	1990
10–24	10.0556	195,600	199,857	198,844	210,235
25–34	4.8611	275,794	332,094	392,091	410,853
35–44	3.2308	130,000	146,598	163,196	192,347
45–54	5.7308	127,017	122,496	127,487	143,473
55–64	0.7179	22,211	23,308	23,306	22,424
65+	0.3333	111,577	121,928	132,438	141,209
Total		862,199	946,281	1,037,362	1,120,541

* Average number of occasions per capita per year, from 1975 survey.
Source: Dippon, 1977.

first that there be time early in the planning process for verbalization of policy concerns—what questions must be answered by policy decisions. Then, these specific questions—often stated quite simply and in detail—should be incorporated into research guidelines. For example, although it seems reasonable to research the reactions of people to crowding in parks, how is such information relevant to the planner or the politician? (Parks Canada, 1976).

SUMMARY

Measurements of recreation participation vary from rough estimates to full counts of visitors to a property. Projections of future use have been numerous, but the methods used vary widely.

It seems desirable to adopt compatible methods for measuring use among all agencies. The Heritage Conservation and Recreation Service has proposed this and has converted federal land visit reports to visitor-days (12 visitor-hours). Although visitor-hour/visitor-day estimates require some effort to obtain, this type of statistic seems to be the most meaningful and most flexible measure available. Further development of sampling techniques is needed to cover a variety of recreation situations.

Predictions of future use are based on reliable data on past and current use and factors that are associated with recreation participation. Three general techniques are used to estimate future participation: extension of trends in past use, use of judgment and experience, and projection of related socioeconomic factors, followed by calculation of use based on relationships with the factors. National and state plans have usually incorporated various forms of the last approach, based on participation studies.

More attention to measuring recreation use seems advisable. Rigorous and reliable sampling techniques will surely become standard operating procedure in the near future in all types of recreation areas.

Literature Cited

ADAMS, ROBERT L., ROBERT C. LEWIS and BRUCE H. DRAKE. 1973. Outdoor Recreation; a Legacy for America: Appendix "A"—An Economic Analysis. Washington: U.S. Dept. of the Interior, Office of Economic Analysis. 239 pp. + appendices.

Bureau of Outdoor Recreation. 1973. Outdoor Recreation; a Legacy for America. Washington, D.C.: U.S. Dept. of the Interior. 89 pp.

BURCH, WILLIAM R., JR. and WILEY D. WENGER, JR. 1967. The Social Characteristics of Participants in Three Styles of Family Camping. U.S. Forest Service Research Paper PNW-48.

BURY, RICHARD L. and JAMES W. HALL. 1963. Estimating Past and Current Attendance at Winter Sports Areas . . . A Pilot Study. U.S. Forest Service Research Note PSW-33. 7 pp.

BURY, RICHARD L. and RUTH MARGOLIES. 1964. A Method for Estimating Current Attendance on Sets of Campgrounds . . . A Pilot Study. U.S. Forest Service Research Note PSW-42. 6 pp.

CHRISTENSEN, JAMES E. and DEAN R. YOESTING. 1973. Social and attitudinal variants in high and low use of outdoor recreation facilities. Journal of Leisure Research 5(spring):6–15.

CLAWSON, MARION and JACK L. KNETSCH. 1966. Economics of Outdoor Recreation. Baltimore: Johns Hopkins Press. 328 pp.

CUSHWA, CHARLES T., and BURD S. McGINNES. 1963. Sampling procedures and estimates of year-round recreation use on 100 square miles of the George Washington National Forest. Transactions of the 28th N. Am. Wildlife and Natural Resources Conference, pp. 457–465.

DIPPON, DUANE ROY. 1977. Forecasting Region Outdoor Recreation Participation Levels with Cohort Analysis. West Lafayette, Ind.: M.S. Thesis, Purdue University. 144 pp.

GREEN, BERNAL L. and H. A. WADSWORTH. 1966. Campers; What Affects Participation and What Do They Want? W. Lafayette, Ind.: Purdue Univ., Agric. Exp. Sta., Research Bulletin No. 823. 23 pp.

HERBERT, MARY ELLEN. 1974. Systems for Measuring Visitor Participation in Interpretive Programs in Indiana State Parks W. Lafayette, Ind.: M.S. Thesis, Purdue University, 106 pp.

HOF, JOHN G. 1978. Estimating National Recreation Demands. Ft. Collins: unpublished Ph.D. dissertation, Colorado State University.

JAMES, GEORGE A. 1966. Instructions for Using Traffic Counters to Estimate Recreation Visits and Use on Developed Sites. Asheville, N.C.: U.S. Forest Service, Southeast Forest Experiment Station. 12 pp.

JAMES, GEORGE A. 1967. Recreation Use Estimation of Forest Service Lands in the United States. U.S. Forest Service Research Note SE-79. 8 pp.

JAMES, GEORGE A., and J. L. RICH. 1966. Estimating Recreation Use on a Complex of Developed Sites. U.S. Forest Service Research Note SE-64. 8 pp.

JAMES, GEORGE A., and T. H. RIPLEY. 1963. Instructions for Using Traffic Counters to Estimate Recreation Visits and Use. U.S. Forest Service Research Paper SE-3. 12 pp.

JAMES, GEORGE A., H. P. WINGLE, and J. D. GRIGGS. 1971. Estimating Recreation Use on Large Bodies of Water. U.S. Forest Service Research Paper SE-79. 7 pp.

LUCAS, ROBERT C. 1964. The Recreational Use of the Quetico-Superior Area. St. Paul: U.S. Forest Service Research Paper LS-8. 50 pp.

MADDEN, DENNIS B. and DOUGLAS M. KNUDSON. 1978. Attendance Methodology. Indianapolis, Ind.: Indiana Department of Natural Resources. 24 pp.

MARNELL, LEO F. 1975. Use of time-lapse photography for estimating river traffic at Ozark National Scenic Riverways. Paper read to Workshop for Outdoor Recreation Researchers and Cooperators, Land Between the Lakes, Kentucky.

MUELLER, EVA, GERALD GORIN and MARGARET WOOD. 1962. Participation in Outdoor Recreation: Factors Affecting Demand Among American Adults. Washington, D.C.: ORRRC Study Report No. 20.

Parks Canada. 1976. Canadian Outdoor Recreation Demand Study; vol. 1: An Overview and Assessment. Waterloo: The Ontario Research Council on Leisure and Federal-Provincial Parks Conference. 119 pp.

SCHREUDER, H. T., G. L. TYRE and G. A. JAMES. 1975. Instant- and interval-count sampling: two new techniques for estimating recreation use. Forest Science 21(1):40–44.

Standard and Poor's. 1977. Leisure-time Basic Analysis. S & P Industry Surveys, pp. L8-L38.

STOVENER, H. H. and L. J. GUEDRY. 1968. Sociological characteristics of the demand for outdoor recreation. Report No. 1 to Annual Meeting of the Cooperative Regional Research Project No. WM-59, San Francisco, California.

U.S. Forest Service. 1979. The 1980 RPA Assessment. Washington, D.C.: U.S. Dept. of Agriculture.

WHITE, TERRENCE H. 1975. The relative importance of education and income as predictors in outdoor recreation participation. Journal of Leisure Research 7(3):191–199.

CHAPTER 24

Financing Recreation Resources

A few years ago, the San Mateo County, California, park system used about $5,000,000 per year. Only three million of that (60 per cent) came from county sources. The rest was the result of astute financial planning.

Among the generous donors of two millions dollars plus much technical and in-kind assistance were the following:

Department of Housing and Urban Development—funds to buy a 5,700-acre park, matched by a special county bond issue.
Land and Water Conservation Fund—for acqustion and development.
California Fish and Game Commission:
   a) Half of fines money for public education about wildlife and for habitat improvement.
   b) Assistance for all county parks that are legally declared as wildlife preserves.
State Aid to Cities.
Neighborhood Youth Corps (U.S. Department of Labor).
Bureau of Land Management—sale of land at reduced price.
Soil erosion funds.
Army Corps of Engineers—harbor and marina assistance.
Reform school and other prisoners—labor for trails and parks.

Ralph Shaw, then director of the San Mateo system, was one of several able administrators around the nation who put together financial packages that add considerably to local capabilities. The art of administering a local, state, or federal agency, or a private business revolves around funding potential.

This chapter describes the principal financial and technical assistance programs available to public agencies. A few are also accessible by private enterprise and nonprofit corporations. It aims to at least partially answer the question of how some agencies can get outside money. Success is partly based on knowledge, partly on circumstance, and partly on intelligent perseverance.

Local Sources of Finance

State and Local Taxes: The basic funding source for a public park and recreation program is from the tax base. Appropriations from general funds are the most common source. Other arrangements include millage taxes, special taxes, and assessments. Usually, only small proportions come from various permits, concessionaire income, rents, and dispensing machine incomes.

Additional funds can be realized from fees and charges for special services, but these usually merely cover expenses of the service. These include instruction, special facilities, rental of equipment or horses, materials, and other payments.

As one of several cases of state and local special taxation, Kansas passed legislation in 1977 to allow local governments to levy a 2 per cent transient guest tax. The tax was levied on gross receipts for sleeping accommodations at hotels and motels. The use of these tax revenues is for convention and tourism promotion. There is a state committee set up to coordinate this work. It is estimated that there will be more than two million dollars available each year, all from travelers.

Bonding: A park and recreation board usually has the authority to float a bond. This is, in effect, taking out a loan to buy or develop land now. It will be paid back by the people who benefit most from it. They pay property taxes to retire the bonds.

Park bonds have often proven to be heavily favored by voters, even in counties that are generally reluctant to approve bonds for other purposes. The plan must be well prepared and the benefits of the park fairly and clearly presented to the voters.

Bonds are used sparingly, for major projects. They are not appropriate sources of funding for operating costs. Most states allow bond issues for parks and recreation purposes, at the state and local level.

A bond is a written acknowledgment or binding of a debt under seal. Its security or collateral is all the property within a municipality or state. That property is subject to a tax levy sufficient to pay principal and interest. States impose constitutional limits on the amounts of bonds (for example, 2 per cent maximum of the total assessed valuation of property in a park district), their purposes, and the procedures necessary for issuance. A municipal bond is usually of 20, 30, or 40 years' maturity. Most bonds are for capital improvements, such as land purchase, construction of buildings and facilities, or general improvements.

In an inflationary economy, the use of bonds has some advantage. Money is borrowed now to add land or facilities for future use. It allows the agency to buy now at prices that may soon go up substantially. These dollars are paid back at face value with inflated, cheaper dollars in the future. The major disadvantage is the cost of legal and bonding services.

Donations: William S. Hart Park in Los Angeles County was the palatial home of the silent-screen Western movie star William S. Hart. He left this estate to the County of Los Angeles as a gesture of gratitude to the people who paid nickels and dimes to view his Western pictures. Recreation at the park provides visitors opportunities to view art of the Old West, objects used in silent motion pictures, and ranch animals. A highlight of the park is a herd of buffalo presented to the county by Walt Disney. Almost daily, school children are taken by bus to Hart Park, where many youngsters have their first introduction to farm animals.

Similar donations have provided numerous recreation facilities. The Rockefeller family donations have enriched many national parks, notably Jackson Hole of Grand Teton National Park and Virgin Islands National Park. Likewise, states and many cities have received gifts of parks, forests, and nature preserves at bargain prices or no cost.

A small city recently acquired a five-acre riverfront park and installed tennis and basketball courts and made a fine fishing area. The total cost was $150,000, but the city park board did not pay one cent of local tax money. Adroit use of the donation of the land by a foundation, matching Land and Water Conservation Fund grants, and careful bidding procedures made it possible.

Partial donations can be realized when a private or corporate seller of future parkland is willing to sell at a price lower than its appraised value. Then, the difference between the appraised value and the transaction price can usually be considered a tax-deductible donation. It can also be considered as part of the local match for Land and Water Conservation Fund grants. Thus, it is possible that a person who sells for $25,000 land that is valued at $35,000 can claim a deduction of $10,000; save the park and recreation board $10,000; allow the community to apply for $35,000 federal matching money.

Often overlooked, the influence of private enterprise on public parks and recreation resources has been profound. The origins of perhaps 50 per cent of America's city parks are in donations or bequests by private citizens. Foundations have contributed vast amounts of funds for recreation areas. Organizations such as the Save-the-Redwoods League, The Nature Conservancy, and the new Trust for Public Lands have helped acquire thousands of hectares of lands for public recreation resources. Speed and flexibility are major characteristics of private action. An individual or a group with financial resources and dedication can act more in accord with a seller's desires than can a public agency. Public or private conservation agencies can achieve numerous advantages from close work with such groups. Some of the prize elements of national, state, and local recreation resources have come about through cooperative efforts.

State Programs

Local agencies have turned to the federal government for assistance, seldom to the states. The state agencies have acted as a funnel and distributor for federal funds. Only a few states have financial assistance programs. New Jersey's Green Acres program is an example. It has aided many communities to expand their recreation estate considerably. When mixed with federal funding, it gives local money considerable leverage.

Missouri and Washington are two other states that pay 25 per cent of costs for acquisition and development. That allows a county to pay 25 per cent of a project that is federally matched at 50 per cent.

Federal Programs

There are many dozens of recreation assistance programs available. Most are federal. Five of the major ones are the following:

1. Community Development block grants for capital and operations.
2. Land and Water Conservation Fund for capital.
3. General Revenue Sharing for capital and operation.
4. Comprehensive Employment and Training (CETA) program for operations.
5. Youth programs for operations.

Federal assistance programs provided $1.2 billion, or 35.4 per cent of all funds used by cities and counties for parks and recreation in the fiscal year 1976 (HCRS, 1978a). That total included $127 million from Land and Water Conservation Fund, $316.7 million from General Revenue Sharing, $132.1 million from Community Development block grants, and an estimated $600 million from CETA (Figure 24.1). In addition, states have used large sums from most of these federal programs plus many others.

PROGRAMS OF HUD

A number of sources of funding or technical assistance for parks and recreation are available from the Department of Housing and Urban Development (HUD). Virtually all are aimed at improving the quality of the living environment in urban areas. The recreation and park phases are usually tied in with housing improvements, frequently in low-income areas. In addition to these, HUD regulates interstate land sales. Included are the following:

1. Community Development Block Grants (it superseded programs formerly called Urban Renewal, Neighborhood Development Grants, Model Cities, Water and Sewer Grants, Neighborhood Facilities

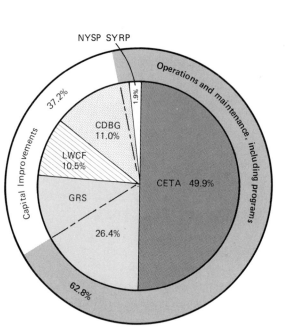

NYSP SYRP

Operations and maintenance including programs

37.2%

CDBG 11.0%

LWCF 10.5%

Capital Improvements

1.9%

CETA 49.9%

GRS

26.4%

62.8%

Figure 24.1 Local park and recreation use of six major grant programs, 1976. (HCRS, 1978a)

LWCF—Land and Water Conservation Fund
CDBG—Community Development Block Grant
GRS—General Revenue Sharing
CETA—Comprehensive Employment and Training Program
NYSP—National Youth Sports Program
SYRP—Summer Youth Recreation Program

Total federal
dollars spent on local
parks and recreation
$1.2 billion

Grants, Public Facilities Loans, Rehabilitation Loans, and Open Space-Urban Beautification-Historic Preservation Grants).

2. Comprehensive Planning Assistance.
3. Community Services for Tenants.
4. New Communities.

Each is described here, based on information from the Department of Housing and Urban Development (HUD, 1978).

Community Development Block Grants: To promote sound community development, HUD awards financial block grants to local governments. These cover many activities, including parks and recreation. They are targeted at lower- to moderate-income neighborhoods, to help offer adequate housing, a suitable living environment, and greater economic opportunities.

About 1,300 metropolitan cities and urban counties are guaranteed an entitlement, based on need calculations that consider poverty, population, and housing conditions. About 1,800 communities qualify for discretionary grants. Title I of the 1974 Housing and Community Development Act (Public Law 93–383), as amended in 1977 (Public Law 95–198), authorized nearly $11 billion for 1978–1980.

The local three-year Community Development Plan is a prerequisite to funding. Communities receiving funds may use them for park acquisition,

Tools for Recreation Administration

construction, site improvements, and facilities. Two features allow use of these funds for payment of the nonfederal share of other federal grant-in-aid programs and partial payment of administration and planning costs of special community development programs.

Relocation costs of families, businesses, and farms for purposes of community development projects can be compensated with money appropriated.

In the first few years, money was allocated in lump sums to local governments for disbursement without project applications. Gradually, more formal application procedures were followed.

Comprehensive Planning Assistance: HUD provides grants of up to two thirds of the cost of many planning and management activities. The grants go to state and local governments for comprehensive planning, covering land use, housing, and community facilities. Participation requires that consideration be given to human and natural resources and improvement of the living environment. The legal authorities are Section 701, Housing Act of 1954 (Public Law 83–560) and Title IV of the Housing and Community Development Act of 1974 (Public Law 93–383).

Community Services for Tenants Program: The program of Community Services for Tenants is aimed at improving resources and programs for a better quality of life for tenants of public housing and HUD-assisted housing. Authorized in the 1937 United States Housing Act (Section 3 of Public Law 75–412), it primarily offers technical assistance. Some financial assistance has come from associated programs from the Departments of Justice and Health, Education, and Welfare. The major recreation activities have been through federal and community agencies providing recreation programs.

New Communities: HUD's Community Development Corporation provides financial and technical assistance to developers of new communities. These may be within central cities, suburbs, or rural areas. The goal is to stimulate careful planning, enhance the environment, and produce viable, economically sound, diversified communities.

The assistance usually has taken the form of up to 80 or 90 per cent guarantees of loans for private developers and to 100 per cent guarantees for public land development agencies. The agency also issues certificates of eligibility to developers who meet the standards but who do not require loan guarantees. These new communities are eligible to receive Community Development block grant funds. This program is fairly young, having been activated by Title VII of the 1970 Housing and Urban Development Act (Public Law 91–609). The results are not yet definitive.

LAND AND WATER CONSERVATION FUND

The single most influential funding program in outdoor recreation was signed into law by the President in 1965. The Land and Water Conservation Fund (LWCF) provides federal monies for acquisition, development, and planning for outdoor recreation.

Money from the fund goes to four major federal land agencies, states, and local public agencies. In addition, the Endangered Species Act of 1973 (Public Law 93–205) authorized the use of Land and Water Conservation Funds for the purpose of protecting endangered or threatened species of fish and wildlife.

The Land and Water Conservation Fund Act of 1965 (Public Law 88–578) was enacted

to assist in preserving, developing, and assuring accessibility to all citizens of the United States of America of present and future generations . . . such quality and quantity of outdoor recreation resources as may be available and are necessary and desirable for individual active participation . . .

Money for the Land and Water Conservation Fund comes from several sources. The original sources of funds were related to recreation: entrance, admission, and user fees from federal recreation areas; motorboat fuel excise taxes, and revenues from surplus land sales. The Act authorized making use charges at federal areas, including the season pass called the "Golden Eagle Passport." When these funds proved inadequate, Congress added a major source of income from off-shore oil drilling leases collected by the Bureau of Land Management.

From 1965 to 1978, the Land and Water Conservation Fund Act has been amended four times for funding purposes. These amendments authorized a maximum annual level for acquisition of land and development purposes. Since 1977, the authorized Fund steadily increased, as can be seen in Table 24.1. Authorization for these funds expires in fiscal year 1989.

The renewal of the Land and Water Conservation Fund Act, signed by President Ford in 1976, authorized expansion of the fund for outdoor recreation and historic preservation over 12 years. It was to go from $300

TABLE 24.1 Authorized land and water conservation fund level and adjusted appropriations.

Fiscal year	Authorized level (million/yr.)	Adjusted appropriations			
		Federal	State	Administrative fund	Total
1965–1968	—	128,507,469	210,835,129	6,910,000	346,252,598
1969–1970	$200	182,418,252	106,770,589	6,411,159	295,600,000
1971–1977	300	1,029,080,000	1,262,665,000	41,643,000	2,333,388,000
1978	600	285,133,000	305,694,000	9,173,000	600,000,000
1979	750				
1980–1989	900				
Total		1,625,138,721	1,885,964,718	64,137,159	3,575,240,598

Source: HCRS, 1978b.

420   Tools for Recreation Administration

Agency	Status through fiscal year 1977			Future estimates	
	Number of tracts	Acres (000)	Cost (000,000)	1978–1983 (000,000)	1984–1989 (000,000)
National Park Service	45,281	977	$ 815	$1,010	
Forest Service	4,177	907	284	752	
Fish and Wildlife Service	512	105	54	478	
Bureau of Land Management	135	6	8	40	
Total	50,105	1,955	$1,161	$2,280	$4,500

Source: HCRS, 1978b.

million in 1976–1977 to 900 million dollars by 1980, the level at which it would stabilize through 1989. Less than a year later, with the urging of President Carter, the act was amended (Public Law 95–42) to authorize raising the ceiling of the fund to $900 million per year immediately for fiscal years 1978 and 1979. That would allow faster action to reduce the land acquisition backlog in the National Park system, wilderness areas, wild and scenic rivers, trails, and national recreation areas.

Federal Share: No less than 40 per cent of the LWCF is allocated to federal recreation lands. In the first 12 years of its existence, the fund provided $1.1 billion for federal acquisition and development, as shown in Table 24.2. The four agencies purchased almost 2 million acres of land for parks, recreation use, endangered species, and other related purposes. In the next 12 years, the agencies hope to spend $6.8 billion more, including some projects not yet authorized by the Congress.

The National Park Service is the biggest single user of LWCF monies. It has spent more than two thirds of the federal share. Reasons are that the Forest Service has some acquisition money under the Weeks Act; the Fish and Wildlife Service has Migratory Bird Conservation Act money, and other sources; and the Bureau of Land Management has not been active in acquiring land. The National Park Service relies almost entirely on the fund for its acquisition programs. Additionally, the Congress has given the park service many new projects that required land purchase.

State and Local Share: To qualify, the state or its subdivision (city, county, township, special district) must meet the following prerequisites:

1. A comprehensive state plan for outdoor recreation is required prior to consideration for financial assistance.
2. A local agency comprehensive recreation plan, approved by the Heri-

tage Conservation and Recreation Service, is required for any money to be assigned to local projects.

3. A project plan serves as the application for funding.

At least half the project cost must come from the state or local agency. This can include actual expenditures by the board from appropriations and bonds or the value of donations of land services. All must be expended, after the project is approved. The agency cannot accept gifts of land and cannot purchase property until after approval, if the value of the property is part of the local match. If Community Development Block Grant money is available, it may serve as part of the local match.

By using the value of donations of land and in-kind services as part or all of the local match, communities have sometimes gained a new park with very little actual cash outlay.

In most cases, states have divided the fund allocation about equally between state properties and local agencies. However, a few states have dedicated almost all of the money to rural state parks (Burdick, 1975). The State of Washington is an example of more equitable distribution.

The Washington State Case: In the state of Washington, LWCF monies are distributed through an Interagency Committee for Outdoor Recreation. State grant funds are combined with federal monies, so they are not easily separable. There were 816 state and local projects funded from 1965 to 1977. These funded projects involved 154 of the 700 agencies in the state that were eligible for funding.

More than $58 million went to the four state land managing agencies for 387 projects. The Department of Game, for example, built boat ramps, bought stream bank easements for fisherman access, and bought wildlife recreation areas. The Department of Natural Resources (forestry) developed primitive campsites, trails, tideland access, and marine areas.

Local agencies received $53 million of matching federal and unmatched state funds for 429 projects. The agencies included 101 cities, 27 counties, 11 port districts, four school districts, three park and recreation districts, one metropolitan park district, two Indian tribes, and one university. Consistently, applications submitted have greatly exceeded the funds available (State of Washington, 1978).

URBANIZATION

Attempts to make the Land and Water Conservation Fund more available to the needs of urban areas have been frequent. Burdick (1975) reported several cases of disproportionate attention to rural areas, partly because of inattention by urban officials. At National Recreation and Park Association meetings and conventions, speakers and participants have often raised the question of meeting urban needs with the fund. The Congress has made some moves in this direction, but the major thrust of the fund has remained to provide monies for purchasing and developing outdoor facilities, with emphasis on conservation of natural areas rather than reclamation of urban spaces. The original purpose of the act was focused on national and state parks, forests, and recreation areas, with some participation by urban agencies. There has been no shortage of valid projects to utilize the money allocated by the Congress each year. There is considerable flexibility in the provisions of the fund, so that many urban parks have been strongly benefited by the matching monies.

An important issue is the use of funds for indoor recreation facilities. Huge chunks of money could be invested in buildings and the associated facilities—enough to require that a whole new approach would have to be taken in obtaining appropriations from the Congress. However, the Fund is limited to outdoor facilities, except for enclosing swimming pools and ice skating rinks in cold climates.

If urban interests are to be funded more completely by the federal government, it would seem appropriate to establish a new program or properly amend the existing fund, rather than to dilute the present limited effort of the fund. The escalation of the LWCF in 1976 to triple its authorization ceiling was one such positive move, partially in response to growing urban pressures. It is curious, however, that there is no Park and Recreation Fund.

Revenue Sharing Funds

In a move to get federal tax monies back to the local government level, the State and Local Fiscal Assistance Act was passed in 1972 (Public Law 92–512). The act appropriated money from the general fund of the United States Treasury to be allocated to local governments (two thirds) and state governments (one third). There are few guidelines as to the manner in which the money is to be spent. Local governments are required to allocate the funds to "priority expenditures," which are usually by local determination, after public meetings to hear suggestions from citizens.

Local government uses include ordinary and necessary operating and maintenance expenses for recreation, environmental protection, public safety, public transportation, health, social services for the poor and aged, libraries, financial administration, and capital expenditures authorized by law. The funds cannot be used to match other federal grant programs.

Direct, unconditional distribution of federally collected tax monies to state and local levels of government was new to the United States in 1972. Andrew Jackson tried it for a year (1836–1837) and then the idea was dropped. Other federal fiscal assistance was available but was earmarked for predetermined purposes. An example of earmarked funds is the Land and Water Conservation Fund, designated only for acquisition and development of outdoor recreation resources, after a *specific* project is approved and conditional upon previously approved state and local plans. These are unique in that the local or state recipient determines how they are to be spent. The original act was altered with 1976 amendments (Public Law

94–488) to stiffen public participation and auditing requirements. However, the program allows maximum local discretion and flexibility in spending the funds to improve delivery of local government services.

The amount of money a jurisdiction receives is determined by formula, favoring low-income and high-tax communities.

Recreation uses of the monies amount to about 5 per cent of the total (Office of Revenue Sharing, 1976). On the local level, recreation uses were 7 per cent of the total; states spent about 1 per cent of their revenue sharing funds on recreation.

Local governments split their uses of the money about evenly between operating and capital expenditures, considering all uses. For recreation uses, however, governments favored capital expenditures by more than two to one (Office of Revenue Sharing, 1976, 1978). States have an even stronger tendency to use recreation money for capital expenditures.

There have been no major changes in spending patterns among the categories of spending since 1972. Public safety, education, and public transportation receive the bulk of the funds.

Curiously, northeastern (3 per cent) and north central (5 per cent) regions spend a smaller proportion on recreation than the southern (6 per cent) and western (10 per cent) governments (Office of Revenue Sharing, 1976). This is approximately inverse to the per capita availability of public park and recreation land.

Labor Department Programs

The Department of Labor has a series of programs that can add workers to the operations of public agencies and nonprofit corporations. The value of this labor has been a major contributor to local and state agencies.

The Comprehensive Employment and Training Act (CETA) contains numerous programs for part- and full-time employment subsidies for selected workers. Some include seasonal workers. Highly motivated professionals can be hired through this arrangement. Only a few have been.

Various and changing summer work programs are offered to employ youth. As part of the Federal Summer Youth Program, the Department of Labor has operated a Summer Recreation Support Program since 1970. The nation's 100 largest cities receive grants each year to help provide recreation programs for children under 13 years of age. The Recreation Support Program is limited to noncapital expenditures, including supplies, small equipment, transportation, and payment of program leaders. Other programs are available through the Department of Labor.

North Carolina Funding Case: Sessoms and Krug (1977) studied financial records of 35 park and recreation departments in North Carolina from 1951 to 1975. They listed for operations expenses (no capital) four sources of revenues:

General funds of the city—yearly average of 39 to 61 per cent.

Special recreation tax levies—16 to 42 per cent.

Fees and charges—varied from 10 per cent in 1951–1952 to 5 per cent in 1974–1975.

Other sources—varied from 8 per cent in 1961–1962 to 31 per cent in 1973–1974.

The largest increase has been in other sources, most of which have been General Revenue Sharing monies, from the U.S. Treasury. In 1974–1975, North Carolina communities spent 10 per cent of the revenue sharing funds allocated to the state for park and recreation purposes. The increasing reliance on federally collected funds has been accompanied by a decrease in other sources, in percentage terms. In North Carolina, the recreation tax levy became less important because of a 1971 law allowing easier access to general fund monies for parks and recreation purposes.

Total recreation and parks budgets have gone up rather markedly. In 1951–1952, the 35 communities spent $2 million, and in 1974–1975, their budgets totaled $27.5 million. This increase was more rapid than population growth and inflationary effects combined. Per capita expenditures ranged from $2.00 to $14.65 over the 25 years. For the period 1967–1975, when data were available, the growth of recreation expenditures was almost three times that of the inflation rate. Also, recreation and parks expenditures became a more important part of the total municipal budgets over this period, rising from 5.4 per cent to 7.7 per cent.

Local park and recreation services have grown significantly over the past quarter of a century. Financial support growth has exceeded the rate of inflation. The proportion of support for parks and recreation from the total municipal budget has increased significantly.

Historic Preservation

Many outdoor recreation areas have an historical connection that can bring in financial assistance.

The nation's concern for historic preservation has been expressed in several laws spaced through the years. In 1906, the Antiquities Act extended protection over antiquities on federal property and empowered the President to set aside National Monuments from the public domain. In 1935, the Historic Sites Act provided for historical units to be managed by the National Park System. It also set up a program for identifying and marking National Historic Landmarks. In 1966, the National Historic Preservation Act (Public Law 89–665) extended the policy of historic preservation to every federal agency and authorized financial assistance to state and local governments, private organizations, and individuals in historic preservation.

Much of the program in the 1966 law was recommended by the United

States Conference of Mayors through their Special Committee on Historic Preservation. The act gives legal recognition to the cultural risks inherent in the constant change of modern society. The forces threatening the natural environment also endanger historical resources. The law does not prevent the destruction of properties. It lists properties worth saving and ensures they will not be destroyed without due process. It requires consideration of whether what is about to be built is of greater worth than what would be destroyed (National Park Service, 1969).

HISTORIC PRESERVATION FUND

The Office of Archeology and Historic Preservation was moved from the National Park Service to the Heritage Conservation and Recreation Service in 1978. It administers the Historic Preservation Fund. The fund provides matching grants for surveys and planning for acquisition and development of historic resources.

Before 1966, most federal historic preservation activities were limited to purchase or recognition and recording of significant properties. Private, state, and local interests had most of the responsibilities for preservation. The 1966 National Historic Preservation Act gave the Secretary of the Interior authority to administer a grants-in-aid program to states (Table 24.3) and the National Trust for Historic Preservation.

The grants-in-aid program gives top priority to National Historic landmarks in clear and present danger of destruction or impairment.

The National Trust is a private, nonprofit corporation chartered by the Congress. It owns and maintains certain nationally significant historic properties. It also assists private and public interests in quick action to achieve preservation. Grants support acquisition, restoration, maintenance, and administration. They also support educational programs, publications, seminars, conferences, consulting, legal services, and feasibility studies.

The National Museum Act of 1966, through the Smithsonian Institution, provides funding of seminars, workshops, stipends for research, training, travel, and intern programs in the United States and abroad. This program is aimed at museums of all types, including those in parks and interpretive centers.

REGISTERS

A number of registers of natural and cultural resources are maintained by the Heritage Conservation and Recreation Service. They are lists of places of national significance, owned by a variety of agencies or individuals. A listing on one of the registers brings prestige and a pledge of protection. There is no funding attached to listing and no change in ownership.

The registers are as follows:

National Register of Historic Places.
Historic Sites Survey.

TABLE 24.3 Historic preservation grants, fiscal year 1977 (dollars).

State	Amount apportioned	State	Amount apportioned
Alabama	309,230	New Hampshire	158,125
Alaska	172,442	New Jersey	221,083
Arizona	145,426	New Mexico	155,088
Arkansas	249,860	New York	525,000
California	525,000	North Carolina	350,075
Colorado	279,246	North Dakota	136,112
Connecticut	463,893	Ohio	378,918
Delaware	187,735	Oklahoma	163,749
District of Columbia	200,277	Oregon	164,998
Florida	199,006	Pennsylvania	469,024
Georgia	264,705	Puerto Rico	157,103
Guam	59,239	Rhode Island	288,290
Hawaii	217,916	South Carolina	314,327
Idaho	146,067	South Dakota	173,720
Illinois	284,642	Tennessee	177,888
Indiana	154,163	Texas	525,000
Iowa	217,741	Utah	136,647
Kansas	141,666	Vermont	194,998
Kentucky	343,391	Virginia	214,988
Louisiana	179,402	Virgin Islands	329,867
Maine	188,045	Washington	220,874
Maryland	405,418	West Virginia	333,675
Massachusetts	525,000	Wisconsin	174,478
Michigan	302,680	Wyoming	181,676
Minnesota	393,614	Trust Territory	141,874
Mississippi	153,047	State & territory grants	13,923,600
Missouri	404,173	National Trust grants	2,544,500
Montana	166,431	Total	16,468,100
Nebraska	187,758	Administrative expenses	1,031,900
Nevada	145,783	Appropriation	17,500,000
		Authorization	24,400,000

Source: National Register of Historic Places, National Park Service (HCRS, 1978b).

Historic American Buildings Survey.
Historic American Engineering Record.
National Register of Historic Landmarks.
National Register of Natural Landmarks.

There are special tax incentives for private, depreciable structures listed on the National Register of Historic Places or located in recognized historical districts. Costs of demolition of historic structures are not deductible. Rehabilitation costs can be deducted over five years. A taxpayer can claim accelerated depreciation for rehabilitated historic structures used for commercial purposes.

OTHER PROGRAMS

Humanities and Arts: In 1965, the National Foundation for the Arts and Humanities was established. It is divided into two virtually autonomous groups.

The National Endowment for the Humanities has provided grants for programming and interpretation through museums, historic parks, archeological areas, cultural programs in parks, as well as a broad range of social science and humanities programs in many other institutions.

The National Endowment for the Arts is concerned with funding performing and creative arts. Programs in local and state recreation areas have been assisted by this program.

The endowments are funded by annual congressional appropriations.

Small Watershed Program (Public Law 566):   The Soil Conservation Service administers a program of technical and financial assistance that often produces important recreational benefits. Ponds and small reservoirs are often part of the watershed control projects developed through the Soil and Water Conservation Districts. They can be developed for recreation and managed under cooperative agreements.

State and Federal Highway Agencies: Highway funds can be used to add bike paths in conjunction with road construction, if the state highway commission approves such use of the funds. Scenic roads and other transportation-related projects may be assisted by certain limited programs of state and federal highway agencies.

SOURCES OF LABOR

Among many labor programs, the following are popular.

College Work-Study pays 80 per cent of eligible students' wages when they are employed by a qualifying agency. Well-qualified and motivated young people can often be employed for the summer and part time during the school year with a low cash outlay.

The Green Thumb program pays older people to work part time on public projects. Planning and supervision are needed for efficient utilization of these experienced workers.

Volunteer programs can be developed with university clubs, scouts, civic clubs, docents, and others. Effective leadership from the park organization is essential for success.

Penal institutions can often provide certain kinds of labor for park development.

ENVIRONMENTAL EDUCATION

When looking for funds for an environmental education program, the administrator might look into federal funds. One possibility is the Environmental Education Act of 1970. The act encourages the initiation and maintenance of environmental education programs at the elementary and secondary school levels to instruct the new curriculum. The act provides training

428

programs for people associated with environmental education and for the planning of outdoor education centers. The act established in the U.S. Office of Education an office of environmental education. This office has an administrator who works with a citizens' advisory council to administer the programs that relate to environmental education.

Funds may be appropriated in the form of grants and contracts to state and local educational agencies for the following purposes, among others:

Support of environmental education programs at the elementary and secondary levels.
Planning of outdoor ecological study centers.
Community education programs.
Preparation and distribution of materials for mass media use.

In addition to the grants to the public education agencies, small grants, not to exceed $10,000 annually, may be made to public and private nonprofit agencies. Applications for grants and contracts must be made to the U.S. Commissioner of Education.

SURPLUS PROPERTY

Federal land is transferable to local park departments at 50 per cent of value for recreation purposes or without cost for historic monument purposes. State agencies, including Soil and Water Conservation Districts, can also receive federal surplus real property. The General Services Administration administers surplus real property transfers through the Heritage Conservation and Recreation Service.

Federal surplus personal property can also be donated to public agencies; nonprofit, tax-exempt organizations; and national youth organizations such as Boy Scouts, Girl Scouts, Boys Clubs, Camp Fire Girls, and the Red Cross. The uses of the property must be for educational or public health purposes. The personal property available as surplus is of great variety, from desks, chairs, and office equipment to machine tools, electronic equipment, boats, and airplanes. The General Services Administration in Washington also administers this program. Surplus equipment and machinery is listed for agencies that wish to make bond and transport it from the point of sale to the park.

NATIONAL PARK SERVICE ASSISTANCE

The NPS cooperates with, assists, and advises other federal agencies, state, and local governments with respect to specific area planning, management, interpretation, protection, maintenance, and operation. The agency provides postauthorization planning assistance for federal water development projects. It also offers planning assistance to HCRS. The NPS conducts studies for the Wild and Scenic Rivers Act and for National Scenic Trails.

Literature Cited

BURDICK, JOHN M. 1975. Recreation in the Cities: Who Gains from Federal Aid? Washington, D.C.: Center for Growth Activities. 48 pp.

Heritage Conservation and Recreation Service. 1978a. National Urban Recreation Study; Executive Report. Washington, D.C.: U.S. Dept. of the Interior. 184 pp.

Heritage Conservation and Recreation Service. 1978b. Federal Outdoor Recreation Land Acquisition—LWCF; Task Force Report. Washington, D.C.: U.S. Dept. of the Interior. 17 pp.

National Park Service. 1969. The National Register of Historic Places, 1969. Washington, D.C.: U.S. Dept. of the Interior.

Office of Revenue Sharing. 1976. Reported Uses of General Revenue Sharing Funds, 1974–1975. Washington, D.C.: U.S. Dept. of the Treasury. 40 pp.

Office of Revenue Sharing. 1978. Fifth Annual Report of the Office of Revenue Sharing. Washington, D.C.: U.S. Dept. of the Treasury. 33 pp.

SESSOMS, H. DOUGLAS and JAMES L. KRUG. 1977. Municipal recreation services in North Carolina: a 24-year analysis. Leisure Sciences 1(1):21–33.

U.S. Dept. of Housing and Urban Development. 1978. Programs of HUD. Washington, D.C.: No. HUD-214-4-PA. 128 pp.

Washington, State of. 1978. 1977 Annual Report, Natural Resources and Recreation Agencies. Olympia. 91 pp.

CHAPTER 25

Land Acquisition and Controls

The recreation resources profession is first a real estate business. This chapter describes the numerous ways that land can be controlled and acquired. They include traditional fee simple ownership and use of easements. Acquisition by mandatory dedication and condemnation are advanced as fair and useful procedures.

These are all becoming important tools to recreation planners, consultants, and managers. Almost every recreation resource administration in the nation is struggling with the concepts of easements, the power of eminent domain, and other touchy issues.

A recommendation in the 1978 urban recreation report (HCRS, 1978) suggested that land be acquired by partial rights only, except in rare cases. The idea was recommended for state and federal governments as well. This is one of many recent signals of a revolution in public recreation resources.

Acquisition Methods

PURCHASE AND LEASE-BACK

An agency purchases a piece of land and then leases it back to the seller for a specified time or for the rest of the seller's life. The lease contains restrictions governing the types of uses and development of the property.

LEASE OR RENT

If an agency is interested in use of a property without ownership, it can pay for temporary use through periodic payment. This may be a good solution for a transition period while more permanent facilities are being acquired or built elsewhere, or for special events. The relatively low annual cost may be helpful to a struggling agency.

OPTIONS

When an agency or individual does not have sufficient money to purchase a piece of land, sometimes an option can be negotiated. This is a low-cost purchase of the right to buy the land in the future. There is a termination date on the option; if it is not exercised (if the land is not purchased) before the expiration date, the seller has the right to put it on the open market. In many cases, options are purchased along with lease agreements, with the prospective buyer paying to use the land for the period before the option expires. The option period allows time to develop capital.

DONATIONS

As mentioned in Chapter 24, donations of land for recreation and conservation purposes are important means of acquisition. In the state of New York, more than 30 per cent of all federal, state, and county parkland has been donated (Stover, 1975). Donations may be by bequest or immediate. There are several advantages of donations, to both donors and donees. The public receives the land virtually free, often in key locations and on lands that have received special care. The donor saves on taxes in several ways. The donation counts as a tax deduction. At the same time, the landowner avoids inheritance taxes, capital gains taxes, and recurring real estate property taxes.

The main reason that donations of land are not more common is possibly that public officials fail to ask (Stover, 1975). Active and continuing inquiry and invitations to donate are a vital part of any growing public land agency. Some park and recreation agencies hesitate to seek donations because of the maintenance costs that follow. Actually, some suitable properties may be almost maintenance-free, if they are designated, at least temporarily, as natural areas, ecology study areas, or other types of undeveloped properties. They can be used for appropriate activities, reserved as open space, or kept as future expansion areas. They may become permanent nature preserves, if this is their highest value. An example of donation is the privately owned Coskata-Coatue Wildlife Refuge (Stover, 1975).

More than 320 ha of sand dunes, salt marsh, and upland on Nantucket Island, Massachusetts, owned by Mrs. J. Allen Backus, Jr. and Mr. and Mrs. Robert W. Sziklas, have been a source of pleasure for almost half a century to the people of Nantucket and visitors to the island.

For more than 40 years, Mrs. Backus, and later Mr. and Mrs. Sziklas, have made their property available for public use. To ensure that public enjoyment of this fine natural area would continue, the owners contracted The Trustees of Reservations, a charitable corporation and one of the country's oldest landowning conservation organizations.

Established by action of the Great Court of Massachusetts, The Trustees is privately administered and operates statewide. As custodian of more than 55 natural areas and historic sites totaling more than 5,600 ha, The Trustees were obviously qualified recipients of the Nantucket property. In December 1974, the owners donated the property to The Trustees.

The donated tract, known as the Coskata-Coatue Wildlife Refuge, is

432   Tools for Recreation Administration

rich with coastal wildlife, finfish, and shellfish. The Trustees of Reservations will protect the integrity of the Coskata-Coatue resources and retain the opportunity for all who come to Nantucket to view the vast scenic resources, delight in the colorful wildlife, and find peace in the historic reminders of nineteenth-century fishermen hauling their boats to shore.

People donate land for many reasons. One of the principal reasons is sentimental attachment to a particular area and a sense of the need for stewardship (sometimes called preservation) of the land.

Jean and Russell Carl donated their Pennsylvania home to the Western Pennsylvania Conservancy when they moved to New Jersey. Summing up the thoughts and reasons for dedicating the proceeds from their home for future acquisitions of special areas, Mrs. Carl wrote:

Because we love the area, and our roots are so deeply embedded here, we want to know that the bounties of what we have harvested here will remain to enrich the leisure hours of many, many other nature lovers in future years. And that we trust the Conservancy to set up in our memory some tract or preserve that will remain invulnerable to the vagaries of changing times such as we see besetting some of the man-created institutions which we might endow otherwise. (The story of a bequest, 1977).

BARGAIN SALE

A bargain sale is a transfer of property at a price less than the appraised fair market value. In most cases of sale to a public agency at a bargain price, the owner has the same benefits he would have from a donation for the value of the price foregone. The seller should make sure the appraisal, survey, and final price are carefully and legally recorded in a manner acceptable to the tax authorities.

A bargain sale is attractive to the seller when 1) he wants to receive some cash from the property; 2) he paid a low cash price for it so would be subject to high capital gains tax on the full property; 3) he has a fairly high current income and, therefore, could use a donated portion of the value as an income tax deduction. The nature of the long-term capital gains tax in the United States allows a seller to keep the receipts equal to the original cost and half of the appreciated profit, without taxes. The other half of the profit is added to the seller's gross income and is subject to tax (unless there are equivalent deductions). If a piece of land is large, the one half of the profit might put him into a higher tax bracket. To illustrate, a person with a $40,000 per year income wanted to sell a forest area. He paid $10,000 for it in 1965. Today, it is appraised at $50,000. If he sold it at the full value, he would not be taxed for the $10,000 or for the first half of the profit of $40,000. However, the last $20,000 would be added to his income to give him a gross income of $60,000. Even if he manages to average this income over several years, his taxes would be markedly higher than if he made a bargain sale and counted the donation as a deduction.

Condemnation

Exercise of the power of eminent domain is called condemnation.

Eminent domain is the long-standing principle under which private land is acquired for public projects for the greater good of the greater number. It may force sale by unwilling sellers, with compensation set by a jury of their peers, if the seller so desires.

The power of eminent domain has a bad name with many people, largely those who are forced to yield their property. The general public should know both sides of the story and understand how the power is used and limited.

Without eminent domain, the nation's highways would twist and turn around corners of properties, skip sections, or not be built at all. A few state roads reveal that the public interest was not paramount when they were built: they have 90-degree turns at mile and even half mile intervals.

Most railroads were granted the power of eminent domain so they could lay tracks on efficient routes. Without this power, there would be few projects for the general benefit, because any single person in the path could block the projects. There would be few reservoirs or other flood control projects, parks, parkways, sewer lines, or power transmission lines.

A key question is whose general good is to be considered? During interstate highway construction, the argument is often heard from local landowners that the big road is not needed—they can get wherever they want to go without it. There are others whose needs and conveniences are considered also—people and enterprises from the locality, the state, and other states who will travel the road. The greater good is not always well represented at local public hearings about the project.

There is no question that the principle of eminent domain involves a conflict between individual and public rights. The principle actually resolves the conflict by stating that the public rights shall prevail in such conflicts, but not at the financial expense of the private individual. Just as private landowners defend their individual rights, the public should also realize and defend its rights to a reasonable extent. The individual who prevails against public projects does so at the expense of the public benefits. Tolerance of this expense varies inversely with the importance of the benefits to the public, with the clarity of the issue and, perhaps regrettably, with the power and expertise of the officials who are representing the public.

Eminent domain is not a public right to be exercised willy-nilly or with a heavy hand. It requires restraint and often is used as a last resort. But it does not require apology. It is a legal, proper, just, and often mutually desirable process to carry out public projects, and it provides a means to acquire land or easements from unwilling sellers, if the project prevails.

Condemnation is often controversial. At least two issues are centers of argument. The first concerns the government's right or need to take a particular piece of property for recreation, forest, or refuge purposes. The

Tools for Recreation Administration

second revolves around the amount of just compensation to be paid. Much of the concern is pretrial worry and imagining what will happen. The landowner sees a land-grabbing government agency that is powerful, remote, and rather uncaring about the plight of an almost defenseless landowner. The agency, with its usually limited funds, may envision the private landowners as profiteers who are trying to hold up the public purse for personal gain.

When the power of eminent domain is enforced through the process of condemnation, the rights to land are involuntarily relinquished. Condemnation is usually employed as an acquisition tool in two cases: when the landowner refuses to voluntarily sell the rights at the price offered and when title to the land is unclear or multiple owners cannot be contacted to clear the title transfer. The latter is often called friendly condemnation.

The use of eminent domain produces a result similar to voluntary sales; the land rights are transferred and the seller is compensated according to fair market value of the land. In condemnation cases, the price is not negotiated between buyer and seller, but set by disinterested third parties— a judge or jury who are advised by court-appointed appraisers.

OUTRIGHT PURCHASE

The purchase of land in fee simple is the most common manner in which parks and recreation properties are acquired. This gives the public or private recreation agency free rein, within reasonable standards, to develop and operate the property. It also gives the agency maximum control over the care and use of the property, allowing the public ready, uncomplicated access to it.

Ownership may be acquired by a public agency through willing buyer-willing seller negotiations or through the use of the power of eminent domain. Both methods are commonly used by local park and recreation departments and by most federal and state agencies. A few agencies avoid the use of condemnation (the implementation of the power of eminent domain) because of a hesitancy to go to court.

A fundamental of all land acquisition proceedings is to determine what the land is worth before making an offer. Most public agencies are required to have such an appraisal made and are limited, in normal circumstances, to paying no more than *fair market value*. That is determined by professional appraisers as the highest price estimate that a property will bring if sold on the open market, allowing a reasonable time to find a purchaser with knowledge of the usefulness and possibilities of the property.

An appraisal can be made by anyone with knowledge of the local real estate market. The most competent appraisers are likely to be members of any of three societies concerned with upgrading the profession—The Society of Real Estate Appraisers, The Appraisal Institute of America, and the American Society of Appraisers (Stover, 1975). In court cases involving condemnation, a judge will often seek the appraisals of three disinterested parties and then the judge or a jury will make final determination of the property value.

An appraisal is essential to any acquisition involving condemnation. It is required for donations and for bargain sales (appraisal paid for by the donor) if the Internal Revenue Service is to accept the value of the donation as a tax deduction. Appraisal is also required when Land and Water Conservation Funds are to be involved in the acquisition or development of a property.

There are three approaches to estimating fair market value: cost, market data, and income methods (Barlowe, 1958). Each is valid and has special value. The cost approach is concerned with estimating the cost to replace property. It is useful for certain accounting applications and internal control, but is not usually applicable in land acquisition. It can be used by the buyer in determining an upper limit in negotiations. Some landowners argue that in condemnation proceedings replacement value should be the criterion for payment. The market data approach compares the property in question with values of similar properties that have recently been sold in the same area. That is the most common approach used in standard real estate appraisals. It does not measure well the special values of a particular property. The income approach first determines the total of future net income from rental of the land, agricultural cropping, or timber harvesting on a sustained-yield basis, depending on the character of the land. The total future income is then discounted to present value, using a standard interest rate. If a farm, for example, is expected to produce an even flow of net returns year after year, the value can be approximated using the following formula:

$$\text{Value} = \frac{\text{annual net returns}}{\text{interest rate}}$$

$$\text{Example: Value} = \frac{\$20,000}{.08} = \$250,000$$

A property that annually produced a net return of $20,000 would be worth $250,000 to purchase, if 8 per cent were considered a reasonable interest rate.

When the property will not return a steady income, the calculation is modified by the particular income and time characteristics involved. This approach may be used for evaluating properties that are about to be developed or rezoned.

Most appraisers find it useful to use at least two and sometimes three approaches. The American Institute of Real Estate Appraisers and several government agencies recommend the use of all three methods (Barlowe, 1958).

Tools for Recreation Administration

LOCAL PARKS—MANDATORY DEDICATION

In 1974, California passed a law, which enabled the legislative body of a city or county to require by law the dedication of land or the payment of fees or a combination of these for park and recreation purposes. The city or county would withhold approval of a final map or plan of the area to be subdivided if the local ordinance were not met. The state law does not set a percentage of the subdivision to be set aside for recreation but requires that the local law define standards for determining the proportion to be dedicated and the amount of fee to be paid in lieu of land. The local legislative body must have a general plan containing a recreational element with principles and standards. The local unit must specify the initiation date of park development and must proceed with development for park and recreational purposes only. Small areas (less than five parcels), industrial, and commercial subdivisions are exempted from mandatory dedication. The local government may require only the payment of fees in subdivisions containing 50 parcels or less.[1]

Such laws forcing dedications by land development applicants are sometimes a condition of granting a zoning variance, issuance of building permits, or approval of subdivision plan maps. It is a relatively inexpensive way for the public to gain parks and open space. It is seen by some land developers as taking without compensation. This allegation has not been accepted in court. However, it is generally assumed that the developer can pass the opportunity cost along to lot purchasers in the subdivision and that the park will make the property more attractive to potential buyers. The procedure certainly is more economical to residents of the area than the alternative of purchasing land after it is built up or partially so. Condemnation would probably be necessary, and park location and acreage could not be acquired as judiciously. Another alternative—acquiring lands for parks before real estate development becomes interesting—is theoretically wiser and less expensive but is quite difficult politically. It is hard to convince voters that rural lands should be purchased for future neighborhood parks when the existing urban areas still may need additional park area closer to home. Various far-seeing local officials have made such precocious purchases. Central Park, then on the outskirts of New York City, was an early example.

The basic premise of the mandatory dedication philosophy is that the subdivision reduces the supply of open land but increases the demand for it, and dedication provides a means to serve the new residents with park and recreation services.

Mandatory dedication procedures help solve the problem of supplying recreation space for new subdivisions. It is economically feasible, even advantageous, for developers to provide space in expensive suburban tracts. It is more of a problem to provide parks in new low- to medium-price develop-

---

[1] Government Code of California §66477.

ments, where the prices are kept low by crowding as many houses as possible onto a site. Even more difficult is the provision of parks in a subdivison that is already made without open space.

A built-in provision for parks in new subdivisions is an open space trust fund, established from a portion of a transfer tax on real estate. By this method, a county or city can acquire public open areas ahead of development or after the need has become evident, when and where it sees fit.

Land Controls

For land to be regularly available for public recreation, it is necessary that it be under some kind of control by a public or private agency committed to keep it available.

Land-use control may be achieved through various devices: regulation through zoning, eminent domain, open market purchase of full title to property, purchase of less than fee title such as easements, leasing, and combinations of these devices. Numerous trails exist on the basis of formal or informal agreements, usually taking the form of free leases.

The purposes of land acquisition may be several, but they basically center around *control of the uses of land*. Traditionally, control implies full ownership of all usual property rights, allowing the owner to develop recreation facilities in any reasonable manner. For many purposes, however, there is little need to own all rights. If an agency wants a scenic buffer or backdrop for a park, trail, or river, the control of the land need be only partial. Ownership of development rights will achieve the same purpose. If the aim is to maintain forest or open space in a community to preserve the rural or forest character, the use of tax incentives or zoning may achieve the goals without any change of ownership. Flexibility in use of techniques may be efficient. Thus, the goal of land acquisition efforts may be thought of as control of the uses of the land. There are several classes of land control, from fee simple ownership to voluntary agreements.

The greatest control comes from fee simple ownership, whereby the recreation business or agency holds full title to the land and its facilities. Variations on fee simple may include ownership of mineral or water rights by outside parties. These often do not transfer to a purchaser of real estate. This is true in many western states, where the owner of downstream water rights may have the power to enter the land of a private or public owner to maintain a reservoir or channel that affects delivery of water. Fee simple ownership is acquired by purchase, donation or bargain sale. It is most appropriate for traditional public and private parks.

Ownership of partial rights provides that the landholder retains the property, but a park and recreation agency holds the development rights or the right to access. There is limited, but specified, control over the

Tools for Recreation Administration

land. Easements and agreements are the two most common types of partial rights arrangements.

Leases or rentals of land are often used in arrangements between a state or local government and a forest industry. Similar arrangements are made with landowners and hunting clubs, private campground concessionaires, or other groups. The terms of the lease are variable, usually allowing the lessee ample right to carry out a full range of activities.

Tax incentives may keep land in open space or natural conditions. In some states, stiff forest classification acts allow owners with dedicated forests to pay only nominal property taxes, as long as the land stays in planned forest management. Farmers and forest owners near cities may be encouraged to keep their lands out of development by assessing their land value on the basis of continuing current use, rather than potential use.

Zoning prohibits certain developments and activities in designated districts of a county. Zoning can sometimes be combined with open space tax incentives to define land uses in an economic manner.

Agreement between an agency and a landowner, with or without monetary renumeration, may also achieve limited control over land use. These may be mutual understandings with landowners, signed agreements to allow hikers to cross land, as with the Appalachian Trail, or restrictive covenants attached to deeds. One of the most binding forms of agreement is the preservation restriction on historic districts or buildings that requires owners to maintain the architectural character of a certain period.

Several of these alternatives are discussed in detail.

EASEMENTS

When George Washington looked out from Mount Vernon across the Potomac, he saw hills and forests on the other side, not supermarkets, parking lots, marinas, and apartment buildings. Today, when a visitor to Mount Vernon looks across the Potomac, forests and water and hills meet the eye, looking much as they did during the historic period that is represented by the house and grounds. The reason the opposite bank has not modernized is that an easement has preserved it in its forested condition. A scenic easement was secured to prevent the development of the land and the river, and to preserve a view and maintain a stand of riverbank forest.

Scenic easements allow land of great scenic value to remain in private ownership, with only the development rights being sold, donated, or leased in the form of an easement held by a government or private body. The party that acquires and holds an easement agrees to leave the land in its natural state to preserve its scenic and environmental protection values. The property owner benefits from the cash received or taxes saved; the public does not have to buy the land but gains from its beauty.

Under a scenic easement, a farm owner could still live on and farm his land, but would have sold his right to build structures, erect signs, subdivide the property, or otherwise develop the land, as specified in the agreement. Every easement can be different. It is essentially a negotiated agreement between the landowner and the holder of the easement. It should specify exactly what rights are involved.

Easements can have a variety of purposes. An easement may prohibit certain kinds of development, such as industrial development, or it may be more detailed to prohibit many specific activities but to permit access across the land. Most recreation, scenic, or conservation easements are negative—that is, they list what cannot be done to the land, such as clearing the trees, dumping, erecting billboards, building apartments. Some are positive wherein the landowner grants permission for certain limited use of the property or a small portion of it, such as the right of the public to cross a corner of the property to reach a river or to follow a hiking trail. It is important to note that public access is not usually implied in a scenic easement. Access is a separate item in any easement, or it may involve a separate easement.

Easements were used for recreation and open space as early as 1893, when Massachusetts authorized the Boston Metropolitan Park Commission to acquire partial rights to land (Whyte, 1959).

They have been used for years for certain public utilities such as power and gas transmission lines. These carry with them the right of ingress and egress to inspect and repair. The landowner may farm beneath the lines or above the buried pipe. County roads and telephone lines are often on lands with an implied easement. The Minnesota legislature requires foresters to consider easements as a tool in the acquisition of public hardwood forests. Counties and cities are using them to guarantee open space. In upstate New York and New Jersey, communities are buying development rights from farmers to keep the land in agricultural uses.

The conservation easement helps reduce land costs when linear-type parks are considered. Trail and river recreation do not require large blocks of land. They are narrow travel routes that benefit from the attractiveness of the surrounding land. To maintain or enhance such paralleling attractiveness, the device of acquiring scenic or conservation easements can be used to keep the land in more or less natural condition. It is, in effect, the landowner's surrender of only the right to alter the scenic quality of the land in question. That may involve the surrender of the opportunity to clear and farm the land, to build homes or cottages on it, or any of a number of activities.

The landowner and the purchaser make a contract that describes their agreement to maintain the land. The contract will spell out the restrictions on the land and the purposes and conditions for which it is to be conserved. If the landowner has special conditions or plans he wants to maintain, he can negotiate these with the recreation agency and make them part of the agreement.

The landowner is, in effect, selling or donating a right to use the land in a certain way or ways. In most scenic easements, the landowner really gives up very little. He has probably kept the area scenic because it is of little value for farming or building. Many farmers and other landowners want to keep the property attractive and rural, so they are pleased to find a way to both preserve the attractiveness of the property and reduce their tax liability.

A purchased easement should be in perpetuity, in most cases. Thus, it would become part of the property description, attached to the deed and carried through title transfers.

If a landowner wishes to seek conservation easement protection on his land, he should first determine the organization or agency that he wishes to hold and administer the easement. National organizations such as The Nature Conservancy, the National Wildlife Federation, and the Audubon Society accept donations of easements. Any government agency with legal authority to accept interests in land may accept or buy easements; these include the National Park Service, state environmental or conservation agencies, and local park districts. Local and regional foundations in the business of preserving land are often excellent recipients and subsequent administrators of conservation easements.

Enforcing the easement is a process that is variable, according to state law and custom. Some states (Connecticut, Maryland, Massachusetts, New Hampshire, California, for example) have passed legislation explicitly recognizing conservation easements and establishing their enforceability. In the states where there is no specific statute, the general rule is that the easement is enforceable if the person or organization to which the easement is given or sold owns real property that will be benefited by the restrictions. This usually refers to real estate that is contiguous to or very near the land on which the conservation easement is placed (Stover, 1975).

Advantages of easements to the grantor can be considerable in real dollar-and-cents terms. Usually, sale or donation of conservation easement rights entitles the landowner to significant tax benefits. Most land is worth something less on the market when development rights have been restricted, so real estate taxes, figured on appraised market value of the land before and after granting of a conservation easement, should be significantly reduced.

Also, a deduction of the value of a conservation easement, donated to a government agency or to a tax-exempt, charitable organization for perpetuity, is allowed by the Internal Revenue Service for federal income tax purposes.

Finally, when a landowner dies, his land is appraised to determine federal and state estate taxes. Because the value of the land protected by easement is less than its fair market value, estate taxes are generally lower, to the degree that the easement limits development.

To illustrate future tax advantages of easements, Stover (1975) quoted Thomas Cielinski of the Maine Bureau of Parks and Recreation:

In Maine, working with conservation easements, we have found there is a definite variation in income tax deductions that takes place. As far as property tax assessments are concerned, property owners don't seem too concerned when we are trying to encourage them to sign a conservation easement about their property taxes going down or very possibly going up. They are interested in the fact that their property taxes probably will not rise at the rate that those of the unprotected land next door will rise. I know of one case where easement property tax stayed at the same level while all other taxes in the town went up anywhere from 25 to 30 percent.

CASE STUDY—CONSERVATION EASEMENT

Mr. and Mrs. Terps owned a 250-acre farm that abutted a state park just outside of Baltimore, Maryland. As suburban sprawl from Baltimore started to move into their community, the real property taxes on the Terps' property started to rise at an alarming rate. Fifteen years ago, Mr. Terps' father had purchased 50 acres of adjoining farmland for $50 an acre. Now, the entire farm had been appraised for tax purposes at close to $1,000 an acre. This appraisal was up from $500 an acre just three years earlier, and Mr. Terps was afraid he would no longer be able to profitably farm the land.

Because the property had been recently upzoned from agriculture to half-acre, single-family residential, several developers approached Mr. Terps with proposals to buy the land and build tract homes. Because the farm abutted a popular state park, Mr. Terps thought that before considering the developers' proposals he should contact the state to see if they had any interest in acquiring his land as a park addition.

The property was separated from the park by a small stream, and both the state and the Terps had always enjoyed this natural boundary. The state had no desire to expand the park, but at the same time, they felt that the development of the Terps' property would have a severe, negative effect on their present park operations. They told Mr. Terps that they would be interested in acquiring his farm as buffer land, but, unfortunately, they did not have any money earmarked for further acquisitions within this particular park.

The state called The Nature Conservancy, and staff members met with Mr. Terps to discuss the land. It became apparent that Mr. Terps had no desire to sell the farm if he could just figure out a way to hold onto the property. The Conservancy asked Mr. Terps if he would be willing to donate a conservation easement on his land to the State of Maryland, giving up his right to develop the land but retaining the option to work the land as a farm as long as he wanted. The farm would remain private property and Mr. Terps would have full control over its use. All the state would have is a negative right in the land that would prevent Mr. Terps, or any future owner, from developing the land. Under Maryland law, the development rights would have value and the property would have to be reassessed in light of the conservation easement. Mr. Terps said he was interested but he would like to see some figures.

The state had the development rights appraised. The appraisal showed that Mr. Terps' land was worth $1,000 an acre, but that comparable farmland was selling for $500 an acre in other parts of the state. Thus, the development rights were worth approximately $500 an acre, or $125,000 for the entire farm.

After much thought, Mr. Terps asked the state to purchase the conservation easement. The state had Land and Water Conservation Funds available and was willing to make an application for 50 per cent of the easement's fair market value. The Bureau of Outdoor Recreation approved a matching grant for $67,500, and Mr. Terps agreed to a bargain sale of a conservation easement on the entire farm to the state.

The Conservancy then recommended a local attorney to advise Mr. Terps on how to use the donation value of the easement to help offset the federal and state capital gains tax he would have to pay on the sale of the development rights. The after-tax effects were quite attractive to Mr. Terps, especially because he had sold something that he never knew he had and the sale had cut his real property taxes in half. The state was, of course, pleased because it had been able to preserve 250 acres of key buffer land without having to purchase the entire property.

Shortcomings of Easements

Difficulties with easements include the following (Schuster, Webster, and Ullrich, 1976):

It is difficult to define the exact rights being acquired and the impact their sale has on the property.

Property-tax assessment is made more complex and difficult.

Easements may be very costly in urban fringe areas where land values are expected to rise rapidly, because the price of the easement is based on the loss of value.

Invalidation of easements commonly occurs early, even if the easement is in perpetuity; short-term easements are often difficult to renew.

Agency-landowner misunderstandings occur, raising questions of validity, especially when the agency attempts to keep its intentions secret.

There is no way for the agency to recoup its outlay if it decides to relinquish the easement.

Landowners are uncertain about the effects of an easement on their property or income taxes, and county and federal tax officials can usually answer that only after the fact of transfer of rights.

Assessors and land acquisition teams have difficulty in appraising partial land values.

A uniform easement deed is difficult to devise unless complicated legal terms and exceptions are included. Each easement will probably require individual negotiation of terms.

Easements are difficult to administer on lands receiving heavy public use.

Easements may not permanently secure lands against development.

Easement enforcement is complex. Most programs are inadequate.

Despite the difficulties, easements are likely to be used increasingly by industry. A scenic easement was negotiated with the Brown Paper Company and other landowners in New Hampshire to protect a 13-mile stretch of scenic river drive. The Androscoggin River is popular for canoeing, picnicking, swimming, biking, camping, snowmobiling, hunting, and fishing. The easement, negotiated on a willing buyer-willing seller basis, has several advantages (Wyman, 1976). It protects highly regarded values that are used by the public, and the public purchases the protection. It allows the landowners to continue with tree harvesting and other business as usual, under terms of the agreement. Finally, the easement forces some of the management of the area onto the state, according to a management plan that defines responsibilities of the public agencies and the landowners.

COVENANTS

Covenants or agreements can be used to keep particular private properties as open space, even though they remain in private hands. The covenant specifies that the land is to remain in a specified condition or that structures that are built meet certain conditions. Such covenants are quite common devices in sales of real estate. For example, a seller may attach to the deed the restriction that any house built on the property will be a single-family dwelling of no less than 1,500 square feet of floor space. The buyer agrees to this by purchasing the land and is legally bound to comply. The covenants usually run with the land, so are passed on to heirs or purchasers.

If a public agency wishes to attach conservation or open space covenants to properties already owned by private individuals, there are three methods it can follow.

1. The landowners can voluntarily agree to attach the restrictions to their deeds in the interests of keeping the land in natural condition and preventing a rise in property taxes, which would occur if the land were to be assessed as a potential subdivision or commercial area.
2. The public agency can pay the present landowner to attach the covenant to his deed.
3. When an important property comes up for sale, the agency purchases it. Then a covenant is legally attached to the deed and the property is resold by the agency to a new individual who accepts the restriction. If the covenant merely prohibits certain future developments, the price will probably be about the same as it was originally.

A conservation covenant may simply state something to the effect that "the property shall always remain in natural forest vegetation along the river, free of industrial, commercial, or further residential development." In all cases, the agency and the grantor of the covenant should consult with an attorney familiar with such agreements.

ENABLING LEGISLATION FOR CONSERVATION RESTRICTIONS

Enabling legislation for the use of restrictions for conservation or historic preservation was passed by Connecticut in 1971. A copy of the Act follows (Stover, 1975).

Public Act No. 173
Connecticut General Assembly, 1971 Session
An Act Concerning Conservation and Preservation Restrictions.
Be it enacted by the Senate and House of Representatives in General Assembly convened:

Section 1. For the purposes of this act, the following definition shall apply: (a) "Conservation restriction" means a limitation, whether or not stated in the form of a restriction, easement, covenant or condition, in any deed, will or other instrument executed by or on behalf of the owner of the land described therein or in any order of taking such land whose purpose is to retain land or water areas predominantly in their natural, scenic or open condition or in agricultural, farming, forest or open space use. (b) "Preservation restriction" means a limitation, whether or not stated in the form of a restriction, easement, covenant or condition, in any deed, will or other instrument executed by or on behalf of the owner of land or in any order of taking of such land whose purpose is to preserve historically significant structures or sites.

Section 2. No conservation restriction held by any governmental body or by a charitable corporate or trust whose purposes include conservation of land or water areas and no preservation restriction held by any governmental body or by a charitable corporation or trust whose purposes include preservation of buildings or sites of historical significance shall be unenforceable on account of lack of privity of estate or contract or lack of benefit to particular land or on account of the benefit being assignable or being assigned to any other governmental body or to any charitable corporation or trust with like purposes.

Section 3. Such conservation and preservation restrictions are interests in land and may be acquired by any governmental body or any charitable corporation or trust which has the power to acquire interests in land in the same manner as it may acquire other interests in land. Such restrictions may be enforced by injunction or proceedings in equity.

Zoning

Lands can be classified by the local government as residential, commercial, industrial, agricultural, and conservation lands. These are often broken down into subclassifications. *Zoning* is a basic approach to assign types of land use permitted or prohibited to a district of a city, county, or town.

The primary use of zoning has been to exclude certain uses in particular areas. Regulation through zoning is one of the most common means of control over private land use. If intelligently applied, it can be very useful for the benefit of the general public. Along rivers or trails or in historic districts or adjacent to scenic or historic parks, zoning authorities can prescribe styles of construction and land use. Scenic or historic districts with architectural standards minimize discordant or monotonous structures. Zoning can assure appropriate uses of waterfronts, trail-side views, or the character of the land adjacent to an important park or wilderness. On federal forest land, wilderness users have successfully required that multiple-use areas that are prominently visible from wilderness areas should be logged with a consideration to protecting the relative naturalness of the view. This is not local zoning, but in effect it is zoning of the national forest through court regulation to protect scenic vistas and enhance the wilderness experience.

In zoned areas, construction, significant changes in land use, or development proposals usually require official permission. Such changes that are approved are licensed through special-use permits issued by the zoning authority.

Land-Use Planning

Land-use planning is interpreted differently by different people. Many urban government officials think of it as zoning and other regulations to guide urban growth. Some federal foresters are primarily concerned with allocation of various forest uses to selected areas and with determination of how much recreation, timber harvesting, wildlife harvest, water, and grazing can be produced.

Ecologists often see land-use planning as requiring a process to determine the ability of land resources to produce goods and services and yet maintain its biological integrity and productivity. More sociologically oriented people tend to emphasize the goal of achieving a livable pattern of land uses that most benefits social welfare.

Farmers and industrialists often decry land-use planning as an unnecessary and socialistic nuisance that restricts their freedom of operation.

Land-use planning and associated management may be all of these things and more. The lack of definition of the process is related to its relative newness as a full-blown policy (although people have been planning uses of land since they were escorted from a garden called Eden) and to the fragmented nature of the decision making process in government and private sectors of free societies.

One definition (Jubenville, 1976) includes the following concepts as modifiers of each other:

Coordination of land uses to meet human needs.

Minimizing environmental impacts by using lands most appropriate for given uses.

Consideration of historical and existing use patterns.

Consideration of the political and economic framework.

Land-use planning involves many compromises. Lands that are highly productive for agriculture are also often highly productive of timber. They may also be good industrial sites.

The guidance of land uses is done by several means. One is pure free market economics, which is the primary determinant of how land is used. Most American farm, ranch, forest, and urban land is used as it is because of economic benefits of those uses to the landowners. Individual decisions, failures, and successes produced much of the order and the complications of current uses. However, the governmental role has always been strong.

The opening of the West was accomplished by giving public lands to anyone who would prove them up. When fraud and abuse of the lands and forests resulted, the federal government took steps to protect the interests of individuals and to establish public forests to ensure that future generations would have trees, water, and wildlife.

America's westward movement was led by people who wanted to get there first. Some of them were trying to find their fortune or a place to survive. Others seemed to be shunning people—moving westward when the neighbors became visible.

Now, migrants to mountains, islands, and rural retreats want to be the last ones there. They want to close their communities or states to newcomers—at least to large numbers of newcomers (Figure 25.1).

The state of Oregon, with a strong feeling for the carrying capacity of the beauty of the state, became famous for its discouragement of migrants from California, starting in the 1960s. Aspen, Colorado, saw a tremendous influx of easterners and Californians during the 1960s. County and city officials tried to take steps to reduce immigration and to control problems of sewage, water, and traffic, which had hit that rural community almost without warning. The people of the state of Colorado voted down the winter Olympics of 1976 with much the same feeling of disgruntlement over the potential rise in population and its problems. The attraction of people to the amenities of scenic country are strong. The impacts of these people are likewise strong. They build houses—sometimes on scenic points and ridges. They demand services. They crowd existing recreation facilities. They also bring considerable money. They enrich real estate firms and many other enterprises.

A key goal of land-use planning is to ensure the long-range productivity of lands through guidance of rational land uses. Another goal is to allow the public interest to sway current uses rather than to allow the most powerful economic factions to determine what is appropriate. The farmer

Figure 25.1 Urban growth sometimes gives people scarcely a chance to touch the earth, even in the suburbs.

whose fields and forests were ruined by chemical from a downwind industrial smokestack and whose house is often fogged in by the white dusty smoke would like to see some controls. The owner of a commercial swimming lake has reason to oppose installation of a landfill on the hill next to his property.

To promote desired land uses, local, state, and, sometimes, federal governments use regulations, fines, and other penalties as well as rewards and tax incentives.

Approaches to Urban Open Space

Green Line Idea: Recreation and open space needs in many urban areas might be met by setting a *green line boundary* around desirable areas, and then defining and administering land use within the area. That reduces the need and cost of acquiring land. The concept is based on the example of New York State's *blue line* in the area administered by the Adirondack Park Agency. Lands in rural upstate New York were set aside to remain forever natural. The park agency is empowered by the state legislature to regulate public and private lands within the blue line boundary.

The green line idea also is derived from early English green belts. The green line areas would encompass identified open space resources containing both public and private lands. Uses of these lands would be planned, regulated, and managed by a state or local ageny set up to protect the natural and cultural values found there.

Federal study has suggested the green line approach for the new Santa Monica Mountains National Recreation Area, close to Los Angeles (National Park Service and Bureau of Outdoor Recreation, 1977). The 200,000-acre area is easily identifiable, rugged, unsuitable for sensible development, and replete with scenic, natural, and recreational values. The area is to be managed by local and state agencies, in cooperation with the National Park Service and private owners. The planned approach involves the following elements:

1. Federal grants to state and local governments, assuming
2. State and local establishment and implementation of land-use controls within the green line area, based on
3. A plan prepared by a commission of state and local officials and approved by the Secretary of the Interior.
4. The state would create an agency empowered to make decisions about land use, which have heretofore been the responsibility of local government, including provisions to preserve the natural and cultural values of the area and to provide increased outdoor recreation opportunities for the nearby urban residents.

Ridgelands Approach: Unlike the green line approach proposed for the Santa Monica Mountains, the *ridgelands approach* leaves the major responsibility for open space preservation with local governments.

Three counties (Bay Area of California), a regional park district (Figure 25.2), and the regional planning association work together as a planning team. The approach is still in the planning stages, describing and evaluating the effectiveness of the full range of land regulatory techniques available to local governments to preserve open space resources. The planning effort shows local government recognition that the large tract of open space cutting across a heavily urbanized area has significant value. Protection of such open space will require cooperative action. These three counties are aiming to achieve that cooperation without involving higher jurisdictions of government.

Urban Rivers Approach: Denver and its suburbs are working on continuous public open space along the banks of the South Platte River and arroyos feeding into it. City, county, state, and federal agencies have been involved.

St. Louis is developing an urban recreation area along the Meramac

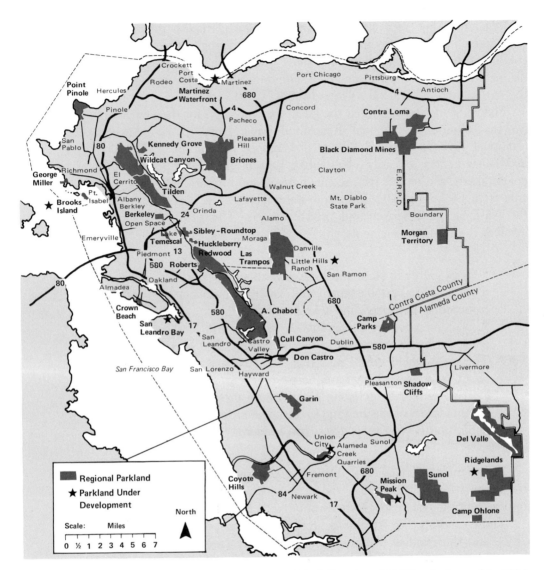

FIGURE 25.2 The East Bay Regional Park District of California, formed in 1934, is now part of the ridgeland approach to open space planning.

River. State, local, and private intiatives are supported by LWCF grants. Starting with a July, 1974 planning grant, a one-year study led to acquisition and development. By mid-1976, 1,600 acres had been added to the existing public ownership of 1,000 acres, largely through private donations and LWCF assistance.

PARKS AS GROWTH SHAPERS

When cities build, expand, or remodel, the controlling infrastructural value of parks, parkways, and trails should be considered. *Infrastructure* is

Tools for Recreation Administration

FIGURE 25.3   Urban sprawl develops along access such as in this small strip city. Strip cities often develop along roads where rural water companies supply water. (HCRS)

a term used by planners and economists to indicate the basic physical facilities of a place. The public infrastructure of a city includes its transportation network, bridges, communication basic service networks, and parks. These factors determine the character and growth pattern of any city, regardless of size. Even small communities (Figure 25.3) are affected by the road pattern. The major determinant of the location of cities in settlement days was proximity to a river or bay. Today, rural housing patterns in some parts of the country are determined by rural water company lines along roads, producing strip cities that are one house deep in otherwise rural areas.

Urban Systems Research and Engineering, Inc. (1976) reports that public facilities—infrastructure investments—influence the pace and pattern of growth and hence the quality of environment. Local public decision makers and citizens should at least be aware of the land use, economic, and environmental consequences likely to follow investment decisions relating to facilities such as water and sewer systems, power supply, roads, mass transit, airports, parks, and recreation areas.

Although little has been done to control design and location of infrastructure, techniques of analyzing and altering design and location could become powerful tools in reducing the negative impacts of unplanned growth. Infrastructure planning would be added to existing tools such as zoning, subdivision regulations, and local planning.

Although the latter often fail during periods of rapid change, the infrastructural investment is frequently the precipitator of the change. Therefore, it can be used to guide land-use changes.

Literature Cited

BARLOWE, RALEIGH. 1958. Land Resource Economics. Englewood Cliffs, N.J.: Prentice-Hall. 585 pp.

Heritage Conservation and Recreation Service. 1978. National Urban Recreation Study; Executive Report. Washington, D.C.: U.S. Dept. of the Interior. 184 pp.

JUBENVILLE, ALAN. 1976. Outdoor Recreation Planning. Philadelphia: W. B. Saunders Co. 399 pp.

National Park Service and Bureau of Outdoor Recreation. 1977. National Urban Recreation Study; Technical Reports, Volume 1; Urban Open Space, Existing Conditions, Opportunities and Issues. Washington, D.C.: U.S. Dept. of the Interior. Var. pag.

SCHUSTER, ERVIN G., HENRY H. WEBSTER and RICHARD D. ULLRICH. 1976. Land-use Controls for Outdoor Recreation Areas. Ames: Iowa State Univ., Ag and Home Ec. Expt. Sta., Special Report No. 78. 24 pp.

STOVER, EMILY JANE (ed.). 1975. Protecting Nature's Estate. Washington, D.C.: U.S. Dept. of the Interior, Bureau of Outdoor Recreation. 123 pp.

The story of a bequest. 1977. Conserve 19(3):1.

Urban Systems Research & Engineering, Inc. 1976. The Growth Shapers; the

Land Use Impacts of Infrastructure Investments. Washington, D.C.: Council on Environmental Quality. 71 pp.

WHYTE, WILLIAM H., JR. 1959. Securing Open Space for Urban America: Conservation Easements. Urban Land Institute Technical Bulletin 36. 67 pp.

WYMAN, BRAD. 1976. Roles and Responsibilities of the Public and Private Sector for Providing Outdoor Opportunities and Resources: Who Provides and How? Paper to National Recreation and Park Association Congress, Boston, Mass.

CHAPTER 26

Interpretation

When a salesman tries to sell a vacuum cleaner, he usually says more than, "It's a cleaning device—want one?" Likewise, when a visitor arrives at a refuge, forest, or park, more is offered than, "Here is nature—welcome!"

The interpreter serves as the host, the guide, and the programmer for visitors to the recreation area. Interpreters play a role in the visitor experience by offering information, activities, and guidance to those who seek it (Figure 26.1). The interpreter does more than say, "that is a butterfly, a bird, or a tree." The butterfly may be the product of a dangerous caterpillar that defoliates trees. The tree may be older than your great-grandmother with many a story to tell. The bird may be a swallow that spends its winters near South American beaches.

The Interpretive Function

The interpreter makes the commonplace or overlooked things become more wondrous. He or she can help the visitor realize what is special about the history of nature of any place and to see the diversity of life as well as the order in it.

The unique quality of a place is a key topic of the interpretive program. The character of a place is what sets it apart or makes it valuable. The reason for the existence of an area is a good starting point.

There are three visitor–oriented objectives to interpretation programming:

1. Tell the story of the place—what the features are all about in relation to the visitor's own experience.
2. Shape the visitor experience on the property by guiding and encouraging uses of the place beyond the standard drive through.
3. Involve the visitor in the place through the interpretive program; get people in touch with the earth in day-to-day life.

Interpretation and environmental education are important tools in the administration and management of recreation resources. Without them,

FIGURE 26.1 Interpretation of natural resources can turn weeds into fascinating plant members of the ecological community. (Hennepin County Park Reserve District)

a park may be little more than a picnic ground, swimming pool, or campsite. With interpretation, the park can be a place of special value that enriches the visitors' immediate experience and helps them discover the richness of life that surrounds them every day.

Values of Interpretation

Interpretation is part of the whole management system. The interpreter is an integral part of the resource management team.

When visitors are understanding and appreciative of the resource, the place requires much less expenditure on the enforcement of prohibitive

FIGURE 26.2 "Interpretation through awareness."—Freeman Tilden. (HCRS)

FIGURE 26.3 A modern nature center at Carver Park Reserve is headquarters for interpreters and visitor activities. (Hennepin County Park Reserve District; photo by Michael Myers Studio)

regulations (Dunmire, 1976). Interpretation includes helping visitors plan the use of their time to best meet their desires. At the start of and during their visits, they can be made aware of the opportunities available in the recreation area. They can be informed of the time, equipment, physical capabilities, and other requirements for engaging in various activities.

Concern for the visitor experience is central to the administration of recreation areas. Hartzog (1974), when Director of the National Park Service, noted that ". . . the effectiveness of park interpretation must be a major concern of all administrators, not just those involved actively in the effort."

The accepted role of interpretation involves revealing the intricacies of the story of a place, encouraging attitudes of respect and concern for the environment, and leading visitors to discover and to think for themselves (Dunmire, 1976). It goes beyond a park, refuge, or forest to help the visitor see the relationships among nature and man in the total environment (Figure 26.2). Many interpretive efforts go from the properties into the schools, churches, and the community at large. Television, radio, and newspaper bring interpretive messages into the home.

Origins of Interpretation

Interpretation is carried on by anyone who guides someone else to a park. It was the fascinating and colorful interpretation of Yellowstone by Jim Bridger that first excited interest in the area. Bridger's accounts seemed so metaphorical that they were not believed.

Formal interpretation in parks originated in the 1920s with first-hand lectures and explanations of the features of several California parks. Previous to this, a number or private resorts offered interpretation of various types, from talks by local fishing experts to learned presentations of natural and historical phenomena by professors hired for the season (Weaver, 1976).

It was from Mr. and Mrs. C. M. Goethe's sponsorship of such lectures that the national park interpretive program developed. They had observed the interpretive process in Switzerland and thought the idea would promote conservation and more enjoyable recreation in the United States. Resort owners around Lake Tahoe booked roving interpreters who eventually were asked to work in California national parks. From these, the interpretive service developed. There are now interpreters in virtually all national parks.

Many state park systems have permanent, year-round naturalists and historians, with seasonal interpreters hired for the summer months. In the past 10 to 20 years, local park and recreation departments have hired many interpreters. Notable among these are the Cook County Forest Preserve District, with six interpretive centers; the East Bay Regional Park District in California; and the Hennepin County Park Reserve District, Minnesota (Figure 26.3).

Reaching the People

A large portion of the population participates in nature walks, according to various studies and Nationwide Outdoor Recreation Plans of 1979 and 1973 (Bureau of Outdoor Recreation, 1973). More than 27 million people participated an average of five to six times per year. There are few activities involving more people in outdoor recreation. The growth since 1973 has been rapid (estimates vary from 30 per cent to more than 50 per cent).

Although every park or forest visitor will not want to take nature walks or attend formal programs, the interpreter can offer them services through written information, exhibits, and other media. Virtually everyone who

FIGURE 26.4 A carpenter at Hopewell Village National Historic Site, Pennsylvania, recreates a bit of the past.

visits a park, forest, or refuge should have ready opportunity and easy access to utilize interpretive materials and programs if they so choose.

The naturalist should not be a remote figure hanging out in the deep forest away from the crowds, available only to the persistent seeker of environmental truth. The interpreter should actively present opportunities wherever the public congregates, in the forms of interpretive labels, exhibits, and presentations (Figure 26.4).

Interpretation, in its broad sense, includes all the possible means to increase a visitor's understanding and appreciation. These include formal, conducted programs, exhibits, publications, signs, television, radio, and newspaper, as well as the informal types of interpretation that may be conveyed by workers in a visitor center or on a lawn crew.

The work of professional naturalists often takes them into schools, broadcasting stations, and before clubs, as well as on the property. Although the refuge, forest, or park is where natural processes may be best demonstrated, the outside work often reaches more people. A TV or radio audience of thousands contrasts with 20 to 50 on a nature hike or 100 to 300 at an evening program. The involvement of the on-site people is greater; a well-prepared mass-media message gets wider but shallower reception.

Interpretive activities started with the lecture and guided walk. These are still used, but modern interpretation also aims to involve visitors as participants, not just spectators. Among the approaches are environmental education, living history, and immersion programs. These promote direct interaction of the visitors with nature, encouraging them to discover on their own and to develop their own feelings for the environment. The former chief of interpretation for the National Park Service has said that the more visitors participate by using all their senses, making their own discoveries, and getting into the thick of a given environment, the more they carry away from the experience. Among approaches to getting visitors involved are a "slough slog" in the Everglades and an ecology float trip in Yosemite (Dunmire, 1976).

Principles of Interpretation

In *Interpreting Our Heritage*, Freeman Tilden has presented six principles of interpretation, summarized as follows:

1. Interpretation relates what is displayed or described to something within the personality or experience of the visitor.
2. Interpretation is revelation based upon information. Build a story into your presentation and incorporate the visitors into your stories. True interpretation deals not with parts but with the historical and spiritual whole.
3. Interpretation is art and can be teachable. The story is the art—

not science. We are all poets and artists to some degree—images are adventures of the imagination. The interpreter must possess the art of speaking and writing.

4. The chief aim is provocation, not instruction. The purpose of interpretation is to stimulate in the reader or hearer a hunger to widen his horizon of interests and knowledge. The national park or monument, the preserved battlefield, the historic restoration, the nature center in a public recreation spot are all places where interpretation blooms and flourishes. First stimulate the visitor's interest, and then stimulate him or her to see and understand.

5. Interpretation should aim to present the whole to the whole man. Toward a perfect whole, the interpreter works for a complete experience, using all five senses. The visitor should leave with one or more pictures in his mind.

6. Interpretation programs for children should use a different approach. Children enjoy using superlatives, such as the largest this, the smallest that. They love to touch objects with their fingers and hands. Challenge their senses. The interpreter can help children relate to phenomena in terms they understand without talking down to them.

Personal and Self-Directed Interpretation

Two categories of interpretive offerings can be identified: *personal* and *self-directed* service. Personal service activities involve face-to-face interaction between the visitors and an interpreter. They include talks, personal slide shows, information services in a visitor center, conducted walks, rides or auto tours, and personal interpretation at a particular point or area in a park. The advantages of personal service include flexibility of information and approach, allowing the interpreter to adapt to conditions and to the audience. The personal contact with an interpreter is important to many visitors. Questions and on-the-spot responses are often preferable to canned facts. The visitor who seeks to discover on his own can benefit from the guidance and personal suggestions of an interpreter who is familiar with the entire property.

Self-directed programs are those that involve printed, graphic, or audio materials used by the visitor at his own initiative. Among activities offered are many kinds of self-guiding nature trails with signs, leaflets, or tape players, markers at points of interest along highways, exhibits, displays, self-directed games, museums, and other devices. These have the advantage of low cost per visitor contact and suitability for dispersed use areas. Visitors can choose the time for a walk or visit and take it at their own pace. They can stop and examine something of interest at great length and skip over other aspects. The individual can enjoy the interpretive experience alone, without suffering the inhibitions or annoyances of being in a large

Tools for Recreation Administration

group. A desire to sniff, taste, or study closely can be indulged without embarrassment.

Approaches to Interpretation

The following three modes of interpretation are examples of the various approaches encountered. They are story-line interpretation, living history, and environmental education.

Interpretation for Casual Visitors

What is sometimes called *story-line interpretation* is used on nature hikes, historic sites, visitor centers, campfire programs, trail leaflets, and roadside exhibits (Brown, 1971). Because it caters primarily to the casual visitor, it must consider the short interest span of most visitors. This limits the subtlety and extent of interpretation. The story line explains what is special about the place and what the visitors can experience there. Deep analysis of environmental relationships is difficult in this rather informal approach to interpretation.

Interpreters often impose limits upon themselves. Brown (1971) observed that story-line interpretation has often been predominately taxonomic and passive-descriptive, with the interpreter serving as a walking textbook. The erudition, naming of things, and canned lectures may intimidate and turn off visitors.

Changes in interpretive approaches emphasize the relationships and processes of ecology and history rather than taxonomy and individual items. It gets people involved with all their senses. This does not mean that personal details are not part of the story. Freeman Tilden (1967), in his classic on interpretive philosophy, notes that stories about individuals and personal events are often best remembered, making the whole event come alive. Use of such stories, woven through the fabric of the big story of the property, helps bring the events home.

Living History

Living history programs bring the human element into environmental interpretation. These are historic role-playing and demonstration programs. They help bring into focus how cultures and societies have been shaped by their environment and how they have affected the natural environment (Figure 26.5).

The goal of living history is not to fool the visitor into thinking he is in the past or that he is observing the real thing, but to help him develop a better sense of the character of the place and to stimulate his thinking in terms of how things must have been for an individual in the total environment and culture. This does not suggest the extreme that the entire environment or culture must be brought to life on the spot, although

FIGURE 26.5 The historic town of Harpers Ferry, West Virginia, comes to life daily with costumed employees.

that has been done in a few well-financed operations such as Colonial Williamsburg. More realistically, it means that a few interpreters dressed in clothing or uniforms suggestive of a period can do much to help the visitor's imagination and to put the time and events into better focus (Figure 26.6). In some historical parks, the guides become authentic museum exhibits with every detail perfect for the time (for example, no watches, eyeglasses of the period, and proper buckles on the shoes). In some parks, the costumed interpreters play strict roles of people in a given time, never breaking character. They must be aware of history in some detail so the events of the future are not known to them. A Civil War soldier would know nothing about Theodore Roosevelt, automobiles, or most western states. In other places, there is no pretense by the guides of presenting authenticity, but there is an attempt to create a general atmosphere or suggestion of an approximate time. The costumed guide is more interactive with the visitors, serving as an explainer of events and conditions, using the costume as an additional interpretive device that lends color and atmosphere to the place.

Tools for Recreation Administration

More than 100 national park properties have incorporated living history in their interpretive programs (Dunmire, 1976). These vary from firing of muskets and cannons to full-scale, full-time, costumed role playing and even dramatic presentations (Figure 26.7). Many state parks and local historical parks also use the technique in varying degrees. In some, the simple but effective process of inviting in a weekend craftsman, spinner, blacksmith, or pioneer gardener can add considerable interest to a visit to a park, as they go about their work and explain the processes to visitors.

One living history program in Rocky Mountain National Park is the Holzwarth Ranch, located on the western side of the park. In 1974, the ranch was sold to the Nature Conservancy and then to the National Park Service by John Holzwarth, Jr., a crusty 73-year-old rancher who took over the property from his German immigrant father. Father and son ran it as a cattle ranch and later as a place for visitors.

Now that the National Park Service has the property, it is interpreting it as part of the history of the West. It is shown to visitors as a working ranch, typical of those along the headwaters of the Colorado River. Visitors are met at the gate by a woman who collects the natural materials of the area to make jellies, jams, and pies. There are two draft horses on the property. Tours through a log cabin built in 1917 are conducted by a woman dressed in period garb—knickers, tall boots, and a loose khaki blouse. She knows all about the Holzwarth family and talks about the life and times in which they lived.

FIGURE 26.6   Living history at Hopewell Village National Historic Site is carried on even in winter time. (NPS)

Figure 26.7 Living history at Lincoln Boyhood National Memorial in Indiana brings to life the cabin and farm of Abe's youth. (NPS)

The log guest cabins, which were part of the former dude ranch, are still clustered around the old homestead. There is an ice house with a sod roof plus pig pens, chicken coops, and other original restored outbuildings. Visitors are served home-baked sourdough bread. In the cabin and around it are treasures of the Holzwarth family that represent those of any pioneer family—wedding pictures, passports, handicrafts, taxidermy, and many other family items. Outside are the farm implements that were used for haying and gardening in that period. This is more than a museum. It is a real ranch, reliving its past for purposes of stimulating, provoking and informing visitors. It is a place where history has come alive.

ENVIRONMENTAL EDUCATION

Many people in urban, industrial areas are unaware of the environmental consequences of their actions. To some individuals and industries, it seems there is no alternative in their day-to-day pattern of living but to consume whatever resources are available, regardless of long-term ecological damages. One aim of environmental education is to present alternative choices in meeting human needs and to describe the consequences of each in terms of the impacts on natural resources.

Environmental education seeks to teach young citizens an understanding of the interdependence between man and his natural environment (Dun-

Tools for Recreation Administration

mire, 1976). Many city children have never walked on clean, wet sand of a beach or hiked through a large forest, even close to home. In urban parks and forests, environmental education can provide exciting experiences and can make a major impact on the thinking and understanding of young citizens.

The Environmental Education Act of 1970 (Public Law 91–516) was designed to stimulate the development of new and improved curricula in public schools to help students better understand the environment. The act established an office of environmental education within the United States Office of Education.

This agency can distribute appropriated funds as grants and contracts to state and local educational agencies for the following purposes: 1) develop curricula; 2) disseminate information relating to curricula; 3) support environmental educational programs at elementary and secondary levels; 4) train adult personnel; 5) plan outdoor ecological study centers; 6) conduct community education programs; and 7) prepare and distribute materials for mass media use. Small grants may also be made to public and private nonprofit groups.

Environmental education is a major effort of private organizations. For example, three educational objectives have been established by the National Audubon Society (Shomon, 1962):

1. To increase knowledge and understanding of the natural world and man's place in it.
2. To develop an awareness, appreciation, and affection for nature.
3. To develop a desire and a will, based upon understanding, to protect, safeguard from harm, and use wisely the living and nonliving resources of the earth important to man. These are the first steps in the development of a geobiotic ethic.

The society's magazine, publications, and films provide one form of education. In-field interpretation is offered through several nature centers and a children's farm. Many state chapters maintain similar facilities.

Volunteers

Interpretation and environmental education programs seem to be very appealing to volunteer workers and organizations. Programs can be enhanced by using docents for museums and well-trained students as weekend or summer guides in outdoor areas. The National Park Service, with a tight job market, works with 9,000 summer Volunteers-In-Parks, who help conduct interpretive programs in order to get experience that may someday qualify them for paying jobs. The Student Conservation Association coordinates volunteer workers.

Local and state parks can often make use of organizations of forestry or history students to help in interpretation. Such work requires considerable coordination, training, and diplomatic guidance from the professional staff, but the rewards of that work are a large corps of interpreters who multiply the efforts of the staff. Many local nature centers offer large programs with a minimal staff that coordinates dozens of talented volunteer guides through the Junior League, historical associations, or "friends of the park" organizations.

Budgetary Support

Interpretation has often faced financial difficulties. When budgets are cut, it is often the interpretive program that receives the axe first. The philosophy is that maintenance and neatness are first priorities in an area, along with supplying basic services to the visitors (Figure 26.8). For some reason, interpretation is not seen as a basic service by some budget directors. However, it would seem that telling the story of a special place—making the significance of the land come alive for the visitor—would be at least an equal partner with the functions of mowing grass and keeping the swimming pool, grocery store, and class A campground in tip-top shape.

Many property managers do not have to be convinced of the value of quality interpretation programs; they see the value every day, with positive

FIGURE 26.8 Visitor centers are keys to interpretation in many parks.

466

reinforcement from visitors. Budget examiners and administrators far from the park or forest are often the hardest to persuade (Dunmire, 1976). They are concerned with cost and return ratios and the consequences of cutting here and there, temporarily. Unfortunately, interpretive program data have not been well recorded and presented to budget controllers. In some cases, such data might be thought embarrassing to the interpretive program, but in most cases, the facts would be quite revealing and supportive. Good records of use could also direct internal allocation of interpretive resources by indicating the types of programs that have low attendance, with some indication of what factors improve attendance (Reyburn and Knudson, 1975).

The Professional Connections

The Association of Interpretive Naturalists and the Western Interpreters Association are the major organizations for professionals in the interpretive field. In Canada, the Canadian Interpreters' Association unites naturalists and historians. Several historical associations are valuable for interpreters involved with cultural interpretation and museums. The national Conservation Education Association focuses primarily on the environmental education aspects of interpretation.

U.S. FOREST SERVICE CASE

Many organizations offer interpretive opportunities. The U.S. Forest Service has a program called the Visitor Information Service (VIS). In the past, the Forest Service had treated interpretation as an activity that was incidental to the many duties of its professional field staff. The VIS was created in 1960 to provide a more intensive interpretive program. It still is rather sparsely spread around the nation and most districts do not have a specialist in interpretation. The objectives of the VIS are to:

1. Developing a better understanding and appreciation of natural resources, products, uses, and activities on national forest lands.
2. Acquainting visitors with recreation opportunities, natural and human history, and activities in the area.
3. Obtaining greater public cooperation in protection against fire, vandalism, stream pollution, and littering.
4. Stimulating curiosity and satisfying the desire for understanding natural resources and their relation to the environment.

Facilities include amphitheaters, visitor centers, wayside exhibits, bulletin boards, and self-guiding trails. Services might include the following list of offerings in any single ranger district: conducted walks and tours; boat tours; winter ski tours; campfire programs; a visitor information center with information, special programs, maps, and basic comfort facilities; ranger stations serving as information centers for local activities; self-guided walks with interpretive signs or leaflets; self-guided auto tours; wayside exhibits; vistas with information to make views meaningful; bulletin boards; and labels on plants.

Interpretive opportunities, recognized in national forests and transferrable to state, county, or corporate forests, include the following:

The many uses of the forests.

The management techniques employed to achieve the various products and uses. There is no need to hide cutting areas if they can be explained and demonstrated.

Recognition of plants, especially those related to wildlife, poisonous plants, and others of special interest, such as the oldest or largest.

Recreation management practices.

The multiple values of firebreaks in providing fire protection, wildlife benefits, and grazing.

Values and fragility of wilderness areas.

Research activities, if visitors would not affect the results.

Archeological, geological, and scenic areas.

Fish and wildlife life cycles, habitat needs, and curiosities.

Historical characters and events of the area.

California Case

California state parks have an active interpretation program. The *Policies, Rules and Regulations* (California State Park and Recreation Commission, 1970) direct as follows:

A high-quality interpretive program is essential to provide a full and rewarding experience to every park visitor and to make available to the people of California an opportunity for greater and deeper understanding of their cultural, historic, and natural heritage, as exemplified in their State Park System.

Interpreters in California state parks are to identify and emphasize the values of primary importance for each park or beach. Secondary values may be recognized, but the key theme or features must be prominent. Regulations suggest that interpretation be creative, objective, and based on fact. Clearly identified legend and myth may be used to develop the color and feeling of an era or event.

Summary

A major objective of park and recreation administrators is to enhance the quality of the visitor experience. Therefore, the director of the National Park Service noted, "I believe interpretation to be one of the most important responsibilities of the National Park Service" (Hartzog, 1974).

The importance of interpretation can be applied to most natural or historic recreation areas. It is a potent tool to enhance the visitor experience and to promote visitor interest in and support of resource management efforts.

The goal of the interpreter is to stimulate the visitor to seek richer experiences in the environment and to be sensitized to natural phenomena.

The techniques include the broad spectrum of environmental education, a great number of activities personally conducted by a naturalist, living history, self-guided facilities, museums, exhibits, and use of mass media.

Aldo Leopold (1966) asserted that the only truly creative activity in recreation is the development of the faculty of perceiving natural processes. That creative function of promoting perception is the goal and the promise of interpretation.

Literature Cited

Brown, William E. 1971. Islands of Hope. Arlington, Va.: National Recreation and Park Association. 194 pp.

Bureau of Outdoor Recreation. 1973. Outdoor Recreation; a Legacy for America. Washington, D.C.: U.S. Dept. of the Interior. 89 pp.

California State Park and Recreation Commission and the Dept. of Parks and Recreation. 1970. Policies, Rules and Regulations. Sacramento: var. pag.

Dunmire, William W. 1976. Stretching recreation dollars through interpretation. In: D. M. Knudson (ed.), Managing Recreation Resources for Century III. West Lafayette, Ind.: Purdue University. pp. 92–100.

Hartzog, G. B., Jr. 1974. Management considerations for optimum development and protection of national park resources. In: Proceedings of Second World Conference on National Parks. Morges, Switzerland: International Union for the Conservation of Nature. pp. 155–161.

Leopold, Aldo. 1966. Sand County Almanac. N.Y.: Oxford University Press. 269 pp.

Reyburn, Jerry H. and Douglas M. Knudson. 1975. The influence of advertising on attendance at park programs. Journal of Environmental Education 7(2):59–64.

Shomon, Joseph J. 1962. A Nature Center for Your Community. N.Y.: National Audubon Society. 40 pp.

Tilden, Freeman. 1967. Interpreting Our Heritage. Chapel Hill: North Carolina University Press. 120 pp.

Weaver, Howard. 1976. Origins of interpretation. In: Grant Sharpe, Interpreting Our Environment. N.Y.: John Wiley & Sons. pp. 23–42.

Managing Forests for Beauty

Foresters have long recognized there is much more to a forest than trees—water, air, soil, forage, wildlife, recreation, minerals. Professional foresters were among the first to integrate the management of all the resources, and to point out that both resource production and resource preservation are needed. But there is a Johnny-come-lately resource which foresters have been slow to recognize and accept in their portfolio of responsibilities. . . . It is the resource of beauty—one of the amenities that helps make for quality of living, and now carries a social and political punch that leaves dollar signs in cost-benefit studies spinning on their axes.   —DEWITT NELSON (1972)

This chapter deals with the philosophy of achieving maximum *total* productivity. It emphasizes techniques of harvesting timber so that the beauty of the forest is retained as much as possible. Techniques reported here are being tested as standard procedure in state, federal, and many industrial forests.

Forest management systems that produce timber while enhancing or maintaining visual values at the same time are important to the land manager. Visual resource management has become an important aspect of timber management by the U.S. Forest Service and state forest managing agencies. Multiple-use forests are under growing demands to produce wood efficiently. They are also under increased scrutiny from an observant, visiting public. Some members of the public are quite vigilant of the scenic beauty and alert to any modifications of the forests.

The recreating public has altered the value system of the forest—sometimes through economics but more often through political expression of their preferences. These owners of the public forest make it clear that they want the forest to look as scenic as possible. The strong love of scenery is counterbalanced by the demands for wood products, so the composite demand is for a mix of beauty with production of timber. Protection of watersheds, production of wildlife, and provision of grazing lands are other demands that must be met on most public forests.

Much has been done toward providing beauty on industrial and public forest lands. The natural scenic qualities of forests, rivers, lakes, and mountains have long drawn recreationists on sightseeing expeditions to lands managed for perpetual forest cover and/or production. By protecting and regenerating forests, the nation has coincidentally managed for beauty.

However, the question goes beyond this. Many environmentalists seem to want beauty in a specific spot today—and tomorrow. They ask that the forest manager do his timber managing with an eye to natural beauty. The forest visitor often asks that cutting operations not be revealed to the esthetic eye.

Beauty seekers decry straight lines, large clear-cuts, harvesting slash, logging roads, erosion, and siltation of waters. They ask that foresters manipulate the resource in a gentle way. Esthetics becomes a constraint or condition of every decision the forester makes. Some users go to the extreme of objecting to any and all manipulation of the so-called natural vegetation. There is a nice philosophical point as to what is natural. It has been said that the condition in which a man first sees an area is its natural condition to him.

Landscape architects have been hired by the Forest Service and other federal agencies to aid in guaranteeing that manipulation of vegetation, for various legitimate reasons, is done in a manner that will keep to a minimum esthetic impacts (Figure 27.1).

Total Productivity

Because public forests are usually managed for many uses, achieving the optimum overall productivity requires careful balancing of the different values, goods, and services. In many parts of a forest, where no single purpose is recognized as preeminent, scenery values must be considered when planning manipulations of the forest cover for timber production, wildlife, or watershed benefits.

All of these uses are interrelated. It is the duty of the forester to blend the uses in such a manner that the final results involve a satisfactory combination. Maximum productivity of one may be deleterious to another. Therefore, maximum output from the *whole* forest may require modification of the output from any *one value*. To maximize total output, it may be necessary to forego some of the timber volume to be removed now in order to provide sustained scenic values, life support values, water regulation, and wildlife.

To achieve the forest's full purpose, the public forest manager cannot think of management objectives and plans based on timber outputs alone. The production of boards and pulpwood is modified—sometimes preempted—by the output of recreational and scenic values, among others.

Basic Analytical Concepts

Elements of visual analysis in the forest landscape are distance, light, topography, form and contrast, spatial definition, observer position, and sequence (Litton and Twiss, 1966).

FIGURE 27.1 The view from the road is very important for timber managers to consider in planning their harvest cuts. (USFS)

Distance can be divided into three parts—foreground, middle ground, and background. In the western United States and Canada, the foreground can be considered the area up to one half mile away. This area is visually critical; it must be well maintained. Screening of some sort is often used in the foreground. The middle ground must blend with the land form; in mountainous areas, it covers the distance between one half mile and five miles away. The background provides texture and contrast to the scenery; it is any distance greater than five miles. Variations of these distances occur, depending upon local conditions of the topography and the vegetation.

Light can be a vital factor in analyzing the landscape, but it appears to be rather flexible. A dark, thick forest is not necessarily more desirable than an open, park-like stand that admits considerable light. People have expressed favor with a wide variety of light conditions in tests that allowed light into the canopy (Rader and Hamilton, 1974).

Topography is correlated with water and the steepness of slope. It affects the viewing distance and the relative impact of cutting patterns. Massive, highly visible mountainsides must be treated with special care, whereas harvest patterns in folded hill and valley country can be tucked out of view. Harvesting on steep slopes presents other problems of soil stability and water retention.

Spatial definition is concerned with the size, shape, and scale of the scene. It relates to the sense of where one is—in a valley, on a mountaintop, on a lake. It relates to the distance of view and the amount of enclosure around the viewer.

The position from which the person views a scene and the sequence of the scenes he views are important factors in the design and evaluation of the landscape manipulations (Litton, 1968).

Visual influences are not the only keys to esthetic timber harvest. The amount of unnatural noise and odor in the air should be taken into account. Water flow and purity should be considered, along with questions of the water's appearance.

Silvicultural Techniques for Visual Resource Management

Silviculture provides the foundation for treatment of the forest. It is defined as the art and science of establishing, growing, and tending stands of trees. Several approaches to silvicultural practice have been developed to reduce the esthetic impacts of logging and to enhance the appearance of the forest. They involve management of travel influence zones; roadside cutting patterns; cutting block design, location, and size; and silvicultural systems for regeneration. Other procedures are described in a continuing series of Forest Service publications on landscape management.

TRAVEL INFLUENCE ZONES

Scenic values of forests are most important in locations such as viewpoints or interpretive stations; along highways and tourist roads; around lakes and reservoirs; in corridors visible from hiking and riding trails; along scenic streams; from developed recreation areas, such as campgrounds, picnic areas, ski slopes; from resorts, towns, urban, and wilderness areas.

In order to minimize esthetic damage for the majority of recreationists, special zones along principal water, road, and trail routes can be established. This is standard practice with some of the large timber-pulp companies (Figure 27.2), state forestry agencies, and the U.S. Forest Service. Within these *travel influence zones,* timber cutting practices are constrained in consideration of the visual quality of the forest. All harvesting of trees or wildlife habitat improvement is done so there is a minimum of visual disturbance. This usually means that trees harvested are marked on a single-tree selection basis. Most of the stand remains intact. The width of the zone varies with topography, timber type, and position of the viewer, among other factors.

The qualities that make a forest scenic are numerous and personal. Among the characteristics of a forest scene that are attractive to most

FIGURE 27.2 Strips of trees adjacent to main highways screen clear-cutting operations in Florida. (U.S.F.S.)

Managing Forests for Beauty

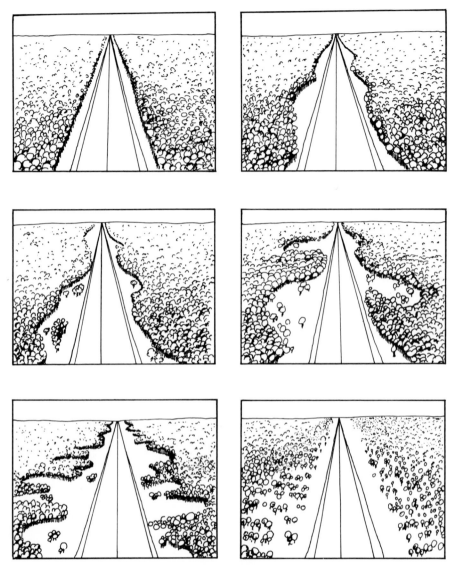

FIGURE 27.3 Six methods of roadside vegetation manipulation. (U.S.F.S.)

people are trees of large diameters and height; views of the forest and topography; variety of textures in different leaf patterns, ground covers, and stand densities; and colors of foliage and flowers. Each of these attributes can be affected by manipulation of the vegetation—opening the stand to stimulate the growth of individual trees, assurance of a variety of species and textures, vista cuttings to allow selected views, and planting or maintenance of colorful trees, shrubs, and herbs along the travel routes and major recreation sites.

Specific approaches also include letting people see *into* the forest, beyond the trees at the edge. This can be done in three ways—by pruning lower branches, thinning the stand, and creating openings. The last may be designed to lead the eye to look into an enclosure, thus inviting visitors to stop and walk into a small open space. Several intensities of cuts along the roadside are illustrated in Figure 27.3.

Vista cuttings are of varying widths, depending upon the shape of the road. Often, by removing just a few trees, dramatic windows can be created, with views of such features as peaks, valleys, lakes, and cliffs. For broad, sweeping views, it is necessary to cut a band of trees from a vantage point. All such cuts next to roads should be done for the primary goal of enhancing the esthetic experience. In many cases, timber values will be minimal and logging costs may be high.

If it is determined to be desirable to clear-cut next to a road, the impact can be lessened by leaving trees on the other side of the road. This offers a sense of scale and an alternative to the starkness of a recent clear-cut.

A sample procedure for logging a roadside stand of trees so as to maintain its esthetic values was outlined by McDonald and Whiteley (1972). They delineated the near view area, extending up to 300 feet back from the road in mixed conifers in the California mountains. They removed 25 per cent of the volume of the stand, and planned on cutting another 25 per cent every 25 years. Diseased, injured, and dying trees were the first to be marked for harvest. Then, each tree was considered on the basis of its impact on the view. Clumps of trees were often left to provide variability in spacing, which required the forester to think beyond the goal of even spacing. Logging and slash disposal were done carefully, to lessen damage to remaining trees and the soil, and to eliminate evidence of slash disposal. Stumps could be no higher than eight inches. Skidding was done to leave the standing trees and shrubs undamaged. Small trees that were damaged were removed. Landings were screened from the highway. Costs were about double those of usual single-tree selection logging jobs, if the narrow strip were considered alone. Benefits included better growing conditions for the remaining stand, rich in high-value pines; future growth is concentrated on these large stems. The chief advantage is that the roadside was attractive after the logging.

CUTTING BLOCK DESIGN

In laying out even-aged timber sales, esthetics become especially important. Large, square clear-cut blocks produce ill will among many environmentalists. The principle is to imitate nature and avoid squares and straight lines. Figure 27.4 shows approaches to clear-cutting block design that avoid the man-made look but produce as much timber as squared-off blocks. Natural openings in the forest are clearings, meadows, landslides, avalanche paths, ridgetops, and areas above the timberline. By simulating these and extending them, the logging operation leaves few unsightly scars.

FIGURE 27.4 In an aerial view of a mountain model, natural forms in cutting blocks on the left side of the mountain contrast with square-sided blocks on the right.

Figure 27.5 illustrates, first, how a mountainside can look after some fairly heavy cutting, designed to blend with nature and, second, how additional cutting can double the area cut and look even more natural. In the second harvest, the old patches are connected and extended along natural lines.

SILVICULTURAL SYSTEMS

As a result of the increased number of visitors to the national forests, a greater part of the population than ever before has had a chance to be exposed to cutting practices. Most visitors are middle-aged, middle-class people on vacation for a few weeks and probably from a large, urban area. In general, they lack any forestry or environmental training and they are quite often appalled upon seeing timber harvest areas. The magazines they have read usually contain nothing but pictures of beautiful green forests, apparently untouched by man. There are numerous reasons why people

Tools for Recreation Administration

A

B

FIGURE 27.5   Harvest openings in A follow more or less natural lines. In B, the second cutting has removed a volume of timber equivalent to that in cut A. By connecting patches, an even more natural appearance is achieved. (Adapted from U.S. Forest Service, 1973)

find clear-cut and other harvest areas objectionable, including the creation of artificial openings, the leaving of uneconomical waste material, the new roads, terraces, and occasional adverse effects on other resources. These have contributed to the controversies about clear-cutting that were especially strong in the late 1960s and 1970s and focused on the Monongahela (Figure 27.6) and Bitterroot National Forests of West Virginia and Montana.

To most people, the forest is seen as unchanging. If a group of trees is cut, there is a sense of something lost. People look at straight roads

FIGURE 27.6   Monongahela National Forest in West Virginia, a center of contro-versy for its forest practices, is a highly popular recreation area and the key to quality water supply of the headwaters of the Potomac River. (USFS)

and straight boundaries of cuts as being ugly and unnatural (Duffield, 1970). Logging roads often have a greater visual impact than does removal of the trees. Roads can remain a visual scar long after the clear-cut areas has grown over. For these reasons, layout of roads must consider the road grade and alignment, allowing them to follow the topography, blending with it rather than contrasting with it.

The forester's view of the conflict about cutting should also be examined. The forester, because of his training, often looks at a clear-cut area differently from the recreational visitor. He does not necessarily evaluate the area and its beauty. He may be more concerned with figuring what method of slash disposal will be used, what species will be planted, or what type of site preparation will be necessary to achieve rapid natural regeneration (Figure 27.7).

When timber harvests are made in public or private forests, several

Tools for Recreation Administration

FIGURE 27.7 Changes in a managed forest over time are seen from a single vantage point in the Bitterroot National Forest, Montana. Top: photo taken in 1909 after logging the Lick Creek Sale area. Center: The Ponderosa pine and Douglas fir had regenerated to this condition by 1938. Bottom: the area after another harvest. (USFS)

methods are available for carrying out the harvest. These can generally be grouped into even-aged methods and uneven-aged methods. These are sometimes combined by making small, uneven-aged patch cuttings that leave the stand with a variety of ages over any large area of the stand, with small, even-aged patches throughout. Environmentalists have fairly consistently advocated uneven-aged arrangement of a forest stand. This may be desirable for no other reason than ensuring the continuous growth of some large, handsome trees in stands of recreational significance. Uneven-aged stands also are less susceptible to damage from biotic enemies, because most injurious species do not attack all age classes of a given tree species (Smith, 1962). Even-aged stands, on the other hand, tend to provide better wildlife diversity, if developed on a fairly small-scale basis. The interface between cut and uncut forests, called *edge* by wildlife ecologists, provides a desirable mix of habitats for many wildlife species. Young sprouts and shrubs provide food and cover that are lacking in the deep forest.

Many foresters consider even-aged management in the clear-cutting of forest stands as beneficial for recreational use and esthetic purposes. Their argument is as follows: Clear-cutting even-aged forests causes some ugliness for a few years after harvest, but such an area can be left to other uses over an extended period of time without further interference. Logging trucks and crews are seen and heard in a given area for a few months, rather than frequently over a period of a few years or the entire rotation length of the forest, as in the selection system. Therefore, the young vigorous forest can remain as a recreation area for many years without the intrusion of logging or other management activities.

There are at least two basic approaches to modifying the silvicultural harvest systems to produce more esthetic effects. One is to cut timber without using the currently common but maligned clear-cut or other even-aged approaches, adopting, instead, modified selection systems or tiny clear-cuts. The second approach is to plan the even-aged harvest cuts so they blend with the landscape and avoid offending the viewers. Both will be used by agencies and industries in the future.

Avoiding clear-cutting entirely is advocated by many preservation groups, partly as an overreaction to the dominance of clear-cuts. In the West in 1970, 60 per cent of the National Forest harvest was by clear-cutting. In the East, 50 per cent of the National Forest harvest was by clear-cutting (Crafts, 1973). In the last 15 years, more than 1,000 lawsuits have been brought against the United States Forest Service, mostly by conservation groups. Protest has been expressed by those opposing clear-cuts. The court decision against clear-cutting on the Monongahela National Forest in 1973 brought considerable disruption to timber operations in several eastern forests. In 1975, a Colorado wilderness group blocked timber management plans on four national forests. An Alaska judge temporarily stopped a 50-year, eight-billion-board-foot sale—mostly to be clear-cut—to one of Alaska's large pulp and paper mills. Those who brought the action belonged to a wilderness group, interested in keeping the forest for their pleasure and emotionally wedded to the idea that clear-cutting is bad (Figure 27.8). The signals are clear.

Anthony Wayne Smith (1976) of the National Parks and Conservation Association has proposed that public agencies use "ecological forestry" to be compatible with esthetic and conservation values. His version of *ecological forestry* is forestry for all values. Ideally, proponents of this method favor light selective cuttings on a short cycle and long rotation with no single final cut. Thinnings are intermediate cuts aimed at controlling the growth of stands through adjustments in stand density. Harvest systems endorsed are individual tree selection, group selection, shelterwood, and small patch clear-cuts. Minckler (1972) and Twight (1976) proposed the same approach under the name *environmental forestry*. Unfortunately, the names suggest that any other system of timber management is somehow not ecological or environmental.

FIGURE 27.8   An experimental 1958 clearcut in the Maybe-so drainage of the Tongass National Forest by Ketchikan Pulp and Paper Company in Alaska. (USFS)

Ecological forestry in the eastern hardwoods calls for intensive forest improvement, maintenance of mixed species, and a high level of managerial skills, probably using a group selection system that removes all trees from one fifth- to one half-acre plots.

The questions of costs and trade-offs always arise and must be dealt with in terms of the alternatives in the long run. Will wood continue to be a structural material or will more energy-demanding substitutes become cheaper? Looking at the other side, will wood again become an important fuel in North America, as it still is in much of the rest of the world? Will intensive silviculture economically produce large quantities of fiber on a relatively few sites, making timber harvest on mountainous areas relatively unimportant? Will demands for esthetics be valued enough to make harvesting by clear-cutting impractical? Or, more likely, how much are we willing to pay for products from timber harvested by single-tree selections, group selection, or small clear-cuts?

From an energy viewpoint, wood is the cheapest material to use. Its likely use in the future will require continued harvesting. The environmentalists cannot practically oppose timber harvest; they have proposed methods of harvesting that respect continuing esthetic values at a cost.

The second major approach involves *modifying even-aged harvest sytems* to make less visual impact. How can clear-cutting be esthetically improved? The basic idea is to design the cut area to harmonize with the landscape. The shape and size of the cutting units should blend with natural openings and topographical lines, as described under cutting block design. In addition, the logging plan can reduce road density. Esthetic distractions can be reduced by promoting slash disposal by scattering rather than windrows, putting mufflers on equipment, and hand planting rather than using machines.

There are many reasons to use even-aged management, only one of which is apparent economics. When the stand is logged all at once, the logger gets a fairly high volume of timber for each time he sets up equipment. Thus, he saves on logging costs per unit of wood removed. On the other hand, in the clear-cutting system, he often has to fell trees that are of no value to him, which may increase the cost per unit somewhat. Other advantages of clear-cutting are that growth of regeneration is not reduced by an overstory, even-aged stands may be burned by prescription to reduce fire hazard and other problems, and, finally, genetically improved materials can be introduced in plantations on high-intensity management areas. Many economically favored species often require light and bare soil to germinate and grow rapidly. Tree planting with machines on flat ground is much easier when the stand is cleaned off and the ground is easily traveled.

The Forest Service restricts clear-cuts to 160 acres, unless the regional forester directs otherwise. In most eastern national forests, the size is down to 20 or 30 acres. Buffer strips along shorelines, streams, and bald eagle nesting trees are standard procedure. The Forest Service reports the volume harvested by clear-cut decreased in the period 1970 to 1975, from 61 per cent to 40 per cent of all timber harvested from national forests.

The Forest Service has had several researchers working on the problems and potentials of improving visual resource management. Bacon and Twombly (1977) and others before them (Noyes, 1967; Rudolf, 1967; Thompson, 1967; Twiss, 1969; Magill and Leiser, 1972) have proposed methods to achieve a desirable balance between scenery and timber. They suggested and tested silvicultural techniques that can produce timber, regenerate the stand, and maintain or even enhance visual interest of forest landscapes (Figure 27.9). Greater scenic diversity can be introduced, along with concomitant biological diversity. Biological diversity can improve ecosystem rusticity and wildlife habitat (U.S. Forest Service, 1973). One approach is to make cuts that taper toward a road. With repeated entries into a stand, blocks are cut intensively away from the road, and only partially as the road is approached. Near the road, individual trees are harvested, but the stand retains the appearance of a forest (Bacon and Twombly, 1977).

There are some problems in developing such guidelines. Not everyone perceives the forest landscape in the same way; that depends on one's background, mood, attitude, and expectation. These psychological variables must be considered in planning for esthetic values. Therefore, considerable study of visual preferences has been conducted to determine the range of visual conditions that is acceptable to the recreating public (Shafer and Rutherford, 1969; Rader and Hamilton, 1974).

The guidelines also face the question of cost to the timber operations. A certain amount of flexibility and potential income are foregone from timber operations to provide the scenic quality and to perpetuate the ecological diversity that is desired. Such trade-offs often require quantification and analysis. Income to a public agency may be reduced as a result of special measures required of the loggers. Thorough studies of costs of alternative logging systems are important. It is easy to accept the argument that a change in logging practice will add costs per unit of production, but, in reality, the claims may be exaggerated.

Guidance for the manipulation of stands can include the visual objectives adopted by the Forest Service (Bacon and Twombly, 1977). These result from combining two inventories: the scenic quality of the land (variety classes), and a measure of people's concern for the scenic quality of the National Forests (sensitivity levels). In general, the higher the scenic quality, the more sensitive a given landscape, and the closer the landscape is to the observer, the more restrictive is the visual objective. The objectives for different tracts of land follow:

Preservation—only ecological changes permitted.
Retention—management activities are not visually evident.

FIGURE 27.9 Opponents of clear-cutting often picture the immediate after-effects (above). After planting and 16 years of growth (below), the same Willow Creek area in Idaho (St. Joe National Forest) looks quite different. (USFS)

Partial retention—management activities remain visually subordinate.

Modification—management activities in foreground and middleground are dominant but appear natural.

Maximum modification—management activities are dominant but appear natural when seen as background.

In the South, where industrial forests look something like row crops grown tall, the forest industries use a variety of techniques to maintain the stands in attractive condition. When planting with machines, they can run the rows parallel to the road, and some of them leave a buffer strip between public roads and cut areas to temporarily screen out unsightly areas. Five or 10 years later, the buffer trees can be removed and the young growth behind it will be attractive. Along the roadways, slash is removed or chopped up and dispersed as much as possible. The possibility of chipping for other forest products enhances the clean-up potential. Where clear-cutting is used, public education and understanding of the method can be developed through explanations and interpretive devices such as roadside signs, trails, and guided hikes. The setting aside of a few demonstration plots will allow the public to return to see the changes in species growth and development as the regeneration has established itself.

SUMMARY

In today's multiple-use and corporate forests, the expanding recreational use of forest land has brought growing objections to forest management practices that detract from the esthetic appearance of the forest. The conflict between sustained yield of timber products and recreational use can be lessened by some management for esthetics, with silviculture as the basic tool.

Commercial timber managers are sometimes under attack because what was once a beautiful recreational forest has been cut between visits of the recreationists. This pressure has resulted in some forest tracts being appropriated for public parks, forever lost as timberland.

Most forest visitors do not know anything about regeneration, working circles, rotations, sustained yield, thinning, and pruning. Therefore, their opinions are based largely on what they see. But what the natural resource manager sees is not what the recreational visitor sees. What one person perceives to be sound management, another may perceive as esthetic degradation and devastation (Wagar, 1974, and Davis, 1976).

It is difficult to make management decisions about a forest without damaging someone's interest. A presidential panel on forest policy recommended that logging practices be established to reduce site disturbances but allow efficient timber harvest, including clear-cutting, under appropriate conditions (Kilpatrick, 1974). The Sierra Club reacted to this report by saying that it was the latest in a long series of actions of the administration on behalf of the timber industry "to rip the country up, no matter what." What aroused the Sierra Club most, apparently, was the reference to clear-cutting. Preservationists have become very active and vocal, and the focus of their objections is disruption of the esthetic scenery of the forest.

Twight (1976), writing for environmentalists, claimed that "our values in forestry have been expressed by striving for higher standards of forest practices regulation. We have sought to guarantee continued productivity of forests, prevent erosion of the basic soil resources, protect water quality in streams, and protect wildlife and esthetic resources which renew the human spirit. When we fear loss of too many values through forestry, the best alternatives often appear to be restrictions on cutting and protection of forest values through parks and wilderness areas."

Prescribing silvicultural practices for scenery values can include a number of techniques, ranging from buffer zoning to sophisticated harvest designs now being tested by the Forest Service and some state agencies. Roadside manipulations can produce varied and interesting driving experiences.

Silvicultural harvesting systems can be modified for esthetic purposes. Clear-cutting may be avoided altogether on mountain slopes that are readily seen by visitors from highways and recreation areas. The shape of timber harvests of an even-aged nature can be blended into the landscape by avoiding straight lines. The edges can follow the tilt of the land, leaving tree cover in saddles and clumps of trees to break up the forest regularity. Edges can be softened by feathering or by cutting the boundary several years ahead of time so that new growth will be well advanced when the stand is finally logged. Any clear-cuttings should be planned so there is a succession of regeneration and age classes that is obvious to the observer. This helps the visitor to see that the cutting does result in regeneration, as well as providing diversity in age classes for esthetic and wildlife values.

Silviculture for beauty is a frame of mind, a sense that vegetative manipulation can enhance wildlife and recreation values, preserve or even restore scenic qualities, and still keep the forest productive of timber, water, and other products. The challenge to the forestry profession is to implement its long-held philosophy of multiple use by skillful, sensitive planning and management, with visual beauty as a major product of the forest.

Literature Cited

BACON, WARREN R. and ASA D. TWOMBLY. 1977. Managing the Visual Resource Through Timber Harvest; Concepts and Achievements. Paper to Society of American Foresters Convention, Albuquerque, Oct. 3.

CRAFTS, EDWARD C. 1973. Foresters on trial. Journal of Forestry 71(1):14–17.

DAVIS, G. D. 1976. Meeting recreation, park and wilderness needs. American Forests 82(3):12.

DUFFIELD, JOHN W. 1970. Silviculture need not be ugly. Journal of Forestry 68(8):464–467.

Kilpatrick, J. J. 1974. Better to cut a tree than let it rot. American Forests 80(1):23.

Litton, Burton, Jr. 1968. Forest Landscape Description and Inventories—A Basis for Land Planning and Design. U.S. Forest Service, Research Paper PSW-49. 21 pp.

Litton, Burton and Robert Twiss. 1966. The forest landscape: some elements of visual analysis. In: Proceedings, Society of American Foresters Meetings, Seattle, Washington, pp. 208–223.

McDonald, Philip M. and Raymond V. Whiteley. 1972. Logging a roadside stand to protect scenic values. Journal of Forestry 70(2):80–83.

Magill, Arthur W. and Andrew T. Leiser. 1972. Growing plants on view landscapes and recreation areas. Guideline 2(5):57, 59–61.

Minckler, Leon S. 1972. Hardwood silviculture for modern needs. Journal of Forestry 70(1):10–17.

Nelson, DeWitt. 1972. Competition, conflict—and confusion. Journal of Forestry 70(7):419.

Noyes, John H. 1967. Timber Harvesting and Forest Esthetics. Amherst: Univ. Massachusetts Coop. Ext. Serv., Publication 440. 19 pp.

Rader, Terry D. and Lawrence S. Hamilton. 1974. Aesthetics Related to Selected Forest Practices. University Park: Pennsylvania State Univ., College of Agriculture Extension Service, Special Circular 183. 12 pp.

Rudolf, Paul O. 1967. Silviculture for recreation area management. Journal of Forestry 65(6):385–390.

Shafer, Elwood L., Jr. and William Rutherford, Jr. 1969. Selection cuts increased natural beauty in two Adirondack forest stands. Journal of Forestry 67(6):415–419.

Smith, Anthony Wayne. 1976. Resources for outdoor leisure. In: D. M. Knudson (ed.), Managing Recreation Resources for Century III. West Lafayette, Indiana: Purdue University, pp. 1–13.

Smith, David M. 1962. The Practice of Silviculture. New York: John Wiley and Sons. 578 pp.

Thompson, Roger C. 1967. Preservation, recreation, and the premise of forestry. Journal of Forestry 65(6):372.

Twight, Peter A. 1976. Environmental forestry: fiber farms or parks? American Forests 82(5):22–23, 50–52.

Twiss, Robert H. 1969. Conflicts in forest landscape management—the need for forest environmental design. Journal of Forestry 67(1):19–23.

U.S. Forest Service. 1973. National Forest Landscape Management, Vol. 1. Washington, D.C.: U.S. Department of Agriculture, Agricultural Handbook No. 434. 77 pp.

Recreation Resource Policy

Wilderness

Throughout much of history, the term *wilderness* has referred to waste places. In the United States, the federal government has declared wilderness to be a positive resource, to be preserved and carefully administered so that the nation's citizens may find solitude and primitive recreation opportunities away from the influence of civilization.

Wandering in the wilderness was not considered a positive experience for the Israelites, except in retrospect. The heritage of laws, customs, and miracles from that 40-year wilderness trek guide the lives of Jews and Christians even today. Christ found rest, inspiration, and trials in the wilderness solitude on many occasions.

The wilderness that was America is part of the cultural history of this continent, often romanticized to the point that hardships are ignored. To recall it and to find peace and inspiration, many Americans visit wilderness areas that are kept primitive by government policy.

Basic Wilderness Facts

The first wilderness area officially established on federal land was in 1924 on the Gila National Forest, New Mexico. The state of New York had declared a large state forest preserve "forever wild" in the late 1800s, but there were substantial differences in the nature of the wilderness. A 1964 law, the Wilderness Act, legally established the National Wilderness Preservation System and provided for additions to it. Wilderness areas in this system are only those approved by the Congress. A wilderness area, once designated, continues to be managed by the agency that was previously responsible for the property. Under the 1964 Act, wilderness areas were designated on lands managed by only three federal agencies: the U.S. Forest Service, which had the bulk of the original system, the National Park Service, and the Fish and Wildlife Service. Recently, lands administered by the Bureau of Land Management became eligible for the system.

In 1975, the Eastern Wilderness Act was signed, allowing selected Forest Service lands east of the 100th Meridian to be included, even though they did not meet the criteria of being essentially free of man's influence.

They are to be allowed to revert to wild conditions. Some of them are smaller than the prescribed 5,000-acre minimum size (islands and similar units excepted), but that size guideline remains in effect.

From time to time, the Congress makes additions to the system, either at the recommendation of the agencies or upon its own initiative. The largest additions to the system are the outgrowth of the Alaska Native Claims Settlement Act, by which national interest lands are assigned to the various land-managing agencies and large portions of these lands are designated as wilderness.

Recreation Resource Policy

History and Policy

Much wilderness has been destroyed. Some had been transformed into parks and public forests. A small portion of that has been designated to remain in or return to wilderness conditions, where man's influence is as minimal as possible. Up to 100 years ago, much of North America was still wilderness pocked with islands of civilization; today, the continent is an ocean of civilization surrounding a few remaining islands of wilderness. These remain as wilderness only because of the will of the people to keep them in that state, despite the best efforts of some individuals and groups to reduce their naturalness.

In these wilderness areas, the processes of nature are to function without the guiding hand of man and without the extraction of resources from them—except for some mining and some grazing.

In 1964, Congress gave permanent and enthusiastic recognition to the concept of wilderness, which had been practiced by the Forest Service for 40 years before. The Wilderness Act (Public Law 88–577) gave new status and formal definition to the idea of setting aside certain public lands for preservation in their more or less natural state, primarily so that man could experience primitive conditions on nature's own terms.

Millions of visitors now troop to the wilderness areas of the nation each year. Their popularity has become such that management of their activities and restriction of their numbers are necessary (Hendee and Lucas, 1973).

The wilderness idea was part of American philosophy for many years before it became reality. Ralph Waldo Emerson, Henry David Thoreau, George Catlin, and many others wrote of the values of contact with and preservation of wild places. Catlin, often credited with proposing the national park philosophy, called for it as a wild preserve where Indians, wild animals, and plants could be left to live without the interference of European-derived civilization. These and other philosophers paved the way by influencing American public opinion. The concept of wildness as a positive value did not totally supplant the drive to clear, settle, and civilize. The preservation of wilderness in some spots, however, did at least become acceptable enough so the establishment of national parks, forests, and wilderness areas was possible.

A landscape architect, Arthur Carhart, and a forester, Aldo Leopold, were the driving forces behind establishment of the first wilderness areas. Carhart was employed by the Forest Service to do recreation planning in Colorado, Michigan, South Dakota, and Minnesota. His work carried him to the Flat Tops area and Trappers Lake in the present White River National Forest. Summer cabins there became a threat to the pristine qualities of the lake and surrounding mountains. He also visited and saw wilderness values in the Quetico-Superior area of southern Ontario and Minnesota.

Carhart wrote voluminous correspondence and reports recommending the preservation of areas such as these in their undeveloped state so that people could enjoy the natural environment in at least some places. Leopold was a forester in New Mexico. He met with Carhart in 1919 and they discussed their mutual interest in saving wild places. The two reinforced each other in the idea that wilderness conditions should be preserved for their ecological, esthetic, and scenic values.

Carhart was successful first, to a degree. In 1920, the Trappers Lake area was designated as a roadless and undeveloped area. The present-day Flat Tops Wilderness Area eventually grew out of that. In the next year, the Superior Roadless Area (now Boundary Water Canoe Area) was established by a policy to limit the road into the area, using boats and canoes as the principal means of travel.

Leopold's enthusiasm for wilderness resulted in the 1924 designation of 574,000 acres in the Gila National Forest for wilderness recreation. The designation was made by the district (now regional) forester Frank Pooler after the development of a policy for protecting wilderness was drawn up by Leopold and Gila supervisor Frederic Winn (Nash, 1967).

These early wilderness designations were the actions of regional forest officers. There was no national policy by the Forest Service and none by the Congress. The Chief of the Forest Service, William B. Greeley, announced his support of the Gila reserve and encouraged further designations in other regions in 1926. Hundreds of foresters agreed with the idea; some called it crazy. The Gila designation was strongly supported by local sportsmen's associations in New Mexico. Public support has been a strong part of the wilderness movement, although other public opinion was adverse to the idea (Figure 28.1).

It was not until 1929 that wilderness policy became official Forest Service policy with the issuance of L-20 regulations, which described procedures for establishing *primitive areas* on national forests.

In 1939, new regulations defined *wilderness areas* as those of more than 100,000 acres and *wild areas* as those of from 10,000 to 100,000 acres. These were designated and managed by administrative decision, without any law. Until 1964, these designated wilderness areas existed only on the national forests. The Forest Service developed and expanded the concept from 1924 to 1964. The agency's pride in its achievement was one reason it opposed passage of the Wilderness Act as unnecessary.

The Congress and supporters of wilderness legislation believed that to adequately protect and manage the areas included in the Wilderness Preservation System it was necessary to define them by law. A wilderness area is assigned a distinctive name, which associates it in the minds of administrators and others with a specific location. Any area included in the system must be delineated by definite boundaries, usually recognizable by physiographic features such as streams or ridges, and readily identifiable on maps. Direct or indirect legal authority for designation and enforcement

Figure 28.1 Dinosaur National Monument's Echo Park and Steamboat Rock (right center) were the scene of a 1955 wilderness defense against dams, leading to public proposal of the Wilderness Act of 1964. (NPS)

of management provisions should be evident. Previous to the Wilderness Act, the national parks and wildlife refuges had large, undefined backcountry areas with variable management policies. The same was true for the Bureau of Land Management until recently. The Wilderness Act directs and authorizes management of designated areas as permanent wilderness. It declared wilderness to be a positive resource, to be managed to provide primitive recreational experiences and other services.

The 1964 Wilderness Act declared it to be the policy of the Congress "to secure for the American people of present and future generations the benefits of an enduring resource of wilderness." The Congress could designate federally owned areas as wilderness to be "administered for the use and enjoyment of the American people in such manner as will leave them unimpaired for future use and enjoyment as wilderness. . . ."

The act defines wilderness as "an area where the earth and its community of life are untrammeled by man, where man himself is a visitor who does not remain." Wilderness is specifically "an area of undeveloped federal

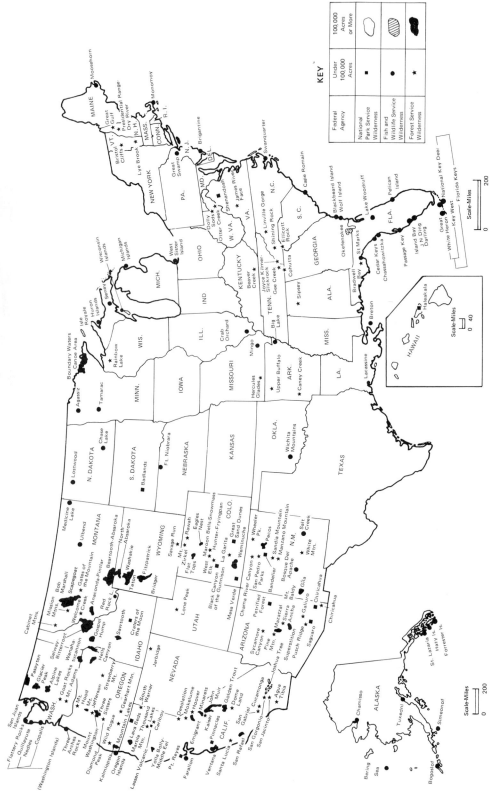

FIGURE 28.2 National Wilderness Preservation System, April 1978.

land retaining its primeval character and influence . . . and which 1) generally appears to have been affected primarily by the forces of nature, with the imprint of man's work substantially unnoticable; 2) has outstanding opportunities for solitude or a primitive and unconfined type of recreation; 3) has at least 5,000 acres of land or is of sufficient size as to make practical its preservation and use in an unimpaired condition, and 4) may also contain ecological, geological, or other features of scientific, educational, scenic, or historical value."

The National Wilderness Preservation System, as of April 1, 1978, consisted of 175 areas classified as wilderness and a total of more than 16.6 million acres (Figure 28.2). The areas are found in National Forests, National Parks, National Wildlife Refuges, and on public land administered by the Bureau of Land Management (Table 28.1).

The Forest Service managed 89 per cent of all federal wilderness land in 1978. If administration-approved wilderness is adopted (including Alaskan proposals), the total Forest Service wilderness would be 9.6 million ha (23.8 million acres) (Figure 28.3). This is 49 per cent of the total of 19.5 million ha (48 million acres).

The National Park Service manages 7 per cent of the present wilderness, but this would increase to 35 per cent if the total proposal of 6.8 million ha (16.8 million acres) of NPS land is designated (Figure 28.4). Likewise, the Fish and Wildlife Service now handles 4 per cent, with a possible total of 3.2 million ha (7.9 million acres) or 16 per cent. After the Bureau of Land Management enters the list with future designations, the proportions will shift somewhat.

The Bureau of Land Management became directly involved in the National Wilderness Preservation System in 1976, with the passage of the Federal Land Policy and Management Act (Public Law 94–579). The BLM had already started to identify some primitive areas through its administrative policy. Its mandate to study and designate Congressionally approved wilderness may have an important expansion effect on the size of the system. It has nearly 50 million ha of roadless areas from which to choose. Three wildernesses, located primarily on National Forest land, contain approxi-

TABLE 28.1 National wilderness preservation system, April 1, 1978.

	Designated		Before Congress	
	Areas	Ha (1000)	Areas	Ha (1000)
Total	175	6,721	89	12,469
Forest Service	106	5,951	25	3,644
National Park Service	17	455	31	5,910
Fish and Wildlife Service	52	295	33	2,915
Bureau of Land Management	3	5	—	—

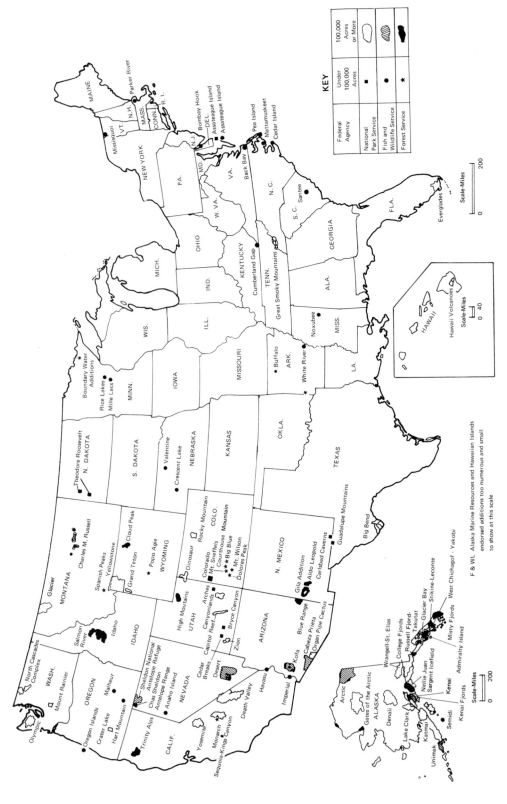

FIGURE 28.3   Administration-endorsed additions to the National Wilderness Preservation System, April 1978.

FIGURE 28.4 Gates of the Arctic National Monument preserves a large portion of the wilderness of Alaska's Brooks Range. This area inspired Robert Marshall to form the Wilderness Society. (NPS)

mately 12,000 acres of national resource land, administered by the Bureau of Land Management.

Opportunities to expand the National Wilderness Preservation System are present within federal land-managing agencies. If all administration-endorsed areas are classified and added to the existing wildernesses, the NWPS would consist of 264 areas containing 2 per cent of all the land in the United States and 6 per cent of the federal property. However, the further study of other lands under the BLM and Forest Service may produce a slightly larger system. It is doubtful that 10 per cent of the federal lands will ever be designated.

Regardless of these figures, the Congress has not defined how large the National Wilderness Preservation System is to be. Resource managers have not received guidelines. It is not possible to know whether allocations to wilderness and other uses are in accordance with overall needs for forest goals and services. That is a major concern of forest industries.

The repeated challenges to Forest Service timber management and sales plans by wilderness advocates have produced confusion and distress.

Wilderness

Figure 28.5 The feeling of wilderness is related to a sense of risk. Bear tracks help legitimize the feeling. (NPS)

Sawmills and other forest products industries have seen their supplies dwindle or be held in doubt in many local situations.

Several years are required for decisions on whether or not to designate specific areas as wilderness. This prompted one industry executive to suggest to a Congressional committee in 1978 that they enact legislation to designate nonwilderness areas.[1] That would allow the Forest Service to manage lands with certainty and without challenges to every management decision.

Piecemeal wilderness designation is exemplified by the Endangered

---

[1] Scott Wallinger of Westvaco Corporation to House Interior Committee on Public Lands, April 28, 1978.

Recreation Resource Policy

American Wilderness Act of 1978 (Public Law 95–237). Sponsors of the bill believed that certain lands were in danger of losing whatever wilderness character they possessed. These identified lands were made "instant wilderness" by the act. Some were of dubious wilderness character.

Currently, there is strong sentiment to save the last of the wilderness (Figure 28.5). Proponents are in an almost desperate struggle to get anything wild into wilderness classification. Saving "primitive" areas of land from road builders, real estate developers, miners, and loggers is their goal. They do not believe that the point of diminishing returns is proximate, but they cannot or will not define that point; it changes with public attitude and time.

Many areas have been nominated by citizens for wilderness study (Figure 28.6). The Forest Service evaluated many of these under an effort called Roadless Area Review Evaluation (RARE), starting in 1972. Criticism and further nominations resulted in an intensive one-year effort in 1977–78, called RARE-II. The goal was to reduce the time of decision for areas that clearly were most appropriate for multiple use. These "wilderness rejects" could be worked back into the timber and other resource management plans. RARE-II examined about one third of the national forests for wilderness potential. Enactment of the recommended wilderness areas by Congress is expected to require several years.

FIGURE 28.6 Mount McKinley National Park and much of the wilderness of the United States occurs in alpine areas. (NPS)

State Wilderness

Nine states have wilderness policy or law that designates certain state properties as wilderness or primitive areas. Two of these have legislation and management policies that meet standards of being equivalent to federal wilderness; California has two areas totaling 39,000 ha (97,000 acres), and New York has 16 areas containing 405,000 ha (about 1 million acres). Eighteen other states have some kind of protection policy or law for natural areas.

State lands are not considered as part of the National Wilderness Preservation System. However, in the two states with equivalent areas, they are counted as representing their ecosystem, in planning for expansion of the national system.

Characteristics of Users

Officials charged with wilderness management must be sensitive to the physical resources. Their esthetic appeal and the value sought by the users become important questions.

FIGURE 28.7   Trail riders in Flat Tops Wilderness, Colorado. (USFS)

FIGURE 28.8　Boundary Waters Canoe Area in the Superior National Forest has been a continuing source of controversy. It was established as one of the first roadless areas by the U.S. Forest Service in 1921. Resort owners and powerboat users have contended with canoeists and wilderness advocates. Mining and logging interests have also entered the fray. (USFS)

Data from 1,950 users in the Pacific Northwest showed that wilderness users were primarily young to middle-aged adults, the majority between 25 and 54 years of age; the 16- to 24-year-olds were also well represented (Hendee, et al., 1968). In terms of educational attainment, 60 per cent were in the top ten per cent of the population. Couples with children visit wilderness areas with far greater frequency than do couples without children; about one half of wilderness use is by small family groups. Many of the other users were traveling with small groups of friends. The most common motive for the visit to the wilderness area was for solitude and escape from the artificiality of cities (Figure 28.7).

This general attitude favoring naturalness of the wilderness area is supported by studies conducted elsewhere. In the Boundary Waters Canoe Area (Figure 28.8), many visitors based their visits on the fascination of the wilderness area (Bultena and Taves, 1961). The underlying theme relates to escape from the artificiality of contemporary environments into more natural settings, untouched by man (Hendee, et al., 1968).

Opposition to wilderness is often based on the loss of derived benefits when an area is secured for limited use. If a given wilderness area were utilized in a more developed recreational atmosphere, some contend the benefits would be increased. That may be true for some individual areas. However, in the context of total recreational opportunities, wilderness is in short supply, whereas highly developed recreation abounds (Wagar, 1974). To maintain the diversity of recreational opportunities desired by the diversity of users, the spectrum of areas includes the maintenance of some areas as wilderness to provide a truly natural experience. In wilderness area recreation, the challenge is to face natural environments on one's own. The assistance of technology and safety devices is left behind. Here is the one place on earth where there is some sane risk—the risk of being alone without ever-hovering, mothering society, without telephone and ambulance in case of injury, without hamburger stands or radio. It is the visitor using his own wits, strength, and judgment in nature. For some, it is a place for finding sanity, stability, and self.

ELITIST ARGUMENTS

One argument that constantly arises when wilderness is proposed is that only the handful of those physically and financially able can enjoy the wild area experience; therefore, there is no justification for setting it up. Roads, chairlifts, and other means are suggested to provide access to "all the people." The argument is specious to anyone who examines it carefully. Obviously, "all the people" won't be interested in visiting the area in the first place.

Wealth is no limitation except as to location. However, the distance to the area would be the same from major cities whatever the level of development within the area. Wilderness travel needn't be expensive. In fact, a large number of young people find it to be an inexpensive form of recreation—certainly cheaper than operating automobiles, buying meals in restaurants, and paying for sleeping accommodations.

Health is a prerequisite to many activities. Is this a reason to reduce the opportunity for challenge to healthy people? Should the rights of the vigorous to have a physical, mental, and spiritual challenge be eliminated so the infirm can see a few more miles of road through formerly wild country? Are there not enough roads now to carry the infirm into former backcountry? Is it necessary to have a road through everyplace that has a bit of naturalness? Must there be a cog railway or chair lift up every mountain? This doesn't make good economic sense.

Actually, the vast majority of the population is financially and physically capable of using wilderness areas. The majority does not choose to visit them, just as the vast majority does not use golf courses, tennis courts,

Recreation Resource Policy

campgrounds, or other specific recreation facilities. Justification of decisions to provide recreation facilities has seldom, if ever, depended upon participation by a majority or even a large minority of the population.

Wilderness experiences are at one end of the diverse spectrum of recreation activities. They offer solitude and individual resourcefulness, both of which would be obliterated if masses of people were present, on foot or in automobile.

Wilderness Management

When conversation lags during a forester's coffee break, a stimulus is the question of how can a wilderness area be managed and still be wilderness. This is most perplexing to a few foresters whose definition of management is confined to manipulation of vegetation.

Wilderness management, as interpreted by the Congress, includes no timber harvesting, no building of structures, no controlled hunting, no roads. The language of the act also implies that man's imprint should not become evident, although trails are allowed. This suggests that management is mainly an effort to control human use of the areas. Keep the wilderness so there is some wildness left. Management involves actively enforcing policies that prevent certain uses. Trail maintenance with hand saws and axes, patrol on foot or horseback, and education of incoming visitors are among the management duties. Keeping the area wild is the key to management. That cannot mean ignoring it.

The Degree of Wildness

When is wilderness wild? The question often faces managers, in many forms. Management policy is the response to the specific issue of how much human interference with natural processes.

Wilderness character is a matter of degrees. The first person who enters a wilderness makes it less wild, to a very small degree. A permanent trail makes travel easier and therefore lessens the truly wild character of an area. If campsites are designated and use of fires restricted to protect wilderness values, the freedom inherent in a wilderness experience is restricted, even though these measures may result in a less damaged environment (Figure 28.9).

There are basic questions faced by the managers and the Congress of how wild wilderness should be. When do human incursions change an area from "wild enough" to "too tame" or "unwild"? The question has been answered only suggestively by the Congress and administrators, despite the apparently strong definitions of the Wilderness Act. From the act, it is clear that wilderness is on the far end of the development scale. From a recreational standpoint, it is intended to provide the most primitive possible types of experiences.

FIGURE 28.9 Restriction of visitors to the backcountry has become a necessity in many of the popular parks. (NPS)

Management issues that will require future consideration include the following:

1. **Horses:** Should horseback riding be allowed in wilderness areas? This traditional use of the area is highlighted by the American Forestry Association's Trail Riders of the Wilderness and various commercial pack operations. Horses and mules are considered part of the frontier experience and were the companions of historic Indian and mountain men. The damage done to meadows where horses graze repeatedly on overnight stays causes wilderness managers distress. Horse travel accelerates erosion on trails, causing severe gullying and washouts on steep slopes and many soils. Restrictions on horses and grazing have been imposed on some wilderness area.

2. **Fishing:** A primitive experience is embodied in catching and eating fish in a remote lake or stream. The nonwilderness aspect is related to the stocking of fish, many of them exotic trout, to increase fishing take. The purity of the wilderness experience is probably not severely hampered for most visitors by the presence of brook trout and the limited fish management activities. Some will insist that some fish management is preferable to a lack of fish. Others will point to the law and concept of wilderness,

Recreation Resource Policy

calling for administration that lets nature take its course, which may include lakes with low fish populations.

3. Hunting: Like fishing, hunting is a survival skill and a typical wilderness recreational activity. The use of increasingly sophisticated rifles with strong scopes and other modern paraphernalia may dilute the experience somewhat, but hauling the bagged animal out by muscle power reminds civilized man of some purposes of his muscular and skeletal structure. Some argue that hunting should not be allowed at all, allowing natural processes to control animal populations. This is feasible if natural predators are present. However, without predators or hunters, populations of deer, elk, and, sometimes, moose grow unchecked until the vegetation is overbrowsed and the herd suffers privation. People concerned about the shooting of individual animals may also be sympathetic to the plight of starving herds, but many are not convinced that hunting prevents overpopulation and starvation.

4. Grazing: Domestic livestock are allowed to graze in many national forest wilderness areas, based on long-term lease arrangements. The same is true on BLM lands and on some of the national park system. As permits expire, it seems appropriate that grazing would be phased out to remove this unnatural element from the wilderness environment. That idea is not popular with ranchers who use the high country meadows and semidesert ranges for a few important months each year, just as they have for decades. Although the grazing lands in wilderness may not be important in total quantity, reallocation of existing permits will cause disruption of patterns and numbers of livestock for each permittee.

Other fundamental questions face wilderness managers. Do we let nature take its course? Do we keep hands off? If so, what does this imply about human use? Can man be allowed to roam freely and uncontrolled in the wilderness environment as a part of nature?

The question of wildness relates to attacks of Southern pine beetle, spruce budworms, fire, and fungi. Should they be allowed to run wild, harvesting the forest naturally? Present policy supports this unless the epidemic threatens adjacent lands.

Natural fires are common in the West. A fire in a wilderness may destroy the forest cover. Should it be allowed to burn out, as long as it can be contained within the wilderness? Some contend that there are so few wilderness areas left, they should be kept attractive. The current policy suggests suppression of man-caused fires and "let-burn watchfulness" for lightning fires.

Wilderness, Science and Recreation

The wilderness philosophy of the United States has always had recreation as a focal point. There have always been arguments that the scientific values of the wilderness were important, but little has been done to preserve large wilderness areas strictly for scientific purposes.

One practical reason for this is politics; the old argument of locking up public lands for science is not very popular, especially if the scientific community is relatively inactive in pursuing studies of wilderness areas, as most of it has been. The principal justification of wilderness is related to recreational experiences of a primitive nature in an environment where one has the feeling of being on his own.

Scientists, however, plead for areas that are truly untouched by man, where natural processes can occur in a human vacuum. This is particularly important to those who study the actions of large animals (Allen, 1976). Unnatural disturbance or harassment can alter animal behavior so as to make observation difficult and conclusions invalid.

It is unlikely that wilderness will be quarantined for scientific studies. Research and recreation will have to be conducted on the same areas. Managers have the duty to ensure that recreation activities keep to a minimum disruption of natural conditions and that the wild character remains.

It is important to note the emphasis on protection of wilderness values. Sometimes, there is a fine line but visitor convenience is not a justification for installing facilities. Visitor safety allows installation of simple bridges and trails, but all other decisions are justified on the basis of protection of wilderness values. Thus, the presence of posts designating campsites in Rocky Mountain National Park is justified because it helps confine use impacts and prevents pockmarked wilderness.

SUMMARY

With the passage of the Wilderness Act, the United States was the first nation in the world to formalize a policy of preserving wilderness. This nation and many others had, of course, established national parks and national forests. The concept of preservation of more or less natural conditions was not new in 1964, or in 1924, but the formal statement of intent to keep certain lands in their wild condition, where man was to be but a transient and light-footed visitor, was new to national politics.

The concept is acceptable to many Americans. Implementation is more difficult and highly controversial. Ever since the wilderness concept was proposed as federal legislation in 1955, there has been organized opposition from the timber industry, mining interests, and cattlemen. The expressed concern has not been against the idea of wilderness, but about the extent of wilderness and the restrictiveness of its management. Wilderness is fine, they claim, as long as it does not lock up timber supply, prohibit mining, or exclude grazing by domestic animals.

Implementation also involves management and use of the resources so that the wild nature of the areas is retained. This involves rationing of use, which creates new questions.

Continuing assignment of federal lands to wilderness has stimulated controversy far out of proportion to the relative extent and productive value of the area. At present, only two to three per cent of the nation has wilderness status. At most, the wilderness system is unlikely to exceed ten per cent of the federal lands.

Literature Cited

ALLEN, DURWARD L. 1976. The worth of wilderness. In: Research in the Parks, Natl. Parks Centennial Symposium. Washington, D.C.: National Park Service, Symposium Series No. 1, pp. 169–181.

BULTENA, GORDON L. and MARVIN J. TAVES. 1961. Changing wilderness images and forestry policy. Journal of Forestry 59:167–171.

HENDEE, JOHN C., WILLIAM R. CATTON, JR., LARRY D. MARLOW and C. FRANK BROCKMAN. 1968. Wilderness Users in the Pacific Northwest—Their Characteristics, Values, and Management Preferences. Portland, Oregon: U.S. Forest Service Research Paper PNW-61. 92 pp.

HENDEE, J. C. and R. C. LUCAS. 1973. Mandatory wilderness permits: a necessary management tool. Journal of Forestry 71(4):206–209.

NASH, RODERICK. 1967. Wilderness and the American Mind. New Haven: Yale University Press. 256 pp.

National Park Service. 1973. Administrative Policies for Historic Areas of the National Park Service. U.S. Dept. of the Interior. 170 pp.

WAGAR, J. ALAN. 1974. Recreation carrying capacity reconsidered. Journal of Forestry 72:274–276.

Corridors as Parks

The Old West has come to the big city. Weekend cowpokes can ride their horses 100 miles on the Sun Circle Trail around and through Phoenix, Arizona. In Oregon, hikers stroll along the banks of the Willamette River or paddle down its gentle waters. Canoeists risk their necks on the rapids of a scenic river just outside of Atlanta.

Elmer Onstott of Missouri (Figure 29.1) and people of all ages test their muscles and endurance on the 3,400-km Appalachian Trail, about 200 of them trekking from end to end each year.

These corridors are set aside for recreation. They are part of a major trend in recreation resource development—turning old corridors into new strip parks.

Much recreation is linear in pattern. It involves travel along a line or in a loop. Among the top recreation activities, about half can be accommodated in linear corridors, including driving for pleasure, walking for pleasure, backpacking/hiking, sightseeing, nature walks, fishing (stream), ORV riding, canoeing, horseback riding, and cross-country skiing. In addition, swimming can be accommodated in a narrow band along streams or lakes and much hunting is done along rivers and riverbank corridors.

Corridors offer an efficient way to provide effective resources for recreation. The land area requirement is low, but the use opportunity is high. Facilities required are few and usually inexpensive.

Environmental corridors represent a special element in the recreation resource system. They serve several important functions. One is providing defined and unhindered access to natural areas, usually by nonvehicular means. The corridor may serve to connect parks to parks, connect parks to cities, connect cities to cities, or to meander along a river or creek with no other purpose than to offer access to an area of scenic or recreational value.

This chapter describes trails, scenic roads, and rivers as recreation resources. They are of growing interest but provide many difficulties for the administrators and planners. Customs related to private land lead to resistance against public trail and scenic river designation. The use of easements and other partial controls are poorly understood by many people.

FIGURE 29.1 Hiking is one of the most democratic of activities, accessible to all ages, rich and poor. (Elmer L. Onstott)

These and other challenges will face professionals in recreation resource work for some time.

TRAILS

England and Wales have a greater length of public trails than the entire United States. Almost all is on private lands. These two sections of the United Kingdom have about one quarter of the population of the United States on a land base that is less than one fiftieth that of its former American colony.

President Lyndon Johnson noted the dearth of American walking places when he proposed the National Trails Act. He remarked on the enthusiasm for hiking despite the severe lack of proper places, calling on the federal, state, and local governments to add to the nation's meager trail system. Despite the encouragement from on high, progress has been painfully slow.

Trails for walking and backpacking are the most numerous. Many of the same routes are used for horses and off-road vehicle riding, although these are separated wherever possible. Bicycle trails are usually paved strips

Corridors as Parks

three to eight feet wide, paralleling roads or other trails. There are actually few independent bike trails; most are parts of city streets or rural roads (Figure 29.2). Some are merely existing roads with "bicycle route" signs posted along them.

An estimate of available, designated trails is shown in Table 29.1. The National Park Service gathered the numbers from all possible sources. The

FIGURE 29.2 The increasing popularity of bicycling has required that special provisions be made to separate bicycle from auto traffic and to provide pleasant surroundings for the bicycle ride. (HCRS)

TABLE 29.1   Trails in the United States, 1978.

	mi	km
Private lands	116,000	187,000
National forests	93,000	150,000
Other federal lands	16,000	26,000
State lands	+36,000	58,000
County and municipal lands	19,000	30,500

Source: Denver Service Center Study, National Park Service.

trails on private lands are particularly significant. These exist under various arrangements, including agreements with Scout groups, agreements or leases with hiking associations or governments, and provision of trails by industrial landowners. The national forests contain many long trails, although much of the system has been usurped by roads. The agency is currently building new trails. The Bureau of Land Management has potential for thousands of miles of trails, requiring only that existing old wagon roads and other routes be brought up to standard, signed, mapped, and officially designated. Nearer to population centers, state and local governments face the more controversial issues of developing trails through various types of land ownership.

BIKE TRAILS

For the Bicentennial of the United States, an organization was formed to promote bicycling trails. Calling itself "Bikecentennial," the group researched, mapped, and marked a 4,500-mile route across the continent, from Astoria, Oregon, to Yorktown, Virginia (Figure 29.3). Then, in 1976, after three years of planning, more than 4,000 people inaugurated this longest recreation trail in the world by riding it. Almost half of them rode the entire length of the Trans-America Bicycle Trail. In the tradition of the Appalachian Trail and other hiking trails, private initiative got the trail idea going and advertised. Most of the $440,000 spent on staff, research, development, and programming came from memberships and trip fees. Only 10 per cent of the group's funding came from corporate, state, and federal grants, including a $26,700 donation from the American Revolution Bicentennial Administration. The group produced guidebooks, maps, and tour programs; they designated 90 overnight facilities and operated tours.

The basic idea behind the trail was to designate a route on existing, scenic back roads, which were maintained and would require no further costs to be used safely for bicycle travel. The trail operates under the shared roadway concept, using state and county highways with low traffic-volume count. The Bikecentennial organization "maintains" the roads by persuading highway departments to improve road shoulders, putting up signs, and making other improvements. Volunteers travel over them to

Corridors as Parks

515

FIGURE 29.3 The Trans-America bicycle trail, started in 1976, follows secondary highways. (Bikecentennial)

update facility listings and maps, check pavement conditions, and otherwise inspect the roadway.

Places for Trails

There are many potential routes for recreation trails, bikeways, and other linear activities. Espeseth (1976) and others have made suggestions that include:

> Abandoned railroads—The DuPage County, Illinois, Forest Preserve District has a 30-mile route, and Wisconsin has two highly popular routes in the Elroy-Sparta trail and the Cross Wisconsin Bikeway. Old streetcar and interurban track routes may also be useful. There is usually considerable red tape in dealing with the railroad companies for recent abandonments.
>
> City streets—Guidebooks and signs make ordinary sidewalks and buildings into interesting historical or architectural tours. Bike lane planning can turn the streets into safe recreational bikeways. Although some safety experts insist on barriers and separated bikeways, rearrangement of painted lines on selected streets in small cities can provide an effective and economical bike lane with little disruption of traffic. Most European cities have separate bike routes parallel to the major arteries.
>
> Roadways in large cemeteries—Often used by bikers, but overlooked

Recreation Resource Policy

by many park and recreation departments, cemetery roads can provide attractive routes, given the cooperation of the cemetery officials.

Canals, ditches and drain ways—Rights-of-way along these water developments are often ready-made hiking, biking, and horseback riding routes. The famous Sun Circle Trail winds 100 miles through Phoenix, Arizona, along canal banks, providing the most spectacular riding opportunities in any city. The state of Illinois has several trails along canals, such as the Illinois-Mississippi (Hennepin) Canal.

Highways—Considerable money is available to the states from federal highway funds to construct parallel rights-of-way for bikes and hikers. Only a few states have chosen to use this opportunity to reduce congestion in their cities.

Levees—Hundreds of miles of flood control levees have been constructed by the Corps of Engineers to protect cities and fields from flooding. Most of these have service roads for access and fairly level tops. They offer interesting views of forests and rivers.

Reservoir shorelines—Trails around reservoirs have often been proposed but seldom developed. For long horseback trips, bike rides, or hikes, they are superb sites. The trail can be in the flooding zone and closed during periods of high water. There are some land control problems that would have to be worked out on projects where incomplete ownership of the shoreline exists.

Power lines and pipeline routes—Utility channels are among the first routes suggested by most planners, because of their obvious cuts through the countryside. Control by the utilities varies considerably, but only in certain spots do the companies have more than a light easement. This means that the land belongs to other people. In addition, the lack of shade discourages some summer uses. Construction costs of bridges and trails may be very high in rugged terrain. However, some excellent routes exist. Indiana built a trail beneath power lines along the inland dunes just south of Lake Michigan. Pacific Gas & Electric Company has built parks, trails, and golf courses on its rights-of-way in urban and rural areas.

Each type of route has special needs for careful planning for safety. There is considerable negotiating required for most of them, as well. Cooperation among the parks agencies and the organizations that control the resources is of critical importance to continuing success. Persistence is required in getting corridor parks established. There seems to be ingrained resistance to establishing anything that is slightly different from previous patterns. People raise many types of real and phantom problems to haunt the efforts of building a place to walk, ride a bike, or ride a horse. Not the least of these is speculation about how people will behave once they start walking or riding. Most landowners are concerned with littering, vandalism, and group behavior. One method of reducing dangers of this type is to provide facilities at strategic distances along the routes—restrooms, picnic tables, and trash cans. Inform trail users of facility locations with maps. Then set up a regular trail maintenance schedule and follow it rigorously. Diplomatic and prompt handling of complaints will help maintain strong relationships.

RAILS TO TRAILS

There are an estimated 15,000 miles of abandoned railbeds in the nation. Of these, the Interior Department has estimated that about 5,000 miles would be suitable for bicycle and hiking trails. Half of these are in the Northeast and Great Lakes states, near population concentrations.

The Railroad Revitalization and Regulatory Reform Act (Section 809) provides funds to help states to convert abandoned rights-of-way to recreation trails. In 1978, 10 projects were funded, after applications of 135 projects. They included a 20-mile bike-hike trail through Baltimore County, Maryland, on the old North Central Railroad line. In Missouri, a spur line of a railroad was converted into a multiuse parkway, trail, and commuter bikeway. In New Jersey, an 11-km segment of the Penn Central Railroad line became a multiuse trail connecting a state park and a battle monument for biking, hiking, and wheelchair use (10 rails-to-trails projects awarded, 1978).

Guidelines and warnings about using abandoned rails, canals, and other transportation routes should be sought and heeded. The red tape and expense is often much greater than seems reasonable (Citizen's Advisory Committee on Environmental Quality, 1975).

National Trails System

The National Trails System was authorized by federal legislation in 1968 (Figure 29.4). Public Law 90–543 was the culmination of a long series of legislative actions that began in 1945. In 1965, President Johnson called for a study of the development of a nationwide system of trails. It was to include metropolitan, rural, and wilderness areas. The young Bureau of Outdoor Recreation, in cooperation with other agencies, conducted the study. In September, 1966, it produced the extensive report, *Trails for America* (Bureau of Outdoor Recreation, 1966).

The report recommended that "a limited number of national scenic trails should be established to provide opportunities of extended foot, horseback, and bicycle trips. . . ." Also encouraged were more trails in federal and state parks and forests plus metropolitan area trails. For the cities and counties, a standard was suggested of 25 miles of foot trails, five miles of bridle trails, and 25 miles of bicycle trails for each 50,000 residents, to be supplied by the local government. For motorcycle riders, local governments were requested to seek 15 acres for each 50,000 residents.

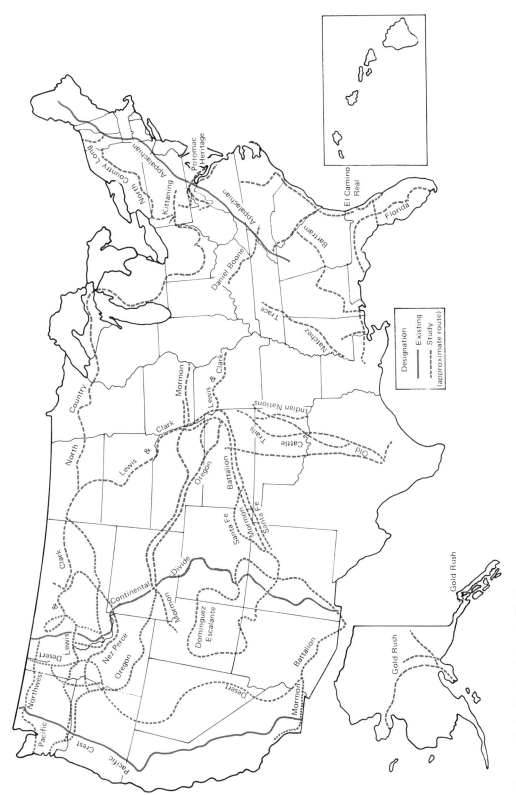

Figure 29.4 National Scenic Trails.

The National Trails System consists of three classifications:

1. National recreation trails, which must be located near urban areas and on federal, state, or local government land.
2. National scenic trails, which are major cross-country trails, administered by the Secretaries of Agriculture and Interior.
3. Connecting or side trails, which provide access to national recreation and scenic trails.

In 1977, President Carter called for the addition of National Historic Trails as a fourth classification.

SCENIC TRAILS

The act creating the National Trails system adopted two 30-year-old trails as its first two scenic members, the Pacific Crest Trail down the Cascades and Sierras and the Appalachian Trail (Figure 29.5).

The 3,400-km Appalachian track along the spine of the eastern mountains was proposed in October, 1921, in the *Journal of the American Institute of Architects* (MacKaye, 1921). The idea was based on trails built by clubs in New Hampshire (White Mountains) and Vermont (the Long Trail). Considerable support came from clubs formed to promote hiking. Early hiking clubs in the East—about 1915—included Appalachian Mountain Club, Green Mountain Club, Fresh Air Club, and Tramp and Trail Club.

By 1921, there were 40 such clubs in and around New York City. New groups were forming rapidly. The Adirondack Mountain Club was one that soon entered into maintenance work on trails (Hiking and Trail-making, 1923). The concept of volunteer labor building and maintaining the trail and its camping shelters is continued even today. The Forest Service aided clubs in completing the trail by 1937. The Appalachian Trail Conference united many clubs in 14 states in an unusual maintenance and improvement program that has helped keep the trail usable to millions of walkers. The trail is within a two-hour drive of nearly 60 per cent of the United States population.

The 1968 act officially established the trail as a federal entity and made the Appalachian Trail Conference a permanent source of representatives to the advisory council of the Secretary of the Interior. The National Park Service is charged with administrative responsibility, in consultation with the Forest Service.

In 1932, the idea of a border-to-border trail along the Pacific Crest was proposed by Clinton A. Clark. A conference was formed to promote the project. By 1937, there were 3,700 km (2,313 miles) open (Archibald, 1951). Traveling from International Monument 78 on the Canadian border with Washington to International Boundary Marker 251 on the Mexican border 64 km southeast of San Diego, the trail traverses some of the most spectacular mountain and desert scenery in the United States. The rugged

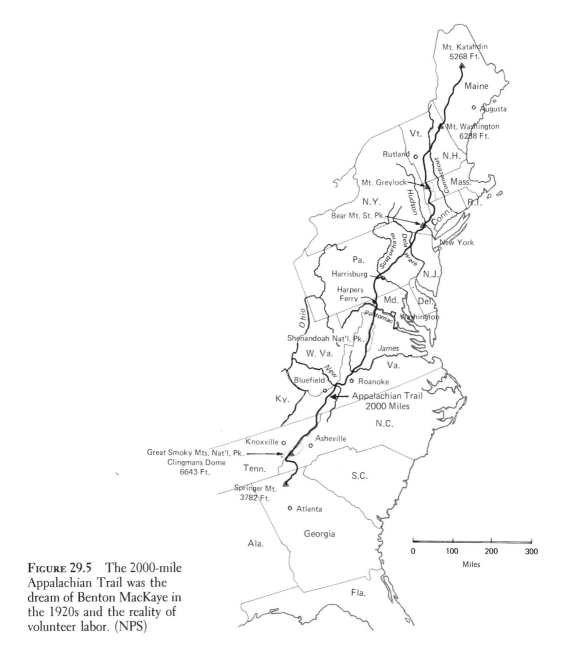

FIGURE 29.5 The 2000-mile
Appalachian Trail was the
dream of Benton MacKaye in
the 1920s and the reality of
volunteer labor. (NPS)

Cascade Mountains of Washington, the soaring Oregon Cascades, Crater
Lake National Park, and the High Sierras make walking a much richer
experience than merely putting one foot before the other. At the southern
end are difficult, but fascinating, desert mountain ranges.

Administration is by the U.S. Forest Service, which controls most of
the land along the route (Table 29.2).

After the first 10 years of the system there were still only two of the

TABLE 29.2   National scenic trails ownership.

Trail	Length		Land		
	km	*mi*	*Federal*	*State*	*Private*
Appalachian	3,400	2,050	34%	23%	43%
Pacific Crest	3,700	2,300	80%	1%	19%
Continental Divide	4,960	3,100			

long-distance National Scenic Trails, the Appalachian and Pacific Crest Trails. Another 16 routes were under study or awaiting Congressional approval. The Congress had been slow to act, but in 1978, finally designated the Continental Divide Trail and authorized work on four long historic trails.

The Continental Divide Trail connects the Canadian border with Silver City, New Mexico, through the Rocky Mountains. It provides wilderness and western history experience for riders and hikers (National Scenic Trails are only for pedestrian and limited equestrian use).

Two other trails have not fared well in Congress. The North Country Scenic Trail of 5,120 km, connecting the Appalachian Trail in Vermont with the Lewis and Clark Trail in North Dakota, travels in a curiously tortuous path through midwestern and northern states. Most of the route would be across private land, a fact that has surely militated against its rapid development.

The Potomac Heritage Scenic Trail would extend for 1,355 km miles along the Potomac River, from Chesapeake Bay through West Virginia and into Pennsylvania. Although the Potomac Trail seemed likely to be easily developed, even it has suffered from a host of inhibitions.

All such cross-country trails face many difficulties in establishment. The Congress and the administrations have expressed enthusiasm for the idea of long trails, but have dedicated neither the money nor the personnel to get the trails built. Without the hard work and dedication of trail clubs, there would be little or no possibility of long hikes across political jurisdictions. The Forest Service and the National Park Service have numerous internal trails. Even these have suffered a history of alternating neglect and cutback versus development and maintenance depending on funds available.

In laying out tentative routes for the National Scenic Trails, planners have apparently tried to avoid large urban areas. This has several advantages, including lower cost of acquisition, fewer landowners to deal with, and more scenic country. There are also some advantages to a trail with urban connections. A trail through urban areas would be accessible to many people who would not have to drive to a distant rural spot to start hiking. Connections with public transportation could save inconvenience and fuel. The poor and the young could use the trail much more readily. There might be little cost in running a route through a city such as Chicago, if planners and hikers were willing to accept the urban environment for the duration. Public sidewalks, canals, and Chicago's famous string of forest preserves could be connected to make an interesting, low-cost trail. There are serious problems related to some farm and suburban areas where land is expensive and difficult to traverse except on roads. Nonetheless, it seems sensible to connect long hiking trails to the cities in some direct way.

Among many long trail projects, the Bureau of Land Management is working on the Dominguez Escalante Trail, which loops through four states in some of the nation's most spectacular mountain and desert scenery.

Long trails are being built in several states. Florida has a project to complete a 1120–km trail from south to north. The longest stretch presently is in the Ocala National Forest. Much of the rest will cross private lands; a lack of commitment to finishing the route has produced discouraging delays and has allowed land costs to rise alarmingly.

State and local trail systems have been started, but there has been considerable difficulty. The public interest and private property interests run afoul of each other. Private landowners have usually made the loudest noises, often convincing elected officials that their rights to control activities on property should take precedence over public opportunities for hiking or riding. Michigan and Ohio trails, pushed more by clubs than by semisupportive government, have been relegated primarily to rural roadways.

Local action is inevitably involved in establishing a National Scenic and Recreation Trails. These trails over private or public land must be open to the public.

RECREATION TRAILS

National Recreation Trails are established by the Secretary of the Interior or the Secretary of Agriculture. They are short or long, usually accessible to urban areas. They may follow stream valleys and floodplains, utility rights-of-way, abandoned railroad or streetcar lines, easement lines, around reservoirs, canal banks, levees, beaches, or other routes. They are for hikers, horsemen, or bicyclists, or combinations of these. Any local, state, federal, or private agency may nominate a trail for entry into the system. It must meet certain criteria of permanence, administration, and national importance to qualify.

Scenic Roads

Ugly roads are often accepted as a necessary price of civilization. The functional but dull roadscape is the natural habitat of the functional monster called the American automobile. The highway can be a work of art. The view from an automobile can be a dynamic play of space and moving forms, of light and texture. The roads can be designed to give the driver-viewer a sense of the proportions and variety of the forest, the hills, and the city. By offering views from different angles, distances, and heights, the road can and does, in some cases, become a source of enjoyment.

Because driving for pleasure is one of the leading outdoor recreation activities, it is surprising that more pleasurable driving areas have not been engineered. Attempts have been made by many counties, some states, and the federal government. The parkway concept, which was popular during the first decades of this century, was an attempt to make driving enjoyable— a sort of mechanized substitute for the old walking promenade or carriage path. Most parkways have been widened and straightened to handle the crush of faster cars. The rapid growth of cities and the automobile's accessibility to most buyers turned the parkway into alternate routes to work. If today one drives the Rock Creek Parkway in Washington, D.C., at a leisurely pace suitable for viewing the beauties of the roadside, he may be the object of protest from the good citizens, arrested for loitering, or accidentally rammed from behind.

To provide for pleasurable driving, a few roads have been designed or redesigned as scenic roads. Several states have scenic roads programs. These are often sponsored by the state highway department in cooperation with the department of natural resources.

On scenic roads, scenery, history, and recreation take precedence over speed and efficiency. Several basic criteria are useful: the route should be of scenic or recreational value; it should be safe to drive at slow speeds; a scenic road should avoid unsightly building and roadside developments; the scenic route takes precedence over speed and directness; it avoids congestion; it eliminates or avoids major crossings on grade; it has few or no access rights; it has a wide right-of-way with little or no frontage land (Jolley, 1969).

Wildlife refuges have used the propensity of people to stay in their cars by providing gravel driving roads with guidebooks and pullouts. The cars act as a sort of blind, allowing people to observe and understand some of the wildlife of the area with minimal effort.

PARKWAYS

Two long national scenic roads are managed by the National Park Service. They are the 500-mile-long parks called the Blue Ridge Parkway and the Natchez Trace. Started in the mid-1930s, they were a hotly debated concept. The Blue Ridge was the object of a tug-of-war between North Carolina (the victor) and Tennessee as to the route (Jolley, 1969). The Natchez Trace is still being completed but has long offered sections as relaxed alternatives to major highway travel (Figure 29.6).

Both roads (and other shorter parkways) are designed for drive-a-while, stop-a-while vacations. Along the routes are facilities for camping, picnicking, hiking, interpretive activities, lodging, and eating.

The corridors on both sides of the parkways are usually narrow. Ease-

FIGURE 29.6   The 500-mile Natchez Trace parallels the route of an important American footpath. (NPS)

ments or purchase of land on both sides of the road keep the landscape pleasant and rural. Uses incompatible with the rustic quality are prohibited.

For the Blue Ridge Parkway, a right-of-way of 100 acres per mile was bought in fee simple plus 50 acres per mile of scenic easements. The average width of the right-of-way strip was set at 1,000 feet, with no portion less than 200 feet in width. Easements were simply to assure customary use of the land, but the restrictions were very strict to prevent hot dog stands, power poles, signs, or other blights on the scenery. The concept of a scenic easement was even less understood in the 1930s than it is now, so confusion reigned among landowners and politicians (Jolley, 1969).

River Corridors

The rivers and streams in the United States cover 5.1 million km (3.2 million miles). About 48,000 km (30,000 miles) are displaced by reservoirs (U.S. Forest Service, 1979).

During the past 10 years, there has been a phenomenal growth in the number of people participating in water recreation activities in the United States. One of the most striking examples of this growth is on the nation's rivers. For example, boating activities have increased 100 per cent during the last decade on the Allagash River in Maine (Figure 29.7), the Pine River in Michigan, and Rogue River in Oregon.

Along with the growth in the number of people using river recreation resources has come a growing interest on the part of administrators, planners, managers, researchers, and the public to learn more about their resources (Anderson, Leatherberry, and Lime, 1978).

Although rivers have long been used for recreation, it was not until recently that they developed a scarcity value for recreation—except in the West, where scarcity is a natural phenomenon. The scarcity became evident from at least two developments—the intensive river-altering programs of the Corps of Engineers, the Bureau of Reclamation, TVA, and the Soil Conservation Service plus the realization in the early 1970s that virtually all of the nation's rivers were polluted.

For many decades, the Congress has maintained a policy of utilizing the rivers for irrigation, power, and navigation. Hundreds of millions of dollars are appropriated each year to stop the flow of rivers for man's purposes. Flood control has been a long-time purpose. Recreational use of new reservoirs is a relatively new justification.

However, recreationists of another sort have begun crying out for a stop to the damming of so many rivers. The Congress, in 1968, balanced its long-time river-control policy with a law that maintains designated streams or portions thereof in their free-flowing state (Figure 29.8). Public Law 90–542, the Wild and Scenic Rivers Act, directed as follows:

. . . certain selected rivers of the Nation, which, with their immediate environments, possess outstandingly remarkable scenic, recreational, geologic, fish and wildlife, historic, cultural and other similar values, shall be preserved in free-flowing condition, and that they and their immediate environments shall be protected for the benefit and enjoyment of present and future generations.

Figure 29.7 The Allagash National Waterway is an element of the National Wild and Scenic River System managed by the state of Maine. (NPS)

The Secretaries of Agriculture and Interior, in presenting the bill to Congress, declared (Bureau of Outdoor Recreation and Forest Service, 1970):

America's rivers flow deep through our national consciousness. Their courses beckoned us to explore a new continent and build a nation, and we have come to know, depend upon and love the rivers that water our land.

We have harnessed many of our rivers, dedicating some to navigation, others to power, water supply, and disposal of wastes. But we have not yet made adequate provision to keep at least a small stock of our rivers as we first knew them: wild and free-flowing.

The Congress endorsed this philosophy, restating it in the law, signed October 2, 1968:

The Congress declares that the established national policy of dam and other construction at appropriate sections of the rivers of the United States needs to be complemented by a policy that would preserve other selected rivers or sections

Corridors as Parks

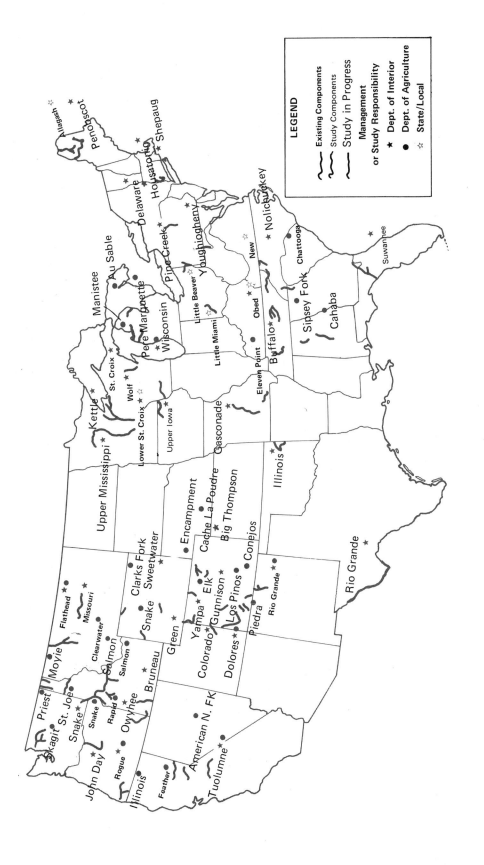

LEGEND

Existing Components
Study Components
Study in Progress

Management or Study Responsibility

★ Dept. of Interior
● Dept. of Agriculture
☆ State/Local

FIGURE 29.8 National Wild and Scenic Rivers System.

thereof in their free-flowing condition to protect the water quality of such rivers and to fulfill other vital national conservation purposes.

Recreation is also specifically mentioned as one of the primary purposes for establishment of the system.

The law urged states to adopt similar programs of river preservation. About 25 states did so and have set aside numerous rivers. The level of protection varies considerably from state to state. State rivers are among the most natural but not necessarily of the quality needed for national designation.

CLASSIFICATION

The federal act established three classifications of rivers in the National Wild and Scenic Rivers System: wild river areas, scenic river areas, and recreational river areas. These are simply classes; the names are more convenient than descriptive of activities.

The wild river segments are truly primitive, on at least four counts. They are unpolluted, inaccessible except by trail, free of impoundments, and have primitive shorelines or watersheds (Figure 29.9). Only a few such primitive and remote rivers remained when the act was passed. Management of these rivers focuses on preservation and enhancement of primitive qualities as the dominant priority. No facilities for recreation, except trails, are foreseen (Table 29.3, page 530).

The scenic rivers or sections are free of impoundments, largely primitive watersheds, and largely undeveloped shorelines, but with road accessibility *in places*. Management emphasizes maintenance of a natural, though somewhat modified, environment. A modest range of facilities for recreation is allowed and perhaps necessary.

Recreational rivers may have been much more affected by man but are still essentially free-flowing. Some past impoundment or diversion is permissible, but such activities are precluded in the future. Development along the shoreline and pollution are permitted. Roads and railroads are usually frequent along the rivers, providing easy accessibility (Figure 29.10).

Management of recreational rivers is strongly oriented to providing for the visitor but maintaining the environment as esthetically pleasing. Recreational river areas usually provide a wide range of readily accessible recreational opportunities, more elaborate and numerous than in the other classifications. The environment may reflect substantial evidence of man's activity.

Classifications are applied to segments of stream, such that the first part of a designated segment may be wild, the second stretch may be recreational, and the third could qualify as scenic, or any combination of these. Few streams in the system are of one classification only. The entire segment must be at least 25 miles long.

The components of the national system in 1977 were those listed in

FIGURE 29.9   Wild and scenic rivers are at their wildest in remote Alaskan valleys where settlements and roads seldom interfere with the free-flowing beauty of the rivers. (NPS)

Table 29.4. Designation of Alaskan rivers adds considerable length and a whole new dimension of wildness to the system.

LEGAL FOUNDATIONS

Water law is extremely complicated. It affects and is affected by scenic river programs. The federal government has a variety of powers and responsi-

TABLE 29.3   Classification characteristics of federal wild rivers.

	Wild	*Scenic*	*Recreational*
Impoundments	None	None	May have had some in past
Pollution	Unpolluted	Not specified	Not specified
Watershed or shoreline	Essentially primitive	Largely primitive and undeveloped	Shoreline may have some development
Accessibility	Trail only	Roads in places	Road or railroad

Recreation Resource Policy

FIGURE 29.10   The Lower St. Croix River is part of the Wild and Scenic Rivers System. (USFS)

bilities for water bodies and streams, defined by the Constitution and the laws and their interpretations through the courts. The basic constitutional powers fall under the categories of the commerce power, the property power, the general welfare power, the war power, the treaty power, and the compact consent power.

The key to these is the commerce power, which relates to regulation of interstate commerce and, thus, to navigable streams and, in most cases, to the flooding potential of their tributaries.

To briefly summarize constitutionally based case law involving the commerce power, navigability in law means navigability in fact. Rivers are navigable in fact when they are used or are susceptible of being used in their natural condition as highways for commerce. The phrase "susceptible of being used in their natural condition" was subsequently interpreted to mean a waterway that could be reasonably improved so as to become available to navigation in interstate commerce. Federal control over navigable waters under the commerce power has been extended to the tributaries of a navigable river in order to protect a navigable river from flood (Great Lakes Basin Commission, 1975):

Corridors as Parks

TABLE 29.4   Components of the national wild and scenic rivers system, 1977.

Rivers: present units in the national system	Administering agency	Miles by classification			Total miles
		Wild	Scenic	Recreational	
1. Middle Fork Clearwater, Idaho (P.L. 90–542—10/2/68)	USFS	54	—	131	185
2. Eleven Point, Missouri (P.L. 90–542—10/2/68)	USFS	—	44.4	—	44.4
3. Feather, California (P.L. 90–542—10/2/68)	USFS	32.9	9.7	65.4	108
4. Rio Grande, New Mexico (Rio Grande Mgt. by Agency) (P.L. 90–542—10/2/68)	BLM/USFS (BLM) (USFS)	51.75 (43.90) (7.85)	— — —	1 (0.25) (0.75)	52.75 (44.15) (8.60)
5. Rogue, Oregon (Rogue Mgt. by Agency) (P.L. 90–542—10/2/68)	BLM/USFS (BLM) (USFS)	33 (20) (13)	7.5 — (7.5)	44 (27) (17)	84.5 (47) (37.5)
6. St. Croix, Minnesota and Wisconsin (P.L. 90–542—10/2/68)	NPS	—	181	19	200
7. Middle Fork Salmon, Idaho (P.L. 90–542—10/2/68)	USFS	103	—	1	104
8. Wolf, Wisconsin (P.L. 90–542—10/2/68)	NPS	—	25	—	25
9. Allagash Wilderness Waterway, Maine (Secretarial designation—7/19/70)	State of Maine	95	—	—	95
10. Lower St. Croix, Minnesota and Wisconsin (P.L. 25–560—10/25/72—27 mi.) (Secretarial designation—6/17/76—25 mi.)	NPS, States of Minnesota and Wisconsin	— —	12 —	15 25	27 25
11. Chattooga, North Carolina, South Carolina, and Georgia (P.L. 93–279—5/10/74)	USFS	39.8	2.5	14.6	56.9
12. Little Miami, Ohio (Secretarial designation—8/20/73)	State of Ohio	—	18	48	66
13. Little Beaver, Ohio (Secretarial designation—10/23/73)	State of Ohio	—	33	—	33
14. Snake, Idaho and Oregon (P.L. 94–199—12/31/75)	USFS	32.5	34.4	—	66.9
15. Rapid, Idaho (P.L. 94–199—12/31/75)	USFS	31	—	—	31
16. New, North Carolina (Secretarial designation—4/13/76)	State of North Carolina	—	26.5	—	26.5
17. Missouri, Montana (P.L. 94–486—10/12/76)	BLM/FWS	72	28	59	159
18. Flathead, Montana (P.L. 94–486—10/12/76)	FS/NPS	97.9	40.7	80.4	219
19. Obed, Tennessee (P.L. 94–486—10/12/76)	NPS/State of Tennessee	46.2	—	—	46.2
Total:		689.05	462.7	503.4	1,655.15

Source: Bureau of Outdoor Recreation

If a stream is found to be navigable, federal power extends over its whole course, including its non-navigable stretches. The power survives commercial disuse due to economic or geographic changes. Use as a navigable stream can be demonstrated in a number of ways, including actual use by any type of vessel, raft or log floating, or by demonstrating its availability for simpler types of commercial navigation such as access to personal or private boats.

The Wild and Scenic Rivers Act limits other federal agencies and licensees. On a designated river, the Federal Power Commission cannot authorize any project, although it is possible to construct dams above and below a designated segment, as long as no reduction in river quality occurs. These limitations also apply to any other federal or state agency dealing with water resources projects. Minerals composing the bank or streambed are withdrawn from mining appropriation laws or leases, but only after the official inclusion of the river in the system (U.S. Senate, 1976).

Presumably, water rights in the West are unaffected. The question of water law is so complex that it must be studied separately. In the United States, there are basically two types of water law—eastern and western. The differences are many and varied, requiring careful legal interpretations. Broadly, western water is so scarce that the water itself is "owned" as soon as it forms a stream. Water rights are acquired by individuals and firms, guaranteeing use rights of a certain quantity per year by that owner. No one upstream from the owner can use up or pollute the water set aside for downstream owners. Thus, a city will have a certain number of acre-feet of water guaranteed (if it rains or snows) from a given watershed. If the city expands and needs more water, it must acquire it from other owners of water rights.

In the East, water law pertains primarily to riparian rights—the water belongs to the individual upon whose land it lies at any moment. So does the land beside and beneath the stream. Thus, access becomes a problem for recreational users, even if the stream is declared as public water. Each state has its own regulations about the status of public waters and navigability. In general, declaration of navigability allows transit of the waters and reasonable access to them. In most states, navigability is an ill-defined term, not necessarily applied to commercial traffic. Recent interpretations seem to allow recreational traffic on the river to constitute navigability, or, at least, to provide evidence that the stream is a public waterway or highway (Figure 29.11). Once this precedent is established, there is little problem of access or transit of the stream.

Administration of Wild and Scenic Rivers

The management of wild and scenic rivers was not prescribed by the establishing act, except that certain limitations are prescribed to the building of structures, and responsible agencies are designated.

FIGURE 29.11   An unusual marked trail is the 99-mile Wilderness Waterway
through the mangrove-covered Ten Thousand Islands in Everglades National Park.
(NPS)

The act calls for individual management plans, within the following
context:

Each component . . . shall be administered in such manner as to protect and
enhance the values which caused it to be included in said system without . . .
limiting other uses that do not substantially interfere with public use and enjoyment
of these values. In such administration, primary emphasis shall be given to protecting its esthetic, scenic, historic, archeologic, and scientific features.

The rivers are administered by the Secretaries of the Interior and Agriculture, through three of their agencies. Involved are the National Park
Service (Figure 29.12), the Fish and Wildlife Service, and the Forest Service. Except where study rivers occur in national forests, the Secretary of
the Interior takes the initiative in conducting studies.

Any component of the systems administered through the National Park
Service becomes part of the national park system. Likewise, those streams
governed by the Fish and Wildlife Service become part of the national
wildlife refuge system. Thus, these components are bound by two legal
documents—the acts of the parks or refuge systems and the Wild and
Scenic Rivers Act. If there is conflict of laws, the more restrictive provisions
apply.

The Secretary of Agriculture, through the Forest Service, may utilize
the general statutory authorities relating to the national forests.

The questions of use by motorboats, types of recreational structures

534

FIGURE 29.12 The Buffalo National River in Arkansas is an original element of the National Wild and Scenic River System. (NPS)

on the shorelines, sanitary regulations, and patrol are left to the administering agency, to be determined by local conditions. As use of these rivers increases, their management will have to include considerations of the following points:

Recreational carrying capacity of the river—how many users can it handle at one time and over one season without impairing its recreational values and other social values. This has become a major management concern in the Grand Canyon and on several Michigan scenic rivers.

Control of users and safety protection, including law enforcement action against trespassers.

Maintenance and protection of the riverbank and other resources at landing sites.

Concentration of overnight users—planning, developing, and maintaining adequate facilities.

Inspection of easements, and liaison with private landowners to protect their privacy and land-use rights.

Provision of interpretive services and adequate maps and river information.

Supervision of concessionaires on some rivers.

The act helped bring into common use the concept of managing corridors of land, particularly recreational travel corridors. It did not, however, make landowners along the streams particularly happy. Many of them have protested federal and, in many cases, state action to designate rivers. Repeatedly, they have expressed fear of creeping government control over their rights.

As in the case of the Blue Ridge Parkway in the 1930s, the concept of scenic easements has not been clearly understood, unless it was carefully explained. The Minnesota river designation program has had success by describing the values and costs of the easements to each landowner on a face-to-face basis. This reduced the confusion of public meetings where vague and inaccurate charges are often raised by dissidents in an atmosphere that defies rational explanation.

The Task Force that studied rivers for the 1979 nationwide recreation plan (Heritage Conservation and Recreation Service, 1978) recommended that river protection should become the rule, not the exception. Instead of looking for worthy or exceptional rivers that merit preservation efforts, the conservation of streams should be considered as a desirable and regular process. The exceptions should be the streams that are not conserved. Unfortunately, the reverse is the case.

Ten years after enactment of the Wild and Scenic Rivers Act, less than 2,000 miles of rivers were protected by the federal program. In addition, less than 5,000 miles were designated under state systems that provide variable levels of protection.

Preservation of river corridors in their natural condition makes good business and economic sense and provides a valuable source of recreation opportunities. Under modern economic conditions and planning concepts, it does not make sense to build in the floodplains and steep slopes along rivers. Most states and localities already have policies that prohibit or at least discourage construction there. Public and private insurance costs for floods can be reduced if the number of structures is kept down in these high-risk areas. A high proportion of historic, cultural, and scenic sites are along river valleys. Because these are in locations that are relatively unsuitable for development, conserving them produces no significant economic loss to society. Preservation of river corridors for recreation and scenery may have several side benefits of great importance. The high-productivity potential of river valleys for wildlife because of their biological diversity is another factor. The Task Force on river preservation for the 1979 nationwide plan (Heritage Conservation and Recreation Service, 1978) summed up the case:

. . . because of their edge effect and the presence of water, they are a nucleus of biologic diversity; because of the action of the river on the land-form, they are a high concentration of scenic and geologic interest; because of their importance as trails and transportation routes in the early exploration of our country, they are a concentration of historic sites; because of this concentration of natural and cultural values and because they are linear, river corridors maximize recreation opportunity.

Water Quality

Most of America's rivers are in sad shape for recreation and domestic purposes, but they are getting better. The primary water quality goal of national policy is "to restore and maintain the chemical, physical, and biological integrity of the nation's water (Public Law 92–500).

Goals of the act were 1) to achieve nationwide applications of secondary treatment to municipal sewage and best practicable technology to control industrial water pollution, by July 1, 1977, and 2) to achieve water quality suitable for fish, wildlife, and shellfish propagation and for full body contact recreation by 1983 (Figure 29.13).

The Council on Environmental Quality (1977) reported that the deadlines were not being met. At mid-1977, only 30 per cent of municipalities had secondary treatment facilities. Industries did much better, with 3,400 of the 4,000 major dischargers complying with the deadline and the rest moving toward compliance. The 1983 fishable and swimmable conditions depend on municipal and industrial actions, but also on elimination of diffuse (nonpoint) sources of sediments and other pollutants. These come from surface runoff from bare agricultural fields, construction sites, roads, urban roofs and streets.

Significant, sometimes dramatic, improvements have been made. The Council on Environmental Quality (1977) recognized 50 water bodies that had greatly improved since the 1960s. They include the Lower Mohawk and Susquehanna in New York, the Ohio in six states, the French Broad in North Carolina, the Escatawpa in Mississippi, the Calumet system in Illinois and Indiana, the Arkansas in Arkansas and Oklahoma, the Houston

Corridors as Parks

Figure 29.13   Rivers, rafts, and boys.

(Texas) ship channel, the Willamette in Oregon, and Gray's Harbor in Washington. Three others are described as follows (Council on Environmental Quality, 1977):

Swimming, fishing, and canoeing are now possible in a 55-mile stretch of New Hampshire's Pemigewasset River. It was in a nuisance condition in the 1960s. Six municipal treatment plants and an industrial waste-water treatment facility were upgraded to allow the summer tourist industry in the basin to flourish.

The Detroit River is one of the nation's best-known successes in water pollution abatement. Fishermen are now catching walleye, pike, muskellunge, smallmouth bass, coho salmon, brown trout, sturgeon, and perch. In the 1950s and early 1960s, it was considered a dead river. It was a dump for sewage, chemicals, oil, acid, garbage, and paper sludge. Much of the shoreline was covered with a quarter-inch film of oil; large grease balls washed ashore. Tons of phosphorus were discharged daily into the river, eventually reaching Lake Erie. The River Rouge, a tributary, was colored orange by acid liquor from steel processors. Aquatic life was drastically diminished and thousands of ducks died each winter after landing on openings in the ice. The Detroit is by no means a clean stream yet, but there have been no major duck kills since 1968. Substantial municipal and industrial pollution control has reduced oil and grease loadings 82 per cent from 1963 to 1975. The oil-covered shoreline is almost clean today, and phosphorus and sewage discharges have been greatly reduced.

Pearl Harbor, Hawaii, is open to the public for swimming, boating, and fishing for the first time since World War II. As recently as the late 1960s, more than four million gallons of raw sewage and 30 million gallons

538

of primary-treated sewage were discharged daily by the U.S. Navy and neighboring municipalities. Osyter beds were contaminated and the harbor was closed to the public. New federal facilities have been constructed. No raw sewage is now being discharged into Pearl Harbor.

The complexity of water quality control is one factor that will require prolonged development and monitoring of discharge systems. The quality of water is related to the presence of industrial and municipal chemical pollutants, soil, bacteria of all types, fertilizers, oil, pesticides, suspended solids, and the amount of dissolved oxygen in the water. Land management is the key to reducing the greatest volume of pollution, which is soil sediment. Erosion from bare fields, roads, construction, and logging sites produce what is called nonpoint pollution. Reduction of obvious pollutants has produced remarkable improvement in the aqueous habitat, but there is a long way to go before national goals of fishable and swimmable water are reached.

SUMMARY

Corridors for recreation offer economical and efficient additions to the recreation estate. Federal and state efforts to provide trails, scenic roads, and free-flowing rivers are becoming increasingly important. The shortage of places to walk, run, and bike in the United States was lamented by ORRRC (1962):

It is something of a tribute to Americans that they do as much cycling and walking as they do, for very little has been done to encourage these activities, and a good bit, if inadvertently, to discourage them. We are spending billions for our new highways, but few of them being constructed or planned make any provision for safe walking and cycling. Many of the suburban developments surrounding our cities do not even have sidewalks, much less cycle paths.

The commission noted that most European nations, with much higher population densities, managed to designate trails throughout their countries, even as the use of automobiles and the building of roads has accelerated. Collective transportation connects with hiking trails, as buses and trains supply places for bicycles. Trails are built from station to station and town to town. In Switzerland and Great Britain, public pathways cross private fields and pastures; they are recognized by common law as being accessible to hikers. One example is the main trail entrance to the Swiss National Park, which leaves the town of Zernez and crosses a large, private pasture before reaching the park boundary. The commission asked, "Why not here?"

The 1968 National Trails Act recognized the need. It did little more than give federal blessing to two long scenic trails and, by now, more than 100 local, state, or federal recreational trails. The 1979 nationwide plan once more called for greater attention to trails. The Bicentennial in 1976 possibly produced more trails than any other effort.

Corridors as Parks

Scenic roads have been established by several federal agencies. Local and state roads have also been designated.

Scenic rivers have been the most successful corridor parks. The federal government and 25 state governments have designated many of the nation's most natural rivers. The management and implementation of these programs have encountered various legal and public opinion difficulties.

The future of corridor park development requires careful attention by administrators, politicians, and citizen groups. The hiker, biker, and river user has long been ignored. It is time that resources were provided in great variety and abundance, accessible to all citizens. Too many Americans have to drive 50 km to find a nice place to walk 5 km.

Literature Cited

ANDERSON, DOROTHY H., EARL C. LEATHERBERRY and DAVID W. LIME. 1978. An Annotated Bibliography on River Recreation. St. Paul: U.S. Forest Service, General Technical Report NC-41. 62 pp.

ARCHIBALD, JANET. 1951. Hitting the high spots. Recreation 45(3):151.

Bureau of Outdoor Recreation. 1966. Trails for America; Report of the Nationwide Trails Study. Washington, D.C.: U.S. Dept. of the Interior. 155 pp.

Bureau of Outdoor Recreation and Forest Service. 1970. Wild and Scenic Rivers. Washington, D.C.: (1970:0–403–700). 29 pp.

Citizens' Advisory Committee on Environmental Quality. 1975. From Rails to Trails. Washington, D.C. 68 pp.

Council on Environmental Quality. 1977. Environmental Quality—1977; the Eighth Annual Report of the Council on Environmental Quality. Washington, D.C. 445 pp.

ESPESETH, ROBERT D. 1976. Linear recreation ways. Parks & Recreation 11(4):26–27, 38–39.

Great Lakes Basin Commission. 1975. Federal Laws, Policies, and Institutional Arrangements. Appendix F20 of Great Lakes Basin Framework Study. Ann Arbor, Michigan. 128 pp.

Heritage Conservation and Recreation Service. 1978. Protection of Outdoor Recreation Values of Rivers; Task Force Report. Washington, D.C.: U.S. Dept. of the Interior. 13 pp. + appendix.

Hiking and trail-making. 1923. Playground 17(2):99, 121.

JOLLEY, HARLEY E. 1969. The Blue Ridge Parkway. Knoxville: Univ. of Tennessee Press. 172 pp.

MacKAYE, BENTON. 1921. An Appalachian trail. AIA Journal 9(10):325–330.

Outdoor Recreation Resources Review Commission. 1962. Outdoor Recreation for America. Washington, D.C. 246 pp.

10 rails-to-trails projects awarded. 1978. Boom in Bikeways 13(2):10.

U.S. Forest Service. 1979. The 1980 RPA assessment. Washington, D.C.: U.S. Dept. of Agriculture.

U.S. Senate, Subcommittee on Environment and Land Resources, Committee on Interior and Insular Affairs. 1976. Hearings on S.158, a bill . . . designating a segment of the New River as a potential component of the national Wild and Scenic River System. 94th Congress, 2nd Sess., May 20, 21.

CHAPTER 30

Preservation, Play, and Production

America's largest outdoor factories are also its largest playgrounds. Its big outdoor museums are also temporary bedrooms and kitchens open to the people.

The forests and ranges of the nation are the producers of wood products, the conservers and dischargers of clean water, and the producers of grass and browse for domestic meat animals and wild game. In these factories, operating on sun and soil power, the recreationist erects his tent or awning, plays his outdoor survival games, and burns his petroleum lamps.

The parks often preserve outstanding scenery and historical mementos and play host to masses of visitors, some of whom are attracted primarily by those features.

Joint offerings of production, preservation, and play are the challenges to recreation resource professionals.

The purpose of this chapter is to further consider the two basic land management policies that govern outdoor recreation areas. These are 1) the *multiple-use policy* on the bulk of the state, federal, and private forest land and 2) the *preservation with use policy* which rules management of most parks (Figure 30.1). The practical implications of these policies are useful knowledge to the practicing professional in parks and recreation.

Multiple-Use Policy

Multiple-use forests and range comprise the bulk of the public land base and much of the private forest land. Recreation is one of many services, blended with management for water, wildlife, wood, and/or grazing.

Multiple use is not just multiple benefits. By that measure, almost any piece of land produces more than one product. Rather, it is a philosophy of land management that leads to active and purposeful measures to produce various benefits from a large land area (Figure 30.2). The multiple-use manager takes steps and makes judgments that balance the total production of the land so as to continually yield the desired combination of goods and services. Emphasis is on the final mix as a whole, rather than on any

FIGURE 30.1   John Muir, advocate of preservation. (NPS)

one of the products, and on achieving maximum yield for the whole over time rather than in any single year.

The following extracts from the Multiple-Use Sustained-Yield Act of June 12, 1960 (Public Law 86–517) describe the Forest Service directive. Similar concepts apply to the Bureau of Land Management and most state forestry agencies.

It is the policy of the Congress that the national forests are established and shall be administered for outdoor recreation, range, timber, watershed, and wildlife and fish purposes. . . . Nothing herein shall be construed as affecting the jurisdiction or responsibilities of the several States with respect to wildlife and fish on the national forests. . . .

Sec. 2. The Secretary of Agriculture is authorized and directed to develop and administer the renewable surface resources of the national forests for multiple use and sustained yield of the several products and services obtained therefrom. In the administration of the national forests due consideration shall be given to the relative values of the various resources in particular areas. The establishment

FIGURE 30.2 Multiple-use lands surround multipurpose Lake Kachess in Washington. Uses include water production and storage, timber production, fish and wildlife production, and many forms of recreation plus power generation from the 35-m-high dam. (Bureau of Reclamation)

and maintenance of areas of wilderness are consistent with the purposes and provisions of this Act.

Sec. 4. As used in this Act, the following terms shall have the following meanings:

(a) 'Multiple use' means: The management of all the various renewable surface resources of the national forests so that they are utilized in combination that will best meet the needs of the American people; making the most judicious use of the land for some or all of these resources or related services over areas large enough to provide sufficient latitude for periodic adjustments in use to conform to changing needs and conditions; that some land will be used for less than all of the resources; and harmonious and coordinated management of the various resources, each with the other, without impairment of the productivity of the land, with consideration being given to the relative values of the various resources, and not necessarily the combination of uses that will give the greatest dollar return or the greatest unit output.

(b) 'Sustained yield of the several products and services' means the achievement and maintenance in perpetuity of a high-level, annual or regular, periodic output of the various renewable resources of the national forests without impairment of the productivity of the land.

Multiple use is a slippery concept. It is difficult to define to the satisfaction of any group of thinking people. Writing regulations for it is, at best, a thankless task; if kept broad, the regulations can be interpreted in many ways, but if made specific, they tend to be ludicrous in their detail and impractical to apply. In the field, application of the concept of multiple use is also difficult. Here, the theory must be implemented. The problems of blending uses are real and must be solved. The problem is not that solutions do not exist, but that different people have varying reactions to the solutions. The manager must artfully blend uses so that the loggers, recreationists, water users, ranchers, and wildlife enthusiasts are all satisfied and so that the agency supervisors agree the solution is suitable.

Compromises characterize the multiple-use forest. Timber production, because of the extensive nature of management practiced and because of the long time required for growth, does not require a great deal of annual manipulation. Therefore, certain other activities can be permitted without a serious sacrifice to timber productivity.

The Public Land Law Review Commission (1970) recognized this as follows:

It takes from 30 to 150 years to produce a harvestable stand of timber. . . . Even though these sites may be administered primarily for timber production, many of them are capable of supporting recreation facilities and use during most of the growing period up to the time of harvest.

There are some sacrifices in the rate of growth of trees, especially on heavily used sites. There is a sacrifice of quality in timber, because of damage inflicted on trees by visitors, soil compaction, and erosion.

A forest can become, and often is, primarily a recreation area, where timber production is relegated to a secondary role or excluded altogether. Emotional attachment of visitors to a place develops a proprietary attitude in public opinion. When public opinion becomes sufficiently strong and widespread, the area may be permanently set aside for recreational use. Further along the scale, public opinion may develop so that even most recreational use will be excluded and the area will be preserved for its natural values and for educational or scientific purposes.

The value of forests has been looked upon differently in different eras. Here are five views of the American forests:

American Indians	The forest was home and nature a force that could be used but not dominated. Small areas could be used up but there was always more.
Pilgrims and pioneers	The forest was a wilderness and the home of a hostile enemy, but produced food, shelter, and export capital. Though it was a necessity, it was recognized that the forest must be reduced by a substantial amount.

Lumbermen	The forest was a timber mine, a resource. It was not yet treated as a renewable resource.
Foresters	The forest is a renewable resource. It must be protected and nurtured; the timber harvest must be rationalized; other uses of the forest were enhanced.
Recreationists	The forest is a service environment. Romantic and esthetic aspects predominate.

Demands on national forests are increasing on all fronts. The U.S. Forest Service (1974) projected the following:

Recreation use would increase 40 per cent per decade. Timber consumption would go up 18–32 per cent per decade. Water withdrawals (nationwide) are to increase 23 per cent per decade. Grazing on forest lands is to go up 12–20 per cent per decade. Mining on forests will rise, especially for coal. Special uses are in heavy demand.

To meet any combination of these increases obviously requires greater efforts in land management and program supervision. This implies more federal resources must be shifted to the Forest Service from other agencies or more tax dollars must come in from the public. At a time when the public appears to be resisting government spending, the agency may find itself in difficulty. The active forest-related groups also are doing little to support federal and state forestry efforts. Polarized opinion about different roles of the forest leaves the managing agencies in the middle of a standoff. Concerted and unified pressure from clients on all sides is needed to secure funds.

Among the many uses of national forests and national resource lands, wilderness has captured public opinion as important and desirable. It is so popular that major land-use decisions are favoring wilderness now. It is not just a few dedicated legislators who are doing it.

What is heard as public opinion about forest management is often disregarded as the loud voices of effectively organized conservation organizations—a few voices of the interested. A recent survey suggests that the opinions heard about wilderness and logging may be fairly representative of general opinion. Opinion Research Corporation of Princeton, New Jersey, conducted a study of Americans' attitudes toward forest recreation use as compared to development for timber. The September, 1977, survey was sponsored by the American Forest Institute, an organization that represents the forest products industry. The survey consisted of interviews with 2,000 members of the general public and 100 selected thought leaders in Washington, D.C. It is important to note that the survey measured attitudes of people, not facts. For example, 20 per cent of the interviewees believed that they have visited wilderness areas; if the sample was representative, many of these had not actually visited officially designated federal or state wilderness areas.

In general, the public opinion sample revealed that the forest industry faced strong opinion in favor of wilderness and against building roads and harvesting increased volumes of timber. After an explanation, both the public and the Washington leaders were offered the choice: increase the yield and sales of timber from our national forests or preserve these trees in their natural state. The results were as follows:

	Public	Leaders
Increase timber sales	28%	36%
Preserve trees	62	38
No opinion	10	7
Both	—	10
Other (some criticism of terminology by leaders)	—	9

The same groups were asked if they favored an increase in timber sales to provide money for road expansion and more public access to national forests:

	Public	Leaders
Favor	29%	15%
Oppose	57	69
No opinion	14	3
Other	—	8

Other surveys show the public is unconcerned about a timber shortage. It seems clear that the industry opposing wilderness on the basis of lost timber production potential finds little sympathy among the public.

There was strong support for wilderness, although the individual's definition of wilderness was not necessarily legalistic. Only 7 per cent said there was too much wilderness, whereas 32 per cent said there was too little. Strongest supporters of more wilderness were males 18 to 29 years old, 51 per cent of whom said there was too little. Overall, 46 per cent of the respondents thought that wilderness area was about right. This does not suggest that they would oppose expansion.

The old elitist argument heard since the 1940s is not given much credence by the public. This argument stresses that only a few select individuals benefit from wilderness areas. Only 3 per cent of the wilderness opponents in this survey accepted the elitist argument. This suggests that the growing popularity of wilderness travel and the wilderness concept have debunked the old elitist argument.

The Opinion Research Corporation advised the American Forest Institute that it did not find sufficient support to warrant a mass communications program to increase public support for greater timber harvesting on federal lands.

Foresters invented multiple use in recognition that forests growing timber products can also be used for other values. A public agency waits for nature to do the growing, with minor assists by professional foresters, but there is little enthusiasm from the public. In most places in the world, the public is somewhat cynical about the wisdom of tying up land for so long to grow a few trees.

Unjust as that attitude may be, it is professionally and politically wise to allow and to promote the use of public forests for other uses. The truth is that there is no way to stop other uses without an unpopular enforcement program. The other uses do little harm to the timber. The choice is whether to grudgingly permit use, as is the case with some industrial owners, or to gracefully and strategically invite hunting, fishing, hiking, camping, riding, watershed development, grazing, and related uses.

In a 1922 report, the District II forester reported that recreational use was occurring in the Colorado forests before the Forest Service took over the land. He then called for strong fiscal recognition of the agency's responsibility toward providing recreation facilities and management.

In the national forest and most state forests, recreation was a use to be allowed from the beginning. Eventually, some recreation management and construction efforts were made. The paramount interest and value of the forests were related to timber products, however. Even in the East, where forests were purchased for their watershed value, foresters tended to consider timber production first. Other uses were multiple, but their multiples were on a lower scale.

That hasn't been bad. Productive timber land is usually quite attractive for recreation. With a little planning of cuts, many wildlife species can benefit greatly from the diversity of a forest under a harvest and regeneration system. Much of the Eastern Wilderness is the result of timber-oriented goals of public agencies that are helping cutover lands to recuperate. The emphasis on timber has taken a turn, however.

Now, it is widely recognized that recreation is the principal use of many national and state forests. Instead of putting timber first and "permitting" other uses, the public is suggesting that recreation may be the prime, or a prime, goal of management, "permitting" timber harvesting as long as it is compatible with recreational, watershed, or other values.

Silviculture, in its academic form, is compatible with this view. In the minds of some practicing foresters, however, silviculture is strictly a timber management technique for timber production. This view ignores the concept that forests are managed for the goals of its owner, or else it assumes that all owners share the same goals.

Efforts at active silviculture for recreation are not new. Foresters have practiced timber harvesting in South Dakota's Custer State Park since the 1950s. Every cut is planned to remove hazardous trees, to leave low stumps that are not readily visible, and to enhance the views. There is special care in campgrounds to not disrupt the sylvan scene, so precious in that wide-open state.

Numerous other parks and forests have planted and cared for seedlings to form a new forest. Considerable planting work done during the 1930s by CCC crews are today being enjoyed by campers and picnickers.

The National Park Service started research on using logging and prescribed burning to restore desired forest conditions in the late 1950s. By the mid-1970s, these were employed actively and extensively in a number of parks.

LEGAL BASES

There is well-established legal recognition that public forests, originally established to prevent timber famine, are to be managed for various uses. The Multiple-Use Sustained-Yield Act of 1960 emphasized the balance of various uses on national forests. The policy had been practiced, more or less, since the beginning of the Forest Service. This has been reinforced in recent planning and management acts and administrative plans. Most states also manage their public forests for several uses.

The Monongahela decision by the courts in 1973 drastically altered timber harvest practices that were distasteful to people who apparently were more interested in appreciative than in consumptive uses of the forests. It should be noted that the point of law was not related to primacy of uses but to the 1897 Organic Act that was too precisely stated for modern management practices. The Congress later changed the old law to allow clear-cutting and to invalidate the judgment. Nevertheless, the point was made, dramatically. Some of the members of the public had distinctly said that it was not "timber first" for them. It was "timber . . . if." The "if" is related to compatibility with scenic and conservation values.

In sum, the objective of multiple-use land management is not to see how many different ways a piece of land can be used. It is to use it so to realize its greatest total benefit over the long run. That is bound to displease those who have a single interest in the forest. Those who benefit from recreation, timber, or grazing often dislike the compromises with other uses. Multiple use creates some of its own pressures. The land manager may find his only praise in Heaven.

Preservation and Use

When Yellowstone was established, it became a preserve and a pleasuring ground at one and the same time. When the National Park Service was established in 1916, the Congress gave it the charge to manage the parks in a way that would conserve the scenery, the natural and historic objects, and the wildlife and, at the same time, to make these resources available for the people to enjoy.

Some people have called the instructions a paradox, a self-contradictory task. Others see it as a simple directive to consider carefully the balance between preservation of the park and accommodations for use, as each decision is made (Figure 30.3). The Congress clearly did not wish to attempt to define precisely how much development was appropriate for each park in the future. It defined the spirit and purpose of the operation of the properties. It kept the decision-making process flexible, without doing the

FIGURE 30.3 Boardwalks make swamps and marshes accessible and interesting to visitors at Natchez Trace National Parkway. (NPS)

Preservation, Play, and Production

thinking for future administrators or policy makers. With every decision, the balancing process must begin anew, in light of accumulated experience and current conditions of park use (Everhart, 1972).

Most professional administrators welcome this generosity of the Congress. They are given the opportunity to choose, to judge, and to implement a broad, yet firm, policy. Most of these decisions are made in consultation with other professionals, with the public, and with politicians. As a result, controversy is likely to seep into the decision making process. Some people can see only one side of the preservation-use equation, opting to push their point of view to its ultimate but appearing to view the other side as already overwhelmingly out of balance. Thus, preservationists often oppose additions of roads, buildings, and conveniences for visitors, on the ground that these erode the natural character for which the park was established. Proponents of development argue that the park is for people, that people tend to visit mostly the places where there are developments, that the park is now undervisited in relation to what it could be with a minor bit of additional development, and that the backcountry of the park is so vast and underused that the proposed developments would have virtually no effect upon it. Both sides are often correct in their arguments.

The preservation–use balance confronts not only national park managers. The national wildlife refuges, state parks, county parks, nature preserves and other recreation areas face the question of how much use is too much use. The objective is to provide parks, not parking lots.

The dispute about how many people can be accommodated is related to how resilient the resource is—its carrying capacity. It is also related to the kind of management it is given. That seems to be a function of agency policy and management sophistication.

Clawson (1974) observed five stages, frequently found in the life history of national parks, which describe the changing attitudes toward their management.

1. Reservation stage: Often in response to a few dedicated people, the government sets aside special areas to protect them from other development. Recently, there has been strong local opposition to new areas being set aside in settled parts of the nation.

2. Early management stage: Low public use and low budgets keep management at minimal levels. Proposals by commercial interests and vandalism are inevitable by-products of the lack of support. Some recent parks and refuges have not suffered under this condition, but the new Alaskan facilities seem destined to have a period of custodial care only.

3. Rising public interest stage: As park visits become easier, the area gains fame through the visitor grapevine and the mass media. New visitors require new appropriations for facilities and personnel. Although the money lags behind the rising visitation, there is rising political support from the

new visitors. First, limitations of carrying capacity may be revealed in this stage.

4. Carrying capacity limit stage: Use of the park approaches, reaches, or exceeds carrying capacity. Excessive use of the park may endanger park resources. Stopgap measures are used to raise carrying capacity, but management methods that guide and limit use are eventually required. Public and bureaucratic resistance to stopping the rising tide of visitors makes the process difficult.

5. Crown jewel stage: Perhaps this stage has not been reached in any nation or state. The national or state parks are managed for their significant features, not as ordinary recreation areas. The other kinds of recreation areas take on greater responsibility for everyday activities.

Appropriateness in Parks

What is appropriate for a park? What kinds of uses should be allowed in parks and what should be excluded?

These are questions that face any park manager. They often give him great cause for concern and difficult times in explaining his point of view to the public. He cannot just react and say, "I don't like that kind of activity; therefore, it shouldn't be here." He needs to have a statement of policy of appropriateness. This must describe what the park's purpose is and what it is trying to do.

Even this cannot resolve all the problems that come up. There's no way to write a policy that specifically lists all things that would be excluded or included in the park. Technology brings new equipment, and new ideas arise among people as to how they might use places. Then it is up to the manager to go back to the basic philosophy and policy and to determine the basis of his stance on any particular use. Perennial questions of appropriateness in parks involve ski areas, campgrounds, new roads and concession sales operations.

For many decades, the true and fitting purpose of a national park has been debated in Yosemite. National Park Service officials and the public have bickered over the appropriateness of hotels, motels, the firefall over the cliff, the automobile, and even bears. On summer mornings of 1975, a group of young men and women stood with hang gliders on a rock ledge thousands of feet above the valley floor. Then, one by one, they jumped off.

The flight that follows takes the gliders on a silent, awesome journey over the valley, sometimes turning toward Yosemite Falls, sometimes toward the 8,000-foot face of Half Dome.

By the time a glider lands in a valley meadow near the Ahwahnee Hotel, it has dropped 1,000 meters. It often leaves the person exhilarated in a way he finds difficult to describe. About 700 flights were completed off Glacier Point in the summer of 1975 with neither incident nor injury, except one scraped knee. Virtually all the participants have complied with the park's safety program, one of the strictest in the nation.

Yet, the National Park Service has banned all hang gliding in national parks and historical areas. In the Federal Register of August 20, 1975, the service proposed that all forms of powerless flight be prohibited within National Park Service lands because such flights are "contrary to the purposes for which these areas were established and contrary to . . . enjoyment of park resource." The National Park Service Director criticized the "spectacular nature" of powerless flights over the Yosemite Valley, claiming they distract other visitors from the natural and historical values of the park.

On the other hand, hang gliders have damaged neither the park's environment nor its resources. The Glacier Point Park Ranger established the park safety program and he checked each person before he began his flight. Although hang gliding's safety record has not been good nationally, at Yosemite there has been a nearly perfect record. Despite these positive points, hang gliding has been deemed inappropriate.

Several other questions of appropriateness have recently been raised by users of the parks and by park managers. Among these are nude sunbathing in Cape Cod National Seashore, rock-climbing in Yosemite and other parks, horseback riding in erodible Rocky Mountain National Park areas, and use of snowmobiles on snow-covered roads in Yellowstone National Park through the winter season. There are certain to be other questions in the future that will tax the imagination and the good sense of the park manager.

Jackson Hole

When decisions are made to adopt new service environments in a local area, care must be taken to foresee that this environment is not self-aggrandizing and irreversible, especially if it is potentially in conflict with other values of the area.

An example is the Jackson Hole airport, in Wyoming, surrounded by the Grand Teton National Park. Frontier Airlines serves the area, bringing in skiers and sightseers on small feeder planes. The regional economy has come to depend upon this technological innovation. Without it, the ski slopes and winter lodging-feeding businesses would probably not survive. However, many environmentalists feel that the airport is, at best, an annoyance and a barely compatible element of the National Park area. But the park and region are locked into the technology. There are relatively few alternative sites in Jackson Hole, which is shared with the elk.

In time, Frontier would move toward jet service from more cities. This requires a longer (double) runway. Because low visibility frequently prohibits landing in Jackson Hole, the next technological extension would become ground-assisted guidance instruments, which can only be justified by more air business and larger facilities. With more invested, there is less likelihood

Recreation Resource Policy

of removal of the airport, regardless of good reasons for recreation policy and land management.

Thus, technology becomes the tyrant, and the medium (the airline) becomes the message. The debate about the Jackson Hole airport extension has cropped up several times over the past 10 years. It is undoubtedly one of those perennial controversies that revolves around the proper roles and emphasis of park lands.

Summary: The Value Question

Recreational, scenic, scientific, and related values of recreation resources are quite different from the commercial values of commodities such as timber. Attempts to formulate environmental values in monetary terms are inadequate for conversion to or comparison with commercial values. The resources manager in a multiple-use or park resource operation is required to develop and maintain an orientation toward resources that differs from one based solely on economic values. The human reaction values to natural resources are of as much importance as are the commodity production values. The professional must be able to recognize all of the intrinsic and inspirational values of the environment and to defend them from destructive or damaging influences of natural or human origin.

The recognition of these values requires sensitivity to human responses to the environment, considering the diversity of people and their experiences. Human values cannot be reduced to tables, numbers, or charted points on a graph. Therefore, they are sometimes avoided or looked upon as unsophisticated. In reality, the lack of sophistication is in the desire to oversimplify values and to imagine that numbers representing environmental conditions are precise abstractions of the ecosystem. The professional who avoids subjective or human value aspects of resource management is abdicating technical judgment to the adding machine and is willing to settle for the easiest answers. True professional sophistication uses the available numbers and adds to them sensitivity to and knowledge of political, social, economic, and biological conditions.

Wise management of natural and cultural resources for recreational purposes must be accompanied by an understanding and sympathetic management of the people visiting the properties. With increasing numbers of visitors, skillful control and management of people will assume greater significance in resource management. Balanced attention to both people and resources is required to protect the very values that are inherent in recreational places.

Management and protection of parks and forests are only part of the professional's job. Interpretation of the resources plays an equally important role in offering the visitor knowledge that leads to fuller enjoyment. This knowledge and sensitivity help reduce actions by the visitors that result in aimless, thoughtless, careless, and even malicious destruction of recreation resources and values.

Literature Cited

CLAWSON, MARION. 1974. Park visits in the coming decades: problems and opportunities. In: Sir Hugh Elliott (ed.), Second World Conference on National Parks. Morges, Switzerland: International Union for Conservation of Nature and Natural Resources, pp. 116–126.

EVERHART, WILLIAM C. 1972. The National Park Service. New York: Praeger. 276 pp.

Public Land Law Review Commission. 1970. One-third of the Nation's Land. Washington, D.C.

U.S. Forest Service. 1974. Highlights of the Environmental Program for the Future. U.S. Dept. of Agriculture, Current Information Report No. 13. 39 pp.

C H A P T E R   3 1

Resource Management Policy

Bears, burros, and boars are giving fits to park managers. So are boors.

The deceptive simplicity of the preservation and use directive for park management only begins to indicate the complexity of park management. There are questions of what to do with fires, with vandals, with the volume of visitors, with concessionaires, and a hundred other problems.

This chapter points out the policy bases for a few of these management problems. It emphasizes people and resource management, especially as they relate to resource-oriented recreation properties.

When speaking of recreation management, there is sometimes confusion. Some people equate management with alteration of natural conditions or manipulation of people. Here, the word is used in its broader sense. Management encompasses a broad range of purposeful decisions, intended to accomplish given objectives. Planned action and planned inaction are both management. Resources may be managed for the production of goods and services, for protection from any impact, or for a combination of both (U.S. Forest Service, 1977).

Recreation resource management must resolve questions of conflicts—user-resource conflicts, user-user conflicts, resource-resource conflicts.

Park resource management operates in the framework and constraints defined by laws, policies, tradition and sense of appropriateness, public opinion, and common sense.

The basic goal of policy toward these problems is to offer high-quality experiences for the visitors plus maintenance and restoration of a high-quality naturalistic environment. Experience and testing are continually advancing the specific methods for management of the complex interactions of recreationist and the environment.

Philosophy of Park Resource Management

The national parks and most state parks were set aside as outdoor museums. They were protected. Fires were stopped as soon as detected. Predators were eliminated to protect the deer and other desirable animals, at least until the 1930s.

The results were slow in revealing themselves, but protection appears to be an insufficient philosophy. Current policy in national park resource management is influenced by a report made in 1963 by an Advisory Board on Wildlife Management (Leopold, et al., 1963). Originally requested to review the problem of excess ungulates (deer, elk, etc.) in some parks, this group of leading wildlife scientists dealt with park management policy for all resources.

They recommended as the primary goal to maintain or restore the biotic associations in a condition that prevailed when the area was first visited by the white man (Figure 31.1).

Restoring the primitive scene offers problems. The goal can only be approached. Wolves and grizzlies cannot easily be reintroduced to parks surrounded by ranches. Exotic plants and animals have found a niche, whereas extinct species have vanished permanently. Nevertheless, the goal can serve as a guide for management.

To implement the goal to achieve preservation requires a diversity of procedures. Manipulation of the vegetation is sometimes required.

Protection will work to maintain climax forests or some desert associations. Grasslands, savannas, and successional forests require periodic treatments resembling natural fires, floods, and winds that periodically arrest or set back succession. Use of the chain saw, tractor, rifle, or flame thrower may be useful, but their use should be hidden from visitors insofar as possible and should not violate the Wilderness Act, passed one year after the committee report.

The committee recommended that management be limited to native plants and animals, discouraging exotics and artificiality. They rejected the European use of artfully fenced enclosures to display animals, saying it is appropriate to zoos, not national parks. Likewise, artificial feeding should be replaced by natural range.

Roads are not part of the primitive scene and should be rigidly prescribed and designed to prevent overdevelopment. "If too many tourists crowd the roadways, then we should ration the tourists rather than expand the roadways" (Leopold, et al., 1963).

Among the various habitat manipulation methods, controlled burning is probably the only method sufficiently inexpensive, rapid, natural, and invisible to allow extensive application.

Other approaches include local reintroduction of native species of plants and animals, use of the bulldozer and disc harrow to initiate desirable changes in plant succession, and control of animal populations within the carrying capacity of the soil, vegetation, and habitats of other native animals. These methods may include natural predation, trapping, and transplanting, as well as shooting excess numbers of animals. The last method is most efficiently done by employees. Public recreational hunting eliminates mostly animals close to the roads, thus reducing viewing opportunities; it has generally proven to be an unsatisfactory means of natural-like population control.

The goal of restoring and maintaining natural conditions requires the use of skills that are not well developed. Research and testing are needed before broad application. Public information and education are vital ingredients. Most of all, it requires active and alert management, using skilled personnel.

Fires in the Parks

As suggested in the advisory committee report, fire is a valuable tool for management.

Efforts to preserve vegetation in parks by protection alone have not usually been successful. That is basically because plants form ever-changing communities. The principle of succession of plant communities is operative, although not always in the exact patterns modeled by ecological scientists. Stately groves of big trees have long been attractive ingredients of parks. Huge trees forming groves of sequoias, redwoods, Douglas-firs, and ponderosa pines have often been set aside in preserves. Their dominance depends upon disturbances such as periodic fires.

Fires are set or allowed to burn in many national forests, parks, and wildlife refuges. Prescribed burning has long been a timber management tool, especially in the South for weeding out young pine stands. Presently, several million hectares of federal recreation lands are managed so fires play a more natural role in the ecosystem. Both prescribed burning and natural fires are part of the program.

The first prescribed burning program in the national parks intentionally set controlled fires in the Everglades in the 1950s. Then the policy was further developed in the 1960s in California. Research in the *Sequoia gigantea* groves of Sequoia, King's Canyon, and Yosemite National Parks revealed two problems. First, there was dangerous buildup of debris and litter on the forest floor, which could turn into raging, uncontrolled fires. Second, the sequoias were not reproducing; they were crowded out by firs, cedars, and other species that benefited from man's protection (Kilgore and Briggs, 1972). These trees had crowns that could carry hot fire from the ground to the crowns of the sequoias.

The history of the sequoia stands suggests that light fires have long been an element of the ecosystem. Biswell (1961) recorded historic observations of Indians setting fires. They annually started fires in the autumn to keep the groves open. This eliminated hiding places for foes with ambush on their minds and enhanced hunting and acorn gathering. An early observer, Galen Clark, said that the clear, open ground expanded considerably

FIGURE 31.1 (following pages) Canyon de Chelly National Monument, Arizona, is managed with Navajo Indians actively farming and grazing in the valley. (NPS)

in Yosemite's Mariposa Grove and Yosemite Valley between 1855 and 1894, when many Indians lived there.

The older squaws handled prescribed burning in those days. They would search out little dry spots of vegetation and would burn them as soon as they appeared. Thus, small fires were always under control and the forests remained open without danger of conflagration. The thick bark of the sequoias, pines, and incense-cedars were fairly good protection against light fires.

Study of burn scars in old sequoias in the Mariposa Grove revealed fires back to 450 A.D. (Biswell, 1961). Recent burns were evident for 1622, 1652, 1690, 1710, 1734, 1742, 1752, 1760, 1775, 1803, 1807, 1809, 1842, and 1862. In the Stanislaus National Forest, a more detailed study of 74 acres showed 221 separate fires between 1454 and 1912, an average of one every two years (Biswell, 1961). Many or most of those fires were apparently started by lightning strikes, according to recent fire records.

John Muir recorded the beauty of early fires in Yosemite in his diary (Biswell, 1961). He reported beautiful, slow fires burning on the tops of the large living trees, cut off from the ground. He studied the way that the tops were lit, finding that ground fires would quickly and harmlessly run up the deep furrows in the trunk, where bristled ends of bark fibers caught fire quickly. The blue flames would run up the bristly furrows to the lightning-shattered top of the tree, where dried leaves, twigs, and cones were easily ignited. Muir found these brief, blue streams of fire and torches in the tops to be beautiful and interesting.

After studying the history of fire and testing controlled burning methods, Kilgore (1972) concluded that fire is essential to the life cycle of the giant sequoias and related ecosystems. Young sequoias prefer bare earth for germination and some direct sunlight for growth. As a park service researcher, Kilgore advocated restoration of fire to its natural role, as nearly as possible, in order to continue to have sequoias over the long run. His ideas were adopted.

The basic elements of fire plans in the Sierra Nevada parks are similar to those used in about 20 other national parks. The theme is using fire to prevent fire. The plan has three elements:

1. Prescribed burning is recognized as a proper tool for forest management and is used to reduce hazardous conditions.
2. An allowable burn from natural causes is established for fires that do not threaten human life or developed properties.
3. Fire suppression and prevention are continued in developed areas and at low elevations.

The second phase of the program is often referred to as the "let burn" policy. It does not involve carelessness with fire; careful and systematic observation and preparedness are used. There are no attempts to extinguish

560

the fire that is burning within the parameters established by a fire plan. As long as the fire is not severely damaging or dangerous, it is probably doing more long-range good than harm. It is part of the natural system and will help keep future fires from becoming major conflagrations by burning up recently accumulated fuel. The fires are allowed to burn only for predetermined, beneficial purposes.

Among other advantages of fires of a prescribed or allowed nature are the following: Fire cleans up overmature stands, letting light in and baring the forest floor, thus promoting growth of tree seedlings. Recycling of wood and its nutrients is hastened. Insect eggs or larvae may be reduced. Spores of many rust and mold organisms are either destroyed or their germination is hampered by the drying out of the site after the fire. This reduces some of the potential for plant disease. Fire may also improve the habitat for some wildlife species by allowing grasses and browse to enter the stand.

A wilderness "let burn" policy was announced and implemented by the Forest Service in the mid-1970s. It was somewhat controversial and continues to cause concern in local areas. An extension of the policy, with more restrictions, was announced in 1978 for the entire national forest system. It marked the culmination of a gradual reversal of policy from the 1930s and 1940s, when a blanket fire protection and prevention policy was adopted. That policy was needed. Burning was rampant. Incendiarism in the South was ruining millions of acres of timber per year. There was little or no science in the firing of the woods. Although fire is a natural element of many forest systems, helpful to certain key species and plant communities, the frequent, indiscriminate burns were wiping out the forest values. Thus, Smokey Bear became a valuable symbol, preaching caution with fire and influencing the thinking of two generations of children.

The current policy incorporates naturally caused fires as a cost-effective way to meet resource management objectives. In all cases—wilderness and timber management areas included—fire is suppressed where it could threaten life, property, or public safety. It is also stopped if it would threaten the resource more than it would help it. The new policy requires more efficient and knowledgeable fire management and alert fire suppression organization.

The new policy also requires that study of the entire forest be undertaken to determine fire management objectives and to delineate fire management areas. Each area is identified according to risks, needed resource management activities and the role of fire in them, recreation uses of the area, scenic values, wildlife values and management problems, watershed, timber, and grazing management needs. Then, neighboring areas are studied to determine needs for protection and public safety. Finally, cost considerations are introduced and the fire management policy for the area is developed.

The basic idea of fire management in preserves is to allow the natural process of burning to re-enter the ecosystem. In overcoming the effects of years of fire suppression, care must be taken to gradually and safely approach restoration of natural conditions.

Bears

Visitors have been engaged in ambivalent liaisons with bears since men decided to invade their domain. The bears are both amusing and feared. Most park and refuge visitors have enjoyed their views of the usually pacific animals.

For years, bears wandered through campgrounds, tipping over garbage cans to find food (Figure 31.2). They were "fed" at garbage dumps. Some parks set up bleachers so visitors could get a glimpse of both black and grizzly bears rummaging through the trash. Handouts along the roads created "bear jams," despite rangers' warnings.

With growing numbers of visitors to the parks, chances of encounters increased. The bears, meantime, were becoming less intimidated by human shouting, waving, and odd noises. Yosemite, Yellowstone, Glacier, Great Smoky Mountains National Parks plus many state parks have had so-called bear problems.

Amidst considerable controversy about continuing private research, the National Park Service took action in Yellowstone in 1968. The major step was to close the dumps to bears. That quickly reduced the number of

FIGURE 31.2 A tip-proof garbage can is not impervious to an insistent bear. (NPS)

Recreation Resource Policy

bears in close regular contact with human food. Campground bears were removed to the backcountry. Visitors were instructed to protect their food.

This led to the necessary removal of a large number of bears in Yellowstone—more than 30 per year in the first few years. A 1973 study committee of the National Academy of Sciences supported the closing of the dumps and recommended that they stay closed and no supplementary feeding be permitted. It recommended that the number of grizzly bears removed be held at 10 per year until the population builds up to the level of about 234 bears in the park and the area around it.

The program's human results have been positive. The number of injuries has dropped off. In 1977, press releases from the National Park Service indicated there were no human deaths caused by bears in all the parks, compared to two in 1976. There were 26 injuries, compared to 44 the previous year.

The National Park Service took the following actions in Yellowstone:

1. Closed garbage dumps to bears, usually by fencing.
2. Enforced regulations that campers store food so that bears cannot get to it.
3. Closed campgrounds and trails where people are likely to encounter bears.
4. Trapped and transplanted bears (17 grizzlies and 287 blacks in 1977) that stay too close to campgrounds, trails, and roadsides.
5. Killed especially troublesome bears (1 grizzly and 25 blacks in 1977).

The alternative measure that is not mentioned and is politically unpopular is to reduce the number of humans who invade the bears' territory. In place of that, hikers and campers are given strict instructions and warnings about behavior in bear country. This also has undoubtedly aided in preventing dangerous situations.

Although injuries and deaths to humans are not desirable, sensational reports of a bear attack seem to be blown far out of proportion. Newspapers give brief mention to the tens of thousands of deaths that result from home and automobile accidents and drownings; seldom does the news reach beyond the local community. Yet, a grizzly bear roughing up an intruder into its home receives nationwide coverage. Editors in New York City dictate that rangers in Montana have an obligation to remove the bear which has become "an unreasonable threat."

The chances of harm from bears are few. In Glacier National Park, in 1976, four of 1,600,000 (.00025 per cent) visitors had unfortunate encounters with bears; three were injured and one died. The death was the third caused by grizzlies since 1913. In the same period, 69 visitors to that park died in other outdoor accidents—36 by drowning, 16 from falls by hiking, and six by falling rocks, trees, or other objects (Cauble, 1977).

To some people, the chance of encountering a wild animal will always

Resource Management Policy

563

be unacceptable; but to others, the image of free-roaming predators is a wonderful indication of the wild and free nature of some of our land. Unfortunately, the grizzly has almost been exterminated in the lower United States by the fearful and by livestock producers.

Perhaps moves to identify and protect critical habitat areas will allow a few to survive. Those who use national forests and parks should be willing to accept the minimal risk created by their intrusion on the bear's home territory, just as they accept the much higher risk of death by collision whenever they venture out in an automobile. The risk cannot be removed without exterminating the great bear and thus reducing the wildness and adventure of the place.

Exotic Animals in National Parks

National Parks have long functioned as sanctuaries for wild animals. The long-standing "no hunting" policy has been controverted only in special cases. As a result, animal populations have been allowed to rise and fall more or less as nature designed. In parks, natural processes are left to occur as they will, except that many natural predators have been reduced in numbers. Some observers of parks are convinced that deer, elk, and even bears know where park boundaries are located; at the first sign of hunting activity, the animals are reputed to step over the line into the protection of National Park Service regulations, leaving hunters on adjacent national forests or private lands empty-handed.

The protective policy has had some other results. It protects any animal that happens into the park. Some of these are feral (domestic, gone wild) and exotic (foreign) animals. In some cases, these animals have become threats to the native species.

Overuse of grazing areas and habitat brought the feral burros of Grand Canyon and Death Valley into prominence in 1976.

Other feral and exotic species that have flourished in state and national park areas include horses, ponies, dogs, cats, goats, boars, English sparrows, rats, ring-neck pheasants, starlings, cattle, chukar, partridge, hares, pigs, mongooses, pigeons, trout, and skylarks.

Hawaiian parks contain feral and domestic goats from local graziers and mongooses, which were once imported from India to combat ship-borne rats.

The 1975 park management policies stated:

Control or eradication of noxious or exotic plant and animal species will be undertaken when they are undesirable in terms of public health, recreational use, and enjoyment, or when their presence threatens the faithful presentation of the historic scene or the perpetuation of significant scientific features, ecological communities, and native species. . . .

To carry out the policy, various strategies have been tried. Shooting large animals seems as economical and humane a method as any available, but its directness seems to offend the sensitivities of some people. For limited populations of large animals, fencing is sometimes successful. Strongly enforced regulations about importation of non-native species is a logical preventative. Live trapping can be used to remove individuals but is hardly a valid or economical approach to handling large populations.

Control of feral and exotic species will continue to be a problem in state and national parks. Removal or control is important if the parks are to meet their mandates as examples of native, natural conditions. Two examples follow.

BURROS

The burros in the Southwest are foraging many thousands of acres in Bureau of Land Management lands, parks, monuments, and elsewhere, including Grand Canyon National Park, Bandelier National Monument, and Lake Mead National Recreation Area. They have no natural enemies, so they multiply swiftly. Burros are ecological invaders—as foreign as Guernsey cows. Their homeland is probably Africa, not Arizona or New Mexico. They were introduced to the Southwest by prospectors in the last century. Then, they were turned loose and they multiplied.

In Grand Canyon, more than 500 burros have eliminated considerable forage needed by native animal life (Figure 31.3). They have damaged Indian archeological sites by dusting themselves in ancient pits once used to roast agave. This is happening in a national park where managers are charged with protecting the native habitat. So the rangers of Grand Canyon thought they were being good environmentalists in ordering some of the burros shot. That caused some people to get sentimental about cute, flop-eared animals being mowed down by government agents. The Wild Horse Association and the Humane Society of the United States intervened to stop the shooting.

The animal lovers focus on the suffering of one animal as the key to human concern with nature. They tend to overlook the fact that less aggressive native animals, especially deer and mountain sheep, are left without food. The true ecologist looks at the whole problem. He asks if it is not better to maintain a balance between species than to let emotionalism for one animal's welfare rule his judgment.

Delay in resolving the burro problem in the Grand Canyon just makes the situation worse. The burros multiply at the rate of about 20 per cent per year. They threaten the food supply and living space of the other wildlife, more each year. There is about a 60 per cent overlap between the diets of burros and desert bighorn sheep and an almost total overlap in range.

The burros' impact on soil and vegetation also affect small mammals

FIGURE 31.3 Feral burros have multiplied, overgrazed, and trampled range plants in Bandelier, Grand Canyon, and Death Valley, where controversy slowed their removal by rangers. Meanwhile, bighorn sheep and other native animals suffer from loss of food sources to the Asian burros. (NPS)

and birds. The burro competes somewhat with mule deer. The growing burro population has the capacity to change the entire ecosystem.

Control methods are headed by shooting—the approach recommended by the National Park Service and wildlife experts. Live trapping and removal are costly. Fencing is not practical or legal in this wilderness area. Doing nothing results in continued, increasing destruction of the natural resources.

BOARS

A Smoky Boar controversy has erupted in North Carolina. Feral boars, freed from a game farm, invaded Great Smoky Mountain National Park in 1940. Now about 2,000 of these European natives roam three quarters of the park. They damage vegetation, root up soil, and cause erosion. Some parts of the land look as if they had been plowed, sometimes as much as 18 inches into the ground.

The National Park Service killed more than 900 of the animals over a period of 18 years and then decided to eliminate as many of them from the park as possible. Several hundred were shot from 1975 to 1977. Citizens of Robbinsville, North Carolina, protested and the attorney general of the state discussed the removal policy with the Assistant Secretary of the Interior. The National Park Service called a moratorium on the shooting. The reason for protest was not out of sympathy for the boars. It was related to the sport of hunting them. Local hunters thought the eradication program would annihilate their game. Just when the eradication program was becoming effective, someone in Washington halted it.

Killing the hogs by shooting is the only economical and effective means of reducing their numbers in the park. Even if they are trapped, moving them out of the backcountry is difficult and expensive. The park service turns over to North Carolina officials any hogs that are trapped close to the road on the North Carolina side of the park. The state wildlife agency moves them to managed hunting areas. The Tennessee Wildlife Resources Agency does not accept hogs from the park any more.

Apparently, some of the problem is related to who has a chance to do the shooting. The National Park Service hired professional hunters and dogs from Georgia, which caused expressions of concern from the North Carolina hunters.

Protecting the Visitors

The problems of legal liability for park users are not confined to private lands. Instead of holding that members of the public are, in effect, on their own land when in a public park, the recreation supply agency is required to take reasonable—usually thorough—measures to protect the visitors from harm (Fig. 31.4). Some of the awards of damages would

FIGURE 31.4 In remote parks and forests, rescue operations become part of the management picture. (NPS)

suggest that the park agency must protect the person from his own foolishness, bravado, and from natural conditions.

Court decisions have ruled that climbers of Mt. McKinley (Denali) and other park visitors are invitees of the National Park Service. This requires considerable precaution, because three climbers die for every 100 who reach the top of McKinley (6,194 m) or nearby Mt. Foraker (5,304 m). In 1976, there were 10 fatalities plus 18 frostbite victims, including five amputation cases. In addition there were nine cases of serious pulmonary or cerebral edema (fluid on the lung or brain).

Recreation Resource Policy

Therefore, the National Park Service takes the following precautions for McKinley climbers:

1. Applications with a medical certificate must be submitted at least two months in advance.
2. The group must take a two-way radio.
3. It must check in and out with park headquarters, where information and precautions are reviewed.
4. The park maintains a rescue team and communications team on duty, including helicopters and associated paraphernalia.

These and other proposed procedures infringe upon one of the chief values of Mt. McKinley National Park—its wilderness challenge where visitors can risk injury and even life. Somehow, the sense of danger and adventure is dulled—and, therefore, also the sense of individual responsibility and judgment—when a doctor and rescue unit are, in effect, sitting on the sidelines, ready to run onto the field when the adventurer stumbles. Surely, the precautions are reassuring to the relatives of the climbers and of inestimable value to the seriously distressed victim. However, they may serve to provide a false sense of security, inviting the incompetent or slightly competent to go beyond their skills. This is indicated by park service estimates that merely requiring that experienced Alaskan guides lead small parties would prevent 53 per cent of the evacuations. The presence of a helicopter in a wilderness area is certainly disruptive and offensive to those who have hiked for several days to escape the sounds and effects of overcivilization, other humanitarian considerations aside.

Human Behavior and Misbehavior

When people come to the parks, forests, and refuges, they bring some of their own problems with them. These range from slovenliness to major criminal tendencies. Even solid, careful citizens occasionally leave their manners behind.

ROWDYISM

Perhaps the single greatest source of annoyance in parks is the behavior of groups of people who bring their festive occasions into a campground. All-night binges are usually controlled by frequent policing or the vigilance of the gatekeeper. Removal of the rowdies should be prompt and rigorous, even if they include the son of a judge. Firm, consistent policies keep trouble to a minimum. Where problems have been persistent, the development of a working relationship with a United States magistrate or other rigorous official to mete our quick and decisive justice will often eliminate the problem within a few weeks.

CRIME IN PARKS

Crime is a worsening problem which the resource management agencies are ill-equipped to handle. Crime has become a serious problem in many parks. Offenses include serious crimes—rape, robbery, auto theft, burglary, and assault. Greater numbers of lesser crimes, mainly drug use, are also reported. Law enforcement has become a major activity of many recreation agencies. State conservation officers are trained policemen who assist on many properties. Sheriffs are often used in private and county parks. Federal agencies have begun to train their rangers in law enforcement.

VANDALISM AND LITTERING

The control and prevention of vandalism and littering are major concerns of many recreation professionals (Figure 31.5). The vandalism of recreation facilities threatens the resource, detracts from user experiences, and ultimately results in the loss of taxpayer support for recreation budgets. These decrease the provision of leisure services for the entire community.

The exact cost of vandalism cannot be calculated. The costs in property destruction could be totaled, but the cost as a social problem has many impacts. The self-image and pride of the community or neighborhood are

FIGURE 31.5 Tidiness and a sense of stewardship are sometimes forgotten by citizens of the world's most advanced civilization. (NPS)

Recreation Resource Policy

damaged in a subtle but important way. Vandalism often involves youths under 18 years of age. They are often arrested and subsequently watched carefully. Their lives are negatively affected by the outgrowth of their own acts. Explicit costs mount into the billions of dollars each year. Littering is committed by all ages and does not produce the social onus of more serious activities.

Vandalism in recreation areas is nothing new. Shortly after Yellowstone was established but before federal control was complete, an official report declared (Sax, 1976):

Hunters have for years devoted themselves to the slaughter of game, until within the limits of the park it is hardly to be found . . . the ornamental work about the crater and the pools had been broken and defaced in the most prominent places. . . . The visitors prowled around with shovel and ax, chopping and hacking and prying up great pieces of the most ornmanetal work they could find; women and men alike joining in the barbarous pastime.

Vandalism, exploitation, threats, and abuse of natural wonders and historical places motivate park establishment, perhaps as often as a calculated need for recreation opportunities. Mesa Verde National Park was established in 1912 because of the urging of several cowboys who saw that hundreds of artifacts were being collected and sold and that the remnants of Indian houses were being destroyed. Yosemite was full of sheep, bark was removed from sequoias for exhibitions, and other abuses motivated visitors to encourage its state park and later national park status. Numerous caves were placed under local, state, or federal jurisdiction in attempts to halt the destruction of beautiful cave features by souvenir gatherers and vandals.

A three-year study of undesirable behavior in forest campgrounds indicated that vandalism at such sites is more extensive than is generally believed (Campbell et al., 1968). Approximately 60 per cent of the vandalism acts observed were directed at campground facilities, 30 per cent at the environment, and 10 per cent at private property. Children in groups of two or three were responsible for most acts of vandalism directed at campground facilities. Individual adults were responsible for most acts of vandalism against the environment; these acts were for entertainment purposes more often than because of ignorance of the rules. More than 80 per cent of the depreciative acts observed were committed when other people were around. In more than 90 per cent of these cases, the acts were ignored completely or at least not reported to the officials. Vandalism left sinks pulled off the walls, mirrors smashed, signs torn down, picnic tables burned, and fireplaces destroyed plus numerous acts of boorishness.

Vandalism may be an expression of a variety of interests or hostilities. There are many types of vandalism, including the following:

Overuse destruction, which often appears to be vandalism but is unintentional.

Conflict vandalism, the expression of a user doing what is most logical and natural, regardless of the designer's intent. There may be associated vandalism from nonusers who desire more facilities or changes in existing facilities to meet individual community needs and customs.

"No-other-way-to-do-it vandalism" such as sitting on a fence because there is no park bench or leaning a bicycle against a tree because there is no bike rack.

Inventive vandalism such as "borrowing" a picnic table plank to make a springboard wedged into the jungle gym.

Curiosity vandalism, such as pulling up a tree to see what the roots look like—with infinite variations. An associated type stems from irresistible temptation or lack of personal discipline—picking flowers or riding motorbikes up and down a steep, grassy hill, producing erosion.

Self-expression vandalism is the most common and the most exasperating to some—graffiti on walls and other public places. Somehow, a desperate attempt to be noticed in the anonymity of modern society is easily but pitifully expressed by writing one's name or message in a public place. More imaginative forms include doing seemingly impossible things such as placing big objects in improbable places for the amazement of friends and other observers.

Spin-off vandalism sometimes occurs when other activities lead to the destruction of property, varying from the baseball through the window without apology to the damaging of facilities (and even bystanders) during a gang war in a park.

Slovenly vandalism is an expression of bad manners through littering and other carelessness. This may be the least destructive but most expensive form.

Malicious vandalism is usually the result of the individual wanting to get back at society or a particular agency or individual for real or imagined mistreatment.

Thrill or dare vandalism arises from the goading of friends or an individual desire for excitement and may be exceedingly dangerous to the individual and to the public.

The motivations for vandalism are complex and impossible to list comprehensively. Many of the acts could be prevented if user needs were recognized and fulfilled in recreation areas. Poor design surely contributes to much inadvertent vandalism. Others are deep-seated problems of the society as a whole and are unlikely to be solved by the design or the programming of an outdoor recreation area.

Vandalism not only reflects many of today's frustrations and anxieties, but it also represents a protest against the design and management of many parks. The law and order mentality and lifestyle that recreation area managers are accustomed to is not typical of many user backgrounds. Recreation professionals need to understand and provide for some unconventional forms of behavior. Deviance is not a type of behavior but is a social label. The roots of crime are often in unequal opportunities and life experiences. Antisocial behavior is often produced by discrimination, indifference, and unjust distribution of wealth (Taylor, 1969). This is not to suggest that vandalism is to be tolerated; perhaps it can be better understood and then prevented.

SOLUTIONS

The frustration produced by vandalism and littering often leads to solutions for the symptom rather than for the cause. Some solutions to vandalism have taken two basic approaches: build something so big, so strong, so durable, and so simple, it can't possibly be torn down; or provide nothing, so there is nothing to tear down.

Much of what is labeled vandalism can be prevented through design. It is one belief that vandalism is an expression of need by users to change existing facilities.

It is commonly assumed that human behavior is not aimless activity but is motivated behavior directed at the achievement of some end or goal. In essence, human behavior is purposeful and meaningful behavior. Both the objective and subjective aspects of the situations in which vandalism occurs must be assessed. Vandalism is often an expression of boredom, discontent, and a feeling of anonymity. Participation and involvement often lead to appreciation and eventual stewardship by participants. The prevention of vandalism and other types of delinquency must involve good law-enforcement, good individual treatment, community pride, and custodial care. But most importantly, it must also involve community approaches to delinquency prevention.

The following methods for controlling loss and damage to property are among those recommended by the National School Public Relations Associations (1975):

Eliminate opportunities and temptations by providing maximum security through design, construction, and policing personnel.

Keep careful records of equipment with an adequate checkout and return system, close supervision of equipment, and routine checks of all valuables.

Request patrolling by police cars; make full use of the protection that is available.

Make the value of the property meaningful to the users by making everyone well acquainted with the property and letting youth participate in the purchasing of equipment.

Provide a top program and equipment backed by specific, simple rules.

Provide activities of specific interest to youth.

Develop good relationships with users by being firm, yet fair to everyone, and show respect for individuals.

> Ask for cooperation from parents and other citizens to report vandalism; follow up on reports.
>
> Know your community parents and work with them to control vandalism.
>
> Open facilities for more hours to let responsible groups use them for special or club functions.
>
> Correct results of vandalism as soon as possible to promote continuing pride in facilities.

An important principle is that neatness breeds neatness and carelessness breeds carelessness. Keep recreation facilities clean and free of evidence of any vandalism, and the users will tend to be inhibited about making the first mark. Robert Moses followed this principle at Jones Beach and other New York public parks. He hired uniformed, college-age persons to clean up after everyone, making the penchant for neatness conspicuous. The result was a relative lack of litter and very low vandalism (Caro, 1974). The same practice is followed in most large amusement parks today.

The practice involves rapid removal of graffiti from all surfaces and quick pickup of can tabs, cigarette butts, paper wrappers, and larger material. Restroom and other walls susceptible to vandalism can be surfaced with materials that are difficult to write upon, such as pebbled or sandy concrete or tile with a hard epoxy finish. These allow easy cleaning.

These approaches require diligent paid employees, sometimes in great numbers. They are practical for high-density use areas.

Other approaches have involved volunteer users in maintaining the area. An example is neighbors "adopting" a small park to maintain on a voluntary but regular basis. Neighborhood pride in the park is produced by neighborhood involvement. Park police in Washington, D.C., developed a successful community police team in the summer of 1977 (Byrd, 1977). Vandalism in the parks had escalated along with more general law enforcement problems. The idea of two officers was to get neighborhood youths involved in beautifying their community parks to increase self-respect, create greater environmental awareness, and decrease vandalism.

The first step in Washington was to gather together a group of children, ages 8 to 13, and acquaint them with each other and with the park police. Then they picked a community park to beautify. They went on outings together to see monuments, memorials, the Capitol, Rock Creek Nature Center; they went swimming, had bicycle safety training, played basketball, and had free lunches from co-sponsor McDonald's restaurants. The mutual giving of time and effort was highlighted by acquaintance with park police operations. The National Capital Park police have some compelling attractions—a dog unit, a horse unit, and a helicopter unit. Most of the inner-city children had never even seen a park police officer close up; now they could pet a horse, ride beside an officer in a helicopter, and meet a police dog on friendly terms. The "cops in green cars" became friends. The eight-week program was not just a party. The children worked. More than

574

60 of them received diplomas and T-shirts designating them as KOPS (Keepers of the Park Service). The neighborhoods involved went from one of high vandalism to no reported incidents during the summer. The children developed pride in their parks and in their whole community, according to Park Service personnel.

In Forest Service campsites, a similar idea has worked experimentally. Even though visitors come only occasionally, they will participate in cleanup programs that are properly organized and offer rewards in the form of badges and pins.

There is no one answer to solve all problems. There are many answers, but probably no final solutions.

Summary

The management of resources and visitors in recreation areas is now in a state of evolution. In the past, much of the approach was custodial for the resources and for containment of the people. Increasingly, there are challenges for active management and programming for rich experiences.

This chapter deals mostly with resource-oriented parks, forests, and refuges. The philosophy of resource management focuses on natural conditions. The tone is set by the 1963 Advisory Committee on National Park Wildlife, which called for maintenance or restoration of natural conditions, but not to the exclusion of some manipulative techniques, including fire. The next year, the Wilderness Act restricted the use of machinery and manipulations in designated wilderness areas. The use of fire as a natural element of the environment is widely accepted now, even in wilderness.

Elimination of exotic animals has run into public opinion problems. Control of bears has been achieved somewhat by closing garbage dumps and cans, as well as shipping out beggar bears. Humans who invade the wildlife domain take a minor risk and require some orientation.

Human damage to natural resources and to each other have made law enforcement a necessary, if distasteful, part of recreation area management. There is a need to study human motives and problems, coupled with energetic prevention programs plus vigorous and just enforcement action. Active interpretation, programming, and other visitor guidance tools are gaining importance in resource/people management.

Inevitably, as more people visit more places, there will be conflicts with the resources and with others. Skillful, active administration is a requisite to efficient supply of outdoor recreation resources.

Literature Cited

Biswell, H. H. 1961. The big trees and fire. National Parks Magazine 35(163):11–14.
Byrd, Earl. 1977. Kops meet cops "close up." The Washington (D.C.) Star. August 21.

CAMPBELL, FREDERICK L., JOHN C. HENDEE and ROGER N. CLARK. 1968. Law and order in public parks. Parks and Recreation 3(12):28–31, 51–55.

CARO, ROBERT A. 1974. The Power Broker. N.Y.: Vintage Books. 1246 pp.

CAUBLE, CHRISTOPHER. 1977. The great grizzly grapple. Natural History 86(7):74–81.

KILGORE, BRUCE. 1972. Fire's role in a sequoia forest. Naturalist 23(1): 26–37.

KILGORE, BRUCE M. and GEORGE S. BRIGGS. 1972. Restoring fire to high elevation forests in California. Journal of Forestry 70(5):266–271.

LEOPOLD, A. STARKER, S. A. CAIN, C. M. COTTAM, I. N. GABRIELSON and THOMAS L. KIMBALL. 1963. Study of wildlife problems in national parks; report to the Secretary of the Interior. Transactions of the 28th North American Wildlife Conference 28:28–45.

National School Public Relations Association. 1975. Violence and Vandalism. Arlington, Va.: 80 pp.

SAX, JOSEPH L. 1976. America's national parks. Natural History 85(8):57–89.

TAYLOR, ANDREW R. 1969. Governing the City, New York: Praeger. 230 pp.

U.S. Forest Service. 1977. Final environmental statement and land management plan for the Monongahela N. F. Milwaukee: U.S. Dept. of Agriculture. 266 pp.

C H A P T E R   3 2

Law and Policy Review

"Ignorance of the law is no excuse" is a dictum applicable to professional resource managers. The same goes for policy as for law.

Knowledge of legal and policy matters is a key tool for any public or private recreation resource administrator. Many laws and policies that affect recreation have been discussed in earlier chapters. An index of federal laws appears at the end of this book (Appendix A). This chapter suggests a systematic study of legal and policy matters, notes the environmental impact study requirements, and then concentrates mostly on two major concerns—questions of legal liability for persons using recreation areas and public participation in policy and planning decisions.

The use of legal documents is not confined to judges and lawyers. With a little practice, any intelligent person can understand the intent and provisions of most laws that affect recreation resource management and funding. These laws should become a working part of the intellectual equipment a professional uses, either as background or for day-to-day interpretation and implementation.

Legal Strategy for Recreation Resource Managers

Orientation to laws and policies should start before the first day on a job and will continue throughout a career. The newly employed person can begin a collection of basic laws and policy manuals immediately. At first, gather and comprehend the "organic" documents that govern the purposes, jurisdiction, and limitation of the public agency or the business entity. Then, read the laws that directly affect current events. A policy manual is usually available and serves as a guide to the goals of management. Current operating practice may differ slightly from some of these policy statements, so instant righteousness on the part of the new employee is ill-advised.

Federal laws appear in three forms: as session laws (Public Law numbers), as statutes, and in the *United States Code*. Recent session laws are available as reprints from congressmen and in *Statutes at Large*. The *U.S. Code* compiles the laws into codified form, showing the current status of all legislation concerning a subject. Old provisions are deleted as new laws or amendments supersede them. *The U.S. Code Annotated* is an unofficial collection of laws, which also contains the legislative history of an act. These documents are available in most major libraries. Policies are listed in the *Code of Federal Regulations* and the *Federal Register,* as well as in agency documents.

State and local laws are also available in most libraries. State laws are found in *Acts of the Legislature* and in state codes or statutes publications.

Businesses are regulated by numerous laws and policies. Few lawyers are expert on all the laws relating to small business. Local and state officials in departments of health and natural resources can be of assistance, as can the Cooperative Extension Service and Soil Conservation Service agents. Personal alertness and advice from other businessmen can be of great help.

A current notebook of laws and policies is a valuable asset to a park and recreation administrator. Of greater value is an intimate knowledge of the laws and their implications, which comes from continued study and application.

Environmental Impact Analyses

The National Environmental Policy Act of 1969 (NEPA) established a process for federal agencies that requires a systematic, interdisciplinary approach for decision making that is visible to the public in an environmental statement. NEPA requires a complete discussion of the management alternatives and their impacts before a major federal action is taken.

The law and its regulations apply to most recreation projects that receive federal funding. Following a well-outlined procedure, the agency first may prepare an environmental impact assessment, which is a short form of the more complex environmental impact statement. If the assessment reveals no major impacts, a further statement may not have to be filed.

The process requires study and description of the effects of the proposed project on the natural resources, esthetics, economy, and social environment, positive and negative. In a way, it forces careful planning and analysis plus documentation of the factors involved.

Public Involvement in Decision Making

There are many great interests on the national forests which sometimes conflict a little. They must all be made to fit into one another so that the machine runs smoothly as a whole. It is often necessary for one man to give way a little here, another a little there. But by giving way a little at present, they both profit by it a great deal in the end.

Recreation Resource Policy

National forests exist today because the people want them. To make them accomplish the most good, the people themselves must make clear how they want them run.

—Gifford Pinchot (1947)

All public lands ultimately are managed by public opinion and by compromise. The need for public input is clear in a time of mounting pressures on public lands. What Pinchot observed is a basic fact of political survival. The key is in how the people can make their desires known to the public officials.

One approach to professional decision making is the use of public input in planning and management decisions. It is used in both private and public employment. A major part of it is listening to what people say and how they say it.

An example is in the several controversies about the use of off-road vehicles (ORVs) on public lands. The facts are not really available to determine potential impacts, number of users, and values of competing uses. The manager must estimate tradeoffs, guess at the consequences, and handle public hearings, where acrimony abounds. The feelings are stronger than any available numbers. The cool administrator must weigh statements in terms of their content and implications to help determine the best of several courses of action.

A key decision left to the professional is when and how to involve the public in planning and other decisions. Some laws and agency policies specify requirements for public input. In most cases, sensitivity to public attitudes, interests, and desires is a key. Awareness requires continuing commitment to keep fully informed on current public interests and attitudes.

Guides for successful public involvement start with attitudes that encourage the free interchange of facts and opinions in a cooperative atmosphere. The following attitudes are among those recommended for employees of public agencies (U.S. Forest Service, 1974).

1. Recognize that public involvement is an essential part of decision making.
2. Discard notions that only professionals can judge actions affecting environmental quality; public concern may well outweigh scientific considerations and cause modification of proposals.
3. Be willing to accept criticism with a positive rather than a defensive attitude.
4. Keep records of public involvement and decision making; it allows full review before making final decisions and is a reference if the decisions are challenged.
5. Realize that involving the public does not relieve agency professionals of the final responsibility for the decision.
6. Give equal consideration to the opinions of past opponents of the

agency and of past supporters; all interest groups are champions of some aspect of good resource management.

7. Allow ample time for public study of issues and the land under question, in preparation for meaningful input.
8. Communicate objectives and procedures for specific issues in early stages of involvement.
9. Inform and involve all publics interested or affected by the issue.
10. After decisions are made, immediately inform all interested parties and the general public.
11. Keep the participation process visible and dignified to maintain public confidence.

Techniques for Public Involvement

There are numerous approaches to getting the public involved in issues. These may range from rather informal field meetings to formal written statements or public hearings. Each type has advantages and limitations in terms of quality of input, adequate involvement of the public, expeditious handling of the process, and public acceptance of the program (U.S. Forest Service, 1974). Alternative techniques are suited to different situations. They may be used alone or in combination.

1. Press conferences and releases: for initial exposure, meeting announcement, and final decision announcements.
2. Public meetings or hearings: open testimony of many people and organizations, usually involving a specific proposal.
3. Workshops: people of diverse viewpoints work in small groups to study data and discuss alternatives on specified issues; best for developing proposals to consider.
4. Advisory and ad hoc committees: selected individuals offer indications of public attitudes through informed opinion; federal agencies must comply with the Federal Advisory Committee Act (Public Law 92–463).
5. Invitational group discussion: allow constructive discussion among involved people for careful planning, analysis, or review of previous public input. These may be consultative visits with key individuals or groups.
6. Questionnaires and response forms: carefully designed to get answers to specific alternatives or opinion issues, these can accompany information documents that describe the plans or alternatives. Prior approval by the Office of Management and Budget is needed for federal agencies.
7. Visits to the site: the group can participate in the issue on the ground; this should be more than a guided lecture.
8. Open house information sessions: as a way to explain issues and

direct people to the site, invite them to drop in and study maps and plans on display, with a person on duty to answer questions.

9. Visits to organizations: representatives speak to service clubs and others to explain the issues and answer questions; this is usually done in combination with other techniques.

Other approaches include serving on committees of other organizations, using outside groups to conduct studies, informing all agency workers of the issues, letters, and regional study committees.

PUBLIC MEETINGS

Public meetings or more formal public hearings are among the most frequent and most frustrating of the methods used. They can turn into shouting matches if not conducted with expertise. They are often looked upon with dread by officers of the agency.

Many agency employees become frustrated by public meetings in which polarized opinions lead to unruly argument rather than reasoned seeking of solutions. Federal wilderness meetings are frequently unproductive, with preservationists setting a hard line for maximum wilderness. People who have other views are often intimidated by strong statements or find themselves taking stands in opposition to the unyielding preservationist view, even when they believe some wilderness would be appropriate. Sometimes the tables are turned, with industry, economic development interests, and laborers dominating meetings to the disadvantage of the pro-wilderness people. When groups are at equal strength, the meetings often become bouts of overstatement.

Following are ten basic facts of life about public involvement.

1. There are almost always people against any proposal; some will be violently against any government proposal.

2. If private land is involved in a public proposal, there will be landowners protesting loudly in their own self-interest, or in the interest of saving the nation from socialism, or in the interest of saving taxes. Their arguments will be emotional and difficult to refute. They will overlook the fact that fair market value is paid for any private land involved in a public project.

3. There are always people who do not believe that tax money should be spent on outdoor recreation.

4. People living near a major project will often be the strongest opponents. They will usually underestimate the value of tourism or recreation to the local economy. On the other hand, local proponents will often tend to overestimate the economic and social values. Feelings against a project are especially strong if it involves a shift in land use that will affect local industry.

5. In most national or state projects, the benefits will be understood

and supported best by people who do not live close by but might use the area for recreation.

6. There are many "publics" with vested or rational interests in social issues. They seek to form public opinion as well as to express their own. Power interests are those accustomed to making decisions that stick and then identifying their interests with the public interest.

7. Public involvement produces foolishness along with valuable suggestions. Among ideas the National Park Service received for the use of Alcatraz Island, a former prison, were a space museum, a nudist metropolis, a gambling casino, a crab factory, and a federal center for tidal, wind, and solar energy development.

8. Congressmen and other elected officials are seldom concerned about the opinions of a majority of their constituents on an issue. They know that the majority is uninformed and unexcited about any particular issue, especially a conservation issue. They are interested in what the concerned minorities think. Elections are won or lost on the basis of support from several minorities.

9. Public expression of interest or disfavor in a project may well mislead decision makers as to the value of a project to a community. Many, if not most, comments on such projects are made without careful study of the project and its total impacts. Misinformation and exaggerated claims excite some people to make strong statements that fly in the face of fact or reason. Immediate reactions are among many factors to be weighed in making decisions.

10. In a controversial case, people react to more than issues; they react to the personalities presenting or opposing the plan, to how the plan is presented, and even to vaguely related recent events.

Most public officials and professionals can be far more effective than they are at eliciting and evaluating public input and participation. It is possible to implement the solutions to tough problems, even in the face of controversy. Most really important projects that have failed could have been implemented if the professionals had followed a systematic approach to planning and evaluating public involvement. Public acceptance of solutions to tough problems never just happens. Unless a big project is managed in a manner to develop that acceptance and support, it has at least an 80 per cent chance of being shelved, no matter what it's all about or how important it is to the well-being of society.

Civil Torts

Suits against landowners by recreationists have become uncomfortably common. Forest industries, other private landowners, and even public lands are susceptible to standing trial for accidents that visitors allege are caused by the negligence of the land administrator. It behooves the manager to understand the levels of liability and to take measures that reduce the risk.

Visitors are entitled to various levels of protection, depending upon the conditions under which they visit the property. They are generally classed as trespassers, licensees, or invitees; the criteria are somewhat flexible and variable from judge to judge.

Trespassers: A trespasser is a person who enters the property of another without permission and not for the benefit of the property owner. The landowner has only minimal responsibility for the protection of the trespasser, taking due care to avoid injuring him, if the trespasser's presence is known. He should be notified to make him aware of dangers. Traps set for the trespasser or intentional shooting at him would make the landowner liable.

Licensees: A licensee is a person who enters a property with the consent—implied or stated—of the owners but not for the benefit of the owner. Examples of licensees are cross-country skiers who receive permission (no fee paid) to use company land or a farm, a person who asks permission to hunt pheasants in a cornfield, or a fisherman who is allowed to cross private land to reach a stream. The landowner is required to warn the licensee of hidden hazards (deep hole, snow-covered stumps, a violent bull) known to the owner. He is required to prevent willful harm to the licensees. Other than these, the owner has few responsibilities for injury to visitors. He is not under obligation to inspect the premises for unknown dangers. The licensee cannot receive damages for injury to himself, his vehicle, or equipment.

Invitees: The invitee class includes any visitor to a public park, forest, lake, refuge, or other recreation area, or a business visitor to a commercial recreation area, or any visitor to industrial or other land for the benefit of the landowner. If both the visitor and the landowner receive mutual benefit, the visitor is usually classed as an invitee. The owner has an obligation to keep the premises (that portion that is designated for recreation use) safe and to prevent injury to the visitor. This requires 1) warnings of danger to the visitor, 2) regular inspection of the premises and facilities, and 3) removal of dangerous conditions or installation of safety measures where practicable.

ATTRACTIVE NUISANCE

The doctrine of attractive nuisance applies to trespassing children. It holds that trespassers who are too young to exercise good judgment about what is dangerous to them must receive special consideration and precautions from the landowner. The standard legal concept that landowners owe no duty to trespassers is thus modified so that they are required to keep premises free from hazardous conditions that could be harmful to child trespassers.

The plaintiff for the child must establish three conditions:

1. The child was a trespasser.
2. The owner should have known that a child would be attracted to the dangerous condition.
3. The dangerous condition was man-made, not natural.

The age of the child with ability to discern danger is set at different levels in different states, some at six years and others as high as 12 years for certain incidents. Some examples of attractive nuisances are unfenced swimming pools and unsafe (for children) walkways over cliffs or canyons.

SOVEREIGN IMMUNITY

The doctrine of sovereign immunity long held the government exempt from suit for personal or property injury. The philosophy was that it is better that an individual should sustain injury or loss than that the public should suffer inconvenience or expense. Since the eighteenth century, when in England it was determined that allowing suit of the government could lead to an infinity of actions, the general rule of thumb was "you can't sue the government." Since 1960, however, the doctrine of sovereign immunity has eroded rapidly. Many cases have been tried and found in favor of individuals against the collective body of taxpayers.

Some of the cases have, at least on the face of them, seemed to richly compensate individuals who intentionally or foolishly violated regulations, common sense, and even warnings. An example is the man who repeatedly did careless leaps from a state park diving tower, despite lifeguards' requests to stop. He finally hit a boat and injured his neck. The resulting paralysis was apparently a key to the jury's award of several hundred thousand dollars paid by the state.

As a result of the decline in sovereign immunity, the governmental agencies must take active preventive and defensive measures to clearly regulate users. In the diving tower case, ejection of the man from the waterfront would have been safer than warnings or polite requests. Unplanned, potentially dangerous trails should be obliterated and clear indication made that the area is closed to walkers. Other specific messages must be made clear to people, especially when use is prohibited on a formerly used area.

Sovereign immunity applied, by extension, to private, nonprofit educational or charitable organizations, including religious organizations. The shift from holding public bodies immune is likely to affect the liability of these organizations.

It seems that the current trend is to socialize individual losses, transferring the financial burden of damages from individuals to society. This seems to be consistent with the trend since at least the 1930s to share the wealth through various government programs aimed (however poorly) at assisting the unemployed and the disadvantaged. The question of liability of "big government" for injuries to "unfortunate individuals" seems to extend the same philosophy into tort liability.

Prevention

The causes of many civil tort suits are maintenance-related problems. Trails, hazard trees, and equipment can cause problems. One suit related to serious injury can drastically affect the financial affairs of any recreation property. A sizable suit can virtually eliminate hope for reasonable profit from a commercial operation. An industry may be discouraged from opening its lands to public recreation use by laws that threaten to cost more in court expenses than is gained in public relations or income benefits. Public agencies are caused serious disruption by such actions.

Three factors are important in public liability: 1) a strongly organized maintenance program that prevents situations contributing to legal negligence and attractive nuisances, and exercises care for the visitors; 2) a reasonably priced but adequate insurance program to comprise a balanced financial risk program; and 3) a thorough knowledge of the liability laws and judgments in the locality. The first is established through rigorous scheduling of maintenance work, frequent and careful inspection, sensitivity to complaints, and alertness to changing conditions inside and outside the property. Neighbors and frequent visitors can be helpful as an early warning system, if dealt with cooperatively.

The whole question of civil tort law is frightening or startling to most natural resource managers. Yet, the issues cannot be left with the lawyers. Careful management is the key. There are always more threats to sue than there are actual cases. The plaintiff must have enough confidence of a return to hire a lawyer. Awareness of the law and taking preventive measures will eliminate most conditions that might lead to suits.

Summary

Demands on natural resources and space are apparently limitless, if considered over the long run. With population increases and an apparently insatiable consumptive appetite, now exhibited only in prosperous nations, there seems to be a desire for goods, services, and land, which, if uncontrolled, would consume the resource base.

Laws and policy are basic guides to controlling the uses and delimiting that which is deemed appropriate. The managerial decision making process requires knowledge of the numerous laws that affect a recreation business or agency. That knowledge can help prevent problems and help bring financial and technical assistance.

The policy of using public input for many decisions is government's way of getting customer reaction. There are many ways of listening to input and analyzing what is heard. None is totally satisfactory, but sensitivity to all the publics aids planning.

Civil law provides that visitors to recreation properties must be protected from accident and harm. Alertness and systematic preventive measures reduce the likelihood of financial risk to public or private recreation land.

Literature Cited

PINCHOT, GIFFORD. 1947. Breaking New Ground. New York: Harcourt Brace Jovanovich. 522 pp.

U.S. Forest Service. 1974. Guide to Public Involvement in Decision Making. Washington, D.C.: U.S. Department of Agriculture. 22 pp.

Private Organizations

Thousands of North American clubs, societies, and leagues influence the policies and operations of outdoor recreation resources. The resource manager and planner is expected to hear and to respond to the organized requests of the Sierra Club, the National Rifle Association, the Chamber of Commerce, the National Forest Products Association, and many others. The professional manager can also receive a great deal of cooperation, direct assistance, and support from these groups.

This chapter describes some of the more prominent national organizations that have been active in affecting recreation resources. There is no attempt to include all groups or to rate them by importance. Some very effective organizations are not listed here.

It is important for the professional to know the goals and methods of these groups. They exert influence on the professional's job, salary, and policies. They can be powerful allies or potent enemies. Sometimes, resource management agencies are caught in the middle of controversies between organizations over uses of the land base. The wilderness designation process has involved numerous controversies among factions on both sides of the question, leaving the Forest Service (usually) somewhere in between to recommend the most appropriate solution. Regardless of the recommendation, the decision will be criticized, often by both sides.

Organizations are not merely groups of people with similar interests. They sometimes take on an energy and life of their own, driven by the dedicated work and enthusiasm of staff members and a few volunteer members. Acting for the usually acquiescent membership, they often plunge into projects with great enthusiasm and vigor.

Although national organizations provide some cohesiveness of policy and finance, most recreation resource issues are fought on the local battle-field, with local proponents and opponents often arrayed against each other under the banner of some *ad hoc* coalition. They may bring in outside reinforcement, but the day-to-day work and effectiveness will be the result of the steady, persistent exertions of the local troops.

Private organizations are vital parts of the American governmental process. They affect industries and private landowners as well as governments. They cannot be dismissed as selfish interests or muddle-headed bleeding hearts although many times their causes are selfish or muddled. Their ideas often won't stand the tests of logic or evidence. Their causes are sometimes clearly not in the best interests of the public. Nevertheless, these organizations are potent forces that have and will continue to stop, delay, or at least complicate projects. They are also invaluable allies that can make difficult projects relatively easy and save the public considerable money and time through the efforts of members.

Many so-called conservation organizations operate on the premise of preservation. Most of them realize that there is no possible way to "preserve" a living community of plants; ecological theory describes a dynamic system that only tends to approach the climax abstraction. The goal is not so much to preserve as to keep it natural—keep man and his machines out.

Conservationists object to careless or apparently imprudent timber-cutting methods. They get caught up in the rhetoric of campaigns to save trees and stop dams, and sometimes become quite strident with agencies charged with harvesting trees and building dams. If the land manager treats them as human beings with legitimate concerns, he will generally find that the objections are against carelessness or disturbance in a particular place of great value to them. This does not mean that they are ingenuous; preservation groups have proven to be sophisticated and tenacious in the political arena.

The overemphasis on preservation is probably born out of enthusiasm and even a sense of desperation. Most of these clubs use the slogan that this is the last chance to keep natural our few remaining islands of naturalness—there is not much time. The way in which "civilization" has torn up the environment suggests that their urgency is warranted.

Types of Organizations

There are at least five kinds of organizations active in the conservation and outdoor recreation movement. One is the action organization, which carries out specific conservation programs. Another kind includes policy or watchdog groups, which spend the majority of their efforts influencing the public, educating legislators, and testifying on positions of policy or law. A third group is the professional society, which, to a limited extent, unites people of related professional interests to transmit ideas, trade information, and guide development of professional interests. A fourth group is the commercial or industry association, often involving purchasers of their products. They promote wise use of the products, seek legislation or judgements that favor their users, and promote goodwill. A fifth type is the sanctioning and coordinating organization, which sets itself up as the arbiter and organizer of competitive sports events. Other groups are difficult to categorize or stand as special types.

There are many other types of organizations that affect recreation resources policy from their specific interests in its outcome. Examples include the Chambers of Commerce, which often support major recreation installations as a boon to local economies; the League of Women Voters which encourages citizen examination of current issues, including recreation; the Conservation Clubs which promote and offer hunting and fishing opportunities; and numerous activity groups such as canoe clubs, camping clubs, and bicycling organizations. Scouts, Campfire Clubs, 4-H, the YMCA, YWCA, YHA's, Boys Clubs, and thousands of church organizations strongly affect attitudes of young people and provide important outdoor recreation resources.

Action Groups

Most organizations in the environmental field refer to themselves as action-oriented. The groups listed in this section, however, are strictly limited to those that expend most of their efforts on land acquisition or management for recreation and open space. The four national organizations described here are examples of groups with different objectives and approaches to increasing resources available for recreation. These groups do not conduct active lobbying programs; they deal with government officials concerning their particular activity, usually in a cooperative relationship. They often appeal successfully to industry and foundations for assistance in their rather quiet, purposeful approach to conservation.

THE NATURE CONSERVANCY
1800 N. Kent Street, Suite 800
Arlington, Virginia 22209

The Nature Conservancy (TNC), a private, nonprofit organization, is one of the nation's largest real estate dealers. Its principal activity is the acquisition of land through purchase, donation, bequest, or easement. The land is then either retained as a TNC nature preserve or passed on to a managing agency of local, state, or federal government, or a private organization. The property is almost always managed as a nature preserve, park, or wildlife refuge.

The general objective of TNC is to preserve and protect ecologically and environmentally significant land and the diversity of life it supports, allowing nature to operate with a minimum of disturbance by man.

The Nature Conservancy often acts as an intermediary in land acquisition. If a donor wishes to act quickly, a gift of land for a public agency through TNC can be handled in a few days. It assures the donor of tax advantages, gives assurance that the property will be managed as a preserve, and leaves details of transferring the property to the public agency up to TNC. This procedure was followed by the Union Camp Corporation when it donated a large portion of the Dismal Swamp as a wildlife refuge. The corporation donated the land to The Nature Conservancy, and received favorable publicity and tax benefits. Then the U.S. Fish and Wildlife Service received the land from The Nature Conservancy. In many cases, TNC is involved in a *reverter clause* arrangement. This is part of the transfer agreement, which provides that the Nature Conservancy holds the right to take title to a preserve donated to another agency or organization if the property is managed in violation of the purpose of the donation. For example, a gift of land to a private college in Indiana has a reverter clause providing that TNC will automatically become the owner should the college attempt to use the land for a building site or other purpose than a natural forest study area.

Because preservation of natural lands is the primary goal, the organization considers it unimportant if some other group manages a particular property, as long as permanency and quality management are assured. Some chapters of the Conservancy prefer to sell most of their lands to public agencies so they can tackle new projects.

TNC operates through a national office for legal purposes, but much of the project work is done through state or sectional chapters. These are largely operated by volunteer members, with a minimal but efficient staff of field representatives.

The first project of TNC was Mianus Gorge, within the New York metropolitan area, in 1954 (Figure 33.1). The organization was founded in 1917, a spinoff of the Ecological Society of America. The origins of the idea can be traced to concerned ecology and biology professors who found few places exhibiting natural processes to take their classes or to conduct research. The group took its present form in 1951, when it was organized as a nonprofit corporation.

Many projects have benefited local, state, and national park, refuge, and forest projects. Such efforts are concentrated on projects where significant natural values can be preserved, and rapid transfer of lands to other managing agencies can be made, with promise of prompt payment.

Examples include a 1,000-acre wildlife refuge purchased for the Lake County, Indiana, Parks and Recreation Department from an owner who wanted to sell before the county could produce the funds. Important portions of the Golden Gate National Recreation Area were acquired through careful negotiation and quick action by TNC with private ranchers. The nature preserves systems of several states have been enriched through actions by TNC.

The Nature Conservancy was the major force behind the development of the ideas that formed the National Heritage program, introduced by President Carter in 1978. A similar program had been developed in Georgia when Carter was governor. The TNC Heritage Program is different from the federal operation but complementary to it. It was tested in 10 states and on Tennessee Valley Authority lands in 1977. It involves an inventory

FIGURE 33.1   Mianus River Gorge Nature Preserve, the first preserve acquired by The Nature Conservancy, is just north of New York City. (TNC)

of outstanding natural and historical areas in public and private ownership. These become potential targets for preservation efforts, based on a set of priorities. Many other states have since entered into Heritage inventory programs through contracts with TNC. They now have identified their state's outstanding resources and have a strategy for preservation.

TNC uses various techniques to protect ecologically and environmentally significant land. The Nature Conservancy:

Private Organizations

1. Purchases lands, using a revolving fund, replenished through fund raising.
2. Accepts gifts of land.
3. Retains and manages 60 per cent of its projects.
4. Works with local, state, and federal governments to identify and protect natural areas.
5. Acquires and temporarily manages land in advance of governmental agencies' ability to do so and then transfers the land to the agencies.

The rationale for saving land areas was outlined by Roush (1977) as four basic premises to protecting natural diversity:

Diversity promotes stability of the ecosystem.
Diversity increases the possibility of future benefits.
Diversity is a source of human delight.
Protecting diversity is an ethical necessity.

The Nature Conservancy in the United States is not to be confused with the government agency of the same name in Great Britain. The American version is a volunteer, private group that operates with no governmental powers. The older British organization is a public agency, responsible for management of scientific reserves and for research and public education about natural values. In some ways, the two organizations have similar purposes, but they act with different authority.

The American organization, in its first 25 years of operations, undertook nearly 1,700 projects involving more than 400,000 ha (1,000,000 acres) of land. It retained 670 of the projects as TNC-managed preserves.

A Canadian TNC was incorporated in 1961 as a national corporation. It buys land and finances other groups in similar efforts. The address is 2200 Yonge Street, 661, Toronto, M4S 2E1, Canada.

DUCKS UNLIMITED, INC.
P. O. Box 66300
Chicago, Illinois 60666

Ducks Unlimited (DU) is a single-purpose organization of unusual character. It is dedicated to the conservation and propagation of North American waterfowl. Its major function is to increase and restore nesting habitat. The organization was an outgrowth of the More Game Birds in America Foundation, incorporated in 1930. Since its founding in 1937 in Washington, D.C., and in 1938 in Canada, DU has provided for the reservation of one million hectares of waterfowl breeding habitat. Because 70 per cent of North American waterfowl nest in Canada, a majority of the DU effort has been in Canada's Prairie Provinces. In its first 40 years, DU spent

$40 million to build 1,347 habitat restoration projects in Canada, comprising about 16,000 km of shoreline breeding habitat. In 1977, the organization spent $9.6 million in Canada to construct 118 new projects, adding 24,000 ha to the existing reserve of one million ha. In 1974, Ducks Unlimited de México, L.C. was formed to round out the North American effort.

Funds come from members—mostly people in the United States interested in duck and goose hunting—and from donations by private enterprise and state governments. Banquets and sales of prints and shotguns provide considerable income. Fifteen states contribute revenues from their state duck stamp programs and other wildlife funds (Whitesell, 1977). The organization reports that 80 per cent of the donations received go directly into habitat improvement. *Ducks Unlimited* magazine keeps members informed of progress.

APPALACHIAN TRAIL CONFERENCE
P. O. Box 236
Harpers Ferry, W. Virginia 25425

The Appalachian Trail Conference (ATC) is an amalgamation of many trail clubs stretched along the 2,050-mile Maine-to-Georgia hiking trail. Formed in 1921 to promote the idea of a long trail and to actually construct it, the group coordinates maintenance of the trail. It produces and sells trail guides and publications. The central office answers numerous inquiries and keeps records of trail use (Figure 33.2).

FIGURE 33.2 Half-way house for end-to-end hikers is Appalachian Trail Conference headquarters in Harpers Ferry.

All trail development and maintenance work is done by volunteers. Each local club is responsible for a section of the trail. It maintains the agreements with private landowners, keeps the trail clear and in good condition, and cleans shelters, rest stops, campsites, and other facilities.

Although changes have been made since the trail was named a national scenic trail, the federal presence is just beginning to be felt. The National Park Service has moved to purchase the route of the trail where it crosses private land. Previously, the private landowners were paid no fee and simply agreed to allow the trail to cross their land. The ATC then had to adjust the route if the landowner changed his mind or a new owner did not agree to the route location. This caused numerous alterations, until many miles were along roads. Where the route crossed public lands, the agencies responsible handled some of the maintenance.

The Conference retains its managerial duties under the new federal administration. It is a legal part of the administrative process.

HORSE-SHOE TRAIL CLUB

This club is one of many local groups that maintain trails connecting with the Appalachian Trail. The 120-mile Horse-Shoe Trail connects Valley Forge Park, near Philadelphia, with the Appalachian Trail near Hershey, Pa. It was laid out in the 1930s by volunteer members of the club for hiking and horseback riding. Youth hostels, stables, and campsites are available along the trail. The club keeps the trail marked and publishes a guidebook.

The Trail Club holds easements for a few portions of the trail, but most of the route exists by revocable permission of the property owners. Where subdivisions have encroached, there has been cooperation by communities and developers to maintain the right-of-way.

BIKECENTENNIAL
P. O. Box 8308
Missoula, Montana 59807

Bikecentennial is a member-supported, nonprofit service organization that promotes bicycle touring. It designated a 4,500-mile bike route along quiet, scenic roads from Washington to Virginia as part of the nation's Bicentennial celebration in 1976. Loop trails for 8 to 15-day trips within Kentucky, Virginia, and other states were developed by the group as its next major project. The group researches routes, establishes overnight facilities, promotes cooperation from the state and county highway departments, and publishes maps and guidebooks. A variety of other booklets and directories plus numerous articles in national magazines help to promote bicycling. Founded in 1973 and incorporated in 1974, the organization receives its funding from individual memberships, trip fees, publication sales, and a small portion from grants.

Regional Action Groups

There are dozens of local, statewide, and regional organizations that quietly but effectively safeguard what is beautiful and wild. They are volunteer groups that have accomplished much but get little publicity.

Many of these have been in operation for decades, since long before the national popularity of preservation. Their action has been to acquire, dedicate, protect, and get governments to acquire special resources.

Their interests in the land were often not for recreation, in terms that most people understand. The land, the forest, the rocks, the river were outstanding, representative, or otherwise worthwhile in their natural state. They valued it and saw that others could benefit from it by seeing it and studying it.

The unselfish nature of most of these groups is typical of volunteerism in conservation. Wealthy and poor give of their funds, time, and land to promote preservation of some special areas. There are sometimes tax benefits, but they do not repay the value of the gifts or the hard work.

Two examples of these regional organizations are the well-known Save-the-Redwoods League and the little-known Society for the Protection of New Hampshire Forests.

THE SOCIETY FOR THE PROTECTION OF NEW HAMPSHIRE FORESTS
5 S. State Street
Concord, New Hampshire 03301

This society is a voluntary, nonprofit organization that promotes wise use of New Hampshire's natural resources. It was organized in 1901 and has aided the state in purchasing lands for forests and parks. It has a small staff for land protection and forestry. Its membership of 5,000 has made remarkable progress in affecting the management of natural resources in New Hampshire.

SAVE-THE-REDWOODS LEAGUE
114 Sansome Street, Room 605
San Francisco, California 94104

Like Ducks Unlimited, Save-the-Redwoods League has a single purpose and has been notably successful in accomplishing it. A nonprofit citizens group formed in 1917 to preserve examples of the redwood forest, it has been a major factor in setting aside portions of the California coastal trees in reserves, state parks, and the Redwood National Park (Figure 33.3). It has received the cooperation of industry, private citizens, and government.

The organization started with five men donating $100 to acquire land. From that modest beginning, the Save-the-Redwoods League has played a major role in the formation of the California State Park system. It began purchasing redwood groves in 1918. In 1927, its urging of the legislature resulted in the establishment of a State Park Commission.

FIGURE 33.3 Private efforts of the Save-the-Redwoods League have combined with industry and state cooperation to preserve redwood groves. (USFS)

In the 1920s, with matching funds from the state of California, the first groves at Humboldt Redwoods, Prairie Creek, and Del Norte Coast were purchased. These, along with Big Basin State Park (1902), became the nucleus of California's Redwood State Parks. Three have become part of the Redwood National Park.

In cooperation with the highway commission, the League also assures preservation of trees and beauty along highways. It now spends $2–3 million of donated money each year to buy redwood forest.

The League solicits donations from wealthy individuals and enterprises. It often doubles the value of private donations through matching arrangements with state and federal grant programs. A Redwood Memorial Grove honoring the person of one's choice can be established by donating $10,000 or more.

In the 1880s, virtually all of the coast redwoods were sold into private ownership for $2.50 to $5.00 per acre. Now the governments and private donations are buying the land back, often in second-growth timber, at prices that range into the thousands of dollars per acre.

Citizen Policy Groups

Many citizen organizations are often referred to as influence groups or pressure groups. They are an integral part of a representative government. Without them, legislators would be voting with relatively little information or feedback from constituents on most issues. They also play a vital role in the conduct of affairs by government agencies. In many cases, the vigilance of these groups has prevented development projects in national parks and national forests. They back up administrators and planners on many projects but may oppose them on others.

Influence groups are often criticized for representing only a small minority of interests. However, because only small fractions of the population are actively interested and informed about any one issue, the interest groups often represent the concerned and informed portions of the public. The land administrator must be alert to their special interests and their tendencies, so he can separate bias from fact and personal economic interest from public interest.

There is also a question of balance among the various points of view represented. For decades, the major groups interested in the policies of the Bureau of Land Management were only the western livestock producers and the mining organizations. These groups promoted their own economic interests with the bureau and in the Congress. Their efforts were rewarded by protective legislation and low grazing fees. Partly because of the pressure of conservation groups and partly because of the philosophy of BLM employees, there has been increasing emphasis on forest conservation, recreation, wildlife, and wilderness preservation.

The value of pressure groups includes at least the following functions:

1. Provide information to decision makers, through research, fact-finding, pictures, films, and other methods.
2. Represent a point of view of a portion of the public, articulating and debating it.
3. Serve as watchdog on the implementation of policies, and help mold policies and interpret them.
4. Force or delay decisions through suits, reviews, and urging.
5. Counterbalance political or agency pressures and inertia.

To achieve these many values, the groups play various roles—watchdog, debater, plaintiff, lobbyist, bill writer, legislative informant and advisor, expert witness, public educator, and researcher.

THE AMERICAN FORESTRY ASSOCIATION
1319 18th Street, NW
Washington, D.C. 20036

Founded in 1875, the American Forestry Association (AFA) is a national conservation organization for the promotion of intelligent management and use of natural resources for a quality environment and the well-being of all citizens. The association strives to increase public appreciation of the part that forests and national resources play in the social, recreational, and economic phases of the nation. The AFA seeks, through its magazine *American Forests* and other ways, to promote an enlightened public appreciation of natural resources.

Its activities include:

1. Sponsorship of national and regional conferences for the improvement of America's forests. The early conferences were vital to the establishment of national forests and the U.S. Forest Service.
2. Horseback, hiking, and canoe trips for members (Trail Riders of the Wilderness).
3. Information service to answer members' questions concerning legislative and government activities dealing with natural resources.

The group has a distinguished record of level-headed, low-key analysis and recommendation of natural resource policy. Although it has taken strong positions on many issues and has led the government into new programs, it does not have a reputation for contentiousness or extreme positions. The organization presents its points of view to the Congress and is treated as a valued source of ideas.

NATIONAL PARKS AND CONSERVATION ASSOCIATION
1701 18th Street, NW
Washington, D.C. 20029

The rallying cry of the National Parks and Conservation Association (NPCA) over its many years of existence is that "our national parks are in danger." It has served as the citizen watchdog and promoter of national parks policy since it was founded in 1919. Stephen Mather, first director of the National Park Service, gave it his blessing and encouragement. The value of the association is reflected in its probing of some of the ticklish questions of political and bureaucratic abuse of the parks. When it appeared that special interests or political policies were interfering with the purposes of the parks, this group has stepped to the fore, with nothing to lose, to expose and lay blame where it thought the fault lay. It has stood for consistency in park policy. Its primary focus in recent years has been on keeping the parks natural. Therefore, it has supported the wilderness designation of large areas and has opposed efforts of concessionaires to expand facilities and services within the parks. A printed summary of an investigation of concession arrangements was the basis of a major controversy. It resulted in the scrapping of plans for some concessions to make major expansions.

The group is a friend of the parks but not necessarily of the National Park Service. If the NPS proposes something that the NPCA believes is against the best interests of the parks, the organization speaks out strongly against the NPS policy. Likewise, NPS inaction begets complaints.

The cornerstone of NPCA is its belief that the natural values and wilderness ecosystems are the greatest assets of the national park system. It has recently entered into other conservation activities, including recommendations on timber harvesting practices, land-use planning, mass transit in parks and cities, wildlife and plant survival (especially endangered species), energy, pollution, and various international conservation efforts.

The NPCA operations involve the following six approaches:

National Parks and Conservation magazine—to members, libraries, and the public.
Government—meetings with resources management agencies.
Litigation—use the courts "when reason fails."
Field network—contact with individuals and organizations for information and representation.
Legislation—testify, on invitation as experts, on conservation issues.
Coalitions—help form coalitions of opinion on major issues, bringing support from such groups as farm and labor organizations.

The 1977 membership was 45,000.

NATIONAL WILDLIFE REFUGE ASSOCIATION
P. O. Box 124
Winona, Minnesota 55987

The National Wildlife Refuge Association, a fledgling nonprofit group, was organized in 1975 to protect the integrity of the National Wildlife

Refuge system. Its membership is open to individuals, organizations, and institutions with interest in increasing public understanding of the National Wildlife Refuge system. As the recreational importance of the National Wildlife Refuges grows, this group may become more prominent, or, like many other conservation organizations, it could slip into obscurity after a noble trial. The causes of success or failure of such organizations are so numerous as to warrant intensive study.

NATIONAL AND PROVINCIAL PARKS ASSOCIATION OF CANADA
47 Colborne Street
Suite 38
Toronto, Ontario, Canada M5E 1E3

The National and Provincial Parks Association of Canada, a nonprofit citizens' group, was founded in 1963 to promote park values and to encourage better management of Canada's national and provincial parks. Through its *Park News* magazine, it educates the public and officials about existing problems and potential solutions in the parks. Its influence has been felt in the recent planning efforts relating to Banff and other townsites within national parks. The organization's 2,500 members tend to favor naturalness in the parks, minimizing human impact.

NATIONAL WILDLIFE FEDERATION
1412 Sixteenth Street, N.W.
Washington, D.C. 20036

The National Wildlife Federation is the nation's largest citizens' natural resource organization. It claims nearly four million members in its associate and affiliate classes.

It was formed in 1936, at the urging of President Roosevelt. Its objectives are broad in the conservation field. With major emphasis on the welfare of wildlife, the group is active in all affairs relating to land use, pollution control, recreation and parks, and energy. The interest in wildlife has led to considerable action in regard to water quality problems.

In 1977, the National Wildlife Federation spent $77 million on its education, information, legislative liaison, litigation, and land acquisition activities. Among the recent land acquisition activities was the purchase of two major bald eagle nesting sites in California and Illinois, in line with the federation's bicentennial eagle project.

Litigation is looked upon as a last resort activity. Suits have been brought recently in regard to wetland protection against highway routes and drainage, clean water act enforcement, and endangered species. Legislative liaison involves all aspects of the environment, including major efforts in regard to the Alaska d-2 lands assignment, selection of minimal-damage gas pipeline routes, bottle disposal, grazing fees on public lands, energy policy, water development projects, international and national regulations protecting porpoises and whales, in addition to a host of state and local regulations.

The educational programs of the National Wildlife Federation are widely used and are among the most popular conservation materials in the nation. Its periodicals include *National Wildlife, International Wildlife, Ranger Rick,* and two free newsletters—*Conservation Report* and *Conservation Notes.* Numerous leaflets explain individual issues or points of view. An annual publication, *Conservation Directory,* provides names and addresses of organizations, agencies, and officials concerned with natural resource use and management. Environmental education aids and an environmental quality index are also available. Training sessions and educational trips are available. The federation publishes one book each year related to wildlife or the problems of its habitat. Television spots and scholarships round out the educational productions.

Membership is by direct subscription to the national organization or through affiliated groups in each state. Many of these affiliates are leagues of conservation clubs, each of which has its own programs and special interests related to wildlife, hunting, fishing, or other environmental emphases. There are 6,000 such affiliated clubs in the United States.

Canadian Wildlife Federation
1673 Carling Avenue
Ottawa, Ontario K2A 1C4

The Canadian Wildlife Federation claims 320,000 members and supporters. It was founded in 1961 to foster understanding of natural processes. It has a program of ecology-based information and education. Research and scientific investigation are sponsored. It publishes *Wildlife Report* and *International Wildlife* magazine as well as special reports about current topics.

Sierra Club
530 Bush Street
San Francisco, California 94108

The Sierra Club is one of the oldest and most famous of the policy groups. It started with John Muir leading Californians on expeditions into the Sierra Nevada mountains. Its official formation in 1892 signaled the election of Muir as its president. Its initial interest in the Sierras led to activities promoting policy to favor preservation in parks and forests. The club's interests expanded rapidly during the 1950s, when it became a truly national group. Its influence on national conservation policy has been profound. One of its purposes suggests an even broader vision: to educate the people of the United States and the world to the need to preserve and restore the quality of man's environment and the integrity of the natural ecosystems of the world.

Its voice is far stronger than its membership of 155,000 would suggest. Many of its members are university-related or professional people who tend to be activists. Their concern is usually based on field work and careful study of the issues, but presentation of views tends to become firm, almost dogmatic, once a position is defined. The organization is respected as a formidable opponent, expert in the use of a variety of techniques and media to promote its point of view.

Nature photography has been one of the club's most effective weapons. Several bills have passed the Congress shortly after large color photographs were placed on the desks of each congressman by the Sierra Club. These include the establishment of Kings Canyon National Park (1940), Redwood National Park (1968), and the North Cascades National Park (1968). The club has been active in the Alaska pipeline and land assignment issues. Its pictures in books and magazines have done much to gain public sentiment for preserving natural beauty.

The Sierra Club took to the courts in the 1960s. Although it had limited success for specific cases, it was a pioneer in gaining standing to sue for a citizen's organization. Since 1966, a series of opinions has recognized injuries other than economic or direct physical damage as sufficient grounds for standing. One of these grounds was environmental damages, related to a suit the Sierra Club instituted against the construction of a Disney Corporation resort on national forest land in Mineral King valley in California (Orren, 1976). For the first time, environmental injury was admitted as a basis for a claim to sue before the Supreme Court. Although the club was denied standing on a technicality, the court affirmed that these types of harms "may amount to an 'injury in fact' sufficient to lay the basis for standing . . ." (405 US 727 (1972), 734). The Mineral King area became part of Sequoia National Park in 1979, stopping any hopes for a ski resort.

The group has served as a lobbyist so often that it forfeited its nonprofit status. The Sierra Club Foundation was set up as a nonprofit organization to handle funding of many of the purely educational activities. The Sierra Club Legal Defense Fund was also established to receive donations and sponsor litigation relating to natural resource issues.

NATIONAL AUDUBON SOCIETY
950 Third Avenue
New York, New York 10022

The National Audubon Society, established in 1886, is a combination of various purposes and activities. It is organized into local chapters that are often nature-study groups. The central interest of the organization relates to bird study, but it branches into all phases of nature and the policies associated with management of natural environments.

The society maintains 45 sanctuaries, one of them covering 26,000 acres. It maintains four summer camps with ecology workshops for teachers and youth leaders. Local and national groups conduct field trips. The Christmas bird census is a major undertaking of the organization.

The national organization has four model nature centers with full programs for children and adults. The national office employes a scientific staff specialized in biology, water resource economics, nuclear physics, ecology, vegetation, ornithology, and environmental policy. The national organization offers expert testimony and conducts campaigns on conservation topics, including rare species protection, wilderness, dams, Alaska oil, clearcutting, and strip mining.

Publications include the colorful, high-quality *Audubon* magazine, as well as newsletters and teaching aids. Its wildlife films are presented at about 1,500 programs per year to about 500,000 people. Some are also presented on television. It works through newspapers, radio, and the distribution of educational materials.

THE WILDERNESS SOCIETY
1901 Pennsylvania Avenue, NW
Washington, D.C. 20006

A potent group of about 80,000 supporters of the dedication of wilderness areas, the Wilderness Society has compiled a remarkable record since its formation in 1935. Robert Marshall, a Forest Service advocate of wilderness, was one of its eight founders. The organization has become involved in local and national conservation issues, but it focuses most of its efforts on promoting federal designation of wilderness areas.

Through its quarterly magazine *The Living Wilderness*, the association promoted high standards for wilderness management during the 1950s. The purity of wilderness was emphasized. The philosophy has changed somewhat. New areas to be added may have man-made intrusions, according to society support for some areas.

In 1955, the society began introducing legislation to establish a law to formally set aside wilderness on public lands. This recognized and included the Forest Service wilderness and added other public lands. After nine years of effort and cooperation from many other organizations, the oft-rewritten wilderness bill became the 1964 Wilderness Act. It stands as the society's signal achievement. Current activities center around the designation of more wilderness, wild and scenic rivers, and critical habitat for endangered wildlife species. Unlike The Nature Conservancy and Ducks Unlimited, this group does not buy land but urges governmental action to preserve lands and urges private landowners to practice conservation.

The Wilderness Society has a national office in Washington, D.C., a field office in Denver, and various regional offices. It works with citizen groups with interests in wilderness preservation and provides individuals with guidance on methods of proposing wilderness study areas. Wilderness workshops were sponsored during much of the 1960s to inform the public about the wilderness act and its implications.

THE IZAAK WALTON LEAGUE OF AMERICA, INC.
1800 N. Kent Street
Suite 806
Arlington, Virginia 22209

The Izaak Walton League of America is a national citizen conservation organization, composed of community chapters, state divisions, and members-at-large working for the wise use and conservation of America's natural resources and for the restoration and maintenance of a high-quality environment. Its aims are to conserve, maintain, protect, and restore the soil, forest, water, and other natural resources of the United States. It also promotes and carries out public education on conservation topics. Its mode of action is primarily through taking positions on issues, lobbying, and using the courts. Many chapters of the league have acquired land for nature preserves. Their endowment funds have aided other groups in conservation-related acquisitions. Izaak Walton Parks are mainly for the use of members but are open for public use as well, with permission. Other lands that are purchased are usually transferred to an appropriate public agency.

Established in 1922 and named after a famous British fisherman-writer, the league has long had an interest in water resource problems. Lately, it has fought excessive manipulation of river channels and many Corps of Engineers reservoir projects. With 300 chapters and some strong legal talents, this group has had a strong influence on the conservation policy of the states and the nation. It publishes *Outdoor America* and various regional newspapers.

NATURAL RESOURCES DEFENSE COUNCIL, INC.
917 15th Street, NW
Washington, D.C. 20005

The Natural Resources Defense Council, founded in 1970, has acted primarily through the courts. Its staff of lawyers and scientists has concentrated on making sure that environmental law is carried out vigorously and aggressively. Among its early efforts was the enforcement of the federal water pollution laws. The group has won landmark court decisions to challenge the practice of clear-cutting (Monongahela case and others), to interdict the shooting of Alaskan wolves from helicopters, and to promote the preservation of dunes along coastal areas.

The council's activities are primarily litigation, administrative prodding, monitoring of government agencies and regulations, research, citizen education, and training lawyers and scientists. The council has served as the court representative for virtually every major environmental organization.

Among its 35,000 members are many of the nation's most wealthy and prominent citizens. The group acts vigorously in defense of what it perceives to be abuses of natural resources. Its aggressive vigilance and effective legal procedures have done much to keep governmental and private resource managers alert.

ENVIRONMENTAL DEFENSE FUND

475 Park Avenue South
New York, New York 10015
(also offices in Washington, Denver, and Berkeley)

The Environmental Defense Fund is a national legal action organization of scientists, lawyers, and economists. Its aim is to protect the public interest in environmental quality, energy conservation, public health, and consumer welfare. That allows action in a wide spectrum, with strongest emphasis on environmental quality. Its best-known tool is litigation through the courts. It also provides technical and policy information to politicians and public agencies. Among its major victories are its part in the ban on DDT, protection of dolphins, resource preservation actions along the Atlantic and Gulf Coast, a part in cancelling plans to build a power plant in Utah that would have caused air pollution in some national parks, and a number of legal actions to enforce air and water pollution regulations. Its support comes from about 50,000 dues-paying members, foundation grants, and individual bequests. It was formed in 1967.

THE GARDEN CLUB OF AMERICA

598 Madison Avenue
New York, New York 10022

The Garden Club of America is subdivided into zones and districts, each containing several member clubs. The local clubs have conservation committees with concerns about natural resource conservation. They conduct local club projects, including land preservation, park improvement, support of or opposition to agency activities, and presentation of educational material to schools and civic groups.

These organizations, as individual clubs and through national officers, have helped influence conservation policy for many years. Their members have served on important local and national commissions. They promoted the formation of greenbelt councils, acquisition of nature study areas, support of various Forest Service policies, and work with other agencies. They have provided nature guides, supplied planting materials for outdoor laboratories, and helped raise money for land acquisition.

Professional Societies

Organizations in this category are seldom in the heat of policy battles. Their members may be involved, but the societies find it difficult to take a stand on specific issues that often are more political than professional. The societies listed represent some of those that are directly involved with recreation problems. As groups, they take broad stands on issues and provide information and guidelines. They serve as expert witnesses or sources of technical information to legislators, business leaders, and government officials. The technical information they transmit to their members through meetings and journals is probably the most valuable service provided.

The National Recreation and Park Association
1601 N. Kent Street
Arlington, Virginia 22209

The National Recreation and Park Association (NRPA) is a nonprofit service organization, dedicated to the wise use of free time, conservation of natural resources, and beautification of the total environment. It is actively concerned with the improvement of park and recreation facilities and programs and more wholesome, meaningful leisure-time activities. It is primarily professional in its membership but also includes volunteer members of local park and recreation boards and other interested citizens.

NRPA was formed in 1965 by the merger of five national agencies concerned with recreation, parks, and conservation. The five groups were the American Association of Zoological Parks and Aquariums, the American Institute of Park Executives, the American Recreation Society, the National Conference on State Parks, and the National Recreation Association.

The new amalgamation was reorganized into five branches. Each branch develops materials and programs of special interest to its members. The member usually belongs to one branch and thereby to the NRPA and receives mailings from the parent organization plus the branch.

Parks and Recreation magazine is the principal vehicle of communication. The group also publishes a newsletter and *Therapeutic Recreation*. The *Journal of Leisure Research* offers current research information on a quarterly basis. NRPA collaborates with the National Park Service in the production of three looseleaf periodicals, *Design, Trends,* and *Grist,* which comprise the Park Practice Program. These present practical and philosophical guidelines for field personnel. A series of *Management Aids* also offer specific guidelines for various park practices. The organization sponsors about 10 workshop programs or schools per year in various parts of the nation as part of its continuing education function.

World Leisure and Recreation Association
345 East 46 Street
New York, New York 10017

Founded in 1956, the World Leisure and Recreation Association seeks to increase the role of leisure and recreation in the emerging world. It is an information exchange service to and between its affiliated organizations and members. It is a central international service agency to aid organizations in all nations seeking to provide recreation service to the people. It is connected to 110 organizations in 80 countries and has credited status with the United Nations. It sponsors exchange programs, facilitating contacts for international travelers. It informs and exchanges ideas instead of promoting them.

Activities include meetings, international travel opportunities for members, a five-issues-per-year bulletin, counseling, and an opportunity for discounts on professional and educational material.

THE WILDLIFE SOCIETY
7101 Wisconsin Avenue, NW
Suite 611
Washington, D.C. 20014

To establish and maintain high professional standards in wildlife management is the goal of the Wildlife Society's 7,000 professionals. Its publications include *The Journal of Wildlife Management, Wildlife Society Bulletin,* and *Wildlife Monographs.*

ASSOCIATION OF INTERPRETIVE NATURALISTS, INC.
6700 Needwood Road
Derwood, Maryland 20855

The Association of Interpretive Naturalists is a professional society, started in the mid-1950s, to bring interpreters in all agencies into greater communication. It includes 1,300 members from the United States and Canada. It sponsors regional and national meetings to exchange information and techniques of interpretation of natural and cultural phenomena to the recreating public. It publishes the *Journal of Interpretation.*

WESTERN INTERPRETERS ASSOCIATION
6986 La Jolla Blvd.
La Jolla, California 92037

The purposes of the Western Interpreters Association are similar to those of the Association of Interpretive Naturalists but specifically include historical, recreational, archaeological, and anthropological interpreters along with those interested in natural history. It was formed in 1967 in response to the growth of the profession and the difficulty of meeting with eastern members of the Association of Interpretive Naturalists. Its periodical is *The Interpreter.*

CONSERVATION EDUCATION ASSOCIATION
% R. W. Presnell
Department of Education
University of Wisconsin-Green Bay
Green Bay, Wisc. 54302

The Conservation Education Association promotes environmental education among teachers and interpreters.

SOCIETY OF AMERICAN FORESTERS
5400 Grosvenor Lane
Washington, D.C. 20014

About 21,000 professional foresters belong to the Society of American Foresters (SAF). It accepts full members who are graduates of accredited forestry programs, as determined by its own accrediting committees. The *Journal of Forestry* and *Forest Science* are the regular means of communication.

Founded in 1900 with Gifford Pinchot as president, the organization is independent of, but often closely associated with, the U.S. Forest Service in its sentiments. The membership is wide-ranging, including many industrial, state, consulting, and educator foresters, as well as employees of various federal agencies.

The SAF does little lobbying; it appears more for expert testimony on technical or policy matters. It has a limited public education program that describes the goals and work of foresters.

American Alliance for Health, Physical Education, and Recreation
1201 16th Street, NW
Washington, D.C. 20036

The purpose of the American Alliance for Health, Physical Education, and Recreation is promoting and developing better programs in health, physical education, and recreation. Publications include *Research Quarterly, Journal of Physical Education and Recreation, Health Education,* and *Update.*

Activities include publication of several books and pamphlets, workshops and conferences, and an insurance plan for its members, most of which are directed toward school and college programs. The membership includes professional specialists and educators with orientation to activities and programming rather than to natural resources.

American Planning Association
1776 Massachusetts Avenue, NW
Washington, D.C. 20036

In 1978, the American Institute of Planners and the American Society of Planning Officials united to form the American Planning Association. Land use and urban planners thus joined formally with appointed and elected officials. The two organizations had long worked closely together. The new organization conducts seminars with community and state leaders, promotes principles of land use planning, sponsors research, provides aid to planners in the form of information and advice on new developments. Publications include *Planning* magazine, *Planning Advisory Service Reports,* and *Land Use Law and Zoning Digest.* As a result of the merger, a companion group was formed to certify professionally trained planners and to accredit qualified university programs. It is the American Institute of Certified Planners.

THE AMERICAN SOCIETY OF LANDSCAPE ARCHITECTS
1750 Old Meadow Road
McLean, Virginia 22101

The American Society of Landscape Architects is comprised of professionally qualified landscape architects. It accredits university programs that meet its standards of excellence. The organization provides information to its members and the public and conducts seminars and meetings, often involving interested citizens. It collaborates with other organizations and agencies in offering advice on land planning problems and excellence in design. Its quarterly magazine *Landscape Architecture,* a newsletter, and bulletin are used for communication.

Commercial Organizations

Many organizations are established through the cooperative efforts of industries or economic interests and are important to the outdoor recreation professional. These groups are often very helpful in providing reliable information on products and new developments. They may be useful in protecting consumers and governments against the poor practices of some members of their industries. Land managers are regularly in contact with representatives of various groups. These range from the American Motorcycle Association to the American Miners Congress. Manufacturers of outdoor recreation equipment are naturally interested in the policies and funding of parks.

On the national level, there are many groups that have influenced laws and policy affecting public lands.

AMERICAN NATIONAL CATTLEMEN'S ASSOCIATION
1001 Lincoln Street
Denver, Colorado 80203

The American National Cattlemen's Association has had tremendous influence on the state legislatures of the West and on the Congress. As might be expected, it promotes the policies that would benefit ranchers and cattle feeders. One reason that federal grazing leases are of long duration and low cost is the effective lobbying of this group. Their power is reflected in the Wilderness Act of 1964, in the provisions allowing grazing to continue in most wilderness areas where it was permitted before. This group has been an efficient spokesman of the cattle industry for most of its existence since 1898. Through 43 state associations and 15 beef registry groups, it represents 300,000 ranchers, breeders, and feeders of beef cattle. It is the central agency for the beef cattle business, providing information, research, promotion, and liaison with legislatures and industry. It publishes a weekly *Beef Business Bulletin.*

American Mining Congress
1100 Ring Building
1200 18th Street, NW
Washington, D.C. 20036

Founded in 1897, the American Mining Congress has 600 members including producers of coal, minerals, and metals, manufacturers of mining equipment, banks, and other financial institutions interested in mining. It keeps members up to date with a biweekly *News Bulletin*, a monthly *Legislative Bulletin*, a monthly *Mining Congress Journal*. It has had strong influence in representing mining interests in the Congress. The prospecting exceptions in the Wilderness Act and some mining activity in national parks can be traced to the efforts of this group.

National Forest Products Association
1619 Massachusetts Avenue, NW
Washington, D.C. 20036

Timber industries are organized in numerous groups. The largest is the National Forest Products Association (NFPA), with a strong lobbying effort, legal affairs program, and a superb educational service program. Films, posters, and teaching kits are available from this group and/or from the American Forest Institute.

The NFPA stands on legislative questions often oppose the position of the Sierra Club and other preservation groups. The NFPA interest is in keeping forests open to multiple uses, including timber harvest. Thus, the wilderness designation of timber land and the expansion of preserve lands at the cost of forest production are serious concerns. *Forest Industries Newsletter* and periodic special reports on current issues are valuable free courses of information on current events.

This group is only one of several lobbying and educational organizations related to land-based industry. Other commercial organizations such as the National Association of Manufacturers, Chamber of Commerce, and labor unions have strong voices but do not concern themselves exclusively with natural resource or recreation issues.

Sanctioners and Coordinators of Activities

Every sport seems to have organizations that set the rules, conduct championship meets, and recognize outstanding performers. A few examples are listed here.

U.S. Yacth Racing Union
1133 Avenue of the Americas
New York, New York 10036

The U.S. Yacht Racing Union coordinates sailboat racing in the United

States, sponsors several championships, and publishes a yearbook, handbook, rule books, racing tables, and information.

The Outboard Boating Club of America
401 North Michigan Avenue
Chicago, Illinois 60611

The Outboard Boating Club of America, with 10,000 members, was established in 1928 to promote better boating opportunities to all Americans. More specifically, it promotes boating safety, better boating laws, and improved boating facilities and equipment.

The club's main activities are centered around promoting boating popularity and safety. It provides public information through booklets, pamphlets, and safety posters. There are approximately 300 local boat clubs affiliated with the Outboard Boating Club. The main publication is *Outboard Boating*.

National Rifle Association of America
1600 Rhode Island Avenue, NW
Washington, D.C. 20036

The National Rifle Association is a private membership organization formed in 1871. It strives to educate people in the safe and efficient handling of firearms, foster the knowledge of and ability to use firearms, promote national defense, law, and order. It promotes hunting and scientific management of wildlife resources, good sportsmanship, and the conservation and wise use of renewable wildlife resources. In recent years it has become prominent as a lobbyist. It publishes *The American Rifleman, Tournament News, The Rifleman Newsletter, Uniform Hunter Casualty Report, The American Hunter,* and *The American Marksman.* Some activities include serving as governing body of the United States competitive shooting; nationwide hunter safety program; and certifying agent for marksmanship and firearms safety instructors, tournament referees, and training counselors.

American Camping Association
Bradford Woods
Martinsville, Indiana 46151

The American Camping Association is a voluntary association of camp owners and agencies who promote and improve camping through certification. The purposes are to establish standards and to maintain a standard of excellence in organized camping. Organized camping is a $2 billion industry in the United States.

The group publishes a monthly, *Camping Magazine.* Its activities are to act as the voice of camp leaders throughout the nation, stimulate high professional standards among camp leaders and camping agencies, and sponsor national and regional conferences for improving leadership and camping programs.

The National Campers and Hikers Association
7172 Transit Road
Buffalo, New York 14221

The National Campers and Hikers Association is a large participant organization that unites mostly trailer campers throughout the nation. Its highly sociable programs include rallies and winter meetings to promote camping and to bring people of like interests together. It has worked with state and national legislatures to seek laws to improve camping conditions and information.

Numerous other organizations affect outdoor recreation. A sampling of the remainder includes the Wildlife Management Institute, International Union on the Conservation of Nature, International Commission on National Parks, Midwest Open Land Association, Conservation Foundation, Bicycle Institute, World Wildlife Fund, National Campground Owner's Association, National Trust for Historic Preservation, and Resources for the Future. In addition, there are numerous industrial and business services, campground guidebooks, snowmobile trail guides and safety tips, and other similar information.

The provision of outdoor recreation resources and services involves interaction with innumerable organizations. The alert resource manager can find considerable goodwill and cooperation among these groups. It is probably inevitable that at some time conflicts will arise with one or more of the interests, but, more often than not, these organizations can help guide policy in a constructive manner.

Literature Cited

ORREN, KAREN. 1976. Standing to sue: interest group conflict in the federal courts. American Political Science Review 70(3):723–741.

ROUSH, G. JON. 1977. Why save diversity? The Nature Conservancy News 27(1): 9–12.

WHITESELL, DALE E. 1977. It's called habitat. Ducks Unlimited 41(5):13, 16.

CHAPTER 34

Future Leisure Environments

When Astronaut Neil Armstrong landed on the moon in 1969, he introduced outdoor recreation to the lunar environment. Soon after arrival, he went for a hike and did some jogging. Next, he wheeled out an off-road vehicle and rode off to do some rock collecting, orienteering, and nature study. Even golf has been tried on the moon.

Earthly recreation on the moon hints at the future importance of leisure-time activities. The nature of the future is the topic of this chapter.

A Look Ahead—From the Past

The toil and chore of life should, as labor-saving devices increase, form a diminishing proportion of the average day and year. Leisure and the higher pursuits will thereby come to form an increasing proportion of our lives.

But will leisure mean something "higher"? Here is a question indeed. The coming of leisure in itself will create its own problem. As the problem of labor "solves," that of leisure arises. There seems to be no escape from problems. We have neglected to improve the leisure which should be ours as a result of replacing stone and bronze with iron and steam. . . .

The customary approach to the problem of living relates to work rather than play. Can we increase the efficiency of our *working* time? Can we solve the problem of labor? If so, we can widen the opportunities for leisure. The new approach reverses this mental process. Can we increase the efficiency of our *spare* time?

—MacKaye (1921)

These thoughts about the future, published nearly six decades ago, still pose questions that must be answered today.

These are important questions for the resource manager to ponder. All land management work must look to the future as well as to the past and present. Changes in the work and subsistence environment produce changes in values and needs associated with leisure environments.

As leisure patterns change, there are new opportunities to serve the public. Development of the potential of individuals is increasingly related to leisure time. Self-satisfaction is more and more a result of skills and experiences developed in leisure time. Providing places and programs for human achievement is the fundamental goal of recreation resource administration.

A Glimpse of the Future of the Common Man?

In the summer of 1978, President Carter and his family took a vacation for two weeks. It epitomizes what is almost available to the common citizen, *sans* Secret Service, aides, and newsmen. He left the White House in a helicopter, changed to a jet that flew him home to Plains, Georgia. After a day or two of fishing, softball, and reading, he flew to Idaho, helicoptered

to a remote national forest outpost, jumped in a rubber raft, and spent four days on the Salmon River, a national wild river. Next, helicopter and jet whisked the group to the Grand Teton National Park for a week of fishing, horseback riding, relaxation, and shuttling back and forth to Yellowstone by air and auto. Then, a quick hop to the jetport, and the family was on its way back to Washington.

Personalized flying gadgets may soon make the short hops economical for many people. The long jet trips are already within occasional reach of perhaps half of the population. The two-week vacation is virtually a minimum for most workers. President Carter's trip was not unlike those taken by many skiers in the winter, with bus service to and from the jetport and movement from one lodge to another as part of the package trip. College students from the South and Midwest can hit the slopes in Colorado cheaply enough to make it a popular Christmas and spring break event. The future is here.

Notes of Warning

Forecasters come in two principal forms—doomsayers and eternal optimists. Both tend toward exaggeration to make a point. A look at both sides is a good start.

It is easy to foresee a bleak future. With growing population making increasing demands on a fixed resource base, many scientists and administrators believe the technology that has improved life will also save mankind from its own undoing, forever. Living day by day, happily expecting new inventions to put off crises, people reproduce and multiply their demands on the earth. A course charted between the inevitable doom and the eternal bliss of technology-hope seems a wise one. Answers are neither easy nor evident.

Control of the population increase and total numbers of people is a primary concern. Continued development of more efficient (not necessarily larger) means for utilizing and reusing resources is vital. Adjustment of the way of life of North Americans is underway. The United States has long used a disproportionate share of the world's production of goods and services. As that production goes up, other nations are increasing their proportions. The United States standard of living may not decrease drastically, but "bigger and better" may become a less important slogan.

Social conditions in small towns and the country are changing rapidly, but stay in balance. Urban living has taken some unpleasant turns, making the national life-style an ugly image. Suburbia has sprawled out over the countryside. In the cities, big guard dogs have replaced poodles and Pekingese as family pets. Handguns have replaced sporting rifles. Apartment houses feature 24-hour security guards and doormen.

Fragmented government has flourished, with some agencies designed to undo what others have done.

Positive Direction

There is hope, however. Business proceeds to meet the needs of people, and government makes occasional sounds about preventing excessive bigness in industry. In the recreation field, private enterprise responds efficiently to the desires of people to use the outdoors for recreation. Firms build facilities, offer lakes and forests for public use, and still manage to make some money.

Also, federal, state, and local governments are listening to the people. Public involvement in decisions about land uses have made the town meeting and "write your representative" common again. The quality of leisure has invaded presidential and councilmanic politics as a key issue. Parks and recreation budgets are of vibrant civic interest.

Water is cleaner than in the past 25 years. It should be cleaner yet within the next 5 to 10 years (Figure 34.1). Value systems that demand a clean and decent environment are prevailing slightly but persistently over those others that saw production at any cost as the goal.

The future for wilderness preservation and natural areas looks promising. With laws protecting such areas and more people enjoying them, the primary problem will be to control use levels so the wild character can be sustained. It is very likely that additions to the wilderness system have reached their peak in the Alaskan public interest lands settlement. Future additions of wilderness will come from arid national resource lands. In the future, lands managed for multiple uses, including backcountry recreation, will become increasingly popular among outdoor recreationists. With an active recreation program, the Bureau of Land Management's vast holdings will surely experience tremendous increases in popularity. A strong, active, action-oriented interpretive effort will be necessary to guide use and to encourage appreciation of these public lands.

Some of the most dramatic increases in recreation resources are likely to be in linear parks. Shorelines, rivers, and trails are in short supply, at least in terms of public accessibility. Much of the legal groundwork has been laid. Implementation has been difficult, primarily because of the need to acquire corridors through private lands either in full or through acquisition of partial rights. Unfamiliarity with the legal alternatives and their implications has been a major stumbling block to landowners and natural resource agencies. With time, these problems should be decreased and the methods will be used appropriately to allow public access along linear travel routes and to waterfronts. Rivers and trails will probably see a large expansion in the East because they are among the most cost-efficient means of providing major recreation opportunities with the least impact on the land base. Also, river valleys are the last vestiges of primitive conditions in much of the eastern part of the nation. They are of diminished value for residents and businesses, with floodplain insurance gone by the wayside. Therefore, they should be attractive recreation places (Figure 34.2).

FIGURE 34.1   The Potomac River has suffered chronic pollution and carries heavy sediment loads, but is gradually being cleaned up to restore its value as a recreational resource.

Americans may always be gadget-conscious, but a back-to-nature move, started in the 1960s by young people, promotes simple living (with some gadgets permitted). As those young people dominate the social structure in the next few years, their interest in less mechanization is likely to continue the current trend toward tent camping and backpacking. A balance between

FIGURE 34.2 River corridor recreation offers the visitor pleasant links with the natural world. Cleanup of the nation's waterways and provision of public access and rest facilities are tasks for the near future.

wheeled camping vehicles and ground tents will probably keep campground managers guessing as to the proper combination of sites. The back-to-nature group, with more education and environmental sensitivity, will require alert interpreters and facilities for hiking, horseback riding, nature study, and photography (Marcin and Lime, 1977).

Future Demand

All predictions suggest growing recreation participation. The fueling factors of recreation demand include growth in population, income, leisure time, and mobility (Clawson, 1974). There appears to be a steady, long-term increase in these social phenomena.

Population growth throughout the world is an alarming, perhaps dangerous, fact. For the near future, at least, it will continue to put pressure on recreation resources. In the United States, even if couples limit themselves to two children, there will be sustained growth of the population for another 20 to 40 years.

Income levels are rising in real terms in North America and in most of the world. That enables increasing proportions of the population to meet subsistence needs and to spend for recreation.

Leisure time is a reality throughout the world. Free time from industrial employment approaches that available to primitive man. Use of leisure is of concern to philosophers and to society as a whole. One major use is for constructive outdoor recreation.

Mobility may continue to be one of the most influential factors affecting the use of natural resources for recreation. The automobile booms after both World Wars revolutionized land use and management. The interstate highway system, near completion, helps families to travel easily and cheaply across the nation. In 1978, people took to the airways in record numbers, with a 20 per cent increase in passengers over the year before, apparently as a result of air fare price competition.

The middle-income recreationist can and will spend a weekend in any park, forest, or refuge of his choice by taking a night flight on Friday and returning Sunday or even on a flex-time Monday. One-week vacations are no longer limited to trips to nearby state parks but may involve a quick tour of Alaska, Mexican beaches, or the Rockies.

As jet vacations increase, there may be interesting pressures for particular recreation facilities. Uniformity, dependability, and comfort in parks will surely be the demand of many. Will the highly mobile recreationists carry backpacks with them into the real backcountry, or will they carry portable cocktail kits that turn motel rooms everyplace into anywhere? Both types are now traveling; which will be accommodated by whom and where? The answers are in the defined roles of the supply agencies.

The Cities as Leisure Environments

If we are serious about conserving both our central cities and our energy resources, then we have to start focusing on recreational facilities, both neighborhood and regional, in our central cities. We must make it a national priority to provide recreational opportunities at home, rather than forcing people to use scarce energy to drive 200 miles to Mt. Rainier.

Wes Uhlman, Mayor of Seattle, in a letter
commenting on the Seattle/Everett/Tacoma
Urban Recreation Study in 1977

The majority of recreation is sought close to home, after work and on one-day outings. Local parks, trails, and waterfronts are the key to providing these local opportunities. The local governments are on the spot. Most have provided weak leadership and financial management. They have surrendered many of their powers and prerogatives to state and federal governments. Through Revenue Sharing, the Land and Water Conservation Fund, and Community Development Block Grants, some initiative has been returned to the local scene. Although the tax collection and basic eligibility requirements are handled by federal agencies, the local government chooses among alternative ways to spend the money. Perhaps, someday there will be a swing back toward more local tax collection and locally initiated programs. The trend in the United States and through the world has not been in the direction of decentralization, however.

The future of cities may be in considerable doubt. Urban planners keep trying to make order out of chaotic conditions. City planning has been going on for some time. Paris, Washington, D.C., Chicago, and Brasilia are among the many planned cities of modern times. All contain beautiful parks and other open space. The Chicago plan originated with the World's Columbian Exposition of 1893, with its public buildings and grounds. Parks and a beautiful environment were important parts of the plan. Burnham and Bennett (1909) made a case for parks in cities that is as relevant now as in 1909:

In establishing a complete park and parkway system, the life of the wage-earner and of his family is made healthier and pleasanter, while the greater attractiveness thus produced keeps at home the people of means and taste, and acts as a magnet to draw those who seek to live amid pleasing surroundings. The very beauty that attracts him who has money makes pleasant the life of those among whom he lives, while anchoring him and his wealth to the city.

Le Corbusier (1929), in his explanation of a 1922 plan for an ideal contemporary city for three million inhabitants, declared that "the whole city is a Park." Even though he was a proponent of efficient internal transport over rectilinear arteries with elevated, fast highways among skyscrapers, he insisted that sunlight reach the ground. Setbacks in residential and commercial areas allow architectural perspectives, gardens, game and sport grounds, terraced roofs, lawns, and groves of trees that play against the massive blocks of buildings. Wavering lines of rivers, patches of forest, and a great park would be parts of the city, not foreign elements on the edge of it. Trees are important to his scheme, because they bring human scale to the cityscape. A tree offers comfort. Le Corbusier calls a tree a caress amid our severe creations. Thus, the architect who is renowned and sometimes cursed for the glass skyscraper of stark simplicity actually saw the city as a park full of light, trees, water, and beautiful perspectives.

Rose (1976) held this idea out as a goal for park and recreation administrators when he called for an attitude of living related to leisure. "When parks are a part of our neighborhoods so that we actually live within parks, then we will truly be in the park business."

Perhaps the idea is a false hope. When Chicago became a city, it adopted the motto *urbs in horto*, a city in a garden, to describe its lakefront and the flowering prairie on three sides of the young community. Soon, however, the "urbs" took over the "horto" with hastily built homes and expanding industry. A city that had once virtually lived within nature found itself searching for patches of ground where something green could grow in some profusion to provide relief from the walls of the city. The results in Chicago are some beautiful lakefront parks of unusual significance, long bands of natural forest preserves winding through the outer parts of the city, and a scattering of large and small park blocks through the neighborhoods. Burnham and Bennett (1909) expressed the philosophy:

He who habitually comes in close contact with nature develops saner methods of thought than can be the case when one is habitually shut up within the walls of a city.

Urban areas can be disliked but no longer ignored. The destiny of the cities is the destiny of the nation. Parks and recreation professionals have often been like foresters—happy to sit in their refuges from the city traffic and noise, enjoying the trees, ducks, and usually friendly visitors, leading the activities they were taught in the white state universities, vaguely wishing they could have enough money to do something for the poor and culturally disoriented people down in the slums.

It is simple political reality that the cities—even the inner cities—should become the concern of those who provide outdoor recreation spaces and programs. There can be no throwaway people in a nation that truly values democracy. The city needs those who understand nature, can see a vision of how to sensibly improve cities, and give themselves to the vision (Montgomery and Popovich, 1974). It is a mission of the parks and recreation professional, including foresters and wildlife experts, to help the city become a more hospitable habitat for people (Myers and Kerr, 1974). At the same time, they can make the country parks more accessible to the city residents.

Recreation for Health

Preventive medicine is likely to become a major responsibility of recreation programming. The *parcourse* trails installed in American parks since 1973 provide stimuli to run and exercise. They use park resources very effectively. In a nation that spends $180 to $200 billion per year on curative personal health, there has been virtually no strategy for preventive medicine or the promotion of health. Sports, educational, and recreation interests have taken the initiative from the health professions in promoting personal health and vigor. Life insurance companies have been major sponsors of preventive medicine and health programs.

Exercise trails, fitness programs, running programs, and many other activities are expected to increase steadily in the near and distant future. Resource managers can safely plan to add trails and exercise facilities for active recreation, as local desires are receptive. Recreation professionals will be asked to take a leadership role in developing facilities and programs for preventive medicine activities.

Risk Recreation

Risk recreation, or high-intensity recreation, has become popular through several private adventure programs. Outward Bound and other challenge programs offer courses for young adults that include rock climbing, canoeing in white water, sailing, backpacking, Nordic skiing, winter camping, and survival hikes. The idea is to go into nature under primitive conditions, risking life and limb in hope of learning something about oneself, about resourcefulness, and about personal reaction to fear and privation. Through these programs, thousands of people each year are discovering the satisfaction of personal success without technology. They also learn about natural processes first-hand and develop an appreciation for keeping a diversity of environments in a primitive state. More appreciative visitors help promote more manageable recreation environments.

Natural Areas

A small porportion of the nation's forests, ranges, and wetlands should be preserved in natural conditions for purposes of scientific reference, gene pool retention, education, public appreciation, and nature study.

The responsibility for such preservation has been accepted by federal, state, and some local governments, some forest industries, private organizations, and individuals. Such areas are designated as wilderness or primitive areas, scenic and scientific reserves, nature preserves, and scenic rivers.

There may always be controversy about preserving natural qualities. John Muir (1912) stated a basic truth when he wrote about the plan to dam Hetch Hetchy Valley:

That anyone would try to destroy such a place seems incredible; but sad experience shows that there are people good enough and bad enough for anything. The proponents of the dam scheme bring forward a lot of bad arguments to prove that the only righteous thing to do with the people's parks is to destroy them bit by bit as they are able.

Preservation of natural areas is part of offering a diverse recreational environment. The case for diversity in outdoor recreation opportunities was expressed well by Jay H. Cravens:

We are not aware, certainly, of all the relationships—or even all the species—which exist in the natural world . . .

During brief moments, inspiration may visit a diligent curiosity: and out of that momentary vision, we construct endless systems to accommodate the homeless and the hungry, the impoverished and the uneducated; we create cities to precise specifications and measure the values inherent in our environment by computer code. But no sooner does the system emerge than the man for whom it was designed disappears.

Yet we continue, somehow persuaded that time alone will produce a workable system. We continue, failing for all our energy and expertise to realize that the system is the individual—changeable, unpredictable, but the system, nonetheless. And to build for anything more or less is, finally, not to build at all.

Only slowly are we learning the real value of alternatives.

Leisure Phenomena Forecast

Among the approaches to forecasting recreation phenomena, statistical projections are most useful for short-term projections. After five years, they are of mostly academic interest, because knowledge of basic causal factors is very limited and innovations will arise to change use or management. Yet, there is need to make facility investment decisions for 20 to 30 years.

Forecasts are needed that consider judgment of future breakthroughs and interactions. They can be assessed only by intuition. Because intuition is unavoidable, a Forest Service study of the future (Shafer, Moeller, and Getty, 1974) sought to systematize the use of intuition. The study used the Delphi technique. That involves the use of the personal insights of a number of informed individuals. The panel of experts does not directly interact with each other. A series of questionnaires is sent to each individual to respond separately. Successive questionnaires include feedback from previous responses, including reasoning to stimulate thinking. The process avoids the debate, pressures, and conformity of committee work, each person thinking and responding independently, but not out of touch.

In the Forest Service study, there were four rounds of responses and summaries. There were 405 experts who participated in all levels. There were 904 initially enlisted.

In general, the panel's view of the short-term future was fairly conservative. Extensions or expansions of existing phenomena were foreseen, but almost no real innovations or changes in direction were predicted. That is remarkable, considering the rapid and drastic changes in technology and social phenomena in the recent decades. The experts did not foresee a controlled, programmed population but one with more freedom of choice. However, some controls within a recreation area might be necessary to maintain the environment.

When the panel was asked to predict beyond the turn of the century, it produced some interesting ideas; many may become reality earlier than that. A few of the more interesting predictions are described.

The only real space-age prediction was that sometime after 2050 the first park will be in operation on the moon. Even before the movie *Star Wars* came out, the panel predicted that laser beams might someday replace bullets in hunting weapons.

A four-day, 34-hour week was predicted for 1985. By 2000, weekends will be distributed throughout the week. That will increase the effective supply of recreation facilities, but will also require careful attention to carrying capacities. Retirement age may average 50 years, with people living to age 100 and starting work at age 25. Leisure will thus dominate life after 2050. Sometime after 2050, people will have an average annual vacation of three months, the panel estimated.

By 2000, weekend travel will commonly cover 500 miles, one-way. Other continents will be common vacation destinations for middle-class Americans.

Leisure Counseling

Information and education efforts will be expanded to improve the quality of recreation experiences. Computers will be used to advise recreationists where to go for recreation activities (already started in leisure counseling). By 1985, industries will offer leisure consulting services for their employees (some do it now).

Industrial recreation for employees may become a matter of public concern. The panel foresaw tax incentives for corporations that include employee recreation facilities in new plants, by 2000.

Recreation real estate will continue to be an important growth market, with most middle-income families owning their own vacation homes by 2030.

Recreation Transportation

By 2000, travel systems in public recreation environments will have minimum physical and visual impacts (Figure 34.3); they will have nonpolluting propulsion systems; most popular recreation areas will be serviced by air. Foot travel may be the only form of transportation allowed within major parks. Technology will create new recreation opportunities and new equipment that will challenge managerial expertise.

The panel of predictors expected that new recreation equipment in common use by 2050 would include hovercraft, jet-powered backpacks, and one-man helicopters. Small, private submarines are expected by the turn of the century.

Urban Recreation

By 2000, the urban area should be attractive and livable, with leisure-use spaces becoming abundant. Pollution from transportation devices will be under control.

Where use is heavy, artificial turf and all-weather bubbles will handle

FIGURE 34.3 Collective transportation has reduced traffic congestion in many recreation areas. (Yosemite Park and Curry Co.)

recreation pressures. By 2020, outdoor recreation areas in the cities will be adequate to keep the majority of residents from having to leave the city for wholesome fun. Overnight camping within the city will be available.

Living structures will be designed to provide safe playgrounds, fields, and miniparks at the foot of every building (Brasilia was designed this way in 1955).

By 2050, it is estimated that 90 per cent of Americans will be living in cities. After 2050, self-contained floating cities and underwater communities will handle new growth.

Management of Recreation Areas

Most panelists believed that the following would *never* occur:

User fees set to cover all costs of providing recreation on public lands.
Only daytime use allowed in public areas.
All rural lands open to public recreation use, regardless of ownership.

However, they believed that, by 2050, robots will assist the manager in park maintenance and public information programs (tape-recorded messages already do much of this work).

Maximum carrying capacities will be assigned to public recreation areas, and use will be kept below capacity levels. Controls on the use of wilderness and remote areas will be widespread to preserve solitude. By 2000, there may be permits for most wilderness users, accompanied by certification of their knowledge and skill of wilderness use.

The last wilderness area, as now understood, will be designated by 2050, and withdrawal of land from wilderness will start. Intensive use and management of wilderness and wildlife will be common in the early twenty-first century.

Dwindling open spaces will require construction of recreation islands. This could provide lucrative opportunities for private enterprise. There may be self-contained underwater resorts, by 2050. Rivers will be constructed for recreation (perhaps along the lines of the whitewater canoe racecourse at the Munich Olympics of 1972).

These are among the prognostications of one large group of experts from various fields related to natural resources management. Will they come true? There seems little doubt that most of these are already on the way. Their exact form and importance will be shaped by events and experience. It seems clear that the importance of outdoor recreation will be greater in the future, whatever its exact form. We are not moving toward a totally indoor civilization without direct contact with nature.

FIGURE 34.4 Public interest in the forest environment is likely to continue to alter approaches to intensive timber management. (USFS)

Professional Futures

People trained in natural resources and recreation education are already working closely together. Their cooperation is important for the future.

Specialization has been the route to efficiency in the United States and probably will continue to be so. Comprehensive understanding of the whole recreation service system is needed by all workers in the field.

Wildlife area managers will find themselves increasingly in the people-serving business.

Timber managers can expect continuing public influence on and review of the methods they use, even on industrial lands (Figure 34.4). Mismanagement of farm woodlots will become a major issue that will require the intensive care of foresters.

FIGURE 34.5 The Ranger's work is always fun. (NPS)

Foresters who deal with the multiple uses of land will be better-rounded, using advanced techniques of management for water, wildlife, timber, and grazing, as well as recreation. Clawson (1978) predicted that "there will be vastly less emphasis on the trees and vastly more emphasis on relationships with people . . ." (Figure 34.5). The use-blending process will be more intensive, requiring the truly coordinated work of several professions.

Recreation resource specialists from forestry, wildlife, and interdisciplinary backgrounds will gradually take over management of most state parks, many county and city park systems, and the federal park system. Wildlife refuges and public forests will increasingly employ recreation resource specialists. The work of these people will be primarily in natural resource interpretation, resource planning, and resource management at the property and system levels.

Recreation program specialists will continue to be vital in urban and volunteer agency work, but their influence should also expand in county and state systems. The blending of program and resource management talents, along with carefully integrated design specialists, gives the park and recreation profession a necessary broad base and interdisciplinary nature.

To serve the complex diversity of human needs through outdoor leisure environments, many talents will have to work together. The challenge is exciting and enormous. The outcome will mold civilization. May God bless our efforts.

Literature Cited

Burnham, Daniel H. and Edward H. Bennett. 1909. Plan of Chicago. Chicago: Commercial Club. 164 pp.

Clawson, Marion. 1974. Park visits in the coming decades: problems and opportunities. In: Sir Hugh Elliott (ed.), Second World Conference on National Parks. Morges, Switzerland: International Union for Conservation of Nature and Natural Resources, pp. 116–126.

Clawson, Marion. 1978. What's ahead for the Forest Service? American Forests 84(1):16–19, 49–50.

Cravens, Jay H. (n.d.). . . . a Little Rebellion, Now and Then. Milwaukee: Eastern Region, U.S. Forest Service. 32 pp.

Le Corbusier. 1929. The City of Tomorrow and its Planning. New York: Payson and Clarke.

MacKaye, Benton. 1921. An Appalachian trail. AIA Journal 9(10):325–330.

Marcin, Thomas C. and David W. Lime. 1977. Our changing population structure: what will it mean for future outdoor recreation use? In: Outdoor Recreation; Advances in Application of Economics. Washington, D.C.: U.S. Forest Service, General Technical Report WO-2. pp. 42–53.

Montgomery, K. and L. Popovich. 1974. Forestry in the city—a convention postscript. Journal of Forestry 72(12):776–779.

Muir, John. 1912. Yosemite. Garden City, N.Y.: Doubleday.

Myers, J. Walter, Jr. and Ed Kerr. 1974. Put recreation where the people are. Journal of Forestry 72(7):411–413.

Rose, Larry L. 1976. People and urban parks. In: D. M. Knudson, (ed.). Managing Recreation Resources for Century III. West Lafayette, In.: Purdue University. p. 49.

Shafer, Elwood L., George H. Moeller and Russell E. Getty. 1974. Future Leisure Environments. Upper Darby, Pa.: U.S. Forest Service Research Paper NE-301. 16 pp.

Federal Laws Related to Outdoor Recreation

This list includes only federal laws basic to recreation resource management. Most have amendments or modifiers which name properties and interpret the basic policy. These are thought to be key acts in this field. There is no attempt here to cover *all* laws that pertain to the agencies and policies. Examination of the U.S. Code will provide a comprehensive view of current laws and amendments.

Each law is identified by name, date of passage, its Public Law number or chapter number, reference to *U.S. Statutes at Large,* and reference to the *U.S. Code.* Some names are in parenthesis to indicate that they are the unofficial but commonly used names for the acts. Initials of the agencies most affected follow appropriate citations.

Public Law numbers are used for acts passed after 1956. Through 1956, laws were formally designated by chapter numbers (e.g., ch. 263). Starting with the 85th Congress, each law was listed by the number of the Congress and the chronological number of the law's approval by the President (e.g., P.L. 84–5).

Students of law and policy can keep posted on recent legislative activity through various government documents and Congressional Quarterly newsletters.

(Bureau of Outdoor Recreation Organic Act)		1963
P. L. 88–29	77 Stat. 49	HCRS
16 U.S.C. 460 L		
Land and Water Conservation Fund Act		1965
P. L. 88–578	78 Stat. 892	HCRS
16 U.S.C. 4601–8		
National Historic Preservation Fund (Title II of Land and Water Conservation Fund Act Amendments)		1976
P. L. 94–422	90 Stat. 1319	HCRS
16 U.S.C. 470		
Housing and Community Development Act		1974
P. L. 93–383	88 Stat. 647	HUD
42 U.S.C. 5307		

Yellowstone National Park Act ch. 24 16 U.S.C. 21	17 Stat. 32	1897 NPS

Yellowstone National Park Act
   ch. 24   17 Stat. 32   1897
   16 U.S.C. 21   NPS

(Antiquities Act)
   ch. 3060   34 Stat. 225   1906
   16 U.S.C. 431 et seq.   NPS

National Park Service Act
   ch. 408   39 Stat. 535   1916
   16 U.S.C. 1   NPS

Historic Sites Act
   ch. 593   49 Stat. 666   1935
   16 U.S.C. 461 et seq.   NPS

National Historic Preservation Act
   P. L. 89–665   80 Stat. 915   1966
   16 U.S.C. 470a   NPS

Golden Gate National Recreation Area Act
   P. L. 92–589   86 Stat. 1299   1972
   16 U.S.C. 460   NPS

(Lacey Act)
   ch. 553   31 Stat. 187   1900
   16 U.S.C. 701; 18 U.S.C. 41 et seq.   FWS

Migratory Bird Conservation Act
   ch. 257   45 Stat. 1222   1929
   16 U.S.C. 715   FWS

Migratory Bird Hunting Stamp Act
   ch. 71   48 Stat. 452   1934
   16 U.S.C. 718–718h   FWS

Federal Aid to Wildlife Restoration Act (Pittman-Robertson Act)   1937
   ch. 899   50 Stat. 217   FWS
   16 U.S.C. 669

Fish Restoration and Management Projects Act   1950
(Dingell-Johnson Act)   FWS
   ch. 658   64 Stat. 430
   16 U.S.C. 777

Fish and Wildlife Act (Fish and Wildlife Service Establishment)   1956
   ch. 1036   70 Stat. 1119   FWS
   16 U.S.C. 742–742j

Refuge Recreation Act
   P. L. 87–714   76 Stat. 653   1962
   16 U.S.C. 460 k-1   FWS

National Wildlife Refuge System Administration Act
(Organic Act)   1966
   P. L. 93–205   87 Stat. 902   FWS
   16 U.S.C. 668dd

O & C Sustained Yield Forestry Act		1937
ch. 876 (P. L. 405 of	50 Stat. 874	BLM
75th Congress)		
43 U.S.C. 1181 et seq.		
Federal Property and Administrative Services Act		1954
(Surplus Property Act) (first passed 1926)		BLM
ch. 263 (P. L. 387)	68 Stat. 173	
43 U.S.C. 869 (Also see: 44 Stat. 741—1926 version and		
80 Stat. 210—1966 amendments.)		
Federal Land Policy and Management Act (BLM Organic Act)		1976
P. L. 94–579	90 Stat. 2743	BLM
(Codification scattered)		
Forest Reserve Act (Creative Act of National Forests)		1891
ch. 561	26 Stat. 1103	USFS
16 U.S.C. 471		
(Organic Administration Act—National Forests)		1897
ch. 2	30 Stat. 34–36	USFS
16 U.S.C. 473–478		
(Weeks Law)		1911
ch. 186	36 Stat. 961	USFS
16 U.S.C. 480 et seq.		
Multiple Use-Sustained Yield Act		1960
P. L. 86–517	74 Stat. 216	USFS
16 U.S.C. 528 et seq.		
Forest and Rangeland Renewable Resources Planning Act		1974
P. L. 93–378	88 Stat. 476	USFS
16 U.S.C. 1600 et seq.		
National Forest Management Act		1976
P. L. 94–588	90 Stat. 2949	USFS
16 U.S.C. 1600 (and scattered)		
(Eastern Wilderness Act)		1975
P. L. 93–622	88 Stat. 2096	USFS
16 U.S.C. 1132		
Watershed Protection and Flood Prevention Act		1954
(Small Watershed Act—P. L. 566)		SCS
ch. 656	68 Stat. 666	
16 U.S.C. 1001–1007		
Federal Water Projects Recreation Act		1965
P. L. 89–72	79 Stat. 213	COE,
16 U.S.C. 460 1–12 et seq.		B. Recl.
Federal Water Pollution Control Act Amendments		1972
P. L. 92–500	86 Stat. 816	
33 U.S.C. 1251		
Coastal Zone Management Act		1972
P. L. 92–583	86 Stat. 1280	
16 U.S.C. 1451 (1972)		

U.S. Mining Act   1872
   ch. 152   17 Stat. 91
   30 U.S.C. 22–47 (related laws scattered in 16, 30, 43 USC)

Wilderness Act   1964
   P. L. 88–577   78 Stat. 890
   16 U.S.C. 1131 et seq.

National Trails System Act   1968
   P. L. 90–543   82 Stat. 919
   16 U.S.C. 1241 et seq.

Wild and Scenic Rivers Act   1968
   P. L. 90–542   82 Stat. 906
   16 U.S.C. 1271 et seq.

National Environmental Policy Act   1969
   P. L. 91–190   83 Stat. 852
   42 U.S.C. 4321–4347

Environmental Education Act   1970
   P. L. 91–516   84 Stat. 1312
   20 U.S.C. 1531

Alaska Native Claims Settlement Act   1971
   P. L. 92–203   85 Stat. 688
   43 U.S.C. 1601

Endangered Species Act   1973
   P. L. 93–205   87 Stat. 903
   16 U.S.C. 1531–1543

Public Lands—Local Government Funds Act or
"Payment in Lieu of Taxes" Act   1976
   P. L. 94–579   90 Stat. 2744   USFS,
   43 U.S.C. 1701   BLM

Major Federal and State Agencies Administering Recreational Resources

Department of the Army

ARMY CORPS OF ENGINEERS
Office of the Chief of Engineers
Forrestal Building
Washington, DC 20314
  Divisions:
  Lower Mississippi Valley: P.O. Box 80, Vicksburg, MS 39180
  Missouri River: P.O. Box 103, Downtown Station, Omaha, NE 68101
  New England: 424 Trapelo Rd., Waltham, MA 02154
  North Atlantic: 90 Church St., New York, NY 10007
  North Central: 536 S. Clark St., Chicago, IL 60605
  North Pacific: 220 N.W. 8th Ave., Portland, OR 97209
  Ohio River: P.O. Box 1159, Cincinnati, OH 45201
  Pacific Ocean: Bldg. 230, Fort Shafter, HI, APO San Francisco 96558
  South Atlantic: 510 Title Building, Atlanta, GA 30303
  South Pacific: 630 Sansome St., San Francisco, CA 94111
  Southwestern: Main Tower Building, 1200 Main St., Dallas TX 75202

Department of the Interior

BUREAU OF INDIAN AFFAIRS
Office of the Director
1951 Constitution Avenue, N.W.
Washington, DC 20245
  Trust responsibility of the United States to Indian tribes, including the protection and enhancement of Indian lands and natural resources through technical assistance in the fields of forest management, water rights, range management, irrigation, soil and moisture conservation and management and mineral resource management.

BUREAU OF LAND MANAGEMENT
Office of the Director
U.S. Department of the Interior
Washington, DC 20240

Administers the public lands, which are located primarily in the western states and which amount to about 60 per cent of all federally owned lands, under multiple-use principles for outdoor recreation, fish and wildlife production, livestock grazing, timber, industrial development, watershed protection, and mineral production including that on the Outer Continental Shelf.

> Denver Service Center (Serves AZ, CO, MT, NM, UT, WY, ID, NV): Denver Federal Center, Building 50, Denver, CO 80225

State Directors:
AK: 555 Cordova St., Anchorage 99501
AZ: 2400 Valley Bank Center, Phoenix 85073
CA: Federal Office Building, Room E-2841, 2800 Cottage Way, Sacramento 95825
CO: Room 700, Colorado State Bank Building, 1600 Broadway, Denver 80202
ID: 398 Federal Building, 550 W. Fort St., Boise 83724
MT: Federal Building, 222 N. 32nd St., P.O. Box 30157, Billings 59107
NV: Federal Building, Room 3008, 300 Booth St., Reno 89502
NM: Federal Building, South Federal Place, Santa Fe 87501
OR and WA: 729 N.E. Oregon St., P.O. Box 2965, Portland, OR 97208
UT: Federal Building, 125 S. State, P.O. Box 11505, Salt Lake City 84147
WY: Joseph C. O'Mahoney Federal Center, Cheyenne 82001
Eastern States Office: Director, 7981 Eastern Ave., Silver Spring, MD 20910

HERITAGE CONSERVATION AND RECREATION SERVICE
Office of the Director
U.S. Department of the Interior
Washington, DC 20240

Administers Land and Water Conservation Fund; evaluates surplus federal real property for recreation use conveyance to State and local governments; is federal focal point for outdoor recreation research, technical assistance, and program coordination; assists with environmental impact statements; coordinates nationwide and state recreation planning.

Regional Offices:
Northeast: Federal Office Building, Room 9310, 600 Arch St., Philadelphia, PA 19106

Southeast: 148 International Boulevard, Atlanta, GA 30303

Lake Central: Federal Building, Ann Arbor, MI 48107

Midcontinent: Building 41, P.O. Box 25387, Denver Federal Center, Denver, CO 80225

Northwest: 915 Second Ave., Seattle, WA 98174

Pacific Southwest: 450 Golden Gate Ave., San Francisco, CA 94102

South Central: 5000 Marble Ave., N.E., Albuquerque, NM 87110

Alaska Area Office: 540 West Fifth Ave., Room 201, Anchorage, AK 99501

BUREAU OF RECLAMATION

U.S. Department of the Interior

Washington, DC 20240

Supervises western states water resource development and use to provide fish and wildlife protection and recreational opportunities; water for farm irrigation, municipal, and industrial use; hydroelectric power; flood control; and other conservation benefits.

Regional Offices:

Pacific Northwest Region: P.O. Box 043, U.S. Court House, 550 W. Fort St., Boise, ID 83724

Mid-Pacific Region: 2800 Cottage Way, Sacramento, CA 95825

Lower Colorado Region: P.O. Box 427, Boulder City, NV 89005

Upper Colorado Region: P.O. Box 11568, Salt Lake City, UT 84111

Southwest Region: Herring Plaza, Box H-4377, Amarillo, TX 79101

Upper Missouri Region: P.O. Box 2553, Billings, MT 59103

Lower Missouri Region: Building 20, Denver Federal Center, Denver, CO 80225

UNITED STATES FISH AND WILDLIFE SERVICE

Office of the Director

U.S. Department of the Interior

Washington, DC 20240

Administers national wildlife refuges and migratory animals.

Regional Offices:

Pacific Region (HI, CA, ID, NV, OR, WA): 1500 Plaza Building, 1500 N.E. Irving St., Portland, OR 97208

Southwest Region (AZ, NM, OK, TX): Federal Building, U.S. Post Office and Court House, 500 Gold Ave., S.W., Albuquerque, NM 87103

North Central Region (IL, IN, MI, MN, OH, WI): Federal Building, Fort Snelling, Twin Cities, MN 55111

Southeast Region (AL, AR, FL, KY, LA, MS, NC, SC, TN): 17 Executive Park Dr., Atlanta, GA 30329

Northeast Region (CT, DE, ME, MD, NH, NJ, NY, PA, RI, VT,

VA, WV): McCormack Post Office and Courthouse, Boston, MA
02109

Alaska Area (AK): 813 D St., Anchorage, AK 99501

Denver Region (CO, IA, KS, MO, MT, NB, ND, SD, UT, WY):
10597 Sixth St., Denver, CO 80225

NATIONAL PARK SERVICE

Office of the Director

Interior Building

18th and C Streets, N.W.

Washington, DC 20240

Regional Offices:

North Atlantic Region: 15 State Street, Boston, MA 02109 (ME, NH,
VT, MA, RI, CT, NY, NJ)

Mid-Atlantic Region: 143 South Third Street, Philadelphia, PA 19106
(PA, MD, WV, DE, VA)

National Capital Region: 1100 Ohio Dr., S.W., Washington, DC 20242
(Metropolitan Washington, DC, including nearby MD, VA, WV)

Rocky Mountain Region: 655 Parfet St., P.O. Box 25287, Denver,
CO 80225 (MT, ND, SD, WY, UT, CO)

Western Region: 450 Golden Gate Ave., Box 36063, San Francisco,
CA 94102 (AZ, CA, NV, HI)

Southwest Region: P.O. Box 728, Santa Fe, NM 87501 (AR, LA, NM,
OK, TX)

Southeast Region: 1895 Phoenix Blvd., Atlanta, GA 30349 (AL, FL,
GA, KY, MS, NC, SC, TN, Puerto Rico, Virgin Islands)

Midwest Region: 1709 Jackson St., Omaha, NB 68102 (OH, IN, MI,
WI, IL, MN, IA, MO, NB, KS)

Pacific Northwest Region: 601 Fourth and Pike Building, Seattle, WA
98101 (AK, ID, OR, WA)

Denver Service Center: (See Rocky Mountain Region)

Harpers Ferry Center: National Park Service, Harpers Ferry, WV 25425

Department of Agriculture

FOREST SERVICE

U.S. Department of Agriculture

Washington, DC 20250

Administers national forests and national grasslands; cooperates with
the state and private owners in the application of sound forest management
practices, in protection of forest lands against fire, and in the distribution
of planting stock; conducts research in forestry and wild land management.

Regional Foresters:

Region 1, Northern: Federal Building, Missoula, MT 59807

Region 2, Rocky Mountain: 11177 W. Eighth Ave., Box 25127, Lakewood, CO 80225

Region 3, Southwestern: Federal Building, 517 Gold Ave., S.W., Albuquerque, NM 87102

Region 4, Intermountain: Federal Office Building, 324 25th St., Ogden, UT 84401

Region 5, California: 630 Sansome St., San Francisco, CA 94111

Region 6, Pacific Northwest: 319 S. W. Pine St., Box 3623, Portland, OR 97208

Region 8, Southern: Suite 800, 1720 Peachtree Rd., N.W., Atlanta, GA 30309

Region 9, Eastern: Clark Building, 633 W. Wisconsin Ave., Milwaukee, WI 53203

Region 10, Alaska: Federal Office Building, Box 1628, Juneau 99801

Forest and Range Experiment Stations:

Intermountain: 507 25th St., Ogden, UT 84401

North Central: Folwell Ave., St. Paul, MN 55108

Northeastern: 370 Reed Rd., Broomall, PA 19008

Pacific Northwest: 809 NE Sixth Ave., Portland, OR 97232

Pacific Southwest: 1960 Addison St., Box 245, Berkeley, CA 94701

Rocky Mountain: Foothills Campus, Ft. Collins, CO 80521

Southeastern: Post Office Building, Box 2570, Asheville, NC 28802

Southern: T-10210 Federal Building, 701 Loyola Ave., New Orleans, LA 70113

Forest Products Laboratory: P.O. Box 5130, N. Walnut St., Madison WI 53705

Institute of Tropical Forestry: University of Puerto Rico, Rio Piedras, PR 00928

Independent Agency

TENNESSEE VALLEY AUTHORITY
400 Commerce Avenue
Knoxville, TN 37902

Develops the natural resources of the Tennessee Valley region for flood control, navigation, power production, fish and wildlife development, outdoor recreation, water and air pollution control, and reservoir ecology. Land Between the Lakes is a major demonstration project for outdoor recreation, environmental education, and wildlife.

Director, Forestry, Fisheries, and Wildlife Development: Norris, TN 37828

Chief, Recreation Resources Branch: Norris, TN 37828
Manager, Land Between the Lakes Project: Golden Pond, KY 42231

State Agencies

These are state natural resources agencies with major recreation responsibilities.

ALABAMA
Department of Conservation and Natural Resources, 64 N. Union St., Montgomery 36109
Forestry Commission, 513 Madison Ave., Montgomery 36130

ALASKA
Department of Fish and Game, Subport Building, Juneau 99801
Department of Natural Resources, Juneau 99811

ARIZONA
Game and Fish Department, 2222 W. Greenway, Phoenix 85023
Land Department, 1624 W. Adams, Phoenix 85007

ARKANSAS
Game and Fish Commission, Little Rock 72201
Department of Parks and Tourism, Little Rock 72201
Natural Heritage Commission, Suite 500, Continental Building, Little Rock 72201
Forestry Commission, 3821 W. Roosevelt, Little Rock 72204

CALIFORNIA
The Resources Agency, 1416 Ninth St., Sacramento 95814
Department of Fish and Game
Department of Forestry
Department of Parks and Recreation

COLORADO
Division of Parks and Outdoor Recreation, 1313 Sherman, Denver 80203
Division of Wildlife, 6060 Broadway, Denver 80216
State Forest Service, Colorado State University, Ft. Collins 80523

CONNECTICUT
Department of Environmental Protection, 165 Capitol Ave., Hartford 06115

DELAWARE
Department of Natural Resources and Environmental Control, William Penn St., Dover 19901

FLORIDA

Department of Natural Resources, 202 Blount St., Tallahassee 32304

Game and Fresh Water Fish Commission, 620 S. Meridian, Tallahassee 32304

Forestry Division, State Capitol, Tallahassee 32304

GEORGIA

Department of Natural Resources, 270 Washington St., Atlanta 30334

HAWAII

Department of Land and Natural Resources, Box 621, Honolulu 96809

IDAHO

Fish and Game Department, 600 Walnut St., Boise 83707

Department of Parks and Recreation, Statehouse, Boise 83720

ILLINOIS

Department of Conservation, 605 State Office Building, Springfield 62706

INDIANA

Department of Natural Resources, 608 State Office Building, Indianapolis 46204

IOWA

State Conservation Commission, State Office Building, Des Moines 50319

KANSAS

Forestry, Fish and Game Commission, Box 1028, Pratt 67124

State Parks and Resources Authority, 503 Kansas Ave., Topeka 66601

KENTUCKY

Department of Fish and Wildlife Resources, Capitol Plaza Tower, Frankfort 40601

Department of Natural Resources and Environmental Protection, 5th Floor, Capitol Plaza Tower, Frankfort 40601

LOUISIANA

Wildlife and Fisheries Department, 400 Royal St., New Orleans 70130

State Parks and Recreation Commission, Baton Rouge 70821

MAINE

Department of Conservation, State Office Building, Augusta 04333

Department of Inland Fisheries and Wildlife, 284 State St., Augusta 04333

MARYLAND
Department of Natural Resources, State Office Building, Annapolis 21401

MASSACHUSETTS
Department of Fisheries, Wildlife, and Recreational Vehicles, 100 Cambridge St., Boston 02202
Department of Environmental Management, 100 Cambridge St., Boston 02202

MICHIGAN
Department of Natural Resources, Mason Building, Lansing 48926

MINNESOTA
Department of Natural Resources, 658 Cedar St., St. Paul 55155

MISSISSIPPI
Game and Fish Commission, 239 N. Lamar St., Jackson 39250
Park Commission, 717 Robert E. Lee Building, Jackson 39201

MISSOURI
Department of Conservation, Box 180, Jefferson City 65101
Department of Natural Resources, Box 176, Jefferson City 65101

MONTANA
Department of Natural Resources and Conservation, 32 S. Ewing, Helena 59601
Department of Fish and Game, 1420 E. Sixth, Helena 59601

NEBRASKA
Game and Parks Commission, 2200 N. 33rd. St., Lincoln 68503

NEVADA
Department of Conservation of Natural Resources, 201 S. Fall St., Carson City 89701
Department of Fish and Game, Box 10678, Reno 89510

NEW HAMPSHIRE
Fish and Game Department, 34 Bridge St., Concord 03331
Department of Resources and Economic Development, Box 856, State House Annex, Concord 03301

NEW JERSEY
Department of Environmental Protection, Box 1390, Trenton 08625

New Mexico

Department of Game and Fish, State Capitol, Santa Fe 87503
State Park and Recreation Commission, P.O. Box 1147, Santa Fe 87503

New York

Department of Environmental Conservation, 50 Wolf Rd., Albany 12233
Adirondack Park Agency, Box 99, Ray Brook 12977
State Office of Parks and Recreation, Empire State Plaza, Albany 12238

North Carolina

Department of Natural and Economic Resources, Box 27687, Raleigh 27611
Wildlife Resources Commission, 512 N. Salisbury, Raleigh 27611

North Dakota

Game and Fish Department, 2121 Lovett Ave., Bismarck 58501
State Parks and Recreation Department, R. 2, Mandan 58554

Ohio

Department of Natural Resources, Fountain Square, Columbus 43224

Oklahoma

Department of Wildlife Conservation, 1801 N. Lincoln, Oklahoma City 73105
Tourism and Recreation Department, 500 Will Rogers Memorial Building, Oklahoma City 73105

Oregon

Department of Fish and Wildlife, 1634 S.W. Alder St., Portland 97205
Department of Transportation, State Parks and Recreation Branch, Salem 97310
Department of Forestry, 2600 State St., Salem 97310

Pennsylvania

Department of Environmental Resources, Box 1467, Harrisburg 17120
Game Commission, Box 1567, Harrisburg 17120

Puerto Rico

Department of Natural Resources, Box 5887, San Juan 00906

Rhode Island

Department of Natural Resources, 83 Park St., Providence 02903

South Carolina

Department of Parks, Recreation, and Tourism, 1205 Pendleton St., Columbia 29201

Wildlife and Marine Resources Commission, Box 167, Columbia 29202
Commission of Forestry, Box 21707, Columbia 29221

SOUTH DAKOTA
Department of Game, Fish and Parks, Anderson Building, Pierre 57501

TENNESSEE
Wildlife Resources Agency, Box 40747, Ellington Agriculture Center, Nashville 37204
Department of Conservation, 2611 West End Ave., Nashville 37203

TEXAS
Parks and Wildlife Department, Reagan Building, Austin 78791
Forest Service, College Station 77843

UTAH
Department of Natural Resources, 1596 Temple, Salt Lake City 84116

VERMONT
Agency of Environmental Conservation, Montpelier 05602

VIRGINIA
Commission of Game and Inland Fisheries, 4010 W. Broad St., Richmond 23230
Department of Conservation and Economic Development, 1100 State Office Building, Richmond 23219
Commission of Outdoor Recreation, 803 E. Broad St., Richmond 23219

WASHINGTON
Department of Game, 600 N. Capitol Way, Olympia 98504
Department of Natural Resources, Public Lands Building, Olympia 98504
State Parks and Recreation Commission, 7150 Cleanwater Lane, Olympia 98504

WEST VIRGINIA
Department of Natural Resources, 1800 Washington St., Charleston 25305

WISCONSIN
Department of Natural Resources, Box 7921, Madison 53707

WYOMING
Game and Fish Department, Cheyenne 82001
Forestry Division, Cheyenne 82001
Recreation Commission, Cheyenne 82001

Index

Important entries are shown in **bold face**.

E

Easements, 22, 220, 280, **439–445**, 525–526, 536

Eastern Wilderness Act, 493,632

Ecological forestry, 483

Ecology, 115, 224, 356–366, 386, 556–562, 564–567, 622–623

Economic impact, 86–90, 94–99, 150, 151

Economic importance of leisure and recreation, 5–6, 11, 82–84, 157

Education, 69, 77

Elected officials, 188–190, 203

Eliot, Charles, 170

Elitist arguments, wilderness, 506–507

"Emerald necklace," 170, 183

Eminent domain, power, 22, 157–158, 393, **434–435**

Employee recreation, industrial, 162–163

Enabling laws, 171, 445

Endangered American Wilderness Act, 502–503

Endangered species, 288–289, 420, 633

Environmental Defense Fund, 605

Environmental education, 285, 381, 428–429, **464–465**, 601, 610, 633

Environmental Protection Agency, U.S., 238, 250, 320, 339 (*see also* Impacts)

Environmental quality, 35 (*see also* Pollution, water; Impacts)

Equipment, recreational, **100–118**, 365–366, 614–615, 617–618

Esthetics, 470–474

Exotic and feral animals, 564–567

Expenditures for leisure, 5–6, 11, 71, 85–86, 88, 619

Experience levels, U.S. Forest Service, 32–34, 349–351

Experience, recreational, **25–39**, 49–50, 365, 457, 459, 505–509

F

Facilities, park, 174–175, 267–270, 306–310, 326, 330

Federal Land Policy and Management Act (BLM Organic Act), 295, 299, 499, 632

Federal Power Commission, 156, 323, 533

Federal recreation resources and programs, 18, 131–132, **235–252**, 253–338, 421, 634–639

Federal Water Project Recreation Act, 320–322, 329, 632

Fee simple acquisition of land, 435–436

Fees for recreation, 144–145, 163, 192, 625

Fertility rates, 60

Festivals, 58

Finance, 414–430
  federal, 290, 421
  local parks, 190–193, 203, 205, 421–425
  private enterprises, 141
  state, 216, 219–221, 226, 229–230, 421–422

Fire, 22, 157, 293, 509, 548, 557–562

Fish and wildlife areas, 207, **218–219**, 278–293, 326, 524

Fish and Wildlife Service, U.S., 240–247, **278–293**, 493, 499, 534, 590, 631, 636

Fishing, 285, 326, 508

Flood control, 323–324

Flood insurance, 324

Flood plains, 127

Florida, 84, 219

Ford, Gerald, 271(illus)

Ford, Henry, 72, 75

Forecasts of recreation, 405–411, 623–628

Forest industry (*see* Industrial recreation landowners)

Forest Institute, American, 610

Forest Service, U.S., 87, 108, 239, 241–242, 246, 258, **303–319**, 383, 467–468, 493–496, 499, 515, 534, 542–548, 632–633, 637

Forests, 207, 222–223, 303–319, 544–545 (*see also* National Forests; Industrial forests)

Franchises, 139

Future, 202–203, 405–411, 613–629

G

Garden Club of America, 605

Geological Survey, U.S., 385

Gila Wilderness, 496

Glen Canyon (Lake Powell), 331–332, 337–338

Goethe, C. M., 457

Governmental responsibility for recreation areas, 17–21, 196, 197–203

Gray, David, 53

Grazing, 313, 509, 545, 597

Great Ponds Act, 207

Green line, 448–449

Green Mountain Club, 520
Group behavior factors, 37, 43–44

H

Habitat, wildlife, 289–293, 301, 328, 537, 592–593
Hang gliding, 102, 272, 551–552
Harrison, Benjamin, 311
Health from recreation, 621–622
Heritage Conservation and Recreation Service, U.S. (formerly Bureau of Outdoor Recreation), 18, 238, **248**, 376, 379–380, 419–423, 426–427, 429, 635
Heritage program, 224, 381, 590
Hetch-Hetchy controversy, 247, 333(illus), 336
Historic Places, National Register, 249, 425–427
Historic Preservation Fund, 426
Historic sites, 130, 231, 249, 425–427, 631
History, living, 461–464
Holzwarth, John, Jr., 463
Horse-Shoe Trail Club, 594
Horses, 508, 513
Housing and Urban Development, U.S. Department of, 149, 417–419, 630
Hunting, 155–158, 285, 509, 593

I

Impacts, economic, 5, 86–99, 150, 151
environmental, 150, 339, 578
monitoring, 115–116, 367
on resources, 41, 317, 356–358
on visitors, 41
zones, 357–358
Income, 69, 70–72, 619
Indian lands, U.S., 242–243
Indiana 212(illus), 354–355
Industrial forests, 15, 17, 153–161
Industrial land donations, 160–161
Industrial recreation landowners
Boise Cascade, 158
Bowaters Southern Paper Co., 154–155
Brown Co., 159
Burlington Northern, 156
California Redwood Association, 153, 159
Connor Lumber Co., 157–158
Gulf and Western, 156
International Paper Co., 156

Louisiana Land and Title, 156
Olin Mathieson, 153
Pacific Gas & Electric Co., 156, 517
Redwood Industry Recreation Areas, 153, 159
St. Regis Paper Co., 154
U.S. Steel, 156
Weyerhaeuser Corp., 155
Industrial recreation lands
leasing, 155, 159–160
motivations, 157–158, 163–164
problems, 159
Industrial societies, 58–59, 68
Influence groups, 393, 545–547, **588, 597–605**, 609–610
Inholdings in parks and forests, 261, 272, 273
Intensity of experience, 36–37
Interpretation, 22, 221, 226, 282–287, 297, 307, 316, **454–469**, 536, 553, 607
Inventory of resources, 384–386
Invitees, 583
Islands, 129–130, 626
Izaak Walton League of America, 604

J

Jackson Hole airport, 552–553
Johnson, Lyndon B., 35, 513

K

Kampgrounds of America, 139
Kennedy, John F., 10
Kings Island Amusement Park, 17(illus), 137
Kruger National Park, S. Africa, 260

L

Labor, U.S. Department of, 424
Lacey Act, 278, 282, 631
Lakes, natural, 129, 151 (see also Reservoirs)
Land acquisition, 22, 86, 90–94, 218–221, 235–236, 273–274, **431–453**, 589–593, 595–597
Land and Water Conservation Fund, 170, 209, 220, 248, 376, 382, 416, **419–423**, 630
Land Between the Lakes, 238, 327–328
Land classification, 343–355

Matheson, Scott, 267–268
McLuhan, Marshall, 6
Megalopolis, 64–66
Memorials and museums, state, 208
Metropolitan park districts, 170, 182–186,
    457 (*see also* Local park areas)
Mills, Enos, 38
Mining, 301–302, 533, 545, 633
Mining Congress, American, 610
Minority preferences, 50–51, 506–507
Mississippi, 219, 220
Mobility, 75–76, 619
Monopolistic competition, 140–141
Morality of leisure, 34
Moses, Robert, 170, 189, 195, 574
Mott Foundation, 177
Muir, John, 247, 336, 542(illus), 560, 601,
    622
Multiple use, 236, 295, 305, 311, 313, **317–
    319**, 470–488, **541–548**, 632
Multiplier effect, 84, 89–90
Municipal water supply, 320, 322

N

National and Provincial Parks Association of
    Canada, 600
National Audubon Society, 441, 465, 602–
    603
National Campers and Hikers Association,
    612
National Campground Owners Association,
    140, 612
National Conference on Outdoor Recreation
    of 1924, 28, 313, 374
National Environmental Policy Act, 250,
    339, 537–539, 578, 633
National Forest Management Act of 1976,
    313–314, 318
National Forest Products Association, 610
National Forests, **303–319**, 401, 493, 495–
    499, 515
    Bighorn, 312
    Bitterroot, 479, 481(illus)
    Daniel Boone, 375(illus)
    Gila, 496
    Inyo, 240(illus), 305(illus)
    Monongahela, 317–318, 479, 480(illus)
    Nantahala, 308(illus)
    Ocala, 523
    Pike, 312
    San Isabel, 312

St. Joe, 486(illus)
    Sequoia, 602
    Shawnee, 239(illus)
    Superior (Minnesota Forest Preserve),
        311, 312, 495–496, 505(illus)
    Tongass, 483(illus)
    White Mountain, 307(illus)
    White River, 312, 495–496, 504(illus)
    Yellowstone Timberland Reserve, 311
National Heritage Program, 249, 590
National Industrial Recreation Association,
    163
National monuments, 121(illus), 246, 258
    (*see also* National Park Service)
National Park Service, U. S., 240, 241, 242,
    245–247, 249, **253–276**, 332, 383–384,
    402, 421, 493, 499, 514–515, 534, 548–
    553, 594, 631, 637
National Park Service areas
    Acadia NP, 255(illus
    Appalachian Trail, 520–522
    Arches NP, 16(illus)
    Bandelier NM, 565
    Big Thicket Ntl. Preserve, 274–276
    Blue Ridge Parkway, 264(illus), 524–525
    Bryce Canyon NP, 265(illus)
    Buffalo Ntl. River, 535(illus)
    Canyon de Chelly NM, 558–559(illus)
    Catoctin Mountain Park, 253
    Cape Cod NS, 199
    Castillo de San Marcos NM, 274(illus)
    Chaco Canyon NM, 276(illus)
    Chickasaw NRA, 252
    Cuyahoga NRA, 198, 199, 262–263
    Death Valley NM, 564
    Delaware Water Gap NRA, 199
    Denali NM, 247(illus)
    Devil's Postpile NM, 259(illus)
    Devil's Tower NM, 121(illus), 258
    Dinosaur NM, 336, 497(illus)
    Everglades NP, 117(illus), 459, 534(illus)
    Fire Island NS, 199
    Fort Necessity Ntl. Battlefield, 271(illus)
    Gates of the Arctic NM, 501(illus)
    Gateway NRA, 199; Gettysburg NHP,
        386(illus)
    Glacier NP, 253, 563
    Golden Gate NRA, 199, 200(illus), 590,
        631
    Grand Canyon NP, 55(illus), 253(illus),
        332, 336, 564–567
    Grand Teton NP, 266(illus), 552
    Great Smoky Mountains NP, 96–97, 567

O

W

Y

Z